PERSONNEL/HUMAN RESOURCE MANAGEMENT

PERSONNEL/HUMAN RESOURCE MANAGEMENT

Second Edition

Terry L. Leap
Clemson University

Michael D. Crino
Clemson University

Macmillan Publishing Company
New York

Maxwell Macmillan Canada
Toronto

Maxwell Macmillan International
New York   Oxford   Singapore   Sydney

To our parents
Henry W. and Barbara L. Leap
Samuel J. and Louise M. Crino

Editor: Charles E. Stewart/Denise Abbott
Production Supervisor: Helen Wallace
Production Manager: Roger Vergnes
Cover Designer: Cathleen Norz

This book was set in Caledonia by Carlisle Communications,
printed and bound by R. R. Donnelley & Sons, Crawfordsville.
The cover was printed by Phoenix Color.

Macmillan Publishing Company
866 Third Avenue, New York, New York 10022

Macmillan Publishing Company is part
of the Maxwell Communication Group of Companies.

Maxwell Macmillan Canada, Inc.
1200 Eglinton Avenue East
Suite 200
Don Mills, Ontario M3C 3N1

Library of Congress Cataloging in Publication Data

Leap, Terry L., 1948-
    Personnel/human resource management / Terry L. Leap, Michael D. Crino. — 2nd ed.
        p. cm.
    Includes bibliographical references and index.
    ISBN 0-02-368521-2
    1. Personnel management.   I. Crino, Michael D. II. Title.
HF5549.L375   1993   92-20064
658.3 — dc20   CIP

Printing: 2 3 4 5 6 7 8   Year: 3 4 5 6 7 8 9 0 1 2

Preface

Employees are our Number One priority at this stage. They will continue to be. If you look after employees, they look after customers. And that's good for shareholders.

—Hugh McColl, Jr., Chairman and CEO, NationsBank

Personnel/human resource management (PHRM) is an exciting and dynamic field. PHRM encompasses such a wide range of topics that an introductory course instructor has considerable leeway as to what he or she may elect to cover during one semester or quarter. The selection and emphasis of specific PHRM topics depend upon the individual instructor's background, research interests, and personal tastes. We have attempted to blend various orientations and interests into a balanced and comprehensive textbook suitable for the many approaches to teaching PHRM.

We have based the structure and content of *Personnel/Human Resource Management*, second edition, on our research and teaching experience in PHRM (more than 30 years between us), our familiarity with current PHRM literature and textbooks, and numerous discussions we have had with colleagues across the country. As the plan for the book evolved, it was decided that a successful addition to the PHRM market must contain several important elements. First, the content should thoroughly cover traditional as well as currently emerging topics. We have included chapters on such traditional topics as job analysis and design, recruitment, selection, and performance evaluation, as well as multiple chapter coverage of compensation and labor relations. Additionally we have included extensive coverage of important emerging topics, such as PHRM in multinational firms, employment at-will, the decline in the power and influence of American labor unions, drug testing, and AIDS, which are likely to impact the workplace significantly in the future. Second, the text should emphasize the need for integration of PHRM into the strategic planning and daily operations of the firm. The importance of the link between corporate strategy, daily operations, and PHRM is emphasized in the introductory and concluding chapters and repeatedly discussed throughout the text. Third, the book must be written in a style that appeals to students without sacrificing the depth necessary to understand major PHRM issues. We believe that some college-level texts have tried to increase student appeal and readability at the expense of important details and relationships. This approach underestimates both the importance of the information and the ability of our students. We have tried to strike a balance between a smooth, easy-to-understand writing style and adequate depth of coverage. Fourth, a book needs realistic and timely examples, vignettes, and case exercises. Many of our examples and illustrations are based on recent PHRM incidents and controversies that have arisen in private and public organizations and were reported in *The Wall Street Journal* and other business periodicals. Fifth, a book needs to be well documented and to reflect the most current literature and major developments in the field. We feel that *Personnel/Human Resource Management,* second edition, is especially strong in this respect. We have incorporated the most recent professional and academic literature (much of it from 1990 and 1991), as well as what might be considered the classics in the PHRM literature. Sixth, a book needs a framework to integrate all of the topics, concepts, and ideas in a meaningful fashion. We have developed a PHRM framework, placed it at the beginning of each major section of the text, and highlighted the appropriate portion for reference. The framework emphasizes the importance of corporate strategy and organizational goals to PHRM and the relationships among the major PHRM functions. We have also given greater attention to the role of supervisors and managers who administer PHRM policies. Finally, a book needs to be visually attractive. We have employed tables and figures throughout the chapters. However, in order to maintain a pleasing and readable presentation, we have resisted the temptation to clutter the margins with notes. Further, we have not overloaded the appendices with an excessive amount of material, preferring to include additional lecture material in the instructor's manual.

To assist the student in comprehending, studying, and retaining the material presented in the text, we have integrated a consistent pedagogical structure throughout. Each part begins with an overview of the topics it covers. Each chapter features a chapter outline, learning objectives, a summary, discussion questions, and brief case exercises.

We recognize that a textbook cannot be all things to all people. For example, some instructors may wish to emphasize topics such as job analysis, recruitment and selection, training and development, performance appraisal, and the motivational aspects of compensation. These same instructors may give less emphasis to employee benefits, health and safety, labor relations, and the legal issues surrounding employee rights and responsibilities. We also recognize that instructors develop a style of teaching that suits their personal preferences, level of student preparedness, and institutional norms. Some instructors emphasize the traditional lecture method in an introductory PHRM course, while others employ case studies, simulations, seminar discussions on current topics, and other methods. We have written a book which we believe can support these alternative teaching methods. There is sufficient detail in the text to allow students to acquire a basic understanding of the various topics. Instructors can choose to expand on selected topics with lectures, confident that the student will have a basic understanding of the remaining topics. It is our belief that this book gives the instructor the latitude to use whatever pedagogical methods he or she desires to improve the students' mastery of PHRM topics, and sharpen their decision-making skills. Several ancillaries are available for the instructor:

- The *Instructor's Manual* contains supplemental lecture material, overhead transparency masters, additional cases, and exercises that may be completed on personal computers using the accompanying software.
- An extensive *Test Bank* of multiple-choice and true/false questions and answers has been prepared by the authors. It is also available as Microtest, a computerized test generator.

Terry L. Leap
Michael D. Crino

Acknowledgments

A number of people assisted us with the writing and publishing of *Personnel/ Human Resource Management*, second edition: Charles Stewart, Denise Abbott, and Helen Wallace of the Macmillan Publishing Company were always available to guide us through the myriad decisions necessary in a project of this type. We also are indebted to a number of colleagues who reviewed all or parts of the manuscript: Charles R. Milton, University of South Carolina; David A. Gray, The University of Texas at Arlington; Gary L. Gordon, The State University of New York—Oswego; and Alan Cabelly, Portland State University.

Karen Stine, Ashland College, made her toxicological expertise available to us as we researched and wrote the material on occupational health and safety. We would also like to recognize two of our graduate assistants at Clemson University who helped us with various parts of the book: Rebecca Ballard and Monica Milasnovich. We would like to thank Acting Dean, Jim Sheriff, of the College of Commerce and Industry, and William H. Hendrix, head of the Department of Management, Clemson University, for providing the work environment and support which enabled us to write this textbook.

T.L.L.
M.D.C.

Brief Contents

Contents

■ PART TWO   *Personnel/Human Resource Planning and
                Staffing   131*

CHAPTER 4
JOB ANALYSIS AND DESIGN   133

■ PART THREE *Developing and Compensating*
              Employees   *287*

CHAPTER 8
EMPLOYEE TRAINING AND DEVELOPMENT   **289**

■ **PART FOUR** *Employee Well-Being and Job Security*   *487*

CHAPTER 13
DEFINING EMPLOYEE AND ORGANIZATIONAL RIGHTS   488

CHAPTER 17
PERSONNEL/HUMAN RESOURCE MANAGEMENT: ORGANIZATIONAL STRATEGY, ETHICAL CONCERNS, AND FUTURE DEVELOPMENTS   679

PERSONNEL/HUMAN RESOURCE MANAGEMENT

An Introduction to Personnel/Human Resource Management

■ LEARNING OBJECTIVES

After reading this introductory chapter, you will

1. Be aware of some of the important issues facing personnel managers.
2. Understand the relationship between the organization's mission, goals, and strategies and the goals and strategies of the personnel/human resource department.
3. Have an overview of the major personnel/human resource management functions.
4. Gain an appreciation of the social, economic, and legal forces affecting personnel/human resource management.
5. Understand the career preparations necessary to enter the personnel field.
6. Understand how the personnel/human resource management function helps the organization to achieve its goals.
7. Become aware of how managers and first-line supervisors administer personnel/human resource policies.

■ INTRODUCTORY VIGNETTE

Quality Personnel Programs at Mars, Inc.

Forget the Japanese. Forget the Germans. The best lessons on management come from Mars.

No, not the planet Mars. But the multibillion-dollar, world-class company known as Mars, Inc., a leader in candy, pet food, rice and other products.

This excerpt comes from *The Wall Street Journal*, and it describes the managerial philosophy and organizational culture of one of the most successful corporations in the world. Mars, Inc., can attribute its huge market share, stratospheric profits, and high productivity to personnel/human resource policies that sometimes border on being radically different from those frequently found in large firms. For example, all employees, including executives, punch time clocks. Private offices and reserved parking spaces are nowhere to be found. The president and senior executives work within walking distance of the production facilities. On any par-

2

ticular day, one of the Mars brothers who own the business is likely to show up and head directly to the production floor. If he finds unclean or unsafe conditions, or if a slightly flawed product is coming off the line, you will hear him barking orders and screaming.

According to *The Wall Street Journal*, employees at Mars have something more than merit and incentive systems. They enjoy a high degree of job security and pay that is pegged at the 90th percentile of the compensation offered by other premier multinational companies. Key managers are given a variety of jobs to ensure that they understand the company from top to bottom. Someone heading up human resources today in a billion-dollar domestic business may be heading up a half-billion-dollar manufacturing venture in Europe tomorrow. It is rare for a general manager not to have done a tour of duty in manufacturing or marketing in at least two business units.

Mars, Inc., is a model of the unrelenting obsession for quality that has become a byword in U.S. businesses. Although quality is dependent on all facets of a corporation—accounting, finance, production, marketing—the role of personnel/human resource management is critical. Hiring the best employees, training and developing them so that they can reach their potential, compensating high-quality employees so that they will remain motivated to achieve at even higher levels, and dealing with the multitude of decisions involving people will be critical over the next decade. The Japanese prime minister who in early 1992 blasted American workers as being lazy and unproductive was, in part, attacking the personnel/human resource management policies of U.S.-run companies.

Companies like Mars force us to realize that we must reconsider what a true quality culture looks like, how businesses should be evaluated, how people should be compensated and treated, the role of senior management, and the development of employees—both managerial and nonmanagereial. The role of the personnel/human resource management field will play an integral role in the ability of U.S. firms to establish a quality focus and become competitive with European and Japanese companies.[1]

> People are our most valuable asset. They must feel secure, important, challenged, in control of their destiny, confident in their leadership, be responsive to common goals, believe they are being treated fairly, have easy access to authority and open lines of communication in all possible directions. . . We need to maximize the benefits of cooperation and teamwork, fusing high technology with human talent, so that we here in the USA and all of our subsidiary and joint venture operations will be in a position to realize our full potential.
>
> *George Willis, CEO, The Lincoln Electric Company*[2]

---

[1]See Craig J. Cantoni, "Quality Control from Mars," *The Wall Street Journal* (January 23, 1992).

[2]Arthur Sharplin, "The Lincoln Electric Company—1989," in Fred R. David, *Cases in Strategic Management*, 3rd ed. (New York: Macmillan Publishing Company, 1991), pp. 331–332.

■ Introduction

Even in an age of high technology, people are still the most important asset to an organization. As used here, *organization* can refer to such diverse enterprises as a Fortune 500 corporation, an NBA basketball team, a community hospital, a Las Vegas resort and gambling casino, or a small auto parts store. An examination of the most successful corporations in the United States and elsewhere will usually reveal that a quality workforce has made the difference between mediocrity and success. Companies such as Delta Airlines, IBM, and Lincoln Electric are classic examples of how well-run personnel/human resource management contributes significantly to corporate success. This book proposes that people (human resources) play a vital role in the success of an organization—whether it is a Fortune 500 firm such as Exxon, a large, privately held textile firm such as Milliken, a state or federal government agency, or a small business with fewer than 10 employees.

The operation of the personnel function is dependent on the broad strategy, policies, and structure of the organization. Small companies have different personnel problems than large companies. Geographically dispersed organizations must address problems that do not plague centralized organizations. Multinational firms face different personnel/human resource management issues than do firms whose operations are local in scope. Manufacturing companies have somewhat different personnel concerns than service companies. A large university teaching hospital, for example, is labor intensive and employs a multitude of professional and nonprofessional personnel across numerous departmental and specialty lines. On the other hand, a capital-intensive firm such as a petroleum refinery employs relatively few workers, and its personnel function are radically different from that of the university teaching hospital.

The board of directors and chief executive officer of an organization will change their competitive postures from time to time. Organizations expand product lines, acquire other companies, and are sometimes acquired themselves through either friendly or hostile takeovers. When a company merges with another or is taken over by a larger firm, employees may be transferred, promoted, or discharged. Whatever strategic or organizational changes occur, the personnel/human resource management department must help facilitate these changes through recruitment, selection, training, compensation, and other personnel functions.

To accomplish the organization's goals and support its strategies, personnel/human resources objectives and strategies must also be developed. Among the more important personnel/human resources objectives are the following:

1. To establish employee recruitment and selection systems for hiring the best possible employees consistent with the organization's needs.
2. To maximize the potential of each employee in order to attain the organization's goals and to ensure individual career growth and personal dignity.
3. To retain employees whose performance helps the organization realize its goals and to release those whose performance is unsatisfactory.

4. To ensure organizational compliance with state and federal laws that are applicable to the personnel/human resource management function.

Industries and companies become known for specific personnel policies or strategies. For example, the U.S. textile industry has a history of paternalism and strong antiunion sentiments. Banking is known for its modest salaries. Companies such as Lincoln Electric and Nucor use lucrative incentive programs to motivate employees to work harder.

The list of personnel strategies is endless. They range from tightly controlling labor costs, encouraging sales and production performance, to enhancing employee creativity. Ultimately, each is designed to help the organization fulfill its mission and objectives. To illustrate, examples of the range of personnel/human resource strategies are listed here. We discuss these and other strategies throughout the text.

1. Recruitment and selection strategies: Some firms wish to promote from within by looking first at their current employees when filling managerial positions. Other companies seek managers from outside the company.
2. Personnel planning strategies: Some companies do little planning for future personnel needs. Others use succession planning and computer simulations to determine the type and number of employees needed.
3. Training and development strategies: Some companies allow employees to learn their skills on the job. Others spend thousands of dollars carefully training employees before they are allowed to assume job responsibilities.
4. Performance appraisal strategies: Some companies use very informal performance appraisals such as occasionally telling an employee how he or she is doing over a cup of coffee. Others use carefully developed appraisals and formal appraisal interviews.
5. Compensation strategies: Some companies pay below the market rate, whereas others pay above. A number of companies offer liberal medical, dental, and hospitalization insurance plans whereas others do not. Some companies use incentive pay, sales commissions, and profit sharing; others pay a flat hourly rate or salary regardless of individual productivity.
6. Employment relations strategies: Some companies adapt an antagonistic posture toward unions; others do not. A company may use a well-defined progressive discipline system or leave disciplinary actions entirely up to the supervisor.

In carrying out these personnel strategies, personnel managers are challenged by a number of complex social, economic, legal, and ethical issues. Here are just a few examples:

1. How can organizations screen applicants to ensure that they have not falsified their educational and work achievements? Unfortunately, many job seekers list college degrees that they have never earned, or jobs that they have not held, in order to make themselves look more attractive to a prospective employer.

2. What can be done to keep the skills of technical and professional employees from becoming obsolete? Many employees possess skills that erode quickly unless they receive periodic training and development.

3. How can the job performance of employees be evaluated or graded fairly? Most college students are sensitive to real or imagined grading inequities that arise at colleges and universities. Unfortunately, the problems associated with evaluations are often worse in the working world, where organizational performance appraisal systems are sometimes poorly designed and lend themselves to subjectivity and bias. Inequities in the way an employee's job performance is evaluated can pose serious legal problems for the organization, as well as financial and career problems for the employee.

4. How important is pay to employees? Under what conditions does money motivate employees to work harder or do a better job? How can a company compensate employees so that effort, job performance, and skills are properly rewarded?

5. Most large organizations provide a wide array of employee benefits such as group life and health insurance, retirement (pension) programs, and disability income insurance. How do such benefits affect the total compensation of managerial and nonmanagerial personnel? What can organizations do to control the rising cost of health care and health care insurance?

6. How can jobs be designed to make work more meaningful? Today, many workers are filling jobs for which they are overqualified. What effect will this dilemma have on individual job satisfaction, productivity, and turnover?

7. The rights of employees are now being tested in the courts, and the following questions are being addressed: Under what circumstances should an employer administer drug tests? Should employees who are known carriers of the AIDS virus be banned from the workplace? Should corporations give less qualified females and racial minorities hiring preference over better-qualified males and nonminorities? Does an employer have the right to discharge an employee for no cause or for a cause that may be morally indefensible?

8. How should a personnel manager deal with labor unions? Federal labor laws prohibit discrimination against employees who support union organizing campaigns. What steps can be taken by a firm whose employees are approached by union organizers? If a union successfully organizes a firm's employees and wins a certification election, what duties and obligations does the employer have toward the union and how will it affect the personnel/human resource management function?

9. How should employers handle difficult employees? What can be done about employees who come to work under the influence of drugs? Should employers assume an obligation to help employees with drug problems? Does an organization have the right to discipline employees for criminal or other unacceptable conduct that occurs during off-duty hours?

These and many more issues and problems challenge personnel/human resource management professionals. Some of the issues just posed lack simple solutions, and it is likely that they will be the subject of debate and controversy for years to come. In some cases the courts will provide solutions; in others, issues may be resolved through the creativity of practicing personnel managers and the research of consultants and academicians.

■ Why Study Personnel/Human Resource Management?

An understanding of personnel/human resource management is important to anyone who works in an organization. Wherever people gather to work, personnel issues become important. Even though few students will take an entry-level position in personnel/human resource management, most will find themselves in a supervisory role where they will make decisions about hiring, compensation, performance evaluation, employee discipline, promotions, and transfers. Supervisors must understand the scope and application of their firm's personnel policies in order to ensure that their everyday personnel actions are consistent with those policies. Additionally, nonsupervisory employees interested in their own compensation, training, and career development should understand the basics of personnel management in order to assess the ramifications of personnel policies on their careers.

■ External Factors Affecting Personnel/Human Resource Management

Personnel managers must often deal with factors that are beyond their control. Certain phenomena such as the nature of the labor force, federal and state legislation, labor unions, physical and behavioral characteristics of job applicants and employees, international forces, the strategy and objectives of the organization, and the threat of corporate mergers and hostile takeovers can directly influence the personnel/human resource management function.

The Labor Force and Cultural Diversity

The U.S. labor force has changed in composition and grown dramatically during the past quarter of a century. Persons previously excluded from the mainstream of meaningful worklife—women, racial minorities, and the handicapped, among others—have experienced higher rates of labor force participation and are no longer relegated to the lowest-paying and least desirable jobs (although race, sex, and other forms of unfair discrimination are still far from being eliminated). Much of this change is due to the protective civil rights (equal employment opportunity) laws. Economic necessity, changing attitudes toward minority groups, the increasing number of single-parent households, higher levels of education, and the gradual aging of the labor force all have an impact on organizational life and personnel/human resource management.

The increasing cultural diversity of the labor force means that personnel managers must develop alternative pay and employee benefit plans to accommodate persons who have different attitudes toward careers and work, lifestyles, and family situations. Single parents may find it difficult to work outside the traditional 8-hour, 5-day work week because of problems with child care arrangements. A number of corporations are providing child care as a major employee benefit. A dual-career couple may not desire to have duplicate health insurance coverage and may desire another employee benefit such as higher retirement benefits in its place. Because the workforce is gradually getting older and the Age Discrimination in Employment Act now makes it possible to avoid mandatory retirement, greater emphasis will be directed to phased retirement programs, whereby an employee gradually reduces involvement with work until he or she is fully retired. These and other personnel issues will arise as the labor force continues to change in size and composition. Trends and issues pertaining to the U.S. labor force are discussed in Chapter 2.

Personnel directors must be cognizant of the many individual differences that exist among employees. Employees have varying job skills, education levels, employment backgrounds, physical abilities, and behavioral and psychological attributes (such as levels of motivation, interpersonal skills, intelligence, motor abilities, attitudes toward work, and personality characteristics). Industrial psychologists and other organizational researchers have studied the effects of individual differences on human performance in various work settings for years and have many valuable insights to contribute.

Physical, behavioral, and psychological differences among individuals have important implications for the design of recruitment, selection, training and development, and compensation programs. Personnel/human resource management outcomes such as employee absenteeism and turnover, job performance, and job satisfaction are all directly related to individual and cultural differences among employees. Chapter 2 analyzes major differences among workers, discusses job motivation and satisfaction theories, and looks at performance-related behaviors such as absenteeism and turnover.

Federal and State Legislation

One of the most important factors contributing to the increased prominence of the personnel/human resource management field is the proliferation of federal and state legislation directly affecting personnel decisions. Federal equal employment opportunity (EEO) laws protect against unfair discrimination based on race, sex, religion, color, national, origin, age, and physical and mental handicaps. State

EEO laws often provide protection equal to or greater than that of federal laws and include protection from discrimination based on sexual preferences, political affiliation, and criminal history. EEO laws are discussed in Chapter 3. The Occupational Safety and Health Act regulates safety in the workplace (see Chapter 14). Compensation laws include not only the minimum wage law, but also laws regulating pension programs, workers' compensation (on-the-job injuries), social security, wage garnishments and child support payments, group insurance and others. Private-sector labor-management relations are regulated by several federal laws (Chapter 15), and public sector labor-management relations are regulated by a patchwork quilt of state and federal laws.

Not only must personnel managers have a basic understanding of these laws, but they must also stay abreast of the major legislative changes and court and administrative agency decisions that affect personnel/human resource management. The situation is complicated by the fact that the initial impact of legal developments is often unclear. As a result, the personnel manager's experience, education, and intelligence are occasionally taxed to determine what effect legal developments will have on the organization.

International Personnel/Human Resource Management

Although this book focuses heavily on personnel/human resource management practices in the United States, few organizations are untouched by some aspect of global competition. Corporations in the United States are constantly looking for new market opportunities in foreign countries. Many U.S. corporations own and manage subsidiaries in foreign countries. Foreign corporations, such as the Japanese automobile manufacturers, operate manufacturing facilities in the United States. There is also a growing cadre of individuals who live and work in countries other than their own.

According to Sheth and Eshghi, understanding and managing human resources in a global environment has become increasingly important for several reasons.[3] First, worldwide communication and information technologies enable us to exchange information rapidly throughout the world. Second, increasing economic and political interdependence exists among countries. During the 1970s and 1980s, much was said and written about Japanese management techniques and their impact on workplace practices in the United States. In 1992, 12 Western European countries merged as a single economy (known as EC'92). These 12 countries have a total population of 320 million. New technologies, reduced regulatory barriers, and improved transportation will increase production, simplify logistics, and cut costs for European-based firms. Companies with subsidiaries in Europe will have to adapt their personnel/human resource management policies to the major political and economic restructuring associated with EC'92. Third, labor legislation, tax laws, wage guidelines, and social customs and mores

[3]Jagdish Sheth and Golpira Eshghi, *Global Human Resources Perspectives* (Cincinnati: South-Western Publishing Company, 1989), pp. vii–xii.

may differ significantly from one country to another. The role of labor unions, for example, is different in Great Britain and Australia than in the United States. Cross-cultural differences among employees within a workplace will create unique personnel/human resource management issues. Personnel/human resource management policies in multinational firms will have to deal with issues such as the following:

1. How are employees recruited and selected for foreign assignments? How must the recruitment and selection procedures that our firm uses in the United States be changed when hiring employees in other countries?
2. What training and development will be required to prepare employees for assignments in foreign countries?
3. How do we compensate employees to induce them to accept foreign assignments? What pay and employee benefits are necessary to ensure that our employees enjoy a reasonable standard of living during their tenure in a foreign country?
4. How do we deal with organized labor in our foreign subsidiaries?
5. What major cultural issues will our employees face during a foreign assignment?
6. Should our corporation use companywide personnel/human resource policies or tailor these policies to specific locales?

Personnel/human resource management issues in multinational firms will be addressed throughout the book.

Labor Unions

Approximately 16 percent of all nonagricultural employees in the United States are unionized. Most European countries have considerably higher levels of union activity. The presence and impact of labor unions are important to both unionized and nonunionized organizations. In the unionized firm, a personnel manager generally devotes a great deal of time to contract negotiations and administration. Although management negotiates with the union only once every 2 or 3 years, much time is spent between negotiations preparing for collective bargaining and administering the existing contract. Less obvious, perhaps, is the concern that personnel managers in *nonunionized* firms often have in regard to unions. Few, if any, top managers desire to have their employees organized by a union. However, poorly designed and administered personnel policies or unfair and capricious treatment of employees by management create an ideal organizing climate for union organizers.

Knowledge of contract negotiations and administration, relevant labor legislation and public policy issues, and the strategy of labor unions is important to the personnel manager who desires to maintain harmonious labor relations. This book devotes a single chapter to labor unions, public policy, and union organizing drives

(Chapter 15). An additional chapter covers contract negotiations and administration (Chapter 16).

■ The Major Personnel/Human Resource Management Functions

Private and public sector organizations are vitally concerned with productivity and cost effectiveness in managing resources. As noted earlier, personnel/human resource management is concerned with the effective use of people in order to attain organizational goals and enhance the personal dignity, satisfaction, and well-being of employees. Personnel departments in most organizations act in a staff capacity by giving advice and performing services for supervisors and employees. In most organizations, the personnel or human resources department establishes policies and coordinates functions such as job analysis, personnel planning, recruitment and selection of employees, training and development, performance appraisal, compensation and employee benefits, labor relations, employee discipline and control, and occupational health and safety.[4]

Job Analysis and Design

Job analysis deals with the determination of specific tasks and responsibilities common to a job or class of jobs (job descriptions) as well as identifying the skills, knowledge, and abilities that the job should possess (job specifications). This

[4]The Bureau of National Affairs, Inc., summarizes the personnel/human resource management functions as follows: *Planning:* Human resource planning, personnel policy formulation, and organizational development. *Staffing:* Recruiting, interviewing, testing, selection, and orientation of new employees; performance appraisal, promotion, transfer, and separation of employees. *Training and Development:* On-the-job training, supervisory training, management appraisal and development, and career planning and educational programs. *Wage and Salary Administration:* nonmanagement and management pay policies, wage surveys, job evaluation, incentive and bonus plans, and executive compensation. *Employee Benefits:* Vacations, holidays, leaves of absence, insurance, retirement benefits, savings and stock plans, profit-sharing programs. *Employee Services:* Tuition aid and scholarship programs, counseling, recreational and social activities, housing and relocation assistance, and parking and eating facilities. *Communications:* Employee attitude surveys, in-house publications, suggestion systems, and community relations programs. *Work Environment:* Safety programs, health and medical services, physical working conditions, and plant security. *Union Relations:* Dealing with organizing efforts, collective bargaining and arbitration. *Personnel Research and Record Keeping:* Compiling facts and figures for personnel planning and compliance with government regulations. See The Bureau of National Affairs, Inc., *Personnel Management: Management Policy and Practice Series* (Washington, D.C.: 1990), Section 251. See also Janet R. Andrews, "Where Doubts About the Personnel Role Begin," *Personnel Journal* (June 1987), p. 84; Eric G. Flamholtz, Yvonne Randle, and Sonja Sackman, "Personnel Management: The Tone for Tomorrow," *Personnel Journal* (July 1987), p. 42, and Margaret Magnus, "Will Someone Please Tell Me Exactly What Personnel Executives Do?" *Personnel Journal* (January 1987), p. 40.

information is vital in the development and validation of selection devices such as application blanks, structured interviews, and tests designed to measure an applicant's ability to perform a job. Properly designed performance appraisal systems also depend on thorough job analyses. Job analysis information is also important in the design of equitable pay structures, training programs, and health and safety programs. Collecting job analysis information can be a time-consuming and arduous task. A number of job analysis methods are currently available.

Job design involves structuring the work so that it can be performed efficiently while providing the employee with a feeling of satisfaction or reward. Many jobs such as assembly line or clerical work can be quite monotonous because of their narrow scope and repetition. Jobs such as those performed by air traffic controllers are so complex and demanding that they create enormous stress and can cause burnout. Still other jobs such as those found in meatpacking and forestry pose physical hazards. Chapter 4 discusses job analysis and design.

Personnel/Human Resource Planning

Personnel planning involves placing the right person in the right job at the right time. Organizations often have fluctuating needs for employees. For example, a leading manufacturer of toys in the United States will employ between 17,000 and 20,000 employees during a calendar year because of the seasonal nature of their business. Other seasonal businesses such as farms, department stores, and resort hotels have peak and slack demands for employees, depending on the time of year. Nearly all organizations experience employee turnover due to resignations, retirements, and discharges. Most organizations have annual turnover rates of less than 5 percent, but occasionally turnover is much higher. Employees also move from one department or job to another by way of promotions and transfers. Firms add and delete product lines, expand some business units, and divest others, all of which means that employees may be transferred, be promoted, or suffer layoffs. At any one time, an organization may find that it has a shortage of employees with certain job skills and an excess of others. Unless organizations are able to project future staffing needs and make provisions to have on hand a sufficient number of employees whose knowledge, skills, and abilities can meet this demand, serious problems may arise.

The personnel planning process involves three essential steps: First, a supply and demand forecast for each job category is made. This step requires knowledge of both labor market conditions and the organization's strategic posture and goals. Second, net shortages and excesses of personnel by job category are projected for a specific time horizon. Finally, plans are developed to eliminate the forecast shortages and excesses. If a shortage of accountants is projected over the next year, then the firm can begin searching for accountants through professional placement firms or recruitment on college campuses. Suppose that a manufacturer of expensive jewelry is opening a new production facility next year and will need diamond-cutting experts to staff the operation. Because of the specialized nature of this business, it may not be possible to find diamond cutters whose technical background and experience are suitable. Therefore, the manufacturer may decide to train and promote current employees to fill these positions.

The careful use of a systematic personnel planning program enables the personnel department to forecast needs, plan for employee succession, staff critical areas, and allow the organization to meet its goals without unnecessary disruptions caused by shortages of personnel. Personnel planning can be facilitated by computer-assisted human resource management information systems and models. Chapter 5 addresses major personnel planning issues and methods for predicting and balancing personnel supply and demand.

Recruitment and Selection of Employees

Recruitment involves assembling a pool of applicants from which employees may be selected. Public and private employment agencies, union hiring halls, advertisements in newspapers and professional journals, and colleges and universities are among the sources from which organizations draw applicants. Selection deals with screening, testing, and hiring the best-qualified applicants from the recruitment pool. Organizations use devices such as weighted application blanks, honesty and polygraph tests, ability and interest tests, reference checks, medical examinations, and other selection predictors to determine which applicants are most likely to perform well if hired. Furthermore, the selection process is complicated by trends such as the increasing number of dual-career couples, as well as the complexities of evaluating and hiring employees for assignments in foreign countries.

The validation of selection instruments entails the use of statistical techniques as well as the knowledge of EEO laws. Incorrect hiring or staffing decisions can be very costly to both the organization and the employee. Selection of an employee who later proves to be unsatisfactory can cost an organization thousands of dollars in recruitment, training, legal, and other fees. Chapter 6 covers employee recruitment and Chapter 7 deals with employee selection.

Employee Training and Development

Training and development programs are designed to improve the knowledge, skills, and abilities of employees. Most personnel/human resource management departments devote a great deal of effort to such programs. Organizations may view workers as an investment in human capital, and in order to achieve an adequate "return" on this investment, corporations must be certain that employees are competent and possess up-to-date job knowledge, skills, and abilities. Some employees already possess the requisite skills when they are hired. However, many employees require periodic training and development to prevent their skills from deteriorating or becoming obsolete. Training and development programs include skill training designed to improve employee efficiency on the job, management development programs whose major purpose is to enhance the decision-making abilities of managers, and career development programs.

Chapter 8 covers employee training and development. Among the topics covered are identifying training and development needs, deciding which training methods work best for particular situations, and evaluating the impact of a training program on employee performance. Many private and public sector organizations spend large sums of money on employee training and development. Unfortunately, many programs fail to achieve the desired results because they are improperly planned, designed, and administered.

Performance Appraisal Systems

Performance appraisal systems involve the quantitative and qualitative measurement of employee performance. Ideally, a performance appraisal system should account for every task, duty, and responsibility of an employee's job, as well as the knowledge, skills, and abilities needed to perform satisfactorily—nothing more and nothing less. This means that performance appraisal systems should eliminate irrelevant factors that may bias the evaluation of an employee's performance. Factors such as personal lifestyles, political beliefs, race, sex, age, religion, and other factors outside the scope of the job should not be reflected in performance appraisals. Nearly all personnel managers would agree that such factors should not be considered, and yet these and other irrelevant concerns do contaminate the performance appraisal process.

Performance appraisal results have a number of important effects on recruitment, selection, training, and compensation. As a consequence, it is important that performance appraisal systems be based on job-relevant criteria, objectively measured, and protected from undue subjectivity and bias. A number of performance appraisal methods are used in private and public sector organizations, each with advantages and disadvantages. Further, performance appraisal is a personnel function that is shared by the personnel department and line supervisors. Although the design of the appraisal system may be the responsibility of the personnel department, it is generally the immediate supervisor who is responsible for the actual appraisal. Supervisors must be trained to administer performance appraisals properly and to understand their importance to both the organization and to the employee. Chapter 9 covers performance appraisal techniques and issues.

Compensation Management

Compensation management is an important and occasionally difficult responsibility for personnel/human resource managers. Because behavioral, organizational, legal, and technical factors all have an impact on compensation systems, pay-related issues are often complex and emotionally charged. An employee's pay not only determines his or her standard of living but is also an indication of his or her personal success and value to society. Therefore, it is important to understand the impact that pay can have on employee motivation and job satisfaction.

Several methods are used to place monetary values on jobs. These methods attempt to create fair, market-competitive rates of pay that will attract, retain, and motivate high-quality employees. The compensation specialist must make a number of important decisions and deal with a number of interesting issues. For example, why does a hospital personnel director decide to pay a nurse working in the intensive care unit 10 percent more than a nurse working in pediatrics? How should superior performance and seniority be reflected in an employee's pay? Should pay be based primarily on productivity, work quality, attendance, conduct, and safety? Do employees deserve compensation for skills they possess that are not immediately useful for the job held? Under what conditions do bonus plans and stock options work best? These and other issues must be addressed by personnel managers who are in charge of compensation programs. Chapters 10 and 11 deal with the theoretical and applied aspects of compensation management.

Employee benefits (also called *fringe benefits*) now comprise a significant percentage of the total compensation expenditures in U.S. firms. Some benefits such as Social Security, unemployment compensation, and worker's compensation are mandated by federal or state law, whereas others are provided by employers and unions. Most employee benefits provide an employee with economic security against risks such as premature death, disability, catastrophic illness, and loss of income through unemployment or disability. Group life, medical, disability, and pension programs are provided by most organizations, and they supplement the benefits provided by Social Security. The administration of the organization's employee benefit programs is generally the responsibility of the personnel/human resource management department. Issues such as what benefits should be provided to employees, the income tax ramifications of employee benefits, and the costs of such programs are important concerns to those responsible for employee benefits. These and other issues are addressed in Chapter 12.

Employee Discipline and Control

A difficult and sensitive personnel/human resource management issue involves dealing with inefficient, incompetent, and troublesome employees. Examples of undesirable employee behaviors include coming to work under the influence of alcohol or drugs, theft, fighting, insubordination, and work rule violations. Personnel managers must understand the importance of due process when dealing with employee disciplinary actions and must have the ability to counsel problem employees. The issue of equitable organizational sanctions for problem employees has received considerable attention because of federal and state EEO laws. Recently, the right of an employer to fire employees for questionable reasons has generated considerable controversy. For decades, the common law doctrine of employment at will has given employers the right to discharge workers for good cause, bad cause, or no cause at all. The employment at-will doctrine is coming under increasing attack in many states, especially for discharges that are contrary to the public interest. Chapter 13 deals with employee and organizational rights. Among the topics discussed are the latest legal issues, progressive discipline systems, and the handling of unusual disciplinary cases.

Occupational Safety, Health, and Well-Being

Employee health, safety, and well-being have become increasingly important concerns. The enactment of the Occupational Safety and Health Act of 1970 (commonly called *OSHA*), the recent prominence of AIDS-related news, the increased incidence of chemical substance abuse, and workplace drug testing controversies are all testimony to this issue. Thus, safety and health issues are not limited to physical injuries that occur on the job. Many employers are attempting, through employee assistance programs, to address a variety of employee health problems such as drug and alcohol abuse and the cumulative effects of exposure to toxic substances and psychological stressors. Additionally, employers are devoting resources to employee wellness programs, thereby encouraging healthy lifestyles. Chapter 14 deals with employee health, safety, and well-being and focuses on traditional concerns as well as some recently emerging issues.

Labor-Management Relations and Collective Bargaining

Labor relations and collective bargaining are primarily concerned with union-management relations. Labor unions represent employees with regard to wages, hours, and working conditions. In essence, a union acts as an agent on behalf of a group of employees who have designated the union as their exclusive bargaining representative. Approximately one fifth of all nonagricultural employees in the United States belong to unions. Personnel/human resource managers are concerned about unions for several reasons. Unionized (or partially unionized) employers must negotiate in good faith with the bargaining representative (union) chosen by employees. The product of union-management negotiations, the collective bargaining agreement, establishes pay scales, hours, seniority provisions, and other working conditions of employees. Once the collective bargaining agreement has been negotiated with the union, personnel managers and supervisors must deal with union representatives almost daily in administering the agreement. Finally, personnel managers in nonunionized firms are usually alert to threats posed by union organizers; they must understand how organizers attempt to unionize a workforce and be cognizant of the legal issues associated with union organizing campaigns.

Personnel managers should have a basic understanding of the American labor movement and the goals, structure, and strategies of unions. In addition, a knowledge of labor relations law is necessary in order to deal better with union organizing campaigns, contract negotiations and administration, and work stoppages. Chapters 15 and 16 discuss union-management relations. Included in the discussion are labor history, labor law, union organizing campaigns, contract negotiations, and administration of the collective bargaining agreement.

■ Major Personnel/Human Resource Management Objectives and Priorities

The personnel/human resource management function is accorded departmental status in most organizations. Like other departments, the personnel department is responsible for achieving specific objectives or outcomes. The personnel/human resource management department can be evaluated on the extent to which it measures up on certain criteria that contribute to the efficient attainment of broad organizational strategies and goals. Production departments, for example, are evaluated on the quantity, quality, and timeliness of their product. Sales and marketing departments are evaluated on the basis of meeting sales goals, and financial and accounting personnel are judged on the basis of controlling costs, staying within budgets, and minimizing tax liabilities. Personnel/human resource managers are judged on the basis of such measures as rates of employee absenteeism and turnover (employee losses through resignations and firings), compliance with personnel-related legislation, on-the-job accident rates, disciplinary incidents and employee grievances, quality of union-management relations, and level of employee job satisfaction. The personnel department has a direct impact on these outcomes. But other factors, such as the quality of employee supervision, the strategy and resources of the organization and the political climate within the organization, also play an important role.

The bottom-line measure of the personnel department's effectiveness is the degree to which it enables an organization to attain its overall goals. Organizational outcomes such as the fulfillment of a firm's strategic choice, cost effectiveness, growth and survival, and social responsibility are all facilitated or hindered by the personnel/human resource management function.

Table 1–1 provides the results of a 1991 survey of 248 companies by the Bureau of National Affairs, Inc. Companies were asked to list their top three personnel/ human resource management priorities. The survey indicates that employee training and development, employee benefit programs, and the recruitment and

TABLE 1-1 Priorities of the Personnel/Human Resource Department

Percent of Respondents

(Number of respondents)	All Companies (248)	By Industry		Non-Business (70)	By Size		By Union Status	
		Manufacturing (106)	Non-Manufacturing (72)		Large (51)	Small (197)	Union (83)	Nonunion (165)
Training and development	40%	37%	49%	37%	39%	41%	37%	42%
Employee benefits	37	35	38	39	37	37	36	37
Recruiting, selection, and placement	36	25	35	56	49	33	35	37
Compensation administration	30	25	31	37	35	28	19	35
Employee/labor relations	26	34	19	20	37	23	55	11
Human Resources Information Systems (HRIS)	17	14	18	21	25	15	19	16
Safety and Health	17	25	13	10	8	19	20	15
Productivity improvement	16	20	15	11	20	15	13	18
Personnel/HR department's role in the organization's strategic plan	16	16	19	13	14	17	12	18
Employee communications	16	19	14	13	10	17	10	19
Restructuring/reorganization	13	16	13	7	8	14	13	12
Human resource planning	9	10	8	7	8	9	6	10
Employee services	4	4	1	6	2	4	2	4
Other	8	10	4	7	8	8	7	8

BNA Publications (Washington, D.C.: The Bureau of National Affairs, Inc., 1991). Reprinted with permission.

selection of employees are the highest priorities of most personnel departments, followed closely by compensation administration and employee-labor relations. Nonmanufacturing firms tended to place the most emphasis on the three primary personnel/human resource management functions, whereas nonmanufacturing and nonbusiness organizations focused more heavily on compensation and labor relations issues. Not surprisingly, unionized companies gave their highest priority to employee-labor relations.

■ The Rising Prominence of the Personnel/Human Resource Management Profession

Until the mid-1960s, many personnel executives were selected for their ability to get along with people. Personnel managers were often assigned to the "people functions" in an organization because they did not have the talent to work in operations, finance, marketing, or other important areas. Companies often staffed the personnel department with managers who did not have professional training or a college education. Primarily because of the factors discussed earlier in this chapter, the personnel/human resource management function now occupies a much more prominent position in most organizations than it did 20 years ago. College business and education schools now offer a variety of personnel management courses, and there is a proliferation of specialized management seminars on a wide variety of personnel topics offered by universities and management consultants.

The personnel/human resource management profession offers two basic career paths. One career path is that of the personnel generalist who works as a plant, division, or corporate personnel manager. Often these individuals enter the field after working in another area of the organization and acquiring a thorough understanding of the corporate objectives, strategy, and culture. The generalist often acquires knowledge of the personnel/human resource management function through experience, executive development programs, and university courses. An alternative career path is that of the personnel specialist who becomes an expert in a personnel area such as labor relations, compensation management, employee benefits, EEO law, or training and development. Personnel specialists often hold advanced graduate or law degrees or have obtained specialized undergraduate education. Many personnel specialists work at corporate or division headquarters where they formulate policies in their respective areas for use by personnel generalists at the plant or division level.

The primary professional association for personnel managers is the Society for Human Resource Management (SHRM). SHRM offers a number of training and development programs for personnel executives and managers, professional accreditation programs, student SHRM chapters in colleges and universities, and a series of publications with news of recent developments in personnel management. Other professional associations for personnel generalists and specialists include the American Compensation Association, the American Society for Training and Development, the American Management Association, the American Psychological Association, the International Foundation of Employee Benefit Plans, and the Board of Certified Safety Professionals. Professional organizations such as these typically offer training programs, publications, and other services to their members. Personnel professionals with an interest in research issues can join the Academy of Management or the Industrial Relations Research Association.

A survey conducted by SHRM and William M. Mercer, Inc., reveals that top personnel executives earn an average total compensation of more than $130,000 (base salary plus bonus). Middle-level personnel managers have an annual income between $49,000 and $63,900. These salaries vary considerably, depending on the organization and its geographic location. Personnel specialists' income also varies, with compensation managers having the highest pay. One survey revealed that labor relations supervisors receive an average income of $93,384, EEO managers $56,800, and branch personnel managers $55,300. However, the salaries of top personnel executives still lag behind those of their counterparts in the financial, legal, and marketing areas of the corporation.[5]

Personnel administrators come from a wide variety of educational backgrounds. College schools of business and industrial and labor relations offer a wide variety of courses, ranging from introductory personnel management to advanced courses in compensation management, labor arbitration, and the legal aspects of personnel. Many of the larger state and private universities offer undergraduate majors or specializations in personnel/human resource management, as well as in labor-management relations. Students attending colleges without extensive course offerings in personnel should consider elective courses in accounting, economics, computer science, industrial and organizational psychology, and sociology. Any course or field of study that will sharpen individual communications skills is also valuable when applying for entry-level personnel positions.[6]

---

[5]The Bureau of National Affairs, Inc., "Salaries, Costs, and Personnel Ratios," *Personnel Management: BNA Policy and Practice Series* (The Bureau of National Affairs, Inc., 1990), Section 251, and The Bureau of National Affairs, Inc., "Pay Policies," *Bulletin to Management* (January 23, 1992), p. 23.

[6]See David Lewin, "The Education and Training of Human Resource Management/Personnel Specialists," in *The Changing Human Resources Function*, Report No. 950 (New York: The Conference Board, 1991), p. 29; "Entry Level Requirements for HR Professionals," *Personnel Journal* (June 1987), p. 124; Thomas J. Bergmann and M. John Close, "Preparing for an Entry Level Position in Personnel," *S. A. M. Advanced Management Journal* (Summer 1980) p. 62, Michael B. Arthur, Lotte Bailyn, Daniel J. Levinson, and Herbert A. Shepard, *Working with Careers* (New York: Columbia University Career Development Publication, 1985); William J. Traynor, *Opportunities in Personnel Management*, 2nd ed. (Lincolnwood, Illinois: VGM Career Horizons, 1983); Tom Jackson and Alan Vitberg, "Career Development Part I: Careers and Entrepreneurship," *Personnel* (February 1987), pp. 12–17.

■ The Personnel/Human Resource Management Department

As previously discussed, personnel/human resource management is normally regarded as a staff function whose role is to serve the organization and help it accomplish its objectives. However, no two personnel/human resource management programs have exactly the same roles and responsibilities. Depending on the size and location of the company, the composition of the workforce, the type of industry, the presence of unions, and the value that top management places on personnel, a typical personnel/human resource management department may be responsible for 25 to 50 functions. For some functions, the personnel department may have full responsibility, whereas in other companies the personnel functions may be shared by other departments and supervisors. For example, some personnel departments take sole responsibility for employee recruitment; in other organizations this function is shared with department heads. In many colleges and universities, the personnel department is responsible for ensuring that the individual academic departments conform to accepted personnel policies regarding recruiting and selecting new faculty members, although the academic departments themselves do the actual recruiting and selecting. Some companies limit the personnel management department's influence to advising managers on matters concerning employees. Others allow personnel to formulate policies and make decisions that have far-reaching effects on the organization.

Figure 1-1 illustrates the organizational structure of the personnel/human resource management function in a large corporation. The chief personnel executive is often a corporate vice-president who is in charge of a group of staff specialists or experts. The vice president of personnel/human resources and his or her staff formulate the organization's personnel policies, engage in research, and keep personnel managers at the plant and division levels apprised of developments that affect their operations. In some organizations, employee benefit programs such as the retirement system may be administered at the corporate level. At the division or plant level, personnel managers and staff provide advice to supervisors on matters such as hiring, training, and discipline. They also perform services such as record keeping, pay administration, grievance handling, and service awards. In addition, they monitor supervisors and employees to ensure compliance with health and safety, wage and hour, and EEO laws.

The importance of the personnel department can also be assessed by the resources devoted to it by top management. In 1990, an estimated $730 per employee was spent on the personnel/human resource function. This amounts to 2.3 percent of the company payroll, or an average of $610,000 annually per organization. As might be expected, these figures vary substantially from one organization to another. In the manufacturing sector there were 1.1 personnel staff members for every 100 employees, whereas the nonmanufacturing sector employed 1.2

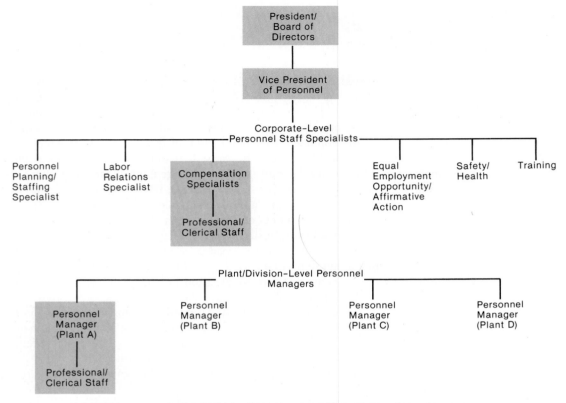

FIGURE 1-1   Personnel/Human Resource Management in a Large Organization

personnel staff members per 100 employees. Both the cost and the staffing ratios tend to decline as the organization becomes larger.[7]

■ The Plan of the Book

This book examines traditional personnel practices and issues, along with topics that are receiving considerable attention by top management, corporate personnel directors, personnel practitioners at the plant and division levels, labor lawyers,

[7]The Bureau of National Affairs, Inc., "The Personnel Department: Salaries, Costs, and Personnel Ratios," *Personnel Management: BNA Policy and Practice Series* (Washington, D.C.: The Bureau of National Affairs, Inc., 1990), Section 251.

academicians, and union officials. Personnel/human resource management is a field filled with change, excitement, challenges, and headaches. Both authors come into frequent contact with practicing personnel professionals, and we have learned a great deal from them. Rarely do these men and women fail to share with us a problem or experience that has been bothering them. Many of them find that there are not enough hours in the workday to finish all the work that comes their way or address all the problems that they encounter.

There is more to personnel management than the practitioners' side, however. Researchers and scholars from colleges, universities, and government agencies such as the U.S. Department of Labor contribute to the growing body of knowledge in the personnel/human resource management field. Nearly all of the social science disciplines have contributed to the development of personnel/human resource management. Between 1900 and 1930, organizations focused on productivity and efficiency and paid scant attention to the well-being of employees. Under the influence of Fredrick W. Taylor and the scientific management school of thought, the worker was viewed as an extension of the machine. Later developments such as the Hawthorne studies, the rise of labor unions, shortages of workers during World War II, the human relations movement, and the civil rights movement of the 1960s shifted the focus to the job satisfaction, motivation, dignity, and personal rights of the employee. Although psychologists, sociologists, and, more recently, legal scholars have contributed to personnel/human resource management, mathematicians and statisticians have been responsible for important developments in the field as well. Nevertheless, personnel management did not emerge as an academic discipline of note until the late 1950s or early 1960s. Since that time, however, the field has grown so rapidly that it is impossible for one person to be an expert in every facet of personnel/human resource management.

This book attempts to provide a balance between the practitioner side of personnel management and the academic side. The previously discussed personnel functions are separate, and yet they are also interrelated. Job analysis, for example, affects recruitment, selection, training, and compensation. Selection predictors cannot be validated without a well designed and properly administered performance appraisal program. The interrelationships among personnel functions are almost endless; we will attempt to illustrate those that are the most critical.

Figure 1-2 summarizes the relationship between the organization's goals, the objectives and functions of the personnel department, and the external environment. It also reflects the organization of this text, which is divided into five parts and roughly follows an employee through an organization from hiring through training, performance appraisal, and so on until he or she resigns, retires, or is terminated. The first part discusses some of the external influences on the personnel department. The second part is devoted to the objective of securing the best qualified employees. The third part concerns the objective of maximizing the

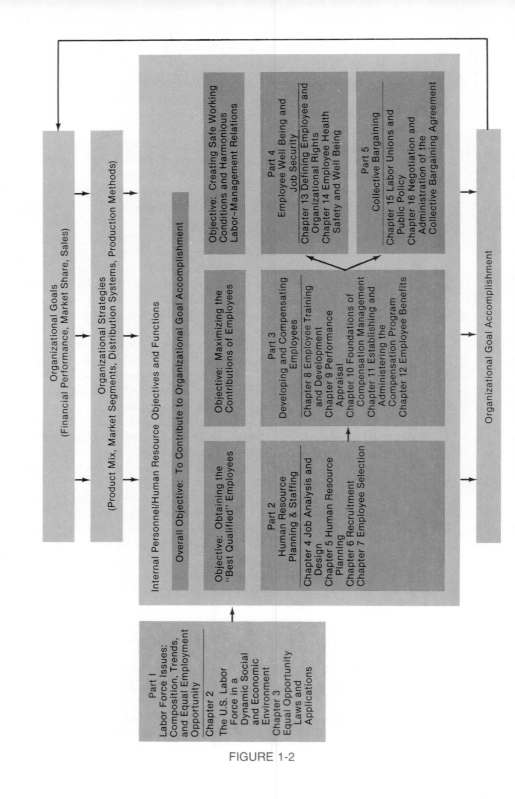

FIGURE 1-2

contributions of the employees, and the fourth and fifth parts deal with the creation of a safe working environment and harmonious working relationships.

■ Questions

1. Discuss four possible objectives of the personnel/human resource management function.

2. Discuss four issues that you believe will challenge personnel managers during the next decade.

3. Why should all employees have a basic understanding of personnel/human resource management?

4. Distinguish between an organization's mission, goals, objectives, and strategies. Why must personnel managers understand the organization's mission, goals, and strategies?

5. Briefly describe each of the following personnel/human resource management functions:

Job analysis and design
Personnel/human resource planning
Recruitment and selection
Training and development
Performance appraisal
Compensation management
Occupational safety, health, and well-being
Employee discipline and control
Labor-management relations

6. What are some of the major personnel/human resource management outcomes?

7. Why is personnel/human resource management regarded as a staff activity?

☐ APPLICATIONS AND CASE EXERCISES

1. A myth that has been perpetuated for years is that a primary qualification for a personnel manager is to like and get along with people. Do you feel that this is an important qualification for the job? What problems might arise if such a qualification were the overriding concern in hiring a personnel manager for a plant that manufactures expensive radios for automobiles? (Note: the plant employs 500 workers ranging from unskilled assembly employees to quality control specialists and electrical engineers.)

2. As any sports fan knows, collegiate sports has become a multi-million-dollar business on many campuses. Based on your knowledge of college football and your understanding of the major personnel functions, describe how a head coach is, in essence, a personnel manager.

3. Because of your knowledge of personnel/human resource management, you have been invited to give an after-dinner speech on the changes that will take place in organizations over the next 25 years. Your audience is especially interested in learning more about how people will be managed in the future and what major social, legal, and economic changes are expected. Prepare an outline of your speech. Use such magazines as *Personnel, Personnel Administrator, Forbes, Time,* and *Newsweek,* as well as newspapers such as *The Wall Street Journal,* to support your answer. (Remember that your audience will be sleepy after their heavy meal, so it is important to keep the length of your talk under 20 minutes.)

4. Find out more about the day-to-day operations of a personnel department by interviewing a local personnel manager. What types of activities occupy his or her time? To what extent are the personnel/human resource functions shared by line supervisors in the organization?

■ Professional Organizations and Information Sources

American Compensation Association
  14040 N. Northsight Blvd.
  Scottsdale, AZ 85260
Purpose: to promote communication with the compensation industry.

American Federation of Labor and Congress of Industrial Organizations (AFL-CIO)
  815 16th St., N.W.
  Washington, DC 20006
Purpose: America's largest federation of labor unions; seek to promote labor.

American Society for Industrial Security
  1655 North Fort Myer Dr. Suite 1200
  Arlington, VA 22209
Purpose: to promote industrial security.

American Society for Training and Development
  1630 Duke St.
  Alexandria, VA 22313
Purpose: membership organization for corporate, education and government trainers.

Association of Training and Employment Professionals
  100 Bidwell Rd.
  South Windsor, CT 06076
Purpose: to promote communication among government training and employment programs.

The Bureau of National Affairs, Inc.
  1231 25th St., N.W.
  Washington, DC 20037

Purpose: An excellent source for publications on all facets of personnel/human resource management.

Human Resource Planning Society
  P.O. Box 2553
  Grand Central Station
  New York, NY 10163
Purpose: to promote human resource planning activities.

International Association for Personnel Women
  5820 Wilshire Blvd.
  Los Angeles, CA 90036
Purpose: to promote professionalism of women in personnel.

International Foundation of Employee Benefit Plans
  P.O. Box 69
  Brookfield, WI 53008
Purpose: information source for employee benefits.

International Personnel Management Association
  1617 Duke St.
  Alexandria, VA 22314
Purpose: to promote better human resource/personnel practices in government.

JAI Press
  55 Old Post Road
  Greenwich, CT 06836
Purpose: research in personnel and human resources management.

Society for Human Resource Management
  606 N. Washington St.
  Alexandria, VA 22314
Purpose: to promote improved human
resource management research and practices.

U.S. Office of Personnel Management
  U.S. Government Printing Office
  Washington, DC 20402
Purpose: to provide personnel literature.

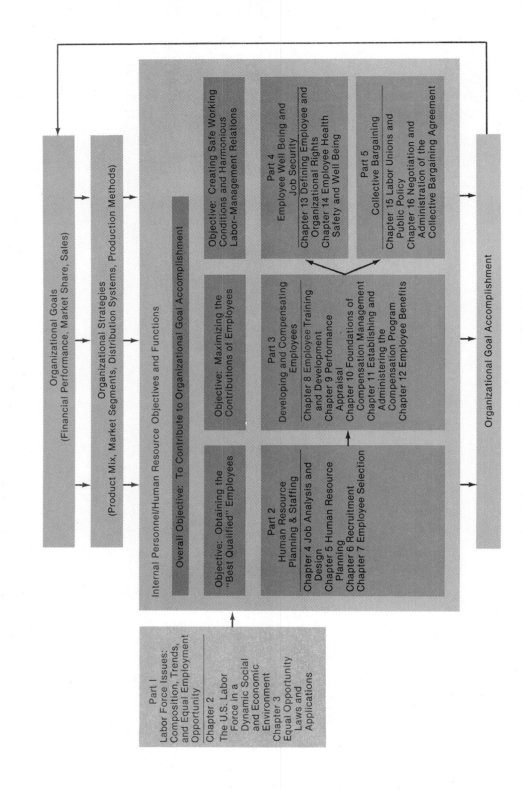

Organizational Goals
(Financial Performance, Market Share, Sales)

Organizational Strategies
(Product Mix, Market Segments, Distribution Systems, Production Methods)

Internal Personnel/Human Resource Objectives and Functions

Overall Objective: To Contribute to Organizational Goal Accomplishment

Objective: Obtaining the "Best Qualified" Employees

Part 2
Human Resource
Planning & Staffing

Chapter 4 Job Analysis and
Design
Chapter 5 Human Resource
Planning
Chapter 6 Recruitment
Chapter 7 Employee Selection

Objective: Maximizing the Contributions of Employees

Part 3
Developing and Compensating
Employees

Chapter 8 Employee Training
and Development
Chapter 9 Performance
Appraisal
Chapter 10 Foundations of
Compensation Management
Chapter 11 Establishing and
Administering the
Compensation Program
Chapter 12 Employee Benefits

Objective: Creating Safe Working
Conditions and Harmonious
Labor–Management Relations

Part 4
Employee Well Being and
Job Security

Chapter 13 Defining Employee and
Organizational Rights
Chapter 14 Employee Health
Safety and Well Being

Part 5
Collective Bargaining

Chapter 15 Labor Unions and
Public Policy
Chapter 16 Negotiation and
Administration of the
Collective Bargaining Agreement

Organizational Goal Accomplishment

Part I
Labor Force Issues:
Composition, Trends,
and Equal Employment
Opportunity

Chapter 2
The U.S. Labor
Force in a
Dynamic Social
and Economic
Environment
Chapter 3
Equal Opportunity
Laws and
Applications

PART ONE

LABOR FORCE ISSUES:
Composition, Trends, and Equal Employment Opportunity

■ Organizations recruit and select employees from a large and diverse labor force. The U.S. labor force consists of approximately 125 million workers who come from a variety of educational and cultural backgrounds. Nearly half of the U.S. workers are female. Workers range in age from 16 to 80 years and older. Some workers possess skills that are rudimentary, whereas others routinely perform extremely complex tasks such as open heart surgery or the monitoring of sophisticated nuclear facilities. From the standpoint of individual earnings, some members of the labor force are paid at the mandated minimum wage, whereas others command salaries in the millions of dollars.

The diversity of the U.S. labor force poses a challenge to personnel/human resource managers, who must recruit, select, train, and compensate employees in a variety of work settings. Chapter 2 provides an overview of the U.S. labor force and discusses the implications of labor force trends for the field of personnel/human resource management. Individual differences in employees, as well as job satisfaction and work performance, are also discussed. Because of the diversity of the U.S. labor force, special attention must be given to the fairness of personnel policies and decisions. Racial minorities and females have been plagued by societal and employer attitudes that have placed them at a disadvantage; they have often been relegated to less desirable jobs even when their skills and experience have warranted more favorable treatment. Chapter 3 focuses on EEO issues and the concept of employment discrimination. An overview of the laws that prohibit unfair discrimination based on race, sex, age, handicap status, and other protected classifications is provided. In addition, some of the major equal employment opportunity issues, such as fair hiring, affirmative action, sexual harassment, and other forms of discrimination, are addressed.

The topics and issues raised in both Chapter 2, The U.S. Labor Force in a Dynamic Social and Economic Environment, and Chapter 3, Equal Employment Opportunity Laws and Applications, have a pervasive impact on all personnel/human resource management functions. The reason these subjects are introduced early in the book is that they have relevance to later discussions of recruitment and selection, training and development, performance appraisal, compensation management, and employee discipline.

The U.S. Labor Force in a Dynamic Social and Economic Environment

■ LEARNING OBJECTIVES

After reading this chapter you should understand

1. The changing composition of the American labor force.
2. The domestic industries likely to experience growth or decline through the end of the century.
3. The importance of considering individual differences among employees when formulating and evaluating personnel policies.
4. The effect of the work environment on employee performance motivation.

■ INTRODUCTORY VIGNETTE

Inland Steel Industries' Commitment to Valuing Workforce Diversity

Inland Steel Industries (ISI) is committed to prepare itself for the workforce of the future. Predictions are that in the year 2000 the workforce will be smaller in number, and dominated by minority and female workers averaging about thirty-nine years of age. This is in striking contrast to the young white male who dominated the American workforce for so much of the twentieth century. ISI has recognized that it must attract and retain qualified minority and female workers in order to survive in the intensely competitive environment expected at the turn of the century. "We must not only recognize the significance of the changes in the work force, but implement specific programs to improve our performance regarding the identification, selection, placement, development, promotion and retention of minorities and females." (Frank Luerssen, Chairman Inland Steel Industries) This means recruitment and selection processes must be designed

This company profile has been drawn from Inland Steel Industries, "Valued for Diversity," *Inland/90*, Vol. 2, Bureau of National Affairs Inc., "One Company's Approach to Valuing Diversity," *Bulletin to Management* (April 29, 1991), p. 48, and Bureau of National Affairs, Inc., "High Potential Workers," *Bulletin to Management* (June 20, 1991), p. 71. See also Taylor H. Cox and Stacy Blake, "Managing Cultural Diversity: Implications for organizational Competitiveness," *Academy of Management Executive*, Vol. 5, No. 3 (1991), pp. 45–54, and Bureau of National Affairs, Inc., "Managing the Diverse Workforce," *Bulletin to Management* (November 22, 1990), p. 376.

to effectively locate, interest and place minorities and women. Training and development programs, compensation plans, performance appraisal and promotion policies must all be capable of unlocking the full potential of the new worker. To do this requires no less than a complete change of the existing corporate culture, a difficult task which should not be underestimated.

"We must and will remove any remaining barriers in the system that make it hard for women and minorities to succeed in their jobs. We have to get to the heart of the institution and create an environment that is not an advantage or a disadvantage to anyone," remarked Bill Lowery, director of personnel and recruiting for ISI, in a recent article in Inland/90, a publication for ISI employees and retirees. He believes that this can be accomplished by ensuring objectivity in all employee evaluations. All those who are responsible for evaluative decisions of all types must become aware of and sensitive to cultural differences in the workforce. ISI is committed to creating the type of racial awareness that can make a difference in the workplace. Management and supervision attend racial awareness workshops which are designed to create racial understanding. "The workshops are built around the belief that bigotry succeeds because white people allow it and black people are powerless to stop it."

ISI also realizes that behavioral change must follow awareness. Inland Steel Flat Products Company, an ISI subsidiary has formed a general focus group to discuss affirmative action in the company, as well as separate focus groups to discuss specific issues facing women and Hispanics. At their once a month meetings the groups discuss relevant issues and plan changes which will bring about an appreciation and valuing of diversity in the workplace. These groups have already created minority and women hiring plans, and have initiated recruiting efforts and a summer intern program.

Corporate affirmative action goals and initiatives are reviewed and implemented by corporate and business unit affirmative action committees. The responsibility for developing a program to fit the needs of its own unique environment rests with each business unit.

These business units are also conducting an inventory of minority and female employees designed to locate, develop career plans for, and encourage promotion of qualified minority workers. Those employees identified as working below expectations will receive special counseling and training. The career progression of women and minority workers will be monitored to ensure proper advancement and development. There have also been an intensification in the recruiting of minorities and women at colleges and universities, and an allocation of foundation funds in a manner consistent with the company's commitment to diversity.

Inland Steel Industries is one of many companies such as IBM, Eastman Kodak, AT&T, Prudential, Xerox, Motorola, USA Today, Hewlett-Packard, and Avon, which appreciate the changes which will be occurring in the composition of the labor force and are committed to ensuring that diversity becomes a competitive advantage for American business.

■ Introduction

American demographics are changing more rapidly than ever. The 1990 census clearly reflects the ethnic mosaic our population has become. There have been and continue to be changes in population characteristics and geographic distribution that will influence significantly the products, organization, and internal operations of American business. In the decade between 1980 and 1990, the Western and Southern states attracted approximately 90 percent of the increase in population, the Northeast became the least populous region of the United States, and our average age increased as the oldest baby boomers entered middle age. The baby bust is upon us, causing a significant decline in the number of younger Americans. The changing geographic distribution of our population has resulted in a shift of political power and influence, with states such as California and Texas gaining congressional representation at the expense of states with declining populations. Minority Americans, numbering between 61 and 62 million in 1990, are likely to wield significant economic, social, and political influence during the next decade. Currently, one in four Americans have African, Asian, Hispanic, or American Indian ancestry, up from one in five in 1980.

American institutions will increasingly experience culture shock as many minority participants bring an unprecedented level of cultural diversity to the social, political, and economic activities in which they engage. Both women and men are reassessing their commitments to family and work, forcing companies to attend to the lifestyles and nonwork responsibilities of their workers. We have discovered that the Pacific Rim countries of South Korea and Japan have become serious international competitors, making us painfully aware when there are shortcomings in the quality of our processes, products, management, and workforce. Western Europe has come together at a level of economic cooperation few would have though possible even a decade ago. We are now faced with a unified European economic force, creating both opportunities and obstacles to international competition. The Eastern European countries that formerly comprised a seemingly unified and politically threatening Communist bloc of countries have moved toward free enterprise and in many cases have abandoned state ownership in favor of private ownership of land and business. East and West Germany now form a unified Germany that promises to become a major economic power during the next decade. Finally, underscoring the incredible pace and scope of recent economic and political change, the Soviet Union no longer exists.

There have been and will continue to be major employment dislocations in the United States as automotive, computer, and retailing companies, to name a few, come to grips with the realities of rapid technological advances, intensified domestic and international competition, changing American demographics, and changing consumer tastes and demands. It is against this backdrop that we will discuss the American workforce in this chapter. We will profile expected changes in workforce demographics and productivity, as well as discuss the individual skills, personal values, and motivation of the American worker—all of which will shape policy at every level of government and industry throughout the 1990s.

The labor force in the United States is defined as all noninstitutionalized persons over the age of 16 who are either working or looking for work. Today the civilian labor force is composed of approximately 125.3 million individuals, who vary considerably with regard to their skill levels, age, race, type of job held, educational level, motivation to work, and income level.[1] Today personnel managers are challenged with recruiting, selecting, training, and motivating employees from among the widest variety of cultural, economic, and social backgrounds ever to participate in the American labor force. To complicate matters further, these employees also have very different interests, values, and attitudes toward work. To meet this challenge, personnel professionals require a knowledge of labor force composition, trends, and issues, in addition to an understanding of individual behavior in the workplace.

■ The Aggregate Labor Force

Consistent with the general population, the composition of the workforce is continuously changing. The various EEO laws that outlaw employment discrimination, to be discussed in Chapter 3, have provided increased opportunities for women, minorities, older individuals, and the disabled. These opportunities have served to draw more people into the labor force. Women, for example, with ever-improving career potential, have steadily increased their representation in the labor force. The lightening of physical demands, achieved in part through technological advances, has increased the attractiveness of employment for older and handicapped individuals. Further, there will be an inevitable graying of the post–World War II baby boomers by the year 2000, and thus of the workforce in general. This section profiles the changes in workforce composition that have been taking place during the 1970s, 1980s, and early 1990s. It also reviews predictions from the Bureau of Labor Statistics on the composition of the labor force in the year 2000.

In 1991, the civilian labor force in the United States was 125.3 million, representing approximately 66.2 percent of the total population.[2] Of that number, 93.2 percent, or 116.7 million people, were employed. Government statisticians estimate that the labor force will reach 141 million by the year 2000. This reflects a projected annual growth rate of 1.2 percent and represents a slowing of the annual growth rate from the 2.0 percent experienced during 1972–1988.[3] Labor force

---

[1]"Current Labor Statistics," *Monthly Labor Review* (May 1991), p. 63.

[2]"Current Labor Statistics," *Monthly Labor Review* (May 1991), p. 62.

[3]Howard N. Fullerton, Jr., "New Labor Force Projections, Spanning 1988 to 2000," *Monthly Labor Review* (November, 1988), p. 20.

composition classifications of traditional importance include age, sex, and race or ethnicity. Each of these classifications is discussed in turn.

Age Composition

In 1972, individuals between 16 and 24 years of age comprised 23 percent of the workforce. In 1986, this group represented 20 percent of the workforce, and it is estimated that by 2000 it will comprise only 16 percent (Fig. 2-1).[4] However, this projection masks a continuing decline through the mid-1990s and a significant increase during the latter part of the decade. In fact, by 1991 this age group had already dropped to 16 percent.[5] The principal labor group, workers from 25 to 54 years of age, is expected to continue to grow. This age group constituted 60 percent of the total labor force in 1972, and government statisticians anticipate that it will represent 72 percent of the labor force by 2000.[6] One key factor in the growth of this age group is the aging of the baby boomers during the 1980s and 1990s.

The percentage of those older than 55 years will decrease until 1995 and then increase to approximately the 1986 level by 2000. Major influences on their par-

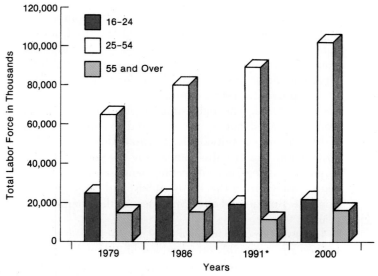

*1st Quarter 1991

FIGURE 2-1   Labor Force Composition: Age Classifications
Source: Bureau of Labor Statistics

[4]Howard N. Fullerton, Jr., p. 19. Also see Lynn R. Offermann and Marilyn K. Growing, "Organizations of the Future," *American Psychologist* (February 1990), pp. 95–108.

[5]Bureau of Labor Statistics, *Employment and Earnings* (May 1991), p. 10.

[6]Howard N. Fullerton, Jr., p. 22.

ticipation in the labor force include increased longevity, prevention of employment discrimination through age and handicap laws, and improvement of safety and health measures through enforcement of OSHA and worker's compensation laws. In addition, technological advances and medical discoveries have eased the physical demands of many jobs. All of the factors listed have contributed to an extension of the average working life by approximately 20 years since 1900.

Sex Composition

Women currently comprise 45 percent of the workforce, and by the year 2000 they will comprise 47 percent.[7] The recent figures (1979–1991), and projections to the year 2000 are shown in Figure 2-2. They reflect the rapid entry of women into the workforce since 1972. Figure 2-3 shows that since the mid-1970s, women have accounted for approximately two out of every three entrants into the labor market.[8] Although women remain concentrated in the traditional female occupations, such as teaching, nursing, and clerical work, they have begun to move into those occupations that were traditionally considered male. More women, including those with young children, have elected to enter the workforce and to remain at work for the same reasons men do: to satisfy personal needs and ambitions and

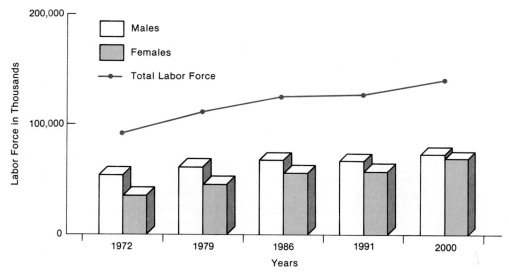

FIGURE 2-2   Labor Force Composition by Sex
Source: Bureau of Labor Statistics

[7]Howard N. Fullerton, Jr., p. 22.

[8]Bureau of National Affairs, "Labor Force Demographics Spur Employee Development," *Bulletin to Management* (July 23, 1987), p. 238.

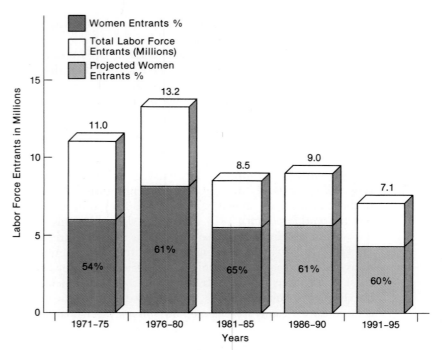

FIGURE 2-3   Women Labor Force Entrants
Source: Bureau of Labor Statistics

to meet financial needs. More and more women find permanent employment both desirable and essential. In addition, EEO laws and the availability of education, training, and child-care centers make entering the workforce an increasingly attractive alternative for women.

Women have increased their participation in education as well. Not long ago, the number of male students in college far exceeded the number of females. With very few exceptions, universities have become truly coeducational. Both male and female participation in higher education has risen sharply since World War II. Currently approximately one third of graduate business degrees and law degrees are earned by women.[9] Since most of those students are between 18 and 24 years of age, the number of young people seeking jobs right out of high school is reduced. Among other things, their delayed entry into the workforce means that more young people will qualify as managerial and professional employees, seeking white-collar rather than blue-collar jobs.

Although women have increased their participation in the labor force, they remain underrepresented in high-paying jobs. In 1990 only 2 percent of women earned more than $50,000 compared to 9 percent of men.[10] Lynn Martin, Secre-

[9]Bureau of Labor Statistics

[10]Mindy Fetterman, "Women Exec's Salaries Fall Short," *USA Today* (June 13, 1990), p. 1A.

tary of Labor in the Bush administration, criticized corporate America for the existence of a "glass ceiling" of subtle attitudes and prejudices that prevents the promotion of women and minorities. Although the glass ceiling is transparent, the results are not. The Department of Labor's study of nine randomly chosen Fortune 500 companies that prompted her remarks found that only 16.9 percent of management positions were held by women and only 6 percent were held by minorities. When top executive positions were reviewed, only 6.6 percent were found to be held by women and 2.6 percent by minorities.[11] Women continue to hold the types of jobs that pay less than male-dominated jobs in spite of the changing mores and laws. Overall, the average pay for men is considerably higher than the average pay for women.[12] Figure 2-4 shows data collected by the Bureau of Labor Statistics on the earnings gap during the years 1979–1991. When reviewing these figures, you should be aware that they represent an aggregation

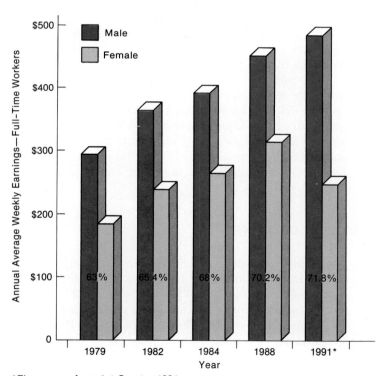

*Figures are from 1st Quarter 1991.

FIGURE 2-4   The Earning Gap, 1979–1984

Source: Bureau of Labor Statistics

[11]Susan B. Garland, "Throwing Stones at the Glass Ceiling," *Business Week* (August 19, 1991), p. 29; and Albert R. King, "Labor's Martin Is Out to Break 'Glass Ceiling'," *The Wall Street Journal* (August 9, 1991), p. B1.

[12]Bureau of Labor Statistics, *Employment and Earnings* (May 1991), p. 10.

across the standard age classifications (16–24, 25–54, and 55 and over) and across many different job types and levels. The earnings gap does appear to be narrowing, although one study indicated that women at the vice-presidential level and above earn 42 percent less than their male peers.[13] Further, according to the Bureau of Labor Statistics, at the beginning of 1991, male managers and professionals outearned women in similar positions by $220 per week. Males averaged approximately $730 per week, while women averaged $510. At this job level, women earned only 69.9 percent of what men earned.[14] The earnings gap is least pronounced for the younger age groups. Women in the 16–24 age group earned 90 percent of what men earned, whereas women 25 and older earned only 72 percent of what their male counterparts earned.[15] Two forces are contributing to a narrowing of the earnings gap. The first is the erosion of the historically limited access for women to high-paying jobs. The second is the gradual recognition that there is an inherent fairness to equal pay for equal work. Although the situation is improving, it should be remembered that sex discrimination was socially, religiously, and legally acceptable for centuries, and the shift to equal access and equal pay for equal work may require several generations' worth of effort to become a reality.

Some information of interest regarding the changing sex composition of the workforce is that according to the Bureau of Labor Statistics, the number of men aged 25–54 who have dropped out of the paid labor force to do housekeeping and/or care for children rose from 61,000 in 1975 to 257,000 in 1990.[16] While this increase is considerable and represents changing values, it is unlikely to be a major trend of consequence to the future sex composition of the workforce. These stay-at-home fathers represent only 2 percent of married parents with children under 18.

Racial or Ethnic Composition

The ethnic composition of the labor force has also been changing. High birth rates and increased immigration to the United States have boosted the number of Spanish-speaking individuals in the workforce. It is estimated that Hispanic workers will increase from 5 percent of the total labor force in 1979 to 10.2 percent by 2000.[17] According to the 1990 U.S. Census, the Hispanic population increased by approximately 7.7 million, or 56 percent, during the 1980s, while individuals of Asian ancestry increased by 107 percent during the same period. Black Americans

[13]Sharon Nelton and Karen Berney, "Women: The Second Wave," *Nation's Business* (May, 1987), p. 18.

[14]Bureau of Labor Statistics, *Employment and Earnings* (January 1991), p. 223.

[15]Bureau of Labor Statistics, *Employment and Earnings* (March 1991), p. 110.

[16]Associated Press, "More Dads Staying at Home with Kids," *The Greenville News* (June 16, 1991), p. 4E.

[17]Howard N. Fullerton, Jr., p. 23.

comprised 10.2 percent of the labor force in 1979 and are projected to constitute 12 percent by 2000.[18] The U.S. Department of Labor's *Workforce 2000* projects that from 1985 to 2000, the workforce will increase by approximately 26 million people. Less than 15 percent of this increase will consist of white males, who dominated the workforce only a decade ago.[19] Figure 2-5 provides insight into the projected demographic characteristics of labor force entrants from 1985 to 2000. Figure 2-6 shows the changes in the racial and ethnic composition of the labor force between 1979 and 1988, with projections to the year 2000.

It is clear from these projections that ethnic and cultural diversity in the workplace will continue to increase. This will call for workplace programs designed to build skills, knowledge, and awareness of cultural differences among employees. If workers are not willing to accommodate and learn from the many cultures that coexist in the American workplace, then misunderstandings and interpersonal

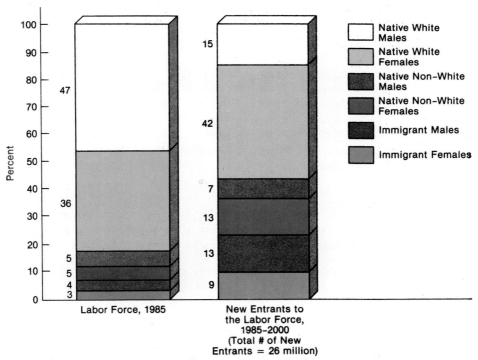

FIGURE 2-5   Distribution of New Entrants to the Labor Force
Source: Bureau of Labor Statistics

[18]Howard N. Fullerton, Jr., p. 23.

[19]The Bureau of National Affairs, Inc., "Charting a Course for Diversity: Society for Human Resource Management Annual Conference," *Bulletin to Management* (July 25, 1991), p. 3.

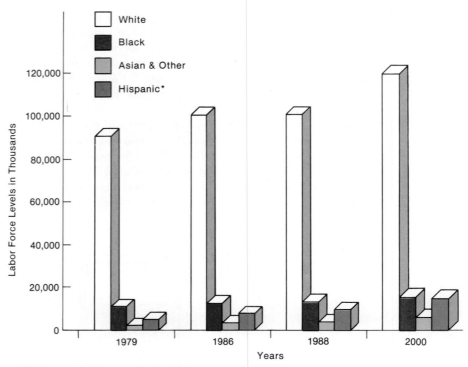

*Persons of Hispanic origin may be of any race.

FIGURE 2-6   Labor Force Composition by Race
Source: Bureau of Labor Statistics

conflict are more likely to occur. The full potential of each employee must be realized in order to increase and sustain high levels of productivity. That is unlikely to happen in an environment of discord, mistrust, and disharmony.

■ Occupational Outlook

Among the various important and interrelated factors that affect the labor market are aggregate private demand for goods and services (including changing consumer tastes), government activities (including fiscal and monetary policies), economic fluctuations (including stock and bond markets), demographic changes (including birth rates and immigration and emigration flows), foreign economic activity (competition, inflation, exports to and imports from the United States, foreign investments, and oil embargos), and technological change.

Technological innovations of significant magnitude have the power to either create or destroy industries. The declining railroad passenger business is an example of a technological casualty, whereas the reverse is true of the still-expanding genetics-related industries. Another aspect of technology is its effect on worker productivity. The introduction of more efficient machinery and methods of operation often results in greater demand and higher wages for workers and greater profitability for the employer. However, technological change may also create the potential for worker displacement when excessive labor costs and human inefficiencies pose barriers to productivity. One major technological influence on the creation and elimination of jobs may be the use of robots. "Robots will displace approximately 4% of the workforce by 1995, but will help create 45,000 jobs," according to a study by the University of Michigan and the Society of Manufacturing engineers. The study predicts that advances in robotics will lead to new jobs for 25,000 maintenance workers, 12,000 programmers, 4,500 supply firm employees, and 3,000 manufacturing jobs. Nearly 90 percent of the employees displaced by robots will remain with their companies, the study suggests, observing that most of these workers will receive lateral transfers to new jobs requiring similar skills. Ten percent will be promoted, 10 percent will be demoted, and only 6 percent will quit or be laid off. The study speculates that the single greatest effect of robotization will be the need for a better-educated workforce. It points out, for example, that the shift toward robotics will mean a scarcity of entry-level jobs requiring no training or experience.[20] Indications are, however, that with the exception of the automotive industry, American businesses have been slow to adopt the use of robots. According to a recent estimate by the Robotic Industries Association, Japan has 176,000 industrial robots to the United States' 37,000.[21] If this trend continues, it will take a number of years before worker displacements dues to robots will approach the University of Michigan estimates.

In mid-1987, the Commerce Department identified seven emerging technologies that will most likely have the greatest economic impact in the next century: plastics, metals and ceramics development, computer development, optical fibers and lightwave processing electronics, genetic engineering, automation, medical advances, and development of ultrathin layers of chemicals.[22] Another technology that may prove to have a significant impact is micromachines. This technology has led to laboratory prototypes of turbines and working gears that are 125 microns in diameter, with gear teeth only 15 microns wide (less than one fifth of the thickness of a human hair). The machine components are created by etching patterns on silicon chips. Developers envision products that include microrobots and machines small enough to enter the human bloodstream for medical treatment.[23]

[20]The Bureau of National Affairs, Inc., "Robots Create and Eliminate Jobs," *Bulletin to Management* (September 5, 1985), pp. 73–74.

[21]Associated Press, "U.S. Being Left Behind in Robot Manufacturing," *Greenville News* (August 5, 1991), p. C1.

[22]"Business Report," *The Greenville News* (June 10, 1987).

[23]William D. Marbach, "A Small World Grows Tinier," *Newsweek* (November 30, 1987), p. 65.

Newly created occupations and industries will provide a different mixture of jobs than before. With the exception of service workers, there will be a shift away from low-skill to high-skill jobs. It is estimated that highly trained workers, who comprised 25 percent of the labor force in 1986, will be needed for almost 40 percent of new job growth between 1986 and 2000.[24] This means that with the exception of service-producing industries (in which a 27 percent increase is forecast by 2000),[25] the future appears to promise the creation of fewer blue-collar jobs.

Table 2-1 shows the fastest-growing and most rapidly declining industries in terms of output and employment opportunities between 1986 and 2000.[26] The changes reflected in Table 2-1 will assuredly affect the composition of available jobs to the end of the century.

TABLE 2-1   Fastest-Growing and Most Rapidly Declining Industries: Output and Employment

Fastest Growing Industries: Output	Most Rapidly Declining Industries: Output
Electronic computing equipment	New farm housing
Arrangement of passenger transportation	Crude petroleum, natural gas
Semiconductors and related devices	Footwear except rubber and plastic
Miscellaneous electronic components	New nonfarm housing
Amusement and recreation services	Railroad equipment
X-ray and other electromedical apparatus	Luggage, handbags, and leather products
Fastest-Growing Industries: Employment	**Most Rapidly Declining Industries: Employment**
Computer and data processing services	Railroad transportation
Outpatient facilities and health services	Footwear except rubber and plastic
Personnel supply services	Metal mining
Offices of health practitioners	Luggage, handbags, and leather products
Credit reporting and business services	Blast furnaces and basic steel products
Legal services	Iron and steel foundries

Bureau of Labor Statistics.

[24]Highly trained workers are those in the following categories: executive, administrative, and managerial workers; professional workers; and technicians and related support workers. See George T. Silvestri and John M. Lukasiewicz, "A Look at Occupational Employment Trends to the Year 2000," *Monthly Labor Review* (September 1987), pp. 46–47.

[25]Valerie A. Personick, "Industry Output and Employment Through the End of the Century," *Monthly Labor Review* (September 1987), p. 32.

[26]Valerie A. Personick, "Industry Output and Employment Through the End of the Century," *Monthly Labor Review* (September 1987), pp. 34, 35.

TABLE 2-2   Fastest-Growing and Most Rapidly Declining Occupations, 1988–2000 (Numbers in Thousands)

Fastest-Growing Occupations	Employment Level		Percent Increase
	1988	2000*	
Paralegals	83	145	75.3
Medical assistants	149	253	70.0
Home health aides	236	391	67.9
Radiologic technologist and technicians	132	218	66.0
Data processing equipment repairers	71	115	61.2
Medical records technicians	47	75	59.2
Medical secretaries	207	327	58.0
Physical therapists	68	107	57.0

Most Rapidly Declining Occupations	Employment Level		Percent Decline
	1988	2000*	
Electrical and electric equipment assemblers	237	134	−43.5
Broadcast technicians	27	19	−29.6
Gas and petroleum plant and system operators	30	22	−26.6
Farmers	1,141	875	−23.3
Stenographers	159	122	−23.3
Railroad brake, signal, and switch operators	37	29	−22.0

* Projected
Bureau of Labor Statistics.

Table 2-2 provides a look at the fastest-growing and most rapidly declining occupations between 1988 and 2000. Notice the rapid predicted growth of employment in occupations requiring specialized training, and in legal and medical services. In all, the Bureau of Labor Statistics predicts that 20 occupations will experience employment growth in excess of 49 percent of the current level by the year 2000, while 20 will decline by at least 17 percent during the same time.[27]

Although these figures are interesting and important, the occupations that are predicted to grow most rapidly are not necessarily those that will experience the greatest increase in the number of available jobs. Table 2-3 shows those occupations that will account for the greatest increases in actual job growth. Note that service-related occupations will contribute the bulk of new jobs through the 1990s.[28]

[27]George T. Silvestri, and John M. Lukasiewicz, "A Look at Occupational Employment Trends to the Year 2000," *Monthly Labor Review* (September 1987), pp. 48, 61.

[28]Robert E. Kutscher, "The Major Trends," *Occupational Outlook Quarterly,* (Spring 1990), p. 7.

TABLE 2-3   Occupations with the Largest Job Growth, 1988–2000 (Numbers in Thousands)

Occupation	Employment Level		Percent Increase (1988–2000)	Number
	1988	2000*		
Salespersons, retail	3,834	4,564	19.0	730
Registered nurses	1,577	2,190	38.8	613
Janitors and cleaners, including maids and housekeeping cleaners	2,895	3,450	19.2	556
Waiters and waitresses	1,786	2,337	30.9	551
General managers and top executives	3,030	3,509	5.8	479
General office clerks	2,519	2,974	18.1	455
Secretaries, except legal and medical	2,903	3,288	13.2	385
Nursing aides, orderlies, and attendants	1,184	1,562	31.9	378
Truck drivers	2,399	2,768	15.4	369
Receptionists and information clerks	833	1,164	39.8	331
Cashiers	2,310	2,614	13.2	304

*Projected.
Bureau of Labor Statistics.

■ Additional Labor Force Issues

Dual-Career Families

The increase in the number of women joining the workforce has translated directly into a rapid and significant decline in the percentage of traditional one-income families. Figure 2-7 shows the changing labor force patterns of families from 1940 to 1988. In 1940 dual-career couples represented only 9 percent of all families, compared to 41 percent of all families by 1988.[29] By 1990 both spouses worked in 57 percent of married family households.[30] That same year, the median weekly earnings for all married couples was $653, in contrast to $880 for married couples where both spouses worked.[31] Although many married women have joined the workforce because supporting a family on a single salary is becoming increasingly

[29]The Bureau of National Affairs, Inc., "Family Workforce Participation," *Bulletin to Management* (April 26, 1990), p. 132.
[30]Married family households with at least one wage earner.
[31]Bureau of Labor Statistics, *Employment and Earnings* (January 1991), p. 219.

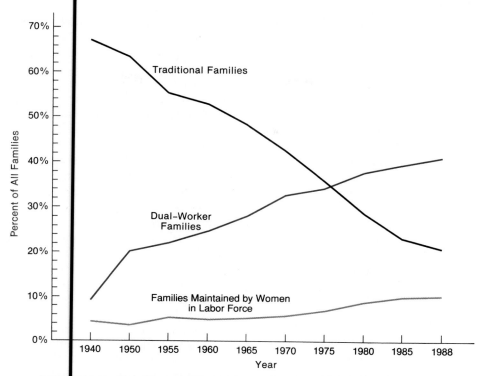

FIGURE 2-7   The Changing Labor Force Patterns of Families, 1940–1988
Source: Adapted from the Bureau of National Affairs, Inc., "Family Workforce Participation,"
Bulletin to Management (April 26, 1990), p. 132.

difficult, statistics do show that a disproportionate percentage of homes and other consumer goods are purchased by these couples.

The participation of mothers with young children in the workforce has pressured employers to become sensitive to a range of issues not previously considered important. For example, more employers are providing day-care and elder-care facilities for their employees. The duplication of benefits when both spouses are qualified to receive benefits from their respective employers has made cafeteria benefit plans an important retention and recruitment issue. Employees with spouses who work are often reluctant to accept transfers without some concession to their spouse's career. This has led to an expansion of the relocation services provided by employers to include career counseling and job placement for spouses. Parental leave for the birth, adoption, or serious illness of a child has become an important concern for many dual-career couples. By 1990, over twenty states had some form of parental leave legislation.[32] More employers are experi-

[32]Cathy Trost, "Survey Fortifies Parental-Leave Backers," *The Wall Street Journal* (August 9, 1990), p. B1.

menting with flexible working hours and part-time employment, in part to accommodate working couples. Some employers are allowing employees to work in
their own homes, using personal computers and fax machines, going to the office
perhaps one day a week. US Sprint has a "FamilyCare" program for its 16,000
employees. This program, developed from employee recommendations, contains
provisions for guaranteeing the loss of a working partner's salary up to $4,000 due
to a Sprint relocation, work schedule flexibility, financial assistance for adoption of
up to $1,000, and child- and elder-care resources and referral.[33]

Other issues are also associated with the increased number of dual-career
couples. Children who come home to empty houses because both parents work
("latchkey" children) are being studied to determine whether they are suffering
psychologically from this time without parental contact and supervision. The
convenience food industry has found business booming because working wives
have less time to prepare meals for their families. The social relationships and
roles within the family have changed as husbands and wives have assumed
responsibilities formerly handled by their spouses. This transition has been
difficult for many couples, increasing the stress and strain on both husbands
and wives.

There are recent indications that the interest of women in joining and remaining in the workforce may have leveled off. More women are delaying entry or are
dropping out of the workforce to have children. Economists and demographers are
studying these recent statistics in order to determine whether a meaningful trend
is developing and if workforce projections need to be amended. If there is a trend,
it could have a significant economic impact by the year 2000. The labor shortage
already predicted for the turn of the century could be made much worse if large
numbers of women decide to stay home.[34]

Labor Force Quality

"What's 45 cents take away 9?" "I don't know, I don't have a calculator."
Two cashiers overheard at a Family Dollar store

New technology, stiff international competition, changes in consumer tastes,
and demographic shifts will cause perverse mismatches between workplace
needs and workforce capabilities. The next 10–15 years threaten that growing
numbers of our working age youth and adults will lack the education and skills
to obtain even their first entry-level job.[35]
William H. Kolberg, President, National Alliance of Business

---

[33]The Bureau of National Affairs, Inc., "FamilyCare at US Sprint," *Bulletin to Management* (October 5,
1989), p. 320.
[34]"Do More Babies Mean Fewer Working Women?," *Business Week* (August 5, 1991), p. 49.
[35]Jeffrey J. Hallett, "Worklife Visions," *Personnel Administrator* (May 1987), p. 59.

> The nation's ability to compete is threatened by inadequate investment in our most important resource: people. Put simply, too many workers lack the skill to perform more demanding jobs.[36]
>
> *Business Week,* October, 1988

And there is little doubt that jobs will become more demanding. We have been told for many years that the quality of our workforce is on a collision course with the job demands of the future. No workforce issue has captured the attention of political, business, and education leaders as has the declining skill level of the American worker. A special commission of the U.S. Labor Department reported that in 1991 more than half of U.S. students were leaving high school without the knowledge or foundation required to hold a good job.[37] A recent survey of over 1,600 companies conducted by the American Management Association found that over one quarter of job applicants lacked basic reading and math skills. The deficiency rate for those tested only for reading skills was 36 percent. Of the surveyed firms, 110 reported applicant deficiency rates above 50 percent.[38] The jobs of the future require a highly adaptive, skilled, and educated workforce, yet we seem ill prepared and reluctant to accept the challenge.

The techniques for measuring the overall quality of the labor force are not sophisticated. Commonly used measures include educational level, skill level, work experience, and the results of various ability and psychological tests. Although years of schooling, grade point average, and previous employment are easy to document, other measures of quality are not. The less tangible factors of personal maturation and motivation to succeed are important yet difficult to assess. Unfortunately, almost every measure of quality provides real cause for concern at the present time.

The Hudson Institute's "Workforce 2000" report contained the information found in Figure 2-8. The Institute looked at the skill levels required for jobs now and in the future, using a scale of 1 to 6.4. Laborers are at 1.2, construction workers at 3.2, marketing and sales personnel at 3.4, and natural scientists and lawyers are at the top skill level. The report predicts that 41 percent of new jobs will be at a skill level of 3.5 or greater (level 4 is the ability to read periodicals and write business letters). This can be contrasted with only 24 percent of currently existing jobs that require a skill level at or above 3.5. Further, there will be almost no growth (4 percent) in the number of jobs requiring the lowest skill levels.[39]

---

[36]*Business Week*, October, 1988, as quoted by the U.S. Department of Labor, "Work-Based Learning: Training America's Workers" (November 1989), p. i.

[37]The Bureau of National Affairs, Inc., "Commission Identifies Necessary Workplace Skills," *Bulletin to Management* (July 1991), p. 209.

[38]The Bureau of National Affairs, Inc., "One Quarter of Job Applicants Are Deficient," *Bulletin to Management* (June 1991), p. 191.

[39]U.S. Department of Labor, "Work-Based Learning: Training America's Workers" (November 1990), p. 3.

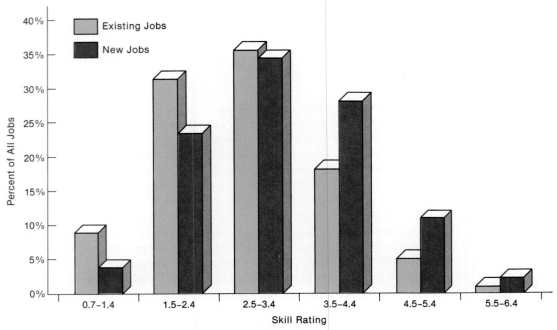

FIGURE 2-8   Job Skill Levels (Skill Ratings by Percentage of All Jobs)
Source: U.S. Department of Labor/Hudson Institute.

Arnold Packer, deputy director of the "Workforce 2000" study, and at the time of the study a senior research fellow at the Hudson Institute, discussed the results of an Educational Testing Service (ETS) survey in *Training and Development Journal* shortly after the report's release. He indicated that ETS surveyed "3,600 people in the 21–25 age group, and found that only 60 percent of whites, 40 percent of Hispanics, and 25 percent of blacks could find information in a news article, and 25 percent of whites, 7 percent of Hispanics, and 3 percent of blacks could follow directions to travel from one location to another using a bus schedule."[40] Packer went on to estimate that in the year 2000 the average American worker will be at a skill level of 2.6 on the previously mentioned skill level scale (level 3 is the ability to read safety rules and maintenance instructions), while the average job will be above the 3.5 level.

The picture becomes even more troubling when one considers that workers need certain basic language and math abilities to be trainable for jobs with higher skill levels, yet there are estimates that as many as 27 million adults are illiterate (basic skills below the fifth-grade level), and perhaps another 45 million are mar-

---

[40]"How Can Business Fight Workplace Illiteracy?" *Training and Development Journal* (January 1989), p. 22.

ginally literate.[41] It has been estimated that 40–42 percent of the entire adult population must receive training of some kind to be brought up to the level of advanced functional literacy necessary to perform the jobs of the future. The American Society for Training and Development (ASTD) calculates the bill to be an additional $15 billion per year over and above the current expenditures for employee training of $30 billion per year.[42] Investments in capital equipment will not yield the expected return unless we have a workforce that can properly use it. "Some of the exporters of equipment, specifically from West Germany and Japan, are no longer selling into the United States their state-of-the art equipment because our people do not have the educational level required to make them trainable on that equipment."[43] Some believe that our problems stem from a general failure of the public educational system to educate and prepare our young people for the world of work. Students, they have charged, have not learned to reason or to think critically.[44]

There are demographic, social, economic, and educational reasons for our current situation. For example, large numbers of non-English-speaking immigrants have joined the American workforce during the last decade, many of whom are illiterate in their native language. An example is provided by the following story concerning the new customer service manager of Britches, a clothing chain in Washington, D.C. He called a meeting of the company's 40 alteration tailors and discovered that 30 of them spoke no English. The company taught the tailors survival English so that they could speak to the customers.[45] Social and economic forces work against students even staying in school. Clemson University's National Dropout Prevention Center has stated that 700,000 students drop out of public schools each year.[46] David Kearns, chairman of Xerox, in a 1987 speech stated that "The American workforce is in grave jeopardy. We are running out of qualified people. If current demographic and economic trends continue, American business will have to hire a million new workers a year who can't read, write or count."

Employers, in part due to disappointment in the quality of public education, have reluctantly had to assume more financial responsibility for educating and training not only the professional, skilled, and white-collar labor that is needed, but the labor for the lowest-level jobs as well. Aetna Life and Casualty in Hartford, Connecticut, reports that in 1988 it spent $750,000 to teach 500 employees basic reading, writing, and math skills.[47] IBM spent more than $20 million on K-12 education projects in 1989 and has committed at least another $52 million over the

---

[41]"How Can Business Fight Workplace Illiteracy?" *Training and Development Journal* (January 1989), p. 18.

[42]"How Many of Your Employees Can Read?" *American Demographics* (April 1991), p. 16.

[43]"How Can Business Fight Workplace Illiteracy?" p. 20.

[44]Allan Bloom, *The Closing of the American Mind* (New York: Simon and Schuster, 1987).

[45]"How Many of Your Employees Can Read?" p. 16.

[46]Personal communication, Clemson University National Dropout Prevention Center.

[47]Ron Zemke, "Workplace Illiteracy—Shall We Overcome?" *Training* (June 1989), p. 35.

years 1990–1995.[48] The vice-president of training and development at Motorola estimated the cost of remedial training (a sixth- or seventh-grade level of reading and math ability) for its U.S. workforce, including paying for training time away from the job, at $35 million over the 3 years 1989–1991.[49] It appears that the solution will require a coordinated effort on the part of private business, educational institutions, and all levels of government. Private business training programs like those at IBM, Aetna Life and Casualty, and Motorola, as well as corporate adopt-a-school, adopt-a-student, and teacher motivation programs, are becoming more common.[50] The U.S. Department of Labor has sponsored studies like "Workforce 2000" and has provided grants to private businesses like Domino's Pizza ($150,000) to develop innovative employee training programs.

There are political initiatives as well. For example, in February 1990 the governors of all 50 states adopted the following six very ambitious goals for the reform of the school system:[51]

1. By the year 2000, all children in America will start school ready to learn.
2. By the year 2000, the high school graduation rate will increase to at least 90 percent.
3. By the year 2000, American students will leave grades 4, 8, and 12 having demonstrated competence in challenging subject matter, including English, mathematics, science, history, and geography.
4. By the year 2000, U.S. students will be first in the world in mathematics and science achievement.
5. By the year 2000, every adult American will be literate and will possess the knowledge and skills necessary to compete in a global economy and will be able to exercise the rights and responsibilities of citizenship.
6. By the year 2000, every school in America will be free of drugs and violence and will offer a disciplined environment conducive to learning.

Consistent with the spirit of the governors' six points, Oregon passed the Oregon Educational Act for the 21st Century in 1991.[52] The act abolished the traditional high school in favor of a "certificate of mastery" in the 10th grade followed by either 2 years of college prepatory courses or a program that combines academic work and on-the-job training, similar to the current German system. Special classes would be available to assist students who fail to receive the certificate on the first try to continue trying for it. The act also calls for the abolition of grades from kindergarten through third grade, grouping students by ability rather

[48]Jack Gordon, "Can Business Save the Schools?" *Training* (August 1990), p. 20.

[49]"How Can Business Fight Workplace Illiteracy?" p. 20.

[50]The Bureau of National Affairs, Inc., "Better Education from Business Involvement," *Bulletin to Management* (April 1988), p. 106. See also, "Job Training by Apprenticeship," *Fortune* (June 29, 1992), p. 16.

[51]Gordon, p. 27.

[52]Associated Press, "Oregon to Revamp Traditional High School," *Anderson Independent-Mail* (July 17, 1991), p. 10A.

than age, and an expansion of the school year from 175 to 220 days by the year 2010. It remains to be seen if private business initiatives, government studies and grants, and such education reform acts as Oregon's will produce a workforce capable of competing in a global economy.

Labor Force Flows

The labor force fluctuations, both long term and short term, are affected by companies' and workers' change of location, consumers' changing tastes, economic fluctuations, shifting government policies and regulations, introduction of new products and technology, employee ambitions and dissatisfactions, employee illness, retirement, and aging, and cyclical and seasonal occurrences. Sometimes these changes are both predictable and desirable; at other times, they are neither. Job changes are either intraoccupational or interoccupational, with the former occurring when employees change employers without changing occupations and the latter occurring when employees shift to other occupations or professions.

Geographic and occupational mobility in the United States has increased since World War II. The increased mobility of labor is the result of geographically expanding organizations, technological and competitive forces, and a broader outlook on life and work by employees generated from increasing education. Workers continue to migrate to the South, the West, and nonurban areas. This migration is due, in part, to the decline of smokestack industries in the East and the movement of high-tech service corporations to those ares of the country.[53] In a sense, labor recruitment has become easier, but mobility has also added to the challenges faced by the personnel department. Uprooting leads to economic and social problems for workers and their families, which can affect efficiency and impose high costs on both the organization and the employee.

Intraoccupational Mobility

Employees change jobs for many reasons. Altered marital status, a higher income or better lifestyle, additional security, and more favorable professional opportunities can all induce a person to change positions. Voluntary intraoccupational mobility, if triggered by the availability of other opportunities, may signify a healthy economy. Involuntary mobility, on the other hand, can indicate economic sluggishness (e.g., layoffs and reductions in the workforce). Increased worker mobility during times of prosperity indicates upward and lateral mobility, which reflects a healthy demand for labor. Excessive lateral mobility may be of concern to the firm, particularly if it is indicative of internal management problems or of noncompetitive wages or salaries.[54] After prolonged periods of recession and layoff, an insufficient number of younger workers may be employed; seniority clauses

[53]Eric G. Flamholtz, Yvonne Randle, and Sonja Sackmann, "Personnel Management: The Tenor of Today," *Personnel Journal* (June 1987), p. 62.

[54]More will be said regarding excessive lateral mobility (turnover) later in this chapter.

tend to protect the older employees. The recruitment of younger people, however, may be necessary to the future performance of an organization because managers are often groomed for long periods before they step in to fill the shoes of retiring executives.

Considerable lateral mobility can be expected in high-demand professional and technical jobs. Professional, technical, and top managerial employees are often scarce because of the extensive education and experience that are generally required. Organizations may increase the compensation offered to persons whose skills are in the high-demand and short-supply areas in order to attract such individuals. Furthermore, organizational pay policies may prevent current employees from receiving generous salary increases. Such policies may force high-demand employees to move to other firms in order to achieve significantly higher levels of income.

Information recently provided by the Bureau of Labor Statistics indicates that mobility among older workers may not be as great as it is among younger ones. Young people may be more intraoccupationally mobile because they have fewer financial ties and assets, fewer family ties (e.g., children), more adventurous attitudes, and more ability to withstand the emotional and physical burdens of change than older persons. As would be expected, younger workers are most mobile; as workers grow older and career paths are selected, mobility decreases.

Interoccupational Mobility

The typical worker 35 years of age or over has become involved in an occupation that will probably engage him or her until retirement. Despite occasional signs of discontent, few workers entertain serious thoughts of changing occupations; in fact, changing occupations usually becomes more difficult and threatening with age. Recent information from the Bureau of Labor Statistics indicates a strong relationship between age and interoccupational mobility. The older the employee, and the longer the tenure with the current employer, the less likely he or she is to change careers. However, because of changing workforce and industrial conditions, there may occasionally be a need to encourage interoccupational movement for certain employees. Technological changes and aggressive competitive forces will continue to characterize the late twentieth century. New products are introduced and new industries develop, while others decline. Although technological changes are favorably viewed as beneficial to society, the short- and even long-term effects can create economic and social hardship for many workers.

Unemployment

The federal government is legislatively committed to full employment. Four percent unemployment, although considered unrealistic by some, is considered acceptable to policymakers. Unemployment of 8 percent or higher, however, is considered politically unacceptable. The changing face of the labor force is characterized by both temporary and permanent unemployment. Workers are displaced by labor-saving machines, new production and management techniques, and plant and equipment obsolescence.

Some unemployment is seasonal, caused by such factors as inclement weather and changes in a firm's business cycle. The construction, canning, and garment industries are examples of seasonal industries that experience peak labor demand followed by considerable unemployment. The economic and social costs of seasonal unemployment have not created as much public anxiety as unemployment based on changing industrial structures, economic downturns (such as the recession of 1990–1992), and technological displacement.

Part-time employment can also be of public concern under certain circumstances. Some segments of the labor force, such as women with children, prefer part-time employment. Seasonal economic changes and business fluctuations may also lead to part-time employment. However, part-time employment may symbolize an era of recession if it is due to the forcing of employees to cut working hours or to develop work-sharing arrangements. Where part-time employment is widespread and involuntary, public officials and firms should be concerned.

Critics argue that labor market statistics fail to account for underemployed workers, that is, individuals who hold jobs that are not commensurate with their education, skill, and experience, such as a college graduate working as a clerk. Statistics also show that the unemployment rate among minorities continues to be higher than average. Figure 2-9 provides unemployment figures for the total civilian labor force, whites, blacks, and Hispanics between 1982 and 1990.

Unemployment remains a serious concern for minorities. The unemployment rate for blacks was 11.3 percent in 1990, about two and one half times that of whites (4.7 percent) and one and one half that of Hispanics (8.0 percent). Generally, EEO laws and affirmative action commitments have not led to statistical equality. Parity has been blocked by continued discrimination, lack of skills, inadequate education, geographic immobility, seniority clauses protecting older white workers, competition among minorities and other equal-employment-protected groups, and periods of recession. Public sentiment concerning reverse discrimination has also added to the relative ineffectiveness of some anti-discrimination laws.

Absenteeism

A great deal has been written about absenteeism and its impact on an organization. Absences occur when an employee fails to report to work as scheduled. Such failure may be due to an employee's inability to come to work (sickness, accidents, or other reasons not within the employee's control) or an unwillingness to report even though there is no legitimate reason that prevents an employee from coming to work. A problem facing supervisors and personnel managers is distinguishing

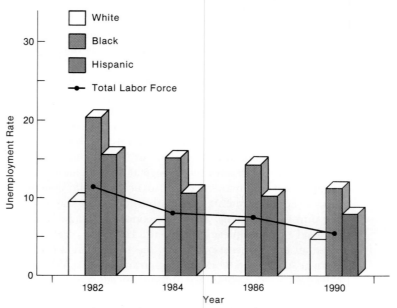

Note: All figures are fourth quarter except 1987, which is second quarter.

FIGURE 2-9   Unemployment Rates, 1982–1990
Source: Bureau of Labor Statistics

between an employee's inability to work and his or her unwillingness to work. The problem is compounded because most employees who fall into the latter category usually provide plausible reasons for their absences and, as a consequence, are considered to be legitimately absent.

Absenteeism rates are commonly computed as follows:

$$\frac{\text{Number of days lost through absences}}{\text{Number of employees} \times \text{number of workdays}} \times 100$$

Most organizations experience average monthly absenteeism rates that range from 1 to 3 percent. The average monthly absenteeism rate has remained fairly constant (1981–2.4 percent; 1984 – 1.9 percent; and 1990 – 1.9 percent.)[55] Although these figures may seem low, it should be remembered that in 1990, 1.9 percent of all scheduled work hours were lost due to absenteeism. The cost of absenteeism may vary considerably from one company to another, depending

[55]The Bureau of National Affairs, Inc., "Job Absence and Turnover," *Bulletin to Management* (March 7, 1985) pp. 3–6; Bureau of Labor Statistics, "Employment and Earnings" (January 1991), p. 232; and The Bureau of National Affairs, Inc., "BNA's Job Absence and Turnover Report— 2nd Quarter 1991" *Bulletin to Management* (September 12, 1991), p. 284.

upon the skill levels of the jobs involved, the interdependency among the jobs, the ability of other employees to cover those who are absent, and whether the absenteeism occurs when an employee's presence is critical. Absenteeism costs may be assessed on the basis of wages or salary paid to the absent employees, lost production or customer service, payroll costs for employing more employees than necessary because of anticipated absences, and supervisory effort required to document absenteeism and rearrange working schedules.

Turnover

Turnover is broadly defined to be the rate at which employees leave an organization. Turnover may be voluntary or involuntary. Voluntary turnover occurs when the employee who has the option to remain with the present employer decides to accept a job elsewhere or leaves the labor force altogether. Involuntary turnover occurs when the employee is discharged or must resign for reasons outside of his or her control (layoffs, illnesses, permanent disability, retirement, death).

Turnover rates can be calculated as follows:

$$\frac{\text{Number of separations}}{\text{Number of employees}} \times 100$$

For most organizations monthly turnover rates range from 1 to 2 percent. The average monthly turnover rate across all companies for the first two quarters of 1991 was less than 1 percent.[56] The overall annual turnover rate across all industries for 1990, for example, was 10.8 percent. Like absenteeism, turnover represents a real expense to the organization. The most common costs include recruiting, selecting, and training replacements and the disruptions caused by temporary vacancies that lead to lost production or higher production costs.

Employees decide to leave an organization for a variety of reasons. These include dissatisfaction with the job (work, compensation, co-workers, supervision, promotion opportunities, and working conditions) and the prospects of better job opportunities elsewhere. Voluntary turnover may be reduced by careful selection and job placement, high-quality orientation and training programs, competitive and equitable pay, and attention to employee job satisfaction.

Involuntary turnover may be reduced through a disciplinary system that emphasizes improving employee problem behavior and a health and safety program that minimizes unsafe working conditions and possible accidents. Employee assistance programs and wellness programs, which are discussed in Chapter 14, can help employees with chemical dependency, as well as financial, psychological, and physical problems, before those problems contribute to involuntary turnover.

[56]The Bureau of National Affairs, Inc., "Median Job Absence and Turnover Rates," *BNA Policy and Practice Series No. 735* (1990), pp. 103–113, and The Bureau of National Affairs, Inc., "BNA's Job Absence and Turnover Report—2nd Quarter 1991," *Bulletin to Management* (September 12, 1991), p. 285.

■ Implications of Labor Force Trends for Personnel/Human Resource Management Functions

Recruitment and Selection

As the labor force becomes more diversified, traditional recruitment and selection devices such as interviews, tests, and biographical information will require more critical analysis. Recruiters must not ignore the fact that older, handicapped, and minority employees may not present themselves through traditional selection channels. Special effort may be needed to ensure that these groups are afforded the opportunity to apply for positions for which they may be qualified. Certain selection tests that are designed to measure aptitudes, abilities, knowledge, and skills may be discriminatory toward particular racial groups and in possible violation of EEO laws (see Chapters 3, 6, and 7). More attention must be paid to selection devices that are valid and reliable predictors of a candidate's potential job performance. An understanding of EEO laws is essential.

Training and Development

Employees who lack general or specific skills because of inadequate education or industrial obsolescence must be trained if they are to be prepared for the increased sophistication of tomorrow's jobs. The diversity of the labor force, coupled with the rapid changes in job demands due to technological advances, will place an increasing burden on company training and development programs. As was discussed earlier in this chapter, considerable cooperation among all levels of government, private enterprise, and the formal education system will be necessary if we are to improve significantly the quality of the labor force and our ability to manage its diversity.

Training and development directors will be required to determine training needs, to develop and use appropriate training methods, and to evaluate their efforts on a timely basis. The futures of individual businesses and of the American economy overall are heavily dependent on the extent to which the training and development function improves and prepares human capital for the challenges of new products, services, technologies, and intense domestic and international competition. Chapter 8 discusses these issues in more detail.

Compensation and Employee Benefits

As the labor force becomes more diversified, it is possible that workers will have different ideas and desires about what constitutes an appropriate compensation package. Younger workers may desire a higher salary or wage and fewer benefits, such as life and health insurance or pensions. Older workers, on the other hand, may prefer benefits in lieu of additional take-home pay. Married persons with working spouses may also prefer fewer benefits if their husbands or wives already have adequate family coverage under an employer-sponsored group life and health insurance program.

EEO laws regulate compensation and employee benefits by prohibiting unfair pay discrimination against women and other protected groups. The concepts of equal pay for equal work, and the more difficult issue of comparable worth, may become even more pressing due to the influx of women into the labor force and to the increased opportunities for women and minorities. Employee benefits such as disability insurance, medical insurance, and pension programs have already endured legislative and judicial scrutiny insofar as sex discrimination is concerned. These issues are examined in greater depth in Chapters 10–12.

Labor-Management Relations

The decline of the steel, rubber, automotive, and other heavy manufacturing industries (with the resultant decrease in the number of blue-collar workers) has been a major factor contributing to the downturn in the percentage of unionized employees in the labor force. Union organizing efforts may be more difficult with a more heterogeneous, technologically advanced, white-collar labor force. For organizations that are extensively organized, the diversity of the labor force may create difficulties at the bargaining table because of the problems associated with satisfying a wider range of employee desires.

Industrial relations specialists and union leaders will need to adjust to a collective bargaining structure that may be more fraught with labor disputes. Collective bargaining agreements may become even more complex as a wider variety of labor and management needs must be accommodated. For example, provisions dealing with technological change, compensation and benefits, job security and layoff arrangements, and career and pay advancements geared to seniority versus job performance merit will probably be the focal points most affected by changes in the supply and demand for labor. These issues are discussed in more detail in Chapters 15 and 16.

■ The Individual Employee

The previous sections of this chapter have focused on the aggregate labor force. The remainder of this chapter deals with the individual employee within the organization. For the individual employee, work or employment serves a number of social and economic purposes. In addition to providing an income, work has always been a place to meet people, socialize, and form friendships. One's social status, class standing, lifestyle, and social contacts are largely determined by one's occupation or profession. Society's evaluation of a person's contributions and worth are generally based on the job he or she holds. Work, in essence, becomes a major source of one's self-esteem and one's standing in the community. Hence, an appreciation of the psychological effects of work on the individual employee should be of concern and interest to personnel professionals. This section presents some basic concepts relevant to how the employee may psychologically interpret the work environment and what organizational efforts can influence that interpretation.

An analysis of the individual employee within the work environment is a complex task. The treatment provided here is necessarily brief and presented solely to create an appreciation for the influence of psychological factors on employee behavior. To appreciate fully the complexities involved, a background in organizational behavior, social psychology, industrial psychology, or sociology is necessary.

Our discussion begins with information on some of the individual differences among employees that are of importance to personnel professionals. We then discuss employee job satisfaction and its effects on individual behavior. A useful theory of individual performance motivation is also presented and is related to many of the personnel functions to be discussed throughout this text. The theories selected for discussion in this section are well respected at the present time, but, like all behavioral science theories, they will be revised when necessary to accommodate new knowledge. They represent research-based hypotheses concerning relationships between people and their work environments.

Individual Differences

Organizations, large and small, are composed of people drawn from our diverse population. These people differ in age, sex, race, religious beliefs, personal values, temperament, intelligence, psychomotor skills, and education, as well as in many other personal characteristics. These differences become important as applicants are compared to one another and decisions are made as to which employees are better suited for various jobs. These individual differences also figure prominently when one considers the motives behind why people work and how they decide where and how hard to work. Behavioral scientists have attempted to observe, understand, and predict human behavior in work settings for many years. As a consequence, many different theories have been proposed to explain work behavior. These theories attempt to relate elements of the work environment and the individual employee's personal characteristics and values to work effort and performance.

Personnel/human resource managers must take individual differences into account when formulating and administering personnel policies and programs. Compensation and employee benefit programs that are acceptable to married employees may not be as acceptable to young, single employees. Older workers are likely to have a different view of career management and retirement programs than do their younger counterparts. In addition, research indicates that males and females may desire both different and similar things from their work and from their employers.[57]

Examples of the impact of psychological, physical, socioeconomic, and other individual differences among employees on the personnel/human resource functions are plentiful, and much more will be said concerning them in the appropriate chapters of this text. The point to be made here is that the successful personnel manager must learn to accommodate both similarities and differences among employees. This accommodation is necessary if one wishes to create rewarding and satisfying working environments and to obtain the most from human resources.

Job Satisfaction and Employee Work Performance

Personnel managers are generally aware of important concepts such as job satisfaction, performance, and productivity. This section briefly reviews the relationship between employee work performance and employee job satisfaction.

Job satisfaction may be conceived of as an employee's attitude toward his or her work, organizational rewards (pay, benefits, and so forth), and the social, organizational, and physical environments in which work is performed. It is possible for a person to have positive attitudes toward his or her pay, negative ones toward the duties that must be performed, and a neutral feeling toward co-workers and employee benefits. Generally, however, individuals who are satisfied with one aspect of their jobs report that they are satisfied with others as well. Thus, most individuals' feelings about their jobs are dominated by a general or global feeling of satisfaction or dissatisfaction.

As one would expect, this global level of job satisfaction is most heavily influenced by the environment. However, one recent study found a biological link as well. This study used identical reared-apart twins to conclude that approximately 30 percent of an individual's overall job satisfaction may be due to genetics, with environment accounting for the remaining 70 percent.[58] This suggests a natural limit to the influence an organization may have on employee job satisfaction and provides an explanation for the similar levels of job satisfaction that an individual experiences across jobs and organizations. Although these findings are intriguing, they are new, and much more research must be done before a truly convincing argument can be made for a genetic basis for job satisfaction.

For decades, surveys indicated that job satisfaction was high for American workers. As recently as 1987, 60–70 percent of American workers described

---

[57]See for example Michael C. White, Michael D. Crino, and Jack Naramore, "Sex Differences and Job Attributes: A Review of the Literature," *International Journal of Management*, Vol. 2, No. 3 (1985), pp. 19–28; Ann M. Morrison and Mary Ann Von Glinow, "Women and Minorities in Management," *American Psychologist* (February 1990), pp. 200–208.

[58]Tori DeAngelis, "Genetics: Part of Job Satisfaction?," *APA Monitor* (April 1989), p. 13.

themselves as satisfied with their jobs.[59] During the recession of the early 1990s, surveys indicated that job satisfaction had declined significantly, especially for managerial workers. Many companies decided to restructure or at least significantly reduce their workforces. This often resulted in large numbers of managerial workers losing their jobs. Many of those who remained employed felt unappreciated, overworked, and expendable.[60] It remains to be seen if this is a long-term trend, but it does represent the first major change in what had been historically high and stable levels of job satisfaction.

Personnel/human resource administrators are interested in a number of issues related to job satisfaction. Two questions of primary importance concern the relationship between job satisfaction and employee behavior (absenteeism, turnover, organizational citizenship, and job performance) and the impact that specific personnel policies can have on job satisfaction. We address the first question in this section and the second in the following section.

The behavioral science literature indicates that the relationship between job satisfaction and absenteeism and turnover is reasonably straightforward. Employees who are dissatisfied with their jobs have both higher than normal rates of absenteeism (voluntary) and resignation.[61] Given our preceding discussion of the costs associated with absenteeism and turnover, these relationships provide ample reason for being concerned about employee job satisfaction.

Consistent with our discussion about differences among individuals, recent evidence has provided insight into the importance of cultural differences for job satisfaction and subsequent employee behavior. The American Psychological Association's Office of Ethnic Minority Affairs has collected data indicating that the higher turnover rates among minorities (10.1 percent for minorities, 7.9 percent for nonminorities) can be traced to a definition of job satisfaction different from that held by the nonminority group. "For non-minorities, satisfaction was associated with the likelihood of career advancement and an objective job appraisal of areas over which they have control. They also took a long-term perspective of the corporation. For minorities, job satisfaction was related to their present situation."[62] According to the conclusions reached in the study, "companies need to review management practices to be sensitive to cultural diversity."[63]

Despite years of research, however, the relationship between job satisfaction and employee performance is not fully understood. Intuitively, it makes sense to believe that a happy (highly satisfied) employee will be the most productive.

[59]See, for example, Associated Press, "Poll Finds Most U.S. Workers Happy with Pay," *Anderson Independent-Mail* (August 22, 1987), p. 38; and The Bureau of National Affairs, Inc., "Insights into Workplace Satisfaction," *Bulletin to Management* (June 30, 1988), p. 208.

[60]John S. McClenahen, "It's No Fun Working Here Anymore," *Industry Week* (March 4, 1991), pp. 20–22, and Anne B. Fisher, "Morale Crisis," *Fortune* (November 18, 1991), pp. 70–80.

[61]Laurie Larwood, *Organizational Behavior and Management*, (Boston: Kent Publishing Company, 1984), p. 153.

[62]Kathleen Fisher, "Minorities Cite Bias as Cause of Turnover," *APA Monitor* (June 1986), p. 38.

[63]Kathleen Fisher, p. 38.

However, the belief that job satisfaction leads to performance has not been strongly supported by organizational research.[64]

More recently, a second position has been advanced that states that performance causes satisfaction. The research evidence currently available makes a somewhat stronger case for this viewpoint.[65] A similar view is that organizational rewards cause satisfaction, and when current rewards are based on current performance, subsequent performance will be affected.[66] Assuming that this proposition is true (and it has considerable support), personnel managers must not only provide rewards that are satisfying to employees, but they must also time or link the rewards to job performance as a means of encouraging future high performance levels. The link between job satisfaction and performance, according to this position, is provided through performance-contingent rewards. The following section presents an important behavioral science theory that deals with the relationships between organizational rewards, job satisfaction, personnel functions, and an employee's motivation to perform.

Performance Motivation and the Individual

The behavioral science literature contains many theories of motivation.[67] One such theory (or model) that places many personnel activities in perspective is an expectancy-based model called the *Perceptual Model of Motivation*.[68] This model is presented in Figure 2-10.

This model was proposed to explain why some people choose to invest more or less effort in their work. To the extent that we understand why people select one

[64]Charles N. Greene, "The Satisfaction-Performance Controversy," *Business Horizons*, Vol. 15 (1972), pp. 31–41; L. W. Porter and R. M. Steers, "Organizational, Work and Personal Factors in Employee Turnover and Absenteeism," *Psychological Bulletin* (1973), pp. 151–176; D. R. Ilgen and J. H. Hollenbeck, "The Role of Job Satisfaction in Absence Behavior," *Organizational Behavior and Human Performance* 19, 1(1977), pp. 18–31. Also see Edward E. Lawler III, "Satisfaction and Behavior" in Barry M. Staw (ed.), *Psychological Foundations of Organizational Behavior*, 2nd ed. (Glenview, Illinois: Scott, Foresman and Co., 1983), pp. 80–96.

[65]See Lyman W. Porter and Edward E. Lawler III, *Managerial Attitudes and Performance* (Homewood, Illinois: Richard D. Irwin, Inc., 1968); Donald Bowen and Jacob P. Siegel, "The Relationship Between Satisfaction and Performance: The Question of Causality," paper presented at the annual meeting of the American Psychological Association, Miami Beach, Florida (September 1970).

[66]David H. Cherrington, H. Joseph Reitz, and William E. Scott, Jr., "Effects of Contingent and Non-Contingent Reward on the Relationship Between Satisfaction and Task Performance," *Journal of Applied Psychology* 55, 6 (1971), pp. 531–536.

[67]Excellent discussions of motivational theories can be found in Marvin D. Dunnette, ed., *Handbook of Industrial and Organizational Psychology* (Chicago: Rand McNally College Publishing Company, 1976), pp. 469–644; H. Joseph Reitz, *Behavior in Organizations*, rev. ed. (Homewood, Illinois: Richard D. Irwin, Inc., 1981), chapters 3 and 4; and Raymond A. Katzell and Donna E. Thompson, "Work Motivation: Theory and Practice" *American Psychologist* (February 1990), pp. 144–161.

[68]Lyman W. Porter and Edward E. Lawler III, *Managerial Attitudes and Performance* (Homewood, Illinois: Richard D. Irwin, Inc., 1968).

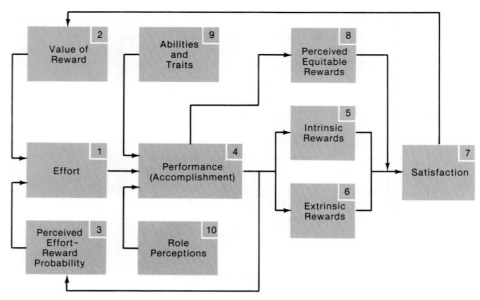

FIGURE 2-10   Perceptual Model of Motivation
Source: L. Porter and E. Lawler III, *Managerial Attitudes and Performance* (Homewood, Illinois: Richard D. Irwin, Inc., 1968)

level of work effort rather than another, we may be able to create an environment that will foster high levels of work effort.[69] According to this model there are two major influences on work effort (box 1 in Figure 2-10). The first (box 2) is the employee's personal estimate of the probability that a given level of effort will lead to a reward (likelihood of organizational reward). This simply means, for example: "If I work hard, how likely is it that I will be rewarded?" The second major influence (box 3) is the degree to which the likely reward(s) is (are) of any personal value to the worker. Combined, they influence whether the employee perceives it to be worthwhile to exert a high level of effort. For instance, if a worker perceives that a great deal of effort will result in valued rewards, that person is likely to put forth that level of effort. On the other hand, if a worker perceives that significant work effort will not result in valued rewards (either because the rewards will not be provided or, if provided, are valueless), it is unlikely that significant work effort will result. This is hardly surprising. What this model offers is not startling conclusions but insight into the influences on an employee when he or she determines what level of work effort to exert.

The first step in understanding why one level of work effort is selected over another requires an examination of how a worker determines the likelihood of organizational reward. The model (Fig. 2-10) indicates that this likelihood is based on two smaller expectations. The first is that high effort, for example, will lead to

[69]It should be understood that we are not attempting to explain effort with great precision. Rather, this model attempts to present the major organizational influences on individual effort.

a high level of performance (box 4). In other words, "If I work hard, how likely is it that I will perform at a high level?" The second expectation or question is "If I perform well, how likely is it that I will be rewarded for it?" (boxes 5 and 6). The answers to these questions, expressed as perceived probabilities, result in the overall expectation of organizational reward (or the effort–reward probability).

If either or both perceived probabilities are low, the resultant overall effort-organizational reward expectation will also be low. In a work environment where employees do not feel that effort will result in reward, few if any employees will work hard. Hence, the personal and organizational influences on these employee expectations are of some interest.

As Figure 2-10 shows, there are two major influences on the employee's expectation that effort will lead to performance. One is the degree to which the employee feels that he or she has the abilities or traits to perform well (box 9). An employee who feels underqualified for the job may not perceive himself as having much chance for success. Another major influence is the role perception of an employee (box 10). *Role perception* refers to how well the employee feels that he or she understands the nature of the job. Employees who are confused by the job demands may have little faith in their ability to perform well. The less well understood the job, the less likely a person is to believe that he or she can perform it well. There are, of course, other influences on this effort–performance expectation, such as the previous level of success attained in this job or similar jobs and the degree to which constraints are placed on performance. Performance constraints include the quality of supervision, tools, raw materials, and other similar environmental limitations.[70]

It is in the best interest of the organization to ensure that employees feel that their effort will affect performance. Certain personnel functions can impact this belief. For example, the organization should ensure that the individuals selected for employment either have the abilities and traits to perform the job well (*selection*) or will be assisted in acquiring such abilities and traits (*training*). Further, a well-written job description (*job analysis*), an employee orientation session (*orientation*), and job-specific training (*training*) may serve to support a high effort–performance expectation.

The remaining expectation deals with the belief that organizational rewards are performance sensitive. This means that different levels of performance will result in different levels of reward. High levels of performance should result in rewards, and those rewards should be greater (in some manner) than the rewards provided for lower levels of performance. If this is not perceived to be true, then there is little reason for an employee to strive for high performance. For example, if promotions within an organization are based primarily on merit (quality of performance) rather than seniority (length of performance), then an employee may be more likely to strive for a high level of performance, knowing fully well that by doing so, he or she is likely to be rewarded with a promotion and the higher pay,

---

[70]See, for example, Robert P. Steel, Anthony J. Mento, and William H. Hendrix, "Constraining Forces and the Work Performance of Finance Company Cashiers," *Journal of Management* (Fall/Winter 1987), pp. 473–482.

benefits, and status that generally accompany promotion. If, on the other hand, promotions are geared to seniority (assuming only acceptable performance), then the employee will realize that a reward will not be forthcoming until the prescribed amount of time needed to fulfill seniority requirements is served. In this situation, improved job performance is to no avail because the promotion cannot be attained until the employee has spent a certain number of months or years on the job.

To maintain a high performance–reward expectation, an organization must first ensure that employee performance is accurately measured (*performance appraisal*). This is because organizational rewards are linked to performance appraisals, and employees must believe that high-quality performance will be reflected in their performance appraisals. Second, the employer should make an effort to ensure that extrinsic (box 6) and intrinsic rewards (box 5) are available to employees.[71]

Extrinsic rewards are such things as base pay, incentive pay, job status, employee benefits, promotions, and gifts of any kind. To the extent possible, these rewards should represent a variety (something for everybody) and should be contingent upon performance. The stronger the performance–extrinsic reward link, the greater the overall performance–reward expectation. There are a number of personnel activities associated with extrinsic rewards in an organization. For instance, *formal compensation programs, promotion policies, seniority systems,* and *collective bargaining activities* are all related either to levels of, or the provision of, extrinsic rewards.

Intrinsic rewards are those rewards that are provided directly to the employee as a function of performing the job. For instance, feelings of accomplishment for a job well done or feelings of satisfaction for succeeding at a task are intrinsic rewards. They are derived directly from job accomplishment itself and are dependent upon the nature of the work a person is doing. Some jobs offer little potential for intrinsic rewards because of their routine, unchallenging nature. Other jobs have considerable intrinsic reward potential. Employers have found that by redesigning jobs (*job design*), opportunities for intrinsic rewards can be greatly increased. The greater the intrinsic rewards potential of a job, the greater the likelihood that an employee will be motivated to perform well enough to receive them. Once again, however, individual differences must be considered, as not all employees desire (or value) intrinsic rewards. Job design (redesign) is discussed in detail in Chapter 4.

We have stated that rewards themselves, as well as the level of rewards, should be linked to performance. Explicit incorporation of the levels of reward is provided in this model by the link between performance and the employee perception of the equitability of the rewards received (box 8). We view our performance-related rewards in two ways: first, by their absolute level and, second, by their

---

[71]Frederick Herzberg, Bernard Mausner, and Barbara Synderman, *The Motivation to Work* (New York: John Wiley and Sons, 1959). Richard A. Guzzo, "Types of Rewards, Cognitions, and Work Motivation," *The Academy of Management Review*, Vol. 4, No. 1 (1979), pp. 75–86.

relative level. The absolute level of reward simply means that $100 is greater than $10 and that we recognize that difference. The relative aspect of rewards states that we view our reward level with reference to the quality of our performance and what we feel that performance is worth. Hence, if we feel that $1,000 is an equitable reward for our work, $500 (even though a tidy sum) will not be considered adequate, and we will not be satisfied with it. One way we determine the appropriate level of reward for our performance is by comparing how other employees have fared under similar circumstances. This between-employee comparison of rewards is quite common. In fact, a well-respected theory of motivation is based upon this comparison process. This theory is called *equity theory* because it deals with how we determine the equitability of our work-reward relationship with our employer.[72] A complete discussion of this theory is presented in Chapter 10. For now, it is important to appreciate that employees will view organizational rewards from both an absolute and a relative perspective, and that both perspectives affect employee satisfaction (and subsequent performance).

The personnel manager is in a position to influence employees' perceptions of equity through careful formulation and application of promotion, compensation, discipline, and labor relations policy. Perceptions of inequity are detrimental to work motivation and job satisfaction, and may ultimately lead to increased absenteeism, turnover, substandard performance, discipline problems, and grievances.

The value (Fig. 2-10) we place on these rewards will be based on our perception of how equitable they are and to what extent they can satisfy our needs.[73] Those rewards that are not perceived by an employee as capable of satisfying current or future needs will not be considered valuable enough to encourage the additional performance effort necessary to acquire them.

The implications of this model are clear. Employers should create an environment where employees know what is expected of them, believe that they are capable of accomplishing what is expected, feel that their personal efforts will affect their performance, and expect valued and equitable rewards for their performance efforts. Personnel activities such as job analysis, selection, job evaluation, training, employee relations, and job design all contribute to such an

[72]A great deal of research has been conducted on this theory. Overall, the theory has proven to be supported by this research. For a complete presentation of equity theory, see J. Stacy Adams, "Inequity in Social Exchange" in L. Berkowitz (ed.), *Advances in Social Psychology* (New York: Academic Press, 1965), pp. 276–299; "Toward an Understanding of Inequity," *Journal of Abnormal and Social Psychology* (November 1963), pp. 422–436; Paul S. Goodman and Abraham Friedman, "An Examination of Adam's Theory of Inequity," *Administrative Science Quarterly* (December 1971), pp. 271–288; and Raymond A. Katzell and Donna E. Thompson.

[73]The various needs that employees may wish to satisfy, and the relationships between these needs and their satisfaction, are subjects of need theories of motivation. Two of the most widely cited need-based theories are Maslow's hierarchy of needs and Alderfer's ERG (existence-relatedness-growth) theory. Discussions of these theories may be found in most industrial/organizational psychology and organizational behavior texts. The interested reader is also encouraged to see C. P. Alderfer, *Human Needs in Organizational Settings* (New York: Free Press, 1972), and A. H. Maslow, *Motivation and Personality*, 2nd ed. (New York: Harper, 1970).

environment. When personnel activities are poorly performed, individual motivation cannot help but be adversely affected.[74]

The Individual and the Work Group

Although the Perceptual Model of Motivation concentrates on employee performance as a personal, individual decision, that is not entirely the case. Peers and colleagues can also stimulate, regulate, and sometimes curtail the productivity and performance of a given employee.[75] A considerable amount of research has been conducted on the behavior and influences of formal and informal work groups.

Formal group relationships are established through the organizational structure. Each person has a specified function within the organization that is (or should be) well defined. Many companies are organizing work around self-managed work groups.[76] These groups are given the responsibility for making a number of decisions regarding the product or service being provided or made by the group. The compensation of all group members is based on how well the group performs. Often these groups are given the additional responsibilities of hiring and enforcing organizational and group work rules. These groups exert considerable influence on the behavior of their members. It is a particular challenge to create effective work groups in organizations that have a diverse workforce and have always encouraged and rewarded high levels of individualized effort. High levels of cooperative effort on the part of well-trained group members are necessary for a self-managed work group to succeed. Also of interest to personnel managers is the role that informal group structures play in employee performance.

Informal groups in the organization consist of spontaneously developed relationships and patterns of interaction between employees. Such groups arise, to varying degrees, in most organizations as the result of specific individual personalities, working arrangements, and other organizational factors. Managers often overlook or are insensitive to the size, magnitude, and effects of this informal organization. As a result, personnel policies may become difficult to administer or, in some cases, may prove counterproductive. The following information concerning informal groups and their effects might prove helpful:[77]

---

[74]For an additional but somewhat different discussion of expectancy theory, see Walter B. Newsom, "Motivate Now," *Personnel Journal* (February 1990), pp. 51–55.

[75]One might incorporate such group influences into the Perceptual Model of Motivation as situational influences on performance, or as work outcomes valued by the employee (e.g., peer group acceptance). There is an advantage in discussing these issues apart from the Perceptual Model, however.

[76]For a complete discussion of self-managed work groups, see Eric Sundstrom, Kenneth P. De Meuse, and David Futrell, "Work Teams: Applications and Effectiveness," *American Psychologist* (February 1990), pp. 120–133.

[77]Ross A. Webber, *Management: Basic Elements of Managing Organizations*, rev. ed. (Homewood, Ill.: Richard D. Irwin, Inc., 1979), p. 118.

1. Group pressures may restrict employee productivity and ambition. Personnel managers must recognize the degree to which this may occur in their organizations and provide incentives that will cope with or alleviate the problem. This should be considered when designing compensation, promotion, and other formal reward systems.
2. Group pressures may make it difficult to implement new personnel policies. Employees are often suspicious of and resistant to changes unless they can clearly understand the reasons and benefits behind such changes. Such resistance is more likely when there is an informal group to support these negative feelings. This demonstrates the need for clear employer-employee communication channels and sound, rational personnel policies.
3. Informal groups often have positive effects, such as controlling absenteeism, enforcing compliance with organizational policies, providing informal on-the-job training, and bringing minor grievances to the attention of management before they escalate into irreconcilable conflicts. Because these effects occur when informal groups understand and share organizational and departmental goals, they are not by definition a problem for the personnel manager.

In summary, two important points are brought out by this discussion. First, personnel managers must recognize that informal work groups can have both positive and negative effects on the management of human resources. Second, personnel policies must be fashioned with the presence of the informal group kept in mind. For example, informal groups are likely to react positively to recruitment from within and resist recruitment from outside policies, or, through informal group pressures, to negate the effects of incentive pay systems when they require behaviors that violate informal group norms.

■ Summary and Conclusions

This chapter has discussed both the aggregate labor force and the individual employee. An understanding of the labor force at both levels is important to the personnel professional.

The labor force is undergoing continual change. Women and minorities are participating more fully in the American workplace than ever before; the workforce is aging as baby boomers grow older and older workers elect to remain in the workforce longer; foreign competition, technology, and legislation have contributed to a reshaping of the workplace and workforce; and some industries are declining while others are experiencing impressive growth. Personnel professionals must be aware of these forces and anticipate their probable impact on the quality, quantity, and demand for human resources. They must plan recruitment, selection, and training programs appropriate to the labor force of the future and the business and legal environments that are likely to exist.

The concepts of performance, job satisfaction, and employee motivation, and the methods by which these factors can be improved are at the heart of any efficiently managed organization. This chapter presents only a brief sketch of the major issues that must be considered when one deals with the individual employee in the work environment. Other important concepts, for example, sources of power and influence, leadership behavior, and conflict resolution, are not discussed here but are usually part of an organizational behavior or industrial psychology course.

A major point of this discussion is that personnel managers must be cognizant of the issues discussed here and the methods that are available for maximizing the performance potential of the organization's human resources while simultaneously maintaining the respect and dignity of the individual. Many of the behavioral facets of personnel management are covered in subsequent chapters on recruitment, selection, performance appraisal, training and development, compensation, and labor relations.

■ Questions

1. What is meant by *quality of the labor force*? How do you think labor force quality should be measured? Do you believe the quality of the American labor force is improving? Why or why not?

2. Many managers believe that happy employees are productive employees. Is this true? What is the logic behind the position that happy employees are not necessarily productive employees?

3. Although groups of employees are typically more alike than different, why should individual differences among employees be important to personnel managers? What personnel functions or activities might be more effectively performed if individual differences among employees are kept in mind?

4. Discuss briefly the changes that have taken place in the composition of the labor force over the past 30 years on the basis of age, race, and sex. How have these changes affected the American culture?

□ APPLICATIONS AND CASE EXERCISES

1. The First National Bank has decided to computerize as many of its operations as possible in order to increase efficiency and customer convenience. One of the first steps was to place automatic teller machines (ATMs) in the surrounding community. The bank has also started a program that expands on telephone banking by allowing the owners of microcomputers to conduct virtually all of their banking business from their homes.

These successes have caused the bank to consider the use of microcomputers or terminals in the homes of their employees so that they may work at home. It is believed that this would allow greater flexibility for employees and reduce the need for office and floor space at the main and branch offices. The personnel director has been asked to develop a report outlining the changes that would be necessary in the bank's personnel policies. For example, what changes would be necessary in the current performance evaluation procedures for these employees as a result of the fact that contact with immediate supervisors would be eliminated? It is clear that technology will stimulate many changes in the bank's current personnel practices as the relationship between work and the individual employee changes.

What effects do you think current and future computer and telecommunications technologies will have on the jobs in (a) a typing pool, (b) a fast food franchise, (c) a university, and (d) a publishing company?

2. Supervisors often complain that they are unable to motivate their subordinates to achieve high levels of performance because of organizational policies. To what extent do you believe that this position is legitimate? What effects do organizational personnel policies have on the performance motivation of individual employees?

3. Research and discuss the causes for unemployment among those under 24 and over 55 years of age. What can be done to reduce levels of unemployment for these two groups?

4. Technology will continue to have a significant impact on the relationship between employees and their work. Select and research two technological changes (e.g., telecommunication, office automation) that you believe will have an impact on the workplace of the future. Discuss how these innovations will affect the nature of work and the relationship between the individual employee and the employer.

3 ■

Equal Employment Opportunity Laws and Applications

■ LEARNING OBJECTIVES

After reading this chapter you will

1. Understand the provisions of the equal employment opportunity (EEO) laws.
2. Appreciate the differences between legal and illegal employment discrimination and the basic concepts upon which EEO laws are based.
3. Be familiar with the manner in which the administrative agencies and courts enforce equal employment opportunity laws.
4. Gain insights into the complexities involved in interpreting and enforcing the EEO laws.

■ INTRODUCTORY VIGNETTE

Breaking the Glass Ceiling in Major U.S. Corporations

The *glass ceiling* is a term used to describe the artificial barrier that has prevented qualified women and minorities from advancing to mid- and upper-level management positions. The New York executive search firm Battalia & Associates conducted a telephone survey of 52 women with the title of partner or vice president (and above) in large companies, law firms, banks, and management consulting firms. The survey results indicate that 69 percent of the respondents do not believe that becoming a CEO is possible. Of the women who indicated an interest in becoming a CEO, one third believe that senior management discriminates against women and 29 percent feel that most firms are unwilling to promote a woman to CEO. A study of nine Fortune 500 companies by the U.S. Department of Labor, Office of Federal Contract Compliance Programs (OFCCP), indicates that the glass ceiling was at a lower organizational level than was previously thought. According to the OFCCP, all of the companies studied had a level beyond which few women and minorities were recruited or promoted. The study indicated three major barriers to advancement:

1. Recruitment and hiring practices at the executive levels excluding women and minorities. Most executive positions are filled through executive

Adapted from The Bureau of National Affairs, Inc., "Stymied by Glass Ceiling," *Fair Employment Practices* (Washington, D.C.: The Bureau of National Affairs, Inc., June 10, 1991), p. 62; The Bureau of National Affairs, Inc., "Promoting Women to Upper Management," *Fair Employment Practices* (Washington, D.C.: The Bureau of National Affairs, Inc., July 19, 1990), p. 86; and The Bureau of National Affairs, Inc., "OFCCP's Glass Ceiling Initiative," *Fair Employment Practices* (Washington, D.C.: The Bureau of National Affairs, Inc., August 29, 1991), p. 102.

search firms and networking (a practice in which executives are hired through personal acquaintances or previous business contacts).

2. Excluding women and minorities from training and developmental experiences that are designed to prepare them for upper-level management positions. The OFCCP found that almost none of the companies kept track of the developmental opportunities, participation on task forces and committees, or special projects and assignments given to women and minorities.

3. A lack of organizational accountability for EEO in higher-level positions.

According to Robert Lattimer of Diversity Consultants in Atlanta, the glass ceiling cannot be broken unless women, minorities, and other diverse groups are allowed to participate in higher-level jobs. The challenge in managing a diverse workforce is to recognize the importance of managing people who are different and who refuse to adopt the models of the predominant group (typically white males in the 40 to 60 age group). Lattimer notes that women in today's workforce are extraordinarily talented and committed to the employer's goals, but they have "no intentions of adopting the white male management style to be successful."

Diversity initiatives at E. I. duPont de Nemours & Company include affirmative action, work and family, and professional development efforts through the corporation's Workforce Partnering Division. In 1986, du Pont named a manager to the full-time job of accelerating the upward mobility of women and minorities into top management and, at the same time, expanded its range of educational offerings.

Charles Thomas, vice president of human resources at the Prudential Insurance Company, states that Prudential's focus is to integrate women into its corporate environment. He notes that women hold 42 percent of the company's management positions, an increase of only 2 percent since the mid-1960s. Although most of the firm's female managers are concentrated in the lower and middle management levels, some are breaking through to the senior level, Thomas says. "Our pipeline for women looks pretty good," he asserts. By 1995, Prudential expects to have women represented at all levels of management. Thomas says the company can no longer afford "to have a work climate where one group is running the show and the other is being excluded."

Advocates for breaking the glass ceiling recommend that the following steps be taken:

1. Top management should make a commitment to improve advancement opportunities for women and minorities.

2. Awareness seminars should be held to show the impact that sexist and cultural stereotypes and attitudes have on the work environment and on the opportunities for women and minorities.

3. Career ladders should allow qualified men, women, and minorities to have equal access to top management positions.

4. Information about job openings should be equally accessible to men, women, and minorities.

5. Clear goals and performance standards should be developed for each job, and objective measures should be used to measure an employee's job performance. Promotion criteria should be free of sexist or cultural biases.

6. Company officials conducting interviews should be selected for their reputation for treating men and women equally. The interview process should be scrutinized so that selection criteria are explicit and do not place women or minorities at a disadvantage.

7. Equally qualified men, women, and minorities should be given equal opportunities for desirable job assignments and tasks. Qualified women and minorities should be placed in visible, critical jobs within the company.

8. Committees that make promotion decisions should avoid gender- or culturally- based criteria in the evaluation of women and minorities.

9. Gender and cultural biases should be eliminated when using performance evaluations to make individual compensation decisions.

■ Introduction

Prior to the enactment of EEO legislation in the early 1960s, little attention was given to the impact that personnel policies had on employees insofar as race, sex, age, handicap status, and other factors were concerned. The passage of federal and state EEO legislation marked an attempt by Congress and state legislatures to eliminate employment discrimination rooted in racial prejudices, sexist stereotypes, and bias toward older and handicapped employees. Since 1964, rulings by administrative agencies and the courts have gradually clarified the meaning of the EEO laws and delineated areas such as the use of selection tests, pay practices, employee benefit plans, sexual harassment on the job, and other concerns that would require careful evaluation by personnel administrators.

This chapter covers the issue of employment discrimination and the federal and state EEO laws. The concepts of unfair discrimination, fair hiring, affirmative action, and reverse discrimination are defined to provide a broad understanding of the impact and purpose of the various federal and state EEO laws. Provisions of each major EEO law are discussed. Finally, the major areas of EEO litigation are examined.

■ The Concept of Employment Discrimination

Discrimination Defined

Personnel/human resource management is by necessity a discriminatory function. Most personnel decisions involve legal discrimination, but a personnel decision may inadvertently result in the violation of an EEO law. When one applicant is hired and another rejected for the same position, a form of discrimination has occurred. If the applicant hired was clearly more qualified for the job in terms of *job-relevant* experience, education, and other criteria, then the discrimination is in all likelihood legal, even if the rejected applicant is a member of a group protected under EEO law.

Illegal employment discrimination is a complex and elusive concept to define. Shortly after the EEO laws went into effect in the mid-1960s, the courts looked at the motives or intent of an employer to determine whether a personnel-related decision constituted illegal discrimination. A personnel policy prohibiting the hiring of qualified blacks or women would be a prime example of intentional, unfair, and hence illegal discrimination. It soon became obvious to the courts that an employer's motives were impossible to ascertain except in instances of the most flagrant unfair employment practices. Today, both intentional and unintentional discriminatory practices may violate the EEO laws if they unjustly and adversely affect a protected group.

Employment discrimination usually occurs in one of two forms: (1) disparate *treatment* and (2) disparate *impact*. The first category to evolve, *disparate treatment,* involves practices such as an absolute refusal to hire blacks, paying a woman a lower wage than that paid to a man for the same work, or discharging a Spanish-surnamed employee for an offense for which other employees are treated with leniency. Many cases of disparate treatment involve intentional bias by an employer who harbors racial, sexist, or other prejudices. Some of these are isolated incidents involving only one or a few employees, whereas others represent a concerted effort by an employer to exclude a specific race, sex, or age group from being hired or obtaining fair treatment.

A second category of discrimination involves policies or practices that have a disparate or adverse impact on a protected group. For example, an employer may elect to hire only unmarried applicants who do not have preschool-age children. Such a hiring policy is likely to have an adverse impact on female applicants who are divorced or unwed because a higher percentage of single mothers have custody of their children than do single fathers. The issue of adverse impact has it origins in the landmark U.S. Supreme Court case of *Griggs v. Duke Power.*[1] The *Duke Power* case involved a situation in which the employer required that all employees

---

[1] *Griggs v. Duke Power,* 401 U.S. 424 (1971).

possess a high school diploma and pass an intelligence test and a mechanical aptitude test in order qualify for the more desirable and higher-paying jobs (known as *inside* jobs, as opposed to general labor and coal handling jobs, which were referred to as *outside* jobs). Both a federal district court and a U.S. court of appeals agreed that the Duke Power Company had not engaged in unlawful discrimination. However, the U.S. Supreme Court reversed the lower court decisions and held that (1) the high school diploma requirement and test scores excluded a higher percentage of black applicants than whites and that (2) Duke Power could not demonstrate that the diploma requirement and test scores were job-related. That is, the company had to show that employees with a high school diploma and "acceptable" intelligence and mechanical aptitude test scores were better employees than those who failed to meet these requirements. Perhaps the most important precedent of the *Duke Power* case is that the Supreme Court held that *a lack of discriminatory intent is not a sufficient defense*.[2] Had the *Duke Power* decision been decided in favor of the employer, the impact of the EEO laws would have been diluted significantly; all an employer would need to do was plead that the discrimination was accidental or unintentional, and no violation of the law would be found.

Illegal discrimination exists when members of a protected group (e.g., blacks, women, persons older than 40) have a lower likelihood of being recruited, selected, promoted, given merit raises, or receiving other favorable treatment, although the probability of their performing successfully on a job is the same as it is for individuals not belonging to a minority group. The term *minority* pertains to groups who have *historically* been plagued by unfair employment discrimination or who are greatly outnumbered by other race, sex, and age groups. Under certain circumstances, white males, who are otherwise historically and statistically considered to be nonminorities, are also protected under the EEO laws.

Equal Employment Opportunity Versus Affirmative Action Obligations

The concept of *equal employment opportunity* means that members of a protected group or class must be employed without being subjected to the various forms of unfair discrimination just discussed. *Affirmative action* represents an obligation for employers holding federal government contracts not only to engage in fair and nondiscriminatory practices but also to make a special effort to recruit, hire, and promote job-qualified members of a preferred or targeted group (typically blacks, females, Vietnam-era veterans, and the handicapped). It is important to note that it is rare for either EEO laws or affirmative action programs to require a firm to favor a worker in a targeted group over a better-qualified nonminority employee.

[2]Robert D. Gatewood and Hubert S. Feild, *Human Resource Selection*, 2nd ed. (Chicago: The Dryden Press, 1990), p. 49.

The underlying rationale of affirmative action programs is to enable *qualified* women, racial minorities, and other targeted groups to catch up and overcome the effects of past discrimination in the workplace.[3] *Reverse discrimination*, on the other hand, involves giving preference to targeted groups, usually by excluding better-qualified candidates who are not part of the preferred group. The Bush administration was opposed to civil rights legislation that proposed to establish hiring quotas, which would force companies to employ a specific number or percentage of minorities. Except under unusual circumstances, reverse discrimination is not legal under EEO law.

The only legislation requiring affirmative action protects the handicapped and Vietnam-era veterans. Nevertheless, employers holding federal contracts (above a specified dollar amount) are required by *federal executive order*[4] to engage in fair and affirmative employment if racial minorities, persons over age 40, and women are underrepresented in a firm's workforce. Affirmative hiring is not required by law or executive order to alleviate religious discrimination. The federal courts have attempted to clarify the meaning of equal employment opportunity, affirmative action, and reverse discrimination, but the concepts often become blurred and distorted in practice.

Employers must agree to fair and affirmative hiring in order to secure and hold business contracts with federal agencies. Companies failing to make a good-faith effort to meet affirmative action goals risk cancellation or denial of future contracts. Although personnel managers, union leaders, and society in general today accept the need for equal employment opportunity, there is some resistance to affirmative hiring and promotion, which is often viewed as unjustified reverse discrimination.[5] Affirmative hiring is currently required for more than 60 percent of the total labor force. Those responsible for the policy and operation of personnel departments must not only be concerned with the EEO laws and executive orders, but must also preserve a sense of equity in the workplace to avoid damaging the morale of employees who perceive themselves as being better qualified than those in the preferred group.[6]

[3]See Susan B. Garland, "The Civil Rights Champion Trying to Mend Bush's Fences," *Business Week* (December 31, 1990), p. 63; J. S. Leonard, "The Impact of Affirmative Action on Employment," *Journal of Labor Economics* (October 1984), pp. 439–463; and Jeanne C. Poole and E. Theodore Kautz, "An EEO-AA Program That Exceeds Quotas—It Targets Biases," *Personnel Journal* (January 1987), p. 103.

[4]Executive orders enacted by the president of the United States do not have the permanence of a law and can be rescinded by the president or succeeding presidents.

[5]James R. Redeker, "The Supreme Court on Affirmative Action: Conflicting Opinions," *Personnel* (October 1986), p. 8; and Betty Southard Murphy, Wayne E. Barlow, and D. Diane Hatch, "Supreme Court Reaffirms Affirmative Action," *Personnel Journal* (September 1986), p. 19.

[6]In 1979, the U.S. Supreme Court ruled in *Steelworkers v. Weber* that reverse discrimination was permissible in order to eliminate a conspicuous racial imbalance in "traditionally segregated job categories" 20 FEP Cases 1 (1979). The original plaintiff in the case was Brian Weber, a white employee, who was denied admission into a union-sponsored training program in favor of black employees who possessed less seniority.

■ An Overview of Equal Employment Opportunity Legislation

Title VII of the 1964 Civil Rights Act, as Amended

Title VII prohibits unfair employment discrimination based on race, sex religion, color, and national origin by federal and state governmental agencies, private firms, nonprofit organizations, unions, and employment agencies operating in interstate commerce.[7] Because the coverage of Title VII is so broad and covers a multitude of organizations, it is perhaps simpler to list the organizations, individuals, and jobs where Title VII does *not* apply:

1. Religious corporations, associations, educational institutions, or societies can limit employment to individuals of a particular religion. Discrimination based on race, sex, or age by religious organizations, however, is illegal.
2. Bona fide, tax-exempt private clubs.
3. Indian tribes insofar as they act as employers.
4. Employers operating in *intrastate* commerce or employing fewer than 15 employees (many state EEO laws cover these firms).
5. Elected state and local officials, their personal assistants, and immediate advisers.
6. Jobs requiring national security clearance. For example, a person's national origin may make it impossible to obtain a government job that requires a top secret security clearance.

Title VII makes it unlawful for an employer to discriminate with regard to hiring, compensation, firing, and other conditions and privileges of employment on the basis of race, color, religion, sex, or national origin. The ban on *race* discrimination is not limited to racial minorities who have traditionally experienced unfair treatment or adverse impact; Title VII also protects members of majority races. In connection with the ban on race discrimination, discrimination based on an individual's skin *color* is also illegal under Title VII. For example, an employer who will hire only light-skinned blacks who physically resemble whites violates Title VII because of the *color*-protected classification. By including both race and color as protected classifications, Congress avoided potential arguments about subtle anthropological distinctions concerning the classification of races.[8]

Sex discrimination is the most frequently litigated charge under Title VII. Many sex discrimination charges are precipitated by stereotypes of male or female behaviors that have been perpetuated for long periods of time. The assumption that females are less capable than males of performing physically strenuous work

---

[7]Public Law 88-352 (1964), as amended.

[8]Commerce Clearing House, Inc., *1986 Guidebook to Fair Employment Practices* (Chicago: Commerce Clearing House, Inc., 1986), p. 8.

is a common stereotype that has been used to ban females from traditionally male-dominated jobs. Discrimination against pregnant women or women with small children is another common form of sex discrimination. Sexual harassment is also a form of sex discrimination because women are forced to endure an unpleasant and tense working environment and may have career opportunities blocked if they fail to yield to pressures for sexual favors.

National origin discrimination occurs when an employer uses an individual's nationality or language as a basis for unfair treatment. For example, an employer who bans a Spanish-speaking employee from a job because the individual's English-speaking skills are poor may be in violation of Title VII unless it can be shown that a good command of English is a necessary requirement for performing the job.[9] When an employer imposes minimum height and weight requirements in order for an employee or applicant to become eligible for a certain job (e.g., police officer), then there may be national origin discrimination against persons of Oriental or Hispanic descent (as well as sex discrimination against women).[10] The protection from national origin discrimination applies to all individuals living in the Unites States, but discrimination based on alien status alone is not protected under Title VII. As a result, an employer may refuse employment to noncitizens.

Religion is also a protected classification under Title VII. Employers normally cannot place hiring bans on employees because of their religious faith. In addition, employers are expected to make "reasonable accommodation" to the religious practices of their employees whenever possible. An employer might, for example, be expected to allow someone of the Jewish faith to have the day off for Yom Kippur, a holiday observed with fasting and prayer. However, the employer is not required to make reasonable accommodation to an employee's religious beliefs or practices if an undue hardship will be imposed on the firm or if the terms of a collective bargaining agreement (negotiated between the employer and a union) will be violated.

In exceptional circumstances, employers are entitled to a *bona fide occupational qualification (BFOQ)* permitting legal discrimination if it is "reasonably necessary to the normal operation" of the business. BFOQs can be obtained if a company can demonstrate that cost, efficiency, or safety is impaired. In addition, BFOQs are limited to religion, sex, or national origin discrimination and are not granted on the basis of race or color. BFOQs might be allowed under the following circumstances:

- A nursing home was granted a BFOQ to discriminate against male nursing aides because the majority of the facility's residents were female.[11]

---

[9]See, for example, *Gutierrez v. Municipal Court*, 51 FEP Cases 435 (1988); *Garcia v. Rush-Presbyterian Medical Center*, 26 FEP Cases 1557 (1981); and *Vasquez v. McAllen Bag and Supply Corp.*, 27 FEP Cases 562 (1981).

[10]Avak Keotahian, "National Origin Discrimination in Employment: Do Plaintiffs Ever Win?" *Employee Relations Law Journal* (Winter 1985), pp. 467–492.

[11]*Fesel v. Masonic Home*, 17 FEP Cases 330 (1978).

- The U.S. Supreme Court held that women can be barred from working as guards in maximum security prisons when their jobs would require them to come into contact with male prisoners.[12]
- A male actor might be rejected for casting in a female role in a Broadway play.[13]
- An employment application of a male might be rejected for the position of female locker room attendant at a health spa.

As a general rule, BFOQs are granted sparingly under Title VII. Except where the issues of morality and decency are involved (such as in the case of the male locker attendant in a locker room for females), customer preferences are not grounds for a BFOQ. For example, an airline could not obtain a BFOQ to ban the employment of female flight officers (pilots) simply because a large number of the company's customers feel safer with a male flight officer in command. A county sheriff violated Title VII by refusing to hire females as deputy sheriffs and correctional officers in an all-male county jail (not a maximum security prison). Ruling that the county failed to show that gender was a BFOQ for correctional officers, a U.S. court of appeals ruled that the employer failed to demonstrate "why it could not accommodate, through the reasonable modification of the facility and job functions, female corrections officers."[14] In the absence of a BFOQ, however, employers must base hiring, promotion, and other decisions on an employee's *individual* qualifications rather than on the general characteristics or stereotypes based on sex or national origin.

The Equal Employment Opportunity Commission

Title VII (and several other EEO laws to be discussed) is enforced by the Equal Employment Opportunity Commission (EEOC). Charges filed with the EEOC are referred for 60 days to a deferral agency if the jurisdiction in which the complaint is filed has a state or local EEO agency.[15] An individual filing a Title VII complaint in Illinois, for example, would first have his or her case referred to the Illinois Department of Human Rights for 60 days. At the end of the 60-day period a charge is automatically filed with the EEOC unless the state or local agency has satisfactorily resolved the case. The EEOC has the authority to investigate and conciliate charges of discrimination. The 1972 amendments to Title VII empower the EEOC to bring action in a U.S. district court against a party who is suspected of violating the act. A charge must be filed in writing with the EEOC within 300

---

[12]*Dothard v. Rawlinson*, 15 FEP Cases 10 (1977).

[13]The Bureau of National Affairs, Inc., *Fair Employment Practices Manual: BNA Labor Relations Reporter* (Washington, D.C.: The Bureau of National Affairs, Inc., 1984), Section 421.

[14]*U.S. v. Gregory*, CA 4, Nos. 86-3121 and 86-3122 (1987).

[15]The purpose of the deferral policy is to support and encourage the operation of state and local EEO and civil rights agencies. It was not intended to entangle those filing complaints with procedural technicalities. The Bureau of National Affairs, Inc., *Fair Employment Practices Manual: BNA Labor Relations Reporter* (Washington, D.C.: The Bureau of National Affairs, Inc., 1985), p. 431.

days of the alleged discriminatory action (180 days if the plaintiff does not first file a charge with the appropriate state agency).

After the charge is filed, the EEOC serves a notice to the accused party (who, in legal terminology, is referred to as the *respondent*). The EEOC then investigates the complaint to determine whether there is reasonable cause to believe that the charge has merit. Under normal circumstances, the EEOC attempts to determine reasonable cause within 120 days. If no reasonable cause for a Title VII violation is found, then the charge is dismissed. Should the EEOC's investigation reveal that a violation of the Act has occurred, it will engage in conciliatory efforts with the respondent in an attempt to resolve the problems listed in the charge. The Director of Compliance notifies the charging party and respondent that a conciliator will meet with them and attempt to reach a solution that is acceptable to both the charging party and the EEOC. If all parties are satisfied with the terms and conditions of the compliance efforts, a Conciliation Agreement is submitted to the EEOC for approval. The EEOC may also help the respondent to avoid future Title VII charges by including in the Conciliation Agreement modifications of employment practices not listed in the original charge. In the event that conciliatory efforts are not successful, the EEOC may bring civil action in an appropriate U.S. district court or it can issue a right to sue letter that allows the charging party to file a suit in a U.S. district court.

The major EEOC compliance actions are as follows:

- *Preliminary relief*, in which an injunction is used to prevent an organization from engaging in discriminatory acts until the complaint can be resolved by the EEOC or the courts. Preliminary relief is usually granted in exceptional circumstances where irreparable harm is likely to occur to the alleged victims of discrimination.

- *Affirmative relief* includes actions such as reinstating workers to their jobs, ordering an employer to promote an employee who has been victimized by discrimination, or granting tenure, seniority, or other favorable employment conditions to an individual who has suffered from illegal discrimination. Actions involving affirmative relief are often enforced through court-approved agreements known as *consent decrees.*
- *Back pay* compensates discrimination victims for lost pay that would have been earned in the *past* had the discrimination never occurred. For example, a woman who is denied a promotion because of illegal sex discrimination may receive back pay to compensate her for the delays associated with remaining in a lower-paying job. Back pay is usually based on the amount that the employee would have earned (plus interest) less any income from outside sources (e.g., Social Security disability payments or income from another job held by the employee while the discrimination case was pending). Back pay may also include lost bonuses, lost overtime to which the employee would have likely been entitled, lost health insurance benefits, and compensation for moving expenses or the repossession of an automobile.
- *Front pay* compensates discrimination victims for the loss of *future* wages. For example, a woman who is denied a promotion because of illegal sex discrimi-

nation may receive front pay to compensate her for lost future income in the event that the higher-paying job (which she failed to receive) is no longer available.

- *Attorney's fees* covering reasonable legal costs may be assessed by the courts against organizations that have been found guilty of employment discrimination.

Prior to the passage of the Civil Rights Act of 1991, remedies were based primarily on the *make-whole* concept. Under this concept, a victim of discrimination is entitled to remedies that would restore him or her to the economic position that would have existed had the illegal discrimination not occurred. The enactment of the Civil Rights Act of 1991 provided for two major categories of damages—compensatory and punitive:

- *Compensatory* and *punitive damages* may be awarded to victims of employment discrimination that is based on sex, national origin, religion, and disability. Under the Civil Rights Act of 1991, victims of the aforementioned types of employment discrimination may collect compensatory damages relating to "future pecuniary losses, emotional pain, suffering, inconvenience, mental anguish, loss of enjoyment of life, and other nonpecuniary losses." Limited punitive damages may also be assessed against organizations as punishment for discriminatory practices. Punitive damages are limited and are based on a sliding scale that is linked to the number of persons employed by a firm. For example, firms with 16 to 50 employees are limited to punitive damage liabilities of $50,000, whereas firms that employ 500 or more workers have a maximum punitive damage liability of $300,000.

The Immigration Reform and Control Act of 1986

The Immigration Reform and Control Act of 1986 (IRCA) is designed to regulate the employment of aliens in the United States and requires that job applicants provide suitable documentation to verify their citizenship status and employability. The act makes it unlawful for employers, employment agencies, and unions to recruit, hire, or refer aliens who are known not to be eligible for employment. An unauthorized alien is one who is not a lawful permanent resident of the United States or is not authorized by the attorney general to work in the United States. Unauthorized aliens who were employed prior to the enactment of the IRCA as well as those referred by public employment agencies (state Job Service) are exempt from the act. The IRCA is enforced by the U.S. Department of Justice, Special Counsel for Unfair Immigration-Related Employment, and each employer must present a sworn statement certifying that the status of each alien has been reviewed. Acceptable documentation that entitles an alien to work in the United States includes a U.S. passport, certificate of U.S. citizenship or naturalization, an unexpired foreign passport with a U.S. employment authorization, an alien registration receipt card (green card), and other documentation acceptable to the attorney general. Employers and others who violate the IRCA are subject to civil and criminal penalties.[16]

Discrimination against otherwise authorized aliens and others on the basis of citizenship or national origin is prohibited under the IRCA as well as Title VII.[17] The IRCA, however, does permit employers to lawfully prefer U.S. citizens or nationals when it is required by law, executive order, or other essential government interest. If an employer can demonstrate that a U.S. citizen (or U.S. national) and an alien are equally qualified based on job-relevant criteria, then preference can be given to the U.S. citizen or national. Discharges and layoffs, however, cannot be based on citizenship status when a citizen and an alien are equally qualified. Title VII violations are possible, according to the EEOC, if employers attempt to reject "foreign-looking" applicants because of their physical appearance or accent or if they institute unnecessary English-speaking job requirements, height requirements, or permit on-the-job harassment of foreign employees.[18]

Studies by the U.S. General Accounting Office (GAO) and the Urban Institute indicate that the IRCA may have caused employers to discriminate against job applicants who look or sound foreign. The GAO's report indicates that 19 percent of the employers surveyed had begun discriminatory practices as a result of the IRCA. According to the Urban Institute, young male Hispanic job applicants were three times more likely than their Anglo counterparts to be treated unfavorably. The GAO believes that employers are discriminating because they do not fully understand the IRCA's provisions and are fearful of inadvertently hiring an undocumented alien. Furthermore, employers are confused about how to determine employment eligibility, and many firms are wary that some job applicants are providing counterfeit eligibility documents.

The IRCA was amended by the Immigration Act of 1990. Amendments to the IRCA include more severe civil and criminal penalties for national origin discrimination. Although companies with 15 or more employees are forbidden to discriminate against persons because of their national origin under Title VII, the IRCA covers firms having fewer than 15 workers. The Immigration Act of 1990 extends protection to seasonal agricultural workers. Under the IRCA, aliens had to declare an intention to become U.S. citizens before they were protected by the act. However, the Immigration Act of 1990 protects persons who have not declared their intention to become citizens. There is currently a proposal to reduce the number of acceptable verification documents from 10 to 2. This move should

---

[16]Robert G. Heiserman, "Employers Face New Challenges Under the Immigration Reform Act of 1986," *The Human Resources Yearbook, 1987 Edition* (Englewood Cliffs, N.J.: Prentice-Hall, Inc., 1987), pp. 11.1–11.6.

[17]Diana Solis, "Double Bind: Employers Who Shun Illegals Risk Discrimination Charges," *The Wall Street Journal* (June 5, 1987), p. 12(W). p. 22(E) , col. 1.

[18]The Bureau of National Affairs, Inc., *Fair Employment Practices Manual: BNA Labor Relations Reporter* (Washington, D.C.: The Bureau of National Affairs, Inc., 1987), p. 421.

reduce employer confusion and make it more difficult for aliens to obtain counterfeit documentation.[19]

The Age Discrimination in Employment Act of 1967, as Amended

The Age Discrimination in Employment Act (ADEA) of 1967 was originally enacted to promote employment opportunities for persons between the ages of 40 and 65. The age limit for protected individuals was raised to 70 in 1978, and then the upper age limit was removed altogether in 1987. Thus the ADEA prohibits age-based employment discrimination against persons who are *40 years of age or older*. The act's purpose is "to promote the employment of older persons based on their ability rather than age; to help employers and workers find ways of meeting problems arising from the impact of age on employment."[20]

Emphasis has been placed on evaluating the working ability of employees in the protected age group, rather than gearing employment decisions solely to age without regard to physical and mental capabilities. To attain this objective, the ADEA covers hiring, discharge, and discriminatory treatment during employment, advertisements reflecting age preference, refusal by employment agencies to refer older applicants, discriminatory treatment by labor unions, and retaliation against employees.[21] The ADEA covers private sector employers affecting interstate commerce with 20 or more employees. Federal and state government employees are also covered, as are employment agencies and labor unions. Enforcement authority is vested with the EEOC. The ADEA permits punitive damages in instances of willful discrimination.

The Rehabilitation Act of 1973

Section 503 of the Rehabilitation Act of 1973, as amended (also known as the *Vocational Rehabilitation Act*), requires that organizations holding federal contracts in excess of $2,500 employ the physically and mentally handicapped on an affirmative basis. If the contract is in excess of $50,000 and the company employs 50 or more workers, the contractor must prepare a written affirmative action program. Section 504 of the act forbids discrimination against handicapped

---

[19]See The Bureau of National Affairs, Inc., "IRCA Amendments," *Fair Employment Practices* (Washington, D.C.: The Bureau of National Affairs, Inc., December 24, 1990), pp. 149–150, and The Bureau of National Affairs, Inc., "GAO Says IRCA Bias; Repeal of Employer Sanctions Urged," *Fair Employment Practices* (Washington, D.C.: The Bureau of National Affairs, Inc., April 12, 1990), pp 45–46.

[20]The Bureau of National Affairs, Inc., *Fair Employment Practices Manual: BNA Labor Relations Reporter* (Washington, D.C.: The Bureau of National Affairs, Inc., 1987), p. 421.

[21]29 C.F.R. 860.50 (1979).

persons by organizations receiving federal financial assistance. Section 501 of the act requires that federal agencies take affirmative action in hiring and promoting the handicapped.[22] Sections 503 and 504 are enforced by the U.S. Department of Labor and Section 501 by the EEOC.

The act's definition of *handicapped individual* is broad and includes "any person who (1) has a physical or mental impairment which substantially limits one or more of such person's major life activities, (2) has a record of such impairment, or (3) is regarded as having such an impairment." For example, a definition such as this protects not only persons with the obvious types of handicaps, such as amputated limbs, impaired vision or hearing, and partial paralysis, but cancer victims, diabetics, and those with a history of heart disease as well.

Although discrimination against handicapped individuals is forbidden and affirmative action is required, there is no obligation to hire persons who are either unable to perform or who are less skilled than employees without handicaps. The act protects only "qualified handicapped individuals" who are capable of performing a particular job with "reasonable accommodation" to their handicap. Reasonable accommodation to an employee's handicap might include modifying job tasks and duties so that they can be more easily performed by the employee, installing ramps for persons confined to wheelchairs, or allowing an employee additional rest or medication breaks.

The Americans with Disabilities Act of 1990

Title I of the Americans with Disabilities Act (ADA) of 1990 (effective July 26, 1992) is a comprehensive statute that expands the coverage and scope of the Rehabilitation Act. Employers engaged in industry affecting interstate commerce that have 25 or more employees are covered under the ADA, along with employment agencies, labor organizations, and joint labor-management committees. Unlike the Rehabilitation Act, a firm is covered under the ADA even if it does not hold a federal contract or receive federal financial assistance. The federal government and government-owned corporations (which are usually covered by the Rehabilitation Act), Indian tribes, and bona fide tax-exempt private clubs all are excluded from ADA coverage. Religious organizations may give employment preference to their own members. The EEOC is responsible for enforcing the act.

Employers may not discriminate against a "qualified individual with a disability" with regard to job applications, hiring, promotions, discharge, compensation, training, or other terms and conditions of employment. The ADA's definition of disability and requirements for reasonable accommodation appear to be quite similar those of the Rehabilitation Act. A "qualified individual with a disability" is one who, with or without reasonable accommodation, can perform the essential functions of the job. It is the employer's responsibility to define the essential

---

[22]Public Law 95-602 (1973). The U.S. Department of Justice held in 1988 that the fear of contagion by employees working with AIDS victims was not grounds for discrimination against those tested as seropositive for AIDS.

functions of a job. Employers are not required to engage in reasonable accommodation if such accommodation will impose a severe financial or operational burden on the company.

The ADA specifically excludes a number of groups from protection. The law amends the Rehabilitation Act to exclude from its coverage current illegal drug users and current alcoholics who cannot perform their job duties or whose employment presents a threat to property or the safety of others. Rehabilitated alcoholics and drug addicts are protected, however. The act also states that homosexuality and bisexuality are not regarded as disabilities. Furthermore, transvestites, pedophiles, and other persons with sexual disorders not resulting from physical impairments are not protected under the ADA. Likewise, compulsive gamblers, kleptomaniacs, and pyromaniacs are not regarded as being disabled under the law. Persons whose jobs involve food handling may be involuntarily transferred to another job if they have certain infectious and communicable diseases that pose a danger to the public.

The ADA allows employers to require medical examinations of employees (and applicants who have already been offered a job) only to the extent that the examinations are job related and consistent with business necessity. The ADA also allows the employer to give voluntary physical examinations in conjunction with employee health programs. All information obtained from a medical examination must be kept confidential. Employee drug testing, however, is not regarded as a medical examination under the act. Thus, the ADA permits employers to test employees for the use of illegal drugs and alcohol in the workplace. The law does not protect employees who are disciplined or fired for on-the-job drug use or who test positive for illicit drugs.

The Civil Rights Act of 1991

After two years of extensive debate, compromises, and threats of a presidential veto, the Civil Rights Act of 1991 was enacted. Although specific details of the act are discussed in subsequent sections of this chapter, several major changes occurred in the way EEO litigation will be handled. First, the Civil Rights Act of 1991 reverses parts of seven U.S. Supreme Court cases whose decisions were handed down since 1988. Second, the act amends parts of Title VII of the 1964 Civil Rights Act, the ADEA, the ADA, and several other laws.

The Civil Rights Act of 1991 has a strong impact on the hiring and promotion of employees. In addition, it makes it possible for certain victims of intentional employment discrimination to collect large sums of money in compensatory and punitive damages. The act also provides for more extensive use of jury trials. In addition, the law requires the EEOC to establish a Technical Assistance Training Institute for covered employers, as well as to provide educational and outreach activities for individuals who historically have been victims of employment discrimination. The Civil Rights Act of 1991 establishes a Glass Ceiling Commission to study barriers to the advancement of women and minorities in the workforce and to recommend ways of reducing these barriers. Section 205 of the act provides for a national award for diversity and excellence in executive management to businesses that have made a substantial effort to promote the opportunities and developmental experiences of women and minorities.

The 1991 law also addresses issues such as on-the-job bias, seniority systems, expert witness fees, persons employed by U.S. firms in foreign locations, and government employee rights. To a large extent, the act was designed to send a message to the U.S. Supreme Court that its decisions in recent years have been too favorable to employers. Many experts also believe that the law creates a friendly legal environment for job applicants and employees who feel that they are victims of illegal employment discrimination. The improved potential for large financial judgments against employers will also increase the number of complaints filed under Title VII, the ADEA, the ADA, and other EEO laws.

The Vietnam Era Veterans Readjustment Assistance Act of 1974

Firms holding contracts with federal agencies in the amount of $10,000 or more must employ Vietnam-era veterans and disabled veterans of all wars on an affirmative basis.[23] Vietnam-era veterans are covered for a 4-year period from their date of discharge (other than a dishonorable discharge). A Vietnam-era veteran must have served on active military duty for at least 180 days between August 5, 1964, and May 7, 1975. Veterans who served on active military duty during this time, not only those who served in Vietnam, are entitled to affirmative employment. Disabled veterans are those with at least 30 percent disability, as well as those discharged for service-related disabilities. Employers are also required to list employment opportunities with local public employment offices, where referral priority is given to disabled veterans and veterans of the Vietnam era. The enforcement of the act requires that a person claiming illegal discrimination file a complaint with the Veterans' Employment Service of the Department of Labor.[24]

Federal Executive Orders

Title VII forbids unfair employment discrimination, but companies doing business with the federal government have the additional obligation of recruiting, hiring, and promoting women and minorities on an affirmative basis. Federal Executive Order 11 246 parallels Title VII with regard to the types of discrimination prohibited (race, sex, religion, color, and national origin). Contractors and subcontractors

[23]James W. Hall-Sheehy, "The Unknown Vietnam Vet Manager," *Harvard Business Review* (May-June 1986), p. 117.

[24]Section 403 of the 1974 act, as amended, 38 U.S.C. sec. 2014. The law appears as last amended by the Veterans' Compensation, Education, and Employment Amendments of 1982, Public Law 97-306, 96 Stat. 1429, effective October 14, 1982.

with contracts in excess of $10,000 must engage in affirmative action, and those with 50 or more employees and contracts of $50,000 or above must develop an affirmative action plan that includes a set of specific results-oriented procedures and goals designed to correct any underutilization of women or racial minority groups in the firm's workforce.[25] Other executive orders apply to age,[26] federal employment,[27] citizenship requirements,[28] handicapped federal employees,[29] and veterans.[30]

Covered employers are expected to make a good-faith effort to correct any underrepresentation of targeted groups (e.g., blacks) in their affirmative action programs. Federal executive orders are enforced by the Department of Labor, with the Office of Federal Contract Compliance Programs (OFCCP) having specific responsibility for ensuring compliance. When a compliance review reveals that a contractor has failed to make a good-faith effort to attain its affirmative action goals, the OFCCP attempts to reach a conciliation agreement with the employer. Organizations with affirmative action obligations may be required to provide back pay, seniority credit, promotions, or other forms of relief to victims of discrimination. The employer is also entitled to a formal hearing before an administrative law judge. If attempts at conciliation are not successful, a contractor may lose its government contracts, have payments withheld, and be ineligible for future government contracts.

The Equal Pay Act of 1963

The Equal Pay Act of 1963,[31] an amendment to the Fair Labor Standards Act, requires equal pay for equal work; sex cannot be a factor in establishing pay differentials. Although provisions of the act do not contain a definition of the meaning of *equal work*, court cases and guidelines indicate the *equal* does not mean *identical*. The precise definition of what constitutes equal work hinges on an analysis of the specific jobs in question to determine whether responsibility, skill, effort, and working conditions are similar (rather than identical). Although pay differentials based on sex are unlawful, they are permitted for reasons of productivity, merit, and seniority. As a result of reorganization of EEO programs at the federal level, the Equal Pay Act is currently enforced by the EEOC. The Equal Pay Act and related issues are also discussed in Chapter 11.

[25]Executive Order 11246 signed by President Johnson, September 24, 1965, amended by Executive Order 11375 (October 13, 1967) and Executive Order 12086 (October 8, 1978).

[26]Executive Order 11141 (February 12, 1964).

[27]Executive Order 11478 (August 8, 1969).

[28]Executive Order 11935 (September 2, 1976).

[29]Executive Order 12125 (March 20, 1979).

[30]Executive Order 11701 (January 24, 1973).

[31]P.L. 88-38, codified as 29 U.S.C. sec. 206(d) (1963).

Equal Employment Opportunity in Multinational Corporations

Since many U.S. citizens work outside the United States, either for U.S.-owned corporations or for firms owned by foreign companies, the issues arises as to what extent such persons may be protected by Title VII, the ADEA, and other EEO laws. In 1991, the U.S. Supreme Court held that Title VII does not apply to American workers who are working outside of the United States. The case involved a naturalized U.S. citizen who worked for Aramco, a private American company. The employee in this case was allegedly the victim of racial, religious, and national origin discrimination, principally by his supervisor in Saudi Arabia.

The Supreme Court's ruling reversed the EEOC's position that Title VII applied to U.S. workers in foreign countries. However, Congress then nullified the Supreme Court's decision when it passed the Civil Rights Act of 1991. Section 12 of the Civil Rights Act of 1991 extends the coverage of Title VII and the ADA to American citizens employed by U.S. companies operating in foreign locations. Section 12 makes Title VII coverage comparable to that of the ADEA, which contains an explicit provision that provides protection to Americans who are over age 40 and work overseas for American companies. However, the Civil Rights Act contains an exemption that allows U.S. companies to avoid applying U.S. law if compliance with Title VII or the ADA would cause the company to violate a law of the foreign country in which it is located.[32]

Foreign-owned firms operating in the United States must also abide by U.S. EEO laws. A federal court ruled that a Japanese firm operating in the United States discriminated by firing American managers while retaining its Japanese managers. The three American managers of a Japanese-owned electronics distributor were terminated during a reduction in force. Although 66 of the firms 89 managers were dismissed during the layoffs, the employer discriminated by "reserving certain managerial positions for employees of Japanese origin," according to the court. The company was ordered to pay the managers $1,482,330 in front pay, $467,650 in back pay, and an additional $467,650 in punitive damages for willful violations of the managers' rights under the ADEA.[33]

State Equal Employment Opportunity Laws and Other Legal Avenues

Nearly all states, as well as many local jurisdictions, have EEO laws that, in some instances, provide a wider array of protection than federal EEO legislation. State laws often cover very small firms normally excluded under federal law; they may

---

[32]Equal Employment Opportunity Commission, *EEOC Policy Guide on Application of ADEA and Equal Pay Act Overseas* (Washington, D.C.: EEOC, March 3, 1989).

[33]*Fortino v. Quasar Co.*, 54 FEP Cases 966 (1990).

expand protection to include certain groups such as AIDS victims, homosexuals[34] and ex-convicts; or they may prohibit certain practices such as lie detector tests in personnel decisions. The most comprehensive EEO ordinance of this kind is Title 34 of the District of Columbia, which prohibits 13 kinds of discrimination, including physical appearance, matriculation, sexual preference, and political affiliation.

Victims of discrimination will occasionally use an earlier civil rights law such as the Civil Rights Acts of 1866, 1870, and 1871. These acts were passed after the Civil War to provide black citizens the same contractual rights and entitlement to legal action as white citizens. Although Title VII is used most often by victims of discrimination, the earlier civil rights laws may be used to obtain larger back pay settlements than provided by Title VII or in instances where Title VII is not applicable (such as when a small employer not affecting interstate commerce discriminates). When a state government engages in discrimination, an individual may seek relief under the 14th Amendment of the U.S. Constitution. Victims of discrimination by the federal government may pursue a remedy under the 5th Amendment. Both the 5th and 14th Amendments ensure equal protection and due process under the law.

Table 3-1 summarizes the major equal employment opportunity laws.

Role of the Courts in the Enforcement of Equal Employment Opportunity Laws

Although administrative agencies, such as the EEOC and state EEO commissions, resolve all but a small percentage of employment discrimination cases, these agencies usually cannot force parties to adhere to a conciliation agreement. When the administrative agencies fail to resolve a complaint or the parties involved are not satisfied with the agency's ruling, the issue is settled in a state or federal court.

For example, when the EEOC does not settle a charge, it can be appealed in federal district court and, eventually, taken to the U.S. Supreme Court. The role of the courts is to examine evidence, interpret the applicable EEO law, andadjudicate the dispute. Decisions by the courts, especially the U.S. Supreme Court, provide guidelines when similar cases arise in the future. Personnel managers, therefore, must not only be cognizant of the various EEO laws, but they must stay abreast of the major court rulings that interpret those laws.

---

[34]Laws that protect against *sex discrimination* do not usually provide protection for *sexual preference* or *sexual orientation*. However, in February 1988, a U.S. court of appeals ruled that the U.S. military could not prevent the re-enlistment of a homosexual whose military record indicated entirely satisfactory performance. Although this case was based on constitutional issues rather than on Title VII, it could conceivably mark the beginning of a broader interpretation of what constitutes sex discrimination.

TABLE 3-1   A Summary of the Major EEO Laws

EEO Law	Major Requirements/ Prohibitions	Organizations Covered	Exemptions	Enforcement
Title VII of 1964 Civil Rights Act	Race, sex, religion, color, and national origin discrimination that is not supported by business necessity	Private organizations with more than 15 employees, employment labor unions, state and federal government agencies	Religious organizations (partial), private clubs, aliens working for U.S. organizations in foreign locations, Indian tribes, organizations with fewer than 15 employees, Communist Party members, jobs requiring a government security clearance, BFOQs for religious, sex, and national origin	Equal Employment Opportunity Commission
Immigration Reform and Control Act	Recruiting, hiring, or referring aliens who are not eligible for employment in the United States	Private organizations, employment agencies, labor unions	Aliens employed prior to the effective date of the act, aliens referred by public employment agencies, aliens possessing proper documentation under the act	U.S. Department of Justice, Special Counsel for Unfair Immigration– Related Employment
Age Discrimination in Employment Act of 1967	Discrimination against persons over age 40 that is not supported by business necessity. Involuntary retirement is prohibited for most employee groups	Same as those covered by Title VII, except that private organizations with 20 or more employees are covered.	Discrimination permitted based on resasonable factors other than age. BFOQs granted for public safety and other reasons	Equal Employment Opportunity Commission

TABLE 3-1   (continued)

EEO Law	Major Requirements/ Prohibitions	Organizations Covered	Exemptions	Enforcement
Rehabilitation Act of 1973	Discrimination against otherwise qualified physically and mentally handicapped persons. Reasonable accommodation to employee's handicap is required	Organizations holding federal contracts in excess of $2,500 or receiving federal financial assistance. Federal agencies are covered	No BFOQs. Employees must be evaluated on an individual basis	U.S. Department of Labor (Sections 503 and 504) Equal Employment Opportunity Commission (Section 501)
Americans with Disabilities Act of 1990	Discrimination against qualified individuals with a disability. Reasonable accommodation is required	Organizations with 25 or more employees affecting interstate commerce, employment agencies, labor organizations, and joint labor-management committees	Persons with various sexual and gender identity disorders not resulting from a physical impairment, compulsive gamblers, kleptomaniacs, pyromaniacs, current illegal drug users, and alcoholics who are unable to perform their jobs in a satisfactory manner	Equal Employment Opportunity Commission
Civil Rights Act of 1991	Amends and clarifies provisions of Title VII, the Americans with Disabilities Act, and other EEO laws	Same as Title VII and the Americans with Disabilities Act	Same as Title VII and the Americans with Disabilities Act	Equal Employment Opportunity Commission

continued

TABLE 3-1   (concluded)

EEO Law	Major Requirements/ Prohibitions	Organizations Covered	Exemptions	Enforcement
Vietnam Era Veterans Readjustment Act of 1974	Affirmative employment of veterans serving in the armed forces between August 5, 1964, and May 7, 1975, and disabled veterans	Organizations holding federal contracts of $10,000 or more	Veterans more than 4 years beyond military discharge and veterans receiving dishonorable discharges	U.S. Department of Labor, Veterans Employment Service
Federal Executive Orders	Affirmative employment based on race, sex (E.O. 11246, 11375, and 12086), and veteran status (E.O. 11701), and handicap (E.O. 12125)	Organizations holding federal contracts of $10,000 or more		U.S. Department of Labor, Office of Federal Contract Compliance Programs (OFCCP)
Equal Pay Act (1963)	Employers must not discriminate with regard to pay on the basis of sex if jobs performed by men and women have similiar responsibility, effort, working conditions, and skill requirements	Federal, state, and municipal agencies. Private sector firms affecting interstate commerce	Pay differentials based on productivity, seniority, merit, or skill relevant to job performance	Equal Employment Opportunity Commission

■ Major Areas of Equal Employment Opportunity Litigation

Recruitment and Selection of Employees

Hiring decisions are based on information gathered from application blanks, interviews, reference checks, and tests. In certain instances, these selection devices unfairly eliminate protected groups (such as blacks) from employment consideration.[35] Until the "Uniform Guidelines on Employee Selection Procedures" (also discussed in Chapter 7) were established as regulations under Title VII, none of the federal EEO laws detailed the dos the don'ts of recruitment and selection. It is often difficult to introduce evidence establishing that a recruitment and selection procedure is intentionally discriminatory, especially when all applicants appear to have been treated equally. Yet by introducing statistical data showing that members of a protected class are not hired as frequently as others, it may be possible to prove that discrimination exists.

In the landmark decision *Griggs v. Duke Power Co.*, mentioned earlier, the U.S. Supreme Court decided that employers using selection devices that had an adverse impact on blacks violated Title VII because it could not be demonstrated that such devices predicted or accounted for successful job performance. The *Duke Power Co.* decision bars the use of employment tests that have a disparate impact upon protected minorities unless the employer can establish business necessity by showing that the selection tests have been properly validated. To ensure proper validation, tests must be geared to a current job description, and there must be a relationship between test scores and employee job performance. In addition, the tests must be periodically rechecked for validity (see Chapter 7 for further discussion.) Employers cannot require more education and skill than are needed for the job if such requirements have an adverse impact on a protected group (unless the employee is being hired to fill a more responsible job in the near future).

The following recruitment and selection practices can result in unequal treatment and adverse impact against protected groups under EEO law:

- Advertising in the help wanted section of newspapers using wording such as *male only, applicants under age 40,* or other terms indicating that members of certain protected groups need not apply.
- Using word-of-mouth recruiting where a company with an all-white workforce enlists the support of employees to recruit job applicants. The problem created by this system is that white employees are more likely to refer only white applicants.[36]
- Making pre-employment inquiries about an applicant's race, religion, or nationality when such inquiries have no relationship to the job.
- Imposing a "residents-only" hiring rule on job applicants. A federal court ruled that such a policy in the city of Harrison, New Jersey, had a discriminatory impact on blacks. Blacks made up only 0.2 percent of Harrison's population, but the town abuts Newark, New Jersey, which has a black population of 60 percent. The city of Harrison had never employed a black municipal worker.[37]

---

[35]David G. Scalsie and Daniel J. Smith, "Legal Update: When Are Job Requirements Discriminatory?" *Personnel* (March 1986), p. 41, and William J. Connelly, "How to Navigate the River of Legal Liability When Hiring," *Personnel Journal* (March 1986), p. 32.

[36]*U.S. v. Georgia Power*, 5 FEP Cases 587 (1973).

[37]*NAACP v. Harrison, NJ*, 53 FEP Cases 1499 (1990).

- Using a minimum height requirement that is not necessary for successful job performance. Minimum height requirements (e.g. a 5-foot, 9-inch minimum requirement for police officers) have an adverse impact on women, Hispanics, and persons of Southeast Asian descent.[38] However, a maximum height requirement of 6 feet, 4 inches by a trucking firm for its drivers was ruled not to be unfairly discriminatory against men.[39] Another trucking firm did not violate Title VII when it refused to hire a woman because she was unable to satisfactorily handle a heavy mechanism used to connect two trailers.[40]
- Refusing to hire job applicants because of previous arrest and conviction records. Antiarrest and conviction record policies have had an adverse impact on black applicants in some instances. Employers may eliminate applicants with criminal records if they can demonstrate business necessity.[41]

Employers may be able to justify an otherwise discriminatory recruitment and selection procedure by convincing the EEOC or the courts that business necessity justifies the practice. Business necessity can hinge on a safety issue. For example, United Airlines would only hire flight officers who had a college degree and at least 500 hours of flight time. A federal appeals court held that such a policy was job related and enhanced safety in an industry where safety is extremely important: "When a job requires a small amount of skill and training and the consequences of hiring an unqualified applicant are insignificant, the courts should examine closely any preemployment standard or criteria which discriminates against minorities. . . . On the other hand, when the job clearly requires a high degree of skill and the economic and human risks involved in hiring an unqualified applicant are great, the employer bears a correspondingly lighter burden to show that his employment criteria are job related."[42] The U.S. Supreme Court supported the New York Transit Authority's policy of denying employment to all current methadone users even though the policy had a discriminatory effect on blacks and Hispanics. The Court sustained the policy on the ground that the safety and efficiency of the transportation system supported the employer's argument of business necessity.[43]

An employer cannot usually demonstrate legitimate business necessity simply because hiring employees from a protected group would pose an inconvenience, annoyance, or extra expense.[44] For example, an employer cannot normally refuse to hire women simply because there are no suitable locker or restroom facilities available for their use. As noted earlier, an employer cannot make a case for

[38]EEOC Decision No. 71-1448.

[39]*Livingston v. Roadway Express*, 41 FEP Cases 1713 (1986).

[40]*EEOC v. Ryder/P*I*E**, 42 FEP Cases 929 (1986).

[41]See *Green v. Missouri and Pacific Railroad Co.*, 10 FEP Cases (1975), and *Richardson v. Hotel Corp. of America*, 5 FEP Cases 323 (1973).

[42]*Spurlock v. United Airlines*, 5 FEP Cases 17 (1972).

[43]*New York City Transit Authority v. Beazer*, 19 FEP Cases 149 (1979).

[44]The Bureau of National Affairs, Inc., *Fair Employment Practices Manual: BNA Labor Relations Reporter* (Washington, D.C.: The Bureau of National Affairs, Inc., 1977), Section 421.

business necessity based on customer preferences for a specific sex or racial group. According to one court, business necessity must be based on a "purpose [that] is so essential to the safe and efficient operation of the business as to override any racial impact."[45]

After 6 years of debate by employers, government officials, and industrial psychologists, the Uniform Guidelines on Employee Selection Procedures were enacted in 1978 to deal with the measurement of adverse impact and employment testing. The Uniform Selection Guidelines adopted a general measure of adverse impact known as the *80 percent rule*, which says that a selection rate for any racial, ethnic, or sex group that is less than 80 percent of the group with the highest selection rate will generally be regarded by federal enforcement agencies as evidence of adverse impact. Thus if a firm hires 60 of 120 white applicants (a hiring rate of 50 percent) and only 18 out of 50 black applicants (a hiring rate of 36 percent), then an adverse impact is said to exist because the selection rate for blacks (36 percent) is less than 80 percent of the selection rate for whites (50% × 80% = 40%). If 21 of the 50 black applicants had been hired (a hiring rate of 42 percent), then no adverse impact would be said to be present. Once adverse impact is documented, the burden of proof shifts to the employer to demonstrate that the employment tests, job interviews, and other methods used in the hiring process are valid and job relevant (this is known as a *prima facie* case).[46] Employment tests should be carefully validated (see Chapter 7).[47] Even when there is no adverse impact against a minority group, the U.S. Supreme Court has held that "Title VII does not permit the victim of a racially discriminatory policy to be told that he was not wronged because other persons of his or her race were hired."[48] When an employer uses specific hiring criteria (such as a minimum height requirement) or selection procedures (such as an employment test) that discriminate against an individual because of sex or race, then the employer may violate Title VII even though there is no adverse impact and the overall selection procedure does not violate the 80 percent rule. A U.S. court of appeals has also held that minority test scores can be adjusted to correct for adverse impact.[49]

Recent Legal Developments Affecting Selection Decisions

The Civil Rights Act of 1991 will have a significant effect on hiring and promotion decisions. The act effectively nullified several U.S. Supreme Court cases involving hiring and promotion practices. At the same time, Congress, under the constant pressure of President Bush, wanted to avoid passing a law that would force

[45]*Robinson v. Lorrilard Corp.*, 3 FEP Cases 653 (1971).

[46]*Washington v. Davis*, 12 FEP Cases 1415 (1976).

[47]In the eyes of the EEOC and the courts, the validity or job relevance of an employment test has little to do with the professional status or reputation of the individuals who designed and administered the test.

[48]*Connecticut v. Teal*, 29 FEP Cases 1 (1982).

[49]*Bushey v. New York Civil Service*, 34 FEP Cases 1065 (1984).

employers to adopt preferential hiring quotas (e.g., hiring a specific number of racial minorities, disabled workers, and women).

Civil rights advocates were concerned that the Duke Power "effect" doctrine would be damaged by the case *Wards Cove Packing Co. v. Atonio.* The case originated in 1974 when Filipinos and Alaska Natives sued three Alaska fish canneries (including Wards Cove), charging that racially biased hiring and promotion practices created racial stratification in the canneries' workforce, housing, and dining facilities. In reversing lower court decisions, the U.S. Supreme Court ruled that the canneries' personnel practices did not have an adverse impact on minorities, particularly for those desiring to hold skilled jobs. The percentage of whites hired by the canneries did not exceed the percentage of whites in the available labor force, and workers were allegedly hired based on their qualifications rather than on their race. It was noted that the predominantly white workers arrived first and were housed together, regardless of race, whereas unskilled laborers arrived later and took the remaining housing. The U.S. Supreme Court also held that racial imbalance in one segment of the workforce does not, by itself, establish a case of adverse impact. Statistics proving discrimination had to be based on the number of qualified applicants available in the labor pool, not on the total number of minorities in the geographic area.[50] The *Wards Cove* case required that an employee claiming bias in hiring must identify the specific employment practice (e.g., an interview or no-spouse rule) that produces the adverse impact on a protected group.

The Civil Rights Act of 1991 (Section 105) softened the impact of the *Wards Cove* decision and should allay the fears of civil rights advocates that victims of discrimination will have a difficult time proving that employer practices are illegal. Under the 1991 law, an employment practice (or group of practices) that results in a disparate impact on a protected class (e.g., blacks) is unlawful if the employer cannot demonstrate that the practice in question is job related and consistent with business necessity. Unlawful disparate impact is also established if the victim of an allegedly illegal employment practice can show that a less discriminatory alternative practice is available and the employer refuses to adopt it. If an employer shows that the challenged practice does not cause a disparate impact, it does not need to prove business necessity. However, a demonstration that an employment practice is legitimate and is based on business necessity is not a defense for intentional discrimination. For example, an employment policy that prohibits the employment of persons who are currently using illegal drugs is justified by business necessity. If a company uses such a policy as an excuse for intentionally discriminating on the basis of race, color, religion, sex, or national origin, it may be regarded as illegal even though it serves a useful business purpose. The Civil Rights Act of 1991 does not appear to address the portion of the *Wards Cove* decision that adopted tighter statistical standards for disparate impact cases.

The Civil Rights Act of 1991 prohibits *race norming* of employment tests. Race norming occurs when the employment test scores of persons in a protected group are altered by adjusting their scores (e.g., adding 20 points to the scores of

---

[50]*Wards Cove v. Antonio,* 49 FEP Cases 1519 (1989).

Hispanic applicants) or using a different cutoff score to provide a certain group with an advantage in the selection process.

Most adverse impact cases have involved *objective* employment criteria that are easily measured. Objective employment criteria include a high school diploma, a certain amount of employment experience, minimum test scores, or a specific height or weight requirement. A U.S. court of appeals ruled that *subjective* criteria may also create an adverse impact on a protected group. In the case of *Watson v. Fort Worth Bank and Trust,* a black female repeatedly lost out to white employees for a promotion to a supervisory position. The bank had no formal performance appraisal system, and promotion decisions were made informally using subjective criteria. Subjective criteria such as "common sense," "good judgment," and "cooperativeness" are difficult to measure but nonetheless important. Although the U.S. Supreme Court remanded the case back to the court of appeals for further consideration, it noted that subjective evaluations from employment interviews or informal performance appraisals could be used as a means to illegally discriminate against protected groups. According to the Court, "We are persuaded that our decisions in *Griggs* [the *Duke Power* case] and succeeding cases could largely be nullified if disparate [adverse] impact analysis were applied only to standardized selection practices."[51]

Subjective employment criteria also came under critical attack in *Price Waterhouse v. Hopkins.* Ann Hopkins, a senior manager at the big eight accounting firm Price Waterhouse, was denied a partnership even though she was highly successful at obtaining major contracts for the firm. Only 7 of the 622 partners at Price Waterhouse were females. The denial of Ms. Hopkins's partnership was allegedly based on her "macho" character. She was described as being overly aggressive, unduly harsh, difficult to work with, and impatient with corporate staff members. Some partners claimed that Ms. Hopkins "overcompensated for being a woman" and advised her to take "a course at charm school." Her candidacy was put on hold, and Ms. Hopkins was told that she should "walk more femininely, talk more femininely, dress more femininely, wear make-up, have her hair styled, and wear jewelry." Both the U.S. district court and the court of appeals ruled that the employer had the right to reject Ms. Hopkins for a partnership if her interpersonal skills were deficient. The U.S. Supreme Court held that an employer is free to make adverse employment decisions against female employees for legitimate business reasons. However, the Court held that gender-based stereotyping had played a role in the firm's decision to deny Ms. Hopkins a partnership. The case was remanded to a federal district court, which ordered Price Waterhouse to offer Ms. Hopkins a partnership and reimburse her for lost compensation (back pay).[52] Cases such as this illustrate the aforementioned problem of the glass ceiling faced by female managers and professionals (see Chapter 2).

The *Price Waterhouse* case is also an example of a "mixed-motive" case that contains both legal and illegal factors affecting an employment decision. The U.S.

[51]*Watson v. Fort Worth Bank and Trust*, U.S. Supreme Court, No. 88-61-39 (June 29, 1988).

[52]*Price Waterhouse v. Hopkins*, U.S. Supreme Court, No. 87-1167 (May 1, 1989) and *Price Waterhouse v. Hopkins*, USDC DC, No. 84-3040 (May 14, 1990).

Supreme Court held that if the employer (Price Waterhouse) could demonstrate that the same action (failure to promote) would have been taken without a discriminatory motive, then the firm could avoid liability for intentional discrimination. However, the Civil Rights Act of 1991 (Section 107) declares that if a victim of discrimination shows that any intentional discrimination motivated an employment decision, then the practice is unlawful even if other lawful factors also motivated the action. However, the 1991 law does not provide a great deal of relief for victims of discrimination in mixed-motive cases. On claims in which the employer demonstrates that the same action would have been taken in the absence of a discriminatory motive, the court may not award damages or require that the victim be reinstated, promoted, or granted monetary damages. The court may prohibit the employer from using such discriminatory factors in the future, a decision that will be of little consolation to the original plaintiff.

The Use of Testers to Uncover Discrimination in Hiring

The EEOC is now allowing the use of "testers" to uncover discriminatory hiring practices. The testers are usually minority group members who pose as job applicants but have no intent of accepting a job offer. If unfair job discrimination is discovered, the testers notify the EEOC. The use of testers is well established legally in housing civil rights cases but is a new tactic in employment discrimination cases.[53] Testers are usually employed by civil rights groups such as the NAACP, but the EEOC has also made plans to use them.[54]

The NAACP filed a classwide race discrimination suit against a Miami department store after testers uncovered evidence of employment bias. Similarly qualified black and white sales job testers visited eight stores to apply for jobs with the sole intention of uncovering illegal hiring practices. Three of the stores allegedly discriminated against minority job applicants. In one instance, a black female law student with extensive work experience was not offered a job, whereas a white female undergraduate student with some experience was immediately offered a position. In another instance, a black college student with some experience was offered a job for two weeks, while a white college student with no experience was offered work for a month.[55]

Some employer groups are criticizing the use of testers. The Equal Employment Advisory Council, an organization representing private companies in employment matters, raises the possibility of legal entrapment and compares the use of testers to the use of wiretaps. There is also the criticism that the use of testers will penalize law-abiding employers who will waste time and money interviewing,

[53]EEOC, *EEOC: Policy Guide on Use of "Testers" in Employment Selection Process* (Washington, D.C.: EEOC, November 20, 1990).

[54]The Bureau of National Affairs, Inc., "EEOC to Use Testers," *Fair Employment Practices* (Washington, D.C.: The Bureau of National Affairs, Inc., December 10, 1990).

[55]The Bureau of National Affairs, Inc., "First 'Testers' Case," *Fair Employment Practices* (Washington, D.C.: The Bureau of National Affairs, Inc., January 21, 1991), p. 2.

testing, and checking references of job applicants who have no intention of accepting a job offer. Furthermore, if a tester is offered a job and then rejects it, other legitimate job applicants may have either become discouraged or found other employment during the intervening time period.[56]

Age Discrimination

Age discrimination cases involving employment are becoming increasingly common as the number of persons over 40 years of age in the labor force continues to rise.[57] Under the ADEA, it is illegal to use age as a reason for refusing to hire, for discharging, or for otherwise discriminating against an individual with respect to compensation or terms and conditions of employment. Employers, labor unions, and employment agencies are normally forbidden to indicate a preference for younger employees (or a prohibition against older employees) in the recruitment and selection of employees. Help-wanted notices that contain terms such as *age 25–35, young man or woman, college student, age 40–50, boy, girl, supplement your pension,* or any other phrase that connotes a preference for a person in a specific age group are likely to violate the act.[58]

Under the 1987 ADEA amendments, which removed the upper age limit of 70, an employee cannot be forced to accept involuntary retirement in accordance with a seniority system or pension plan.[59] Employees may, of course, retire voluntarily and companies may offer financial inducements for early retirement. If an employer makes layoff or reduction-in-force decisions based on an employee's seniority, performance, skills, job content, or location, then the decision is probably permissible under the ADEA. However, an employer may violate the ADEA if (1) an employee's age is a primary consideration in determining whether an individual will be subject to layoff, (2) a company denies severance pay to workers over age 40 during layoffs because the older workers are eligible for a pension, whereas the younger workers are not, (3) an employer offers an older employee early retirement but makes it obvious that the employee will be terminated if the retirement "option" is rejected, or (4) an employer targets workers over age 40 for

[56]The Bureau of National Affairs, Inc., "Criticism of 'Testers'," *Fair Employment Practices* (Washington, D.C.: The Bureau of National Affairs, Inc., March 4, 1991), pp. 20–21.

[57]Between 1981 and 1987, the number of age discrimination complaints increased by a factor of 2.5. During the last quarter of 1986, age discrimination cases represented about 18 percent of the EEOC caseload. The Bureau of National Affairs, Inc., *Fair Employment Practices: Summary of Latest Developments* (August 6, 1987), p. 96. See Douglas F. Seaver, "Terminating Older Workers: The Million Dollar Gamble," *Personnel Administrator* (June 1984), p. 16, and Charles P. Bird and Terri D. Fisher, "Thirty Years Later: Attitudes Toward the Employment of Older Workers," *Journal of Applied Psychology* (August 1986), p. 515.

[58]The Bureau of National Affairs, Inc., *Fair Employment Practices Manual: BNA Labor Relations Reporter* (Washington, D.C.: The Bureau of National Affairs, Inc., 1987), Section 421.

[59]Jeanne Saddler, "Early Retirement Plans Encounter Court Challenges," *The Wall Street Journal* (June 16, 1987), p. 1(W), p. 1(E), col. 5.

layoff because older employees have higher pay and benefit costs than younger workers.[60]

Several groups of employees are exempted from the ADEA's retirement restrictions. Executives who work in high policymaking positions may be involuntarily retired at age 65 if they have served in this position for 2 years or more and are entitled to an annual retirement benefit of at least $44,000. Public safety personnel such as police officers, fire fighters, and prison guards may be hired or retired in accordance with local laws and retirement programs until 1994.[61] This exception applies to public safety personnel who come into daily contact with potentially dangerous and stressful situations, as well as those in administrative positions. A third exception to the retirement provisions of the 1987 ADEA amendments involves tenured college professors. Tenured employees at colleges and universities may be forced into retirement at age 70 until 1994.

There are several reasons for prohibiting the involuntary retirement of employees. Congressional intent to base an individual's right to be employed only on the basis of physical and mental abilities rather than on age necessitates the ban on mandatory retirement. The abolishment of mandatory retirement for nearly all occupations affects approximately 800,000 workers over age 70, and the U.S. Department of Labor estimates that 200,000 additional older workers will remain in the workforce by the year 2000 because they are no longer required to retire at age 70.[62] Another reason given for the elimination of mandatory retirement is that organizations and society benefit from the skills and experience possessed by older workers. Older workers have also been characterized as being responsible and productive employees. The greater concern for individual health and fitness and the sedentary nature of professional, managerial, and clerical jobs make it likely that many workers will be capable of working on a full- or part-time basis well beyond the age of 70. The removal of the age 70 limit of the ADEA will provide a financial benefit to the Social Security program. Social Security benefits paid to today's retirees are supported by payroll taxes levied on workers who are *currently* employed. By allowing employees over age 70 to continue working, fewer Social Security benefits are paid out and more payroll taxes are accumulated; this relieves some of the financial burden that currently plagues the Social Security program.[63]

Age discrimination cases often involve controversy over an employee's physical and mental fitness to work. The ADEA permits legal employment discrimination

[60]See *Wilson v. Firestone Tire & Rubber Co.*, CA 6, No. 89-3801 (1991); *Shager v. Upjohn Co.*, 53 FEP Cases 1522 (1990); *Cancellier v. Federated Department Stores*, 28 FEP Cases 1151, (1982), *cert denied*, U.S. Supreme Court, 31 FEP Cases 704 (1983); *Graefenhain v. Pabst Brewing Co.*, 44 FEP Cases 180 (1987); *EEOC v. Westinghouse*, 50 FEP Cases 988 (1989); and *Herbert v. Mohawk Rubber Co.*, 49 FEP Cases 1051 (1989).

[61]Cynthia Pola, "Age Bias Legislation Exempting Police, Fire Approved by Congress," *Nation's Cities Weekly* (October 20, 1986), p. 8.

[62]Commerce Clearing House, Inc., *New Mandatory Retirement and Maximum Age Benefit Rules* (Chicago: Commerce Clearing House, Inc., 1986), p. 8.

[63]*Ibid.*

in cases where the discrimination against persons over 40 years of age is based on "reasonable factors other than age." Physical fitness requirements geared directly to the job would be an acceptable exemption, especially if physical inability or poor health poses a significant threat to production or safety. Although the burden of proof is often on the employer to justify discriminatory treatment, jobs involving public safety make it easier for employers to legitimize discrimination. In cases involving the ADEA and bus drivers, bus line officials were not required to evaluate each driver over age 40 to determine whether he or she could safely operate a bus. Rather, the court recognized that medical examinations could not always detect health problems in older drivers and a blanket prohibition of hiring drivers over 40 was upheld.[64]

A number of cases have arisen in the airline industry.[65] A Federal Aviation Administration (FAA) regulation requires that airline and corporate pilots retire at age 60, and several court cases have upheld this policy.[66] However, there is no age 60 retirement limit for flight engineers who do not actually fly the aircraft; requiring flight engineers to retire at the same age as airline pilots is a violation of the ADEA.[67] A U.S. court of appeals also ruled that experimental test pilots for a helicopter manufacturer could be retired at age 55.[68]

The courts have mixed opinions on the issue of mandatory retirement for law enforcement personnel and firefighters. A U.S. court of appeals ruled that Missouri's mandatory retirement age for highway patrol officers and a maximum hiring age for patrol officers and radio operators were legal.[69] Similar decisions were rendered in Massachusetts and Rhode Island.[70] In a case involving campus police officers at the University of Texas Health Science Center, a U.S. court of appeals ruled that an upper age limit of 45 for new offers was a BFOQ under the ADEA. The court agreed with the university's contention that the age limit was justified because "older individuals lack the acute physical and mental agility and stamina required to serve effectively as rookie campus police officers" and because "younger officers . . . 'relate' better to college-age students."[71] Other courts have ruled that the mandatory retirement of law enforcement personnel and fire fighters is not permitted under the ADEA. For example, the U.S. Supreme Court has held that Baltimore, Maryland, firefighters could not be involuntarily retired at age 55. Similarly, the federal courts have struck down the mandatory retirement

---

[64]*U.S. Department of Labor v. Greyhound Lines, Inc.*, 9 FEP Cases 58 (1975), and *Usery v. Tamiami Trail Tours*, 12 FEP Cases 1233 (1976).

[65]"TWA Discriminated Against Older Pilots," *Monthly Labor Review* (March 1985), p. 49.

[66]*Johnson v. American Airlines*, 37 FEP Cases 1883 (1985); *EEOC v. Boeing Co.*, 40 FEP Cases 292 (1986); and *El Paso Natural Gas Company*, 39 FEP Cases 1206 (1985).

[67]*Western Airlines v. Criswell*, 37 FEP Cases 1830 (1985). Some airlines allow pilots who reach age 60 to transfer to a flight engineer's job if openings are available.

[68]*Williams v. Hughes Helicopter, Inc.*, 42 FEP Cases 1035 (1986).

[69]*EEOC v. Missouri Highway Patrol*, 36 FEP Cases 401 (1984).

[70]*Mahoney v. Trabucco*, 36 FEP Cases 464 (1984), and *EEOC v. City of Providence*, 41 FEP Cases 906 (1986).

[71]*EEOC v. University of Texas Health Science Center at San Antonio*, 32 FEP Cases 944 (1983).

policies that affected Wisconsin firefighters and Pennsylvania state troopers. In these cases, the state or municipality failed to demonstrate that older firefighters and state troopers were incapable of performing their jobs safely and competently.[72]

The ADEA may also be violated if a younger employee is given preference based on age, even though the younger employee is older than 40.[73] Two employees, both aged 62, demonstrated that the action taken against them amounted to a violation of the ADEA, although they were replaced by persons older than age 40. An employer cannot necessarily rely on customer preferences in favoring a younger employee over one who is older. A 51-year-old disc jockey was fired and replaced by a 33-year-old when the radio station decided to change its programming from "easy listening" to "middle of the road" music. A jury awarded the discharged disc jockey nearly $200,000 in lost benefits and double damages because the radio station management willfully violated the ADEA.[74]

Employment decisions such as those pertaining to promotions, layoffs, or compensation that are made under the terms of a bona fide seniority system do not violate the ADEA as long as they are not used to evade the purpose of the act. However, the ADEA prohibits involuntary retirement even if it is done in accordance with a seniority plan. Furthermore, the ADEA does not prohibit an employer from providing lower benefits for older workers (except for health care benefits) in accordance with a bona fide employee benefit plan. A plan that prohibits the hiring of persons older than 40 or mandates retirement at a specific age is not normally regarded as a bona fide plan.[75]

In the 1989 case *Public Employee Retirement System of Ohio v. Betts*, the U.S. Supreme Court ruled that bona fide employee benefit plans such as retirement plans or group life insurance and health insurance were exempted from the ADEA.[76] Congress nullified the *Betts* ruling by enacting the Older Workers Benefit Protection Act of 1990 (OWBPA). The OWBPA prohibits discrimination against older workers in all employee benefit programs except when an age-based reduction in employee benefit plans is justified by significant cost considerations. The act regulates early-retirement programs and does not allow an employer to discriminate with respect to severance pay on the basis of age. The OWBPA amends the ADEA and allows older employees to waive their rights under the Act as long as the waiver is "knowing and voluntary." An employee may decide to waive his or her rights under the ADEA in order to accept an early retirement or

[72]*Johnson v. Mayor and City of Baltimore*, U.S. Supreme Court, 37 FEP Cases 1840 (1985); *Orzel v. Wauwatosa, Wis., Fire Department*, 33 FEP Cases 440 (1983); and *EEOC v. Pennsylvania*, 44 FEP Cases 1470 (1987).

[73]Phillip Longman, "Age Wars: The Coming Battle Between Young and Old," *Futurist* (January–February 1986), p. 8.

[74]*Rengers v. WCLR*, CA 7, No. 86-1548 (August 4, 1987). Also see *Brown v. M&M/Mars*, 50 FEP Cases 497 (1989).

[75]The Bureau of National Affairs, Inc., *Fair Employment Practices Manual: BNA Labor Relations Reporter* (Washington, D.C.: The Bureau of National Affairs, Inc., 1987), Section 421.

[76]*Public Employees Retirement System of Ohio v. Betts*, U.S. Supreme Court, 50 FEP Cases 104 (1989).

exit incentive such as severance pay. Under the OWBPA, the waiver must be in writing, it must specifically refer to the employee's ADEA rights, and the employer must allow the employee 21 days to decide whether to accept an exit incentive or other termination program. In addition, the employee has a 7-day period in which to revoke a signed waiver. Because of the OWBPA's complexity and the fact that it is still untested in the courts, the impact of the act remains unclear.[77]

Employment of the Handicapped

There is increasing evidence that the handicapped can perform a variety of jobs competently, reliably, and often at little inconvenience to the employer. Pizza Hut has instituted a "Jobs Plus" program through local community rehabilitation agencies and plans to hire at least 3,000 Jobs Plus workers by 1993.[78] A report issued by the American Federation for the Blind reveals that visually impaired employees are working in every major employment field.[79] The handicapped have also seen their employment opportunities expanded because of the proliferation of microcomputers in organizations.[80] Hearing-impaired workers are recruited and trained by the FBI as fingerprint examiners.[81] An analysis of court cases and labor arbitration decisions indicates that persons with handicaps and health-related problems are often not hired, passed over for promotion, or discharged because personnel directors and supervisors fear that efficiency, insurance costs, and safety rules will be jeopardized. Handicapped workers may not be evaluated fairly if management fails to evaluate employability on an individual basis. Erroneous employability evaluations may be made if only one or two criteria associated with an employee's physical or mental handicap are considered. A multitude of factors often determine whether an employee is able to continue working. Although the nature of an employee's disease or handicap may have a significant bearing on his or her employability, the rate at which an employee's health is likely to decline, the frequency of acute episodes requiring hospitalization, the individual's capacity for recovery and improvement, and the presence of other complicating diseases or impairments must be considered. Individuals also vary in their ability to cope with

[77]The Bureau of National Affairs, Inc., "Waivers of ADEA Rights," *Fair Employment Practices Manual* (Washington, D.C.: The Bureau of National Affairs, Inc., 1991), Section 421.

[78]The Bureau of National Affairs, Inc., "Commitment to Hire 3,000 Workers with Disabilities," *Fair Employment Practices* (Washington, D.C.: The Bureau of National Affairs, Inc., July 5, 1990), p. 80, and "Disabling Legislation," *Fortune* (June 15, 1992), p. 160.

[79]The Bureau of National Affairs, Inc., *Fair Employment Practices: Summary of Latest Developments* (Washington, D.C.: The Bureau of National Affairs, Inc., July 9, 1987), p. 85.

[80]The Bureau of National Affairs, Inc., *Fair Employment Practices: Summary of Latest Developments* (Washington, D.C.: The Bureau of National Affairs, Inc., June 11, 1987), p. 73.

[81]*Disabled USA*, No. 4 (Washington, D.C.: U.S. Government Printing Office, Superintendent of Documents, 1985). Cited in The Bureau of National Affairs, Inc., *Fair Employment Practices: Summary of Latest Developments* (Washington, D.C.: The Bureau of National Affairs, Inc., June 12, 1986), p. 71.

disabling conditions and health problems. Age and educational and social factors often play a vital role in determining employability.[82]

The nature of the job to be filled by the handicapped employee must be carefully analyzed. Factors such as the amount of physical effort required by the job and the frequency and duration of rest pauses dictate whether an employee with health problems can remain employed at his or her present job or should accept a transfer to a less taxing job. Exposure to toxic agents and environmental hazards that may aggravate an employee's health problem, potential emergency situations posing abnormal physical and mental stress, the safety of others, and the ease with which workflow, scheduling, and equipment alterations can be made to accommodate disabled employees are all relevant to assessing employability.

Employers are not required to hire inefficient and unreliable employees simply because they happen to be physically or mentally handicapped. Rather, the Rehabilitation Act and the ADA require employers to seek out and hire competent handicapped employees. The law does not provide BFOQs, thereby requiring employers to consider *individually* the employee's ability to perform a specific job.

Reasonable accommodation to the physical and mental limitations of qualified employees must be made under the Rehabilitation Act and the ADA unless the employer can demonstrate undue hardship. Under the Rehabilitation Act and the ADA, it is discriminatory to fail to remove architectural and communication barriers in buildings when such removals are "readily achievable" without major difficulty or financial hardship. Newly constructed facilities must be accessible and usable by individuals with disabilities, except where the structure of the facility makes such accommodations impractical. According to a survey conducted by The Bureau of National Affairs, Inc., more than 80 percent of responding organizations employ individuals with disabilities and 78 percent of these firms have taken measures to aid the performance and advancement of disabled workers. Survey results indicate that the most prevalent disability among employees is hearing impairments (56 percent), followed by visual impairments (39 percent), speech impairments (33 percent), confinement to a wheelchair (27 percent), mental handicap (27 percent), and mental illness (13 percent). The survey results imply that measures to aid the performance or advancement of employees with disabilities are usually modest and do not pose a financial hardship to the employer. Such measures include special or modified work station equipment, job restructuring, transfers, and flexible work schedules. The most frequently mentioned structural modifications to accommodate the disabled were designated parking spaces, special restroom equipment, and wheelchair ramps.[83] A custodial worker employed by the U.S. Postal Service suffered from depression, which in part was caused by his job. A federal district court ruled, however, that the Postal Service was not

[82]Terry L. Leap, *Health and Job Retention: The Arbitrator's Perspective*, Key Issues No. 26 (Ithaca, New York: ILR Press, Cornell University, 1984).

[83]The Bureau of National Affairs, Inc., "Special Survey Report: Employment and Accommodation of Individuals with Disabilities," *Fair Employment Practices* (Washington, D.C.: The Bureau of National Affairs, Inc., January, 1991).

obliged to transfer him to a clerical job in order to help him alleviate his depression.[84] In determining the extent of the employer's accommodation obligations, business necessity and financial costs are considered. Typical accommodation measures might include making facilities readily accessible to persons in wheelchairs, modifying job design and equipment to accommodate an amputee, and altering work schedules for employees requiring specialized medication or treatment. The U.S. Mint in San Francisco was ordered by a federal court to hire a rehabilitation specialist after it unlawfully fired five handicapped workers for failing to meet production quotas. Although the five handicapped employees worked through coffee breaks in an attempt to maintain production standards, they were unable to do so and were discharged. The court held that the employer must show "the impossibility of reasonable accommodation without undue hardship." The Mint was ordered to hire the rehabilitation specialist, who would determine whether reasonable accommodations or reassignments were possible for handicapped workers who could not meet production standards.[85]

Employers may not use tests or other selection standards that screen out handicapped persons unless the test is job related and alternative unbiased job-related measures are not available. Employment tests must be administered in a manner to ensure that applicants or employees with sensory, manual, or speaking impairments are not placed at a competitive disadvantage, unless, of course, such skills are necessary for the job. The use of physical examinations or health-related inquiries in hiring or promotion decisions must be limited to an applicant's ability to perform job-related functions.

The Rehabilitation Act and the ADA do not limit protection to employees who have obvious handicaps such as amputated limbs, total or partial blindness, or deafness, or those who are confined to a wheelchair. Persons with conditions such as epilepsy,[86] contagious diseases,[87] sensitivity to cigarette smoke,[88] and diabetes[89] may also be covered under federal law. The law also covers individuals who have a record of physical or mental impairments as well as those who "are regarded" as being handicapped even when a handicap does not exist. Persons who have been mentally restored through psychiatric treatment are a prime example.[90] Cancer victims who have been successfully treated and have a low probability of remission are also covered. A former cancer patient rejected by the San Francisco Police Department won a $184,000 settlement. The candidate for the police force

[84]*Carty v. Carlin*, 39 FEP Cases 1217 (1985).

[85]*American Federation of Government Employees v. Baker*, 43 FEP Cases 1393 (1987).

[86]*Reynolds v. Brock*, 43 FEP Cases 1077 (1987).

[87]In *School Board of Nassau County, Fla. v. Arline*, 43 FEP Cases 81 (1987), the U.S. Supreme Court ruled that persons with contagious diseases are not automatically excluded under the Rehabilitation Act. This decision may herald protection for AIDS victims under the Rehabilitation Act of 1973.

[88]*Vickers v. Veterans Administration*, 29 FEP Cases 1197 (1982).

[89]*Bentivegna v. Department of Labor*, 30 FEP Cases 875 (1982).

[90]"Accommodating Mentally Restored Federal Workers," *EAP Digest*, Vol. 6, No. 1 (Troy, Michigan: Performance Resource Press, Inc., 1986).

had passed all the required tests but was rejected because he had been diagnosed with testicular cancer 2 years earlier.[91] Presumably, previous victims of heart attacks would also be covered under the law. Employees with heroin addiction,[92] fear of heights,[93] or left-handedness,[94] however, are not regarded as being handicapped under federal law.

In recent years, considerable controversy has arisen as to whether AIDS victims are regarded as disabled under federal law. The U.S. Justice Department has taken the position that persons infected with the AIDS virus are protected under the Rehabilitation Act. Since the ADA has adopted the same definition of disability as the Rehabilitation Act, AIDS victims will also be protected under that law. AIDS victims whose jobs require that they handle food cannot be fired, since there is no evidence that the AIDS virus can be transmitted through the handling of food. Employers must provide reasonable accommodation to employees who have AIDS, and such individuals may not be isolated from customers or fellow employees because they have the disease. Although AIDS cannot be transmitted through the normal social contacts of the workplace, special provisions may be made for health care workers who run the risk of transmitting or acquiring the AIDS virus through contact with patients.[95]

Reverse Discrimination

Reverse discrimination can be defined as granting preference in employment to members of a group that, in the past, had been subjected to unfair discrimination. Until 1979, discrimination in favor of blacks or females whose qualifications were deemed to be less impressive than their white or male counterparts was generally regarded as a violation of Title VII. In the landmark case *Steelworkers v. Weber*,[96] however, the Supreme Court ruled that private employers can legally give special preference to black workers to eliminate a "manifest racial imbalance" in jobs historically dominated by whites. The *Weber* case involved an agreement between Kaiser Aluminum and the United Steelworkers union whereby 50 percent of the openings in a Kaiser plant craft training program were reserved for blacks. Kaiser and the Steelworkers agreed to continue this arrangement until the percentage of black craft workers in the plant approximated the percentage of blacks in the local labor force. The Supreme Court held that the benign quota system "falls within

[91]The Bureau of National Affairs, Inc., *Fair Employment Practices: Summary of Latest Developments* (Washington, D.C.: The Bureau of National Affairs, Inc., March 5, 1987), p. 30. Also see The Bureau of National Affairs, Inc.,"Employees with Cancer Fight for Life, Fight for Jobs," *Fair Employment Practices Manual* (Washington, D.C.: The Bureau of National Affairs, Inc., April 26, 1990), pp. 51–52.

[92]*Heron v. McGuire*, 42 FEP Cases 31 (1986).

[93]*Forrisi v. Bowen*, 41 FEP Cases 190 (1986).

[94]*De la Torres v. Bolger*, No. 85-1375 (February 5, 1986).

[95]The Bureau of National Affairs, Inc., "AIDS Discrimination," *Fair Employment Practices Manual* (Washington, D.C.: The Bureau of National Affairs, Inc., 1990), Section 421.

[96]*Steelworkers v. Weber*, 20 FEP Cases 1 (1979).

[the] area of discretion left by Title VII for private voluntarily adopted affirmative action plans designed to eliminate conspicuous racial imbalance in traditionally segregated job categories, since purposes of [the] plan mirror those of Title VII without necessarily trammelling [the] interests of white workers."[97]

Several cases following *Weber* clarified a number of unanswered questions raised by the 1979 case. First, when an employer has been guilty of flagrant discrimination, a court may order affirmative race-conscious relief such as minority hiring goals. In a 1986 case, the U.S. Supreme Court ruled that an order that is "narrowly tailored" to promote a governmental "compelling interest" does not violate the constitutional rights of nonminorities.[98] One year later, the high court upheld a federal district court's order requiring the State of Alabama to temporarily promote equal numbers of blacks and whites on its state police force because "strong measures" were required in light of the state's "long and shameful record of delay and resistance." The Supreme Court held that the promotion quota did not violate the rights of white state troopers who would have their promotions delayed but not eliminated.[99] A race-conscious plan of relief can benefit individuals who were not prior victims of discrimination.[100] In a California case, the U.S. Supreme Court ruled that the promotion of a woman ahead of a man who had scored slightly higher on a promotion examination did not violate Title VII. Santa Clara County, California, was attempting to use a voluntary plan to eliminate traditional imbalances in its workforce, and a candidate's sex was but one of a number of factors evaluated in the promotion process.[101]

The issues associated with court-ordered affirmative action and reverse discrimination were complicated in 1989 when the U.S. Supreme Court ruled that white employees may challenge consent decrees years after they have been approved by a court. A consent decree is a voluntary settlement between parties to a discrimination suit that is approved by a court. In 1974, the U.S. Justice Department sued the city of Birmingham, Alabama, on behalf of black employees who claimed race discrimination by the city in municipal hiring and promotions. Ten years later, the U.S. Supreme Court allowed a group of white Birmingham firefighters to sue on the basis of reverse discrimination. Thus, affirmative action that is taken in good faith by employers and the courts may later be subject to legal

[97]*Ibid*, p. 1.

[98]See the Bureau of National Affairs, Inc., *Fair Employment Practices Manual: BNA Labor Relations Reporter* (Washington, D.C.: The Bureau of National Affairs, Inc., 1989), Section 421, and *Sheet Metal Workers Local 28 v. EEOC*, 41 FEP Cases 107 (1986). Also see *U.S. v. Chicago*, 52 FEP Cases 402 (1990).

[99]*U.S. v. Paradise*, 43 FEP Cases 1 (1987). See Ted Gest, "A One-White, One-Black Quota for Promotions," *U.S. News and World Report*, Vol. 102 (March 9, 1987), p. 8, and Stephen Wermeil, "Supreme Court, in 6-3 Vote, Backs Hiring Goals to Correct Sex Bias; Ruling May Pressure Firms to Boost Employment of Women, Minorities," *The Wall Street Journal* (March 26, 1987), p. 3(W), p. 3(E), col. 1.

[100]*Fire Fighters Local 93 v. City of Cleveland*, 41 FEP Cases 139 (1986).

[101]*Johnson v. Transportation Agency, Santa Clara County*, 43 FEP Cases 411 (1987). See Bob Martin and Stephanie Lawrence, "Personnel Directors Respond to Reaffirmation of Affirmative Action," *Personnel Journal* (May 1987), p. 9. Also see *Conlin v. Blanchard*, 51 FEP Cases 707 (1989).

challenge by persons who were not involved in the original suit. According to the U.S. Supreme Court, a person "cannot be deprived of his legal rights in a proceeding to which he was not a party." This decision created additional controversy regarding affirmative action and reverse discrimination cases by making it possible to litigate indefinitely over consent decrees.[102] The Civil Rights Act of 1991 (Section 108) significantly reduced the level of uncertainty in such cases by prohibiting challenges to consent decrees by individuals who had a reasonable opportunity to object to the decree or whose interests had already been adequately represented by another party.

The U.S. Supreme Court has struck down preferential layoff plans that alter collectively bargained seniority systems. Employers may follow bona fide seniority systems when laying off workers (last hired, first fired) even when there is an adverse impact on recently hired blacks and women.[103] Similarly, the Court refused to approve a provision in a public school teachers' collective bargaining agreement that would have caused tenured nonminority teachers to suffer layoffs before less experienced minority group teachers. The Supreme Court claimed that such a plan would violate the constitutional rights of white teachers and was not permissible even though the plan was attempting to compensate for past societal discrimination and the school board was trying to provide teacher role models for minority students.[104]

Sexual Harassment

One of the most controversial issues surrounding the working conditions and job rights of females is the problem of employment-related sexual harassment.[105] In late October 1991, the nation's attention was riveted to the Senate Judiciary Committee hearings that probed Oklahoma law professor Anita Hill's allegations of sexual harassment by U.S. Supreme Court nominee and former EEOC chairman Clarence Thomas. The hearings involved extensive testimony by Ms. Hill, Mr. Thomas, and numerous other witnesses, most of whom appeared to be credible and knowledgeable of the circumstances surrounding the case. Mr. Thomas ultimately won confirmation to the Court, but the episode makes several important points about the subtleties and difficulties associated with sexual harassment in the workplace. First, both the victim and the alleged perpetrator of the sexual harassment in the workplace may suffer serious personal trauma and irreparable damage to their careers (regardless of how the case is resolved). Second, behavior that constitutes sexual harassment is often difficult to define with any degree of

---

[102]*Martin v. Wilkes,* 49 FEP Cases 1641 (1989).

[103]*Firefighters Local Union No. 1784 v. Stotts,* 34 FEP Cases 1702 (1984).

[104]*Wygant v. Jackson Board of Education,* 40 FEP Cases 1321 (1986).

[105]Alan M. Koral, "Social Invitations, Strict Liability, and Sexual Harassment," *Employment Relations Today* (Spring 1986), p. 13.

precision. Although aggressive sexual behavior such as attempted rape is obviously illegal, other behaviors such as a male supervisor asking a female coworker for a date or using sexually explicit language in her presence may or may not violate the law. Third, perpetrators of such misconduct often confront the victim when no other witnesses are present. The case often is reduced to the word of one person against the word of another, and the parties often have radically different accounts as to what was done or said to precipitate the case.

Unwelcome sexual advances, requests for sexual favors, and other verbal or physical conduct of a sexual nature constitute sexual harassment when (1) submission to such conduct is made either explicitly or implicitly a term or condition of an individual's employment, (2) submission to or rejection of such conduct by an individual is used as the basis for employment decisions, or (3) such conduct has the purpose or effect of substantially interfering with an individual's work performance or creating an intimidating, hostile, or offensive work environment.[106] These three factors are published as part of the EEOC's guidelines on sex discrimination, and the tenor of the guidelines is reflected in Title VII litigation involving sexual harassment.

Although the federal courts have not been completely united in their treatment of sexual harassment complaints, three conditions must normally be met for the plaintiff to receive a favorable judgment in an EEOC hearing or a federal court. First, the plaintiff must show that the sexual harassment is gender specific. That is, one sex (usually female) must be treated unfairly, while the opposite sex is unaffected. The most common type of sexual harassment occurs when a male supervisor makes advances toward a female subordinate. Also, a female soliciting sexual favors from a male or a homosexual making overtures to someone of the same sex would probably be viewed in a similar vein under Title VII. The key is that one sex is singled out for mistreatment, while the opposite sex is not. However, it appears that no Title VII violation would exist if a bisexual employee sexually harassed members of both sexes because there is no gender-specific discrimination.[107] A second, and perhaps more important, condition needed to pursue a sexual harassment case successfully under Title VII is that a sexual advance must be linked to a subsequent unfavorable personnel decision or result in an unsavory working atmosphere or relationship. Incidents of sexual harassment that occur at off-duty social functions also violate Title VII if there are ramifications in the workplace. For example, a supervisor who makes an unwelcome sexual proposition to a subordinate at a social function is likely to be in violation of Title VII if the subordinate's refusal to accede later causes problems at work.[108] Third, the sexual harassment must occur with either the explicit or tacit approval of the

---

[106]Equal Employment Opportunity Commission, "Guidelines on Discrimination Because of Sex," Section 1604.11 (November 10, 1980). 29 *C.F.R.* 1604.

[107]This point was noted in the footnote of a sexual harassment case. To date, this issue has not been tested in the courts. See *Barnes v. Costle*, 15 FEP Cases 345 (1977), footnote 55.

[108]The Bureau of National Affairs, Inc., *Fair Employment Practices Manual: BNA Labor Relations Reporter* (Washington, D.C.: The Bureau of National Affairs, Inc., 1987), Section 421.

employer. An employer is legally obligated to investigate and eliminate problems of sexual harassment precipitated by supervisors, co-workers, and even customers.

Two major types of sexual harassment cases have evolved. One is known as a *quid pro quo* case in which an employer requires sexual favors in return for job-related benefits such as a promotion or pay raise.[109] A second type of sexual harassment case is one involving a *hostile working environment* in which the employee suffers no "economic" or "tangible" injury. Thus, victims of sexual harassment have legal recourse even though the harassment does not lead to firing, denial of promotion, or loss of other economic benefits.

The first sexual harassment in employment case to be heard by the U.S. Supreme Court was the 1986 case of *Meritor Savings Bank v. Vinson*.[110] The case involved an employee, Mechelle Vinson, who was hired by the Meritor Savings Bank in the Washington, D.C., area. During her 4 years of employment at the bank, Vinson claimed that she was "constantly . . . subjected to sexual harassment" by her supervisor, Sidney Taylor. Although her promotions at the bank were based only on her job performance, she claimed that she had sexual intercourse with Taylor approximately 40 to 50 times over the 4-year period. Taylor denied the sexual activities with Vinson, as well as any sexual advances toward her. In making its ruling in the *Vinson* case the Supreme Court made the following points:[111]

- Title VII forbids sexual harassment in situations where the employee suffers no economic or job loss (hostile environment cases).
- In order to constitute sexual harassment, the conduct must be sufficiently severe or pervasive to alter the victim's working environment and create an abusive atmosphere on the job.
- Although Vinson voluntarily engaged in sexual activities with her supervisor, the Court held that *voluntariness* is not a defense for the employer; the crucial question is whether the sexual advances are *unwelcome*.
- A victim's sexually provocative speech or dress may be relevant in determining whether she regarded the sexual advances as unwelcome.[112]

Although the *Vinson* case involved sexual advances and activities, other forms of employee conduct such as offensive and unwanted touching and a pattern of

[109]*Henson v. City of Dundee*, 29 FEP Cases 787 (1982).

[110]*Meritor Savings Bank v. Vinson*, 40 FEP Cases 1822 (1986). See "Supreme Court Hears Sexual Harassment Case," *Monthly Labor Review* (September 1986), p. 39; and Frederick L. Sullivan, "Sexual Harassment: The Supreme Court's Ruling," *Personnel* (December 1986), p. 37.

[111]The Bureau of National Affairs, Inc., *Fair Employment Practices Manual: BNA Labor Relations Reporter* (Washington, D.C.: The Bureau of National Affairs, Inc., 1990), Section 421. For a detailed analysis of these points , see EEOC, *EEOC: Policy Guidance on Sexual Harassment* (March 19, 1990).

[112]Such evidence is admissible in court at the judge's discretion. An employer may be liable for sexual harassment by *requiring* that an employee wear provocative clothing that encourages supervisors, co-workers, or customers to engage in sexual harassment. See *EEOC v. Sage Realty Corp.*, 24 FEP Cases 1521 (1981).

lewd, obscene, and suggestive comments may also constitute sexual harassment. However, jokes, graffiti, and posters that convey a sexual message may imply sexual harassment. A federal court ruled that calendars and posters that stereo-typed women as sex objects amounted to illegal sexual harassment. After a female shipyard welder complained about pornography in the workplace, she and other female employees were subjected to harassment by male co-workers. The co-workers laughed openly at the women and began to bring more sexually provoc-ative material to work. One manager remarked that the shipyard was a "man's world" where foul language was allowed. The male workers claimed that they had a constitutional right to display sexually provocative posters at work. The court, however, ruled that the posters and foul language create "a barrier to the progress of women in the workplace" and that women "do not belong . . . [and are] wel-come in the workplace only if they will subvert their identities to the sexual stereotypes prevalent in that environment."[113] However, if it can be demonstrated that a woman contributed to the vulgar atmosphere through her own behavior, then the court may rule that sexual harassment did not occur.[114]

Recent cases indicate that the EEOC and courts are applying a "reasonable woman" test to determine whether certain conduct constitutes sexual harassment. In a 1991 case, the U.S. Court of Appeals in San Francisco ruled that sexual harassment was defined as what a reasonable woman would consider sufficiently severe or pervasive to "alter the conditions of employment and create an abusive working environment." The case involved a female Internal Revenue Service agent who was upset by frightening and bizarre "love letters" sent to her by a co-worker. Although the agency transferred the co-worker, he filed a grievance and was moved back to his former job near the woman he harassed. A U.S. district court subsequently dismissed the case, but the U.S. Court of Appeals ruled that women may have a justifiable fear that "even a mild form of harassment may be a prelude to violent sexual assault." According to the court, a sex-blind reasonable person test would tend to be male-biased and ignore the perspective of women. The court added that by focusing on the perspective of the female victim rather than on stereotyped notions of society, women will be able to participate on an equal footing with men.[115]

A federal court held that a supervisor who promoted an employee with whom he was sexually intimate may be liable under Title VII for damages to deserving candidates who were bypassed for promotion.[116] However, another federal court ruled that Title VII should not be expanded to include "sexual liaisons" and "sexual attractions"; to do so, they said, would put the EEOC and courts into the position of policing intimate relationships.[117]

---

[113]*Robinson v. Jacksonville Shipyards*, USDC MFla, No. 86-927-J-12 (1991).

[114]*Weinsheimer v. Rockwell International*, 54 FEP Cases 828 (1990).

[115]*Ellison v. Brady*, 54 FEP Cases 1346 (1991).

[116]*King v. Palmer*, 39 FEP Cases 877 (1985). See Cathy Trost, "The Boss's Girlfriend Gets the Job, But That Isn't Sex Discrimination," *The Wall Street Journal* (March 3, 1987), p. 1(W), p. 1(E), col. 5.

[117]*DeCintio v. Westchester County Medical Center*, 42 FEP Cases 921 (1986). Also see *Drinkwater v. Union Carbide Corp.*, CA 3, No. 89-5418 (1990).

Personnel directors should establish a policy that explicitly forbids sexual harassment not only by supervisors but also by co-workers. The EEOC guidelines emphasize that a supervisor's actions will be especially suspect, regardless of whether the employer knew or had reason to know that sexual harassment was taking place. Co-workers or agents of the employer who engage in sexual harassment can also be a source of liability to the firm, although it must be demonstrated that the employer had prior knowledge of such actions. The guidelines further state that prevention is the best tool for elimination of sexual harassment and that emphasis should be placed on expressing strong disapproval, developing appropriate sanctions, and informing employees of their right to complain if subjected to sexual advances in connection with their employment.[118] One company responded to a sexual harassment complaint by placing a written statement in the harasser's file, delaying his promotion and salary increase, limiting his contact with female employees, and threatening to fire him for any future misdeeds. Despite providing the sexual harassment victim with two weeks of leave and offering to pay her for counseling, she resigned and sued under Title VII. The U.S. Court of Appeals ruled that the woman was not forced to resign and, in fact, did not give the employer's remedies the opportunity to work.[119]

Pregnancy and Sex Discrimination

A number of cases have arisen regarding the employment rights of pregnant women. Some cases have involved management's refusal either to hire women who are pregnant or to allow expectant mothers to remain on the job. Other cases have dealt with the fairness of health care insurance and disability leave plans toward pregnancy. In recent times, attention has been given to the right of pregnant women or women in their childbearing years to perform work that exposes them to hazardous chemicals.

The Pregnancy Discrimination Act of 1978 (an amendment to Title VII) requires employers to view pregnancy and related conditions in the same vein as other disabilities and medical conditions.[120] For example, the following types of discrimination are illegal under the Pregnancy Discrimination Act:[121]

- Refusing to hire or promote an otherwise qualified pregnant woman who is physically able to perform a job.

---

[118]The Bureau of National Affairs, Inc., "Conducting Sexual Harassment Investigations," *Fair Employment Practices* (Washington, D.C.: The Bureau of National Affairs, Inc., July 19, 1990), p. 85. Donald W. Caudill and Regina M. Donaldson, "Is Your Climate Ripe for Sexual Harassment?" *Management World* (July-August 1986), p. 26.

[119]*Paroline v. Unisys Corp.*, 52 FEP Cases 845 (1990).

[120]P.L. 95-555 (1978) added a new section, Section 701(k), to Title VII.

[121]The Bureau of National Affairs, Inc., *Fair Employment Practices Manual: BNA Labor Relations Reporter* (Washington, D.C.: The Bureau of National Affairs, Inc., 1987), Section 421.

- Requiring a pregnant employee to remain on leave for a stipulated period of time before being allowed to return to work.
- Providing a health or disability policy that does not cover pregnancy or imposes a high cost to employees for such coverage.
- Limiting pregnancy coverage to married workers and excluding maternity benefits to unwed mothers.
- Identifying the sex of the person whose insurance policy is responsible for paying health insurance claims. In the case of a working couple where both spouses have their own group health insurance coverage, a woman's health insurance plan required that when two health insurance plans cover a dependent, the expenses of the dependent are the primary responsibility of the husband.[122]

However, the Pregnancy Discrimination Act does not require the employer to establish health and disability programs where none previously existed. There is also no requirement for employers to pay for health insurance benefits covering abortions except where the life of the mother would be endangered if the unborn child were carried for the full term of pregnancy or where medical complications have arisen from an abortion.

The act places emphasis on individual evaluation of an employee's ability to work rather than on blanket personnel policies applicable to all pregnant women. Thus, employers are prohibited from terminating or firing women solely because of pregnancy. The Pregnancy Discrimination Act also bars employers from imposing mandatory leaves for women at some arbitrary point, such as at the end of the fifth month of pregnancy.[123] Furthermore, it protects their reinstatement rights, including credit for previous service, accrued retirement benefits, and accumulated seniority. An employer must have a nondiscriminatory reason for discharging or demoting pregnant employees. Reasons such as excessive absenteeism, unsatisfactory job performance, or other legitimate reasons that do not unfairly single out pregnant employees can be used as grounds for discharge or demotion without violating Title VII. For example, an unwed pregnant employee was fired by the Omaha Girls Club. The woman was hired as a role model for teenage girls. Since a primary mission of the club was to discourage teenage pregnancies, the court ruled that a BFOQ was permissible and could be used to discriminate against unwed pregnant women.[124]

In addition to protecting the job security rights of pregnant women, the Pregnancy Discrimination Act does not permit employers to discriminate between men and women with regard to employee benefits, such as medical, hospital,

---

[122]*Reinforcing Iron Workers Local 426 Health and Welfare Fund v. Michigan Bell Telephone Co.*, 90-CV-70590-DT (1990).

[123]This issue was initially addressed in *Cleveland Board of Education v. LaFleur*, 6 FEP Cases 1253 (1974).

[124]*Chambers v. Omaha Girls Club*, 45 FEP Cases 698 (1987).

accident, life insurance, and retirement benefits. Different benefits cannot be accorded to head of households or principal wage earners, since this practice is likely to have an adverse impact on women and bears no relationship to job performance. It is also unlawful for an employer to offer greater benefits to the spouse of a male employee than would be provided to the spouse of a female employee.

Many states have also enacted laws or adopted regulations that prohibit discrimination based on childbirth or pregnancy. Some states have passed laws or regulations that specifically address maternity leave and job reinstatement rights of mothers after childbirth. A few states have provided additional protection for pregnant women by requiring employers to grant a period of leave and reinstatement after childbirth.[125] The legitimacy of these statutes withstood challenge in the U.S. Supreme Court's decision in *California Federal Savings and Loan v. Guerra*.[126] A California statute requires that employers grant up to 4 months of unpaid leave to pregnant workers and guarantee reinstatement to the same or comparable job upon their return. The employer, California Federal Savings and Loan, claimed that the state statute conflicted with the Pregnancy Discrimination Act because it favored female employees and did not afford temporarily disabled males comparable protection. The U.S. Supreme Court noted that the Pregnancy Discrimination Act and the California statute shared the goal of promoting EEO and "allows women, as well as men, to have families without losing their jobs." In handing down its decision, the Court noted that an employer is "free to give comparable benefits to other disabled employees." Data compiled by The Bureau of National Affairs, Inc., and the Society for Human Resource Management show that there is a wide gap between the amount of parental leave offered by employers to new mothers and new fathers. The EEOC suggests that employers seeking to comply with Title VII adopt leave policies that distinguish between disability leave for medical reasons and parental leave. For example, an employer might provide up to 6 weeks of medical disability (with proper documentation from a physician) for a woman who suffers pregnancy-related medical problems. The company might then offer 4 weeks of parental (nonmedical) leave for both the mother and the father.[127] According to the U.S. Department of Labor, Bureau of Labor Statistics, however, 18 percent of U.S. employees at companies and organizations with 100 employees or more were offered unpaid paternity leave in 1989,

[125]The Bureau of National Affairs, Inc., *Fair Employment Practices Manual: BNA Labor Relations Reporter* (Washington, D.C.: The Bureau of National Affairs, Inc., 1987), Section 421.

[126]42 FEP Cases 1073 (1987). See Aaron Bernstein, "Business and Pregnancy: Goodwill Is No Longer Good Enough," *Business Week* (February 2, 1987), p. 37, and Amy Wilentz, "Garland's Bouquet: A Landmark Supreme Court Ruling Supports Pregnancy Leave," *Time* (January 26, 1987), p. 14.

[127]See The Bureau of National Affairs, Inc., "Unequal Parental Leave for Men Discriminates," *Fair Employment Practices* (Washington, D.C.: The Bureau of National Affairs, Inc., May 27, 1991), p. 60, and The Bureau of National Affairs, Inc., "Mothers' Leave Open to Challenge by Fathers," *Fair Employment Practices* (Washington, D.C.: The Bureau of National Affairs, Inc., December 24, 1990), p. 151.

whereas 1 percent were offered paid leave. Although paternity leave is being offered, many men are reluctant to take it for fear that it may jeopardize their careers.[128]

In 1991, the U.S. Supreme Court unanimously ruled that women who are otherwise qualified may not be barred from jobs that might be hazardous to their reproductive system or unborn children. In *United Auto Workers v. Johnson Controls*, the Court reviewed the legitimacy of a fetal protection policy of an automobile battery manufacturing firm. Johnson Controls had adopted a policy that prevented all women (except those who had medical verification that they were unable to bear children) from jobs involving lead exposure. Lead is a primary ingredient in battery manufacturing and poses a health risk to unborn children. Although a U.S. court of appeals had ruled earlier that Johnson Controls's fetal protection policy was reasonable and in the best interests of industrial safety, the U.S. Supreme Court disagreed. "The bias in Johnson Controls' policy is obvious," the Court stated. Even though lead has been found to pose a danger to the male reproductive system, male employees at Johnson Controls were given the option to decide whether to expose themselves to the risk, whereas female employees were not. An explicit gender-based policy of this nature constitutes sex discrimination, the Court said, and Title VII "prohibits an employer from discriminating against a woman because of her capacity to become pregnant unless her reproductive potential prevents her from performing the duties of her job." The Court also said that "decisions about the welfare of future children must be left to the parents who conceive, bear, support, and raise them rather than to the employers who hire those parents." As a result of this case, firms whose production processes involve employee exposure to chemicals have been rescinding fetal protection policies, and some companies will undoubtedly require that employees sign waivers that will absolve the employer of future liability for damage to their employees' reproductive systems or birth defects in their children.[129]

Retirement Programs and Sex Discrimination

Pension plans pose equal employment opportunity problems due to differences in the average life expectancy of men and women. Women, on the average, live 4-5 years longer than men, so that retirement benefits are paid to women for a longer period of time. As a result, pension plans are more costly for women than for men

---

[128]The Bureau of National Affairs, Inc., "Most Fathers Aren't Taking Paternity Leave When Offered," *Fair Employment Practices* (Washington, D.C.: The Bureau of National Affairs, Inc., October 29, 1990), p. 128.

[129]*United Auto Workers v. Johnson Controls*, 55 FEP Cases 365 (1991). Also see The Bureau of National Affairs, Inc., "Fetal Protection Ruling," *Fair Employment Practices* (Washington, D.C.: The Bureau of National Affairs, Inc., April 1, 1991), p. 31, and The Bureau of National Affairs, Inc., "Fetal Protection Case Aftermath," *Fair Employment Practices* (Washington, D.C.: The Bureau of National Affairs, Inc., April 15, 1991), p. 37.

if other factors such as income, age at retirement, and number of years' participation in the retirement plan are held constant. To counteract "actuarial reality," one of two approaches has traditionally been taken: either reduce the monthly retirement benefit to female retirees (assuming equal contributions to the pension plan are made by or for each sex during their working years) or increase the required contribution for women so that equal male-female benefits can be paid upon retirement.

Pension plans requiring unequal contributions or paying unequal benefits because of sex have both been held to violate Title VII. This position has been upheld by the courts, not only where females receive inferior benefits,[130] but also in circumstances where males are shortchanged.[131] In *Los Angeles v. Manhart*, the U.S. Supreme Court held that an employer who required females to make larger contributions than male employees to a retirement program violated Title VII. The Court also noted that sex is only one factor affecting longevity. Other factors, such as smoking, drinking, obesity, and personal health habits, have traditionally not been considered in computing pension benefits and the level of contributions needed to fund a retirement plan adequately.[132] As is the case with other personnel practices, individual factors rather than the class characteristics of men and women must be taken into account. It was also held that a retirement program that pays women a smaller retirement benefit than that received by men is illegal (assuming that other factors are equal).[133]

Fortunately for pension plan administrators, none of the court rulings have required restitution of past contributions or other forms of retroactive relief.[134] A 1986 ruling by a U.S. court of appeals held that a plan using sex-based mortality tables does not have to grant women the same monthly benefits that they would have received had they been men, but rather that the plan must *equalize* monthly retirement benefits between men and women.[135] In June of 1988, the U.S. Supreme Court reversed a lower federal court ruling that had required the State of Florida to pay $43.6 million to male state workers after it continued to use sex-based mortality tables contrary to the *Manhart* decision. A U.S. Department of Labor study estimates that this ruling will save public and private employers nationwide $817 million to 1.26 billion a year.[136]

Under the Retirement Equity Act that went into effect in 1984, a pension plan must, among other things, allow a 1-year maternity or paternity leave without penalizing the employee for a break in service.[137] Although the act does not

---

[130]See, for example, *Bartness v. Drewrys U.S.A., Inc.*, 3 FEP Cases 1218 (1971); *Henderson v. State of Oregon*, 11 FEP Cases 1218 (1977); and *Peters v. Wayne State University*, 20 FEP Cases 1621 (1979).

[131]*Fitzpatrick v. Bitzer*, 12 FEP Cases 1586 (1976).

[132]17 FEP Cases 395 (1978).

[133]*EEOC v. Colby College*, 18 FEP Cases 1125 (1978).

[134]This applies to pension contributions collected after August 1, 1983.

[135]*Norris v. Arizona Governing Committee*, 41 FEP Cases 820 (1986).

[136]*Florida et al. v. Hughlan Long*, U.S. Supreme Court, No. 86-1685 (June 22, 1988).

[137]Public Law 98-397 (1984).

explicitly favor women, it was passed by Congress in the interests of working women and older women. The act allows employees to take up to 5 years of leave without suffering a break in service for pension accrual purposes. In addition, the minimum vesting age was lowered from 21 to age 18 (see Chapter 12 for a discussion of pension vesting). These provisions are especially beneficial for younger women who wish to take a leave of absence for child care. The act also contains provisions designed to protect the rights of the dependents of working spouses. For example, the written consent of a spouse must be obtained before a worker may waive survivor benefits (e.g., retirement benefits that are paid to a wife in the event that her husband dies after retirement). In addition, retirement payments must be made to the spouse of fully vested workers who die before retirement. These provisions are especially helpful to older women whose husbands predecease them.

The Concept of Reasonable Accommodation and Religious Discrimination

EEO cases pertaining to religion usually involve the issue of reasonable accommodation by the employer to a worker's religious practices and beliefs.[138] Most complaints have centered on employees seeking to observe their Sabbath. In *TWA v. Hardison*, the Supreme Court decided that an employer's duty to accommodate an employee's religious observance was limited.[139] *Hardison* involved a job assignment system governed by a union contract. The Court indicated that neither employers nor unions are obliged to take steps inconsistent with an otherwise valid collective bargaining agreement. In essence, an employer is under no obligation to impose an undesirable shift preference on employees of other religious faiths in order to accommodate the religious practices of a specific employee. *Hardison* holds that an employer does not have to find substitute or replacement workers if such accommodation would require more than a minimal cost. The U.S. Supreme Court has also ruled that an employer is not required to accept the type of accommodation specifically requested by the employee; any reasonable accommodation stipulated by the employer is acceptable.[140]

Title VII takes a broad view on religious beliefs and activities. A religion is not restricted to the conventional practices commonly encountered in the United States; rather any sincere or meaningful belief (including atheism) is protected even though it may be illogical or incomprehensible to others. Moral or ethical beliefs held by an individual regarding what is right or wrong are also protected from religious discrimination. However, employers must keep the workplace free from religious bias or intimidation by employees who insist on imposing their

---

[138]William L. Kandel, "Religious Accommodation After *Philbrook: De Minimus* Reduced," *Employee Relations Law Journal* (Spring 1987), pp. 690–697.

[139]14 FEP Cases 1697 (1977).

[140]*Ansonia Board of Education v. Philbrook*, 42 FEP Cases 359 (1986).

religious beliefs on others.[141] Employers who require mandatory prayer meetings may violate Title VII and an employer who fires a worker because of differing religious beliefs is also guilty of intentional discrimination.[142] Religious institutions and educational institutions affiliated with a religious group often have more leeway insofar as religious discrimination is concerned, especially when leadership positions are involved. Marquette University, a Jesuit-controlled institution, did not violate Title VII when it refused to hire a woman in its theology department because of disagreements with her religious views.[143]

The line between reasonable and unreasonable accommodation is somewhat blurred, but court decisions have delineated several basic factors that are weighed in determining whether employers have made reasonable efforts to accommodate an employee's religious beliefs. They include the nature of the job,[144] the size of the firm,[145] the effects of transferring an employee to a different job,[146] the effects of accommodation upon the morale of other employees,[147] and the degree of cooperation given by the employee in accepting the employer's offer to change jobs or workshift.[148] The employer can generally reject an accommodation if it results in undue hardship because of scheduling problems or expenses associated with a transfer or shift change that requires the payment of overtime or a higher wage rate. An automobile parts salesperson refused to work Saturday because of her religious beliefs. When her employer was unable to accommodate her schedule, she filed a complaint under Title VII. However, a U.S. court of appeals ruled that the employer could not accommodate her without extra expense and significant administrative problems.[149] A company's requirement that an indivdual be a Moslem to perform the duties of a helicopter pilot in certain parts of Saudi Arabia is a legitimate BFOQ according to a federal district court. Saudia Arabian law forbids non-Moslems from entering holy areas, and those caught violating this law are beheaded. Thus safety considerations justified a BFOQ in this instance.[150] The transfer of a Sikh machinist who refused to shave his beard for religious reasons did

[141]EEOC Decision No. 72-1114, 4 FEP Cases 842 (1972); *Spratt v. County of Kent*, 39 FEP Cases 911 (1985); and *Baz v. Walters*, 40 FEP Cases 173 (1986).

[142]EEOC Decision 91-1 (1991) and *Blalock v. Metal Trades*, 39 FEP Cases 140 (1985).

[143]*Maguire v. Marquette University*, 40 FEP Cases 167 (1986).

[144]*Weitkenaut v. Goodyear Tire and Rubber Co.*, 10 FEP Cases 513 (1974); *Olds v. Tennessee Paper Mills*, 11 FEP Cases 350 (1974); and *Roberts v. Hermitage Cotton Mills*, 8 FEP Cases 315 (1974).

[145]*Claybaugh v. Pacific Northwest Bell Telephone Co.*, 5 FEP Cases 719 (1973), and *Drum v. Ware*, 7 PEF Cases 269 (1974).

[146]*Ward v. Allegheny Ludlum Steel Corp.*, 11 FEP Cases 594 (1975), and *Dixon v. Omaha Public Power District*, 10 FEP Cases 1052 (1974).

[147]*Cummins v. Parker Seal Co.*, 13 FEP Cases 1178 (1976); *Johnson v. U.S. Postal Service*, 8 FEP Cases 371 (1974); and *Reid v. Memphis Publishing Co.*, 11 FEP Cases 129 (1975).

[148]*EEOC v. Universal Manufacturing Corp.*, CA5, No. 89-7097 (1990), and *Chrysler Corporation v. Mann*, 15 FEP Cases 788 (1978).

[149]*Wisner v. Truck Central*, 40 FEP Cases 613 (1986).

[150]*Kern v. Dynelectron*, 33 FEP Cases 255 (1983).

not violate Title VII. In the course of his employment, the machinist was exposed to toxic fumes, and his beard interfered with the snug fit of a respirator.[151] In late 1990, the Occupational Safety and Health Administration (OSHA) revoked a 12-year-old agency rule that had exempted certain workers from wearing hard hats. In 1978, OSHA had passed a hard-hat exemption for members of the Old Order Amish and the Sikh Dharama Brotherhood. In changing the exemption, OSHA stated that the federal health and safety law is a "neutral, generally applicable regulatory law" and must be observed regardless of one's religious beliefs.[152] A company refused to hire an applicant for a truck-driving position because he used peyote, a hallucinogenic drug, in ceremonies of the Native American Church. Although a federal district court claimed that using hallucinogenic drugs was a protected religious practice, the employer did not violate the religious accommodation requirements of Title VII because of legitimate safety concerns.[153] The argument that employee morale will be lowered if an employer accommodates an employee for religious reasons has been viewed, by itself, as being inadequate to demonstrate undue hardship.[154] Although employers can look to various court decisions for guidance, the EEOC has issued a set of "Religious Discrimination Guidelines."[155] The guidelines discuss the use of voluntary substitute employees, flexible scheduling, lateral transfers and job changes, and criteria useful in defining "undue hardship" on the firm. A Seventh-Day Adventist was fired after refusing to work on Saturdays. A U.S. Court of Appeals ruled that she was entitled to reasonable accommodation even though she was promoted into the job knowing that she might be required to work on Saturdays.[156] However, another Seventh-Day Adventist who worked for an airline as a flight attendant was fired after she refused to work on two consecutive Saturdays. A federal district court held that the flight attendant did not cooperate with the company in reaching an accommodation.[157]

■ Summary and Conclusions

This chapter has presented the major legal developments involving the application of EEO law. Given the dynamic nature of the area, this discussion represents only a snapshot photograph of a rapidly changing scene. Nevertheless, several trends

---

[151]*Bhatia v. Chevron, U.S.A.*, 34 FEP Cases 1816 (1984).

[152]The Bureau of National Affairs, Inc., "Religious Exemption Withdrawn," *Fair Employment Practices Manual*, (Washington, D.C.: The Bureau of National Affairs, Inc., December 10, 1990), p. 147.

[153]*Toledo v. Nobel-Sysco*, 41 FEP Cases 282 (1986).

[154]*Roberts v. Hermitage Cotton Mills*, 8 FEP Cases 319 (1974).

[155]29 C.F.R. 1605 (amended November 1, 1980), amended 1988.

[156]*Proctor v. Consolidated Freightways*, 41 FEP Cases 704 (1986).

[157]*Hudson v. Western Airlines, Inc.*, USDC Calif., Case No. CV 83-2367 (1987). Also see *Ackerman v. National Railroad Passenger Corp.*, USDC SFla, 86-0746 (1990).

are apparent. First, the EEO issue is here to stay. As long as organizations engage in discriminatory practices that are unfair to protected groups, the enforcement agencies and courts will continue to have an impact on personnel policy. The liberalized compensatory and punitive damages that are available under the Civil Rights Act of 1991 will also encourage additional EEO suits against private and public sector organizations.

Second, it is likely that the EEO rights of older employees and the handicapped will receive increasing attention. As medical science cushions the adverse effects of age and health-related problems and technological changes lessen the physical demands of the job, more employment-related decisions in these areas will be challenged. This trend will accelerate as the number of less physically demanding white-collar jobs increases and the labor force participation rate of older employees continues to rise. The passage of the ADA expands EEO protection to a larger number of disabled individuals.

Third, the intense interest in the working rights and conditions of women should continue. The emphasis is clearly on achieving parity between men and women in all facets of employment, as witnessed by the recent litigation on equal pay and comparable worth issues (see Chapter 11) and by the attention given to sexual harassment, employee benefit programs, and pregnancy and employment, among others. At the same time, there is recognition that a conflict may exist between a woman's rights and possible exposure in certain occupations and industries to toxic substances harmful to the female reproductive system.

Fourth, although a large proportion of the cases in the past have involved entry-level or lower-level jobs, the 1990s will bring increasing attention to EEO problems in upper-level management positions. Recent attention by the EEOC to sex discrimination and dead-end promotion channels (the glass ceiling), coupled with the generally increasing levels of education, seniority, and relevant job experience of working women, will result in litigation focusing not only on suitable entry-level jobs but also on the upward mobility of women in organizations.[158]

Finally, controversy will continue to build regarding sex discrimination in compensation practices. With EEOC hearings, professional conferences, and involvement by the National Academy of Sciences providing the forum for highlighting various views, the basic tenets of long-accepted job evaluation plans and compensation structures will be questioned (see Chapter 11).

Although a number of complex issues have been surveyed here, the essence of this chapter is twofold. First, personnel adminstrators must be aware of the myriad

---

[158]Charles C. Fischer, "Toward a More Complete Understanding of Occupational Sex Discrimination," *Journal of Economic Issues* (March 1987), p. 113, and "Up Against a Glass Ceiling: Gender-Related Barriers Still Exist," *Management Review* (April 1987), p. 6; Paul E. Stephan, "The Career Prospects of Female MBA's," *Business* (January-March 1987), p. 37; Madeline Heilman and Richard F. Martell, "Exposure to Successful Women: Antidote to Sex Discrimination in Applicant Screening Decision?", *Organizational Behavior and Human Decision Processes* (June 1986), p. 376; Peter Dubno, "Attitudes Toward Women Executives: A Longitudinal Approach," *Academy of Management Journal* (January 4, 1985), p. 15; and Barry Z. Pozner and Gary N. Powell, "Female and Male Socialization Experiences: An Initial Investigation," *Journal of Occupational Psychology* (March 1985), p. 81.

EEO laws, administrative regulations, and prominent court decisions. Second, each personnel policy and practice should be periodically evaluated to determine whether it operates unfairly against a specific race, sex, age, handicapped, or other protected group. EEO laws generally require that employees be evaluated on an individual basis (except when BFOQs are authorized). As a general rule, employment decisions that are made on an individual basis are better than those based on broad assumptions about a specific race, sex, or age group. Given the potential costs in terms of time and money devoted to litigation, back-pay awards, and adverse publicity, EEO issues should be approached in a preventive manner, with emphasis placed on recruiting, selecting, compensating, and treating employees in a way that maximizes the relevance of job performance and minimizes the attention given to factors not directly applicable to the job. Table 3-2 summarizes some of the primary concerns that EEO laws present for the major personnel/human resource management functions.

■ Questions

1. What is the major objective of each of the following EEO laws?
- Title VII of the 1964 Civil Rights Act
- Civil Rights Acts of 1991
- Immigration Reform and Control Act of 1986
- Age Discrimination in Employment Act of 1967
- Rehabilitation Act of 1973
- Americans with Disabilities Act of 1990
- Vietnam Era Veterans Readjustment Assistance Act of 1974
- Equal Pay Act of 1963

2. What does the Age Discrimination in Employment Act (ADEA) provision "factors other than age" mean insofar as hiring and employment rights are concerned?

3. What do the ADEA amendments of 1987 say about mandatory retirement?

4. Explain the concept of *reasonable accommodation* under the Rehabilitation Act of 1973 and the Americans with Disabilities Act of 1990.

5. What is the difference between the concepts of affirmative action and reverse discrimination?

6. Outline behaviors that can constitute sexual harassment in the workplace.

7. What is the basic purpose of the Pregnancy Discrimination Act?

8. Describe an employer's obligation to accommodate the religious beliefs of an employee.

□ APPLICATIONS AND CASE EXERCISES

1. A female bartender at a nightclub was approached by her supervisor, who made sexually suggestive remarks to her. She responded to the supervisor's conduct in foul language of her own. When the incident was reported to the nightclub owner, he discharged not only the supervisor, but also the female employee. The female bartender filed a complaint under Title VII. Discuss why you believe she will either win or lose the case.[159]

[159]*EEOC v. FLC & Brothers Rebel, Inc.*, 44 FEP Cases 362 (1987).

TABLE 3-2   Major EEO Issues for Personnel/Human Resource Management

Job analysis	Comprehensive, accurate, and current job analyses form the foundation for recruitment, selection, performance appraisal, compensation, and other personal/human resource management functions.
Personnel planning	Planning to ensure compliance with affirmative action obligations.
Recruitment and selection	Recruitment patterns that avoid excluding minority job candidates. Establishing job requirements based on business necessity. Selection methods (application blanks, reference checks, etc.) that do not have an unfair adverse impact on protected groups.
Training and development	Entrance requirements that do not have an adverse impact on protected groups. The use of training programs to eliminate racial imbalances in skilled jobs.
Employment conditions	Maintaining a working environment that is free of racial, sexual, or other types of harassment. Enforcing safety rules, grooming standards, and disciplinary measures on an equitable basis without regard to race, sex, religion, age, or other protected classification. Reasonable accommodation to an employee's religious beliefs or handicap status. Promotion and layoffs made in accordance with a bona fide seniority plan or other equitable basis that does not create an unfair advantage for a protected group. Avoidance of involuntary or compulsory retirement of employees (regardless of age). Equitable treatment of pregnant employees regarding working conditions.
Performance appraisal	Designing job-relevant appraisal systems that are free from contamination (e.g., evaluating someone's political beliefs or sexual orientation). **Ensuring that performance appraisals are made objectively, without regard to race, sex, religion, color, national origin, handicap status, and the like.**
Compensation	Complying with the equal pay act provisions—"equal pay for equal work." Comparable worth—paying the same for different jobs that have the same value to the organization or society. Pay decisions such as the application of sales commissions or determination of pay increases that do not have an unfair adverse impact on a protected group.
Employee benefits	Treating pregnancy on the same basis as other disabilities. Gearing retirement benefits to unisex mortality tables.

2. A woman who had coached both boys' and girls' sports was the only teacher to bid on a vacancy for head football coach. The school principal appointed her to the position, but the deputy superintendent of schools revoked the appointment and reinstated a temporary male teacher who had served as the football coach the year before. The female teacher sued. Do you believe that sex should be a BFOQ for hiring a head football coach? Discuss.[160]

3. The Baylor College of Medicine excluded two anesthesiologists who were Jewish from a surgical team sent to staff a hospital in Saudi Arabia. The college rejected the doctors because they were Jewish and would be unable to obtain visas to enter the country. Physicians participating in the program received twice the salary that they would have earned in the United States. The rejected doctors sued under Title VII on the basis of religious discrimination. Do you believe that the doctors are entitled to back pay? Would their inability to obtain a visa to enter Saudi Arabia be grounds for a BFOQ?[161]

4. A 51-year-old employee sued his company, claiming that it refused to promote him to an assistant manager's job because of his age. He quoted a company vice-president as telling him that the firm was looking for a younger person to fill the position. A jury awarded the employee double damages because the employer committed a willful violation of the ADEA. Do you agree? What impact are double damages likely to have on age discrimination cases?[162]

5. An employee who had concealed her epilepsy out of fear of being denied a job was hired as a clerk-typist. A few months later, she suffered an epileptic seizure at work; this was later followed by two additional seizures. She subsequently received a series of unsatisfactory performance evaluations that led to her dismissal. Do you believe that her rights may have been violated under the Rehabilitation Act of 1973? Discuss.[163]

[160]*Oates v. District of Columbia*, 44 FEP Cases 639 (1987).

[161]*Abrams v. Baylor College of Medicine*, 42 FEP Cases 806 (1986).

[162]*Lindsey v. American Cast Iron Pipe Co.*, 43 FEP Cases 143 (1987).

[163]*Reynolds v. Brock*, 43 FEP Cases 1077 (1987).

■ The Firing of a Pregnant Security Guard

The Old Dominion Security Corporation operates a security guard service for various public and private organizations. In 1979, the company hired Terry Williams as a security guard. Shortly after being hired, Mrs. Williams earned a degree from a private security guard training program at Thomas Nelson Community College and began working at Old Dominion's contract sites. During 1981, the company stationed Williams at the New Hope Towers apartment complex in Newport News, Virginia. During this time, the employer learned that Mrs. Williams was pregnant and expected to deliver during the last week of November 1981.

On several occasions between July and October 1981, the operations manager, Louis Cappino, and an immediate supervisor, Miller Rush, requested that Mrs. Williams resign and return to work after the birth of her child. Williams consistently refused and asserted that her pregnancy did not interfere with the execution of her job responsibilities. In September, after the company began pressuring her to resign, she obtained a physician's certificate that stated that her medical condition did not prevent her from working as a security officer. On October 31, 1981, Howard Blackmon, general manager at Old Dominion Security Corporation, telephoned Mrs. Williams and instructed her not to report to duty because of her pregnancy. Mr. Blackmon explained that Williams could return to duty after the birth of her child. However, Mrs. Williams was then formally terminated on November 9, 1981. She subsequently filed charges against the Old Dominion Security Corporation under Title VII.

Questions

1. The company normally allowed employees suffering from temporary disabilities to remain absent from work for one pay period and to return without formally reapplying. Does Mrs. Williams's pregnancy constitute a temporary disability? Should the same practice apply to Mrs. Williams as it does to other Old Dominion employees who are temporarily disabled?
2. The company contended that Mrs. Williams could not safely perform her duties as a security guard. They claimed that the work environment at the apartment complex where she worked required that she be able to detain suspected troublemakers until the police arrived, as well as to help tenants in distress. However, none of these crises had ever arisen. Does the company have a right to speculate on what events might occur that would make it difficult for Mrs. Williams to perform her duties?
3. Security guards often have to work during the evening and on the midnight-to-morning shifts. Could Old Dominion argue that they do not want to hire female guards with newborn children because of the difficulties of finding suitable and reliable child care arrangements (which would present absenteeism and tardiness problems)?

■ Mandatory Retirement at Delta Airlines

Delta Airlines is a large international air carrier operating a variety of aircraft. Delta's fleet of jumbo jets is composed primarily of the

Lockheed L-1011 series. This aircraft requires three crew members on the flight deck (cockpit): a captain, a first officer (copilot), and a second officer (flight engineer). The captain and first officer fly the aircraft, and the flight engineer sits behind the captain and first officer and monitors a side-facing instrument panel. Although many flight engineers are licensed pilots, they do not operate the flight controls. The Federal Aviation Administration (FAA) prohibits any person aged 60 and older from serving as a captain or first officer on a commercial flight. The FAA, however, has not established a mandatory retirement age for flight engineers.

Joseph Iervolino was employed by Delta Airlines as an L-1011 captain until his 60th birthday. Five months before his retirement, Iervolino requested a transfer to the position of flight engineer so that he could continue working for Delta beyond age 60. Delta denied Iervolino's request, and he was retired on his 60th birthday. The airline based its refusal to transfer Iervolino to a flight engineer's position on two grounds: (1) its policy of prohibiting captains from transferring to flight engineer positions (known as a *two-step downbid*) qualified as "a reasonable factor other than age" within the meaning of the ADEA and (2) the under-age-60 qualification for the position of flight engineer is a BFOQ reasonably necessary to the safe transportation of passengers. Iervolino filed charges against Delta under the ADEA.

Delta Airlines argued that a two-step downbid from captain to flight engineer would cause "role reversal" problems when a former captain who was accustomed to flight command duties was placed in a subservient position and required to take orders from younger, less senior captains and first officers. Delta did, however, allow one-step downbids from captain to first officer and from first officer to flight engineer. The airline felt that two-step downbids would pose safety problems. Expert testimony indicated that when former captains serve as flight engineers, the role of the crew members may become confused or ambiguous and former captains serving as flight engineers may intimidate other crew members during an emergency. Several pilots also testified as to the potential problems that could result from former captains serving as second officers. Delta also argued that because an individual pilot may not be aware of any difficulty in his transition to a flight engineer position until *after* a problem occurs, it is impossible to predict which captains would have difficulty making the transition and which would make the change with ease.

Iervolino contended that a flight engineer's normal duties are less critical to the safety of a flight than are those of a captain or a first officer. He cited the FAA's reluctance to impose an age-60 involuntary retirement on flight engineers as evidence that flight engineers have rarely been the cause or a factor in commercial aircraft accidents. He also introduced evidence that 485 flight engineers over the age of 60 (including 134 former captains) were serving on other airlines. This argument was bolstered by testimony from several former captains who were serving as flight engineers; they claimed that they had experienced no difficulty in safely performing their duties.

Delta argued that certain age-related diseases such as heart attacks, stroke, and susceptibility to adverse drug reactions become more prevalent at or around the age of 60 and that medical science cannot predict who will be victims. Iervolino countered that Delta could screen its flight engineers on an individual basis for potentially disqualifying medical conditions. He pointed out that Delta relied on FAA-mandated medical examinations to assess individually the ability of flight crew members to perform their jobs safely and efficiently. Iervolino claimed that Delta had permitted pilots to return to flight duty following the diagnosis of serious medically disqualifying conditions. He also pointed out that Delta has a system of proficiency checks designed to ascertain whether crew members can perform the required duties in a safe and proficient manner.

Questions

1. Summarize the arguments presented by both Iervolino and Delta Airlines. If you were a member of the jury presiding over this case, how would you evaluate each argument?
2. In most EEO cases, obtaining a BFOQ is very difficult. Do you believe that the requirements for obtaining a BFOQ should be relaxed in cases where public safety is an issue? What evidence should be presented to obtain a BFOQ in Delta Airline's case?
3. What factors favor Iervolino? As a possible future passenger on a Delta flight in which Mr. Iervolino could be the flight engineer, do you believe that airline safety would be compromised if the courts favor his position?

■ The Psychology Professor Who Was Denied Tenure

Dr. Martha G. Thomasko was employed as an assistant professor in the psychology department at Coastal Carolina College, a 4-year institution within the University of South Carolina system. Dr. Thomasko was hired by the college in 1971 as a part-time instructor. One year later she was promoted to the position of full-time assistant professor (she was also the first female Ph.D. at Coastal Carolina College) and began serving on a career path commonly known in higher education as a *tenure track*. With an acceptable record of

teaching, research, and public service, Dr. Thomasko could reasonably expect to become eligible for tenure in approximately 5 years. The granting of tenure is a milestone in the career of a faculty member and generally ensures permanent job security.

Dr. Thomasko's service as an assistant professor at Coastal Carolina College was marked with high and low points. She served as head of the psychology department and, in 1974, was granted permission to open an office for the practice of clinical psychology. However, her teaching methods and inaccessibility outside of class provided the basis for complaints from students to the administration. In early 1974, a committee was formed to study grievances brought by students regarding Dr. Thomasko's teaching methods and procedures.

On September 26, 1976, Dr. Thomasko applied for tenure and a promotion to the rank of associate professor. According to Paul Stanton, Associate Director and Dean of Academic Affairs at Coastal Carolina College, promotion and tenure decisions are based on a faculty member's teaching effectiveness, scholarship, and community service. Tenure decisions are made independently by a promotion and tenure committee and an administrative committee. If the two committees agree on their decision to promote and tenure a faculty member, then the decision stands. When the committees do not agree, they hold a joint meeting to resolve the issue. Both committees voted to deny promotion and tenure to Dr. Thomasko. The reasoning behind their decision was that Dr. Thomasko did not spend an adequate amount of time with students and faculty members.

On March 8, 1977, Dr. Thomasko formally appealed to a faculty grievance committee. In a letter dated April 25, 1977, the grievance committee denied her appeal. Dr. Thomasko then filed a charge of discrimination against the University of South Carolina system with the EEOC. She claimed that she was a victim of sex discrimination and national origin discrimination because of her Hungarian-German ethnic background. In addition, Dr. Thomasko also claimed that she had suffered pay discrimination while employed at Coastal Carolina College. In the latter claim, she stated that she was denied a salary equal to that of male professors who possessed the same qualifications and seniority.

Questions

1. How should Dr. Thomasko proceed in order to demonstrate that she was a victim of sex and national origin discrimination?

2. In making tenure decisions, college and university administrators often do not use strict guidelines or well-defined criteria. What problems could this pose when charges are brought under Title VII?

3. Although Dr. Thomasko was denied tenure in 1977, her case was still in the federal courts in 1986. Because civil cases often take years to settle, what impact does this have on the individual filing charges and the organization that must defend itself against such charges?

4. What must Dr. Thomasko do in order to demonstrate that she was a victim of sex-based pay discrimination?

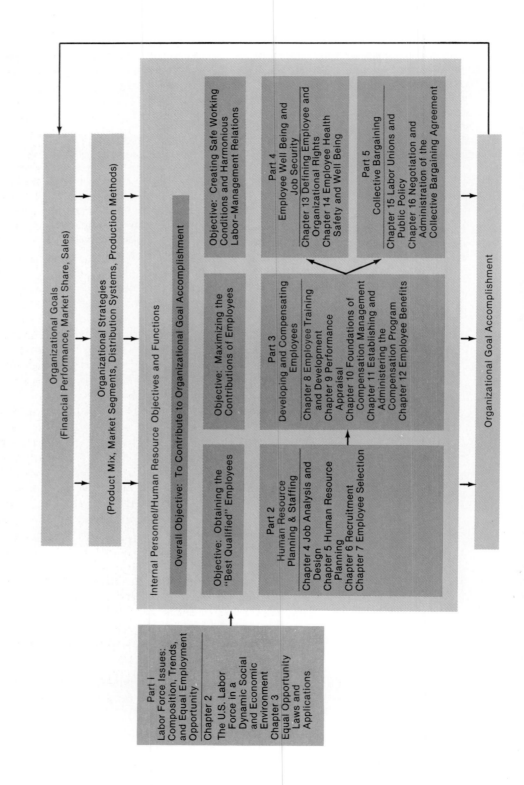

Organizational Goals
(Financial Performance, Market Share, Sales)

Organizational Strategies
(Product Mix, Market Segments, Distribution Systems, Production Methods)

Internal Personnel/Human Resource Objectives and Functions

Overall Objective: To Contribute to Organizational Goal Accomplishment

Objective: Obtaining the "Best Qualified" Employees

Part 2
Human Resource Planning & Staffing

Chapter 4 Job Analysis and Design
Chapter 5 Human Resource Planning
Chapter 6 Recruitment
Chapter 7 Employee Selection

Objective: Maximizing the Contributions of Employees

Part 3
Developing and Compensating Employees

Chapter 8 Employee Training and Development
Chapter 9 Performance Appraisal
Chapter 10 Foundations of Compensation Management
Chapter 11 Establishing and Administering the Compensation Program
Chapter 12 Employee Benefits

Objective: Creating Safe Working Conditions and Harmonious Labor-Management Relations

Part 4
Employee Well Being and Job Security

Chapter 13 Defining Employee and Organizational Rights
Chapter 14 Employee Health Safety and Well Being

Part 5
Collective Bargaining

Chapter 15 Labor Unions and Public Policy
Chapter 16 Negotiation and Administration of the Collective Bargaining Agreement

Organizational Goal Accomplishment

Part I
Labor Force Issues: Composition, Trends, and Equal Employment Opportunity

Chapter 2 The U.S. Labor Force in a Dynamic Social and Economic Environment
Chapter 3 Equal Opportunity Laws and Applications

PERSONNEL/HUMAN RESOURCE PLANNING AND STAFFING

■ People and the jobs they perform are the lifeblood of the organization. Part Two consists of four chapters that focus on placing the right people in the right jobs at the right time. Such a simple objective is often complex and may involve a number of important considerations. Chapter 4, Job Analysis and Design, provides the foundation for most of the personnel/human resource management functions. Job analysis information helps in the personnel planning process, defines what qualifications are needed for applicants who wish to fill a particular job, provides input into the content of employee training programs, and determines the rate at which different jobs are compensated. The way in which a job is designed also affects the ability of an employee to perform the job in a safe and efficient manner.

Personnel/human resource planning is addressed in Chapter 5. As organizations grow in size, they may expand their product and service lines. In such instances, proper personnel planning ensures that an organization is not left with a shortage of critical personnel or an abundance of employees with obsolete skills. Personnel/human resource planning involves analyzing a firm's competitive environment in order to develop realistic forecasts of labor supply and demand. In fact, the personnel planning process is a constant balancing act between an organization's current supply of employees and the employees it will need to conduct its business in the future.

Once an organization's staffing levels are established through the personnel/human resource planning process, the process of employee recruitment begins. Recruitment involves assembling a pool of applicants, or prospective employees. In many instances, companies recruit from external resources such as employment agencies, college campuses, and newspaper advertisements, to name a few. However, a firm may also recruit internally by tapping the talents of its current employees. Promotions and transfers represent internal staffing methods. The types of employees needed by a firm (as determined by the personnel planning process) dictate what recruitment sources will be used. Chapter 6 provides a detailed discussion of the major recruitment sources.

Once an organization has assembled a pool of applicants, it must have a means for selecting those who are best qualified. Chapter 7, Employee Selection, discusses the use of tools such as application blanks, reference checks, employment interviews, psychological tests, honesty tests, and others. These devices are known as *selection predictors,* and organizations often use them without knowing whether they are effective in screening out and selecting the best-qualified employees. The characteristics of validity and reliability in selection predictors are discussed in Chapter 7, along with the costs associated with making selection errors.

■4

Job Analysis and Design

■ LEARNING OBJECTIVES

After reading this chapter you should understand

1. The importance of job analysis to other personnel functions, such as personnel planning, recruitment, employee selection, performance appraisal, training, compensation, discipline, health and safety programs, and labor-management relations.
2. The various methods by which job analysis information can be collected, as well as the strengths and weaknesses of each method.
3. The important elements of job descriptions and specifications.
4. The various approaches to the design of jobs, and the underlying philosophy of each.

■ INTRODUCTORY VIGNETTE

Aid Association for Lutherans—Designing Work Around Self-managed Work Teams

Aid Association for Lutherans (AAL) is an 84-year-old nonprofit fraternal society that is both a charitable organization and a fiercely competitive insurance company selling life, health, and disability income policies to members of Lutheran congregations. It has an asset base of $6 billion and more than 1,900 field agents and ranks among the top 2 percent of U.S. life insurers. Like other life insurance companies, AAL operates at a low margin of profit and tries to do all it can to minimize costs. On August 14, 1987, AAL began an experiment that broke new ground in the insurance industry, cut costs, increased productivity by 20 percent, and decreased case-processing time by 75 percent. The experiment was nothing short of a complete reorganization of the insurance operations. Five hundred clerks, at the stroke of noon, on August 14, 1987, simultaneously moved their belongings to newly assigned work areas. Self-managed work teams had become a reality. These teams were designed to operate without layers of management. In fact, 55 supervisory jobs were eliminated over the next few years. Under the old system, an application for insurance would go to either the medical or life insurance sections, and then on to the support

This profile was drawn from John Hoerr, "Work Teams Can Rev Up Paper-pushers, Too," *Business Week* (November 28, 1988), pp. 64, 67, 72.

services section for such things as billing and policy loans. Complex cases would bounce among the sections for an average of 20 days, with some getting so lost that it took 30 days to locate them. Field agents were less than happy when information was delayed and customer applications and claims were temporarily misplaced. Now, with a regional organization and teams that can perform all of the 167 tasks that were formerly done across all three sections, cases average only 5 days. Field agents now deal with only one team, developing personal relationships, and they are secure in the knowledge that someone they know, as opposed to an anonymous bureaucrat, is processing their request. Team members schedule their hours, rotate jobs, and assign themselves tasks. Along with this redesign of work has been a redesign of the compensation system. A pay-for-knowledge system that encourages the acquisition and application of new knowledge was instituted in 1989. There are still a number of problems to be solved, including a continuing reduction in force, but AAL's employees acknowledge that service, productivity, and teamwork have all increased markedly.

◾ Introduction

The managerial functions of planning, organizing, directing, and controlling are well known and generally accepted as defining the primary responsibilities of managers. The organizing function refers to the organization of work and is of particular interest as we look at job analysis and design. Organizing includes, among other things, the determination of the proper grouping of tasks and responsibilities into jobs.[1] Once tasks and responsibility are organized into jobs, it is unrealistic to assume that those jobs will not change as time passes. Organizations must chart their course through an ever-changing environment. Customers' needs change, technologies change, the company's strategic plan changes, and human resources change as people come and go. These changes may be radical and abrupt or subtle and evolutionary. Regardless, they will affect the work that must be done and the allocation of that work to jobs and people. Therefore, independent of the approach a firm may take to the design of jobs (to be discussed later), it is likely that some changes will take place in every job. Further, it is very important for a company to document formally the tasks and responsibilities allocated to each job. Aside from the need to ensure that all the work is allocated as management wishes it to be, there are many other personnel functions, such as recruitment, selection, training, and compensation, that require up-to-date

[1]Managerial organizing extends far beyond the grouping of tasks and responsibilities into jobs. It includes, when appropriate, the allocation of work and responsibilities into companies, within a company into divisions, within a division into departments, and within a department into jobs. There are many different strategies for the organization of jobs, departments, and divisions. When the allocation of work and responsibilities occurs at the company, division, and department levels, we refer to the process as *organizational design*. When the allocation is at the job level, we refer to it as *job design*.

documentation of job content. As new jobs are created and as job content is altered, the documentation must reflect these changes. Typically, two documents are prepared for each job. One document, the job description, describes the content and context of the job. The other, the job specification, states the minimum personal attributes necessary to perform the job. Job analysis is the process of gathering information about the job and using it to write the job description and specification.

Designing a job refers to the process of deciding what combination of tasks and responsibilities should be allocated to it. There are different approaches to the design of jobs.[2] First, the organization of work within a company can follow traditional lines. You have probably noticed that secretaries have similar jobs across many companies. When this occurs, it is based upon the assumption that certain tasks and responsibilities are customarily "secretarial" in nature and should be grouped together. A person skilled in secretarial tasks is then assigned to perform the work. Traditional job design of this nature has evolved over many years, and there is much to recommend it. It is consistent with expectations that people have about how work should be organized, there is a ready group of qualified individuals who can be recruited to perform it, and it draws upon well-established and time-tested relationships among tasks, responsibilities, required skills, and jobs.

A job that has tasks and responsibilities that cut across the familiar secretarial and managerial jobs might require a very different and less commonly available combination of skills. This unique combination might create problems in recruitment and selection, as well as in the determination of the appropriate rate of pay. However, the deliberate addition of managerial responsibilities to the traditional secretarial job may also have some benefits. For many individuals the traditional secretarial job may be considered dead-end, boring, and repetitive. Those who consider it such might not be motivated to perform it very well. The deliberate addition of elements of managerial work might make the job more interesting and challenging, and create a positive motivational force within the individual. This second approach to job design is less concerned with the traditional organization of work and instead emphasizes the *psychological* impact work has on the person performing it.

A third approach emphasizes the organization of work for *maximum efficiency*. This approach is concerned with finding the best combination of physical movements, tools, and tasks to maximize productivity.[3] It is most often used for production or manufacturing and similar factory jobs requiring less personal judgment, decision making, and education. A firm may decide to use all three of these approaches. Different ones would be used for different jobs or job levels. All three approaches are discussed later in this chapter.

[2]See Michael A. Campion, "Interdisciplinary Approaches to Job Design: A Constructive Replication with Extensions" *Journal of Applied Psychology,* Vol. 73, No. 3 (1988), pp. 467–481, for a different perspective on approaches to job design. This article discusses the mechanistic, motivational, biological, and perceptual/motor approaches. These approaches parallel the psychological (motivational) and maximum efficiency (mechanistic, biological, perceptual/motor) approaches discussed in this chapter.

[3]See, for example, R. M. Barnes, *Motion and Time Study: Design and Measurement of Work,* 7th ed. (New York: John Wiley & Sons, Inc., 1980).

We begin our discussion of job analysis and design by looking at the job analysis process. Specific uses of job analysis information, data collection methods, and problems and errors associated with using job analysis information are discussed. We then review the various approaches an organization may take to the design of work.

■ Job Analysis

A key element in any personnel/human resource management program is job analysis. The job analysis process results in two essential documents: the job description and the job specification. As mentioned earlier, job descriptions summarize the duties, responsibilities, working conditions, and activities of a particular job. Job specifications outline employee qualifications such as education level, job-related experience, knowledge, skills, or abilities that are required to perform a given job.

Figure 4-1 summarizes the job analysis process and provides an initial look at the various uses to which the job description and specification may be put. To provide an overview of the job analysis process, we review it briefly at this point. A more detailed discussion follows in subsequent sections of this chapter.

Supervisors or other management personnel may recommend that certain jobs they supervise be analyzed. This recommendation is based upon the belief that the job has undergone significant change in its content and that the current documentation is no longer accurate enough to support related personnel functions. Jobs may also be analyzed on a set time cycle or when the organization plans to conduct a review of its compensation system (job evaluation). The job evaluation review is conducted to ensure proper base compensation for employees; not surprisingly, the essential first step is to ensure that all job descriptions and specifications are accurate.

After the jobs have been selected for analysis, information must be gathered concerning the content of the job. The personnel/human resource department must make a number of decisions regarding this data collection. First, the type of data should be decided upon (e.g., physical working conditions, use of machines, tools). Second, the method of data collection to be used must be selected from among many possible methods. Third, the individual who will be responsible for the analysis must be selected. These decisions are discussed in detail later in this chapter.

The information collected must then be processed into the job description and specification. At this point the information may be in a variety of forms. Depending upon the data collection method selected, the information may be encoded in scannable forms, written questionnaires, or notes and tape recordings of interviews. Further, some of the information may not be useful or accurate, and it must be edited from the information used to develop the job description. The end result of this processing will be the job description. Based upon the job description, the personnel department will decide (infer) what qualifications are needed to perform the job satisfactorily. To be sure, recommendations will be gathered during

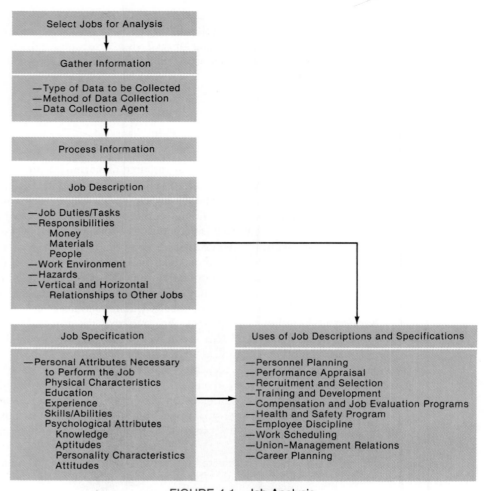

FIGURE 4-1   Job Analysis

the job analysis process from knowledgeable people on the necessary qualifications, but it is the ultimate responsibility of the personnel/human resource department to decide on those qualifications and to ensure that they are appropriate to the job content. Table 4-1 provides an example of a job description and specification for an administrative assistant in the Department of Agricultural Communications at a land grant university. The percentage associated with each task in the job description represents the distribution of job incumbent time across the various tasks.

After the job description(s) and specification(s) have been prepared, they may be used to support the many personnel functions illustrated in Figure 4-1. Each step in the job analysis process just outlined is discussed in more detail in the following sections.

TABLE 4-1   Job Description and Specification—Administrative Assistant

Job Description

Job Purpose: Provides administrative support for the Director of Agricultural Commuications. Coordinates activities and provides administrative support for the Department of Agricultural Commuications. The department provides the people of South Carolina with public service information supplied by the Clemson University Cooperative Extension Service and the South Carolina Agricultural Experiment Station.

Job Tasks:

1. Duties of administrative assistant   50%
   - Keeps Director's calendar, coordinating his meetings with other departments, makes appointments, coordinates department meetings.
   - Prioritizes Director's incoming mail.
   - Represents the Director at administrative meetings at his request.
   - Composes routine correspondence for the Director and other staff members.
   - Makes reservations and other travel arrangements for the Director.
   - Prepares travel and expense reports for department members.
   - Establishes and implements office procedures.
   - Preserves confidentiality of sensitive information, including personnel performance appraisals, wage/salary information, and budget matters.
   - Composes a monthly department report circulated to deans and directors in the College of Agricultural Sciences, the CU Cooperative Extension Service, and the South Carolina Agricultural Experiment Station.
   - Authorizes office equipment and supply expenditures at the university bookstore and Communications Center. Authorizes state vehicle requests.
   - Coordinates recruiting and hiring of five to seven student assistants for the department's administrative, publications, and studio areas. Supervises and trains the student assistant assigned to the administrative area.
   - Responsible for training department members in new computer software and equipment use as necessary.
   - Performs other duties as required (e.g., researches and estimates total equipment needs and costs to relocate and establish the Department of Agricultural Communications, including art studio, editorial and administrative offices).
2. Manages office: 15%
   - Defines departmental operating needs and selects/recommends appropriate office equipment and business machines.
   - Reviews and corrects as necessary to ensure the accuracy of university forms completed by department members before submission through appropriate channels.
   - Orders and disburses supplies.
   - Accepts and certifies office supply and equipment deliveries from state and local vendors.
   - Answers department telephone and responds to routine inquiries.
   - Maintains and updates department files.
   - Updates and maintains extensive mailing lists for dissemination of information and varied correspondence.

continued

TABLE 4-1   (continued)

Job Description (continued)

3. Uses a dedicated word processor (Motorola/FourPhase) and IBM personal computer; keyboards, formats, proofreads, and prints news releases, columns, administrative reports, manuals, general office correspondence, meeting agendas, and speeches. Edits for grammatical and syntactical errors.   13%

4. Responsible for final preparation and distribution of approximately 300 news releases per year written by Extension and Experiment Station editors, in compliance with strict time deadlines necessary for release of timely information. Dissemination of this material is accomplished through the use of an electronic telecopier, Teleram communications equipment, IBM personal computers, or the U.S. Postal Service. Maintains extensive up-to-date resource of news releases and news clippings for use by departmental staff and to service inquiries.   20%

5. Assigns technical contribution numbers and maintains comprehensive permanent record of technical contributions (research articles submitted for publication in scientific journals) written by scientists in all departments of the College of Agriculture for the South Carolina Agricultural Experiment Station.   2%

Supervisory Responsibilities
(1) Student Assistant II

Comments
Acts as liaison between Director/department and deans, directors, department heads, and other administrators on a regular basis. Deals with many campus offices in regular execution of duties. Daily use of Motorola/FourPhase word processor, IBM personal computer, 10-key calculator, photocopier, bulk folding machine, IBM Selectric typewriter, and information systems/telecommunications equipment (telecopier and electronic Teleram Portabubble).

Completed work is reviewed only for overall effectiveness. Employee exercises considerable independence and discretion, with the exception of budget and personnel matters.

Job Specification

Excellent understanding of English grammar, syntax, and spelling. Time management/organizational skills essential to meet frequent, variable deadlines. Knowledge of modern office practices. Keyboard skills, including calculator, data terminals, and corrected typing speed of 50 wpm.

Knowledge of word processing principles and ability to learn different types of software in order to train department members in their use.

Must possess ability to work without supervision.

These types of knowledge, skills, and abilities can be accquired through a college degree and 1–2 years of relevant experience or a high school diploma, formal office management training, including English composition, and 4 years of relevant experience.

Job Analysis Information and Its Relation to Other Personnel Functions

Figure 4-1 illustrates the pervasive influence of job analysis on the personnel/human resource management function. Table 4-2 provides specific examples of where job analysis information becomes especially useful.[4]

The list of specific uses of job analysis information depicted in Table 4-2 is not exhaustive. However, it illustrates the need for and importance of maintaining

TABLE 4-2   Relationship Between Job Analysis Information and Personnel/Human Resource Information

Personnel/Human Resource Function	Specific Uses of Job Analysis Information
Personnel planning	Delineating types and qualifications of employees needed to fill personnel needs
	Establishing computer-based skills inventory systems
	Employee succession planning program
Performance appraisal	Establishing and measuring performance criteria
Recruitment and selection	Developing selection predictors
	Validating selection predictors
	Ensuring compliance with EEO legislation in recruitment and selection activities (interviewing, testing, etc.).
	Ensuring compliance with Americans with Disabilities Act
Training and development	Assessing training needs
	Measuring the effects of training programs on job performance
	Selecting training methods
	Establishing promotion channels/career paths
Compensation programs	Job evaluation
	Incentive program standards
	Comparable worth analysis
Health and safety programs	Preventive safety analysis
	Accident and occupational disease analysis
Employee discipline	Establishing work rules and procedures
Work scheduling	Predicting and controlling the need for overtime
	Analyzing the feasibility of flexitime and other unique work schedules
Union-management relations	Wage negotiations
	Grievance administration
	Bargaining unit determination

[4]See also Philip C. Grant, "What Use Is a Job Description?", *Personnel Journal* (February 1988), pp. 45–53; Stephen L. Guinn, "Objective Placement Through Job Analysis," *Employment Relations Today* (Summer 1988), pp. 127–130; and Richard J. Mirabile, "The Power of Job Analysis," *Training* (April 1990), pp. 70–74, for additional discussions of the many uses of job description information.

thorough, up-to-date job documentation. Once an effective job analysis program is established and maintained, many troublesome personnel problems either become much less difficult to resolve or disappear entirely. For example, a firm plagued with employee turnover may discover, after investigation, that a poorly administered compensation program is at fault. Consider the case in which employees perceive that a firm's pay rates and increases are unfair. Further investigation might reveal the following problems:

1. The firm has no specific standard for measuring the value of specific jobs or the performance and contributions of its employees. This discovery, in turn, may reveal that
2. The firm's job analysis program is (a) nonexistent, (b) out-of-date (i.e., not reflective of current jobs), or (c) poorly conceived (e.g., vague, poorly written, biased, or inaccurate).

This firm must first establish proper documentation of its jobs through job analysis and then base its base compensation and performance appraisal systems on that documentation. Other organizational symptoms that might be at least partially caused by poorly conducted job analysis include poor placement of employees, excessive absenteeism, inadequate training and development programs, and employee accidents, among others. Many of the uses for job analysis information are discussed in detail throughout this text. The importance of job documentation (description and specification) for the various personnel functions is discussed in the following chapters: human/resource planning—Chapter 5; recruitment and selection—Chapters 6 and 7; training and development—Chapter 8; performance appraisal—Chapter 9; compensation programs—Chapters 11 and 12; employee discipline—Chapter 13; health and safety programs—Chapter 14; and labor-management relations—Chapters 15 and 16. The emphasis placed on job descriptions and specifications in this text should indicate the importance of the job analysis process to an organization.

Selection of Jobs for Job Analysis

As discussed earlier, the selection of the jobs for job analysis is the first of a number of important decisions that must be made. A job may be selected because it has undergone undocumented changes in job content and the personnel functions that depend upon accurate documentation cannot be properly performed. In these circumstances the request for analysis of a job may originate with the employee, supervisor, or manager. When the employee requests an analysis, it is usually because new job demands have not been reflected in changes in compensation. Employees' salaries are, in part, based upon the nature of the work they perform. As the work changes, compensation appropriate to the job may also change. Supervisors and managers may also request analysis to determine appropriate compensation, but they may also be interested in formally documenting necessary changes in the recruitment, selection, and training for the job.

Some organizations establish a time cycle for the analysis of each job. For example, a job analysis review may be required for all jobs every 3 years. The assumption is that over an extended period of time it is likely that job content for many jobs will change, causing current documentation to become inaccurate. A typical approach would be to request all employees and supervisors to review job descriptions with the purpose of selecting those that are no longer accurate.

New jobs must also be subjected to analysis in order to establish the documentation necessary to determine appropriate compensation, recruitment and selection strategies, and performance appraisal instruments.

Job Analysis Data Collection

Three major issues must be addressed when planning the collection of job analysis data. First, what type of job analysis information (data) is needed? Second, what method(s) should be used to collect the information? Third, who should collect and provide the information?[5]

Types of Job Analysis Information

A potentially wide range of information on a specific job may be obtained. The exact type and scope of information procured, however, will depend on both the intended uses of the job analysis information and the time and budget constraints imposed on the organization. Major types of job analysis information are depicted in Table 4-3.[6]

Based on the preceding discussion, it becomes apparent that Parts I–III of Table 4-3 form the basis of the job description, whereas Part IV provides the foundation for the job specification.

Methods Used to Collect Job Analysis Information

A number of methods have been used to collect job analysis information.[7] Each method has certain advantages, disadvantages, and points of emphasis that must be kept in mind. Employers should consider the use of multiple methods of data

---

[5]See Ernest J. McCormick, "Job and Task Analysis," in Marvin D. Dunnette (ed.), *Handbook of Industrial and Organizational Psychology* (Chicago: Rand McNally College Publishing Company, 1976), pp. 651–669.

[6]Ernest J. McCormick, pp. 652–653.

[7]A review discussion of many alternative data collection methods is presented in Patrick M. Wright and Kenneth N. Wexley, "How to Choose the Kind of Job Analysis You Really Need," *Personnel* (May 1985), pp. 51–55.

TABLE 4-3   Types of Job Analysis Information

  I. Work Activities
       A. Description of work activities (tasks)
            1. How a task is performed
            2. Why a task is performed
            3. When a task is performed
       B. Interface with other jobs and equipment
       C. Procedures used
       D. Behaviors required on the job
       E. Physical movements and demands of the job
 II. Machines, Tools, Equipment, and Work Aids Used
       A. List of machines, tools, etc. used
       B. Materials processed with items listed in II.A
       C. Products made with items listed in II.A
       D. Services rendered with items listed in II.A
III. Job Context
       A. Physical working conditions
            1. Exposure to heat, dust, toxic substances
            2. Indoor versus outdoor environment
       B. Organizational context
       C. Social context
       D. Work schedule
       E. Incentives (financial and nonfinancial)
 IV. Personal Requirements
       A. Job-related attributes (requirements)
            1. Specific skills
            2. Specific education and training
            3. Work experience (related jobs)
            4. Physical characteristics
            5. Aptitudes

collection because it is unlikely that any single method will provide all the information necessary to document a job properly.

Observation of Tasks and Job Behavior.   Through observation, trained job analysts can systematically gather information on the tasks, responsibilities, and working conditions associated with specific jobs. Observation is a well-accepted method of gathering information on unskilled, manual jobs but is less practical for jobs involving considerable thought, creativity, or analytical abilities, as these are difficult to observe and document. Analysts must be trained to gather observations over the entire set of employee job behaviors. Observing only a few job behaviors will result in a distorted view of the job content. Further, some employees are less receptive to being observed than others. They may feel threatened or intimidated by the analyst. The careful selection and training of analysts and their proper introduction into the workplace will help reduce many problems associated with observation.

Interviews with the Job Incumbent.   Persons performing a job are obviously in a good position to describe what they do, as well as the qualifications needed to perform their duties in a competent manner. Several biases may contaminate information from this source, however. They include inaccurate responses based on how the job incumbent feels the information will be used, the temptation to overstate the skills and qualifications needed to perform the job, and overreliance on a single person in obtaining important job information. Many of these biases can be eliminated by gathering the information from several job incumbents or interviewing them as a group. Further problems may result if the individual conducting the interview is not experienced or skilled in interviewing techniques. The following list of appropriate and inappropriate behaviors for job analysis interviewers contains some useful suggestions.[8]

- Do not take issue with the employee's statements. When the employee makes a statement concerning job duties and relationships, do not take exception to the statement. Record it and, if necessary, edit it out when writing the final job documentation. When you take issue with employee statements during the interview, the employee may become argumentative, defensive, or hostile. The level of cooperation will drop, and valuable information concerning the job may be deliberately withheld or distorted.
- Do not take sides on issues concerning employer-employee grievances or conflicts. A common behavior by an employee who disagrees with the employer over job duties is to enlist the sympathy or support of representatives from management or personnel. You may hear such statements as "Don't you think that it is unfair that I am asked to do this?" Agreement in any form will most likely be used to support the employee's position in the future. Disagreement will embroil you in the conflict, to the disadvantage of objective and complete data collection.
- Do not show any interest in the wage classification of the job. Employees are especially sensitive to a job analysis that may affect their compensation. References to the wage classification of the job may alarm employees and cause them to exaggerate or otherwise mislead you regarding their job duties.
- Behave professionally throughout the interview. Be polite and courteous, avoid talking down to the employee, and avoid being influenced by your personal prejudices.
- Do not criticize or suggest any changes or improvements on organization or methods or work. Your job is to gather information. Any criticism of the current way the employee is performing the job is likely to generate a defensive and hostile reaction from the employee. As indicated earlier, that is not the type of atmosphere conducive to gathering objective, accurate job information.
- Be sure that you request the permission of the supervisor before you talk to an employee. This is not only a matter of courtesy; the supervisor is responsible for

[8]The list is drawn from Ernest J. McCormick, *Job Analysis: Methods and Applications* (New York: American Management Association, 1979), p. 39.

the time of the employee. It would be unprofessional of you not to recognize that fact.

● Verify job information with someone else who is familiar with the job. This is especially important when the information contains many technical, unfamiliar terms.

Questionnaires and Checklists.   There are numerous standardized questionnaires and checklists that are valuable in job analysis. Questionnaires generally require the job holder or trained job analyst to describe job functions, responsibilities, and skills in narrative form. The more open-ended the requested responses are, however, the more susceptible this method is to inaccurate response contamination, such as was described in the section on interviewing. Checklists are more structured and often lend themselves to relatively easy, yet comprehensive statistical analysis through computer programs designed to accompany the checklist.[9] Examples of well-established job analysis questionnaires and checklists include the Position Analysis Questionnaire (PAQ),[10] the Management Position Description Questionnaire (MPDQ),[11] and Functional Job Analysis (FJA).[12]

Unlike other, more open-ended questionnaires, the PAQ provides a tool for quantitatively describing the various aspects of a job. A checklist of 182 job elements were rated from 3,700 different jobs. Through the statistical technique of factor analysis,[13] the original 182 job elements were reduced to 30 job dimensions, which were then classified under 6 major categories.[14]

With each major division depicted in Table 4-4, questions are coded for computer analysis. The job incumbent or analyst is then required to provide a subjective estimate (based on a 5-point scale) of the extent of use, amount of time involved, importance, possibility of occurrence, and applicability to the various job divisions and components within a division. Obviously, the PAQ is lengthy and

[9]For an excellent discussion and illustration of job analysis methods, see Richard W. Beatty and Craig Eric Schneier, *Personnel Administration: An Experiential/Skill Building Approach* (Reading, Massachusetts: Addison-Wesley Publishing Company, 1981), pp. 68–100.

[10]See E. J. McCormick, P. R. Jeaneret, and R. C. Mecham, "A Study of Job Characteristics and Job Dimensions as Based on the Position Analysis Questionnaire (PAQ)," *Journal of Applied Psychology,* Vol. 56 (1972), pp. 347–368, and E. J. McCormick, *The Position Analysis Questionnaire* (West Lafayette, Indiana: Purdue University Press, 1979).

[11]W. W. Tornow and P. R. Pinto, "The Development of a Managerial Job Taxonomy: A System of Describing, Classifying, and Evaluating Executive Positions," *Journal of Applied Psychology,* Vol 61 (1976), pp. 410–418.

[12]See S. A. Fine, "Functional Job Analysis: An Approach to a Technology for Manpower Planning," *Personnel Journal* (November 1974), pp. 813–818, and U.S. Department of Labor, Employment Service, Training, and Development Administration, *Handbook for Analyzing Jobs* (Washington, D.C.: U.S. Government Printing Office, 1972).

[13]Factor analysis is a statistical technique used for examining the intercorrelations within a data set. Broadly speaking, it addresses the problem of analyzing the interrelationships among a large number of variables (in our case, job components or divisions) and then explaining these variables in terms of their common underlying dimensions.

[14]See Ernest J. McCormick.

TABLE 4-4   Position Analysis
Questionnaire Job Divisions

---

1. Information Input
   a. Sources of job information
   b. Discrimination and perceptual activities
2. Mediation Processes
   a. Decision making and reasoning
   b. Information processing
   c. Use of stored information
3. Work Output
   a. Use of physical devices
   b. Integrative manual activities
   c. General body activities
   d. Manipulation/coordination activities
4. Interpersonal Activities
   a. Communications
   b. Interpersonal relationships
   c. Personal contact
   d. Supervision and coordination
5. Work Situation and Job Context
   a. Physical working conditions
   b. Psychological and sociological aspects
6. Miscellaneous
   a. Work schedule, method of pay, apparel
   b. Job demands
   c. Responsibility

---

time-consuming, but it represents an excellent means of obtaining a wealth of valuable job analysis information.

The MPDQ, although developed and applied in a fashion similar to that of the PAQ, consists of a set of job description factors that characterize management-level positions. These factors include the following:[15]

1. Product, marketing, and financial strategy planning
2. Coordination of other organizational units and personnel
3. Internal business control
4. Products and services responsibility
5. Public and customer relations
6. Advanced consulting
7. Autonomy of action
8. Approval of financial commitments
9. Staff service
10. Supervision

[15]See W. W. Tornow and P. R. Pinto.

11. Complexity and stress
12. Advanced financial responsibility
13. Broad personnel responsibility

Each of these factors is accompanied by a brief description, and can be used in analyzing and evaluating managerial jobs.

FJA is a procedure originally established by the U.S. Training and Employment Services (USTES). It is used to develop job descriptions and specifications and forms the basis for the current *Dictionary of Occupational Titles*, a well-known publication that furnishes standardized job descriptions for nearly all jobs in the U.S. economy.[16] The job analysis procedure used in FJA is predicated on the assumption that *work functions* for each job involve a relationship to data, people, and things. Furthermore, FJA assumes that the involvement of people in each of these areas can be viewed in a hierarchical fashion (Table 4-5). In addition to work functions, FJA provides a quantitative method for assessing the *work environment, machines and tools,* and *worker traits.*

The questionnaire/checklist methods briefly described here represent three of the better-known methods for collecting job analysis information. Other highly suitable standardized questionnaires include the Hay Plan,[17] CODAP,[18] work sampling,[19] Results Oriented Description, and Dimensions of Managerial Positions.[20]

Other Methods Used to Collect Job Analysis Information.   In addition to the methods just described, alternative means are available to collect job analysis information. These methods may be used either by themselves or in conjunction with other methods. Examples of such methods include conferences with supervisory personnel and participant logs (diaries) completed by the job incumbent. Other potentially valuable sources of information about jobs include equipment design blueprints and data, films, photographs, and even maintenance records.[21] Such sources often provide unobtrusive measures of job duties, responsibilities, and qualifications.

[16]Employment and Training Administration, U.S. Department of Labor, *Dictionary of Occupational Titles,* 4th ed. (Washington, D.C.: U.S. Government Printing Office, 1977). Although many generalized job descriptions are provided in this publication, it should be emphasized that they are general descriptions and would be inadequate for describing specific jobs in specific organizations.

[17]Charles W. G. Van Horn, "The Hay Guide Chart-Profile Method," in Milton L. Rock (ed.), *Handbook of Wage and Salary Administration* (New York: McGraw-Hill, 1972).-

[18]Raymond E. Christal, *The United States Air Force Occupational Research Project* (Human Resources Laboratory, Occupational Research Division, Lackland Air Force Base, Texas, January 1974).

[19]See Donald J. Schwartz, "A Job Sampling Approach to Merit System Examining," *Personnel Psychology* (Summer 1977), pp. 175–185.

[20]See Elmer Burack and Robert D. Smith, *Personnel Management: A Human Resource Systems Approach* (St. Paul, Minnesota: West Publishing Company, 1977), p. 289.

[21]See Ernest J. McCormick, pp. 653–654.

TABLE 4-5   Worker Function Hierarchy of Functional Occupational
Classification of the USTES

Data	People	Things
0 Synthesizing	0 Mentoring	0 Setting up
1 Coordinating	1 Negotiating	1 Precision working
2 Analyzing	2 Instructing	2 Operating–controlling
3 Compiling	3 Supervising	3 Driving–operating
4 Computing	4 Diverting	4 Manipulating
5 Copying	5 Persuading	5 Tending
6 Comparing	6 Speaking–signaling	6 Feeding–Offbearing
	7 Serving	7 Handling
	8 Taking instructions–helping	

Persons Responsible for Collecting Job Analysis Information

The persons responsible for collecting job analysis information ultimately influence the accuracy, thoroughness, and cost of gathering such information. Therefore, it is important that these persons be selected carefully and, if necessary,
trained in the use of questionnaires, checklists, interviews, or observational
techniques.

Most job analysis projects rely on one of three types of individuals: trained job
analysts, supervisors, or job incumbents. Table 4-6 summarizes the advantages
and disadvantages of each.

In essence, certain trade-offs must be made regarding time, cost, and accuracy
when selecting persons to collect job analysis information. Trained analysts generally offer the greatest objectivity and standardization, an important point when
job specifications are being designed to withstand scrutiny by the EEOC or the
courts for job relatedness (see Chapter 3). However, supervisors and job incumbents may be able to provide more in-depth information at less cost, although bias
and less standardization are more likely to occur.

The selection of a particular method of collecting job analysis information and
of the person(s) to be involved depends on two important factors. First, what is the
purpose of the job analysis? Second, what is the state of the current job analysis
program?

Purpose of the Job Analysis Program

Previously, it was mentioned that job analysis plays a broad and vital role in the person-
nel/human resource management program. However, certain aspects of the personnel
operation often need more attention than others.

If, for example, the recruitment and selection program is weak, the methods
such as the PAQ or FJA administered by a trained analyst may provide a good
foundation for establishing and validating selection criteria (see Chapter 7). The

TABLE 4-6   Selecting Persons for Data Collection:
Advantages and Disadvantages of Alternatives

Persons Collecting Job Analysis Data	Advantages	Disadvantages
Trained analyst	Objectivity is maximized Consistent reporting of information Expertise in job analysis method used	Expensive May overlook certain intangible aspects of a job because of lack of familiarity
Supervisor	Familiarity with jobs being analyzed (greater depth of information and familiarity with intangible aspects of a job) Fast data collection (possibly)	Need to train supervisor for effective job analysis Severe time burden imposed on supervisor Objectivity may be reduced (especially if supervisor feels that current employees are overworked) Less standardization of information
Job incumbent	Greater familiarity with job Fast data collection Less expensive (unless each employee receives job analysis training)	Problems with response patterns due to ambiguity in job analysis questionnaire Employee may neglect to report certain job duties Very poor standardization of data Restrictive job sample (unless other employees in same job also analyze their job)

PAQ, Hay Plan, and MPDQ have been successfully used in designing and administering equitable compensation programs.

It should be remembered that most of the job analysis methods described here are capable of providing a useful data base. The key to successful job analysis may not lie as much in selecting a specific job analysis technique as it does in selecting well-trained, objective persons to gather and analyze the information.

State of an Organization's Current Job Analysis Program

If an organization's job analysis program is antiquated or nonexistent, then considerable time and money must be spent to rectify the situation. Such a situation may require the use of a full-time project manager or consultant who selects a job analysis method, supervises the data collection, and is responsible for analyzing the information and writing the job descriptions and specifications.

For organizations with a well-established job analysis program, it should be remembered that job analysis information provides only a snapshot of a particular job. Jobs change over a period of time due to technological innovations, organizational restructuring, and changes in products, among other reasons. Thus, well-administered job analysis programs provide a built-in system for periodically reassessing jobs. This reassessment may be done expeditiously through observation or interviews, or by using a brief questionnaire or checklist. Unlike performing job analysis from scratch, keeping the program up-to-date is a much less expensive and time-consuming endeavor.

Processing the Information into Job Descriptions and Specifications

Once job analysis information has been collected, the next step is to place it in a form that will make it useful to those charged with the various personnel functions. Several considerations arise with respect to constructing job descriptions and specifications. First, how much detail is needed? Second, can the job analysis information be expressed in quantitative terms, qualitative terms, or a combination of both? Third, what means are available for developing job specifications once the duties, responsibilities, and work environment have been delineated?

Degree of Detail

Job descriptions and specifications may vary in length from several sentences to several pages. For example, Table 4-7 and 4-8 contain a job description and specification for an airline pilot; one is brief, whereas the other is extensive.

The job analysis depicted in Table 4-7 presents a thumbnail sketch of a Boeing 727 captain's job, but little information can be extracted that would be useful to the personnel manager. A far more comprehensive job description and job specification is needed in order to be of use in recruitment, selection, training, compensation, or labor relations matters. Table 4-8 provides such a description, which is patterned after the framework provided by the PAQ (see Table 4-4).

Table 4-8 provides considerably more detail than the original job description and specifications found in Table 4-7. As a result, more information is available to personnel specialists who must subsequently design recruitment, selection, training, compensation, and other programs. Of course, more detail may be added if time and money are not serious constraints. Although longer job descriptions and specifications provide additional information, the marginal value of such additional information may not warrant the effort and expense.

TABLE 4-7   Job—Captain: Boeing 727

Job Description: Plan and acts as a pilot in command of Boeing 727 flights carrying passengers and a crew of eight members.

Job Specifications: Possess an Air Transport Rating and a Boeing 727 rating, and meet current experience requirements as set forth by the Federal Aviation Administration (FAA) and the airline.

TABLE 4-8 Job—Captain: Boeing 727

I. Information Input
   A. Sources of job information
      1. Operations manuals: Boeing 727 including weight and balance, fuel systems, hydraulic systems, electrical systems, jet engine operations, emergency procedures, pressurization systems, and NAVCOM systems.
      2. Weather reports provided by Flight Service Stations: radar summary charts, weather depiction charts, area forecasts, terminal forecasts, winds aloft forecasts, PIREPS, NOTAMS, AIRMETS, and SIGMETS.
      3. FAA *Airmans Information Manual* and pertinent FAA regulations.
      4. Instrument approach plates, SIDS, STARS, low-altitude en route charts, high-altitude en route charts.
   B. Discrimination and perceptual activities
      The job incumbent must be able to utilize the information outlined in 1.A in planning, executing, and terminating a flight that is both safe and within the regulations set forth by the FAA. These activities include
      1. Determining whether the airplane is mechanically safe for operation by checking weight and balance, and pertinent aircraft systems, either through visual inspection, analysis of aircraft instruments, or collaboration with the flight engineer.
      2. Analyzing weather information, instrument departure, en route and approach procedures to ensure safe and timely departure and arrivals in accordance with airline schedules.
II. Mediation Processes
   A. Decision making and reasoning
      1. As pilot in command, all decisions made by the job incumbent must be adhered to by the crew and passengers.
      2. Decisions made in emergency situations require both rapid and excellent judgment, often under stressful conditions.
   B. Information processing
      The job incumbent must be able to analyze and integrate the information set forth in 1.A. An understanding of interrelationships among this information is vital. For example, the relationship between certain weather conditions and the feasibility of executing specific instrument approaches must be understood.
   C. Use of stored information
      See 1.A and II.B.
III. Work Output
   A. Use of physical devices
      1. Airplane control systems
      2. NAVCOM systems (VOR, DME, ILS, LOC, ADF, NDB, SDF, LDA, compass locator, PAR, OMEGA, LORAN, etc.)
      3. Emergency equipment
      4. Flight and engine instruments
      5. Radar
   B. Integrative activities
      1. Use of information in I.A in connection with the physical devices in III.A.
      2. Operations coordination with the appropriate FSS, clearance delivery, control towers, departure and approach control, ARTCC, and airline flight and maintenance personnel.

TABLE 4-8   (continued)

C. General body activities
   1. Use of both hands and feet for reaching, turning on switches, and manipulating flight controls.
   2. Acceptable level of physical and medical fitness required to meet standards for a First-Class Medical Certificate.
D. Manipulation/coordination activities
   Smooth and accurate operation of flight controls, instruments, and systems.
IV. Interpersonal Activities
   A. Communication
      Effective air–ground communications with those listed in III.B.2.
   B. Interpersonal relationships, personal contact, supervision, and coordination
      1. Clear delineation of duties and responsibilities among other crew members in order to provide efficient and safe operations of aircraft.
      2. As pilot in command, decisions made by the job incumbent carry final authority unless he or she becomes unable to perform duties during flight, in which case the first officer assumes command.
      3. Reports directly to the Director of Operations.
V. Work Situation and Job Context
   A. Physical working conditions
      Airline cockpit, pressurized cabin, normal heat and light, no exposure to toxic substances, radiation, or fumes.
   B. Psychological and sociological aspects
      Periods of high mental stress during adverse weather conditions, heavy air traffic conditions, and equipment malfunction. During such periods, proper delegation and teamwork among flight crew members are essential.
VI. Miscellaneous
   A. Work schedule
      Both day and night hours, approximately 15 working days per month.
   B. Method of pay
      Salary based on seniority, domestic versus overseas routes, supplemental compensation for travel expenses, pension, and group life and health insurance.
   C. Apparel
      Uniform provided by airline.
   D. Responsibility
      Ultimate responsibility for passenger safety, compliance with FAA regulations, and safe and proper use of aircraft.
   Job Specifications
      1. Hold the Air Transport Rating and current First-Class Medical Certificate.
      2. Have a minimum of 500 hours of flight experience in a Boeing 727 or simulator.
      3. Have at least 50 hours of flight time in a Boeing 727 within the previous 3 months that must include:
         a. Ten instrument approaches in a Boeing 727
         b. A review of in-flight emergency procedures
      4. Have received within the previous 6 months a proficiency flight check by a designated examiner in all phases of Boeing 727 operations.

Some organizations create job descriptions using standard task components. The analyst simply reviews the inventory of component descriptions and builds the job description by combining those appropriate to the content of the job. The application of computer technology makes this process more efficient, since many component descriptions can be stored, retrieved, and combined quickly and easily. Organizations using this approach believe it to be useful for jobs with frequent and rapid changes in content.[22]

Form of Job Analysis Information

Job analysis information may be expressed *qualitatively* in a fashion that is typically verbal and consists of narrative descriptions such as those provided in Tables 4-7 and 4-8. Qualitative job analysis information must be written clearly and precisely.

In addition to the qualitative form, job analysis information may be *quantitative*. Examples of this might include unit sales or production output, error rates, size of the work group, noise levels, and so on. Quantitative measures lend themselves to establishing standards for validating selection devices (Chapter 7) and measuring performance criteria (Chapter 9). Quantitative job analysis information is often used in conjunction with qualitative information.

Establishing Job Specifications

Job specifications (education, experience, and other characteristics or qualifications required of the job incumbent) are derived from a combination of three sources. First, qualifications for certain jobs are required by law. In order to pilot an airliner in the United States, for example, one must hold an Air Transport Rating, which requires 1,500 hours of flight experience, a very high level of flying proficiency demonstrated through written and flight examinations, good moral character, and a minimum age of 23. Airlines may require considerably higher qualifications, but the federal government has provided minimum standards that all airline pilots must meet. Numerous other jobs also require that certain legal standards such as licensing requirements be met.

A second type of job specification is based on professional tradition. University-level professors must generally hold a Ph.D. or an equivalent degree if they are in a tenure-track position. Whether the possession of a Ph.D. is essential to effective teaching or research is debatable, but it is, nevertheless, a well-established requirement in the United States. Other professions such as law, medicine, and dentistry have legal as well as traditional job specifications or requirements. Likewise, members of skilled craft trades have traditionally been required to meet certain skill levels and apprenticeship requirements before being admitted to their respective trades.

[22]See K. L. Aho, "Understanding the New Job Analysis Technology," *Personnel* (January 1989), pp. 38–40, for a discussion of this approach.

A third type of job specification involves establishing certain standards, traits, or characteristics that are deemed to be essential to the successful performance of a particular job.[23] This approach depends upon the judgment of the employer. The employer infers the job specification from the job description, often using personal attribute information gathered from job incumbents and supervisors during the job analysis process. For example, a life insurance company may decide that sales personnel need certain levels of psychological attributes to be effective on their jobs. The company might then require applicants to pass certain types of psychological tests. A radio assembly firm, after reviewing the job description of an assembler, may require a certain level of manual dexterity (an ability that can be measured) of its assemblers. Secretarial applicants may be required to demonstrate typing speeds in excess of 100 words per minute. Applicants seeking a specific managerial position may be required to possess at least 3 years of successful experience in a similar position. Personal attribute requirements or job specifications such as these must be directly related to the job description (job relevant). Ideally, such requirements should be subjected to validation studies, a topic to be covered in Chapter 7.

■ Job Design

In the introduction to this chapter we briefly discussed three approaches to the organization or design of work. The first was a traditional approach, the second sought to maximize the efficiency of the worker, and the third emphasized the psychological impact of work on the individual worker. All three approaches have a long history and have much to recommend them. This section reviews each in turn and discusses additional changes in the design of work, such as team building and alternative work schedules.

Traditional Job Design

As discussed in the introduction to this chapter, the traditional approach to assigning job duties emphasizes the commonality or similarity of particular jobs across organizations. Secretaries do secretarial tasks, accountants do accounting tasks, and so on, for most of the jobs in the organization. What is most characteristic of this approach is the reliance on what is customary in the determination of job content. The *Dictionary of Occupational Titles* contains standardized job descriptions for many jobs in the American economy. These descriptions and specifications embody this approach. Specific individuals may have somewhat different tasks, but for the most part, the jobs resemble the standardized

[23]For an excellent analysis of the measurement of human abilities, see Ernest J. McCormick and Daniel Ilgen, *Industrial Psychology,* 7th ed. (Englewood Cliffs, New Jersey: Prentice-Hall, Inc., 1980), pp. 145–180.

description. This approach to the design of work has many advantages. It considerably simplifies recruitment, selection, and compensation. It is consistent with employee expectations and formal commercial training and education programs as well. Further, the traditional organization of work has developed over many years, and it has proven acceptable to many organizations.

Maximum Efficiency and Job Design

When employers are particularly concerned with production efficiency, industrial engineers are often consulted. They study and analyze hand, arm, and other body movements, tools, and the physical relationships among tools, individual workers, and raw materials, as well as assembly or construction activity sequences, in order to maximize the efficiency of the production process. They attempt to simplify and standardize the job in order to make it possible for all employees to meet predetermined levels of production. This approach has its origins in the scientific management movement in the early part of this century.[24] Critics, although appreciating the usefulness of time and motion studies, charge that the design of work should not be controlled by the simple notions of efficiency, simplification, and standardization. They contend that "The psychological components of time and motion studies are very important. Whenever these are overlooked—and they often are—these studies become ineffective tools in the hands of fools."[25] Their position is that human and machine must function together. An efficient machine does not necessarily yield a productive human-machine relationship. This appreciation has led to the development of an area of study known as *human factors psychology* or *engineering psychology*.[26] This approach includes such concerns as human mental capabilities and limitations, especially those regarding the attention and concentration requirements of jobs.[27] More recently a new term, *ergonomics*, has characterized the study of humans and the work environment. Ergonomics has met with considerable success in designing the work environment to reduce fatigue, errors, eyestrain, and muscular and psychological stress. The emphasis of ergonomics is not so much on job content as it is on the design of the workplace. Issues such as the height of office chairs, the brightness and best degree of angle for computer screens, and other physical and psychological relationships between employees and office automation are considered. The performance of State Farm clerical workers improved 15 percent when their work stations were made ergonomically acceptable. Office workers' performance at Detroit Blue Cross/Blue Shield improved by 4.4 percent, and a telemarketing group reported an increase of 10–80 percent on final sales closings when they

[24]Frederick W. Taylor, *The Principles of Scientific Management* (New York: Harper, 1911).

[25]Milton L. Blum and James C. Naylor, *Industrial Psychology* (New York: Harper & Row, 1968), p. 572.

[26]The distinction between human factors psychology and engineering psychology has begun to blur. Engineering psychology once referred only to the design of machines.

[27]Michael A. Champion, "Interdisciplinary Approaches to Job Design: A Constructive Replication with Extensions," *Journal of Applied Psychology*, Vol. 73, No. 3 (1988), p. 468.

installed ergonomically enhanced furnishings and improved their lighting and acoustics.[28]

Psychological Issues and Job Design

There is little question that major economic benefits resulted from designing jobs to maximize efficiency. American industry became much more efficient and productive, with both employers and employees prospering. Over time, however, an appreciation developed that employees wanted more from work than simply economic rewards. They also wanted to experience job satisfaction and a sense of accomplishment from their work. This sense of accomplishment and job satisfaction, along with other similar reactions, were labeled *intrinsic rewards*, in contrast to financial or *extrinsic rewards*. Intrinsic rewards by definition came from the job itself; hence, the more challenging and enjoyable the job, the greater the available number of intrinsic rewards. Standardization and simplification of work limited the intrinsic rewards by reducing the working independence of the employee, by requiring low skill levels (and offering no likelihood of improving those skills), and by resulting in boring and monotonous work.[29]

Several major job design efforts were considered by behavioral scientists and employers to enhance employee productivity and job satisfaction. Three earlier efforts—job enlargement, job rotation, and job enrichment—are discussed, as well as a more recent approach.[30] Job enlargement, job rotation, and early job enrichment programs, although dated from a theoretical perspective, remain of interest because they represent different phases in the attempt to affect the psychological relationship between the employee and his or her work.

Job Enlargement

Job enlargement involves expanding the number of tasks or duties assigned to a given job. However, the additional tasks or duties typically require no new skills and are more similar to than different from the previous ones. The job has undergone only *horizontal* expansion, so that a previously monotonous job remains monotonous (only on a larger scale than before). Frederick Herzberg, a pioneer in job design, has characterized job enlargement as simply "adding zero to zero,"[31] meaning that one set of boring tasks (zero) is simply added to another set of boring

[28]M. Franz Schneider, "Why Ergonomics Can No Longer Be Ignored," *Office Administration and Automation* (July 1985), p. 28.

[29]Robert T. Golembiewski, *Men, Management, and Morality: Toward a New Organizational Ethic* (New York: McGraw-Hill, 1965).

[30]For a complete discussion of the evolution of job design interventions, see Andrew D. Szilagyi, Jr., and Marc J. Wallace, Jr., *Organizational Behavior and Performance*, 3rd ed. (Glenview, Illinois: Scott, Foresman and Co., 1983), pp. 124–159, and J. Barton Cunningham and Ted Eberle, "A Guide to Job Enrichment and Redesign," *Personnel* (February 1990), pp. 56–61.

[31]Frederick Herzberg, "One More Time: How Do You Motivate Employees?" *Harvard Business Review* (January–February 1968), p. 89.

tasks (zero). It should not come as a surprise that job enlargement has met with limited success in its attempt to alter the psychological relationship between employees and their work.

Job Rotation

Job rotation also represents a horizontal change in the job. Rather than adding tasks of a similar nature to the job (as with job enlargement), job rotation requires that a given employee alternatively perform a number of different, but unfortunately similar, jobs. The rationale is that as different jobs require different skills, the intrinsic reward potential of the job will increase. Professor Herzberg has characterized this approach as merely "substituting one zero for another zero."[32] Like job enlargement, this job design strategy has had a limited impact on employee motivation and productivity.

Job Enrichment

Job enrichment also attempts to change the relationship between the worker and the job. Whereas job enlargement and rotation involve horizontal alterations to the work performed (similar tasks are added to an existing job), job enrichment involves vertical loading (adding intrinsically rewarding or satisfying components to the job). Vertical job loading may entail greater responsibility, greater autonomy and self-regulation, a greater variety of tasks, and additional feedback on job performance.

Early job enrichment attempts were often based upon the dual-factor theory of motivation.[33] This theory states that two different sets of factors are present in the workplace. One set of factors can create employee dissatisfaction with the job (hygiene factors). Such factors include company policies, pay, and quality of supervision. When these factors are not at acceptable levels, employees are dissatisfied and act accordingly. When these factors are at acceptable levels, employees are not motivated to perform well but, rather, are simply not dissatisfied. (It is interesting that although these factors can cause employee dissatisfaction if absent, they do not cause job satisfaction if present.) A different set of factors, it was hypothesized, would cause employees to be satisfied with their jobs (motivators). These factors were intrinsic to the job and included such things as achievement, responsibility, and accountability. Hence, it made sense to provide just enough of the hygiene factors to prevent job dissatisfaction, and to provide a number of the motivators to motivate employees. Job enrichment, then, became characterized by vertical job loading as responsibilities and other such intrinsic factors were added.

As the dual-factor theory became less widely accepted as a modern theory of work motivation,[34] there remained evidence that job enrichment could neverthe-

---

[32]Frederick Herzberg, p. 89.

[33]Frederick Herzberg, pp. 83–92.-

[34]The dual-factor theory of motivation has been criticized by psychologists for a variety of reasons. These reasons centered on the research methodology used by Herzberg to collect data in support of the theory.

less accomplish a great deal. Different theories were proposed to explain the successes of job enrichment activities. The job characteristics model of motivation is one of the theories that has gained some degree of acceptance. This strategy offers a different, yet compatible, view of how job enrichment or vertical job loading can increase job motivation for employees.[35]

Figure 4-2 presents this theoretical model. According to this theory, a job can cause three psychological states to exist within a worker: experienced meaningfulness of work, experienced responsibility for work outcomes, and knowledge of the work results. To the extent that these states are created in an individual, personal and work outcomes such as internal work motivation, performance quality, job satisfaction, absenteeism, and turnover are affected. These critical psychological states are created by certain aspects, or core dimensions, of a job (skill variety, task identity, task significance, task autonomy, and feedback). Jobs can be described in terms of similarities and differences along these core dimensions. The theory states that an enriched job has high levels of these core dimensions, and they in turn create high levels of the critical psychological states in employees. Hence, the degree to which a job is enriched (has motivating potential) can be estimated by reviewing the levels of the core job characteristic dimensions (measured by a questionnaire, the Job Diagnostic Survey). Should these levels indicate that there is potential for enriching the job, and the employer feels a need to do so, the implementation concepts (presented in Figure 4-2, and discussed in Table 4-9) may be used.

Personnel practitioners can use the framework in Figure 4-2 to diagnose jobs that may have low levels of job motivation or satisfaction potential. If low levels of job motivation and satisfaction are found and if they are related to the tasks and structure of the job, then the implementing concepts depicted in Figure 4-2 can be used to alleviate the difficulties.[36]

Employers should be aware that not all jobs can be, or should be, enriched. It is a mistake, for example, to assume that all employees desire enriched jobs. Employees differ in many ways, and these differences translate into different expectations and reactions to the workplace. For example, enriched jobs may allow employees to feel challenged by their work and to experience a sense of accomplishment when that work is completed. These outcomes are important to employees who value such intrinsic rewards.[37] Employees who value these

[35]J. R. Hackman, G. Oldham, R. Janson, and K. Purdy, "A New Strategy for Job Enrichment," *California Management Review* (Summer 1975), p. 62.

[36]See J. R. Hackman et al. for a complete discussion of the diagnostic tools used.

[37]It is noteworthy that the research on the relationship between perceived task scope and employee performance yields contradictory and inconclusive results. See Ricky W. Griffin, Ann Welsh, and Gregory Moorhead, "Perceived Task Characteristics and Employee Performance: A Literature Review," *The Academy of Management Review* (October 1981), pp. 655–664. Also see J. Richard Hackman, "Is Job Enrichment Just a Fad?" *Harvard Business Review* (September–October 1975), pp. 129–139; M. Fein, "Job Enrichment: A Re-evaluation," *Sloan Management Review* (Winter 1974), pp. 69–88, cited in John M. Ivancevich, Andrew D. Szilagyi, Jr., and Marc J. Wallace, Jr., *Organizational Behavior and Performance* (Santa Monica, California: Goodyear Publishing Company, Inc., 1977), pp. 154–155.

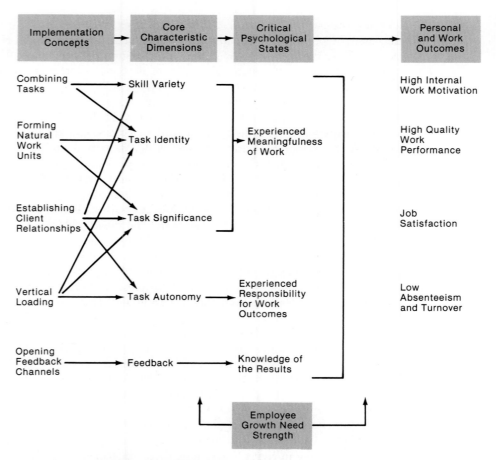

FIGURE 4-2   Job Characteristics Model of Motivation
Source: The Regents of the University of California. Reprinted from the *California Management Review,* Vol. 17, No. 4. By permission of The Regents.

intrinsic rewards have a high growth need. They wish to be challenged by their jobs. When intrinsic rewards are valued, enriched jobs will motivate employees. When intrinsic rewards are not valued (low growth need strength), employees will neither seek nor be motivated by enriched jobs. In fact, some employees may resent enriched jobs. For this reason, an employer must be convinced that a job can be enriched, and that such enrichment would be welcomed by employees, prior to instituting a job enrichment program.[38] Furthermore, the technological nature of a specific production or work process (e.g., an assembly line,

---

[38]Roger L. Anderson and James R. Terborg, "Employee Beliefs and Support for a Work Redesign Intervention," *Journal of Management* Vol. 14, No. 3 (1988), pp. 493–502.

TABLE 4-9   Implementation Concepts

Combining tasks	Existing and fractionalized tasks are put together to form newer and larger modules of work.
Forming natural work units	Providing a sense of "ownership" and continuing responsibility for an identifiable body of work.
Establishing client relations	Encouraging and enabling employees to establish direct relationships with clients.
Vertical loading	Responsibility and controls that formerly were reserved for high levels of management are added to the job.
Opening feedback channels	Providing means by which a worker can learn about his or her performance *as the job is accomplished*.

tank feeding system), may not make it physically or economically feasible to enrich certain jobs.[39]

Other Changes That Also Affect the Content or Context of Jobs

Employers have also changed the content or context of jobs through the use of quality circles, team building, self-managed work teams, and alternative work schedules. Each of these changes provide for greater involvement of the individual worker in the specifics of his or her job. We will discuss these changes in this section.

Quality Control Circle

The quality control (Q-C) circle is an intriguing and successful practice that is found in Japanese management and is increasingly being used in American industry (where, according to recent estimate, there are currently Q-C programs involving over 1 million employees).[40] Q-C circles have been used in Japan to achieve high-quality productivity and increased employee morale—all at a relatively low cost.

In Japan, a Q-C circle typically consists of between 2 and 10 employees who are permanently assigned to that circle. However, all employees (temporary, part-time, and at all levels) are encouraged to participate. The task of each Q-C circle is to identify any problems that fall within the scope of its work. Once a problem is identified, circle members suggest methods of correction.

[39]See Hugh J. Arnold and Robert J. House, "Methodological Extensions to the Job Characteristics Model of Motivation," *Organizational Behavior and Human Performance*, Vol. 25 (1980), pp. 161–183, and Brian T. Loher, Raymond A. Noe, Nancy L. Moeller and Michael P. Fitzgerald, "A Meta-Analysis of the Relation of Job Characteristics to Job Satisfaction," *Journal of Applied Psychology* Vol. 70, No. 2 (1985), pp. 280–289.

[40]The Bureau of National Affairs, "Quality Circle Problem Perusal," *Bulletin to Management* (April 11, 1985), p. 8; and Thomas R. Miller, "The Quality Circle Phenomenon," *SAM Advanced Management Journal* (Winter 1989) pp. 4–12.

A primary distinctive factor of Q-C circles is management's investment in teaching production-level employees managerial problem-solving skills. In essence, Q-C circles are designed to enrich the entire work environment, not just the job. Perhaps the greatest purported contribution of the Q-C circles is the dignity provided to the individual employee, regardless of job level. Unlike other management improvement schemes, Q-C circles are not designed to provide instantaneous changes in job satisfaction or employee attitudes. Q-C circles permit employees to play the roles of planner and engineer, as well as worker. In the United States, these functions have been traditionally separated, perhaps to the detriment of the organization in some instances.

Q-C circles are thus a very broad form of job enrichment. Unlike many job enrichment efforts, however, Q-C circles attempt to equate increasing productivity with increasing employee income. Whether Q-C circles will be successful in the United States remains to be seen.[41] However, if cultural attitudes toward work and managerial decision making can be somewhat modified, Q-C circles may represent an extension of current job enrichment practices.[42]

Team Building

Team building recognizes that individuals work in an interdependent manner within an organization. Individuals work with others in their own work groups and with those in other work groups. To the extent that this interdependence requires integration of effort and the sharing of a common goal or set of goals, team building can provide a necessary common sense of direction and identity. The ultimate purpose of team building is to improve the effectiveness of the integrated effort of the group members.

Team building may take advantage of a number of techniques, such as role playing or role analysis and problem-solving sessions among the principals. Regardless of the technique used, it accomplishes its purpose by setting common goals for its members, analyzing the way work is performed by the group members, examining the way the group functions (its processes—group norms, decision-making behaviors, interpersonal and individual-group communication patterns, and effectiveness), and examining the interpersonal relationships among its members.[43]

---

[41]Two personnel researchers have concluded that the success of quality circles in the United States will be limited until organizations move beyond Japanese Q-C manuals and provide appropriate human relations skills training for Americans. See Larry R. Smeltzer and Ben L. Kedia, "Training Needs of Quality Circles," *Personnel* (August 1987), pp. 51–55.

[42]William Ouchi, *Theory Z: How American Business Can Meet the Japanese Challenge* (Reading, Massachusetts: Addison-Wesley Publishing Co., 1981), pp. 261–268.

[43]R. Beckhard, "Optimizing Team-Building Efforts" *Journal of Contemporary Business*, Vol 1, No. 3 (1972), pp. 23–32, as found in W. Warner Burke, *Organization Development* (Boston, Massachusetts: Little, Brown, and Company, 1982), p. 268.

Self-managed Work Teams

Self-managed work teams, also known as *self-directed, employee-participative, semiautonomous,* or *modular work teams,* exist at a greater level of employee involvement than Q-C circles and work groups as we have discussed them so far. Although elements of Q-C circles and team building are present with self-managed work teams, they are different enough to make it useful to discuss them separately. Employers hope that by designing work around a group of five to eight employees and then allowing the group a great deal of freedom in completing the work, employee productivity, satisfaction, and product or service quality will improve. Self-managed work teams are given many managerial responsibilities, thereby creating real change in the nature of the work performed. Teams are self-scheduling and have one member, the team coordinator, who handles administrative details. Fewer supervisors are needed, and those who remain perform a facilitating role rather than a supervisory one. Although not all self-managed work groups do all of the following tasks, many are responsible for safety and housekeeping maintenance, assignment of work to team members, working with internal and external customers and suppliers, stopping production or work in progress to address quality concerns, routine equipment maintenance, implementing process improvements, and selecting production/work methods. Some teams even select, discipline, and, when necessary, terminate their own team members. All of this requires a real commitment by management and employees, extensive training in communication skills, statistical quality control, conflict resolution, work flow/process analysis, selection techniques, disciplinary policies, a knowledge of EEO law, appropriate production- or service-related knowledge and skills, and a reward system that encourages team effort and productivity.

While many organizations have successfully implemented self-managed work teams, others have been less successful. The radical change in corporate culture that is sometimes necessary before self-managed work teams can succeed is more difficult for some companies than for others. Resistance from employees and supervisors, inadequate training, incompatible reward systems, and unsupportive management are some of the more common reasons for failure.[44] This approach to the design of jobs is growing more popular and enjoying more success each year. Part of this popularity is due to the increased interest in *total quality management,* which, among other things, requires flexibility of response and the empowerment of employees.[45] Experience has shown that both of these can be accomplished by self-managed work teams. As the successes and failures of more companies contribute to our understanding of self-managed teams, we will become more sophisticated in their implementation and the likelihood of their success will be increased.

[44]The Bureau of National Affairs, Inc., "Teaming Up for Success," *Bulletin to Management* (February 7, 1991), p. 40.

[45]The Bureau of National Affairs, Inc., "Focus on Quality," *Bulletin to Management* (May 2, 1991), p. 136.

Alternative Work Schedules

The most popular alternative work schedule for full-time employees is flexitime. In general, flexitime (or gliding time) allows an employee to set his or her own hours within certain limitations. Organizations using flexitime request employees to work certain core hours every day. An example might be from 10 A.M. to 2 P.M. Employees may then work the remaining hours before or after the core time, at their option. This flexibility appeals to employees who may have personal demands on their time in the mornings or afternoons. Employees, knowing that they have the ability to schedule their own work time, may feel more in control of their work lives. If an employer can accommodate flexitime and the employees wish to have it, there is reason to believe that no adverse consequences will result and that productivity and satisfaction gains are possible.[46]

Additional types of flexible work schedules have also been designed and are listed here. At the present time, little is known about their possible popularity or probable impact on employee morale or productivity.[47]

1. Flextour: Management defines the days to be worked and the number of hours per day. Employees choose the starting times.
2. Maxiflex: Management defines the work to be done. Employees choose the days, times, and number of hours.
3. Flexshift: Employees define the days and hours they prefer. Management sets up a matching schedule that fits the schedules preferred by workers.

Some organizations allow employees to elect four 10-hour days (4/40) as opposed to five 8-hour days as their work schedule. This is referred to as a *compressed* or *modified* workweek. Although this increases the length of the workday, it allows the employee to have a greater block of time to spend on personal pursuits.[48]

Job sharing is a relatively new approach that can accommodate those employees who wish to work on a part-time basis. Many employers are willing to divide a full-time job between two individuals. This provides a full-time "person" for the organization but part-time work for the two employees involved. The flexibility of job sharing is attractive to employees who wish more free time than a full-time job

[46]V. E. Schein, E. H. Maurer, and J. F. Novak, "Impact of Flexible Working Hours on Productivity," *Journal of Applied Psychology* Vol. 62, No. 1 (1977), pp. 463–465.

[47]See James E. Bailey, "Personnel Scheduling with Flexshift: A Win/Win Scenario," *Personnel* (September 1986), p. 62.

[48]Simcha Ronen and Sophia Primps, "The Compressed Work Week as Organizational Change: Behavioral and Attitudinal Outcomes," *Academy of Management Review* (January 1981), pp. 61–74. The results of a limited survey of readers (97 companies) on alternative work schedules is reported in Hermine Zagat Levine, "Alternative Work Schedules: Do They Meet Workforce Needs? Part 1," *Personnel* (February 1987), pp. 57–62. This survey indicates that permanent part-time help is the most popular alternative (75 percent), followed by flexitime (36 percent), staggered hours (30 percent), compressed work week (24 percent), job sharing (16 percent), short work weeks (12 percent), and job rotation (1 percent).

would allow or who have alternative uses for their time.[49] It is an especially useful way to provide employment to people who wish to spend a portion of their day with their children. Husbands and wives have shared the same job, as have complete strangers. As employers find it more difficult to find qualified employees, this might prove to be a useful way to interest persons who do not wish full-time employment in the firm.

In December 1986, Northeast Utilities established a job-sharing program. The scope of the program was limited to 50 pairs of employees. All employees are allowed to participate except those in supervisory or management positions and those covered by union contract. Jobs can be split in any manner that is acceptable to the supervisor and the job-sharing employees. Hence, alternative weeks, days, split days, or months are all acceptable alternatives. Employees may find their own partners, or the job may be posted for interested applicants. Northeast Utilities will also advertise for outside applicants if no employee is interested in the split position. Job sharers who work at least 20 hours per week are personally eligible for health care benefits, but family benefits must be purchased by the employee. Holiday pay, vacation pay, and educational benefits are split equally between both employees.

Thus far everyone involved, supervisors and employees alike, are very satisfied with the program. The company believes its image among employees has improved, productivity and morale have increased, and sick leave and personal time use have decreased, as have absenteeism and turnover. In addition to women with young children, Northeast Utilities has also noticed that job sharing appeals to employees who are approaching retirement age, or who wish to pursue their education. In all, Northeast Utilities officials are very satisfied with the job sharing program.[50]

Although much has been said and written about job design and alternative work schedules, much remains to be said and written. Several major factors emerge from the current literature and experience, however, that are relevant to those interested in personnel/human resource management:[51]

1. Whenever possible, the job should allow a worker to feel personally responsible for a meaningful portion of his or her work. Jobs that provide task autonomy and control to the employee increase personal responsibility for successes and failures that occur.

2. Jobs should be structured to allow employees to perform tasks that are perceived as being worthwhile and meaningful. Behavioral scientists use terms such as *task identity* (an employee is assigned specific responsibilities for certain duties), *task variety* (a variety of skills and duties are incorporated into a

[49]Walter L. Polsky and Loretta D. Foxman, "Can Job Sharing Work for You?" *Personnel Journal* (September 1987), pp. 30–33.

[50]Bureau of National Affairs, Inc., "Job Sharing: Two-in-One Techniques," *Bulletin to Management* (October 22, 1987).

[51]Edward E. Lawler III, *Motivation in Work Organizations* (Monterey, California: Brooks-Cole, 1973), p. 158.

job), and *task significance* (a job is perceived as having an important impact on the organization, other people, or society) to assess the meaningfulness of a specific job.

3. The job should provide feedback about what is accomplished. A feeling of personal satisfaction is difficult to achieve, even on an otherwise well-designed job, unless task feedback is provided. Feedback may originate either from the accomplishment of the task itself or from other individuals, such as the supervisor, co-workers, or customers.

4. Not all employees will react positively to opportunities for increased responsibility and autonomy, and it is the responsibility of the personnel manager to ensure that such employees are matched with the types of jobs that they desire.

■ Summary and Conclusions

Job analysis forms the foundation for nearly all personnel/human resource management functions. Therefore, it is important that a great deal of time and effort be spent in designing a job analysis program, collecting the data, and writing job descriptions and specifications so that they are useful to personnel specialists. Although a solid job analysis program does not guarantee a trouble-free personnel operation, it can go a long way toward *preventing* many of the problems that can arise. Furthermore, should problems arise, a high-quality job analysis program may provide the necessary solutions.

Given the limited information contained in this chapter, it is difficult to appreciate fully the importance of job analysis at this relatively early stage in a personnel management course. For this reason, the role of job analysis is continually reemphasized in subsequent chapters of this book. Specific applications of job analysis are mentioned throughout as a means of reinforcing what has been said here.

From an administrative standpoint, job analysis can be a slow, tedious process. Nevertheless, its importance in documenting the organization of tasks and responsibilities at the job level is significant.

Job design is the philosophy with which a firm approaches the organization of work. A company can allocate duties and responsibilities consistent with common practice and tradition. An emphasis on efficiency, standardization, and simplification might require the services of an industrial engineer. An industrial psychologist, on the other hand, would provide a company with insight into how an individual would react to jobs at a psychological level. All three approaches can coexist within the same company and each has much to recommend it. The effect that work organization has on the economic health of the company and the psychological health of the employee should not be underestimated.

■ Questions

1. Review the suggestions for job analysis interviewing presented in the chapter. Describe why each suggestion is important for gathering valid information.

2. What unique problems might arise if you were gathering data for a job analysis of managerial jobs (as opposed to unskilled or semiskilled positions)?

3. Discuss the sources of error that can distort or render job analysis information inaccurate.

4. What are the differences between job rotation, job enlargement, and job enrichment?

5. Research a personnel function (e.g., EEO, labor relations, compensation, recruitment, etc.). Describe the importance of job analysis to this function. Provide specific contributions of job analysis to the function you have selected.

6. This chapter discussed three different approaches to the design of jobs. What are these approaches? What is each trying to accomplish? Are these methods compatible?

☐ APPLICATIONS AND CASE EXERCISES

1. Metal Parts, Inc., has grown considerably during the last 5 years. Laurie Nichols started the company with two employees and contracts for $60,000 in gross sales. The company now employs 65 people and is expected to have gross sales of $1,250,000 this year.

   During the early years, it was always clear what was expected from each employee. Everyone knew how to do everything and was often called upon to do exactly that. This is no longer true, and it is apparent to Ms. Nichols that each employee must be given a clear set of general guidelines as to what duties the employee must perform.

   In addition, it is becoming increasingly difficult to hire employees without having a clear understanding of exactly what the individual will be doing. Applicants seem reluctant to join the firm without some information about their probable job duties, and it is difficult to know exactly what skills prospective applicants should have without knowing in some detail what they will be doing.

   Ms. Nichols has decided to write job descriptions and job specifications for her firm. It is her belief that such documents will clear up any misunderstandings among employees regarding responsibilities, help to organize better the work that must be done, to inform prospective employees about their probable job duties, orient new employees, and help to make better selection decisions.

   A small business consultant has outlined a number of decisions that she must make. These decisions include determining whose responsibility it will be to gather the data and write the descriptions and specifications (Laurie Nichols, a consultant, supervisors, or the job incumbents), how the data will be gathered (observation, questionnaire, or interview), and how detailed the descriptions and specifications should be.

   Ms. Nichols is currently considering these job analysis issues but has a number of questions about how each will affect the final results.

   a. What recommendations would you make to her regarding the most appropriate individuals and methods to be used for data collection?

     b. What approach to the design of jobs do you believe Laurie Nichols should consider? Explain your answer.

2. Conduct a job analysis interview with someone who is employed full time. Using the information gathered during the interview, write a job description and specification for the job. Show these to the individual you interviewed and discuss with him or her the accuracy of your description and specification.

3. Contact an organization that has self-managed work teams. Discuss the transition from the previous organization of work to the present team approach with a member of the personnel department and a member of a work team. Do both individuals feel the same way about the change? What problems were encountered during the transition? How well are the current teams working together? Do you think that the use of work teams is an improvement for this organization? What general opinions have you formed regarding work teams from this exercise?

Human Resource Planning

■ LEARNING OBJECTIVES

After reading this chapter you should understand and appreciate

1. The importance of personnel planning to the organization.
2. The effect of internal and external organizational factors on the personnel planning process.
3. How an organization can develop forecasts of personnel needs (anticipated demand).
4. Methods by which an organization can stay abreast of and assess its current and anticipated pool of employees (personnel supply).
5. How various personnel functions are used to reconcile and balance personnel supply and demand.
6. The application of quantitative models and management information systems in personnel planning.

■ INTRODUCTORY VIGNETTE

Corporate Downsizing and the Changing Economic and Political Environment

During the latter part of the 1980s, a number of American companies previously known for stable and secure employment environments made major reductions in their workforces. Although recessionary pressures contributed to the timing of these reductions, they also occurred in response to the economic realities of intense international competition, changing social forces, and the increasing pace of technological innovation. These organizations decided that previous products, processes, and organizational structures had to be changed in order to remain competitive. Along with these decisions came associated human resource considerations. Some of the most prominent American-owned companies in the United States concluded that a reduction in their workforces was required. U.S. Steel dismissed 15,000 employees after closing six major plants and reducing its workforce in 24 other facilities.[1] AT&T cut its workforce by

---

[1] Joanne Marshall-Miles, Kerry Yarkin-Levin, and Marilyn K. Quaintance, "Human Resources Planning, Part 1: In the Public Sector," *Personnel* (August 1985), p. 22.

45,000, and Eastman Kodak and Chevron reduced their workforces by 10 and 15 percent, respectively.[2]

The 1990s have seen a continuation of corporate downsizing. By 1991 advances in microcomputer technology had eroded the markets for large computer systems. In late 1991, IBM announced its fourth major reorganization in 5 years in response to slow sales and declining profits. The reorganization gave more autonomy to its divisions as a means of improving their competitive positions. The reorganization also required an approximate reduction of 20,000 positions in the United States and Europe. Unisys Corporation, as a result of its restructuring, eliminated 10,000 jobs associated with deemphasized product and market areas, unnecessary layers of management, and staff positions at corporate headquarters. Sears Roebuck, in an attempt to reduce operating expenses and provide quicker customer access to account information, announced a $60 million expenditure on 28,000 computerized cash registers in 1991. These cash registers allow clerks on the sales floor to access credit account information and answer customers' questions regarding credit limits, balances, and payment history. At the time of the announcement, Sears indicated that it would save approximately $50 million in annual operating expenses. It also resulted in a planned reduction of 6,900 clerical jobs.[3] Early in 1992, General Motors, faced with falling profits—the company's average loss on every one of the 3.5 million cars and trucks made in North America during 1991 was $1,500—falling sales, and falling productivity, was another prominent American company to announce a commitment to restructuring and rethinking of its products and processes.[4] This rethinking had significant human resource planning implications. Based upon its restructuring, production process changes, and product line decisions, General Motors announced that 74,000 white-collar and blue-collar employees would be terminated by the middle of the decade. This represented approximately 17 percent of General Motors's 1992 North American work force.

Political forces also influenced the human resource requirements of many companies during this time. The end of the cold war resulted in a significant reduction of B-2 stealth bomber production. Northrop, which derived half of its $5.5 billion in revenues from B-2 work in 1991, was faced with a need to rethink its strategy, products, and human resource requirements. United Technologies Corporation, a major defense contractor, announced a restructuring in 1992 that would close or consolidate 100 plants and eliminate 13,900 jobs. The Defense Budget Group, a Washington, D.C.-based research group, estimated that during the first half of the 1990s over 1 million defense industry or defense-related private sector jobs will have disappeared.[5]

[2]Kirkland Ropp, "Downsizing Strategies," *Personnel Administrator* (February 1987), p. 61.

[3]Harris Collingwood, "In Business This Week," *Business Week* (January 20, 1992), p. 42.

[4]Alex Taylor III, "Can GM Remodel Itself?", *Fortune* (January 13, 1992), pp. 26–34.

[5]Rick Wartzman, "Defense-Based Regions Cope with Post-Cold War Era," *The Wall Street Journal* (January 17, 1992), p. B4. See also, Lee Smith, "Coping with the Defense Build-down," *Fortune* (June 29, 1992), pp. 88–93.

■ Introduction

Organizations, whether public or private sector, regardless of size or strategy, function in an uncertain and changing environment. Thoughtful planning has become essential for any organization that hopes to prosper during the 1990s and into the twenty-first century. All managerial planning activities, including those involving human resources, must be fully coordinated. Human resource planning must take place at every level, including strategic planning. Just as a manufacturing firm must consider the financial structure, physical plant, available production technology, and levels of raw materials necessary to meet planned production, it must also consider the number of people and types of skills necessary to support the production, distribution, and marketing of the product. Human resource planning explicitly considers the levels and types of human resources necessary to ensure the success of the company's strategic plan. Human resource planning includes the estimation of how many qualified people are necessary to carry out the assigned activities (personnel demand), how many people will be available (internal supply), and what, if anything, must be done to ensure that personnel supply equals personnel demand at the appropriate point in the future (reconciliation process). Planned production levels cannot be realized if the number of skilled production people available is insufficient to provide adequate support. When the supply of qualified personnel falls short of the need (demand), deliberate actions must be taken to increase the number of people to whatever level may be necessary. The company may wish to recruit and hire additional employees or to train, transfer, or promote current ones to meet the predicted personnel demand. Conversely, if there are more people working in the production unit than are necessary to meet production levels, the organization must consider activities to reduce personnel to the appropriate level. This might be accomplished by transferring extra employees to departments where shortages are predicted, by attrition (not replacing employees who leave for various reasons), by laying off employees temporarily or permanently, or by using one of a number of methods to reduce the number of hours worked by employees in that department. The need for these actions must be anticipated in advance so that there is sufficient time to perform them properly, with minimum disruption to the activities of the company and the lives of the employees involved. General Electric announced in late 1987 that a cut of 500 salaried jobs at its main engine-building plant was necessary to remain competitive with other companies in the industry. To minimize the disruption to the company and employees, the cut took place through layoffs, voluntary resignations, attrition, and retirement incentives.[6] The Stroh Brewery Company spent more than $2 million during a 13-month-long transition program for 1,159 employees. These employees were terminated as a result of excess production capacity acquired through a 1982 merger with the Joseph Schlitz Brewing Company. At the end of the 13 months, 98.3 percent of the

---

[6]"The Business Report," *The Greenville News* (September 1, 1987), p. 1D.

employees had been prepared for and placed in other jobs.[7] The DuPont Company, desiring to reduce its workforce by 6,500, offered an early retirement program in 1985. As an incentive, Dupont added 5 years to both length of service and age (thereby increasing the potential retirement benefits) for employees who took this early retirement offer. To the surprise of the company, 11,500 employees accepted the offer. Dupont has filled the unexpected openings primarily with retrained and reassigned employees.[8]

Throughout the 1990s, companies will increasingly find that the business environment will force an integration of human resources into the strategic planning process. In the future, it will not be possible to treat human resource planning as an ad hoc activity conducted independently by multiple decision makers throughout the organization. Human resource planning must be a coordinated activity directed at the accomplishment of the organization's strategic plan.

This chapter discusses human resource planning as a coordinated and focused activity. It examines the factors affecting this planning, such as the strategy of the organization, environmental uncertainties, time horizons, and forecasting information. It considers the nature of the human resource planning process, with an emphasis on forecasting personnel needs (demand), assessing personnel supply, and reconciling the supply and demand for human resources.

■ Factors Affecting Personnel Planning

Strategic Organizational Decisions

The process of strategy development involves defining an organization's business in terms of the products and services it will provide. In addition, management defines the organization's competitive posture and overall concept or image. Once the direction is set for the organization, the product and service levels to be offered are determined, and the competitive posture is developed (how it will deal with the competition), the firm must turn its attention to the resources needed to succeed.

In 1985 Packard Bell's founder, Benny Alagem, decided to pursue a strategy of mass merchandising personal computers. He believed that the personal computer would become a commodity purchase. Consumers, he reasoned, wanted a personal computer complete with software and all operating systems preloaded, that they could get at a low price at a convenient location, and that could be simply turned on and used. He needed to create reliable hardware and software products, find financial support, arrange production facilities, work out the distribution channels, and secure the necessary engineers, technicians, production staff, and sales force to make it happen. Following this strategy, Packard Bell grew from an

---

[7]See Joseph J. Franzem, "Easing the Pain," *Personnel Administrator* (February 1987), pp. 48–55, for a complete discussion of this program.

[8]The Bureau of National Affairs, Inc., "Trends," *Bulletin to Management* (April 25, 1985), p. 7.

idea in 1985 to $1 billion in sales by 1992. It became the third largest player in the U.S. personal computer market after IBM and Apple. To accomplish this, Mr. Alagem created a workforce of 850 employees with the right combination of skills, knowledge, and ability to carry out the strategy he envisioned 7 years before.[9]

Environmental Uncertainties

Human resource managers rarely have the luxury of operating in a stable, predictable environment. Political, social, and economic changes affect all organizations. Chapter 1 of this text discussed some of the major changes that have occurred in the human resource management field. Further, marketing, production, and technological, as well as competitive factors, have an impact on organizations. For example, rising fuel costs during the early 1970s had a devastating effect on companies manufacturing large recreational vehicles. Airlines have been forced to deal with the effects of deregulation, keen competition, and rising fuel costs. The automotive industry has been adversely affected by foreign competition, production inefficiencies, tight financial constraints, and rising labor union demands.

Environmental uncertainties must be considered in planning human resource needs. Human resource planners deal with such uncertainties by carefully formulating recruitment, selection, training, and development policies and programs. Balancing mechanisms are built into the human resource management program through succession planning, promotion channels, layoff, flexitime, job sharing, retirement, and other personnel-related arrangements.

During the early 1990s, declining sales and considerable economic uncertainty caused many companies to reduce workforce size and to restructure themselves into leaner, more flexible organizations. They believed that too many employees and overly bureaucratic structures added to costs and reduced their ability to respond quickly to the changing business environment. As this downsizing and restructuring occurred, corresponding business opportunities were created for other companies. Microsoft Corporation found that as firms reduced their workforces, remaining employees were asked to work smarter. This increased the demand for Microsoft's personal productivity improvement software. Consequently, during a period of economic uncertainty and widespread downsizing, Microsoft increased its staff of programmers, technical consultants, and clerical workers by over 30 percent.[10]

Planning Horizons

Another major factor affecting human resource planning is the time horizon. Short-term forecasts and plans may be as short as 6 months to 1 year, whereas long-term forecasts may range from 3 to 20 years. The exact definition of short- as

[9]Larry Armstrong, "How Packard Bell Broke Out of the Pack," *Business Week* (January 27, 1992), p. 88.

[10]Michael J. Mandel, Michael Oneal, Deborah Fowler, Zachary Schiller, and Michael Schroeder, "Microsoft's Personnel Explosion," *Business Week* (January 13, 1992), p. 58.

TABLE 5-1   Degree of Uncertainty and Length of the Planning Period

Short Planning Period— Uncertainty/Instability	Longer Planning Period— Certainty/Stability
Many new competitors	Strong competitive position
Rapid changes in social and economic conditions	Evolutionary rather than rapid social, political, and technical changes
Unstable product/service demand	Strong management information systems
Changing political/legal environment	Stable demand patterns
Small organizational size	Strong management practices
Poor management practices (crisis management)	

Adapted from Elmer H. Burack and Nicholas J. Mathys, *Human Resource Planning: A Pragmatic Approach to Manpower Staffing and Development*, rev. 2nd ed. (Lake Forest, Illinois: Brace-Park Press, 1987), p. 129.

opposed to long-term human resource planning depends on the degree of uncertainty encountered in an organization's environment. For firms existing in a very unstable, dynamic environment, such as that found in the information processing industry, planning horizons may not exceed 1 year. On the other hand, organizations operating in relatively stable environments, such as state universities, may have time horizons that enable effective planning to span years.

Table 5-1 summarizes key factors that affect uncertainty and the length of the human resource planning horizon. In general, the greater the uncertainty, the shorter the useful planning period for the organization (and vice versa). The factors listed in Table 5-1 are among those that will either increase or decrease the human resource planning horizon, depending on the nature of the organization, its environment, and current managerial capabilities and practices. It should also be noted that these factors are interrelated. For example, small organizations are likely to experience greater uncertainty and, as a result, shorter planning periods.

Type and Quality of Forecasting Information

The information used to forecast human resource needs originates from a multitude of sources. A major issue in human resource planning is the type of information that should be used in making forecasts. Closely related to this issue is the quality of information used. Table 5-2 illustrates the types and levels of forecasting information useful to human resource planners.

The essence of human resource planning is to determine where the organization is going and what human resources are needed to fulfill the strategic plans established by top management. The quality and accuracy of the human resource planning information listed in Table 5-2 depend upon the clarity with which the organizational decision makers have defined their strategy, organization structure, budgets, production schedules, and so forth. In addition, the personnel/human resource department must maintain well-developed job analysis information and

TABLE 5-2   Levels of Human Resource Planning Information

Strategic Information	General Organizational Information	Specific Information Necessary for Personnel Planning

Product mix
Customer mix
Competitive emphasis
Geographic limits of
   the market
	Organizational structure
	Information flows
	Operating and capital
	   budgets
	Functional area objectives
	Production schedules
	Distribution channels
	Sales territories
	Production processes
	Level of technology
	Planning horizons
		Job analysis
		Affirmative action programs and
		   guidelines
		Skills inventories
		Management inventories
		Available training and
		   development programs
		Recruitment sources
		Labor market analysis
		Compensation program
		EEO laws
		Retirement plans
		Turnover data

human resource information systems that provide accurate and timely data. Generally speaking, organizations operating in stable environments are in better positions to obtain higher-quality (comprehensive, timely, and accurate) information because of longer planning horizons, clearer definition of strategy and objectives, and fewer disruptions.

Nature of Jobs Being Filled

Human resource planners must also consider the types of jobs to be filled in the organization. Job vacancies occur as a result of employee turnover (resignations, discharges, retirement, deaths), promotions, and the creation of new positions. Major concerns pertaining to the types of jobs to be filled are sources of new employees, the possibility of training and developing current employees to fill vacant positions, the ease or difficulty of finding suitable employees, and the time horizons involved.

Jobs involving little or no skill are typically easy to fill on short notice, although in some areas of the country this is no longer true. On the other hand, very technical, professional, or specialized positions may require an extensive search spanning months or even years. Therefore, it is of benefit to the organization to anticipate vacancies as far in advance as possible in order to provide sufficient lead time to ensure that suitable candidates are obtained. Furthermore, a knowledge of where certain types of candidates are most likely to be found is also important. For example, a university may seek a faculty member with specific research and teaching capabilities. The hiring of such an individual may mean directing several years of recruitment effort toward a select few universities whose doctoral candidates have received an education in this particular area. Rarely can such positions be filled within a short period of time.

■ The Human Resource Planning Process

People, jobs, time, and money are the basic ingredients in any human resource planning process. In its basic form, human resource planning involves forecasting personnel needs, assessing personnel supply, and reconciling supply and demand through various personnel-related programs. As previously discussed, the human resource planning process is affected by the organization's strategic management decisions and environmental uncertainties. These two factors, in turn, determine the length of the planning horizons, the type and quality of information available to human resource planners, and the nature of jobs to be filled. Figure 5–1 illustrates the human resource planning function and the factors that shape this personnel activity.

It should be noted that human resource planning is a dynamic, ongoing process. This is particularly true in organizations that must be ready to "turn on a dime" and operate, survive, and adapt under uncertain environmental conditions. Intermediate and long-term strategies and objectives are often altered, and, as a result, human resource plans must be revised to accommodate such changes. Therefore, human resource demand forecasts and assessments of supply must be continuously monitored so that adjustments can be made in the programs designed to reconcile the supply of and demand for human resources.

Forecasting Human Resource Needs (Demand)

Human resource demand is the term used to describe the total human resource needs of an organization for a given time period. The precise nature of an organization's demand depends on a number of factors. Once these factors are delineated, methods for forecasting can be designed and implemented. External factors include competition (foreign and domestic), the economic climate (such as the stock market crash of 1987 and the recession of 1990–1992), laws and regulatory bodies, and changes in technology. Internal factors include budget constraints, production levels, new products and services, and organizational structure.[11]

Despite the proliferation of mathematical models and prescriptions in the field of human resource planning, there are no hard-and-fast rules for forecasting. Short-range forecasts usually grow out of normal budgetary processes. Human resource budgets and projections are generally based on estimates of workloads (production schedules, patient loads, expansions or contractions in operations). Conversion ratios that translate workload data into personnel demand estimates may be used for a short-range demand forecast. For example, as sales increase by a certain percentage, a manufacturing concern may determine that the number of employees in certain departments or divisions must also increase. Likewise, a

[11]Elmer H. Burack and Nicholas J. Mathys, *Human Resource Planning: A Pragmatic Approach to Manpower Staffing and Development*, rev. 2nd ed. (Lake Forest, Illinois: Brace-Park Press, 1987), p. 121.

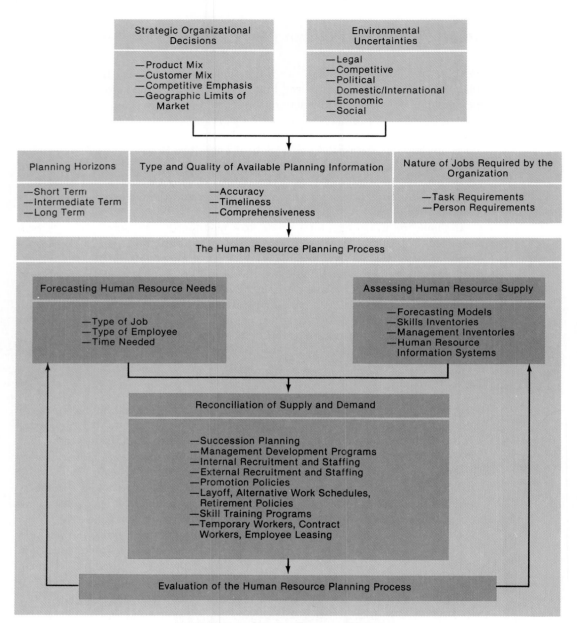

FIGURE 5-1   Human Resource Planning

hospital administrator may decide that a 10 percent increase in patient load will entail a 10 percent increase in nursing staff, an 8 percent increase in laboratory and x-ray personnel, and a 2 percent increase in maintenance, ancillary, and administrative employees.

The use of conversion ratios provides only a rough approximation of the number of employees required and may indicate very little about the types of personnel needed. It is important that an organization carefully define not only the number of workers needed by the entire organization, but also the type required at various levels, departments, and locations. Job analysis information is helpful in this respect, because it defines the educational, experience, and skill requirements of future employees.

Long-range human resource forecasting is more amenable to mathematical and statistical models. This has been particularly true in recent years as new mathematical techniques have been developed and high-speed computers used to rapidly analyze large amounts of human resource planning data. Unlike forecasting short-term human resource needs, which generally involves a fine-tuning operation to ensure that specific vacancies are filled, long-term forecasts are more general in nature.

Mathematical models used in human resource forecasting are based on selected key variables that affect the organization's overall human resource needs. Some mathematical models contain both internal and external variables. For example, a model incorporating the following factors might be used to forecast overall employment in an organization[12]:

$$E_n = \frac{(L_{agg} + G)\frac{1}{X}}{Y}$$

where

E_n is the estimated level of personnel demand in n planning periods (e.g., 5 years).

L_{agg} is the overall or aggregate level of current business activity in dollars.

G is the total growth in business activity anticipated through period n in today's dollars.

X is the average productivity improvement anticipated from today through planning period n (e.g., if $X = 1.08$, this means an average productivity improvement of 8%).

Y is a conversion figure relating today's overall activity to the human resources required (total level of today's business activity divided by the current number of personnel). It reflects the level of business activity per person.

The major purpose of this model is to predict E_n, the level of human resources necessary in n periods. Prior to plugging numbers into the model, estimates of G, X and Y must be made. Such estimates may be based on the previous experiences of management, as well as on future strategic choices to which the organization's decision makers are committed.

[12]See Elmer H. Burack and Robert D. Smith, *Personnel Management: A Human Resource Systems Approach* (St. Paul, Minnesota: West Publishing Company, 1977), p. 128.

It should be emphasized that the application of a human resource (employment) forecasting model depends heavily on obtaining accurate estimates of total growth (G), average productivity improvement (X), and conversion ratios (Y), (e.g., one employee per $50,000 in sales). In order to obtain estimates of these parameters, separate statistical techniques may be used.

An illustration may make the prediction model (aggregate planning model) more understandable. If we wish to estimate the number of salespersons necessary in 2000, we may use the relationship between sales and the number of salespersons we have today as a starting point. Assume that we currently have $1,000,000 in sales today (L_{agg}). Further, assume that by 2000 our sales will increase by $500,000 in today's dollars $(G,$ dollars adjusted for inflation), that there will be no increase in productivity $(X = 1.0)$, and that each of today's employees can support $50,000 worth of sales (X). If we substitute these values into the formula, we obtain

$$E_{2000} = \frac{(L_{agg} + G)\frac{1}{X}}{Y}$$

$$E_{2000} = \frac{(\$1,000,000 + \$500,000)\frac{1}{1.0}}{\$50,000}$$

$$E_{2000} = \frac{(\$1,500,000)\,1}{\$50,000} = 30 \text{ salespersons}$$

Another quantitative approach, linear regression analysis, may also be used to estimate the human resources necessary at a future point in time, based upon a business factor such as sales, output, or services rendered. For example, if a collegiate school of business is expanding, it is likely that more faculty will be needed. If there has been a satisfactory relationship in the past between the size of the faculty and the number of students enrolled, linear regression may be a useful method for estimating the number of faculty needed for expansion. Assume that the information in Table 5-3 is accurate. Note in the exhibit that as the business school grew in the past, more faculty members were considered necessary, and were hired. An alternative to the tabular approach to this information would be to graph the corresponding past number of faculty and past number of students. Figure 5-2 presents this information in Plot 1. You can clearly see the relationship we noticed in our review of Table 5-3 between the number of faculty and the number of students. The point labeled 1993 represents both the 1,107 students enrolled in 1993 and the 60 faculty who were supporting that enrollment.

Linear regression allows us to calculate a straight-line equation that summarizes the information found in Plot 1. Plot 2 shows the straight line that best summarizes the past relationship between the number of faculty and the number of students. Using the statistical technique known as *linear regression*, the equation for that straight line is calculated to be

$$Y = 7.234 + 0.0397X$$

where

Y is the number of faculty
X is the number of students enrolled

When this linear regression equation is used for human resource planning into the future, Y becomes the *predicted* number of necessary faculty, and X becomes the *expected* student enrollment. We simply take advantage of the historical relationship summarized in the equation to predict future need levels of faculty.

If we wish to estimate the number of faculty needed in 2000 (see Table 5-3), we may substitute the expected 2000 enrollment into the equation. Since X is the expected student enrollment the equation with substituted values becomes

Y (number of faculty necessary in 2000) $= 7.234 + 0.0397 \ (1400)$

$Y = 7.234 + 55.58$

$Y = 62.8$ or 63 faculty members

Another approach to determining the number of faculty members required in 2000 involves using the graph in Figure 5-2: locate the estimated number of students in 2000 on the X axis (1400), plot a vertical line up to the regression line, and then plot a horizontal line over to the Y axis, reading the necessary number

TABLE 5-3   Historical Relationship Between
the Number of Students Enrolled and the
Number of Supporting Faculty

	Year	Number of Students	Number of Faculty
	1981	200	15
	1982	250	20
	1983	345	24
	1984	378	25
	1985	400	23
	1986	456	25
	1987	504	27
	1988	546	26
	1989	750	30
	1990	809	33
	1991	837	39
	1992	928	45
	1993	1107	60
Estimated enrollment in	2000	1400	???

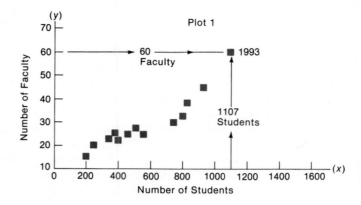

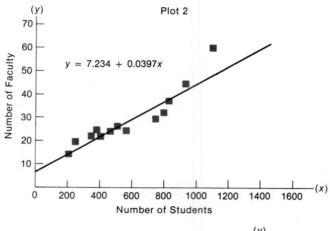

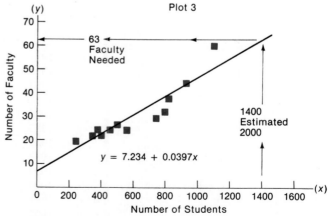

FIGURE 5-2   Linear Regression

of faculty from the Y axis (see the dotted line in Plot 3). If your graph is precise, you will read the same value for the necessary faculty (62.8) as you would get using the above equation.[13] The entire process depends upon the accuracy of your estimation of student enrollment in 2000. If the estimate of likely student enrollment in 2000 is inaccurate, then the prediction based upon it is less likely to be accurate.

The quantitative approaches presented here (conversion ratios, aggregate planning model, and linear regression) represent only three of the many methods that are available.[14] Those models used to predict personnel demand share common characteristics. They are built upon existing or past relationships between some business factor and employment levels in the organization. As a consequence, the accuracy of their predictions is dependent upon the strength of the relationships, how accurately these relationships are captured by the models, and the degree to which the relationships hold, or remain true, in the future. Predictions based upon poor or loose relationships, inaccurate representations (models) of the relationships, or relationships that are dated and will not remain true in future time periods will be inaccurate. The application of such models in highly complex situations becomes even more difficult because of the large number of factors (variables) that must be considered.[15]

---

[13]When using linear regression it is very important that the equation accurately summarize the past relationship between the two variables. How well the straight line equation summarizes the relationship can be reflected in another statistic called the correlation coefficient (r). This statistic ranges from -1.0 to $+1.0$. The larger the absolute value of the coefficient, the better the equation fits the relationship. The sign of the coefficient indicates the direction of the relationship between the two variables. A positive sign indicates that higher values of one variable are associated with higher values of the other. A negative sign indicates that lower values of one variable are associated with higher values of the other. The correlation coefficient for the data in Table 5-3 and Figure 5-2 is $r = +0.94$. The high absolute value of the coefficient indicates that the equation fits the data very well, and the positive sign of the coefficient means that as student enrollment increases, the faculty needed to support the change also increase. More is said concerning the correlation coefficient in Chapter 7.

[14]Examples of mathematical-statistical models used in personnel planning can be found in David J. Bartholomew, Andrew F. Forbes and Sally I. McClean, *Statistical Techniques for Manpower Planning* (New York: Wiley, 1991).

[15]The use of any mathematical model requires knowledge about the underlying assumptions and limitations of that particular model. For example, linear regression models make certain assumptions about linear inequalities and the normality of the distribution of its variables. The use of statistical planning tools under conditions that violate a model's basic ground rules may render the operation useless.

Another factor that must be considered is the cost of using mathematical models versus the benefits derived. The use of such models often requires considerable expertise, available only through consultants procured at considerable expense for the task. No model is a perfect predictor of future events or requirements. An issue that must be addressed is whether the purported accuracy (or inaccuracy) of the model is worth the dollar expenditures needed to design the model. Unfortunately, the value of such models is not known precisely until time and resources have been committed to its design and use.

Persons attempting to take a quantitative approach to human resource planning should have strong backgrounds in statistics, operations research or management science, and computer science. Equally important, the quality of information used to generate estimates and predictions from these models must be timely, accurate, and carefully collected.

Some organizations use group estimation to obtain long-term forecasts. The complexity of organizations and the environments in which they must exist make forecasting input from numerous individuals, each of whom is an expert in his or her facet of the organization, especially useful. Although the group estimation models used may vary somewhat, most of them involve the following:[16]

1. Selecting a variety of specialists or experts throughout the organization who possess knowledge or expertise relevant to the personnel forecast.
2. Identifying key forecasting concerns, variables, problems, and developments through scrutiny of the organization's strategic posture.
3. Developing a list of specific human resource forecasting questions or issues that must be addressed by the group.
4. Designing a system such as a questionnaire that will enable each specialist or expert to have unfettered and, perhaps, anonymous input into the forecasting process.
5. Once input is received and placed in an organized form, the group leader attempts to gain a general agreement on the personnel forecast.

Forecasting Human Resource Supply

Human resource planners must consider both the external supply (employees available for hire in the organization's geographic workforce) and the internal supply (the organization's current employees) of personnel. External supplies of personnel are important for two reasons. First, the normal attrition of employees through voluntary turnover, retirement, illness, death, and discharge may require the organization to look to employment agencies, colleges and universities, and other sources to replenish lost personnel. Second, organizational growth and diversification creates the need to use external sources to obtain additional numbers and types of employees. Human resource planners must be cognizant of available sources of employees. Chapter 6 discusses the various types of external recruitment sources, the types of employees that an organization is most likely to obtain from each source, and the respective advantages and disadvantages of these sources.

The internal supply of personnel is influenced by changes that occur to employees over a period of time as the result of training and development programs, promotion policies, and job-related experiences that contribute to the shifting of personnel within the firm. Environmental factors such as changes in local wage rates and the competitive posture of rival organizations may have an impact on employee turnover if employees leave (for greener pastures). Changes in retirement legislation also alter the internal supply of personnel as older workers reevaluate their plans and objectives. As employees leave or are transferred or promoted to new positions within the organization, vacancies must be filled. Many organizations look first to internal sources of personnel to fill these needs.

[16]See Fred Woudenberg, "An Evaluation of Delphi," *Technological Forecasting and Social Change* (September 1991), pp. 131–151.

It is important for human resource planners to anticipate and pinpoint changes in personnel supply. Various methods are available for doing this. A relatively straightforward method is presented in Figure 5-3.

Figure 5-3 provides an analysis of gains and losses of personnel for a particular job, word processor, in a hypothetical organization. The sources of losses and gains are enumerated and projected for a specific time period (e.g., a fiscal year). Total losses (42) are then subtracted from the current personnel level (250) and total gains added (22) to determine the expected level of personnel at the end of the planning period (230). This figure must then be viewed in conjunction with the anticipated demand for word processors in order to determine whether or not adjustments will be necessary (reconciliation of supply and demand) to ensure that supply will equal demand.

A major concern associated with the approach taken in Figure 5-3 is how the determination of the number of losses (transfers, resignations, discharges, promotions, and so forth) and gains (promotions and transfers) is made. In certain cases such as transfers, promotion, and retirements, it is possible to make very accurate estimates and projections because specific employees have been earmarked for promotion and transfer or have announced their retirement plans. Estimates of losses due to resignations, discharges, or demotions must be made through individual or group judgments or by examining past turnover ratios. It should be

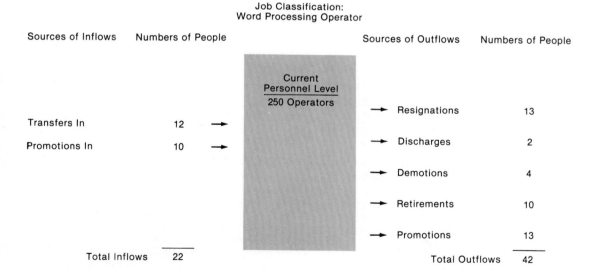

Job Classification:
Word Processing Operator

Sources of Inflows	Numbers of People		Sources of Outflows	Numbers of People
		Current Personnel Level 250 Operators		
			Resignations	13
Transfers In	12		Discharges	2
Promotions In	10		Demotions	4
			Retirements	10
			Promotions	13
Total Inflows	22		Total Outflows	42

Current Personnel Level − Losses (Outflows) + Gains (Inflows) = Internal Supply of Word Processors
250 − 42 + 22 = 230

FIGURE 5-3   Estimation of Internal Supply for a Particular Job. Job Classification: Word Processing Operator

remembered that resignations (voluntary turnover) are often affected by labor market conditions, the organization's promotion policy, and job vacancies within the organization. Therefore, if these factors change, loss ratios based on previous experience may not be reliable indicators of future turnover.[17]

Although human resource planning is concerned with having an adequate number of employees to fill positions within the organization, it is equally concerned with providing the right type of person for the job. A major function of human resource planning is to examine the skills and capabilities of current employees in light of the organization's short- and long-term strategic posture.

Skills inventories are used to collect and assess information on the competencies, skills, and potential of current employees. Information derived from skills inventories form the basis of promotion, transfer, layoff, and training and development decisions. In essence, skills inventories provide an information base for monitoring an employee's potential contribution to the organization, making informed personnel-related decisions, and, in general, assessing the organization's human resources.[18]

Whereas skills inventories specify certain skills such as the ability to weld, keypunch, or operate a machine, management inventories are somewhat broader based. Management inventories may focus on an employee's managerial experiences, successes or failures, and potential to assume more responsible managerial duties. Both skills and management inventories may be merged into a single inventory system, or they may be kept separate. Regardless of the type of inventory used, several important reasons for using skills and management inventories in personnel planning emerge.[19]

1. To ensure an adequate number of properly prepared managers to meet projected needs.
2. To expand the career advancement possibilities for individuals by providing a formal, organizationwide inventory.
3. To ensure objectivity and fairness in considering managerial personnel as candidates for a current or anticipated vacancy.

Human resource information systems (HRIS) provide a means of collecting, summarizing, and analyzing data germane to human resource management. In-

---

[17]Another well-accepted method for estimating internal supply is the use of a Markov model. This method uses historical information on the personnel movements that take place during a typical planning period. Data are collected or reviewed for a number of years in order to estimate the likelihood that persons in a particular job will remain in that job or be transferred, promoted, demoted, terminated, or retired. Thus the historical flows of the personnel (transitions) through the organization are represented by probabilities. These probabilities are arranged in a *transition matrix*, and future personnel flows are estimated on the basis of this matrix. See Michael Sampson, "A Markov Chain Model for Unskilled Workers and the Highly Mobile," *Journal of the American Statistical Association* (March 1990), pp. 177–181.

[18]See Richard A. Kaumeyer, Jr., *Planning and Using Skills Inventory Systems* (New York: Van Nostrand Reinhold Company, 1979).

[19]James W. Walker, *Human Resource Planning*, p. 262.

formation requirements associated with the personnel function are numerous. For example, assessing the personnel supply involves keeping track of employees throughout the organization. Recruitment, selection, training and development, career management, compensation, and labor relations programs also require timely and accurate information for decision making. Furthermore, personnel reporting requirements of governmental legislation can be time-consuming, expensive, and cumbersome endeavors without an HRIS that provides rapid retrieval and consolidation of pertinent data.

As a means of assessing personnel supply, HRISs enable organizations to store skill and management inventory data in a manner suitable for personnel planning use. Many firms establish computer programs that provide easy access to this information.[20] Components of a human resource data base might include some or all of the information listed in Table 5-4.[21] Specific uses of an HRIS in assessing personnel supply include the following:

1. Examining the capabilities of current employees to fill projected vacancies within the organization.
2. Pinpointing positions whose incumbents are expected to be promoted, retired, or laid off.
3. Delineating specific jobs or job classes that have unusually high rates of turnover, discharge, absenteeism, and performance or discipline problems.
4. Examining the age, racial, and sexual composition of various jobs and job classes to determine whether potential EEO liabilities may lurk on the horizon, as well as monitoring affirmative action programs and compliance efforts.
5. Anticipating recruitment, selection, training, and development needs to ensure the timely placement of qualified persons in job vacancies.

Given the state of the art in information technology, HRISs can be quite elaborate and expensive. Personnel administrators and planners who are attempting to design or evaluate a specific HRIS must be cognizant of its cost-benefit ratio, the existing coordination between the computer and human resource management departments, the potential for duplication of information within an organization, and the degree of sophistication desired.[22] Table 5-5 summarizes the range of sophistication available in HRISs. A very sophisticated system would be needed to maintain all of the information depicted in Table 5-4.

[20]Bill Leonard, "The Myth of the Integrated HRIS," *Personnel Journal* (September 1991), pp. 113–116.

[21]Dale Yoder and Herbert G. Heneman, Jr., *ASPA Handbook of Personnel and Industrial Relations: Planning and Auditing PAIR* (Washington, D.C.: The Bureau of National Affairs, Inc., 1976), pp. 2-66–2-68. See Chapter 2.3 of this book by Glenn A. Bassett.

[22]Sources of information on human resource information systems can be found in Michael J. Kavanagh, Hal G. Gueutal, and Scott I. Tannenbaum, *Human Resource Information Systems: Development and Application* (Boston: PWS-Kent Publishing Company, 1990).

TABLE 5-4   Components of Human Information Data Base

PERSONNEL DATA

Name
Pay number or Social Security number
Sex
Date of birth
Physical description of employee (height,
  weight, etc.)
Names, sex, and birth dates of dependents
Marital status
Employee association participation
Minority group classification

RECRUITING DATA

Date of recruiting contact
Responsible recruiter or interviewer
Source of candidate referral (newspaper ad,
  employment agency, etc.)
Date of referral of candidate or application to
  interested management
Names of supervisors or managers referred to
Date of interview(s)
Date of offer of employment
Date added to payroll
Reasons for selection/rejection of candidate
Test scores of interviewer ratings
Number of jobs open for which candidate was
  potentially qualified

WORK EXPERIENCE DATA

Names and locations of previous employers
Prior employment chronology
Military service
Job skills possessed
Product line experience
Managerial or supervisory experience
Foreign languages spoken, written, read
Publications authored
Special skills or hobbies of potential value to the
  business
Patents held
Elective governmental positions
Security clearances held
Date considered for apprenticeship or other
  special training
Reasons for elimination from consideration for
  apprenticeship or other special training
Dates of, type, and reason for disciplinary action

LENGTH OF SERVICE/LAYOFF DATA

Date hired by employer (actual or adjusted for
  lost service)
Seniority date (if different from date of hire)
Date of layoff
Last pay rate
Recall status

EMPLOYEE ATTITUDE/MORALE DATA

Productivity/quality measures
Absenteeism record
Tardiness record
Suggestions submitted (usually to formal
  suggestion plan)
Grievances
Anonymous inquiries/complaints
Perceived fairness of management practices
  regarding employees
Perceived fairness and soundness of
  management philosophy
Attitudes about credibility/honesty of
  management
Attitudes toward work, pay, supervisor, etc.

UNION MEMBERSHIP DATA

Union membership/representation status
Controlling union contract
Union officer status
Dues checkoff status

LOCATION/CONTACT DATA

Home address
City and state
Zip code
Home phone

OPEN JOBS OR POSITIONS DATA

Job request control number
Job title
Position or job code
Educational requirements
Experience requirements
Permissible salary range
Date by which position must be filled

WORK ENVIRONMENT DATA

Average educational level of co-workers
Average salary of co-workers
Number of job openings in component

TABLE 5-4   (continued)

Percent employees terminating employment (for some standard period)

Accident frequency and severity rates for position or company

Relative frequency of job changes in company

Manager's or supervisor's age

Manager's or supervisor's years of supervisory experience

Selection or inheritance of employee by present manager

Relative frequency of manager's or supervisor's disciplinary actions

Manager's or supervisor's tendency toward strict or lenient rating of employees

EDUCATIONAL DATA

College degree, high school diploma, level of educational attainment

Field of degree

Date of degree

Schools attended

Special employer-sponsored courses completed

Professional licenses held

COMPENSATION/WORK ASSIGNMENT DATA

Exempt/nonexempt or hourly/salaried classification

Current salary or pay rate

Date of current salary level

Date and amount of next forecast salary/pay increase

Previous pay rates and dates effective

Previous dollar and percent increase and dates of increase

Organizational reporting level

Position title

Supervisor/individual contributor status

Job code

Hours worked

Premium time hours worked

PERFORMANCE EVALUATION/ PROMOTABILITY DATA

Personal interests

Work preferences

Geographical preferences (for multiplant operations)

Level of aspiration

Rank value of contribution in current work group

Special nominations and awards

Appraisal reports

Date of last appraisal

Growth potential as rated by manager

Previous promotions considered for, and dates of consideration

Dates of demotion

Reason for demotion

Date of last internal transfer

Present component and work assignment

Geographical location of work assignment

Office phone

Emergency notification

BENEFIT PLAN DATA

Medical and/or life insurance plan participation

Pension plan participation

Savings plan participation (U.S. savings bonds, etc.)

Pay for time not worked (vacation, illness, lost-time accidents, personal time off, death in family, jury duty, military reserve duty, etc.)

Tuition refund plan participation

SEPARATION FROM PAYROLL DATA

Date of removal from payroll

Reason for leaving

Forwarding address

Name and address of new employer

Amount of pay increase obtained with new employer

Eligibility for rehire

SAFETY/ACCIDENT DATA

Noise level (in decibels) in work area

Exposure to noxious fumes or chemicals on job

Record of injury (date of accident, date reported, record of medical attention given, name of attending physician)

Classification of injury (disabling or nondisabling, days of work lost, lost time charged)

continued

TABLE 5-4   (continued)

Physical limitation resulting from injury
Worker's compensation claim data
Amount of overtime worked in component

POSITION/JOB HISTORY DATA
Job or position ID number
Job or position code
Date job or position was established
Permanent/temporary classification of job
Identity of past incumbents in the job
Dates of change in job incumbents
Dates of vacancies in positions
Type of change involved for each person leaving
   the position (newly hired, lateral transfer,
   promotion from another position)

If a promotion, identity of position promoted
   from
Location of job in organization structure
Manager of supervisor to whom position reports

LABOR MARKET DATA
Analysis of local personnel availability
Unemployment level by skills, occupation, age,
   sex, etc.
Predicted future manpower needs
Identification of scarce and surplus manpower
   pools
Wage and salary, shift differentials, etc.

Adapted from Glenn A. Bassett, "PAIR Records and Information Systems," in Dale Yoder and Herbert G. Heneman, Jr., eds., *ASPA Handbook of Personnel and Industrial Relations: Planning and Auditing PAIR* (Washington, D.C., The Bureau of National Affairs, Inc., 1976), pp. 266–268.

TABLE 5-5   The Range of Sophistication of HRISs

Unsophisticated	Relatively Unsophisticated
Manually oriented	Semiautomated data storage and retrieval
Limited personnel and employment data (education, experience, biographical)	Expanded data (appraisals of current and potential performance)
	Basic management reports
	Limited access throughout the organization

Relatively Sophisticated	Sophisticated
Semi- or fully automated	Automated
Capable of making essential personnel planning calculations and projections	Capable of a wide range of personnel calculations and projections
Expanded information file (individual interests, job preferences, behavioral and self assessments)	Expanded information file
	Cost-benefit assessments
	Data base for personnel research and development

Adapted from Elmer H. Burack and Nicholas J. Mathys, *Human Resource Planning: A Pragmatic Approach to Manpower Staffing and Development*, rev. 2nd ed. (Lake Forest, Illinois: Brace-Park Press, 1987), p. 249.

Reconciliation of Human Resource Supply and Demand

Once an organization's personnel needs (demand) are determined and the current supply of employees is assessed, then personnel supply and demand must be reconciled or balanced. Reconciling supply and demand is largely a matter of planning, timing, and use of various personnel-related programs to achieve the desired results.

Succession Planning

Succession and replacement planning involves preparing specific candidates (current employees) to eventually succeed present job incumbents who expect to leave or be transferred, promoted, or retired in the near future.[23] The key to succession planning is to develop an accurate profile of the requirements needed to fill the job (using job analysis information), select a candidate who appears to meet the requirements of the job or who has the potential to become qualified for the job, and take specific steps to prepare the candidate to fill the anticipated vacancy through training and development programs.

Figure 5-4 illustrates a management replacement chart. Replacement charts are often used to identify employees who will serve as possible replacements for a particular job incumbent. Notice that each position is currently occupied by an employee (e.g., President—J. Carlson) and has two potential replacements for that employee (e.g., B. Stevens and M. Sloane are possible replacements for the current president). Each replacement employee is rated on his or her promotability for that position. That rating is placed by the employee's name and explained in the coding scheme at the bottom of the figure. If the chart indicates that no one is prepared to assume the duties of a particular position, management must either act to prepare current employees (through management development programs) or to hire a new employee capable of assuming the position in the event of a vacancy.

Management Development Programs

In order to ensure that current employees have the special skills necessary to assume managerial positions in the future, organizations have created programs to develop such skills. These management development programs take advantage of a variety of training opportunities, both internal and external to the company. Employees may attend university classes, special conferences sponsored by professional organizations, or training sessions conducted by consultants. Often training programs are complemented by transfers to different geographic locations and

---

[23]For an excellent discussion of succession and replacement planning, see James W. Walker, *Human Resource Planning*, pp. 274–307. A number of interesting examples of succession planning in a variety of companies may be found in Richard B. Peterson, "Latest Trends in Succession Planning," *Personnel* (August 1985), pp. 47–54.

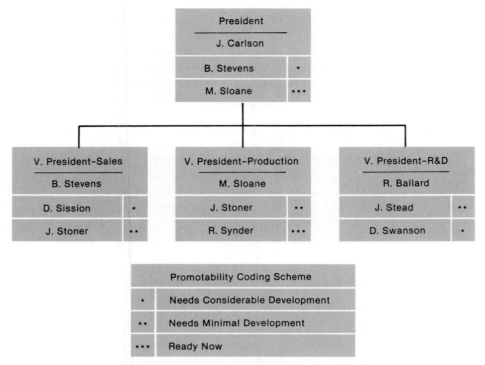

FIGURE 5-4   Managerial Replacement Chart

by functional areas such as marketing, finance, and production. The overall purpose of management development programs is to have personnel capable of assuming managerial positions when they become vacant. These programs are often used in conjunction with succession planning activities. Chapter 8 will discuss managerial development in more detail.

Internal Recruitment and Staffing

Organizations may wish to fill nonmanagerial vacancies with current employees. This may be a matter of standard policy or a strategy to correct fairly large human resource supply and demand imbalances. Often a company will allow any current employee to apply for an job opening elsewhere in the firm. These openings are advertised within the organization and may be applied for by any employee who feels qualified. It may also be the case that the firm has reorganized itself, perhaps closed a plant, and has many extra employees in some positions and too few in others. The extra employees may be recruited to apply for vacancies at other nearby plants or at plants across the country. Skill training programs, discussed later, help prepare employees for job changes. These programs can be coordinated with internal recruitment activities to ensure that employees are qualified to move to other positions in the company. Chapter 6 will discuss internal recruitment in greater detail.

External Recruitment and Staffing

Predicted human resource shortages can be filled by recruiting people from outside the firm to apply and take positions within the company. Typically this allows the firm to take advantage of large numbers of applicants in order to select the most well qualified. Chapter 6 will discuss external recruitment in greater detail.

Promotion Policies

Promotion policies are designed to fill positions as they open with current employees ready to take on additional responsibilities. These qualified employees may be located through internal recruitment or selected from a list of those considered ready by the company. Promotions typically create an opening at a lower level as the employee moves up to the higher position. Management development and skill training programs can be coordinated with promotion policies to ensure that employees are prepared for promotion.

Layoffs, Alternative Work Schedules, and Retirement Policies

Layoffs, retirement policies, and the use of alternative work schedules (flexitime, a 4-day, 40-hour week, part-time work, overtime, shortened workweeks, job sharing) all represent potential means of reconciling personnel supply and demand. Layoffs and retirement policies are typically used to reduce the number of employees. During the early 1990s Digital Equipment, IBM, and Eastman Kodak used early retirement programs to assist in their planned reductions in force. The idea is to make retirement as attractive as possible so that employees will elect to retire earlier than they had originally planned, rather than continue as full-time employees. Alternative work schedules can increase the flexibility of the organization to meet temporary shifts in personnel needs. Overtime can help the company avoid hiring additional employees, and shortened workweeks, part-time work, job sharing, flexitime, and other work schedules can help the company avoid layoffs. It should be mentioned that alternative work schedules are not used solely to reconcile supply and demand. As discussed in Chapter 4, they are often used to accommodate employee lifestyles and work schedule preferences.

Skill Training Programs

Human resource supply and demand can be balanced by using skill training programs to prepare managerial and nonmanagerial employees to perform certain tasks or jobs. For example, if a firm decides to automate certain aspects of its operations, additional training may be necessary to ensure employee competence.

Similarly, current employees can be trained either on an in-house basis or through a training program to develop skills needed to assume a new job within the organization. The use of skill training programs may partially or totally eliminate the need to recruit new employees from the outside.

Possible advantages of training current employees to fill new and more rewarding vacancies include improved morale, reduced uncertainty regarding employee reliability and performance, reduced turnover, and lower recruitment costs. The use of skill training programs in this manner involves the same type of planning and analysis that applies to succession planning. Chapter 8 will discuss training in greater detail.

Temporary Workers, Contract Workers, and Employee Leasing

The methods discussed previously all deal with individuals holding more or less permanent positions with the company. There are alternative methods of reconciling personnel supply and demand using individuals with only a temporary relationship with the firm. Many retail organizations use temporary employees during periods of high product or service demand. The Christmas season is an example. Another example is the use of large numbers of construction workers during short construction seasons on specific projects. Contract workers are used when special skills are needed on a limited basis or for a limited amount of time. Recent examples include management and financial consultants hired for specific activities such as mergers, downsizing, and reorganizations.

Employee leasing is a relatively new human resource planning activity. Rather than hire workers itself, a firm leases employees from a leasing company. The leasing company is responsible for hiring, record keeping, disciplining, paying, and terminating the employees. The company signs a lease for a specific period of time, requiring the leasing firm to provide workers and perform most personnel support activities for them. Leasing is most often used to remove the burden of performing those support activities from the company and to allow the firm to adjust the size of its workforce with greater ease without having to lay off or hire workers. This allows the firm to reduce its personnel support staff and avoid the many reporting responsibilities that accompany the hiring or termination of full-time employees. This is possible because the workers are not employees of the company itself, but rather employees of the leasing firm. Some companies have converted their workforces from permanent employees to leased employees through agreement with an employee leasing firm. To the extent that a firm has more planning flexibility and is better able to manage the size and skill composition of its workforce, employee leasing is a method of reconciling personnel supply and demand.

It should be remembered that adjusting the supply and demand sides of an organization's human resources "ledger" involves balancing employee surpluses and shortages, as well as timing the flow of workers into various jobs and parts of the organization. The specific methods used to achieve these objectives will depend on whether the organization is expanding, moving in new directions (e.g., new product lines and services), remaining the same in overall size, or possibly becoming smaller, perhaps due to changing economic conditions.

■ Summary and Conclusions

Human resource planning enables the organization to pursue its strategy and fulfill its mission by ensuring that the right employees are placed in the right job at the right time. The literature dealing with human resource planning discusses numerous techniques, mathematical models, and factors affecting the process. Perhaps the most important point that can be made regarding human resource planning is the need to attempt *systematically* to forecast personnel demand, to assess supply, and to reconcile the two. In addition, it must be remembered that human resource planning is an ongoing process, an especially important point in rapidly changing organizations where strategic plans must be frequently revised.

Human resource planning involves all personnel functions, but recruitment, selection, and employee training and development are involved more than most. Organizations that fail to do an adequate job of human resource planning may find that they have a tendency to make more than their share of incorrect hiring, promotion, transfer, and related decisions. The motivation for effective human resource planning is to help managers anticipate and deal with the demands of a changing business environment. Effective human resource planning systematically predicts human resource needs and ensures that the necessary adjustments in recruitment, selection, training, and other personnel functions are made.

■ Questions

1. Discuss the external factors and environmental uncertainties that might affect the human resource planning activities of the following organizations:
a. A collegiate school of business
b. A professional football team
c. A marketing consulting firm (small business)
d. A large urban hospital
2. Planning decisions must often be made on the basis of incomplete or imperfect information. What types of information problems might the organizations listed in Question 1 experience?

3. Evaluate the usefulness of mathematical models to determine the long-run demand for a firm's personnel. What advantages would such a model have? What problems might be encountered in the practical application of this model?
4. When assessing personnel supply and demand, why might a general knowledge of the material presented in Chapter 2, "Today's Labor Force," be of value to personnel planners?
5. Discuss the role of recruitment, selection, and training in human resource planning.

☐ APPLICATIONS AND CASE EXERCISES

1. Using the aggregate planning model predict the number of salespersons needed by the Saltzburg Company in 5 years under the following conditions:
   a. Current sales are $2,450,000.
   b. Current salespersons number 245.
   c. No change in productivity is expected during the next 5 years.
   d. Additional sales should reach $1,000,000 (in today's dollars) in the next 5 years.

2. The Executive Umbrella Manufacturing Company wishes to estimate the number of production personnel necessary to meet new production standards (367,000 units). A management science consultant has calculated the following regression equation based on past relationships between production personnel and production levels:

$$Y = 15 + 0.001\,X\ r = +0.90.$$

   where

   Y is the number of production workers.
   X is the number of units of production.
   r is the correlation between the number of production workers and the units of production.

   Based on this equation, how many production workers will the Executive Umbrella Manufacturing company need?

3. Warren Stokes, a supervisor for Real Time Cola, is considering the request of the personnel manager for a forecast of likely vacancies in his work unit over the next few years. Warren is not sure how to comply with this request. He knows that vacancies will occur in his 20-person group over that period of time. He can also see the need for this type of information because the company must ensure that there are always enough people with the right skills to meet the firm's contractual obligations. Further, it does make sense to ask supervisors at Real Time Cola what their opinions might be. Warren is convinced that there are predictable patterns of such job changes over the last few years that can be used to support these estimates.
   a. Do you agree with Warren that supervisors can provide useful estimates of likely vacancies in their work units?
   b. What types of personnel changes are likely to occur over the planning period?
   c. Which of these changes will be the most difficult for supervisors to estimate accurately?

4. Contact a local retail company that uses large numbers of temporary workers. Interview someone in the human resources department about how the company estimates its personnel needs for those periods when such workers are hired. Does the company use mathematical models? What business factor does the company use, if any?

Recruitment

■ LEARNING OBJECTIVES

After reading this chapter you should understand

1. The importance of planning in the determination of a recruitment strategy.
2. The strengths and weaknesses of various recruitment methods.
3. The differences between internal and external recruitment and when each should be used.
4. The need for and methods of evaluating the recruitment process.
5. Recruitment in a fair-employment environment.

■ INTRODUCTORY VIGNETTE

Apple Computer, Inc.

Ever since that Super Bowl Sunday in 1983 when Apple Computer, Inc. advertised the Macintosh® for the first time by showing hordes of businessmen walking over a cliff in mindless lockstep devotion to rival machines and companies, Apple has been known for some of the highest-quality product advertising in the business. Who has not seen an Apple product ad in the college newspaper or in business and popular magazines? The familiar format—a photograph at the top of the page, an attention-grabbing headline immediately below it, and "polished and pithy text" in the lower half of the page—always promises interesting reading. Apple has developed a creative method of merging its familiar product advertising with its recruitment activities. Reasoning that familiar ads get attention, Apple has made extensive use of its high-profile logo—an apple with a bite out of it, slogan—"The power to be your best"—and product ad format in its recruitment ads. The familiar layout, logo, and slogan capture the attention of potential recruits. By using this approach, the corporate image is embedded in every recruitment ad, taking advantage of the good will and positive image that the company have built up over a number of years. Apple's recruiting ads have been award-winning classics. The photographic images and accompanying headlines were attention grabbers—a monster with the headline "Mac Monsters," designed to appeal to the playful nature of computer hackers who might

Most of the information contained in this profile was taken from Jennifer Koch, "Apple Ads Target Intellect," *Personnel Journal* (March 1990), pp. 107–114.

be interested in writing software, or a picture of five people of equal status at a meeting with the headline "Find the finance person in this ad," designed to demonstrate that finance people are close to the action at Apple and are considered important members of the team. In the copy accompanying its recruitment ads, Apple emphasizes the ability of people to use their talents in a supportive environment, to accomplish extraordinary things—"At Apple Computer, we've created a research environment made of space. And we've equipped it with all the powerful tools you'll need to help change the future of computing"; "Fill this space with something we've never imagined. And we'll fill your life with more opportunities than you ever thought possible." Apple's recruiting materials have always had the ability to interest exactly the type of people that Apple wants to excite. This is no accident, but rather the end result of a carefully thought-out strategy requiring a consistency of format, text quality, and theme, regardless of the positions being advertised. The marketing division sets the tone and the conditions for logo placement (lower right-hand corner), trademark colors, typeface, and slogan, but the specific content of the ad is up to the recruiting manager and the advertising agency. Apple's recruiting ads are designed to be "clean, honest, witty," and a bit playful. The next time you see an Apple Computer, Inc., recruiting ad, realize that there is a well-developed corporate-level strategy behind it.

■ Introduction

Human resources are the most important assets in an organization. It is with people that quality performance begins and ends. Recruitment often represents the first contact that a company has with potential employees. It is through recruitment that many individuals will come to know a firm and eventually decide whether they wish to work for it. A well-planned and well-managed recruiting effort will result in high-quality applicants, whereas a haphazard and piecemeal effort will result in mediocre ones. Quality employees cannot be selected when quality candidates do not know of job openings, are not interested in working for the company, and do not apply. Recruitment should inform qualified individuals about employment opportunities, create a positive image of the company, provide enough information about the jobs so that applicants can make comparisons with their qualifications and interests, and generate enthusiasm among the best candidates so that they will apply for the available positions. This includes candidates from outside of the organization (external recruitment), as well as current employees interested in different jobs within the company (internal recruitment).

Our discussion in this chapter will emphasize a systematic approach to internal and external recruitment and will include details on the legal environment, selected recruitment methods, and the issues that affect the internal/external recruiting mix. It is not realistic to assume that all organizations take a systematic approach to recruitment.[1] Those that do, however, recognize the integral role recruitment plays in realizing the organization's strategic plan. This chapter concentrates on recruitment from the employer's perspective. The appendix at the end of the chapter discusses recruitment from the job candidate's point of view.

Estimates of recruiting costs per hire averaged about $3,000 in 1990. This includes hires at all levels (professional and managerial hires are the most expensive) and advertising costs, recruiter and candidate travel, referral bonuses, agency/search firm fees, relocation costs, and the recruiter's salary and benefits.[2] All indications are that recruitment is becoming increasingly important to, and expensive for, American business. Kentucky Fried Chicken, confronted with declining numbers of employable youth, high rates of employment and stiff competition for hourly workers where it needs to recruit and hire during the late 1980s, was forced to take what still must be considered a very creative approach to recruiting.[3] Kentucky Fried Chicken had experienced a 40 percent vacancy rate in management positions and as much as a 100 percent turnover rate for some positions. New advertisements focusing on the advantages of working for Kentucky Fried Chicken, recruitment outside of the geographical areas where the stores are located, and recruitment of military retirees, teachers, displaced homemakers, older workers, and the handicapped greatly increased their applicant pool. Mobile Kentucky Fried Chicken recruitment vans appeared at concerts, special events, and new store sites. The company had much success with "call-in" open houses, where candidates were screened over the phone and invited for same-day interviews. These efforts were coupled with an active retention program that tried to improve the quality of working conditions for current employees.[4] As jobs become more dynamic, the labor force more diverse, skill requirements more demanding, and the legal environment more complex, the need for systematic, professionally managed recruitment will grow.

Figure 6-1 depicts the recruitment process. It begins with a determination of the organization's current and anticipated (short- and long-run) personnel needs and a decision to reconcile supply and demand through recruitment. As you will recall from Chapter 5, there are a number of ways to estimate personnel needs. Combining relevant job descriptions and specifications with estimated needs provides the personnel/human resource department with specifics as to how many individuals with particular combinations of skill, experience, education, and other personal attributes are needed. These specifics are critical to recruiting, because all subsequent activities will be committed to accomplishing them.

---

[1]Recruitment need not be conducted solely by the personnel/human resource department in order to be systematic. In some firms recruitment is conducted by individual departments under the general supervision and policies of the personnel department.

[2]The Bureau of National Affairs, Inc., "HR Performance Factors Examined," *Bulletin to Management* (June 20, 1991), p. 192.

[3]The presentation on Kentucky Fried Chicken is drawn from The Bureau of National Affairs, Inc., "Recruitment and Selection Strategies," *Bulletin to Management* (July 23,1987), pp. 2–3.

[4]See also Brad Ragaglia, "Raise Your Retention Rate," *Managers Magazine* (September 1991), p. 17.

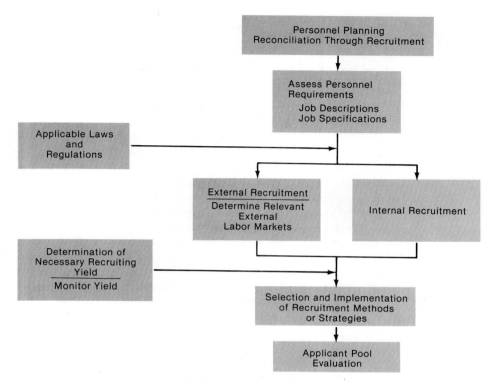

FIGURE 6-1   Recruitment

Regardless of whether the company elects to recruit from internal or external sources, its recruitment activities must be designed and implemented in a manner consistent with all relevant laws and regulations. Of particular significance are those laws and regulations that deal with the discriminatory employment practices discussed in Chapter 3. When considering EEO laws, the basic question to be asked is whether the recruiting method itself (e.g., newspaper advertisement) or the way the method is used (e.g., newspaper advertisement copy) has any potential to restrict the pool of applicants for other than job-related characteristics. Candidates should not be discouraged to apply for a position because of their sex, physical or mental disabilities, race, age, or other characteristics, unless such characteristics are related to job performance. If employer recruiting discourages application for these reasons, however subtly (e.g., advertisements where minorities are unlikely to see them), there is potential for violating the law. In addition, from a practical perspective, it makes little sense to discourage potentially qualified individuals from applying. This limits the size of the qualified applicant pool and may result in inferior applicants becoming inferior employees.

We first discuss the particulars of external recruitment and then turn our attention to internal recruitment.

■ External Recruitment

Determination of External Labor Markets and Recruiting Yield

Individuals who have certain combinations of qualifications in common may be considered to belong to the same labor market. For example, individuals with managerial or certain types of professional skills and experience (although varying in the particulars of that experience and skill) may be considered part of the same labor market (or segment within the entire labor market). Labor market classifications vary in the personnel literature, but some common ones are blue collar, clerical, professional and technical, and managerial. In this classification scheme, blue collar includes skilled and semiskilled workers (e.g., auto assembly line), clerical includes office support personnel (e.g., secretary), professional and technical include specialists such as accountants, engineers, and scientists, and managerial includes professional management personnel. Because the various labor markets require different recruiting approaches, it is important that they be targeted in advance. Another important concern is the intensity of the recruitment effort for particular job openings. Historical recruitment data may help with this determination. Historical data may indicate that for the position of computer programmer, to have 10 new hires (anticipated personnel needs), 50 individuals must be made offers (and hence be qualified in every respect). Similarly, it may be that only half of the individuals selected for further screening (e.g., interviews, testing) will be found sufficiently qualified to merit job offers. Further, to find the 100 applicants deserving of additional attention, historical data indicate that 600 applications must be elicited from interested individuals and reviewed. It should also be mentioned that many more than 600 individuals must be made aware of the organization's need for computer programmers in order to generate those 600 applications or letters of interest. Based on this information, the firm can estimate how much publicity, interest, and attention it must generate among candidates for the job.

As with many organizational activities, timing may also be important. For example, not only may it be necessary for this firm to hire 10 computer programmers, but it may also be essential that they be at work by a particular date, corresponding, for example, to the start of a new project. In those cases, a firm may bring together the historical data and a timetable to form a set of time-based recruiting goals. Looking at the computer programmers example, if the firm needs them on the job in 3 months it might be necessary to have 400 applications by the end of the first month and an additional 200 applications by the end of the second. Similar time-based goals will be established for interviews and job offers so that the 10 programmers will be on the job when needed. Also, recruiting yields (e.g., how many applications received) at various points should be monitored and compared to these goals to ensure that recruiting does not fall behind schedule.

Methods of External Recruitment

Once the labor markets and recruiting yields have been determined, the best means for contacting, informing, and creating interest in potential applicants must be selected. The firm may select one or more recruitment strategies to accomplish this. A recruiting strategy consists of a plan combining recruitment personnel, resources, and recruiting methods. As previously indicated, the recruiting strategy must be designed and implemented in a manner consistent with all relevant laws and regulations.

There is no single combination of resources and methods that will work well for all organizations or, for that matter, across all labor markets, or even within a labor market.[5] Research and experience have shown that particular methods are more effective for some types of jobs and potential applicants than for others. Employers must keep four questions in mind: What are the recruitment goals? Who are the people we want to reach? What message do we want them to receive? How can the message best be delivered?[6]

Table 6-1 lists various methods employers use to contact external applicants.[7] We discuss each in turn.

Professional or Trade Associations

Many associations provide placement services for their members. These services may consist of compiling descriptive text on, or listings of, job-hunting members and their qualifications and providing access to members during regional or national conventions. Further, many associations publish or sponsor trade journals or magazines for their membership. These publications often carry classified advertisements from employers interested in recruiting their members. The Society for Human Resources Management, an organization of personnel professionals, publishes a monthly magazine, *Personnel Administrator*. The magazine contains articles of interest for its membership, advertisements for personnel-related products and services, and employment advertisements. Accountants, engineers, MBAs, and many other professionals have similar associations and publications.

Professional or trade associations are especially useful for attracting highly educated, experienced, or skilled individuals.

Print and Electronic Media Advertisements

According to The Newspaper Advertising Bureau, Inc., $2.18 billion is spent annually on help wanted newspaper advertisements.[8] Many unskilled, semi-skilled, skilled,

---

[5]The Bureau of National Affairs, Inc., "Cost Effective Recruiting." *Bulletin to Management* (October 25, 1990), p. 344.

[6]Bernard S. Hodes, "Planning for Recruitment Advertising," *Personnel Journal* (May 1983), p. 380.

[7]Some researchers make a distinction between sources of applicants and methods useful for those sources.

[8]Margaret Magnus, p. 56.

TABLE 6-1   External Recruitment Methods

Professional or trade associations
Print and electronic media advertisement
   Newspapers
   Magazines
   Special publications
   Electronic media
Employee referral
Public employment service
Private employment agencies
Executive search firms
Special events
Campus recruiting
Vocational guidance counselors
Self-initiated walk-ins and write-ins
Computer data bases

clerical, administrative, and entry-level managerial job openings are routinely advertised in daily newspapers.

Employers use newspaper advertisements for many reasons. Job openings can be announced quickly; advertisements can appear within 1 or 2 days. They are fairly inexpensive compared with other methods, and more than one position can be included in the same advertisement. Newspaper advertisements reach many people in a short period of time and, depending upon the newspaper, can reach a very representative sample of job candidates. This is an important practical and equal employment concern. Further, newspaper advertisements offer flexibility to employers. Employers may request that applicants apply for employment in person, send their resume and salary requirements through the mail, or telephone the personnel office during prescribed hours on certain days. An out-of-town employer can put an advertisement in the newspaper, arrange an interview schedule by mail or telephone, travel to a city for the interviews, and invest only 1 day on the road in that city.[9] Organizations may choose to advertise a position without identifying themselves. These advertisements are called *blind advertisements* and usually request interested applicants to send a letter or resume to a post office box. These types of advertisements are useful when the organization does not want applicants to show up in person to apply for a job. If a position is likely to draw many applicants, some organizations prefer to review the qualifications of each applicant before any face-to-face contact is made.

The composition of printed advertisements requires care because the attractiveness or cleverness of the advertisement may have a significant impact on its effectiveness. Borders, attention-grabbing graphics, and interesting and informative copy make a big difference in the effectiveness of an advertisement.[10] Many

[9]Margaret Magnus, p. 56.

[10]John P. Bucalo, "Good Advertising Can Be More Effective Than Other Recruitment Tools," *Personnel Administrator* (November 1983), pp. 73–79.

recruiters create new advertisements by simply changing a few words from previous, and sometimes not very effective, advertisements. The copy must satisfy the desire of job hunters to know particular information about the job and its compensation.[11]

The composition of printed advertisements also requires care in order to ensure that no violation of EEO laws and regulations takes place. Some newspapers and magazines have policies that reject advertisements that may lead to violations of the law. The *Atlanta Journal-Constitution* has a list of acceptable and unacceptable phrases for classified advertisements with reference to the age and sex of applicants. The paper's policy is violated by the following: *Attention June Graduate, College Dropout, Maximum, 2–5 years' experience, recent veteran, recent graduate, student 16–65,* and *youthful staff,* along with any reference to gender that is unrelated to the job conditions. The paper will publish the following list of phrases: *retired, mature couple, minimum age 18, over 21, trainee,* and *veteran.* The difference between the two lists is apparent. The first serves to cap the possible age of applicants in violation of age discrimination laws, while the second does not. Many classified advertisements are prepared by recruitment advertisement firms that specialize in writing attention-getting copy that conforms to applicable laws. These firms will also recommend publication outlets for the advertisements that will provide the best market exposure.[12]

During our discussion of professional associations, we indicated that many associations publish membership magazines or trade journals that accept employment advertisements. These are of special importance for job positions that require special skills, education, and experience. As is true of all advertisements, these must be cleverly and professionally created, capture the candidate's attention, provide specifics about the position and company, and motivate the candidate to apply.

News magazines such as *Time* and *Newsweek* have developed the ability to deliver different advertisements to regional target markets. This has led employers to advertise in these magazines for professional people and recent college graduates. News magazines also publish special college issues each year that are distributed at no cost on campuses across the country. These special issues can be important for recruiting college students. *Business Week* publishes *Careers* magazine, which is available to college students free of charge. This publication contains high-quality career advice, and, to the advantage of employers and college students alike, employment advertisements. Other useful outlets for recruitment advertisements include *MBA, The Black Collegian, Graduating Engineer,* and *The Minority Engineer.*

---

[11]In a survey, respondents indicated that employees look for different things in first and subsequent jobs. Pay is the most important issue to experienced employees, whereas advancement opportunities, benefits, and potential to use a wide range of skills were most and equally important to first-time employees. It is likely that perspective employees would wish to see this information. See Edward D. Bewayo, "What Employees Look for in First and Subsequent Employers," *Personnel* (April 1986), pp. 49–54.

[12]Virginia Hall and Joyce Wessel, "Age and Sex Discrimination in Classified Advertisements Is Illegal in the U.S.," *The Atlanta Journal-Constitution* (July 2, 1989), p. 39.

When employers are recruiting for experienced personnel, the decisions to change jobs and relocate are likely to be family decisions. For this reason, some recruitment advertisements are written to attract the family as well as interest the job candidate. An example is the advertisement placed by IOMEGA, a manufacturer of cartridge disk drives, for engineers to work in Ogden, Utah. Since engineers were not plentiful in Utah, IOMEGA decided to emphasize quality of life and family considerations. In the body of an ad entitled "24 Things to Do in Ogden, Utah" the following text appeared: "Ogden is a community that has safe streets, clean air and water, schools that kids can walk to, affordable housing, all the things most of us grew up taking for granted . . . and can't seem to find these days."[13] The advertisement was so successful that in spite of the prominent placement of IOMEGA in the advertisement, the Ogden Chamber of Commerce asked permission to use the ad to promote tourism.[14] An interesting aspect of the advertisement was the use of a coupon. A job candidate could clip out, fill in, and send in a coupon requesting additional information on working for IOMEGA and Ogden, Utah. These coupons are appearing more often as employers realize that they present an easy way for a job candidate to make contact. The coupons are less intimidating than a formal letter of interest to the personnel director and the preparation of a resume, so more job candidates are willing to indicate an interest in the firm.

Many companies are turning to special publications as a recruitment method. These include special employment issues of newspapers and magazines, regional and national employment newspapers, and company brochures for direct mailings. These ads and brochures often contain coupons or, in some cases, an abbreviated or complete employment application blank to be filled out and sent in. Martin Marietta Corporation's Baltimore division needed experienced professionals, few of whom seemed to be reading the standard employment advertisements. They contacted a firm specializing in direct mail recruiting campaigns that prepared a mailing list of 10,000 prospects in targeted geographical areas. The materials included an attractive, eye-catching outer envelope, an attention-getting brochure describing Martin Marietta's technological successes, job descriptions of open positions, the geographical location, company relocation policy, employee benefits, and a reply card requesting the applicant's name, address, telephone number, present position, and college degree. An efficient process was developed to ensure that as the cards came in, the company was immediately able to establish telephone contact with promising applicants. If these applicants had the qualifications and interest necessary, they were then sent a resume questionnaire or requested to send a resume. The idea behind the resume questionnaire was to appeal to the inactive applicant who might not have had a completed resume. The manager of employment at Martin Marietta was very pleased with the response, citing a higher than average response rate, resulting in cost-effective hires.[15]

---

[13]Alan Halcrow, "Anatomy of a Recruitment Ad," *Personnel Journal* (August 1986), p. 65.

[14]Alan Halcrow, p. 65.

[15]The example discussed was taken from Rick Stoops, "Direct Mail: Luring the Isolated Professionals," *Personnel Journal* (June 1984), p. 34. See also Margaret Magnus, p. 57, for a discussion of direct mailing recruitment efforts.

Effective advertising can provide an employer with a real "advantage by creating or reaffirming a positive corporate identity, pinpointing the merits of employment with the company placing the ad, and appealing to each employee's pride in his or her talents. That advantage is easily lost, and even reversed, if those efforts are undermined by poorly written copy, ambiguous format, ineffective placement, or inappropriate artwork."[16]

The use of electronic media in recruitment has also increased. Computer data bases containing information on and for potential applicants have been used for many years and will be discussed later in this chapter. Radio, cable TV, and electronic bulletin boards have all proven to be effective competition for the printed medium.[17] College recruiters, for example, have begun to use college radio stations to broadcast well-timed ads at graduation or enrollment periods.[18] Radio ads are often less expensive than newspaper ads and can be very effective in the college labor market. All indications are that the use of electronic media in all forms will become more common.

Employee Referral

Often when current employees hear of job openings in their firm, they will inform their friends or relatives and encourage them to apply. Such referrals frequently result in high-quality hires for the organization. In the past, many firms had rules prohibiting family members from working together. One reason was to prevent close interpersonal relationships from unfairly affecting personnel actions. More recently, the hiring of family and friends of current employees through referral has become recognized as an inexpensive way to obtain loyal and dependable new employees and has been encouraged. Current employees know both the organization and their friends and relatives well enough to avoid recommending a poor match to either. Further, to do so could jeopardize their status with the firm, as well as their relationships with the individuals they referred.

Heavy dependence on employee referrals may cause problems, however, because employees are likely to refer someone fairly similar to themselves. To the extent that the current workforce is not representative of the racial, religious, and sex composition of the relevant labor market, unfair hiring practices may result.[19]

Public Employment Service

The United States Training and Employment Service (USTES) of the U.S. Department of Labor coordinates State Employment Service offices (state unemployment offices) in all of the states and in some territories of the United States. These

[16]Margaret Magnus, "Ad Vantages," *Personnel Journal* (August 1986), pp. 59–79.

[17]The Bureau of National Affairs, Inc., "Recruiting a Changing Workforce," *Bulletin to Management* (April 4, 1991), p. 104.

[18]The Bureau of National Affairs, Inc., "Cost-Effective Recruiting," *Bulletin to Management* (October 25, 1990), p. 344.

[19]The Bureau of National Affairs, Inc., "Auditing the Recruitment and Selection Functions," *Bulletin to Management* (February 14, 1991), p. 2.

agencies list all those individuals out of work who are eligible and wish to receive unemployment compensation, as well as many first-time or less steadily employed job seekers. The forced nature of registration at these agencies in order to receive unemployment benefits has created a negative impression of their usefulness as a source of new hires. Employers sometimes claim that the individuals sent from state agencies have no real interest in employment and are attending interviews in order to retain their eligibility for unemployment benefits. Further, most mid-level or higher managerial, administrative, or professional job openings are unlikely to be filled through these agencies. Some states, however, have attempted to upgrade the image of their employment services for such mid-level positions by opening separate offices expressly for such applicants. Public employment agencies are an excellent source of blue-collar and hourly workers, however. In addition, many standard skill tests (for example, spelling and typing), may be administered and scored by agency employees for the convenience of the hiring organization.

Private Employment Agencies

Private employment agencies can serve as an excellent source of qualified applicants for a wide range of job openings. These agencies typically specialize in the skill level or profession of the applicants that they provide, and they charge fees to either the applicant or the organization (fee paid) for successful placements. Such fees vary from established fixed fees to percentages of the successful applicant's yearly salary.

Advertisements for these agencies are directed at both employers and applicants and may be found in a variety of periodicals. Daily newspapers, specialized newspapers, and other trade or professional publications all carry advertisements for these agencies. From the employer's perspective, these agencies are a ready source of qualified applicants. This prescreened pool of applicants results in a more efficient selection process by reducing the number of unqualified individuals who must be evaluated by an employer. This, in turn, saves the employer time and money.

Situations where an employment agency's services may be desirable include the following:[20]

1. The employer has found it difficult in the past to generate a pool of qualified applicants.
2. The employer's need for only a few people, or an irregular demand for new hires, would make an elaborate recruitment capability inefficient.
3. The organization has a critical need to fill a position quickly.
4. The recruitment effort is aimed at individuals who are currently employed. This is especially true during a time of tight labor markets.
5. The company has limited experience in the local labor market.[21]

[20]Stephen Rubenfeld and Michael Crino, "Are Employment Agencies Jeopardizing Your Selection Process?" *Personnel* (September–October 1981), pp. 70–77.

[21]Bruce S. Algar, "How to Hire in a Hurry: Meet Increased Demands for Personnel," *Personnel Journal* (September 1986), p. 86.

Thus far, only the positive side of these agencies has been discussed. Unfortunately, there is a less positive side that may be shown to both applicants and employers. Applicants may be charged fees well in excess of the service provided. Further, some agencies have been known to charge applicants fees for simply representing them, with no guarantee of successful placement. Many states have begun to regulate such practices, and although they still may be encountered, they are becoming less common. From the employer's perspective, the use of employment agencies may prove to have hidden costs. When employment agencies are used by a firm, those agencies become the employer's agent in the labor market. Discriminatory behavior on the part of the agency may result in unknowing discriminatory hiring practices by the employer. The responsibility for such behavior remains that of the employer.[22]

The following steps have been recommended to employers to minimize the possibility of discriminatory behavior on the part of employment agencies and to maximize the usefulness of such agencies:[23]

1. The employer should provide the agency with thorough and complete job descriptions and job specifications. The better the agency understands the employer's needs, the better the result will be.
2. The employer, not the agency, should specify the predictors used by the agency. Tests, application blanks, and interview formats all should be a proven part of the employer's selection process. At the least, the devices used by the agency should be reviewed and approved by the employer.
3. Where possible, an employer should review the files of applicants rejected by the employment agency as not qualified. This review can reveal important information about the nature of the agency's selection process and can provide valuable data in the event of a legal challenge to the fairness of the employer's selection process.
4. When possible, a long-term relationship should be established with an agency or group of agencies. In addition, it may be advantageous to have one individual act as liaison between the employer and the agency and to have one contact within the agency responsible for that employer. Visits to the agency by the employer, as well as agency visits to the employer, would also contribute to mutual understanding and efficient working relationships.

Executive Search Firms

Executive search firms direct their efforts toward finding high-level managerial and professional talent for organizations. Their fees are rather high (sometimes as much as 33 percent of a year's salary for the successful applicant, plus expenses), but they provide a specialized service that may require personnel skills not

[22]The Bureau of National Affairs, Inc., "Auditing Recruitment and Selection Functions." *Bulletin to Management* (February 14, 1991), p. 4.
[23]Stephen Rubenfeld and Michael Crino, pp. 70–77.

available in the employer's own personnel department. Further, it is often said that the best talent is already employed. To the extent that this is true, executive search firms may provide high-quality talent by "raiding" or luring employees away from other organizations. (These firms are sometimes called *headhunters* because of this behavior.) Such tactics are often better left to such firms than to an employer's own personnel/human resource department. These agencies may also serve as a useful source for highly qualified minority applicants. Such applicants may not be available from other sources more routinely used by the firm.

Executive search firms have become very important in the fluid market for executive talent. Spencer, Stuart, & Associates, an executive search firm, found a new CEO for the $16 billion RJR Nabisco, Inc., at a $500,000 fee, and in 1 year alone found CEOs or presidents for Pillsbury, General Signal, New England Electric, The Rockefeller Foundation, MONY Financial, and Mastercard International. Heidrick & Struggles, Inc., placed PepsiCo Inc.'s John Sculley at Apple Computer and Paul G. Stern, former president of Unisys Corporation, in Northern Telecom Ltd.'s CEO job.[24] The top ten executive search firms had total combined revenues of over $800 million in 1988.[25] There will be increasing dependence on executive search firms throughout the 1990s as more organizations go to the outside to fill their major positions.

As with private employment agencies, some potential hazards for both the employer and applicant may exist. Applicants may request confidentiality and not receive it, while employers may find themselves raided by the same headhunter they recently used. However, these agencies have begun to regulate themselves (The Association of Executive Recruiting Consultants' Code of Ethical Practices), and as a consequence, such potential has been reduced in recent years.[26]

Special Events

On occasion, an employer may wish to recruit applicants at special events such as job fairs. These events usually represent infrequent opportunities to appear with other hiring firms under the sponsorship of a nonprofit, well-respected third party. Job fairs may be sponsored by a chamber of commerce, educational institution, or government agency (such as the local unit of the Veterans Administration). Sometimes they are restricted to individuals somehow affiliated with the sponsoring agency (e.g., students), or specialized (attendees for industry-specific positions that are recruited and screened before the fair) but more often are open to the community.[27] These special events not only offer a potential source of applicants

---

[24]John A. Byrne, "The New Headhunters," *Business Week* (February 6, 1989), pp. 64–71.

[25]Dyan Machan, "The Clients Are Restless," *Forbes* (July 10, 1989), p. 114.

[26]See Robert LoPresto, "Ethical Recruiting," *Personnel Administrator* (November 1986), pp. 90–91, for an interesting article providing guidelines on ethical behavior for executive search firms.

[27]The Bureau of National Affairs, Inc., "Job Fairs: Good Way to Fill Job Openings," *Bulletin to Management* (May 3, 1990), p. 137.

for the employer but may also serve as a good public relations gesture. They represent an opportunity for an employer to become better known in the community and to link that employer's name with a well-respected sponsor.

In addition, some organizations may hold open houses for the community. Current employees are encouraged to invite family and friends, and invitations to attend are extended to local personalities and the community at large. These open houses provide an opportunity to demonstrate community involvement, as well as to make employment possibilities more obvious and attractive to attendees.[28]

Motorola, Inc., has had very positive experiences with open houses in recent years. The company advertised on radio stations, ran half-page ads in local newspapers suggesting questions for prospective employees to ask to help them decide if they wanted to work at Motorola, and scheduled the open houses between 5 and 8 P.M. on weeknights so that working applicants could attend. Information packets were prepared outlining what the applicant could expect after the event, and applicants were invited to leave resumes and applications at the open house. Selected applicants were screened by phone and then invited for an employment interview.[29]

Campus Recruiting

Many entry-level professional and managerial jobs require a college degree. Perhaps the best source of college graduates is the college campus. Each year employers spend thousands of dollars to send recruiters to college campuses around the nation. Campus recruitment programs account for more than 50 percent of the "college-educated talent hired each year."[30] Campus recruiters serve two functions. They act as the organization's representatives to individuals who typically have no firsthand knowledge of the firm, as well as first-level screening agents for the organization. Thus, they are part of both the recruitment and the selection processes. As recruiters they must present a favorable, yet realistic, view of the organizations they represent and the jobs for which they are recruiting.[31] To the extent that they fail in this regard, qualified individuals may choose to apply elsewhere. As part of the selection process, college recruiters must ensure that their recommendations concerning those interviewed are as objective and as job related as possible. The common practice of sending recent graduates back to their respective campuses often works to the disadvantage of the employer. Such graduates are seldom well enough informed to act as representatives of and information

[28]The Bureau of National Affairs, Inc., "Cost-Effective Recruiting," *Bulletin to Management* (October 25, 1990), p. 344.

[29]The Bureau of National Affairs, Inc., "Cost-Effective Recruiting," *Bulletin to Management* (October 25, 1990), p. 344.

[30]Thomas Bergmann and M. Susan Taylor, "College Recruitment: What Attracts Students to Organizations?" *Personnel* (May–June 1984), p. 34.

[31]The Bureau of National Affairs, Inc., "Recruitment Practices Rated," *Bulletin to Management* (November 28, 1991), p. 371.

agents for organizations that they themselves have just joined. Nor are they sufficiently skilled to evaluate objectively the qualifications of peer group applicants. Research has shown that college graduate applicants prefer well-informed, professional, objective, well-mannered, honest and sincerely interested interviewers. Recruiters who are rude, arrogant, aloof, unprepared, or overworked create very unfavorable impressions.[32]

A great deal has been written in an attempt to assist organizations in getting the most from their college recruiting efforts. Two experts in the field have proposed that college recruiting has four stages—needs analysis, program development, implementation, and evaluation.[33] These stages resemble the steps in the recruiting model presented in Figure 6-1 and are presented in Figure 6-2. A review of the model reveals how systematically experts suggest an organization should approach the recruiting effort on college campuses.[34] It should be emphasized that the various stages depicted in the model involve a coordinated effort among all of the departments in the company with personnel needs. Recruitment activities represent a shared responsibility between the human resources department and all other departments in the organization.

There are several things that attract college students when selecting companies for interviews. Among the most important are the company's reputation in its field, the advancement opportunities offered, and the company's overall potential for growth.[35] Because these areas are important to college students, campus recruitment materials should emphasize them. Further, college students rely heavily upon the campus recruiter, company brochures, and campus placement office notices for information about the company.[36] If the company wants a competitive advantage, the recruiter should be as well trained as possible in conducting *recruitment* interviews (as opposed to other types of interviews), and materials should be as well written and informative as possible.

The plant visit is another important step in campus recruitment.[37] Most companies invite only the most promising recruits, so it is important that these applicants have a favorable experience. Candidates should have an opportunity to ask candid questions and receive frank answers, as well as meet individuals with whom they may work. Many candidates prefer not to be met at the airport, since they do not consider themselves presentable at that time. They also prefer to be left alone the night of their arrival in order to prepare themselves for the next day.

[32]The Bureau of National Affairs, Inc., "Recruitment Practices Rated," *Bulletin to Management* (November 28, 1991), p. 375.

[33]D. Chiacci and C. Knapp, "College Recruitment from Start to Finish," *Personnel Journal* (August 1980), pp. 653–657.

[34]See also The Bureau of National Affairs, Inc., "Cutting Campus Recruitment Costs," *Bulletin to Management* (July 19, 1990), pp. 2–3.

[35]Thomas Bergmann and M. Susan Taylor, p. 37.

[36]Thomas Bergmann and M. Susan Taylor, p. 38.

[37]Clearly the site visit is part of both recruitment and selection. We discuss the use of interviews as a method for collecting selection information in Chapter 7.

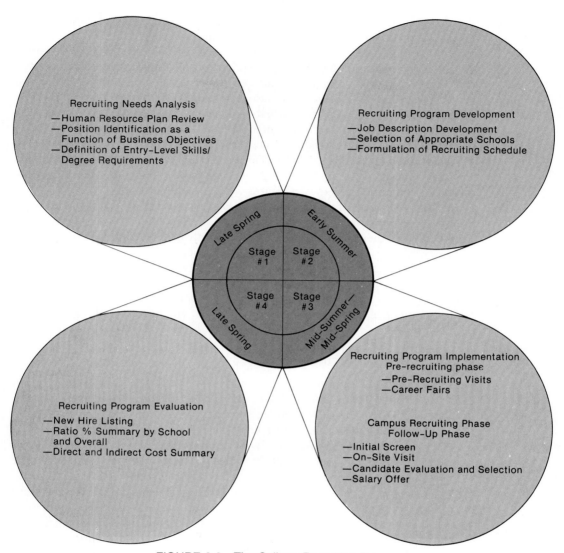

FIGURE 6-2   The College Recruiting Process
Source: D. Chiacci and C. Knapp, "College Recruitment from Start to Finish," *Personnel Journal* (August 1980), p. 657. Reprinted with the permission of *Personnel Journal,* Costa Mesa, California; all rights reserved. Copyright August 1980.

This does not mean that the job candidate should be ignored. Organizations that leave additional information on the company, the geographical location, and the events of the next day at the hotel desk create a favorable impression on job candidates. It might be reasonable to leave the particulars of the arrival day up to the applicant. Individuals who reacted unfavorably to their site visits seemed to be those who had been asked to do unexpected and non-job-related activities during their visits. In particular, candidates who are asked to take psychological tests during the site visit react most negatively to the experience.[38] Superior job candidates will have more than one site visit invitation. The candidate will have to do his or her best to juggle site visits and job offers. Because of the candidate's inexperience in this area, many times the company that acts first receives priority. For this reason, the firm should be prepared to act promptly in inviting and conducting the site visit. When delays are necessary the candidate should be told, so that he or she will not interpret the delays as an unfavorable decision. During these delays it would be helpful if the company contacted the candidate with an offer to answer any questions, provide additional literature, or simply to express continuing interest.

Informal contact with university professors may also prove useful to an organization. Some instructors will willingly provide the names of superior students. Employers may then contact those students directly to determine their interest and perhaps schedule a preliminary on-campus interview. When a firm is interested in using this approach, professors should be provided with extensive, up-to-date, and professionally prepared information for themselves and their students. This method can be especially important when there is competition among employers for a limited number of highly trained graduates (e.g., engineers, accountants).

Vocational Guidance Counselors

Vocational guidance counselors are professionals who assist individuals in selecting careers compatible with their abilities, interests, and values. They may be found in high schools, vocational schools, universities, government agencies (e.g., the Veterans Administration), and occasionally may be affiliated with private employment agencies. Employers are typically most interested in contacting those counselors employed in high schools and vocational schools, since they come in contact with large numbers of young people just before they enter the workforce. Making these counselors aware of employment and career opportunities available to their graduating students within the organization can result in a significant number of applications for employment. In addition, school vocational guidance counselors may invite the firm's representatives to discuss career opportunities with the student body at special events, such as career days, or in academic classes when appropriate. These individuals are significant links to many young people as they prepare to enter the workforce.

Self-initiated Walk-ins and Write-ins

Some applicants either write directly to the organization or simply present themselves to the personnel/human resource department to express an interest in

---

[38]Thomas Bergmann and M. Susan Taylor, p. 42.

employment. The willingness of an organization to consider such applications is important for a number of reasons. Firstly, they represent a good source for many unskilled and semiskilled applicants interested in full- or part-time work. Second, they provide an opportunity to add individuals to the applicant pool who might not have been targeted by other methods but may nevertheless be qualified for employment. Third, failure to accept such applications may result in unintended discriminatory hiring practices. This might result from the failure of the other recruitment methods to generate interest in that segment of the community likely to make a self-initiated application.

Computer Data Bases

Third parties have created a business opportunity for themselves by providing an up-to-date applicant data base for employers.[39] These firms solicit resumes from job candidates using the many methods available to employers. They enter applicant data into the data bank, maintaining and updating it as necessary. An employer pays a fee for access to the data bank, reviews the applicant information, and contacts applicants who may be interested in employment. This approach is not very popular, but it is still too soon to make any predictions about its long-term success as a recruitment method.

College recruiting has seen the development of a number of specialized computer data bases. The most common type, the resume data base, requires students to enter information about themselves into a data base that is then edited and made available to employers on a subscription basis by the company providing the service. Another approach, electronic want ads, puts students and alumni in electronic contact with employers. One company that provides this service is Career Counseling Network. Company profiles and job openings are sent to selected colleges and universities and are then accessed by interested students at workstations set up on the campuses. Each job listing is updated on a weekly basis, and the subscribing company decides the campuses to which their information is to be sent.[40] If the system is interactive, students and employers can send messages regarding the job openings to each other on a computer network.[41] A third type of data base, occupational and company description, provides information on companies and occupations at a general level. It may contain a description of a company, the name of its top personnel officer, sales and earnings, a rating of its salaries and benefits, and the outlook for the company and the industry, or it may simply contain information on many different private and public sector careers. The latter type of data base could be used by students to find occupations that

---

[39]Rod Willis, "Recruitment: Playing the Database Game," *Personnel* (May 1990), p. 24.

[40]The Bureau of National Affairs, Inc., "Computers Aiding College/University Recruiting," *Bulletin to Management* (March 1, 1990), p. 65.

[41]Bob Berkman, "Electronic Career Information Services: What Are Your Choices?", *Career Futures* (Winter 1991–1992), p. 28.

meet a stated set of criteria such as salary level or educational requirements.[42] Additional information on these data bases may be found in the appendix following this chapter.

Enhancements

On occasion, incentives are coupled with the use of some of the methods just discussed. For example, premiums or bounties may be paid to current employees for every successful applicant that they recommend. This has the effect of making employees more interested in recruiting for the firm. Similarly, incentives may be offered to applicants if they accept the job they are offered. For example, the various branches of the military have enlistment bonuses for noncommissioned and commissioned ranks. The individual, after enlisting or reenlisting and, depending upon the chosen specialty (e.g., computer programmer) or profession (e.g., physician), is provided with a monetary bonus or a supplemental salary above that commensurate with the given rank.

Some firms offer a spouse relocation service to interest prospective applicants from dual-career families.[43] This relocation service might be handled by the personnel/human resource department or by an outside consultant. More than one-half of American corporations offered some form of re-employment services to spouses of transferred employees by the early 1990s. Depending on the specifics of the program, this inducement can add $500 to $2,500 to the cost of each transferred employee. The need for this type of program will continue to grow as more families become dual-income families. It has been estimated that 75 percent of employee transfers involve two working spouses.[44] U.S. West provides working partners with a choice of a self-guided workbook with audiotapes or $2,500 to apply to job search costs. Compaq Computer participates in a consortium of Houston, Texas, companies that circulate spouse resumes among themselves. Companies also appreciate the usefulness of housing assistance for employees as a recruiting tool. Some companies subsidize the mortgage interest rate in order to ensure that employees will not suffer higher rates if they come to work for or are transferred to another geographical location by the firm. The makers of Arm & Hammer baking soda, Church & Dwight, make direct loans to employees for down payments on homes. If the employee stays at the company for 5 years, the loan is forgiven. When housing costs are too high or not enough housing exists, some firms build homes on company-owned property and sell them at cost to employees. As a general rule, any activity that will reduce the financial risk of selling and buying a home will capture the interest of potential employees.

[42]Bob Berkman, p. 32.

[43]The Bureau of National Affairs, Inc., "Recruiting a Changing Workforce," *Bulletin to Management* (October 4, 1990), p. 320.

[44]Virginia Hall and Joyce Wessel, "Spouse Relocation Is a Plus for Transferees," *The Atlanta Journal Constitution* (June 10, 1990), p. 37R.

Other companies use their entire package of employee benefits as recruiting enhancements, including educational support, flexible work schedules, and pro-rated benefits for part-time workers. Dependent care programs that provide on-site or reimbursement for child care and elder care are also being used to attract applications.[45] Corning, Inc., located in Corning, New York, has tried to create programs that will improve the quality of life for its employees and then uses those programs for employee retention and recruitment. It has gone to considerable lengths to meet the needs of minority employees and those of the families of all employees. Corning's programs include training for managers on subjects relating to a diverse labor force, elder care, day care, flexible work scheduling, offering shuttle flights to New York City for employees who need a big-city fix, convincing local radio stations to play music more enjoyable to minority employees, and training local barber shop personnel on proper hair care for its black employees.[46] Zale-Lipshy University Hospital in Dallas, Texas, offers nurses 3 months of paid leave, while retaining full benefits and full-time employment status, after 9 months on the job. Nurses have indicated that the policy interested them because it shows that the hospital "is an institution that is looking for ways to make life better for its nurses." Using posted advertisements at local libraries and super-markets, employee referral, and job posting, Key Bank of Eastern New York recruits those who would like a work schedule that corresponds exactly to the vacation schedule of the local school system. All employees on the special sched-ule are considered full-time employees, retaining benefits and receiving prorated pay throughout the entire year.[47]

Regardless of the incentive offered, the desired effect is to increase the interest level of prospective, but as yet unconvinced, applicants in order to encourage them to apply for, and eventually accept, the position.

Evaluation of External Recruitment Methods

From the employer's perspective, the quality of the recruitment program may be evaluated in different ways.[48] Ultimately, all the methods of evaluation come down to the suitability of the applicants generated for the positions, given the resources expended. Suitability may be measured by the percentage of total applicants found to be qualified, the number of qualified applicants relative to the number of

[45]The Bureau of National Affairs, Inc., "Recruiting a Changing Workforce," *Bulletin to Management* (April 4, 1991), p. 104.

[46]The Bureau of National Affairs, Inc., "Corning Enhances Quality of Life to Attract Workers," *Bulletin to Management* (August 23, 1990), p. 271.

[47]The Bureau of National Affairs, Inc., "Recruiting and Retaining Nurses: Innovative Strategies," *Bulletin to Management* (November 29, 1990), p. 377, and The Bureau of National Affairs, Inc., "Summer-Off Program Attracts Working Parents," *Bulletin to Management* (June 14, 1990), p. 185.

[48]John P. Wanous, *Organizational Entry* (Reading, Massachusetts: Addison-Wesley Publishing Com-pany, 1980), p. 62.

available positions, the quality of the subsequent performance for new hires (also used to evaluate the selection process), and the turnover rate of new hires overall and by recruitment source. Of course, the costs of recruitment must be considered for whatever measure is used in order to determine the efficiency of the overall process and of the various methods employed. The cost of campus recruitment ranges from $1,500 to $6,000 per hire, yet some firms and recent research question the quality of individuals hired using this recruitment method.[49]

Another important dimension in evaluating the success of the recruitment effort is the degree to which the applicant pool is representative of the community or the relevant labor market. The composition of the applicant pool should provide an opportunity for participation for all types of individuals. It should represent a cross section of the various groups found n the community or in that portion of the community qualified to perform the job. A neutral and valid selection process may appear discriminatory if applied to a nonrepresentative applicant pool.

A great deal of research has been directed toward evaluating the various recruitment methods or sources. Considering the importance of recruitment to the organization, this should not be surprising. Additional research has indicated that the recruitment method is also related to job performance and absenteeism, as well as work attitudes.

Regardless of the evaluation criterion used by an organization, the personnel/human resources department must clearly demonstrate that resources were efficiently used for external recruitment.

■ Internal Recruitment

In order to better understand what internal recruitment is, it must be distinguished from internal staffing. Internal staffing involves the actual selection of employees for promotions, demotions, transfers, and layoffs. Such decisions are often made without the active and voluntary participation of current employees. Internal recruitment, on the other hand, involves generating active, voluntary participation. Internal recruitment is a process designed to create sufficient interest among current employees to cause them to indicate formally an interest in a given position. The positions applied for may represent promotions, transfers, and perhaps on occasion, demotion (assuming that less attractive alternatives may be imposed by the organization).

Methods of Internal Recruitment

Job Posting

The most common method of generating a pool of internal applicants is through job posting. Job posting is often a requirement in unionized firms. It requires that

[49]Thomas Bergmann and M. Susan Taylor, p. 35, and The Bureau of National Affairs, Inc., "Cutting Campus Recruitment Costs," *Bulletin to Management* (July 19, 1990), pp. 2–3.

management post or otherwise circulate listings of available job openings, although there may be upper-level limits to the jobs that may be posted (e.g., managerial jobs may not be posted). The listings provide information contained in the job description and job specification, as well as information concerning compensation. Employees indicate their interest formally, either through their immediate supervisor or through the personnel/human resource department. Job posting allows employees to evaluate job opportunities relative to their skills, attributes, experience, interests, and career objectives. The personnel/human resource department must sort through the accompanying paperwork and make every attempt to find the best-qualified applicant (whether internal or, in some situations, a combination of internal and external applicants). Employees must feel that positions will be given to those best qualified, and that their interest in the position will not compromise their relationships, status, or future in their current jobs. It is clear to employees that not everyone who indicates an interest in another position will be placed in it. As a consequence, there should be a good faith understanding between employer and employee that participation in the job posting program is encouraged and that the best-qualified applicant will receive the position in question. In some organizations, the job posting program is coupled with a skills inventory. This inventory of employee skills, attributes, and performance data is used to match current employees with the requirements of the job openings. These selected employees are then invited to apply for the position.

National Semiconductor in Santa Clara, California, has developed a sophisticated job posting process for its employees. Reasoning that a high-quality, easily accessible job posting system is necessary for employee career progression, the firm has gone to great lengths to make detailed information available on every job opening. It has abandoned the traditional posted sheet of paper in favor of an electronic posting process whereby an employee using a desk computer can search for job openings using key words like *manager* and *process engineer*. Employees are encouraged to select a career path and to examine the postings for openings that would move them along those paths. Certain general policies control the process; for example, an employee must have been in his or her current position for at least 12 months. Managers are encouraged to support the career progression of their employees, as employees are considered an organizational resource. No permission is required for employees to examine the openings or to apply for those they find interesting. However, if an employee is selected for an interview, the manager in the employee's current department must be informed. National Semiconductor wants to send the message to employees that its job posting process is designed to support their careers in the firm, and that they are encouraged to seek more responsibility and to take an active part in their own development and career progression.[50]

Informal Methods

Job posting is a formalized process of advertising available positions to employees. It also establishes the means by which employees can express an interest in being

[50]Milan Moravec, "Effective Job Posting Fills Dual Needs," *HRMagazine* (September 1990), p. 76.

considered for those positions. Many organizations have not formalized that process. For example, the grapevine may provide information about anticipated openings within the firm. A well-placed indication of interest by an employee may result in his or her securing that position. Unfortunately, the less formalized the process, the more likely it is that organizational politics and issues other than employee qualifications will decide who receives or does not receive a particular position.

Evaluation of Internal Recruitment

As is true of external methods of recruitment, formal internal recruitment must be evaluated. This evaluation appears to be less formalized and focuses on the degree of employee participation, as well as the quality of those employees choosing to participate. Of equal importance, but more difficult to measure, is the impact of internal recruitment on employee morale. It allows employees to feel more a part of the organization and to express an interest in advancement or improvement to management. Further, the position in which an interest has been expressed can serve as a performance-related reward. Potential negative impacts on employee morale and/or performance stem in large part from employees' perception of the organization's enthusiasm for participation, their immediate supervisor's reaction to a requested move, the openness of the program to all qualified employees, and the objectivity and quality of the decision-making or selection process.

■ External and Internal Recruitment

The extent to which an organization uses internal applicants as opposed to external applicants to fill positions should reflect a carefully considered policy decision. For example, the relationship between the use of internal candidates and EEO must be explicitly considered. External recruitment provides an opportunity for future employees to represent all population groups at all levels in the organization. At a minimum, an overdependence on internal recruitment may delay the entry of some groups into higher-level positions in the organization (assuming past under-representation). Internal recruitment can work to the organization's advantage in a number of ways. For example, internal applicants know the organization better, have a performance history within the organization that can be examined, may be more motivated if securing positions with the organization is performance based, and depending upon the position, may be less expensive than external applicants. Retention rates may be improved.[51] Unfortunately, two major problems may occur with internal recruitment: a lack of creativity in problem solving caused by organizational inbreeding ("we've always done it this way") and an increase in

---

[51]Mansour Sharifzadeh, "Internal Hiring: The Sensible Approach to Filling Positions," *Supervisory Management* (August 1990), p. 4.

political behavior among employees if it is perceived that such behavior may secure a desirable job opening. Further, organizations must be committed to helping employees gain the experience and skills necessary for other positions within the firm. This may require additional training programs or management development programs. Such programs must be available, if necessary, in order to ensure that employees are truly competitive for positions and that they do not perceive internal recruitment for higher-level positions as an empty gesture on the part of the organization.

◼ Summary and Conclusions

Recruitment is the process that generates the pool of applicants (both internal and external) from which future employees are drawn. The quality of the applicant pool will directly affect the quality of new employees. This chapter has reviewed the recruitment process by discussing the steps in the process, the sources or methods of reaching potential applicants, the methods of evaluating those sources, the legal environment within which recruitment takes place, and the advantages and disadvantages of external and internal recruitment.

A systematic approach was emphasized throughout the chapter because of the importance of recruitment to the firm. Although the recruitment process should be ongoing, its intensity will vary during the year, subject to institutional cycles (e.g., college graduations), economic conditions, and organizational policy decisions (e.g., expansion of product line). Regardless of current need, a firm should maintain contacts with individuals and organizations that have helped the firm interest qualified applicants in the past.

Some concluding comments about professionalism and recruiting are in order. Individuals who apply in good faith deserve ethical and responsible treatment by recruiters. When recruiting for a company, put yourself in the applicant's shoes, be knowledgeable (know the job and your organization), keep an open mind in the resume screening process (a resume is rarely a fair image of the applicant), and use the interview to gather information, not to verify a premature conclusion. Respond to applicants as individuals rather than through a form letter, describe the job candidly, let applicants know where they stand (if you can), establish an efficient method for responding to letters of inquiry and resumes on a timely basis, return phone calls, and let applicants know ahead of time what they can expect during a company site visit.

◼ Questions

1. This chapter has discussed some of the effects that internal and external recruitment may have on the behavior and beliefs of individual employees. Briefly explain why these effects may take place and why they are important to a firm.

2. An organization may select from among a number of methods for recruiting applicants, such as newspaper advertisements, college recruiting, and employee referrals. Which would you recommend for the following jobs: assembly-line worker, dishwasher, personnel director, university professor?

3. Discuss the external recruitment model presented in this chapter. Be sure to discuss each step in the model and explain its importance to the success of recruiting.

4. Private employment services can be very useful. Explain when these services can be helpful and the steps an employer can take to ensure that they are used effectively.

☐ APPLICATIONS AND CASE EXERCISES

1. An organization for which there are always more applicants than job openings may consider recruitment an unnecessary expense. What dangers do you see in this strategy?

2. Select five classified advertisements from your local newspaper and evaluate their effectiveness. Rewrite them to make them more effective.

3. Kathleen Roman, the personnel/ human resource director for Platte Corporation, has come to the conclusion that the firm has not been getting the better students from the college campuses that have been visited. Platte Corporation currently has recent graduates go back to their own campuses to conduct employment interviews for entry-level management positions. This is based upon the belief of the last personnel/human resource director that recent graduates are better able to develop a rapport with current college students. Other firms send older, more experienced interviewers to these campuses, and, as a consequence, appear to be more successful in their recruiting efforts.

   Ms. Roman is now considering a complete review of the recruitment practices of the firm in order to ensure that appropriate methods are being selected and effectively used. She believes that the first step is to review all of the methods available and to determine when, and for which labor market, each is most effective. This seems to be a difficult job, and she is wondering if it can be done at all.

   What recommendations would you make to Ms. Roman to improve the firm's college recruiting for entry-level management positions? Explain your recommendations.

4. Contact an employment agency in your community and arrange to interview a member of the professional staff. Generate a list of interview questions that will determine the operating procedures of the agency and the nature of the companies for which it recruits. Using the steps listed in the text to maximize the effectiveness of employment agencies, determine whether they are followed in this agency. What is your general impression of this agency and of employment agencies in general?

Recruitment:
The Applicant's View

The chapter has concentrated on recruitment from the organization's perspective. This appendix takes the applicant's view. In particular, it discusses recruitment and selection issues that concern the recent college graduate considering his or her first professional position. On occasion, issues discussed in this appendix are also discussed in the following chapter. When that happens, the discussion in the appendix will be brief, and particular attention should be paid to those sections in the next chapter.

When you are involved in a job search for a professional position, every aspect of your behavior during the job search says something about you to the prospective employer. The quality of your research on the company, the goals that you have set for yourself, and your cover letter, resume, and personal appearance will all be considered. The best advice that can be offered is to behave professionally in every regard. If you expect to be offered a professional position, you must create a professional impression. Resume and application blank misspellings and typos, and careless speech and dress, will send a clear signal that you have not matured to the point where you can accept the responsibility of a professional position.

Before making initial contact with any company, preliminary research is suggested. You should first seriously consider what you wish to obtain from your first job. Decide what combination of travel, training, responsibility for financial and/or human resources, pay, benefits, or specific industry experience you are seeking. While it is unlikely that any job will offer the perfect combination you wish, when an offer comes, and one will, you should be prepared to evaluate it objectively. The best preparation is to have thought about your needs at your leisure, rather than under the time pressure usually accompanying a job offer. Further, you will find that many interviewers will expect you to share your job expectations with them. You will not create a favorable impression if you need to grope for answers to basic questions.

You should take candid stock of your strengths and weaknesses, and likes and dislikes, as they would relate to likely jobs. A number of self-help career guides are available in commercial bookstores. These materials provide structured methods for this self-appraisal. This kind of assessment should help provide insight into what types of jobs you feel competent to do and what job content and situations you would prefer. Although it may not seem important now, before you have a job, a bad match between your needs and a job can be disastrous. Your state of mind, job performance, and career success can all be adversely affected by a bad mismatch in your first professional job.

Researching industries and firms in which you may have an interest is also highly recommended. Initially, a preliminary research effort is all that is necessary. Future research should become more intense as you narrow your list of potential employers. Reviewing industry and company profiles in business magazines and newspapers such as *Business Week, Forbes, Fortune, The Wall Street Journal, Careers, National Business Employment Weekly* and its college edition, *Managing Your Career, Time, Newsweek,* and *U.S. News and World Report,* all popular publications readily available in public libraries, would be useful. Your research should extend back a few years. One or two issues will not provide enough information or perspective. Additional information on specific companies can be found in annual reports and company recruitment brochures. Table 6A-1 lists some additional publications that may be of value in your research. Many of

TABLE 6A-1   Information Sources on Companies and Industries

Type of Source	Publication	Publisher
General guides	*Business Information Sources*	University of California
	How to Find Information About Companies: The Corporate Intelligence Sourcebook	Washington Researchers Publishing
Manuals and handbooks	*Standard Industrial Classification Manual*	U.S. Government Printing Office
	The Almanac of American Employers: A Guide to America's 500 Most Successful Companies	Contemporary Books
Directories	*Million Dollar Directory*	Dun and Bradstreet, Inc.
	Standard and Poor's Register of Corporations, Directors, and Executives	Standard and Poor's Corporation
	Wards Directory of 55,000 Largest U.S. Corporations	B. H. Ward
	The Career Guide: Dun's Employment Opportunities Directory	Dun's Marketing Services
	Moody's Industrial Manual	Moody's Investors Service
	Moody's Over-the-Counter Industrial Manual	Moody's Investors Service
	Moody's Bank and Finance Manual	Moody's Investors Service
Statistical information	*Value Line Investment Survey*	A. Bernhard
	Moody's Handbook of Common Stock	Moody's Investors Service
	Dun and Bradstreet's Key Business Ratios	Dun and Bradstreet
	Standard and Poor's Industry Surveys	Standard and Poor's Corporation

these will be available through the campus placement service, at major university libraries, and at specialized business libraries. A recent, more high-tech approach to your research and preparation is the use of commercial computer software packages. These packages can help you identify prospects, select target companies, figure out how to contact them, write your resume, prepare yourself for an interview, and negotiate a job offer.[52] Companies with which you interview will expect that you have some knowledge about their products or the services they perform, and the future prospects for the company and industry. Firms will be especially interested in your knowledge of their recent successes, products, and associations with your university (scholarships, donations, job fair participation, advisory boards).

At some point you will need to make contact with prospective employers. There are a number of ways that you can do this. You can use the campus placement office, write employers directly, hire or use a private employment agency, answer advertisements in newspapers or magazines, attend special events, register with or use a computer data bank, make informal contact through friends or professors, use networking,[53] or any combination of these approaches.

Many campus placement offices will maintain a standard information form for students and provide them to interested employers. You may be asked to list your major, courses taken, grade point average, job experiences and career interests, and work and academic references, among other things. This service can be very helpful, as you may have your personal information and qualifications called to the attention of many firms that you might not be able to contact successfully any other way. You should neatly type the form and ensure that the information is complete, accurate, and grammatically correct. It is certainly not to your advantage to create an unfavorable first impression with prospective employers, and a sloppy, poorly written, incomplete, handwritten form will do just that. Any personal, professional, or academic references listed should have already agreed to serve as a reference. This courtesy is essential. Further, each reference should be given a copy of your college transcript, resume, and the completed placement form, so that he or she will have complete information available if contacted by an employer. After reviewing your placement form, and assuming that it created a favorable impression, you may receive an invitation for a campus interview from a company. Campus interviews are discussed later in this appendix.

On occasion, you may wish to take the initiative and make contact by writing a company directly. If you are answering an advertisement from a magazine or newspaper, or following up on a suggestion from a friend or contact within the company, be sure to refer to the advertisement or the person involved. As always, your letter should create as favorable an impression as possible. It should show an understanding of the company, the job, and the reasons you would be a good

---

[52]See, for example, The Bureau of National Affairs, Inc., "Computers Aiding College/University Recruiting," *Bulletin to Management* (March 1, 1990), p. 65.

[53]See, for example, Tony Lee, "Networking," *Managing Your Career* (Spring 1992), p. 27.

choice. It is very important that the letter be addressed to the appropriate person within the company. Letters addressed to the incorrect person, or to no one in particular, do not work to your advantage. Enclose an attractive and well-written resume, preferably targeted to that company's needs. Resume writing is discussed later in this appendix.

You are certain to see advertisements placed in magazines and newspapers by private employment agencies. There are a number of reasons that going to a private employment agency would be sensible for you. If you are considering relocating to a city where you have no personal or professional contacts, a private employment agency can be your best approach. If you have limited time to conduct your own job search, especially if you are already employed, you may wish to turn it over to professionals. Although private employment services can work for you, a few cautions are in order. Reconsider your involvement with an employment agency when you experience the following circumstances:[54]

1. You are requested to sign a contract quickly. Some agencies may ask you to commit yourself before you have even seen an employment agent. Never sign anything, except an application blank, unless you take it home, read it, and understand it. Consult a knowledgeable friend or lawyer, if necessary.
2. The agency asks you to pay a fee for representation. This request is sometimes in fine print and will take a complete reading of the contract to be discovered. Consider that under these conditions you are dealing with an agency that cannot get employers to pay for its services and employers who do not think the job is important enough to pay a fee to fill.
3. Some agencies will offer additional services, such as resume writing assistance and employment counseling, at an extra charge. Although the charge for any single service may seem modest, before you are done you may find yourself in debt "for as much as $3,000."[55]
4. A terrific-sounding advertisement will be placed in the paper. You call, and it was just filled. Although it is possible that a terrific job was just filled, these advertisements are sometimes placed as a come-on. The idea is that you can be convinced to come in anyway and look over the positions they do have. The current inventory of jobs will be far inferior to the one advertised.
5. You may be requested to take a typing test. If you are interested in a professional position, do not take the test. If you agree to the test, you are partway down the path to taking a job far different from the one you originally wanted.
6. You may be requested to go on interviews for jobs far below the level you are seeking. This agency is most likely interested in its fee, not your career plans.
7. You may be asked for information about other interviews that you have had. This is often a clever way of finding out about job openings. You may find that

---

[54]This list is based on Rita Stollman's article, "The Truth About Employment Agencies," *Business Week's Careers* (Spring–Summer 1987), pp. 64–66. See also Bob Weinstein, "Should You Employ an Employment Agency?" *Career Futures* (Graduation 1992), pp. 39–41.

[55]Virginia Hall and Joyce Wessel, "Costly Executive Marketing Firm May Do Little But Take Your Money," *The Atlanta Journal-Constitution* (January 28, 1990), p. 41R.

your information results in the agency's sending someone else to interview and compete with you for the job. It might prove wise to keep your previous job search information to yourself.

In this chapter, we have discussed the various data base services that may help you in your job search. You will recall that they fall into three categories: resume data bases, electronic want ads, and occupational and company description data bases. Some of the resume data bases charge a fee for registration, while others are supported by private companies and require no fee. You should evaluate the exposure your resume will receive against the fee charged. The company providing the service should be willing to discuss the number of employers likely to see your information, and the nature of the industries and jobs involved. Electronic want ads are usually available through computer networks or online services. The fees to use these services consist of either a sign-up charge for the network you select or an online service charge incurred only while the service is being used. If the data base is interactive, it will allow you to correspond directly with the companies listing job openings. The third type of data base is actually a library of information on companies, industries, and occupations. It may offer an advantage over the traditional library resources to the extent that you can quickly narrow your search to those entries that meet certain criteria you have set down. For example, you may be interested in chemical companies that offer starting salaries for accountants of over $25,000 per year, located in the Southwest. It is usually easier to generate a list of these companies when you can do so electronically. Table 6A-2 contains information on a number of the data bases available. Before selecting any data base that may charge a fee, be sure to know what you are paying for and investigate the company offering the data base to ensure that it is legitimate.

Regardless of the method you use to make contact with an employer, if you are interested in a professional position, you will eventually need a resume. There are many opinions about resume content and appearance. You will find suggestions ranging from the use of odd colored and sized paper to attention grabbing graphics. Our suggestion is to prepare an attractive, well-presented, well-printed, professional looking resume. Professional looking resumes do not come in odd colors, or in odd sizes, unless prepared for graphics design or similar creative jobs. For most jobs that you would be interested in, they are typeset or offset printed on high-quality, white bond paper. If you can create letter-quality originals easily, so much the better.

Recruiters have limited time to spend reviewing resumes. One estimate is that a manager or personnel director spends only 20 seconds on average scanning a resume.[56] This is not an unreasonable estimate when you realize that although resumes are written one by one, they travel in bunches, usually arriving in response to an ad or other announcement of an opening or at particular times of the year.[57] You want your resume to stand out, but in a positive manner. Your resume

[56]The Associated Press, "Resumes: The Best Are Flawless, Concise, Custom-Made," *The Atlanta Journal Constitution* (July 22, 1990), p. 43R.

[57]Mark Satterfield, "Identify, Work to Overcome Rejection," *The Atlanta Journal Constitution* (September 2, 1990), p. 27R.

TABLE 6A-2　Electronic Career Information Services

Charge to Student	Database Name	Publisher Resume Databases	Address
Yes	Career Placement Registry (CPR)	Plenum Publishing Co.	Career Placement Registry, Inc. 3202 Kirkwood Highway Wilmington, DE 19808 (302)998-0478
No	KINEXUS	Information Kinetics, Inc.	Information Kinetics, Inc. 640 North La Salle Street Suite 560 Chicago, Il 60610 (800) 828-0422
No	Connection	Peterson's	Peterson's 202 Carnegie Center P.O. Box 2113 Princeton, NJ 08543 (800) EDUDATA
		Electronic Want Ads	
Yes[a]	Adnet Online	Adnet Online	Adnet Online 5987 East 71st St. Suite 206 Indianapolis, IN 46220 (800) 543-9974
No	Career Network	College Employment Association	College Employment Association 3125 Dandy Trail Indianapolis, In 46214 (800) 229-6499
		Occupational and Company Descriptions	
No[a]	Corporate Jobs Outlook	Corporate Jobs Outlook	Corporate Jobs Outlook P.O. Drawer 100 Boerne, TX 78006 (512)755-8810
No[b]	Guidance Information System	Houghton Mifflin	Houghton Mifflin Software Division One Memorial Drive Cambridge, MA 02142 (617) 252-3155

[a]The charge is for the network connection or online service only.
[b]The service is available through college placement offices.

The information contained in this table was taken from Bob Berkman, "Electronic Career Information Services," *Career Futures* (Winter 1991–1992), pp. 25–32. The inclusion of this information in the table implies no endorsement by the authors. All information is subject to change and should be verified as necessary.

should reflect professional potential and competence. It should contain as much information as necessary to alert the recruiter to your management potential, skills, knowledge, experience, and career intentions. Unfortunately, this is easier said than done. As a consequence, there is no shortage of resume writing advice. We do not attempt to cover all the information you should have before writing your resume, but there are some points that you should consider. Keep the length of your resume to one or two pages. There are many knowledgeable individuals who insist that the resume should be confined to a single page, but equally competent ones allow that a two-page resume, when necessary, is acceptable. Our advice is to use two pages if you feel it necessary. Two pages filled with irrelevant material will not make you popular with recruiters. However, a resume with substance that requires two pages will represent you well. Typically you will want to include the following information in your resume: personal information (name, address, phone number—nothing else is necessary), job objective (better than a career objective, make it appropriate to the firm receiving the resume), results-oriented work experience (What did you accomplish on that job?), education, honors, university and social activities, and references ("References available on request" would be fine if you prefer not to list names). When you write business correspondence, and that certainly includes resume writing, there are accepted standards. Your writing should be clear, precise, and to the point. Additional verbiage, unclear language, and misused terms all work against you. When presenting your leadership or other relevant employment experiences, university and social activities, use action words. Proper grammar, spelling, and consistent formatting are also essential. Write more than one draft of your resume. After each draft is written, wait a few days or more, then reread and rewrite it. You might be surprised how much your resume will improve after a few additional drafts.

Some organizations will accept your resume but will still ask you to fill out an application blank. Most application blanks ask for similar information: dates and particulars of education (major, years, schools and universities) and work experience (company, immediate supervisor, starting salary, ending salary, job title, job duties, reasons for leaving, permission to contact present employer), name, address, legal working status (citizen, work visa), Social Security number, and personal references (names, addresses, occupations). Chapter 7 discusses application blank information that an employer might be prohibited from asking. The legality of some of these questions may depend on the state in which the employer is located. You may not have the opportunity to fill out the application blank at home, so prepare the information in advance and carry it with you when visiting a firm. This preparation will help you quite a bit when you need to fill out an application blank unexpectedly.

Depending upon whether the companies in which you are interested have campus recruiting efforts, you may be requested to meet with them on campus or to visit them. For the purpose of discussion, we are assuming that you will have a campus interview, followed, if appropriate, by a site visit. The campus interview is a face-to-face opportunity for you to create a favorable impression and gather information about the company and the job. In general, as imposing as it may sound, you can assume that you will be evaluated on the basis of what you say, how you say it, what you ask, how you look, and how you behave. In the midst of this, do not lose sight of your need to evaluate the company and job. Research will help you ask good questions and provide good responses to the questions asked of you. We are not suggesting that you overprepare yourself. Ask yourself what you want to know about the company and the job. Literally prepare a list of questions. Research the company and try to answer as many of these questions as possible. That will prepare you to discuss the company and reduce the information that you will need to gather during the interview. Those questions that you do ask will not appear to be trivial ones that could have been answered through your own research. Think about how to ask those questions skillfully so that you will obtain the information you need without seeming aggressive, threatening, or negative. To prepare for the questions you may receive, look over one of the many "frequently asked campus interview questions" lists. Think about how you would respond to them and why they would be asked. Do not memorize your answers. They will sound as rehearsed as they are. Your delivery will be stilted, and your ability to think on your feet will be justifiably questioned. Also, look over your resume and application blank and think about the questions you might be asked about the information contained in them. Your appearance and body language will also say something about you. You should dress well for your interview. Your dress and grooming should be neat and enhance your professional appearance. If you are uncertain about how to dress or what your grooming should accomplish, go to a library or bookstore and read some of the many books on business clothing and grooming. You should consider how employees of the company are known to dress, and dress to the conservative side of the acceptable range. You can assume that flashy jewelry, cheap throw-away pens or pencils, and poorly fitting, soiled, wrinkled, colorful, and loud clothing are not acceptable. Although we do not recommend rehearsing your answers to possible interview questions, we do recommend that you study your appearance and body language on video tape. Have a friend tape you as you answer standard interview questions. "Why do you want to work for us?" or "Why should we hire you?"[58] This kind of practice will help you understand and improve your body language. Behaviors such as fumbling, chewing, smoking, fidgeting, and failure to make eye contact, will not enhance your professional image. This exercise has become a standard management training technique for executives likely to be interviewed by the press.

A sign of early success in your job search is an invitation to visit the company for an interview. Schedule the visit at a time that is convenient for you. Typically, this visit will take place during the school year when you have many other obligations. You should be prepared to make your own flight arrangements through a travel agent and pay for or charge the fare. This will not always be necessary, but

---

[58]Gabrielle Solomon, "A Day in the Life of an On-Campus Recruiter," *Managing Your Career* (Spring 1991), p. 22.

it is not uncommon for a company to ask you to make travel arrangements and submit your expenses after the trip has been completed. Hotel accommodations are usually arranged by the firm. Company personnel will make reservations and charge room expenses to a company account. Keep a good record of all of your expenses, including receipts. You may need them when requesting reimbursement from the company.

It is standard practice to introduce you to many company employees during your interview day. The interviewing process from the employer's perspective is discussed in Chapter 7. This is useful information for the job candidate as well.

One type of interview that you may encounter is the stress interview. The purpose of the interview is to see how you react when the unexpected happens. The interviewer may act hostile or bored, ask aggressive, pointless, or negative questions, make negative statements ("I don't know why we are interviewing you; your record isn't very impressive."), fail to say anything for long periods of time, and make hostile, impatient, or frustrated facial expressions as you speak. The purpose of a stress interview is to throw you off balance and unnerve you. We find little to recommend the stress interview, and yet employers continue to use them. Justifications include a desire to see how you will react to stressful situations that you might encounter on the job, to help recruiters differentiate among many candidates who are more alike than different, and to get past the rehearsed and predictable answers of job candidates.[59] The best advice is to retain your composure. After all, it is not meant to be personal; it is just a strategy. Do not wonder why a particular question was asked; it may not have a specific purpose. Just answer it as best you can. Keep your sense of humor and do not start speaking until you have given some thought to your answer. There is no reason for you to rush into an answer, and a reflective pause can be very useful. Also, it is better to say you do not know than to talk off the top of your head when you are given a surprise question.[60] In sum, do not be intimidated, do not take the negative approach personally, and do not be thrown off balance.

Although it is not common, a company may ask you to take a psychological test, a drug test, or an honesty test during your plant visit without advance warning. You should realize that this is a possibility. If you find this disturbing, it is worthwhile to inquire about the agenda for your visit or ask directly if you should be prepared to take selection tests. You can always decide not to go on the visit.

Salary offers are often the result of a number of important considerations for the company.[61] It will first check the range of starting salaries for similar positions offered by its competition and decide whether it wishes to offer salaries above, at, or below the average. Salaries that are too high can result in discontent for current

[59]For good advice on how to deal with a stress interview see Sandra L. Davis, "How to Handle a Stress Interview," *Business Week's Guide to Careers* (March–April 1985), pp. 27–29.

[60]This discussion draws from Sandra L. Davis, pp. 27–29.

[61]William H. Corwin, "Staying Afloat in Salary Waters," *Managing Your Career* (Spring 1991), pp. 26–27, 35. See also Chapters 10–12 for additional information on compensation decisions.

employees who may have fallen below market rates of pay during their tenure at the firm. Salaries below the average may result in the loss of important talent, as decisions will be made to go elsewhere. You can establish your market worth by carefully reviewing statistical information available at the university's placement office and any number of nationwide surveys of salary offers to new graduates. In addition, information may be available from alumni and competitors. Be aware that companies will most likely not consider firms outside their specific industry as competitors. It may be that the starting salary offer you received from a firm in an unrelated industry will not be considered relevant in your negotiations with a particular company.

Some recruiters will ask you about salary requirements at the initial interview. Others will wait until the site visit or after they have decided to make you a job offer. Your answer to this question should be based on your research. You should know the range of pay for the position for which you are interviewing. The best advice is not to underprice yourself. If you get the job, you may regret your starting salary. The most reasonable response is in terms of the range of pay—for example, "I understand that the starting salary range for this position is $17,000 to $20,000. Based on my qualifications, I would like to start near the top of the range." In the event that you have not prepared yourself for a question regarding your salary requirements, it is best to ask for a few days to think it over. During that time you can do the research regarding an acceptable salary for the job that you should have done before the interview.

It is possible that a job offer will come in at a lower salary or in a less desirable location than you had wished. This is when your decision will be difficult. If you have thought through what is important to you, this decision will be easier to make. Be aware that if you presented extremely flexible job requirements during the process ("I don't mind travel." "I have no problem relocating anywhere in the world."), the company may well base its offer on your statements. The company has every right to be disappointed and surprised when you turn down an offer that meets your stated job requirements. It is unlikely that the company will be willing to be flexible at that point. For this reason, think through your job requirements before the process starts. Be realistic about what is really important to you, and be honest with the company when you are asked.

A final note on ethics and honesty. Recruiters are becoming more sensitive to dishonest behaviors, including exaggerated statements of accomplishment found on the resume or made during the interview. Of special concern is an individual's academic record as it relates to cheating. Students who were caught cheating during their academic careers are not likely to impress campus recruiters. In fact, some recruiters will only interview on campuses renowned for student integrity. Those universities that have academic honesty or honor codes, and seem to create an atmosphere where personal integrity is valued, contribute greatly to the subsequent employability of their graduates.[62] Companies may also check applicants for criminal convictions and look for records of alcohol and drug abuse. It should

---

[62]Diane Cole, "Companies Crack Down on Dishonesty," *Managing Your Career* (Spring 1991), pp. 8–9.

go without saying that regardless of how much pressure is created by conflicting timetables for firms you are interested in, you should be honest in your dealings with all of them. If you need more time, ask for it. Under no circumstances should you accept a position and then refuse to honor your commitment because something better turned up. Make arrangements so that all of the better positions can be fully investigated before you accept any position.

7 ■

Employee Selection

■ LEARNING OBJECTIVES

After reading this chapter you should understand

1. The basic assumptions underlying the selection process.
2. The means used by employers to ensure that these assumptions are met.
3. The strengths and weaknesses of the most common methods of gathering employment information from applicants.
4. The major requirements of EEO regulation as it relates to selection.

■ INTRODUCTORY VIGNETTE

Japanese Auto Companies and the Selection of American Workers

Getting a job at Toyota's Georgetown, Kentucky, plant involves a good deal more than showing up at the plant gate. The plant produces Toyota Camrys and assembles engines. A battery of paper-and-pencil tests, simulation exercises, and interviews are required for even the most menial job. According to one successful job candidate who was hired as a manager in quality control, going through 25 hours of selection procedures "shows a commitment to working for Toyota." The extensive selection procedure is based on Japanese management's concern about the job commitment and versatility of American workers, the emphasis that the company places on teamwork and loyalty, and their fear of labor unions.

Toyota promised to favor Kentucky residents in hiring for the projected 3,000 jobs in the plant. Many job-hungry residents viewed Toyota as an economic savior and, as a result, the company was flooded with approximately 90,000 applications. Unfortunately, this selection ratio did little to help the poorly educated and chronically unemployed worker. To narrow the field of applicants, Toyota employs a minimum of 14 hours of testing, which is administered on Toyota's behalf by state employment offices and Kentucky State University.

The information on Toyota was drawn from "It's Tough to Get a Job at Toyota's Kentucky Plant," *The Wall Street Journal* (December 1, 1987), pp. 1, 31. The information on Mazda and Diamond-Star was drawn from William J. Hampton, "How Does Japan Inc. Pick Its American Workers?," *Business Week* (December 3, 1988), pp. 84, 88.

The initial tests cover math, manual dexterity, "job fitness," and technical knowledge. Work simulations are then used to assess an applicant's problem-solving skills. There are also mock production lines to test assembly skills, speed, individual tolerance for monotony and repetition, and alertness. Only 1 applicant out of 20 makes it to a panel interview conducted by various Toyota departmental representatives. For applicants who successfully complete the selection process, the final steps are a physical exam and a drug test.

"By then," says personnel manager Dewey Crawford, "we're going to know more about these people than perhaps any company has ever known about people." The extensive selection procedure received high marks, according to Toyota officials. Noriyoshi Ohyra, a veteran trainer for Toyota, claims: "I was very much worried." But he discovered that the trainees are "hard-working and dextrous."

Much the same approach is apparent at Mazda's assembly plant in Flat Rock, Michigan, and at Diamond-Star Motors Corporation, a joint venture between Mitsubishi Motor Corporation and Chrysler Corporation, in Normal, Illinois. About 54 percent of applicants wash out of the selection process at Diamond-Star, where they are confronted by a barrage of written, medical, and drug tests similar to Toyota's. Mazda does the same thing in their five-step screening process. Like Toyota, both companies use work samples to test the applicant's ability against actual job requirements. Applicants for assembly-line jobs are asked to install auto parts like heaters, fans, and hoses on a mock production line. Applicants for the position of group leader are asked to train employees (actors working for the company) on simple jobs and to work through an in-basket of memos—responding to all of them within a specified period of time. This elaborate testing of applicants doesn't come cheap, with Mazda and Diamond-Star both spending about $13,000 to select each employee in their U.S. plants.

Are these companies as obsessed with testing when selecting Japanese workers in Japan? The answer is no. In Japan they believe the school system does their screening for them. "In the United States, the companies believe, they have to start from scratch."

■ Introduction

During the last three decades, economic, political, and social forces have made employers increasingly interested in refining their selection process. Intense domestic and international competition has demanded that American firms do everything possible to eliminate inefficiencies and continually improve their products. These activities require a creative, skilled, and dedicated human resource base. It is through a firm's selection decisions, made one at a time, that this base is created. The quality of employees has never been more important.

Fair employment legislation at every level of government—federal, state, and local—requires that employers select employees without putting protected groups of applicants at an unfair disadvantage. This commitment to ensure fairness also requires a sophisticated understanding of how a firm makes its selection decisions.

This chapter discusses the selection of employees. Particular attention is paid to the logic of the process and the methods employers use to gather and evaluate information on applicants. We will discuss the assumptions that underlie any selection decision, as well as the quality, usefulness, and fair employment implications of various types of information, including psychological tests, handwriting analysis, personal and professional references, and body fluid testing.

■ The Selection Process

The purpose of any selection process is to discriminate fairly among applicants. A firm must be able to separate applicants who will perform well as employees from applicants who will not. Various means may be used to support this determination. For example, psychological tests, samples of work that would be performed if hired, and even "gut reactions" have been used with differing levels of success. The belief is that as applicants differ on the various predictors (e.g., psychological tests), they will differ in their work performance as employees.

Figure 7-1 presents an overview of the selection process. The first, or information-gathering, stage uses various methods to determine the extent to which an applicant possesses the qualifications necessary to perform well on the job. Applicants, particularly external applicants, are largely unknown quantities. Before a decision can be made as to their potential performance, more must be known about their job-related abilities, skills, knowledge, and psychological and physical attributes. Although it is every bit as important to have complete information on internal applicants as on external applicants, organizations typically do not need to gather as much information on them because of their history of employment with the firm. Whatever information is gathered by the employer is then used to differentiate applicants from one another. The employer will know which of the applicants has the highest measured or reported level of education, experience, intelligence, mechanical aptitude, or other job-related attribute. Using that information, some estimate of likely future job performance for each applicant can be made. Selection decisions are then based on these predictions. Although the figure indicates that the internal and external applicant pools are combined for selection decisions, some employers will continue to treat the two pools separately. This is usually done when an employer wishes to select internal applicants (if qualified) over external ones. Hence, the employer will not turn to the external applicant pool until all qualified internal applicants have been placed.

Although it may seem that the selection process as presented is more characteristic of large organizations than small ones, that is not the case. A manager of

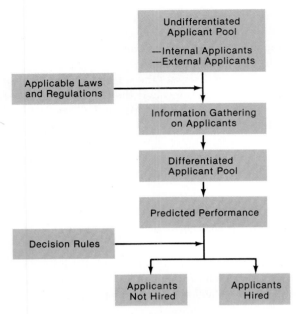

Figure 7-1   Selection

a shopping mall boutique who wishes to fill an opening for a night cashier would first decide what personal attributes a successful cashier would need (job specification). After reviewing the job description, the manager might decide that the cashier needs to be a high school graduate, have cash register skills, get along with people, and be honest. The manager would most likely collect information on applicants using an application blank and a personal interview. He or she would review the application blank for level of education (high school graduate), previous experience (cash register skills), and any other information considered relevant. An interview might be used to collect additional information that the manager believed was necessary, including perhaps an applicant's level of interpersonal skill, and to follow up on information provided on the application blank. Once all the information is collected, the manager would use it to predict the probable success of each applicant and to make a decision as to which one would be the best choice. Thus, although smaller businesses are less likely to have elaborate and formal testing and information gathering methods, the steps in the selection process are the same as for larger firms.

Although the entire process is rather straightforward, it is dependent upon certain assumptions. The most important of these assumptions are as follows:

- The information collected on the applicant's attributes (i.e., experience, aptitudes) is accurate.
- The information collected is related to likely job performance.
- The information collected can be used to make an accurate prediction of job performance for each applicant.

The testing of these assumptions is critical to ensuring that the selection decisions made are both effective and fair. To the extent that any one or all of these assumptions are violated, the entire process is compromised. One can think of the process as a chain of events linked together by these critical assumptions. As is often heard, that chain will only be as strong as the weakest link. It is therefore understandable that society and employers have focused a great deal of attention on them. The following discussion elaborates on these assumptions and presents the methods currently used to examine whether they are met.

■ Assumptions

Accuracy of Applicant Information

Whenever information is gathered on applicants, that information must meet certain standards. It must be both reliable (consistent) and accurate (valid). *Reliability* in this context refers to the extent to which the information is stable or consistent. For example, if an employer requests information from another organization about an applicant's past performance, that employer would expect that the information provided would be the same regardless of who provided it. Further, it would be hoped that the information provided would be an accurate or *valid* representation of that employee's performance. Information may be reliable but may not necessarily be accurate (valid). An examination of employee records may always yield the same information, but that information may be inaccurate. The extent to which the reliability and validity of information is a problem for an employer differs across the various types and sources of information gathered. For example, information provided by an applicant on his or her physical health may be less reliable and/or valid than similar information provided by a competent physician.

The validity of information used in the selection process is an extremely important issue. Predictions of likely job performance are not an exact science. There is considerable potential for error. Predictions using inaccurate information are compromised from the start.

There are three general reasons for a lack of accuracy in the information gathered on applicants. The first is that the source of the information does not know the correct information. For example, applicants may not really know their state of health. These inaccuracies, although real, are unintended. When applicants are confronted with a request for information that they are uncertain about, it is common for them to provide their best guess. For the employer, who must predict job performance using that information, it is likely that a guess will not be good enough.

The second reason is deliberate misrepresentation. Such deliberate misrepresentation is not just true of information from applicants themselves. On occasion, references, interviewers, and past employers have been known to provide invalid information for their own purposes. Typically, however, the greatest problem with deliberate inaccuracies involves data provided by the applicants themselves. Such misrepresentation has required employers to verify self-reported employment data, educational background data, conviction records, and similar standard resume or application blank information. This is done by requesting transcripts of university work; evidence of certifications or special training programs; examining police records; and other third-party corroboration. A failure to seek third-party corroboration has resulted in universities hiring bogus Ph.D.s, hospitals hiring bogus M.D.s, law firms hiring bogus lawyers, and business and government organizations hiring unqualified individuals.

The third reason for inaccurate information concerns the methods of gathering the information. If application blanks are poorly designed or vaguely worded, applicants may be confused and may unintentionally provide poor-quality information. The same may be said for haphazardly conducted and subjectively evaluated employment interviews. Significant potential for this type of problem exists with tests designed to measure psychological attributes as well. In fact, the issues of reliability and validity are so important with reference to psychological testing that a field of study called *psychometrics* has evolved to examine these and related issues. Although many aspects of psychological measurement are very sophisticated, there are some basic concepts essential to understanding the usefulness of psychological tests for selection purposes. A detailed discussion of reliability and validity as they relate specifically to psychological testing is presented later in this chapter. In short, the employer must be able to depend upon the accuracy of the applicant's information regardless of the source of that information. It is worth the effort to minimize inaccuracies in those data.

Applicant Information and Job Performance

One way to ensure that the information collected on applicants is related to probable job performance is to collect selection information only on those attributes listed in the job specification. The relationship between the information collected by the employer and the applicant's probable job performance should be initially established by the job specification. As discussed in Chapter 4, there are three sources of applicant qualifications (job specification). Some qualifications are required by law. An employer may assume that society's interests are served when such qualifications are included in the job specification. Other qualifications are based on professional tradition. The job relatedness of these qualifications has a professionwide, historical acceptance. This does not mean that such qualifications will remain unchallenged forever, but rather that current belief and practice across employers support their inclusion. Still other qualifications depend on the judgment of individual employers regarding their relationship to job performance.

Employers should attempt to link qualification requirements based on tradition and employer judgment directly to the duties found in the job description. It makes practical sense to do so. Applicants rejected because they lack unnecessary qualifications may have been effective employees. A skill requirement may be set when the job description includes duties that demand that skill.[1] Justifying a relationship between an attribute and particular job duties is sometimes straightforward and sometimes difficult. It is easier to present a logical case for a skill or knowledge requirement than it is for various psychological attributes. Typing skills may be logically associated with typing duties for various clerical jobs. However, the relationship between personality characteristics and job duties may not be as obvious. For all personal attribute requirements, and especially for those that are psychological in nature, logical arguments should be supported by statistical analysis if possible. Statistical support for including an attribute among the job requirements, and hence for gathering information on it from applicants, can be obtained by demonstrating that performance levels vary with the levels of the personal attribute. This requires that the organization be able to quantify both personal attribute levels and performance levels. An example would be a manual dexterity requirement. If it can be shown that individuals with greater degrees of manual dexterity perform better as employees, then a statistical case might be made for its inclusion as a job requirement. Further, a justification for manual dexterity information to be gathered and used for prediction purposes during the selection process may be made. It should be kept in mind, however, that prior to any attempt to relate manual dexterity and job performance, it must make sense, given the job description, to relate the two. A purely statistical argument, without the supporting evidence of a relevant duty or task in the job description, may prove to be spurious and hence inadequate for useful prediction. In addition, should the relevance of a given job qualification be legally challenged, a purely statistical argument may not survive that challenge. Figure 7-2 illustrates how an employer might relate attribute information (mechanical aptitude) to job performance. Keep in mind that for this statistical analysis to be meaningful, we must have accurate information on both the attribute and job performance. We will discuss the validity of various types of information and information sources later in this chapter. Chapter 9 examines the problems associated with developing valid job performance measures.

Two different approaches are commonly used by employers to determine whether a statistical relationship exists between a job qualification and job performance. These approaches are labeled *predictive validation* and *concurrent validation*. Taken together, they are said to examine the *criterion-related validity* of the job qualification information. Both approaches require that quantified attribute (predictor) and job performance (criterion) data be gathered on an individual basis for a number of persons.[2] These data are then examined and analyzed to see if a relationship exists between the degree to which an individual meets a

---

[1] This underscores the importance of a thorough job analysis prior to establishing applicant qualifications.

[2] This chapter takes the position that any information gathered on applicants is gathered because it is related to the qualifications necessary for the job. When this information is used for prediction, it is called a *predictor*. As a consequence, for our purposes, any predictor used in the selection process should be traceable to a job specification.

One way to determine whether a relationship exists between a particular applicant attribute and job performance is to examine the degree of correspondence between attribute scores and job performance evaluations. An illustration would be if we determined logically that mechanical aptitude was necessary for effective job performance. We might give a mechanical aptitude test to a group of employees and compare the aptitude test scores to their performance levels. Assume that we get the results below:

Employee	Aptitude Test Score	Performance Evaluation
G. Barland	43	7
E. Andler	26	4
D. Cartwright	57	10
E. Stephens	32	5
J. Ulman	27	5
J. Mosel	60	10
A. Nash	51	9
H. Pyron	22	3
L. Burkey	30	4

An easy way to visualize the degree of correspondence is to graph the aptitude test scores against the performance evaluations, as shown here.

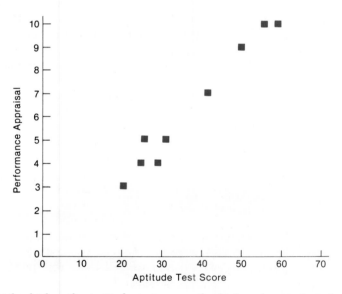

Note that the higher the aptitude test score, the higher the employee's job performance. In order to verify this relationship we can use a statistical test. If the statistical test is consistent with our visual assessment of the relationship, then we have additional support for the inclusion of mechanical aptitude in the job specification. The statistic we use is the correlation coefficient. When we use the correlation coefficient to show the degree of correspondence between attribute (predictor) and job performance (criterion), we call it the criterion-related validity coefficient.

FIGURE 7-2   Plot of Job Performance and Aptitude Test Scores

job requirement (or possesses an attribute) and the job performance of that individual. The statistic that is calculated and used to test whether a relationship exists is the correlation coefficient. Correlation coefficients are discussed in Figure 7-3, as well as in most introductory statistics textbooks. The differences between predictive and concurrent validation involve the individuals selected for the validation study and the timing or sequencing of data collection.

In predictive validation an employer first determines the degree to which applicants possess the attribute or qualification of interest (perhaps by administering a psychological test). The employer then hires all of the applicants, or a random sample of them (assuming that there are limited positions), without regard to probable performance on the job. After these new employees have been on the job long enough for their current performance levels to realistically indicate their long-term performance levels, the employer evaluates their performance. Performance may be measured by an examination of the employee's safety record, absenteeism record, a job knowledge test, or supervisor performance appraisal ratings, depending upon which performance dimension the employer wishes to predict. By calculating the degree of correlation between attribute scores and performance scores, the employer determines whether the attribute is related to job performance. The greater the degree of correlation, the better the case for including the attribute in the job specification and the more useful the attribute will be in predicting job performance for applicants. The predictive approach is considered an excellent way to demonstrate a relationship *(to validate the predictor)* between a personal attribute and job performance. However, this method may occasionally prove to be too costly or otherwise impractical for use. Applicants who might not otherwise be hired because of concerns about their probable job performance may need to be hired as part of the validation study. As a consequence, the result may be a group of substandard employees, thereby increasing those costs associated with poor employee performance.

Further, limited job openings may significantly reduce the number of applicants who can be hired and thus participate in the validation study. If too few individuals are available for the study, a statistical analysis cannot be conducted and the relationship cannot be estimated. Some employers have modified the logic of predictive validation somewhat by rejecting those applicants for employment (and therefore the validation study) who have a low likelihood of success. This modification reduces the potential costs of hiring inferior employees solely for the purpose of the validation study. However, it also reduces the information that may be gained from the validation study by not testing the complete relationship between predictor and job performance. Because no applicants with a low likelihood of successful job performance are included in the study, the job performance range over which the relationship may be studied has been restricted.[3]

A potentially less costly method is concurrent validation. An employer measures the attribute and performance levels at the same time (concurrently), using a group of current employees. A statistical relationship between the attribute and

---

[3]The likely result from this restriction of range is that the correlation coefficient (validity coefficient) will be underestimated.

The correlation coefficient is a statistic that can represent the degree to which plotted data such as those in Figure 7-2 are on a straight line. The absolute value of the coefficient can range from 0 to 1.0. The closer to 1.0 the correlation coefficient is, the closer to a straight line the data are, and the better the justification for including the attribute in the job specification. This figure represents the mechanical aptitude and performance data presented in Figure 7-2. Note that we have now put a straight line through the data so that we can see the relationship more clearly. The data are very close to the straight line. This is reflected by the correlation coefficient (*r*) or .99.

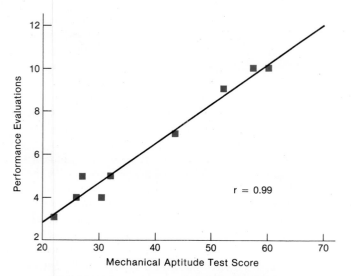

FIGURE 7-3a   Positive Correlation Coefficient

The correlation coefficient can have either a positive or negative sign. A positive correlation coefficient means that as mechanical aptitude increases, performance levels increase, as is seen in Figure 7-3a. A negative correlation would mean that high levels of mechanical aptitude are associated with low levels of performance. Our line would look like the one here, and our correlation coefficient would have a minus sign (r = −0.83), indicating a negative correlation.

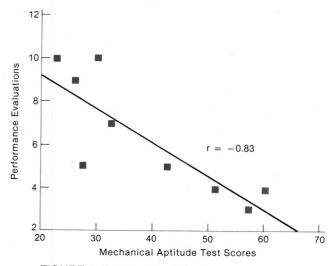

FIGURE 7-3b   Negative Correlation Coefficient

current performance is taken as support for the inclusion of the attribute in the job specification.[4] The illustration in Figure 7-2 is an example of concurrent validation because the mechanical aptitude and performance data are gathered from current employees. Although this method does not have the potential costs associated with hiring unsuitable employees that predictive validation may have, it does not offer as clear an understanding of the relationship between the attribute and job performance for applicants. For example, current employees may not resemble the applicant pool. Hence, will the relationship found for current employees also be true for applicants? Also, the performance of current employees may range from average to excellent, thereby failing to test the strength of the relationship between attribute and performance at lower levels of performance (restriction of range). Further, the motivation to provide information regarding the qualification may differ between applicants and current employees. Applicants desire the position, whereas current employees may not treat the process seriously, or may fear that the information may jeopardize their current or future status with the firm. In addition, current employees have experience in the firm, and the effect of that experience on the statistical relationship cannot be estimated accurately. For these reasons, the relationship found for current employees may not be representative of the relationship between the qualification and job performance for applicants. Employers should be aware of these potential problems and, to the extent possible, should attempt to eliminate or minimize their impact. However, concurrent validation can be very appropriate, and its intelligent use should not be discouraged. In fact, some personnel researchers feel that the long-felt inferiority of concurrent validation has been overstated, and that it may be used with confidence.[5]

For many years employers believed that each employment predictor (attribute) that could be statistically validated (criterion-related validation) needed to be validated separately for every job for which it was to be used. In fact, employers felt that separate validation studies were necessary for even the same jobs when those jobs were located in different communities or drew applicant pools of different racial or ethnic backgrounds. Early evidence indicated that differential validity (different validity coefficients for different groups) was a common enough problem with selection predictors to merit different validation studies for different groups. Unfortunately, however, the ability to generalize the results of a validation study across locations for particular jobs, across similar jobs within an organization, or across organizations is very important to employers. Such an ability would significantly reduce the costs associated with validating selection predictors. Fortunately, recent studies have provided strong support for validity generalization by shedding doubt on previous research, which indicated that criterion-related

---

[4]Some employers, rather than conduct what may be an out-of-sequence performance appraisal for concurrent validation, will use the most recent past performance appraisals for current employees. This process has been referred to as postdictive validation. See Stephen Rubenfeld and Michael Crino, "The Uniform Guidelines: A Personnel Decision-making Perspective," *Employee Relations Law Journal*, Vol. 7, No. 2 (1981), pp. 105–121, for a discussion of postdictive validation procedures.

[5]Gerald V. Barrett, James S. Phillips, and Ralph A. Alexander, "Concurrent and Predictive Validity Designs: A Critical Reanalysis," *Journal of Applied Psychology*, Vol 66, No. 1 (1981), pp. 1–6.

validity was situation specific (validity specificity). In fact, this more recent research clearly demonstrates that "test validities are broadly generalizable across applicant populations, geographical locations, and jobs and that even 'gross changes' or differences in job tasks do not destroy validity [criterion-related validity].[6] The American Psychological Association gave validity generalization a measure of support in its published professional standards for testing as early as 1985, yet it remains a controversial concept among industrial psychologists and the courts.[7]

Usefulness of Applicant Information

The third assumption deals with the usefulness of applicant information to predict job performance. This refers to all of the information gathered by various means, including interviews, application blanks, psychological tests, and any other predictor (or attribute measure) used by the organization. This entails using statistical methods of prediction when possible or using nonstatistical means when they are not.

Usefulness of a Single Predictor

Employers are often interested in the usefulness of information gathered from a single predictor (e.g., a single test or test battery). This is especially true when the employer is considering the addition of that predictor to the current selection process. Although some estimate of the usefulness of additional information may always be made over the long run by examining the after-the-fact improvement in decision making, it is sometimes possible, when a predictor's criterion-related validity coefficient (see the previous discussion of criterion-related validity) is known, to make that estimate in advance of its use.

When employment decisions are made, only four outcomes are possible. If the information on the applicant is favorable (there is a good reason to believe that the applicant will be successful) and he or she is hired (positive selection decision), the new employee may prove to be successful (*true* positive) or unsuccessful (*false* positive). If the applicant is rejected (negative decision), that decision may be correct because he or she might have failed on the job (*true* negative) or incorrect if the applicant would have done well on the job (*false* negative). The terms *true and false positives* and *true and false negatives* are very important in selection. From a firm's perspective, there is a desire to minimize the number of false positives (people who are hired and later fail on the job). From society's point of

---

[6]Douglas D. Baker and David E. Terpstra, "Employee Selection: Must Every Job Test Be Validated?" *Personnel Journal* (August 1982), p. 604. The major contributors to this research are Frank L. Schmidt and John E. Hunter. Their research has been published in a well-known series of articles. Among these articles are "The Future of Criterion-Related Validity," *Personnel Psychology*, Vol. 33 (1980), pp. 41–60, and "Development of a General Solution to the Problem of Validity Generalization," *Journal of Applied Psychology*, Vol. 62, No. 5 (1977), pp. 529–540. The interested reader is also encouraged to consult Virginia R. Boehm, "Differential Prediction: A Methodological Artifact?" *Journal of Applied Psychology*, Vol. 62, No. 2 (1977), pp. 146–154.

[7]Chris Lee, "Testing Makes a Comeback," *Training* (December 1988), p. 56.

view, there should be a minimum of false negatives (people who are incorrectly predicted to fail). In particular, it is critical that no group of minority applicants systematically and disproportionately appear in a firm's false negatives. That would mean that even though minority applicants would perform well, they are being rejected at a higher rate than majority applicants. (More is presented on disproportionate rejection rates later in this chapter.)

Figure 7-4 shows how these four selection outcomes might appear in graphical form. The graph has four quadrants (I, II, III, IV) created by the performance level considered satisfactory by the organization (horizontal line) and the predictor score above which applicants will be hired (cutoff score—vertical line). Individuals in quadrant I are those who had acceptable predictor scores (to the right of the

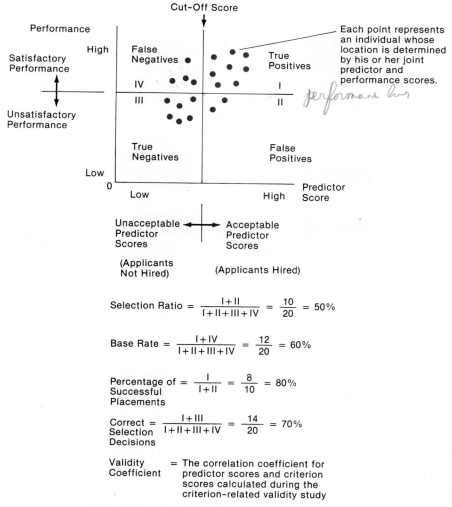

$$\text{Selection Ratio} = \frac{I+II}{I+II+III+IV} = \frac{10}{20} = 50\%$$

$$\text{Base Rate} = \frac{I+IV}{I+II+III+IV} = \frac{12}{20} = 60\%$$

$$\text{Percentage of Successful Placements} = \frac{I}{I+II} = \frac{8}{10} = 80\%$$

$$\text{Correct Selection Decisions} = \frac{I+III}{I+II+III+IV} = \frac{14}{20} = 70\%$$

Validity Coefficient = The correlation coefficient for predictor scores and criterion scores calculated during the criterion-related validity study

FIGURE 7-4 The Effectiveness of a New Predictor

vertical line), and satisfactory subsequent performance (above the horizontal performance line). These people are *true* positives, unlike those in quadrant II, who, after being hired, did not perform well (*false* positives). Similar logic can be used to understand quadrant III (*true* negatives) and quadrant IV (*false* negatives).

The percentage of applicants selected for a position is called the *selection ratio*. This ratio can be expressed in terms of the quadrants as well (keeping in mind that we are really representing the number of individuals in a quadrant by the respective quadrant number). The selection ratio is the number of people selected (vacancies filled [quadrants I, II]), divided by the total number of applicants (quadrants I, II, III, and IV). The example provided in Figure 7-4 is a selection ratio of 50 percent. The smaller the selection ratio, the more favorable it is for the firm. For instance, a selection ratio of 10 percent means that only 1 of every 10 applicants needs to be hired. On the other hand, a selection ratio of 90 percent means that 9 out of every 10 applicants must be hired. It is difficult to be very selective when almost all applicants need to be hired in order to fill open positions.

The percentage of current employees considered satisfactory is called the *base rate*. This rate refers to the percentage of individuals selected *in the past* who have proven successful on the job. It can be represented by dividing the total number of individuals above the satisfactory performance line (quadrants I, IV) by the total number of individuals (quadrants I, II, III, IV). The example provided in Figure 7-4 presents a base rate of 60 percent. This means that if all applicants are hired (using *past* selection devices), 60 percent of them would turn out to be satisfactory (those in quadrants I and IV). This sets the stage for the most important concept: the degree to which the current base rate of 60 percent can be improved by using a new predictor. The idea is that by taking advantage of the relationship between predictor (test score) and criterion (performance), and assuming some selectivity in hiring (selection ratio less than 100 percent), we should be able to improve the quality of our current selection decisions (base rate). The stronger the relationship between predictor and criterion (validity coefficient), and the more selective a firm can be (selection ratio), the more a given base rate can be raised by using the selection device. Figure 7-4 shows that using this predictor, and hiring 50 percent of the applicants (everyone in quadrants I and II), the percentage of people hired who will perform successfully rises to 80 percent (quadrant I divided by quadrants I + II). This means that rather than only 60 percent of this firm's new hires performing satisfactorily, 80 percent will. Depending upon the expense of using this predictor, the firm may gain considerably from its adoption. (Figure 7-5 shows the relationship between selectivity and improvements in the base rate.) A firm need not go through the elaborate calculations just discussed in order to determine how useful this predictor will be. The relationships between base rate, selection ratio, and validity coefficient are so stable that tables have been developed that can be used to determine the new base rate. Table 7-1A provides one example from this set of tables. A firm determines which table to use based upon the current base rate (there are different tables for different current base rates). The example in Table 7-1A (Taylor-Russell Table) is for a firm with a base rate of 70 percent. The firm finds the correct column in the table by locating its selection ratio. It can then locate the row by finding the validity coefficient for this new

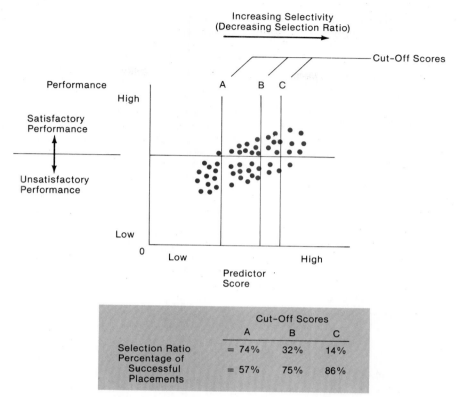

FIGURE 7-5   The Effect of the Selection Ratio on the Percentage of Successful Placements

predictor. (There are many more columns and rows in the actual tables.) If the firm had a selection ratio of 20 percent and a validity coefficient of $r = 0.5$, the new base rate would be 91 percent. The firm can then decide whether this increase from 70 percent to 91 percent is cost effective. If it is, then the device will be adopted. However, if it costs more to use this device than it saves by preventing incorrect selection decisions, the firm will not adopt it. This relationship between the usefulness of the selection device and its cost is often labeled the *utility of* the device. This refers to the savings and/or productivity gains from the use of the device when compared to the costs.[8]

[8]Some very interesting research on the utility of selection devices has been conducted. This research illustrates methods of calculating the dollar value of the productivity gains resulting from the use of valid selection devices. See Frank L. Schmidt, John E. Hunter, R. McKenzie, and T. W. Muldrow, "Impact of Valid Selection Procedures on Work-Force Productivity,"*Journal of Applied Psychology*, Vol. 64, (1979), pp. 609–626; and Frank L. Schmidt, John E. Hunter, and K. Pearlman, "Assessing the Economic Impact of Personnel Programs on Workforce Productivity," *Personnel Psychology*, Vol 35 (1982), pp. 333–347. A more sophisticated statistical model based on contributions from accounting, utility theory, psychometric techniques, Markov processes, labor economics and present-value analysis has been developed and presented in Jean C. Wyer, "A Stochastic, Psychometric Valuation Model for Personnel Selection Systems," *Decision Sciences* (Summer 1988), pp. 700–707.

TABLE 7-1A   Taylor-Russell Table
Proportion of Employees Considered Satisfactory = 0.70

Validity Coefficient	Selection Ratio					
	0.05	0.20	0.30	0.60	0.80	0.95
0.05	0.73	0.72	0.72	0.71	0.71	0.70
0.50	0.96	0.91	0.89	0.82	0.77	0.72
0.95	1.00	1.00	1.00	0.98	0.86	0.74

This is an abbreviated version of the complete table presented by H.C. Taylor and J.T. Russell, "The Relationship of Validity Coefficients to the Practical Effectiveness of Tests in Selection: Discussion and Tables," *Journal of Applied Psychology*, Vol. 23 (1939), pp. 567-578.

TABLE 7-1B   Lawshe Expectancy Table
Proportion of Employees Considered Satisfactory = 70

Validity Coefficient	High $\frac{1}{5}$	Next $\frac{1}{5}$	Middle $\frac{1}{5}$	Next $\frac{1}{5}$	Low $\frac{1}{5}$
0.15	77	73	69	69	62
0.50	91	82	73	62	42
0.75	98	91	78	57	25
0.95	100	100	93	52	4

This is an abbreviated version of the complete table presented by C.H. Lawshe, R.L. Boda, and G. Auclair, "Expectancy Charts, III: Their Theoretical Development," *Personnel Psychology*, Vol. 11 (1958), pp. 545-599.

The Taylor-Russell tables provide insight on how useful a new predictor may be; however, they do not provide directly useful data on making selection decisions on an individual-by-individual basis. The Lawshe Expectancy Tables (See Table 7-1B), can be used for this purpose. These tables are also based on the stable relationships between the validity coefficient, selection ratio, and current base rate. As with the Taylor-Russell tables, a firm finds the correct table to use based upon its current base rate. In Table 7-1B, that base rate is 70 percent. Again, as with the Taylor-Russell tables, the proper row is selected based upon the validity coefficient of the selection device. The major difference is in selecting the correct column in the table. This column is based upon the relative applicant score on the predictor. For instance, if the applicant's score is in the top 20 percent, the correct column would be the first one (High 1/5). If the validity coefficient is 0.75, the table entry of 98 represents this applicant's chances out of 100 of being successful. These data are sometimes presented in graphical form as in Figure 7-6. This bar graph corresponds to the entire row from Table 7-1B (Lawshe Expectancy Table) for the validity coefficient of 0.75. The top bar (98 percent) represents the table entry just discussed. The additional bars correspond to the subsequent table entries of 91, 78, 57, and 25. A personnel employee simply determines the ap-

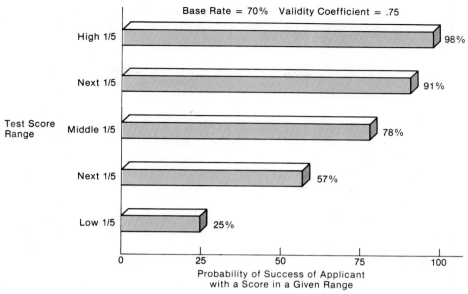

FIGURE 7-6   Individual Expectancy Chart

plicant's relative score, finds the correct table or expectancy chart, and determines the statistical probability of success for the applicant. If that probability is high enough, the applicant will be hired.

Combining Information from Multiple Sources

Organizations may elect to combine information in different ways in order to arrive at their selection decisions. Three general ways of combining information are multiple hurdles (also called *successive hurdles*), the compensatory approach, and a combination of the two.

The *multiple hurdles* approach assumes that acceptable levels of each job qualification are known. For example, the number of years of experience, physical condition, or personality characteristics that an applicant needs to do the job is known. It is also assumed that an applicant needs to possess all of the attributes in question (at acceptable levels). The logic of this approach is to examine each applicant with reference to each attribute in sequence. If an applicant possesses the first attribute, then he or she will be examined for the second. At any point where an applicant does not meet the standard for an attribute, that applicant is rejected. Applicants meeting the standards for all attributes are considered qualified for the job.

The *compensatory approach* is statistical in nature. Working from the data and relationships found during criterion-related validity studies, organizations combine predictors into an overall prediction equation. In other words, each prediction device that has a statistical relationship with job performance is combined with other similar predictors. These combined predictors are then used to predict job performance with equations such as the following:[9]

$$\text{Predicted job performance} = 0.7 + 0.5 \times \text{years of experience}$$
$$+ 0.75 \times \text{IQ test score}$$

It is clear from this equation that for a given predicted job performance rating, more years of experience may compensate for a lower IQ score and vice versa. Because one predictor score may be used to offset lower scores associated with another, this approach is called *compensatory*.

The combined approach requires that only applicants who qualify (multiple hurdles) will have their performance predicted by a prediction equation such as the one just presented (compensatory approach). This approach is often used for admission decisions to graduate school. Minimum grade point averages and achievement test scores are usually established as a means for determining who is eligible to apply for admission. A predicted graduate grade point average, based on a prediction equation, will determine who is actually admitted.

■ The Equal Employment Opportunity Environment

Although the Civil Rights Act was passed in 1964, and the first set of Equal Employment Opportunity Commission (EEOC) Guidelines on Employee Testing was published in 1966, the current definition of unfair discrimination was delivered in a decision by the U.S. Supreme Court in 1971. This decision was the first time that the intent to discriminate was considered of secondary importance. Of primary importance was whether or not discrimination had actually taken place. This decision was handed down in the *Griggs v. Duke Power Company* case discussed in Chapter 3.

You will recall that the Duke Power Company was sued by Willie Griggs and other Duke Power employees for denying them certain jobs because they lacked a high school diploma. The employees charged that a high school diploma was not necessary for the position. The court ruled that even though a high school diploma (and certain standardized test scores) were required of all applicants regardless of race, the effect was to deny a disproportionate number of blacks the position. Hence, the *intent* to discriminate was not as important as the basic *impact* of the selection process. Further, unless the employer could show that the "employment practice which operates to exclude negroes" is job related, the "practice is prohibited." This decision created the concept of adverse impact, which is discussed later. In 1988, the U.S. Supreme Court expanded the doctrine set forth in *Duke Power* and held that employment decisions based on subjective measures from

[9]This equation has the same form as that presented in the regression analysis example in Chapter 5.

employment interviews and performance appraisals could be illegal if they had an adverse, although unintentional, impact on a protected group.[10]

The Uniform Guidelines

The Uniform Guidelines protect the rights created by Title VII (Civil Rights Act of 1964, as amended), Executive Order 11246 (as amended), and various other federal laws.[11] (A flow chart of these guidelines is presented in Figure 7-7).[12]

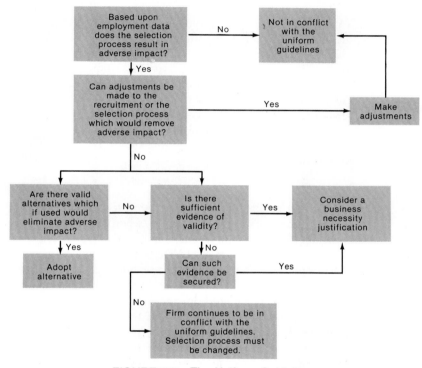

FIGURE 7-7   The Uniform Guidelines

[10]Justice Burger, *Griggs v. The Duke Power Company,* as found in James Ledvinka, *Federal Regulation of Personnel and Human Resource Management* (Boston; Kent Publishing Company, 1982), p. 41. The Supreme Court has made it clear that the current definition of unfair discrimination covers employment decisions based on objective tests, as well as subjective information from sources such as interviews and recommendations. *Watson v. Fort Worth Bank and Trust,* US Supreme Court, No. 86-6139 (June 29, 1988).

[11]Stephen Rubenfeld and Michael Crino, p. 106.

[12]For a much more complete flow chart and discussion of the uniform guidelines see Stephen Rubenfeld and Michael Crino, pp. 105–121, and The Bureau of National Affairs, Inc., "Selection Procedures," *Fair Employment Practices* (1991), Section 421.

Following the flow chart in Figure 7-7, employers who use selection devices (selection tests and other applicant qualifications) that screen out a disproportionate number of women or minorities must eliminate this adverse impact or provide a business necessity or job-related argument supporting their use. An employer may discover that the adverse impact is due to poorly trained selection personnel or a flawed recruitment process. In these instances, adjustments can be made to bring the firm into compliance. Should such adjustments not be possible, the firm has two basic choices: eliminate adverse impact by using an alternative selection procedure that is equally valid or present strong and significant validity data, evidence that no valid alternative procedure exists, and a convincing argument that without the procedure the firm would suffer (business necessity justification).[13]

A primary concern for employers is the method that the courts will adopt to define adverse impact. Depending upon the definition chosen, an employer may or may not be found in violation of the law. Although there are a handful of definitions of adverse impact, the two most common appear to be the 80 percent rule of thumb and the population/workforce comparison.[14]

The first is presented in Table 7-2 and requires that selection rates for minorities and majority groups be calculated and compared. Assuming that membership in a minority group does not affect job success, the rates at which applicants are selected from the minority and majority groups should be equal. Employers are allowed, under this definition, to have a minority selection rate of as little as 80 percent of the majority selection rate before a determination of adverse impact is made.

The second definition compares the percentage representation of a minority group in the organization (or job) to the percentage representation of that group in the relevant workforce. A concern when this definition is used is how the relevant workforce is defined. For example, what skills and what geographical area define the relevant labor market? The way the relevant workforce is defined may have an important effect on whether or not organizational representation of minority groups is sufficient to avoid charges of adverse impact.

Although we have defined discrimination in aggregate terms, such as selection rates for protected groups, even when there is no adverse impact against a minority group the U.S. Supreme Court has ruled that "Title VII does not permit the victim of a racially discriminatory policy to be told that he or she was not wronged because other persons of his or her race were hired."[15]

We have reviewed the assumptions most critical to the selection process, as well as guidelines for ensuring the fairness of selection decisions. We now review the most commonly used means for gathering applicant information and evaluate the

---

[13]Different forms of validity may be presented, for example, criterion-related validity, content validity (to be discussed under proficiency and competency tests), and construct validity (to be discussed under psychological tests).

[14]Robert J. Haertel, "The Statistical Procedures for Calculating Adverse Impact," *Personnel Administrator* (January 1984), pp. 55–58. See Chapter 3 for additional discussion of the Uniform Guidelines and of adverse impact.

[15]*Connecticut v. Teal*, 29 FEP Cases 1 (1982). See also the discussion on the recruitment and selection of employees in Chapter 3.

TABLE 7-2   Adverse Impact

80% Rule

$$\text{Selection rate (SR)} = \frac{\text{Number of hires}}{\text{Number of applicants}}$$

$$SR_{\text{Minority}} = \text{Selection rate for minority group}$$

$$SR_{\text{Majority}} = \text{Selection rate for majority group}$$

If:

$$\frac{SR_{\text{Minority}}}{SR_{\text{Majority}}} \geq 0.80 \qquad \text{No adverse impact}$$

$$\frac{SR_{\text{Minority}}}{SR_{\text{Majority}}} < 0.80 \qquad \text{Adverse impact}$$

Example

$$SR_{\text{Minority}} = \frac{10 \text{ hires}}{100 \text{ applicants}} = 0.1$$

$$SR_{\text{Majority}} = \frac{100 \text{ hires}}{150 \text{ applicants}} = 0.67$$

$$\frac{SR_{\text{Minority}}}{SR_{\text{Majority}}} = \frac{0.1}{0.67} = 0.15$$

$$0.15 < 0.80$$
$$\text{Adverse impact is present}$$

extent to which they may contribute to a successful and fair selection process. Special attention is paid to how they may be used effectively, as well as their relationship to federal and state laws and regulations that have created the current atmosphere of equal employment opportunity.

Data-Gathering Methods

Application Blanks

Application blanks provide an opportunity for an employer to gather a good deal of information about an applicant in a short period of time. An application blank is one of the two most common methods used for collecting applicant information.

The pre-employment interview, which is discussed later in this chapter, is the other. Certain issues must be addressed when discussing this method of data collection. The first has to do with the accuracy or validity of the information provided by the applicant. This is a problem shared with other methods of data collection. As discussed earlier, third-party corroboration is often used to assess the validity of this information. To emphasize the importance of honesty in the provision of application blank information, some employers request applicants to sign a statement that the responses that have been provided on the application blank are true under penalty of immediate dismissal if found to be false.

The second issue deals with information that may or may not be requested of applicants. Although Title VII does not directly prohibit questions relating to race, color, religion, sex, or national origin, the EEOC will react with suspicion to employers' claims that such information, when requested prior to hiring, is not used in the selection decision or when used, is a BFOQ. Although the ADEA permits date of birth or age to be asked on applicant application forms "provided the question does not conceal a discriminatory purpose," requests for an applicant's age will also be viewed with suspicion.[16] Many state agencies have issued guidelines that expressly forbid questions regarding the applicant's sex, religion, conviction record, and race, among others.[17] Employers should review the appropriate guidelines for their state. Perhaps the best advice is to avoid requesting any such information that cannot be shown in a convincing fashion to be related to job performance and, if necessary, to be a BFOQ or a business necessity.

The Americans with Disabilities Act (ADA), discussed in Chapter 3, has also prohibited inquiries on an application blank or during a pre-employment interview regarding an applicant's physical or mental condition. Even the generic question "Do you have any physical or mental conditions that would prevent you from performing your job functions?" is prohibited. No inquiry of this type may be made until the applicant has been offered a position. That position may be made contingent upon a satisfactory medical exam, however, so the employer need not hire someone who is not physically or mentally capable of performing the job.[18]

Table 7-3 presents some application blank inquiries that have proved troublesome to employers in the past. It should be kept in mind when reviewing Table 7-3 that, with the exception of inquiries regarding physical or mental health, the extent to which an inquiry proves to be a problem will be due to applicable state laws and regulations and the use to which the information is put.

A third issue of importance is the way in which an organization uses application blank information to predict job performance. Many employers have found that application blank information may be combined to create a weighted score for each

---

[16]See Michael Levin-Epstein, *Primer of Equal Employment Opportunity* (Washington, D.C.: The Bureau of National Affairs, Inc., 1987). Issues of what employers actually do ask, and whether they are risking serious legal problems, are discussed in articles such as Julia Woo, "Job Interviews Pose Rising Risk to Employers,"*The Wall Street Journal* (March 12, 1992), p. B1.

[17]Carl Camden and Bill Wallace, "Job Application Forms: A Hazardous Employment Practice," *Personnel Administrator* (March 1983), pp. 31–32.

[18]David Warner, "Rules on Medical Tests for New Hires," *Nation's Business* (August 1991), p. 29.

TABLE 7-3 Pre-employment Inquiries

Subject	Troublesome Inquiries
Marital and family status	Questions concerning pregnancy
	Inquiries regarding whether the applicant is married, single, divorced, or pregnant
	Information on child care arrangements
	Number and age of children
Age	Requirement that applicant provide age or date of birth or produce proof of age
Sex	Sex of applicant (unless it is a BFOQ)
Race	Race of applicant
Birthplace	Birthplace of applicant or applicant's parents, spouse, or other relatives
	Any inquiry into national origin
Religion	Applicant's religious faith or affiliation, church, parish, pastor, or religious holidays observed
Military record	Type of discharge
Photograph	Requirement that applicant submit a photograph at any time prior to hiring
Conviction, arrest, and court record	Inquiries relating to arrests or requests for applicant conviction record if not substantially related to functions of a particular job
References	Requiring submission of a religious reference
	Requesting reference from applicant's pastor
Physical or mental health	Asking if the applicant has any physical or mental conditions that would prevent them from performing their job functions

Adapted from Clifford M. Koen, Jr. "The Pre-employment Guide," *Personnel Journal*, (October 1980), pp. 826-828. Reprinted with the permission of *Personnel Journal*, Costa Mesa, California; all rights reserved. Copyright October 1980, and from David Warner, "New Rules on Medical Hires," *Nation's Business* (August 1991), pp. 29-31.

applicant. As shown in Table 7-4, weights are assigned to application blank items (response categories) based on the item's ability to discriminate the superior (current or past) employees from the inferior ones on a performance dimension of interest (e.g., tenure with the organization). Scores are calculated by summing the weights.[19] These scores may be validated using criterion-related validation

[19]Biographical information blanks (BIBs) may be weighted in much the same way. The primary difference between BIBs and standard application blanks is the extensive amount of personal life history information requested by BIBs. See Karl W. Kuhnert and Craig J. Russell, "Using Constructive Developmental Theory and Biodata to Bridge the Gap Between Personnel Selection and Leadership," *Journal of Management*, Vol. 16, No. 3 (1990), pp. 595–607, for a discussion of the usefulness of biodata in predicting leadership effectiveness for selection. See Edwin Fleishman, "Some Frontiers in Personnel Selection Research," *Personnel Psychology*, Vol. 41 (1988), pp. 685–688, for a discussion of biodata research in general.

TABLE 7-4   Weighted Application Blanks

Application Blank Information	Number of High Performers[a]	Number of Low Performers[b]	Total	Percent High[c]	Weight[d]
High school graduate[e]					
Yes	45	10	55	82%	8
No	12	23	35	34%	3
	57	33	90		

[a]This column states the number of current employees who are high performers and who are (45 employees) and are not (12 employees) high school graduates.

[b]This column states the number of current employees who are low performers and who are (10 employees) and are not (23 employees) high school graduates.

[c]This column states the percentage of high school graduates who are high performers (82%) and the percentage of non-high school graduates who are high performers (34%).

[d]This column states the weight to be given an answer of yes (8 points) and no (3 points) to the high school graduate question. The points reflect the percentages listed in the adjoining column (82%/10 = 8.2, or 8 points, and 34%/10, or 3 points).

[e]This question is one of many questions that might be asked on an application blank. The total score that an applicant receives would be the sum of the weights associated with his or her answers to the entire series of questions on the application blank.

strategies (predictive or concurrent). Using the correlation coefficient calculated in the validation study, the usefulness of the information can be determined. An employer may then choose to use the scores for predictions on individual applicants. One firm, after instituting a weighted application blank as part of its selection process, reported that 6-month turnover was reduced from 80 percent to 26 percent.[20]

However, considerable caution must be exercised when using weighted application blanks. The temptation to include all types of information in order to increase the overall predictive power of the application blank may result in violation of EEO laws. One way a firm may find itself in violation of the law would be to include information in the total score that would be prohibited or suspect if used alone (e.g., age or sex of the applicant). Even if such information is not used alone, the employer must be sure that the use of weighted scores does not discriminate against protected groups (adverse impact). This might occur even when no questionable inquiries are used. An illustration might be the use of a seemingly innocent question concerning hometown population. If more favorable scores were received by individuals who grew up in small towns, then members of most minority groups, who reside in larger cities, would be at a disadvantage. In order to minimize the likelihood that problems will occur, two personnel specialists have suggested that only application blank data that have a content directly related to

[20]Daniel G. Lawrence, Barbara L. Salsburg, John G. Dawson, and Zachary D. Fasman, "Design and Use of Weighted Application Blanks," *Personnel Administrator* (March 1982), p. 47.

job performance be included in the statistical analysis used to derive the weights.[21]

References

Either personal or professional references may be requested from applicants. Personal references are useful in verifying personal history information such as the length of residence in a given community or the general reputation of the applicant. There should be a genuine concern for the applicant's right to privacy and a clear need to know whenever personal information is collected. When personal information must be collected, such as when the applicant must qualify for a security clearance from the federal government, the rights of the applicant should be respected. Fortunately, most firms do not require detailed information of this nature. Typically, personal references are requested only to verify that they have known the applicant for a given period of time and have no reason to believe that the applicant is unsuitable for a position.

Professional references have to do with past employment history. They consist of information that verifies an applicant's application blank data, work performance, absenteeism, and the like. Firms can check references themselves or hire an outside company to do the checking.[22] Regardless of who does it, it is very important to verify employment data. Personnel specialists estimate that 90 percent of hiring errors probably could be eliminated by proper reference checking.[23] In a survey of its members, the National Association of Corporate and Professional Recruiters found that 81 percent made reference checks before offering a job.[24]

It has been estimated that as many as 30 percent of all resumes contain at least one major fabrication. One company that investigates applicants has stated that up to one fourth of the MBAs checked by the company are fraudulent.[25] Common fabrications include exaggerated educational accomplishments and past job responsibilities. Many mail order diploma factories advertise in popular magazines and offer advanced degrees for life experiences for a given amount of money. The FBI has estimated that there are 100 diploma factories in the United States selling 10,000 to 15,000 phony degrees per year.[26]

[21]Larry A. Pace and Lyle E. Shoenfelt, "Legal Concerns in the Use of Weighted Applications," *Personnel Psychology*, Vol 30 (1977), pp. 159–166.

[22]The Bureau of National Affairs, Inc., "Trends," *Bulletin to Management* (October 29, 1987), p. 351. See also Kathryn Hudson, "Reference Checking? Hire a Hand," *Insight* (February 1, 1988), p. 45.

[23]Timothy D. Schellhardt, "What Personnel Offices Really Stress in Hiring," *The Wall Street Journal* (March 6, 1991), p. B1.

[24]Jolie Solomon, "Reference Preference: Employers Button Lips," *The Wall Street Journal* (January 4, 1990), p. B1.

[25]The Bureau of National Affairs, Inc., "Rooting Our Ringers," *Bulletin to Management* (March 28, 1985), p. 8.

[26]Ellie McGrath, "Sending Degrees to the Dogs," *Time* (April 2, 1984), p. 90.

Not only is it more likely that an ineffective employee will be hired if references are not checked, but issues of negligent hiring are also involved. Under certain circumstances, an employer may be liable financially when reasonable care was not exercised in the selection of an applicant. Checking references is considered part of exercising reasonable care. So long as permission is granted by the applicant, the information requested is job related, is true to the best of the reference's knowledge, and is not used in a discriminatory fashion, it should be gathered and considered in the selection decision. If applicants do not wish their current employers contacted, and many do not, you should make their employment probationary until you can verify the information regarding their current jobs.[27]

Individuals providing reference information must be careful not to violate the rights of the applicant. Although federal employees are protected from disclosure of employment data without their permission, there is no federal legislation protecting private sector employees. A number of states have attempted to protect a current or former employee's right to privacy. Because legislation varies from state to state, it is wise to review the appropriate state privacy acts prior to the disclosure of information regarding current or past employees. Further, an employer should ensure that the permission of the former employee has been secured for release of the requested information. Only the information for which permission has been granted should be released.[28]

A number of successful defamation lawsuits have been brought against employers who provided more than factual information in references. Many companies have policies that forbid employees from giving a reference. A survey of 80 human resource managers found that 41 percent of their companies had such a policy.[29] When an applicant loses a job opportunity because of comments made by a former employer, those comments had better be factual. Disclosing secondhand information or gossip about a former employee opens the firm to lawsuits. One applicant, who lost a job offer because his former employer disclosed negative information based on gossip, won $250,000 in a lawsuit.[30] An employer who, during a reference check, characterized a former employee as a "classical sociopath," as a "zero,"

---

[27]The Bureau of National Affairs, Inc., "Meeting Staffing Needs," *Bulletin to Management* (June 13, 1991), p. 177.

[28]On some occasions permission from the employee may not be sufficient to protect an employer from legal action for the release of negative information. If the employee has been dismissed for disciplinary reasons, and fails to secure new employment because of the release of that information by the employer or himself, the employer may be subject to legal action. This seemingly strange state of affairs is due to the fact that the disciplinary discharge may not have been for good cause. An employer must be prepared to defend the legitimacy of the dismissal under these circumstances, even if it is the employee personally who discloses the negative information. Employees may feel compelled to provide the negative information if requested to do so, and should be protected from losing an employment opportunity because of an unjust dismissal. See Peter A. Susser, "Compelled Self-publication: Expanding Employers' Liability for Defamation," *Employment Relations Today* (Spring 1987), pp. 75–81.

[29]Patricia Amend, "Job References Hard to Come by These Days," *USA Today* (February 2, 1990), p. 10B.

[30]The Bureau of National Affairs, Inc., "Job Reference Ramifications," *Bulletin to Management* (March 21, 1991), p. 88.

and as disliked by office personnel paid $1.9 million for the privilege. However, although high-profile, high-award cases are interesting, most employers who give references will not be involved in a lawsuit. Nevertheless, to minimize the legal risk, "employers should provide references in good faith, without malice or reckless disregard for the truth," containing only accurate, job-related information to the proper party in the requesting firm.[31]

Interviews

The employment interview is one of the most commonly used means of collecting information about job applicants.[32] Employers may require a single or multiple employment interviews. There may be one or multiple interviewers present at each interview. A multiple interview strategy usually begins with a brief preliminary interview designed to eliminate those applicants clearly unsuited for the position. The remaining applicants will receive additional consideration during a second, more in-depth interview, usually at the organization's personnel offices. A final interview may be required of applicants not eliminated during the second interview. Should a third interview be required, it is usually with those individuals with whom the new hire will work. Despite the considerable expense involved in interviewing, the interview, as commonly conducted, remains a highly suspect way of predicting applicant job performance. There is considerable evidence that interviews may not predict job performance all that well. This raises three rather important questions: First, if interviews are not especially effective predictors of applicant job performance, why are they used so extensively? Second, why is it that interviews are not very effective predictors of job performance? Third, what ways are available to improve the predictive validity of applicant interviews? The remainder of this discussion addresses these questions.

As previously stated, despite their rather poor track record, interviews remain one of the most common means for gathering information on applicants. This is true for a number of reasons. For one, many organizations don't realize that their interviewing is not effective. They have never evaluated it. They just assume that their interviewing is effective and continue to do it. When all interviewed applicants are basically qualified for the job, it is more difficult to notice that interviewing is making little additional contribution to predicting job performance. Another reason is that some employers cannot bring themselves to hire someone without seeing him, talking to him, and taking his measure. They want to be sure that the applicant would fit in as an employee, and believe they can best decide

---

[31]The Bureau of National Affairs, Inc., "Job Reference Ramifications," *Bulletin to Management* (March 21, 1991), p. 88.

[32]The popularity of employment interviews ensures that there is no shortage of advice on how to conduct one. See, for example, The Bureau of National Affairs, Inc., "Interviewing with Insight," *Bulletin to Management* (August 30, 1990), p. 280; The Bureau of National Affairs, Inc., "Guidelines for Interviewing," *Bulletin to Management* (May 9, 1991), p. 139; Robert L. Dipboye, *Selection Interviews: Process Perspectives* (Cincinnati, Ohio: South-Western Publishing Company, 1992).

this during an interview. That may or may not be true. The reality is that many of us think we are better at sizing people up than we are.

In order to understand why interviews, as often conducted, lack predictive validity it is necessary to examine the dynamics of the interviewing process (Figure 7-8). As can be seen in Figure 7-8, there is potentially a great deal of information that can be gathered about any applicant. Some of that information is relevant to the applicant's job qualifications (e.g., aptitudes, past work history) but most of it is not (e.g., taste in foods, hobbies). Applicants are willing to disclose only a portion of this total information. Most typically, information viewed as irrelevant, personal, or information that may reflect poorly on them will be withheld. Using whatever information is provided by the applicant in reply to interview questions, the interviewer forms a mental picture of the applicant. This image is then compared to what the interviewer views as the image of the successful applicant. Based upon this comparison, an evaluation of an applicant's performance potential is made by the interviewer. It is apparent then that the quality of the process is heavily dependent upon the accuracy of the images in the mind of the interviewer. In turn, the accuracy of those images is dependent upon the information available about the applicant and the position, as well as the way in which that information is combined in the mind of the interviewer.

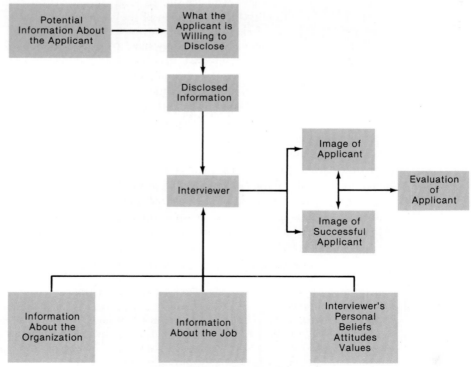

FIGURE 7-8   **Interview Dynamics**

These dynamics should provide some insight into the most significant problems with interviews as they are currently used in organizations:[33]

- Lack of uniformity
- Lack of objectivity
- Failure to understand the limitations of the interview
- Lack of training for the interviewer

Of the problems just cited, the lack of training for interviewers is the most significant, and, in fact, contributes to the others. Very often interviews are conducted by managers on a part-time basis, or by junior members of the organization being groomed for more responsible positions. In either case little is invested in providing training in interviewing skills. Worse yet, interviews may be conducted by individuals with brief organizational tenure, who know very little about the organization or even about the position for which they are conducting the interview. Hence, the information used by these individuals to form their image of the successful job applicant (stereotype) may be both limited and inaccurate. Further, untrained individuals are more likely to include irrelevant information, be swayed by personal biases (lack of objectivity), or succumb to typical interviewer errors. These errors include overemphasis on first impressions and negative information, tendency to favor applicants who are similar (e.g., in sex, attitude, or race) to the interviewer, and allowing the impression of the most recent past interviewee to affect the evaluation of the current interviewee (contrast effect).[34] This lack of training also contributes to a misunderstanding of what type of information may be gained effectively during an interview. For example, a great deal of effort has been expended in the attempt to validly measure psychological attributes either through psychological tests (as discussed later in this chapter) or through clinical evaluation by trained psychologists. Nevertheless many interviewers are convinced that they can accurately assess a variety of personality characteristics in applicants after interviews of rather short duration. In actuality, it is highly unlikely that interviewers can make such determinations; this contributes significantly to the lack of predictive validity for interviews.

In addition, the more an interview is dependent upon the personal judgment of untrained interviewers, the less likely it is that the interviews for an organization will be uniformly conducted. Uniformity of interviews is essential in order to effectively compare applicants to each other on job-relevant attributes. This uniformity of information from interviewers is called *interrater reliability* and is important when organizations rely upon many interviewers in the field.

[33]This list is drawn from Thomas L. Moffatt, *Selection Interviewing for Managers* (New York: Harper & Row Publishers, Inc., 1979). See also Michael M. Harris, "Reconsidering the Employment Interview: A Review of Recent Literature and Suggestions for Future Research," *Personnel Psychology,* Vol. 42 (1989), pp. 691–726.

[34]For a complete discussion of the professional literature associated with these errors, see Frank Landy and Don A. Trumbo, *Psychology of Work Behavior*, rev. ed. (Homewood, Illinois: The Dorsey Press, 1980), pp. 204–206.

The remaining question of those previously stated involves improvement of the interviewing process. How exactly can organizations generate useful information using the interview, and how can that information be used to effectively predict applicant job performance? The answer appears to be the structuring of the interview, coupled with the training of the interviewer. Structuring of the interview means that the content and format of the interview are provided to the interviewer and, therefore, do not depend upon the interviewer's personal judgment. Training can prevent the common interviewer errors just discussed and ensure that the interview is conducted as it was intended by the organization. In addition, an interviewer should be trained in how to prepare for an interview. This includes how to review applicant data (e.g., application blank, resume), as well as job analysis data. Together these two steps will systematize the interviewing process. The interview should be structured around the content of the specific job or similar groups of jobs. This is accomplished by basing the questions and information required of the applicant upon a complete understanding of the personal attributes necessary for the successful performance of a given job. A thorough job analysis is, of course, a necessary step.[35] The organization must then be realistic about which of the attributes can be evaluated by an interview, or series of interviews. For example, the measurement of intelligence is best left to professional psychologists, but the abilities to plan and organize may be accurately assessed during a structured interview by a trained interviewer. Assume that a particular job requires the "ability to structure employees in the correct methods/ procedures for performing maintenance/service tasks by demonstrating, coaching, and providing feedback on their performance.[36] Questions in the structured interview might include

- "Tell me how you trained workers to do their job."
- "What methods of training have you found useful with operators and/or mechanics?"

Interviewers can be trained to look for particular elements or content in applicant responses. Interviews can be very useful in collecting information and predicting applicant job performance. Exactly how useful they will be depends upon the care taken in structuring the interview around a job analysis and training the interviewers.

---

[35]Recent studies have found that the predictive validity of interviews is improved when the interview is structured, and based on a job analysis. See M. A. Campion, E. D. Pursell, and B. K. Brown, "Structured Interviewing, Raising the Psychometric Properties of the Employment Interview," *Personnel Psychology*, Vol. 41 (1988), pp. 25–42, and W. H. Wiesner and S. F. Cronshaw, "A Meta-Analytic Investigation of Interview Format and Degree of Structure on the Validity of the Employment Interview," *Journal of Occupational Psychology*, Vol. 61, (1988), pp. 275–290. Additional research indicates that the use of a structured panel interview (two or more interviewers) shows promise of improving predictive validity even more. See P. L. Roth and J. E. Campion, "An Analysis of the Predictive Power of the Panel Interview and Pre-Employment Tests," *Journal of Occupational and Organizational Psychology*, Vol 65. (1992), pp. 51–60.

[36]Robert Bloom and Erich P. Prien, p. 84.

Employment Testing

Employment tests have proven to be an effective method of collecting important job-related information on applicants. As with the collection of any personal information, potential misuse and violation of personal privacy are paramount concerns. However, employment test information, when collected according to recommended test procedures, when kept confidential, and when used appropriately, is unlikely to violate the personal privacy of applicants.[37] Further, the issue of fairness is always important when using employment tests to make selection decisions.[38] Before using an employment test, employers should investigate the company providing the test, the fair employment history of the test, the litigation history of the test, and the reputation of the test among testing professionals.

Most of the forms of information discussed in this chapter may be considered employment tests to the extent that scores may be generated that reveal something about the applicant (allowing inferences to be made about potential job performance).[39] Some discussions of employment tests in the human resource literature include structured interviews, application blanks, assessment centers, and tests of motor and physical abilities. We have chosen to discuss them separately. Further, many employment tests, such as integrity tests and proficiency tests, may be classified as forms of psychological assessment, although we will not discuss them as such. We have chosen to focus on tests that are designed to measure cognitive abilities (general mental ability and various aptitudes), personal interests, and personality characteristics[40] in the discussion of psychological assessment. We will discuss integrity tests and proficiency tests separately within this section.

Psychological Assessment

There is little question that psychological attributes such as intelligence, mechanical or mathematical aptitude, and analytical reasoning are related to success for certain jobs. Questions arise as to whether a particular psychological attribute is

---

[37]The Bureau of National Affairs, Inc., "Behavioral Testing: Invasion of Privacy?," *Bulletin to Management* (June 7, 1990), p. 178.

[38]Some fairly popular employment tests, including the Department of Labor's General Aptitude Test Battery (GATB), have required *race norming* in order to avoid unfair discrimination. When test scores were race normed, they were adjusted for different subgroups of applicants. This was considered necessary when a subgroup of applicants performed less well on the test but equally well on the job. The Civil Rights Act of 1991 bans the adjustment of employment test scores on the basis of race, color, religion, sex, or national origin.

[39]Richard D. Arvey and Robert H. Faley, *Fairness in Selecting Employees*, 2nd ed. (Reading, Massachusetts: Addison-Wesley Publishing Company, 1988), pp. 90–91.

[40]It remains to be seen if personality tests will be classified as medical examinations under the ADA. If they are, they will be subject to the same requirements as information regarding the physical condition of the applicant. See Chapter 3 and the Physical Examinations section in this chapter for a discussion of those requirements.

necessary for a particular job (or group of jobs), whether that attribute can be reliably and validly measured in an applicant, and whether measurement scores of that attribute can be used in a nondiscriminatory fashion to predict job performance.[41] These are not easy questions, and, as a consequence, many employers abandoned the use of psychological tests in the late 1970s. Because of recent increased confidence that these questions can be intelligently addressed, psychological testing is once again considered a useful method for collecting data on applicants. During the discussion of the assumptions underlying the selection process, it was stated that the information collected on applicants should be reliable and valid. Reliability was defined as the consistency of the information, and validity was defined as the accuracy of the information. These issues are of critical importance when considering the adoption of psychological tests for selection purposes. The reason is that with psychological testing (of the type being discussed here) we are trying to generate information on an unobservable attribute. One can neither see nor touch intelligence, for instance. We might say that particular behaviors are a reflection of intelligence or the lack of it, but intelligence itself is unobservable. The concept of intelligence was literally "created" in order to explain certain differences in the behavior of different individuals. Hence, general intelligence (and other similar psychological attributes such as aptitudes) are both made up and forever unobservable. You can see the problem in stating that a made up psychological attribute is critical to the performance of a job, and that even though it cannot be directly observed or measured, we intend to make selection decisions based on the degree to which an applicant has it. Fortunately, psychologists have developed certain direct and indirect means for estimating the reliability and validity of instruments designed to measure these psychological attributes (often called hypothetical constructs). These means were developed over an extended period of time and are considered the central issues in the area of study called psychometrics.

As with the other information that has been discussed thus far, reliability, as it relates to psychological testing, also refers to consistency, which means (1) consistency within a particular measurement instrument, or *internal consistency* (e.g., consistency among questions or items within an IQ test), (2) consistency between two versions of an instrument or *parallel forms* (e.g., Form A and Form B of the IQ test), and (3) between two administrations of the same instrument, or *test-retest reliability* (giving the IQ test twice to the same person).

Thus, reliability may represent three different forms or types of consistency. It is important to know which type of reliability has been established for a psycho-

---

[41]There is some question regarding the use of personality tests such as the Minnesota Multiphasic Personality Inventory (MMPI) and the California Psychological Inventory (CPI) as employment tests. These tests contain questions dealing with sexual preference and religious beliefs that are considered by some to be invasive and potentially discriminatory. The Court of Appeals of California, First Appellate District, Division Four, ruled that the portions of the tests containing such questions are inappropriate for use to select security guards. However, the Uniform Guidelines on Employee Selection do not require that each item of a selection test be validated against performance when summary scores will be used to make the selection decision. The issue of whether asking particular questions constitutes an invasion of privacy when the answers are confidential and buried in summary scores remains open.

logical test being considered for use. For example, if the psychological test is designed to measure only one personality attribute, the internal consistency estimate of reliability would provide insight into how well that is being accomplished. This is because the internal consistency estimate indicates how the items within a test relate to one another. If an organization is interested in using two forms or versions of a psychological test then it becomes important to demonstrate that the two forms provide consistent information and can be used with similar results. This means that a parallel forms estimate of reliability would be useful. If the attribute being measured is stable over time (i.e., an applicant with a high mechanical aptitude now should have a high aptitude next month as well), an employer might wish to know that the aptitude test scores are stable over time (as is the aptitude). This would mean that the test-retest estimate of reliability would be of importance. Reputable professional test developers, from whom psychological tests may be purchased, provide this information to prospective purchasers.

Reliability is estimated using the correlation coefficient. As with criterion-related validity, the greater the correlation coefficient, the better. One significant difference does exist, however. The correlation coefficient used to estimate criterion-related validity could be either positive or negative; what was important was its absolute value and whether it made theoretical sense. For the reliability estimate the correlation coefficient *must* be positive. Otherwise, the information is extremely inconsistent. This is true regardless of the type of reliability you are estimating.

Assuming that the information is consistent (reliable) in the fashion appropriate to the organization's needs, the second question to be asked is, "How can we be sure that this psychological test measures the attribute it claims to measure?" This is an extremely important issue for psychological measurement. This type of accuracy of measurement is called *construct validity.* This distinguishes it from the validity (or veracity) of information such as years of schooling, height, sex, and salary history. It makes clear that the issue is the degree to which the test measures a psychological construct (or attribute). This can only be established indirectly. There are various methods for estimating the construct validity of psychological tests, but a presentation of those methods is beyond the scope of this discussion. Suffice to say that prior to adopting *any* psychological test for selection, the employer must be provided with information supporting the construct validity of the test. Without such information, the use of a psychological test is risky, and very possibly counterproductive. Further, unless such information can be secured, the use of the test would be indefensible in a court of law, should a legal challenge be raised against its use.[42]

---

[42]The sale of many psychological tests is restricted to qualified professionals with a clear, stated need for them. Once the tests have been sold, the purchaser is obligated to administer them, score them, and interpret them in a manner consistent with the test developers' instructions. To do otherwise would very likely violate standard accepted ethical practice, compromise the reliability and validity of the test, and significantly reduce the defensibility of the test if presented with a legal challenge. This is so important that the American Psychological Association has provided guidelines for the administration and use of psychological tests. This information may be found in American Psychological Association, Society of Industrial and Organizational Psychology, *Principles for the Validation and Use of Selection Procedures* (Dayton, Ohio: The Industrial Organizational Psychologist, 1987).

Interestingly, the term *construct validity* may also be used to describe the relationship between a psychological construct such as intelligence, and job performance. When it is used in this manner, it is assumed that the construct is being reliably and validly measured and the issue is whether a logical case can be made for the psychological attribute to be included in the job specification. There is a danger in relying solely upon this type of argument in that the employer is not freed from proving that scores on the measure of the psychological attribute are correlated with job performance.[43] This proof will require a criterion-related validation study.

One form of personality assessment, handwriting analysis, has not yet met the reliability and validity standards of professional psychologists. The analysis of handwriting is called *graphology* and is not new. However, there has been a significant increase in its use in both the United States and Europe, since the mid-1980s. One article estimated that 85 percent of European firms used graphology to make employment decisions,[44] and another article in *The Wall Street Journal* indicated that major American firms, including Fortune 500 companies, were using it. *The Wall Street Journal* also cited statistics indicating that firms specializing in graphology were seeing major increases in their business.[45]

Employers who use handwriting analysis make the assumptions that the technique is reliable and valid. There is no evidence, other than anecdotal, that these assumptions are true. Employers point out that a sample of handwriting can be collected in a few minutes and analyzed inexpensively ($25–$200). They contrast handwriting analysis with other forms of personality assessment that may take hours and cost as much as $1,000. What is rarely pointed out is the long history of research supporting the reliability and validity of those other forms of personality assessment. Currently, among personnel psychologists, there is a universal lack of respect for handwriting analysis as a way of measuring personality characteristics. The future of graphology as a source of information for selection decisions is an open question. There is little doubt that graphology will continue to be used. What is uncertain is whether it will gain respectability among professional psychologists.

Integrity Testing

Employers are interested in assessing the integrity of applicants for two general reasons: to evaluate the credibility of information provided at the time of application and to determine whether the applicant can be trusted in the workplace. We have discussed the importance of using accurate information in the selection process but have not considered honesty as part of the job specification. One estimate by the Chamber of Commerce puts the amount of workplace theft at $40

---

[43]This issue is discussed in Stephen Rubenfeld and Michael Crino, p. 120.

[44]Chris Lee, "Testing Makes a Comeback," *Training* (December 1988), p. 52.

[45]Michael McCarthy, "Handwriting Analysis as a Personal Tool," *The Wall Street Journal* (August 25, 1988), p. A19.

TABLE 7-5 Early Lie Detection Technology

The need to tell the guilty from the innocent has always been with us. Stories of early lie detection technology have become part of folklore. One such example is that of a Persian King who had a magic donkey. This donkey could tell a guilty person from an innocent one. The king would ask those accused of a crime to go, one by one, into a dimly lit room where the magic donkey was waiting. Each was instructed to pull the donkey's tail, and was told that if they were guilty the donkey would bray. If an innocent person pulled the donkey's tail it would remain silent. One by one the accused would go into the room and emerge again. In no case did the donkey bray. Yet, without fail, the king would determine who was guilty and who was not. It seems that the donkey was not magic, and could not bray no matter how much its tail was pulled; the king had covered the donkey's tail with graphite. Those who were innocent pulled the donkeys tail with confidence, and emerged from the room with dirty hands. Those who feared the donkey because they were guilty walked into the room, hesitated for a moment, and walked out—with clean hands. The king's job was to see who had dirty hands and who had clean ones.

Adapted from Chris McCurry, "The Business of Truth," *APS Observer* (July 1989), p. 14.

billion annually.[46] Employers, especially in businesses where the opportunity for employee theft is great, have a real need to consider the honesty of future employees. The issue is not whether employers are justified in their concern over honesty but rather whether they can assess it accurately without violating the privacy of applicants.

A number of methods have been developed to help employers determine who is trustworthy and who is not. All of the methods are controversial. They include lie detectors, voice stress analyzers, paper-and-pencil integrity tests, credit report checks, and personal and professional references.

Since the passage of the Employee Polygraph Protection Act in 1988, lie detectors can no longer be used by most private employers for selection purposes. However, if employees provide security services for a business where "cash in effect constitutes the inventory or stock in trade" or manufacture controlled substances, then lie detectors may be used.[47] Estimates vary as to the accuracy of lie detector tests. Specifically, when used for screening applicants, lie detector tests "have not been studied with any kind of scientific rigor or control."[48] The American Psychological Association's Council of Representatives went on record as supporting the Employee Polygraph Protection Act, stating that the tests produce "an unacceptable number of false positives."[49]

Voice stress analyzers examine the frequency characteristics of an individual's voice when under stress. Attempts to determine the accuracy of this method have

[46]"Should You Tell All?," *Parade Magazine* (May 27, 1990), p. 5.

[47]Bureau of National Affairs, Inc., "Final Polygraph Rules Issued," *Bulletin to Management* (March 7, 1990), p. 65.

[48]Chris McCurry, "The Business of Truth," *APS Observer* (July 1989), p. 14.

[49]John Bates, "Agency Sounds Alarm on Work Test Technology," *APA Monitor* (December 17, 1987), p. 16.

met with little success. Usually, in accuracy studies, the voice stress analyzer is compared with lie detector results. Voice stress analyzers are not popular, and with inexpensive alternatives such as paper-and-pencil tests are not likely to become so.

Personal credit reports as a means of assessing the personal integrity of applicants have become very popular. Employers believe that "knowing how an applicant handles bills, loans, and other financial obligations helps predict whether he or she is likely to steal, sell company secrets or otherwise act irresponsibly on the job."[50] Shortly after the passage of the Employee Polygraph Protection Act, credit-reporting agencies began to experience a boom in sales. Equifax, Inc., of Atlanta sold 350,000 reports to 15,000 employers in 1989, and 1990 sales were much higher.[51] At about $5 per report, they seem inexpensive to employers who are concerned about dishonest and illegal activities. When a credit report is the basis for an applicant's being denied employment, the Fair Credit Reporting Act, enforced by the Federal Trade Commission, requires employers to inform the applicant and to furnish the name of the agency providing the report. However, it seems that many firms are not complying with the act. Consequently, applicants are turned down for employment without any knowledge of the real reason. If their credit report has inaccurate information, and estimates are that as many as 33 percent of credit reports do, applicants have no opportunity to appeal an employer's decision or to correct the information.[52] Employers using credit reports and not complying with the act, are risking law suits from applicants and the Federal Trade Commission.[53]

There are questions regarding the ability of credit reports to predict dishonest behaviors on the job. Most supporters, convinced that people who have had financial problems are more likely to engage in dishonest activity or drug use, can only cite anecdotal evidence to support their position. Moreover, there is little consistency as to what information employers find most useful. Congress is considering legislation to require permission from an applicant before a potential employer may request credit report information. Without legislation limiting access to credit report information, there will continue to be serious concern regarding applicants' rights to privacy.

Employers have turned to paper-and-pencil integrity tests because of their ease of use, inexpensive price ($7 to $15), and relative lack of organized opposition. Integrity tests have had a long history. During the early to mid-1980s, many different types of integrity tests were developed and marketed. More recently, two distinct types of integrity tests have become popular. These test types have been labeled *overt* and *personality oriented*. Overt tests ask questions about past

---

[50]Gilbert Fuchsberg, "More Employers Check Credit Histories of Job Seekers to Judge Their Character," *The Wall Street Journal* (May 30, 1990), p. B1.

[51]Gilbert Fuchsberg, p. B1.

[52]Diane Duston, Associated Press, "Consumers Get More Power Over Credit Agency Records," *Anderson Independent* (March 7, 1992), p. 8C.

[53]Gilbert Fuchsberg, "Use of Credit Reports in Hiring Draws a Caution," *The Wall Street Journal* (November 7, 1990), p. B1.

thefts or attitudes toward honest versus dishonest behaviors.[54] Surprisingly, many people will simply admit theft when asked about it directly.[55] Personality-oriented tests do not ask directly about theft but measure such characteristics as employee reliability, deviance, social conformity, wayward impulse, dependability, and hostility to rules.[56] Some tests have combinations of both overt and personality questions.

Paper-and-pencil integrity tests that claim to measure attitudes and personality characteristics should be held to the same standards of reliability and construct validity as other psychological tests. All integrity tests, whether overt or personality based, should have criterion-related validity and should be examined for fairness. To this point, they have not been held to those standards. In 1986, Massachusetts banned the use of honesty tests along with polygraph tests. Since then, other states have considered doing so. In 1990, the Office of Technology Assessment of the U.S. Congress concluded that it was impossible to gauge the validity of honesty tests since 95 percent of the research on them was done by the for-profit companies that sell them.[57] The American Psychological Association provided qualified support to written integrity tests in its 1991 report, "Questionnaires in the Prediction of Trustworthiness in Pre-Employment Selection Decisions." However, it went on record as stating that "Promotional claims for honesty tests, as perhaps for all other procedures used for pre-employment screening, vary from the circumspect to the fraudulent." The Association also acknowledged that much more high-quality research on the reliability and validity of honesty tests was necessary, and suggested that employers use alternatives to "prevent or discourage theft" before resorting to the tests.[58] The Association recommends that if an employer decides to use an honesty test, it do so with caution. It further advises employers to combine the test results with other information before making a selection decision, avoid making pass/fail judgments, ensure that only qualified people administer the tests, safeguard the confidentiality, privacy, and informed consent of testees, and use only tests that meet the standards for the publication, sale, and use of psychological measures.[59]

Proficiency or Competency Tests

Proficiency or competency tests as we will discuss them here include general reading, spelling, and math tests, specific job skill tests or job knowledge tests

---

[54]Paul Sackett, Laura R. Burris, and Christine Callahan, "Integrity Testing for Personnel Selection: An Update," *Personnel Psychology*, Vol 42. (1989), p. 491.

[55]Ed Bean, "More Firms Use 'Attitude Tests' to Keep Thieves off the Payroll," *The Wall Street Journal* (February 27, 1987), p. B1.

[56]Tina Adler, "Integrity Test Popularity Prompts Close Scrutiny," *APA Monitor* (December 1989), p. 7.

[57]Bureau of National Affairs, Inc., "Continuing Debate Over Honesty Tests," *Bulletin to Management* (April 25, 1991), p. 128, and Christina Robb, Boston Globe, "Just How Honest Are Honesty Tests?," *Anderson Independent* (April 10, 1991), p. 2B.

[58]The Bureau of National Affairs, Inc., "Continuing Debate Over Honesty Tests," *Bulletin to Management* (April 25, 1991), p. 128.

[59]Bureau of National Affairs, p. 128.

(e.g., using specific word processing or spreadsheet software programs), and general work samples (i.e., using multiple job skills).

There has been an increasing interest in the use of competency tests over the last decade. According to the American Management Association, about 50 percent of American companies use competency tests.[60] This increased interest can be traced to a number of things coming together at the same time. Confronted with the declining levels of basic literacy and math skills in the United States, employers can no longer assume that applicants have adequate levels of language and math skills. Recent fair employment legislation has emphasized that employers should use job-related information to select employees. Generally, it is much easier to show the job relatedness of actual samples of the work than for a psychological test. The number of jobs requiring the use of specialized computer programs is increasing dramatically. For many employers the ability to use a personal computer is not enough. It has become important that the applicant be competent with the particular programs used in the company. Consequently, firms like Educational Testing Service, publisher of the Scholastic Aptitude Test, have begun to offer software competency tests for programs like Wordperfect, Displaywrite, Lotus 1-2-3, and Microsoft Word.[61]

Competency tests of reading and math have a long history of research and use in our educational system. There is widespread confidence about what they show concerning the reading and math skills of an applicant. When a question is raised about their use in selection, it is usually about the minimum level of competency required by an employer. What sometimes happens is that an employer will simply set a minimum educational level, say, 10th grade, without really relating that level to the demands of the job. Much as with the high school diploma requirement of the *Duke Power* case discussed in Chapter 3, there may be fair employment implications in the minimum level selected.

Specific skill tests have a long history of use as well. The ability to use a complicated machine like a lathe is often a job requirement. It makes sense that an employer would test an applicant for any skill that requires considerable training or experience to master. A test of important job knowledge, especially when that knowledge is highly specialized or complex, also makes sense. Many professionals take tests of this type, administered by an organization such as the American Medical Association, as a means of certifying their specialized competency. Employers may request applicants to take a test to show their knowledge of safety regulations, for example.

General work samples simply extend the logic of the specific skill test. An applicant is given a sample of work and asked to do it. Buried in that sample of work are usually a number of job requirements demanding a variety of skills. The employer infers that the competency shown with the work sample is an indication of likely competency on the job.

---

[60]Gilbert Fuchberg, "Pencils Sharp? E.T.S. to offer Employee Tests," *The Wall Street Journal* (June 13, 1990), p. B1.

[61]Gilbert Fuchberg, p. B1.

Computer-based simulations may be considered to be a form of work sample if the competencies required for playing the simulation are the same as those required for the job. In-basket exercises, such as those used by Mazda,[62] may also be considered a form of work sample. Applicants are required to review and make decisions on a number of issues similar to those required on the job. They are provided with an in-basket filled with intra- and interdepartmental memos and company reports dealing with employee problems, customer relations, or other issues relevant to the position. They must work through the in-basket, making decisions about the issues and communicating those decisions in brief memos to appropriate personnel. A group of qualified evaluators (often composed of industrial psychologists) then reviews the contents of each applicant's out-basket. Based on assessments of the skill, judgment, and knowledge demonstrated by the applicant during the exercise, decisions are made about how well he or she would perform on the job.

One term often used with reference to work samples is *content validation*. This refers to the similarity of content between the behaviors required in the work sample and those required on the job.[63] When a work sample has been content validated, it refers to the compelling logic that the similarity of content between the work sample and the job is high. The greater the correspondence, the better. This point is significant because the lower the direct correspondence between the two sets of behaviors (work sample and actual job tasks), the less an employer can rely on content validation to support the use of a given work sample.[64]

As with any information used for making selection decisions, an acceptable level of work sample performance (cutoff score) must be established. This cutoff score should be considered carefully. If it is possible to quantify the results of a work sample, then the organization may wish to conduct a criterion-related validation study.[65]

Physical Examinations

The ADA, discussed in Chapter 3, greatly limits the use of any form of physical examination or inquiry as a pre-employment screening device. For example, an

---

[62]See "Japanese Auto Companies and the Selection of American Workers" at the beginning of this chapter.

[63]There are a number of important discussions of content validation that should be recommended to employers considering content validation of work samples or tests: Robert M. Guion, "Content Validity: Three Years of Talk—What's the Action?" *Public Personnel Management,*" Vol. 6, no. 6 (1977), pp. 407–414; Lawrence S. Kleiman and Robert H. Faley, "Assessing Content Validity Standards Set by the Court," *Personnel Psychology,* Vol 31. (1978), pp. 701–713; Robert Otteman and J. Brad Chapman, "A Viable Strategy for Validation; Content Validity," *Personnel Administrator* (November 1977), pp. 17–22. Despite common statements to the contrary, content validation should not be considered inferior to criterion-related validity as a means for establishing the job relatedness of a test or work sample.

[64]Robert D. Gatewood and Lyle E. Schoenfelt, "Content Validity and EEOC: A Useful Alternative for Selection," *Personnel Journal* (October, 1977), pp. 520–524.

[65]John E. Champion, "Work Sampling for Personnel Selection," *Journal of Applied Psychology,* Vol 56 (1972), pp. 40–44.

applicant may be asked whether he or she can use a computer for 8 hours a day, but no inquiry may be made regarding back or eyesight problems, and no physical examination may be conducted until a conditional employment offer has been made. An offer of employment may be withdrawn if a physical examination reveals that the applicant cannot perform the specific "essential job functions" required by the job, even with reasonable accommodation to his or her physical condition. Physical screening of body fluid samples for chemical substance abuse prior to an offer of employment is allowed by the act, however.

Physical Attributes and Motor Skills

There are three general, overlapping categories of information regarding physical and motor attributes and abilities: information on general physical attributes such as height and weight; information on motor skills such as eye-hand coordination and manual dexterity; and information on illness and disabilities such as cancer, diabetes, chemical dependencies, and impaired vision or hearing. Aside from hard-to-diagnose illnesses, medical examinations are believed to provide valid information on an applicant's physical condition. Although it does happen, there is seldom controversy over the accuracy of medical information. Controversy does exist, however, regarding the usefulness and fairness of using physical information for selection purposes. Many general physical attributes are correlated with age, sex, national origin, or race. If an employer makes selection decisions based on such information, it is possible that discriminatory hiring practices may result. For example, one employer required all production employees to be at least 5 feet 5 inches tall. The EEOC stated that this physical requirement eliminated many more women and Spanish-surnamed American men than white men. This adverse impact could not be justified by a business necessity defense, and hence the employer was forced to eliminate the physical requirement.[66] Similar physical attribute requirements such as weight are subject to the same need for proof of performance relatedness and business necessity.

Some jobs clearly require specific levels of motor skills or physical abilities.[67] For example, an employer may need information on eye-hand coordination, manual dexterity, balance, physical strength, and flexibility. Some tests of these physical characteristics are part of work samples, while others may be specific tests designed by professionals (e.g., industrial psychologists). Information from these tests must be held to the same standards of reliability, validity, and job relatedness as all other information, especially when failure to meet the minimum standards may be the result of a disability covered under the ADA. Employers must remain sensitive to inadvertent discrimination in hiring. Just as height and weight requirements may affect various applicant groups differently, so might requirements based upon this type of information (e.g., physical strength requirements).

[66]Howard J. Anderson, p. 48.
[67]Edwin A. Fleishman, pp. 692–696.

Under the ADA, physical data that indicate an illness such as cancer, AIDS, or heart disease cannot be used to support a negative employment decision unless the condition is directly related to an inability to perform essential job functions. Further, applicants who can currently perform the job, but who have disabilities that may result in an increased risk of injury on the job cannot be denied employment based on that increased risk.[68]

Genetic Screening

Genetic testing may be useful in determining whether an individual has a predisposition to any number of serious diseases. "It is expected that researchers will identify genes which contribute to the development of Alzheimer's disease, alcoholism, coronary artery disease, the different forms of cancer, and virtually every other illness."[69] Does that mean that employers may test applicants to determine whether they may in the future develop an expensive or performance-compromising disease? The answer is no. Aside from the fact that "genetic tests are poor predictors of disease and even poorer predictors of disabling illnesses,"[70] this type of pre-employment screening violates the ADA. Genetic information is not related to an individual's current ability to physically perform essential job functions.

A related issue is when individuals, because of genetic traits, may be more likely to develop an adverse reaction or an occupational disease when exposed to workplace chemicals, substances, or pollutants. Employers may wish to refuse employment to applicants on the basis of these genetic traits. This denial of employment is also prohibited under the ADA. The American Medical Association, recognizing the limited predictive validity of genetic tests, recommends that all applicants simply be made aware of any genetic susceptibilities that might increase their workplace risk. Applicants can then decide if they wish their private physician to examine them and if they wish to accept a position with such risks. According to the American Medical Association, there are very limited conditions under which an employer may deny employment based on genetic traits. These limited conditions include all of the following: the genetic test is highly accurate; the disease spreads very rapidly (so that irreversible illness would occur before monitoring could detect a problem); the applicant provides informed consent for the testing; the workplace cannot be made safe; and there are clear data to indicate that the genetic abnormality results in a very high level of susceptibility to occupational illness. It remains to be seen whether an applicant can be denied employment legally even under such restrictive conditions.

[68]David Warner, p. 29.

[69]Council on Ethical and Judicial Affairs, American Medical Association, "Use of Genetic Testing by Employers," *Journal of the American Medical Association* (October 2, 1991), p. 1827.

[70]Council on Ethical and Judicial Affairs, American Medical Association, p. 1827.

Body Fluid Testing

The testing of body fluids, such as blood and urine, is an understandably contro-versial method of gathering employment information. The issues of individual rights and employer needs are difficult to balance. The laws and regulations de-scribed in Chapter 3 are particularly relevant here, as are the Federal Drug-Free Workplace Act and the drug-testing rules of the Defense Department and the Department of Transportation (see Table 7-6).[71]

Somewhat different issues are raised with the testing of an applicant's, as op-posed to an employee's, body fluids. Applicants do not have as many rights as employees when it comes to body fluid testing. Applicants have not yet developed a relationship with the employer, and no collective bargaining agreements or expressed or implied contractual obligations exist for them, as they might for employees.[72] The issue of an individual's right to privacy is relevant for both applicants and employees. However, the employment rights of an applicant are far fewer and are legally defined primarily in terms of federal, state, and local laws and regulations. These laws and regulations are typically designed to protect defined applicant subgroups from systematic employment discrimination. So long as body fluid testing does not create such discrimination, and the state in which the testing takes place does not have a specific law prohibiting it, a company is within its rights to deny employment on the basis of those tests. It is for this reason that the growth of applicant drug testing among employers has been so rapid and has met with comparatively few legal challenges.

A study published in the *Journal of the American Medical Association* provided a measure of support to those employers using pre-employment drug testing. During the period from September 1986 to January 1989, 4,964 applicants for the U.S. Postal Service were tested for drug use. "The Postal Service hired 2,537 of those applicants without regard to the test results, which were kept secret, and the performance of the entire group was followed for more than a year. It was found that marijuana users were twice as likely to be fired, 85% more likely to suffer in-jury on the job, and 55% more likely to be involved in an accident than nonusers. Absenteeism among users was 7.1%, compared to 4% for those who tested neg-ative. Results for cocaine users were similar, except that their absenteeism rate was 9.8%, and they were no more likely to be fired than non-users."[73] Employers who test applicants for drugs indicate that they have seen a decline in the number

---

[71]Although the Federal Drug-Free Workplace Act act does not require pre-employment drug testing, it encourages it by requiring all government contractors to certify their workplaces as drug-free. See The Bureau of National Affairs, Inc., "Employee Drug Testing Escalates," *Bulletin to Management* (May 23, 1991), p. 154.

[72]Robert T. Angarola, "Drug Testing in the Workplace: Is It Legal?" *Personnel Administrator* (Sep-tember 1985), p. 88. See also Rusch O. Dees, "Testing for Drugs and Alcohol: Proceed with Caution," *Personnel* (September 1986), p. 55.

[73]Ron Winslow, "Study May Spur Job-Applicant Drug Screening," *The Wall Street Journal* (Novem-ber 28, 1990), p. B1.

TABLE 7-6   Blood Type and Personality

Although unlikely to be taken seriously in the United States, some Japanese companies test applicants' blood as a means of assessing personality characteristics. Employers who do this testing believe that a person's blood type can provide insight into his personality. According to this theory, a person with Type A blood is cautious, eager to please, indecisive and a conformist; Type B—decisive, known for originality and versatility, occasionally obnoxious, and stands out in a crowd; Type O—team leaders, confident and cool-headed, meets challenges with courage but may become domineering; Type AB—complex, mysterious with a tendency to eccentricity. Estimates state that as many as one third of Japanese businessmen use blood type in selection decisions, either formally or informally. There is no way of knowing how often information on applicant blood type is used for employment decisions in Japan. The fact that blood type might be used at all is more than a little interesting.

Adapted from Associated Press, "Theory Claims a Person's Blood Reveals Personal Characteristics," *The Greenville News* (June 16, 1991), p. 9E.

of positive tests over the years. When Commonwealth Edison Company began testing in the early 1980s, it found a positive rate of 16%; by the early 1990s that rate had dropped to 4 percent.[74] This is attributed to the reluctance of drug users to apply for jobs where they know they will be tested.[75] Based on that reasoning, some employers have begun to put "Drug-Testing Employer" at the end of classified ads.[76] Many employers feel that they must test for drugs simply because those who use drugs will apply for employment where they will not be tested. This would make it more likely that employers who do not test for drugs would have a larger than normal number of drug users among their applicants.

The identification of those who abuse chemicals is usually accomplished through the examination of body fluids (urinalysis, blood tests). These fluids are usually screened for evidence of previous drug use. Urine tests, particularly chemical assay tests called EMIT, are most commonly used. These are relatively inexpensive tests ($15–$20) and lend themselves well to the mass testing that is necessary. When a urine sample tests positive, an additional test is called for before the employer should be notified. The most common second test is the gas chromatography–mass spectrometry test, which can detect the molecular "fingerprints" of the drugs. "A sample of urine, moving through a column of absorbent material, is vaporized, separating compounds according to their chemical and physical properties."[77] This test, unlike the EMIT, eliminates cross-reactivity

[74]Ron Winslow, p. B1.

[75]The Bureau of National Affairs, Inc., "Drug Testing: Laboratory Rating," *Bulletin to Management* (September 6, 1990), p. 281.

[76]Jolie Solomon, "Drug-Testing Firms Eschew Pop Quizzes," *The Wall Street Journal* (September 8, 1990), p. B1.

[77]William Hoffer, "Business' War on Drugs," *Nation's Business* (October 1986), pp. 23–24.

errors[78] and is considered to be 100 percent effective, not counting mislabeling or mishandling problems. Such testing was formerly rather expensive, but the increasing volume of tests has brought the costs down to below $50. Urine samples that test positive at this point are reported as positive test results to the employer. The sample is typically kept frozen for up to 1 year so that any applicants who challenge the test may be provided a sample of the urine for testing in a certified laboratory of their choice.

Suggestions for pre-employment drug testing programs include the following:[79]

1. If any applicants for a job are to be tested, all applicants for that job should be tested.
2. Testing should be conducted without regard to race, sex, religion, or national origin.
3. Provisions should be made for follow-up testing when necessary.
4. Applicants should be warned that drug testing will be required.
5. The body fluid samples must be protected against mishandling and possible contamination.
6. Each applicant should be assured of the confidentiality of results.

There is considerable and justifiable concern over the use and abuse of drugs, alcohol, and other chemical substances in our society. Chapter 14 discusses this concern in detail, as well as drug testing problems and policies for current employees. The emphasis is on the protection of the health, safety, and well-being of employees in the workplace. A positive approach is advocated—employee rehabilitation rather than punishment. The present discussion has focused on employer programs to screen for drug use among applicants. These programs seek to eliminate the incidence of workplace drug use and to improve workplace safety by preventing the employment of identified drug users.

AIDS is discussed in detail in Chapter 14 as a health and safety concern for businesses. At the present time, pre-employment AIDS testing is prohibited under the ADA. Likewise, after a job offer has been made and a physical examination conducted, a negative employment decision may not be based solely on a determination that the applicant has AIDS or tests positive for the AIDS virus. An AIDS-based refusal of employment must be based upon a current inability to perform the job. This inability to perform will in all probability be obvious.

---

[78]Contac, Sudafed, and various decongestants may register as amphetamines, cough syrups containing dextromethorphan can register as opiates, some antibiotics appear as cocaine, Datril, Advil, and Nuprin mimic marijuana, and some herbal teas test positive for cocaine on the tests. See Anne Marie O'Keefe, "The Case Against Drug Testing," *Psychology Today* (June 1987), p. 35, and David Wessel, "Evidence Is Skimpy That Drug Testing Works, But Employers Embrace Practice," *The Wall Street Journal* (September 7, 1989), p. B1.

[79]Many of these points may be found in Jan P. Muczyk and Brian P. Heshizer, "Managing in an Era of Substance Abuse," *Personnel Administrator* (August 1986), p. 100.

Assessment Centers

The use of assessment centers has grown considerably during the last decade.[80] They have become one of the most popular means for gathering information on applicants for supervisory and managerial positions. An assessment center is a central physical location where applicants may come together to have their participation in job-related exercises evaluated by trained observers. The principal idea is to evaluate management applicants over a period of time (1 to 2 ½ days) by observing (and later evaluating) their behavior across a series of selected exercises or work samples. Applicants are requested to participate in in-basket exercises, leaderless work groups, computer simulations, role playing, and similar activities designed to require the same attributes for successful performance as the actual job. After recording their observations (*not evaluations*) of applicant behaviors, the assessors meet to discuss those observations. The decision regarding the performance of each applicant is based upon this discussion of observations. The result is typically a rank ordering of applicants. This rank ordering can then be used with whatever other information is considered appropriate to make selection decisions.

As with any of the information gathering methods discussed thus far, the reliability, validity (accuracy), and predictive validity of the information are dependent upon the particulars of an organization's implementation of the assessment center. That is, the job relatedness of the attributes to be evaluated, the job relatedness and attribute relatedness of the exercises used, the richness and value of the information provided by the exercises, the usefulness of the information, the training and experience of the assessors, and the procedures governing the final assessment are all important considerations when an assessment center is evaluated.[81] There is evidence that the reliability, content validity, and predictive validity of assessment centers are sufficiently high to merit their serious consideration for selection purposes.[82] In addition, the courts have had a generally favorable impression of the fair employment consequences of using assessment

---

[80]A document of considerable historical importance to the assessment center literature is D. W. Bray and D. L. Grant, "The Assessment Center in The Measurement of Potential for Business Management,"*Psychological Monographs*, Vol. 80 (1966), No. 625. This monograph presents the results from the Bell System's Management Progress Study. This was a longitudinal study lasting 8 years. The results from this landmark study encouraged the use and serious study of assessment centers, and is partly responsible for the increased popularity and respectability of assessment centers.

[81]William C. Byham, "How to Improve the Validity of an Assessment Center," *Training and Development Journal* (November 1978).

[82]It should be noted that there is controversy regarding the method used to establish the criterion-related validity of assessment centers. Critics state that the performance measure used, promotions received, is more a reflection of organizational politics than level of performance. See J. J. Turnage and P. M. Muchinsky, "A Comparison of the Predictive Validity of Assessment Center Evaluations versus Traditional Measures in Forecasting Supervisory Job Performance: Implications of Criterion Distortion for the Assessment Paradigm," *Journal of Applied Psychology*, Vol. 70 (1984), pp. 595–602.

centers.[83] As assessment center use has increased, so has the misuse of the logic of assessment centers. Some employers wish to elevate a rather haphazard series of behavioral observations, paper and pencil tests, and interviews, to the status of assessment centers. The Third International Congress on the Assessment Center Method has developed a set of minimum standards (Standards and Ethical Considerations for Assessment Center Operations) and requirements for assessment centers. Among the most important are the following:

- Multiple techniques (e.g., in-basket exercises, leaderless groups) are used.
- Multiple assessors, who have been trained prior to participating in a center, evaluate the results.
- Judgments resulting in a personnel decision are based on pooled data (provided by multiple assessors and techniques).
- The overall evaluation of applicant behavior is made by the assessors at a time separate from the observation of the behavior, and only after all observations from all assessors have been presented and discussed (pooled).
- All exercises used have been pretested and are known to provide reliable, objective, and relevant behavioral information about dimensions, attributes, characteristics, or qualities determined to relate to relevant job behaviors.

■ Alternatives to the Traditional Selection Process

Traditionally, the responsibility for hiring an employee has been shared by the human resources department and the manager of the department where the individual will work. The human resources department may assist in recruitment activities, collecting information on applicants, comparing applicants against minimum hiring standards, and ensuring that the hiring process is consistent with fair employment legislation. The final hiring decision is often made by the manager in charge of the department where the individual will work. In recent years, two alternatives to this traditional process have appeared. The first, employee leasing, makes the actual hiring of employees unnecessary. A firm simply leases part or all of its workforce from an employee leasing company. These employees are not leased on a temporary basis but rather as full-time, long-term help. The employee leasing company is responsible for all of the personnel functions relating to the workforce. The client company no longer needs to recruit, select, keep records on, or compensate any of its workers.[84]

---

[83]For a discussion of the legal status of assessment centers see Frederic D. Frank and James R. Preston, "The Validity of the Assessment Center Approach and Related Issues," *Personnel Administrator* (June 1982), pp. 87–94. These authors present court cases based on content validity arguments that support the legality of assessment center use. See also, Ann Howard, "An Assessment of Assessment Centers," *Academy of Management Journal*, Vol. 17 (1974), pp. 115–135. This is an interesting and complete discussion of assessment centers. It reviews the history, supporting psychological theories, and relevant research on assessment centers.

[84]The Bureau of National Affairs, Inc., "Employee Leasing: Surviving and Growing," *Bulletin to Management* (December 3, 1987), p. 392.

The advantages to employee leasing are considered significant. The client is relieved of many administrative burdens, as well as the need to employ specialized human resource people. Further, employees laid off by the client are sent to another client company as opposed to losing their employment altogether. Some companies have converted their own employees to leased help literally overnight. An arrangement is made with a leasing company to hire all of the firm's employees and to lease them back immediately to the firm. It is clear that companies that lease workers see a real cost advantage in doing so. Smaller firms are more likely to lease their workers. These firms are less likely to have the expertise to understand and comply with the many government regulations and paperwork requirements concerning employees. Further, the costs of medical insurance for smaller firms that may wish to provide it can be prohibitive. All of these concerns become the responsibility of the firm that actually employs the leased workers. One expert has estimated that the total annual revenue of employee leasing companies will grow from the modest $104 million realized in 1980 to $16 billion by the year 2000.[85]

The second alternative to the traditional hiring process is team hiring. The increasing popularity of self-managed work teams in American firms was discussed in Chapter 4. Many of these self-managed teams have accepted the responsibility for selecting new team members. Whereas management made the hiring decision in the past, now the team members might recruit, interview, and select their own coworkers. The specifics of this process are different from firm to firm. Some teams may not recruit or conduct the initial screening of applicants. In those situations, the team selects new workers from among a group recruited and pre-screened by management. Other teams have the responsibility for the entire process, from recruitment to final hiring.[86] The continued movement to self-managed work teams by American companies ensures that team hiring will become more common.

Although it may not seem obvious, the assumptions presented earlier in this chapter are every bit as important for these alternatives as for the traditional process. Whether a firm is leasing workers or using team hiring, accurate, job-related information on applicants is still necessary. The responsibility for the collection, analysis, and use of applicant information simply shifts to the leasing company or the team members.

■ Summary and Conclusions

No personnel function has attracted the outside attention of society and the courts more than employee selection. Society's interest is in ensuring the fairness of the process. Organizational attention has focused on compliance with appropriate state and federal laws and the degree to which their selection decisions provide

---

[85]Paul Scelsi, "The Employee Leasing Remedy," *Management World* (January 1987), pp. 14–15.

[86]John Newstrom, Mark Lengnick-Hall, and Stephen Rubenfeld, "How Employees Can Choose Their Own Bosses," *Personnel Journal* (December 1987), pp. 1–4.

competent employees. This chapter briefly reviewed the legal framework creating the equal employment opportunity environment. It also presented the most critical assumptions underlying the selection process: the assumptions of accurate applicant information, valid job specifications, and the ability to use collected information to predict job performance. Some of the methods employers use to commonly verify that the assumptions are met were also examined. Among the methods discussed were corroboration of applicant information, psychometric examination of psychological tests, criterion-related validation, and the Taylor-Russell and Lawshe expectancy tables.

A variety of sources for applicant information were also presented. Among them were application blanks, references, interviews, psychological tests, and work samples. Our emphasis has been on the quality and usefulness of the information for improving selection decisions. The controversies surrounding honesty and body fluid testing were also outlined and discussed. The future of these tests is uncertain as we attempt to define and balance applicant civil rights with the employer's need to know.

■ Questions

1. This chapter stressed three assumptions considered critical to the selection process. Briefly discuss these assumptions and explain their importance. What additional assumptions do you think are made when we gather and process information on, and make decisions about, applicants?

2. In spite of ample evidence that employment interviews are not very useful in predicting future employee performance, employers continue to use them extensively. What do you feel the reasons are for this? What suggestions would you make to an employer who insists that no person will be hired without a personal interview?

3. Although from a statistical standpoint a predictor may be useful (i.e., an employer can make better selection decisions with it than without it), it may not have a very high level of utility. Explain the difference between the usefulness and the utility of a selection device.

4. Psychological tests are often useful for predicting how well an applicant will perform if hired. What questions should an employer ask before any psychological test is adopted as a part of the selection process?

☐ APPLICATIONS AND CASE EXERCISES

1. The Uniform Guidelines for Employee Selection offer protection against employment discrimination to certain groups of applicants. What requirements or provisions of the Uniform Guidelines do you feel are of most importance to employers? Evaluate the argument that the Uniform Guidelines are unnecessary, since any firm that discriminates against a group of applicants for non-job-related reasons will suffer in the marketplace because the best qualified employees will not be hired.

2. A salesperson has approached you with an inexpensive, easily administered paper-and-pencil honesty test. She claims that the test will reduce employee theft by 50 percent if it is used when making selection decisions. Would you buy the test? How would you "test" the test to see if it meets the standards for applicant information discussed in the chapter? How would you examine the claims of a 50 percent reduction in employee theft?

3. The Felt Corporation has relied upon its first-line supervisors to recruit, interview, and select new employees for its own work units. Over the past few years it has become apparent that some supervisors seem to be far more successful than others at selecting employees who maintain high performance levels and who elect to remain with the organization for longer periods of time. After a series of interviews with the supervisors, it was found that those who were most successful had carefully conceived selection procedures, whereas those who were least successful approached the process in a haphazard manner, basing their decisions upon their first impressions of the applicants and the results of their own favorite psychological tests.

   Michael Tatsuoka, the general manager, is now considering what should be done next. The current situation could be allowed to continue, but the turnover and low productivity that have resulted have been too costly. In addition, he is concerned about the equal employment implications of the current approach to selection. Clearly something must be done.

   What do you recommend that Mr. Tatsuoka do to improve the selection process? Be specific in your recommendations, and justify each one of them.

4. Reread the profile on the selection of American workers by Japanese auto companies at the beginning of this chapter and do the following:
   a. Suggest a strategy that the Toyota plant might use to validate its selection procedures.
   b. Job experience is normally regarded as a positive factor in most hiring situations. However, one Toyota official claimed that experience may actually hinder a candidate's success on the job. Comment.
   c. The job fitness test asks candidates whether they agree with statements such as "It's important for workers to work past quitting time to get the job done when necessary" and "Management will take advantage of employees whenever possible." Discuss the merits of such questions. How relevant are psychological tests for routine factory jobs?

PART TWO INTEGRATIVE CASES

■ Employment Growth in the Temporary Help Industry

The answer to flexible personnel planning for many corporations may lie in what has become known as the *temporary help industry.* Although still small in overall terms, with approximately 750,000 workers, the industry almost doubled in size during the mid-1980s. Indications are that rapid growth will continue through the mid-1990s.

The temporary help industry comprises establishments primarily engaged in supplying personnel to client businesses on an "as needed" basis. Temporary workers are under the supervision of the client business, but they are on the payroll of the temporary help agency. Temporary help companies recruit and screen applicants, check references, administer employment tests, and even train new temporary help. Once an employee is hired, the temporary help agency handles Social Security taxes, unemployment insurance, and other employee benefits.

A company may resort to temporary help agencies when faced with peak business periods or during the summer months when many permanent employees are on vacation. Temporary help may also enable companies to avoid costly overtime payments to permanent employees. Companies with expensive employee benefits packages may use temporary help to reduce medical insurance and retirement plan costs. Temporary help can be used as a hedge against economic uncertainty; when business slows, temporary workers are returned to their agencies. In a similar vein, temporary workers who prove unsuitable are simply replaced by the client business.

Office workers such as secretaries, typists, and clericals comprise the largest segment of the temporary help industry. The industrial segment of the market include laborers, material handlers, and food workers who are unskilled and work at low rates of pay. The medical market within the temporary help industry consists of registered nurses, licensed practical nurses, orderlies, and attendants. Engineers and technical workers are also employed on a temporary basis to help client companies with special projects.

Questions

1. How can temporary help agencies alleviate problems of personnel planning?
2. Do you believe that temporary help agencies can be expanded to include a wider variety of help than is currently being used? What advantages and disadvantages are there to working as an employee in a temporary help agency?
3. Some temporary help agencies also serve as employment agencies, that is, if you are satisfied with the temporary employee, you may hire that person on a permanent basis. What impact would this arrangement have on the recruitment and selection process?

■ The Selection Decision That Went Awry

Lee Bruecher was an airline pilot with a pleasing personal appearance and a questionable background as an aviator. Airline pilots are required by Federal Aviation Administration (FAA) regulations to pass numerous written, medical, and flight tests before being certified to act as a captain or first officer. Airlines supplement these requirements with their own rigorous training programs that include addi-

This case is based on an article by Max L. Carey and Kim L Hazelbaker, "Employment Growth in the Temporary Help Industry," in *The Human Resources Yearbook: 1987 Edition* (Englewood Cliffs, New Jersey: Prentice-Hall, Inc., 1987), pp. 62–8.69.

tional written and flight tests. Although Mr. Bruecher passed the requisite tests, he did so only after several failures. Airline pilots face a highly competitive job market, and the slightest question about a job applicant's ability or safety record is usually sufficient grounds for disqualification. However, Lee Bruecher's good luck turned into a personal tragedy for 26 passengers who were killed when Continental Airlines' flight 1713 crashed shortly after takeoff from Denver's Stapleton Airport in November 1987.

Mr. Bruecher was hired by Continental Airlines after a company personnel officer told a secretary to pluck, at random, some applications from a filing cabinet. His positive attitude and pleasing personal appearance undoubtedly helped his employment prospects. However, a closer look at his personal history would have revealed a darker side to his personality and his capabilities as a pilot. Between 1983 and 1987, he was convicted of nine moving violations while driving his automobile. Most of these violations involved speeding. His Texas drivers license was suspended in 1984–85 because he was regarded as an "habitual violator." Lee Bruecher's record as a pilot also raised a number of questions about his knowledge and competency. He barely passed the written examination for his private pilot license and failed the initial written test for his instrument rating. Knowledge of instrument flying is a critical skill for any professional pilot. He later failed a flight test that was designed to test his competency as a multiengine pilot because he failed to react properly when faced with a simulated emergency. Furthermore, the FAA designated examiner claimed that Mr. Bruecher was totally disoriented while trying to operate the aircraft solely by reference to the flight instruments. After failing to pass the test on a second attempt, he was fired from Able Aviation. He subsequently applied for a job at Rio Airlines, a small commuter airline in Texas, but he failed Rio's flight test.

Mr. Bruecher later applied for jobs at American Airlines and Continental Airlines. He was rejected by American after the company contacted Able Aviation and learned of his flight test failure in Texas. Continental Airlines also did a background check through a Los Angeles security firm. At the security firm, a college student working on a summer job began making phone calls. When Able Aviation was contacted, a different Able employee described Bruecher's work as "very good." Lee Bruecher concealed the fact that he had been fired by Able Aviation and told Continental officials that he left Able because of his desire to advance his career. The Los Angeles security firm also told Continental that Mr. Bruecher had a valid driver's license, but they failed to uncover information on his driving record or his history of poor performance on FAA written tests for pilots. Furthermore, pilots who had flown with Bruecher in the past were not contacted by either the security firm or Continental.

Mr. Bruecher subsequently passed Continental's required tests and began working as a DC-9 copilot. After 9 days of flying experience in the jet airliner, he was involved in the fatal crash in Denver. The National Transportation Safety Board attributed the crash, in part, to Continental's inadequate screening of Lee Bruecher's personal and professional background. Lee Bruecher's inability to pilot an aircraft on instruments was largely responsible for the crash.

Questions

1. What steps should Continental have taken to obtain a more complete profile of Lee Bruecher's background?
2. Continental acknowledged that Bruecher had failed previous written and flight tests but argued that these failures were irrelevant since he later passed the required tests. Evaluate this argument.
3. What impact should a person's off-duty behavior (such as Bruecher's poor driving record) have on a selection decision?

Condensed from William M. Carley, "Slipping Through: How a Marginal Pilot Landed at a Big Airline and Made a Fatal Error," *The Wall Street Journal* (January 19,1991), p. A1.

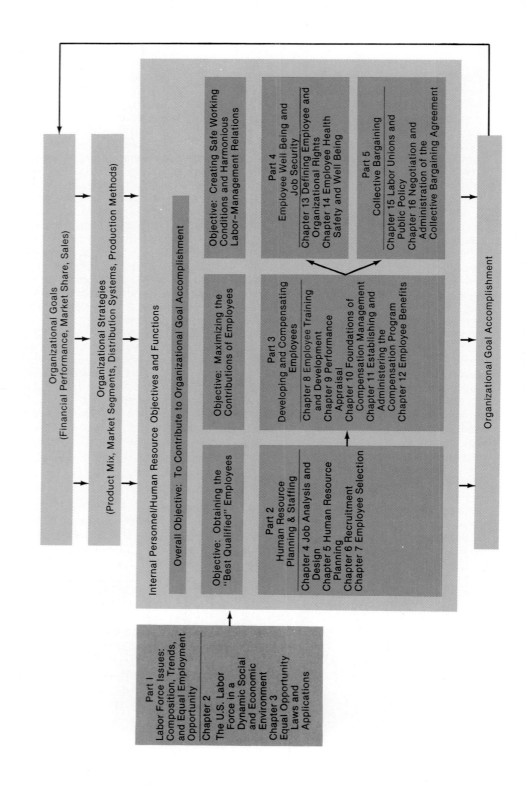

Organizational Goals
(Financial Performance, Market Share, Sales)

Organizational Strategies
(Product Mix, Market Segments, Distribution Systems, Production Methods)

Internal Personnel/Human Resource Objectives and Functions

Overall Objective: To Contribute to Organizational Goal Accomplishment

Objective: Obtaining the "Best Qualified" Employees

Part 2
Human Resource Planning & Staffing

Chapter 4 Job Analysis and Design
Chapter 5 Human Resource Planning
Chapter 6 Recruitment
Chapter 7 Employee Selection

Objective: Maximizing the Contributions of Employees

Part 3
Developing and Compensating Employees

Chapter 8 Employee Training and Development
Chapter 9 Performance Appraisal
Chapter 10 Foundations of Compensation Management
Chapter 11 Establishing and Administering the Compensation Program
Chapter 12 Employee Benefits

Objective: Creating Safe Working Conditions and Harmonious Labor–Management Relations

Part 4
Employee Well Being and Job Security

Chapter 13 Defining Employee and Organizational Rights
Chapter 14 Employee Health Safety and Well Being

Part 5
Collective Bargaining

Chapter 15 Labor Unions and Public Policy
Chapter 16 Negotiation and Administration of the Collective Bargaining Agreement

Part I
Labor Force Issues: Composition, Trends, and Equal Employment Opportunity

Chapter 2
The U.S. Labor Force in a Dynamic Social and Economic Environment
Chapter 3
Equal Opportunity Laws and Applications

Organizational Goal Accomplishment

DEVELOPING AND COMPENSATING EMPLOYEES

■ Once an employee is hired, the organization's concern shifts to developing individual competence and potential on the job. Every year organizations in the United States spend billions of dollars in employee training and development. Training and development expenditures of this magnitude represent an investment in human capital that, if properly conducted, will reap valuable returns to the company. Employee training and development is a primary concern of the personnel/human resource management function and is discussed in Chapter 8. The concepts of learning, assessment of training needs, the strengths and weaknesses of different training methods, career planning, and the evaluation of training and development programs are discussed.

Performance appraisal, the topic of Chapter 9, is one of the most pervasive personnel/human resource management functions. Typically, performance appraisal systems are designed by the personnel department and administered by supervisors. The results of performance appraisals are used to assess employee strengths and weaknesses, define training and development needs, distribute rewards such as promotions and pay increases, validate selection predictors, and provide supporting documentation when terminations and other disciplinary actions become necessary. Chapter 9 discusses the major issues associated with the design and administration of performance appraisal programs. These issues include establishing the proper performance criteria, rater selection and training, the various performance appraisal methods, and conducting postappraisal interviews.

Rewarding employees for their efforts is the primary function of compensation management. Chapter 10 discusses the behavioral, economic, and legal foundations of compensation. Issues such as the motivational effect of money, pay equity, and the impact of pay policies on individual job choice and organizational effectiveness are addressed. The design and administration of a compensation program are discussed in Chapter 11. Organizations are often concerned with wage and salary surveys and job evaluations in order to ensure that compensation programs keep pace with labor market conditions and are equitable in the eyes of employees. Many companies use individual and group incentives to encourage superior job performance. Problems also arise in designing compensation packages for executives, and employees working in foreign locations. A recurring problem with compensation management is the issue of sex discrimination in pay practices. Chapter 11 discusses all of these topics in detail. In recent years, employee benefits have become an integral part of the compensation package in most organizations. Chapter 12 focuses on the use of employee benefits in dealing with the major financial risks faced by persons during their careers. In addition, the provisions, terminology, and issues associated with the most popular employee benefits—group life and health insurance, retirement programs, and others—are discussed.

■ 8

Employee Training and Development

■ LEARNING OBJECTIVES

After reading this chapter you should understand

1. The importance of training to the accomplishment of organizational goals.
2. The variety of ways employees and organizations benefit from training.
3. How to determine organizational and individual training needs.
4. The components of a systematic and effective training program.
5. The importance of trainee characteristics, especially motivation and ability, to the success of a training program.
6. How to select and evaluate outside trainers for your training programs.
7. How to assess the effectiveness of your training program.
8. The questions to ask before instituting a career planning program.

■ INTRODUCTORY VIGNETTE

Manpower, Inc.: Free Training Is Good Business

To anyone familiar with the temporary help industry, Manpower, Inc., is well known. Manpower has over 43 years of experience in placing temporary help and has 1,450 offices in 33 countries. What makes Manpower the topic of this profile is not its size but its aggressive solution to a serious problem. Like its competitors, Manpower was faced with the challenge of finding a steady supply of computer-literate persons for temporary placement. Yet, with an ever-increasing and rapidly changing hardware and software base, how could a temporary help agency offer people skilled in all of the software programs used by potential clients? To make matters worse, when a client was provided with skilled temporary help, it often hired the person full time, and the temporary help agency lost its entire training investment.

The strategy Manpower developed was based on a number of realizations. One was that 35 to 40 percent of their training temps would be hired away by their clients. Manpower decided to accept this as a cost of doing business, reasoning that each temp lost to a client company was an opportunity to strengthen good will. Manpower also realized that trying to advertise for temps skilled in brand new software would not be an effective long-run strategy. It is impossible, over the long run, to wait for a client to identify a software skill, and then to place an ad and quickly hire someone with that skill. Manpower decided to

This profile was drawn from Joseph Oberle, "Manpower, Inc.," *Training* (March, 1990), pp. 57–62.

assume the responsibility of preparing temps on the many programs available, as far in advance of clients' needs as possible. This decision required a time-efficient, inexpensive, and easily understood method of training temps. It also required a steady stream of new employees to replace those hired away by client firms.

The company invested over $15 million to research and develop a computer-based hardware and software training system called *Skillware.* Trainees are given instruction booklets and placed in front of a computer to work through a set of programmed exercises. The exercises allow the trainee to work at his or her own pace and teach only the skills necessary to solve actual office problems. A Skillware facilitator is available to answer questions, and special support manuals are provided for the trainees when they go out on jobs as temps. Skillware has proven to be a method equal to the training task. Employers are excited about the skill level of the temps and impressed by the support documentation prepared for on-the-job use—so impressed, in fact, that clients have asked for copies of the documentation for their own staffs to use. As a good will gesture, Manpower provides the documentation.

The next concern was to generate a steady stream of new employees to replace those hired away. Manpower's advertisements offering up-to-date computer training free of charge took care of that concern. Anyone who qualifies can learn the software absolutely free. This is a strong incentive to answer the Manpower ad. Manpower does not pay trainees while they use Skillware, but estimates the cost at $100 per trainee for a typical 2-day training program. Temps are encouraged to continue to learn different software and hardware systems on their own time. Because of Skillware's ease of use and its obvious self-development benefits, many temps are doing exactly that. Manpower has created a system whereby its product—temporary help—is continually improving itself at a minimal cost on a voluntary basis.

Agreements have been reached with IBM and other computer companies to provide advance copies of new programs and updates to Manpower. This allows Manpower to prepare employees in advance of clients' needs. The Skillware program is continually being updated, requiring Manpower to spend approximately $3 million per year to keep it current.

The early recognition of continual training as an answer to ever-changing technology put Manpower well ahead of its competition. In another move that left the rest of the temporary help industry behind, Manpower opened offices in every Economic Community country and translated Skillware into nine different languages—in preparation for the expected needs of the post-1992 Economic Community. Free training has been good business for Manpower, Inc.

■ Introduction

In 1991 private sector employers spent an estimated $43.2 billion providing approximately 36.8 million employees (31 percent of the total civilian labor force) with 1.2 billion hours of formal training and development.[1] Most organizations pay employees for 100 percent of the time they spend in training (82 percent of total training hours take place on company time).[2] This represents a significant investment in the human resources of this country. This chapter discusses why industry believes such a large investment is necessary, who receives the training, the content of training programs, and how training is conducted and evaluated in the corporate classrooms of America.

The primary impetus for training and development is change. Advances in technology and knowledge are rendering many skills obsolete, while at the same time developing needs for new ones.[3] There have been comic remarks that a college degree should be written in disappearing ink, since technical material has an ever-decreasing half-life (the time it takes for one half of the material to become obsolete). A recent analysis of corporate training programs sponsored by The Conference Board[4] cited one training director who remarked that since the half-life of an engineer is about five years, "a twenty-five-year-old graduate will have to be reeducated eight times in the course of a forty-year career."[5] Nor is engineering the only profession experiencing this continuing need for reeducation. Virtually all workers who draw their expertise from a knowledge base (e.g., physicians, computer technicians) will find it challenging to keep pace with advances in this knowledge base during their careers. The impact of technology has affected the training needs of other levels of workers as well. Typists must now become word processor operators, using micro, mini, and mainframe computers in their daily work. They must master a constantly changing software base that may include electronic mail, word processing, spreadsheet, desktop publishing, graphics, and data base management programs. Cashiers are leaving simple mechanical cash registers behind, as computerized cash registers make it possible to check on the customers' credit history, keep track of inventory, and maintain sales records for departments and stores. As automation continues, competition between union and nonunion firms intensifies, and self-managed work teams grow in number, job specialization will be redefined, with narrow skill distinctions among employees that were once considered necessary and important losing their meaning. This will result in considerable *cross-functional training*. This type of training will broaden an employee's range of skills to accommodate the new job demands.

---

[1]Chris Lee, "Who Gets Trained in What—1991," *Training* (October 1991), p. 48. As impressive as these numbers are, they represent a reduction from the year before. The recession of 1989–1992 forced many companies to reduce training expenditures.

[2]Jack Gordon, "Where the Training Goes," *Training* (October 1986), p. 50.

[3]The Bureau of National Affairs, Inc., "Productivity/Competitiveness," *Bulletin to Management* (July 19, 1990) p. 6. See also Brenda Bell, "Illiteracy: It's Cheaper to Train Them," *Supervisory Management* (September 1991), pp. 4–6.

[4]The Conference Board is a well-respected independent nonprofit business research institute. It has been conducting research on business problems for over 70 years.

[5]Seymour Lusterman, *Trends in Corporate Education and Training*, The Conference Board, Report No. 870, 1986, p. 2.

Change is not always due to advances in knowledge and technology; it also accompanies career advancement. A career spanning 40 years will require proficiency in a number of different positions. Each position will require somewhat different skills, abilities, and knowledge. Many companies anticipate these changing personal requirements and provide appropriate training throughout an employee's career.

As companies are merged, new corporate strategies and products developed, and the rules of international and domestic competition rewritten, change at all levels of a firm becomes inevitable. Under these circumstances, training becomes a strategic tool as employees and management become prepared to take advantage of this change and turn it into profitable opportunity. American business will need fresh, innovative approaches in order to accomplish this, and it is likely that training and development will play a major role. Change will also mean major displacements of workers. An illustration is the more than 17,000 employees who will lose their jobs by the mid-1990s as General Motors continues to reduce its workforce. Consecutive years of slow sales due to intense foreign and domestic competition, coupled with high production costs, forced General Motors to reorganize its production facilities in an attempt to increase efficiency. Ironically, new highly automated production facilities installed by General Motors failed to realize their potential because of a failure to educate the workforce prior to their installation.[6] According to Roger Smith, the company's chairman and chief executive officer, "We found out that automation isn't the be all end-all. It's the skills of the people that are still your limiting factor."[7] It is unlikely that the 17,000 GM workers losing their jobs will be reabsorbed into the automotive industry. Most will find that retraining will make it possible for them to return to the labor force.

Social and demographic forces create changes in the workplace as well. An illustration is the increasing importance of older workers to American industry. According to the American Association of Retired Persons, there are currently 49 million Americans above the age of 55. In 35 years this figure will increase to 91 million.[8] As discussed in Chapter 2, this is due to changes in our standard of living (more people are surviving into old age) and the baby boom of the mid-1940s and 1950s. Overall American industry will come to rely more and more on an ever-aging labor force. This will require deliberate efforts to utilize fully the older worker. Days Inn of America, The Travelers Corporation, Control Data, Kelly Services Inc., AT&T, and others have responded to this challenge by retraining older workers.[9] Rather than stand by as older workers' skills become obsolete, these companies have taken the responsibility of ensuring that they are properly prepared for the new technologies flooding the workplace.

---

[6]Bill Powell, Bill Turque, and Rich Thomas, "General Motors in Reverse," *Newsweek* (September 7, 1987), p. 43.

[7]Bill Powell, Bill Turque, and Rich Thomas, p. 43.

[8]Robert Bove, "Retraining the Older Worker," *Training and Development Journal* (March 1987), p. 77.

[9]Robert Bove, p. 77. See also The Bureau of National Affairs, Inc., "Older Workers Getting the Job Done" *Bulletin to Management* (May 30, 1991), p. 167.

Training should be not viewed, as is often the case, as an activity apart from other organizational activities. Many organizations continue to treat training as an afterthought. In these firms training has become reactive—a series of ad hoc fix-it activities separated from, rather than integrated with, other organizational functions. Under these conditions it is little wonder that training does not contribute much to an organization's goals. As General Motors discovered, the human asset is of primary importance in retaining our competitive edge. Training prepares human resources to accomplish the organization's strategic plan. As a company moves into the future, the success of any initiatives taken depends upon the ability, commitment, and motivation of the human resources involved. There is clearly an important role for training in ensuring the preparation of management and labor alike.

■ Training, Development, and Education

Training is the creation of an environment where employees may acquire or learn specific, job-related behaviors, knowledge, skills, abilities, and attitudes. If one wishes to make a distinction between training and development, it would be that training is directed at helping employees perform better on their current jobs, whereas development represents a future-oriented investment in employees. Development is based on the fact that an employee will need an evolving set of knowledge, skills, and abilities to perform well in the succession of positions encountered during his or her career. The career-long preparation of an employee for this series of positions is what is meant by employee development.

Many discussions of training emphasize a difference between training and education. When this distinction is made, training programs are considered to be designed to limit possible employee responses to those behaviors preferred by an employer. Such responses may be preferred for a variety of reasons. They may be more efficient, safe, or simply consistent with the organizational goals or philosophy. For example, if an unsafe situation develops (e.g., a chemical spill), an employee may be trained in the most appropriate ways of coping with it. The intent is to have the employee react only in certain ways without hesitation. It is in this limitation of responses that training differs from education. Education is considered a means by which the range of possible employee responses is increased rather than reduced.[10] Education represents a broadening of the individual so that he or she may be prepared to assess a variety of situations and select the most appropriate response. Although many unskilled, semiskilled, and skilled positions primarily require training, supervisory and management positions require elements of education. Recently there has been a blurring of the distinction between training and education. As more and more employees are called upon to

[10]See, for example, Bernard M. Bass and James A. Vaughan, *Training in Industry: The Management of Learning* (Belmont, California: Wadsworth Publishing Company, 1969), p. 73.

exercise judgment and to choose among alternative solutions to job problems, training programs have sought to broaden and develop the individual through education. For instance, employees in enriched jobs, self-managed work teams, and/or employees in the service industries may be required to make independent decisions regarding their work and their relationships with clients. Hence, organizations should consider elements of both education and training when planning their training programs. Although the maintenance of this distinction between training and education may be useful, it is not emphasized in this chapter. Rather, aspects of both education and training are assumed to be a part of organizational training programs.

Table 8-1 provides information, by job category, on who is receiving corporate training. This information was gathered by *Training* magazine in a survey of training in America. More than 1,600 organizations of all types are represented in the survey. As can be seen, more than 60 percent of those organizations providing training provide middle management, professional, and executive training. Although only 35 percent of organizations provide production worker training, more people (10.2 million) receive that type of training than any other. Salespeople, professionals, and production workers are exposed to more hours of training (approximately 37–39 hours per year) than other workers. Overall the information

TABLE 8-1   Who Gets the Training

Job Category	Organizations Providing Training (%)[a]	Mean Number of Individuals Trained[b]	Projected Number of Individuals[c]	Mean Number of Hours Delivered[d]
Salespeople	42	51	3.3	39
Professionals	61	65	6.1	37
Production workers	35	189	10.2	37
First-line supervisors	72	33	3.7	34
Middle managers	77	24	2.8	33
Executives	65	8	.8	33
Senior managers	57	12	1.1	33
Customer service people	50	71	5.4	29
Administrative employees	62	37	3.5	16.6

[a]Percent of organization that provide training to people in these categories.
[b]Average number of individuals trained per organization.
[c]Total number of individuals trained in all organizations (in millions).
[d]Average hours of training per individual.

Adapted from Table 1—Who Gets the Training—in Chris Lee, "Who Gets Trained in What." Abridged with permission from the October 1991 issue of TRAINING Magazine. Lakewood Publications, Minneapolis, MN. All Rights Reserved. All data are from organizations with 100 or more employees that provide training to employees in the listed categories.

TABLE 8-2   General Types of Training

Types of Training	Percent Providing[a]
Management skills development	87
Technical skills/knowledge	86
Supervisory skills	83
Communication skills	81
Basic computer skills	78
New methods/procedures	74
Customer relations/services	72
Executive development	69
Clerical/secretarial skills	68
Personal growth	65
Employee/labor relations	57
Sales skills	55
Wellness	54
Customer education	47
Remedial basic education	37

[a]Percent of all organizations of over 100 employed providing each type of training.

Abridged with permission from the October 1991 issue of TRAINING Magazine. Lakewood Publications, Minneapolis, MN. All Rights Reserved. All data are from organizations with 100 or more employed that provide training to employees in the listed categories.

provides an interesting and reasonably complete picture of who receives training, and how much training they receive.

Table 8-2 presents information on the general types of training provided by organizations. Consistent with the number of organizations providing middle manager and executive training, more organizations provide management skills/ development training than any other type of training. Keep in mind that some organizations have little if any need for some types of training. A real estate agency, composed of semi-independent agents, may only provide sales skills and technical skills/knowledge training. There is no need to provide employee/labor relations skills. This information is also drawn from the *Training* magazine survey cited above.

■ The Training Process

Figure 8-1 presents important steps in the training process. An organization must first assess its objectives: What business are we in? What product or service do we wish to provide to customers? At what level of quality do we wish to provide this product or service? Where do we want to be in the future? Once the firm, and other organizational units (e.g., departments) have answered these and similar

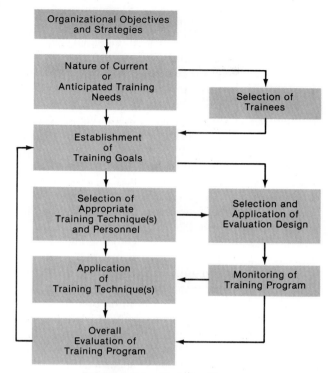

FIGURE 8-1   Training Process

questions, an assessment of human resource requirements should be undertaken. Can our human resources provide the skills, knowledge, abilities, and other personal attributes that are necessary? To the extent that they may lack these attributes, training may be required. The assessment of training needs is perhaps the most important step in the process. It is from this needs assessment that the entire training process will flow. If the organization does not accurately determine its needs, the training process will be inappropriately directed. Methods of needs assessment are discussed later in this chapter, both for the organization as a whole and for individual employees.

After needs have been assessed, trainees must be selected and training goals established. Trainees should be selected with care, ensuring that they and the organization will benefit from their inclusion in the training program. The training goals should ensure that the assessed needs will be served. It is very important that these goals be fully integrated with the organization's human resource training needs. The entire training program will be designed to accomplish these goals; consequently it is important that as training goals are accomplished, the organization's objectives are served.

Once training goals have been established, it is necessary to determine how to conduct the training. This includes the selection of training techniques (e.g., lecture, case study) and trainers (human resources staff, outside consultants) for the program. Additionally, employees' ability should be considered when designing the training program. The intellectual difficulty of the materials used, the organization of the program, the time period (or pace) provided for learning, the level of self-discipline required, and the methods or techniques of instruction should all be sensitive to the ability level of the participants.

At the same time, the means to evaluate the program must be established. Evaluating the effectiveness of a training program (accomplishment of training goals, improved job performance, and accomplishment of organizational objectives) cannot be a haphazard activity. There must be a systematic means for determining the degree to which the program has done what it was designed to do. The means selected for evaluation must be sensitive to the type of training conducted (e.g., communication skills, production skills, initial employee orientation), the training techniques used (lecture, audiovisual, seminar), the training program goals (attitude change, increased knowledge of organizational procedures, skill acquisition), and the initial training needs. The formal evaluation must be directly related to the original program goals.

As training is being conducted, provision must be made for ensuring that the program is proceeding as planned. Without monitoring the training process, it is possible that a well-designed training program may be conducted improperly or otherwise fail to accomplish its goals. It is not practical to allow a program that has gone off course to continue uncorrected. Monitoring allows a training program to be improved before it fails.

The last step in the model is the formal evaluation of the training program. This evaluation must be directly related to the original program goals. If it does not directly address these goals, it does not provide enough information to evaluate the training program. Evaluation involves a comparison of what was accomplished during the training program with what was intended (goals). When appropriate, the comparison may involve statistics. The following discussion reviews each of the steps just outlined in greater detail.

Needs Assessment

The fact that the personal literature is filled with hundreds of articles dealing either in whole or in part with training needs assessment is testimony to its importance.[11] Needs assessment for human resources occurs at two levels. Train-

[11]Irwin L. Goldstein, *Training in Organizations: Needs Assessment, Development and Evaluation* (Monterey, California: Brooks/Cole, 1986). Some informative articles are Gale E. Newell, "Organizing a Successful Management Needs Analysis," *Journal of Systems Management* (June 1981), pp. 30–33; Joe Thomas and Peter J. Sireno, "Assessing Management Competency Needs," *Training and Development Journal* (September 1980), pp. 47–51; John J. Leach, "Organization Needs Analysis: A New Methodology," *Training and Development Journal* (September 1979), pp. 66–69; Henry Langford, "Needs Analysis in the Training Department," *Supervisory Management* (August, 1978), pp. 18–25; Karen L. Vinton, Arben O. Clark, and John W. Seybolt, "Assessment of Training Needs for Supervisors," *Personnel Administrator* (November 1983), pp. 45–51; and Clark L. Wilson, "Assessing Management and OD Needs," *Training and Development Journal* (April 1980), pp. 71–76.

ing needs can be assessed for an individual employee or for employees taken as a group. When training needs are assessed at the group level, it is considered an organizational needs analysis. To illustrate, if a firm decides to install a new computer system in its main office, it would first determine the level of skill necessary to use the system and then determine whether the relevant group of employees had the requisite skills. The determination of employee skill levels is called a *skills inventory*. A skills shortfall (more skills are necessary than exist in the skills inventory) might indicate a need for training.

A skills inventory is an estimation of the types of skills possessed by employees and the number of employees possessing those skills. The skills included in a skills inventory are those that the firm has reason to believe are of importance at the present time or are likely to be of importance in the foreseeable future. A skills inventory may be generated and maintained in a very structured and formal way (e.g., skill tests and computerized employee data bases) or may be an informal assessment on the part of management. Regardless of the depth and formality of the inventory process, its purpose is to inform the firm of its current skills position. Using this current (and in some cases predicted) estimate, the firm will compare skill needs to the skills inventory. This procedure resembles the reconciliation process of human resource planning discussed in Chapter 5. On the basis of this comparison, the firm may determine if there are any current or predicted shortages in particular skill areas. These shortages may be resolved by either the current or future hiring of employees with the necessary skills or through the use of training programs. The failure of General Motors to ensure the preparation of its workers for high-tech automobile manufacturing resulted in the removal of millions of dollars worth of equipment from a car assembly plant in Lansing, Michigan, in mid-1987. The high-tech equipment, which had resulted in increased production costs, was replaced by a traditional conveyor belt.[12]

Training needs assessment can take place at the individual level as well. Analysis at this level is based upon either a comparison of current employee performance to organizational performance standards (performance discrepancy) or a comparison of anticipated employee skill needs to current skill levels. Figure 8-2 demonstrates the performance discrepancy process. Figure 8-3 depicts the

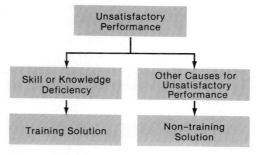

FIGURE 8-2   Performance Discrepancy Needs Analysis

[12]Bill Powell, Bill Turque, and Rich Thomas, p. 42.

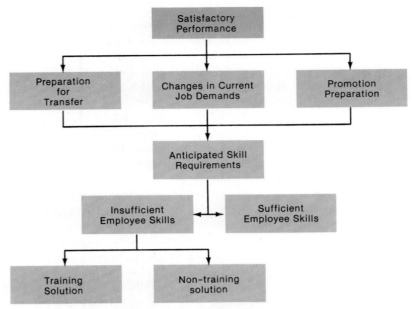

FIGURE 8-3   Anticipatory Needs Analysis

anticipatory assessment process. Performance discrepancy assessment requires that some measure of performance be taken for an employee. That performance appraisal is then compared to the appropriate performance standards. A discrepancy indicates that further analysis is necessary. This additional analysis should reveal whether the performance problem is due to a skill or knowledge deficiency (or other trainable deficiency) or to another problem. The organization may have made a poor selection decision that cannot be salvaged through additional employee training. The employee may have a chemical dependency or personal problems that adversely affect performance. Supervision may be inadequate or the job may have been poorly designed. In any case, it must be determined whether training can improve employee performance. To the extent that training can improve performance, the organization should consider providing it to the employee (assuming that the cost is reasonable). Other options available to the firm include the transfer of the employee to a position for which he or she is better suited (placement/transfer option) or termination due to poor performance. This is the performance discrepancy approach to individual level needs assessment.

An equally important perspective is based upon an *anticipation* of the skills an employee may need in the future. Skill demands will vary as jobs undergo changes and employees progress in their careers. Although changes in employee jobs will invariably result from the dynamic nature of job content and interpersonal relationships, they are becoming more common as technology is brought into the workplace. Changes require that employees be prepared through training and development. Employees may also require training and development to prepare them for career progression. This training can take many different forms. It may range from the relocation and rotation of an employee through various departments and plant locations to the formal executive MBA programs at major universities. Regardless of the specifics of the training effort, it must be based upon a systematic analysis and comparison of current employee skills to those considered necessary for the new position or, in the case of career progression, the series of anticipated positions.

Individuals may also require new skills because of possible job transfers. Although job transfers are rather common as organizational personnel demands vary, they do not necessarily require elaborate training efforts. Employees commonly require only an orientation to the new facilities and jobs. Recently, however, economic forces have required significant retraining efforts in order to assure continued employment for many individuals. Jobs have disappeared as technology, foreign competition, and the forces of supply and demand change the face of American industry.

Methods of Gathering Needs Analysis Data

In order to compare current employee knowledge, skills, and abilities (KSAs) with those that will be needed in the future, two types of information are required. The first has to do with the KSAs necessary to perform the job, and the second indicates the degree to which employees or a particular employee has or needs these KSAs. This information may be collected in a number of ways. Some of these methods work equally well for organizational and individual assessment and include the following:[13]

1. *Advisory Committees.* An organization may seek to establish one or more advisory committees to review job skill demands and the quality of current training and selection programs relative to those demands. These committees may be composed of management personnel and employees. The membership of these committees should be determined by who can best provide the appropriate insight.
2. *Job Descriptions, Job Specifications Task Analyses.* These documents can be reviewed in order to determine which KSAs were considered necessary by a formal job analysis.
3. *Work Sampling.* This refers to the systematic observation by a trained analyst of the job as it is being performed. Like the observational method of job

---

[13]This list is drawn from Michael L. Moore and Philip Dutton, "Training Needs Analysis: Review and Critique," *Academy of Management Review* (July 1978), pp. 532–545; Thomas J. Dilauro, "Training Needs Assessment: Current Practices and New Directions," *Public Personnel Management* (November-December 1979), pp. 350–359; and John W. Newstrom and John M. Lilyquist, "Selecting Needs Analysis Methods," *Training and Development Journal* (October 1979), pp. 52–56. Somewhat different approaches to needs analysis can be found in Leslie Rae, *How to Measure Training Effectiveness* (New York: Nichols Publishing Company, 1986), and S. V. Steadman, "Learning to Select a Needs Assessment Strategy," *Training and Development Journal* (October 1980), pp. 56–61.

analysis, this method has drawbacks. The major drawback is that the analyst must spend sufficient time observing the employee(s) to capture a truly representative picture of the tasks performed, the skills necessary, and the skill level of the employee(s) involved.

4. *Actual Performance of the Job.* In this method of data collection, a trained analyst actually performs the job. From this experience the analyst determines the KSAs required for proficiency. This method can provide useful data for very straightforward jobs. However, the higher the organizational level or the more complex the job, the less useful this method will be. Job analysts are not capable of performing all jobs in the company, especially those that require significant levels of specialized KSAs. Nor is it always possible for the analyst to remain with a job until all possible tasks are performed. There are some jobs in which particular tasks, although important, are performed rarely.

5. *Attitude Surveys.* These are useful for gathering general information on employee satisfaction and other attitudes. These surveys seldom provide information in sufficient detail for the design and planning of training programs, but they can offer information on employee perceptions of the workplace, including current training efforts, promotion preparation, retraining programs, and the like.

6. *Performance Appraisals.* Depending upon the degree of detail and job relevance of the appraisal, this source of information can be very valuable. Employees who consistently fail to perform certain tasks satisfactorily may require training in order to do so. This was discussed as performance discrepancy needs assessment.

7. *Performance-related Documents.* These include productivity reports, absenteeism records, turnover reports, and other performance indicators. These documents are usually collected as a routine part of organizational data collection and can provide insight into areas where training may be necessary.

8. *Questionnaires.* Questionnaires may be given to employees, supervisors, and any other organizational personnel who might be able to provide useful data. These questionnaires may be very detailed and directly address perceived training needs, useful training techniques, and program content. An example of the results from such a questionnaire is seen in Table 8-3. These results are based upon a questionnaire distributed to 976 participants of management and supervisory development seminars. They represent those training needs considered important by at least 50 percent of those questioned.

9. *Skills Tests.* These tests provide an assessment of current employee skill levels. Test results are then directly compared with established skill requirements for the various positions.

10. *Client or Customer Feedback.* This source of information is very valuable, as it represents feedback from those upon whom the firm depends for success. It can also be sufficiently detailed to be of direct use for training planning.

11. *Exit Interviews.* Many employees who are leaving the organization are willing to provide candid assessments of organizational deficiencies. Included among these potential deficiencies may be the current selection process and the preparation provided by training programs.

TABLE 8-3   Rankings of Management Activities
for Which Perceived Training Needs Exist

Management Activity	Percentage Declaring Need
How to use forecasting methods for effective planning.	58
How to use innovation and creativity to maximize plans and organizational objectives.	57
How to base plans and actions on clear, accurate knowledge of company objectives.	57
How to formulate effective plans for achieving organizational objectives.	57
How to promote improvements through effective planning.	56
How to anticipate difficulties and blocks in achieving organizational objectives.	55
How to process long-range planning results.	54
How to select personnel resources to maximize efficiency.	52
How to anticipate difficulties to be overcome in achieving objectives of the organization.	51
How to maximize effectiveness by integrating personnel interests with corresponding positions.	50
How to recognize the individual motivational needs of your subordinates.	63
How to persuade and influence subordinates to support and cooperate in reaching objectives.	58
How to provide opportunities for the professional development of subordinates.	56
How to plan and conduct meetings.	53
How to encourage subordinates to submit ideas and plans.	53
How to integrate task objectives and maintenance objectives to form a team management approach.	52
How to guide subordinates by commendation of good performance and frank discussions of below-standard performance.	50
How to integrate your subordinates' training needs with a personal development plan.	56
How to prepare a personal development plan.	53
How to conduct disciplinary sessions with employees.	53
How to interview potential employees utilizing established job-related criteria.	51
How to control anxiety and feelings of tension.	51
How to handle self-apathy and loss of motivation.	51
How to rejuvenate from a fatigue and stress stage.	51

From Marilee S. Neihoff and M. Jay Romans, "Needs Assessment and Step One Toward Enhancing Productivity," *Personnel Administrator* (May 1982), p. 36. Reprinted with the permission of HRMagazine (formerly *Personnel Administration*). Copyright © 1982, The American Society for Personnel Administration, 606 North Washington Street, Alexandria, VA 22314.

Two human resource researchers have evaluated some of the methods of needs analysis according to the following criteria: employee involvement, management involvement, time required, relative cost, and the degree to which the data can be quantified. Their research results appear in Table 8-4. Although no single method emerges as clearly superior, this research does provide a perspective on the differences among the various methods. Trainers may find that such a systematic examination of methods will allow for more directly useful data collection in their organizations. It has been suggested that the use of multiple methods would allow one method to offset the weaknesses of another.[14]

Selection of Trainees

As training needs are assessed, the particular groups requiring training are also determined. For example, if clients state that customer service employees are not able to locate records and service their accounts quickly and accurately on the phone, then the target employee group is obvious. On occasion, not all employees in a target group are selected for training. One reason is that not all employees may need the training (particularly if performance discrepancy logic is used). Another reason is that some employees may not be expected to participate in transfers or employee career development programs. For example, when training

TABLE 8-4 Contingency Model of Needs Assessment Methods

Method	Incumbent Involvement	Management Involvement	Time Requirement	Cost	Relevant Quantitative Data
Advisory committees	Low	Moderate	Moderate	Low	Low
Assessment centers (external)	High	Low	High	High	High
Attitude surveys	Moderate	Low	Moderate	Moderate	Low
Exit interviews (by personnel department)	Low	Low	Low	Low	Low
Observations of behavior (by trainer)	Moderate	Low	High	High	Moderate
Performance appraisals	Moderate	High	Moderate	Low	High
Performance documents	Low	Moderate	Low	Low	High
Questionnaire surveys and inventories	High	High	Moderate	Moderate	High
Skills tests	High	Low	High	High	High

From John W. Newstrom and John Lilyquist, "Selecting Needs Analysis Methods," *Training and Development Journal* (October 1979), pp. 52-56. Copyright © 1979, *Training and Development Journal*, American Society for Training and Development. Reprinted with permission. All rights reserved.

[14]S. V. Steadman, p. 60.

is directed to the development of supervisory or managerial employees, some employees may not be part of the group that the organization wishes to develop.

Selection for training programs should explicitly consider the ability of the employee to master the material and to use it subsequently. This is not only an important motivational issue but also an important efficiency issue. A training program, like any organizational endeavor, requires the efficient use of resources. Employee failures in the training program itself or on the job after training represent not only personal failure and frustration but wasted organizational resources as well. To the extent that careful selection will make the program more successful, it should be considered. Of course, any evaluation of success should consider the objectives of the program. For example, if the objectives deal with the skills necessary to run a sophisticated, expensive, and complex computer system, the careful selection of trainees is essential. In contrast, if one of the program objectives is to make as many employees feel valued by the organization as possible, the *inclusion* of an employee in the program may be more important than the learning that takes place while the employee is there. Under those conditions, ability requirements for the training program become less important.

A related and important issue is the extent to which the selected employees in the training program are motivated to succeed. Trainee motivation is an essential ingredient in the training process. Individuals who are not committed to learning in the training program can defeat the most well-designed effort. Unfortunately, poorly motivated trainees are common enough to be a problem for most companies. Perhaps the single most common reason for a lack of trainee motivation is the absence of an actual or perceived link between success in the training program and success and rewards on the job. When this link can be established for trainees, a firm is more likely to see trainees committed to learning in the program and to transferring that training to the job. This means that, during training, trainers should focus on the objectives of the program and integrate those objectives with known trainee objectives as early as possible. Actual evidence of the benefits that have accrued to fellow employees as a consequence of the training program would be useful at this point as well. If it is not possible to demonstrate an integration of objectives, or to provide evidence of actual benefits to similar employees, then perhaps the organization should reevaluate the need for the program.

When the firm finds it necessary to select participants for training programs from among its employees, and when that training is necessary for career progression in the company, attention should be directed to ensuring the fairness of the selection process. The equal employment ramifications of training programs will be discussed in greater detail later in this chapter.

Establishment of Training Goals

The goals of the training program must be directly related to the needs determined during the needs assessment phase. Table 8-5 provides an example of needs-based training goals. These goals are for newly hired word processing operators. It is

TABLE 8-5   Training Goals

Knowledge Objectives	
Knowledge objectives refer to an understanding or awareness of particular information.	
Subject	Knowledge Objectives
Disk management	1. Describe the company's system for organizing and labeling data files. 2. Describe the company's storage policies for text files of differing levels of importance. 3. Describe the company's procedures for maintaining backup data files.
Skill Objectives	
Skill objectives refer to a proficiency or expertness at doing something.	
Subject	Skill Objectives
Document creation (using ZIPPO integrated programs)	1. Create a basic text document. 2. Alter the text document by changing the margins to 2.75 inches, changing the font to Alpha font, underlining the headings, and using boldface text for the subheadings. 3. Create a graphics document. 4. Create a simple 100-entry, five-column spreadsheet. 5. Integrate the graphics and spreadsheet into the text document.

assumed that when these goals are met, the training needs will be met and the word processor operators (the relevant human resources in this case) will be prepared to accomplish the established organizational goals. Further, the training goals in this example are clear, and it will be possible to evaluate the extent to which the trainees (and program) have accomplished them. Vague goals, or goals stated in purely emotional terms (e.g., improved job satisfaction), are not as easy to measure, and consequently it is more difficult to assess the impact of training accurately. This relationship between the establishment of training goals and the eventual need to evaluate the degree to which the goals have been accomplished is depicted in Figure 8-1.

Selection of Training Techniques and Personnel

Once training goals have been established, decisions must be made on the training techniques and the personnel to be used in the program. These decisions can directly affect whether training goals can be achieved. For instance, supervisors must occasionally write warning letters to employees who violate company work rules. To be effective, these warnings must be well written and detailed enough to support subsequent disciplinary actions when warranted. If warning letters prepared by supervisors have been poorly written and have consistently failed to support subsequent disciplinary actions, a *performance discrepancy* exists. We realize that supervisors must write higher-quality disciplinary warning letters. An analysis and comparison of the required skills to those possessed by the supervisors may reveal that they lack basic writing skills and that they do not understand the type and degree of detail necessary in a warning letter (knowledge). This *needs analysis* gives us an idea of what the *goals* of the training program should be. At the end of the training program, supervisors (*selected trainees*) should have basic writing skills and possess the knowledge necessary to write warning letters of acceptable quality and detail. To continue our example through the entire process, decisions must also be made concerning *who* will conduct the training (e.g., human resources staff, external consultant) and what *training methods* are to be used (e.g., lectures, films, or reading materials). We can *evaluate* whether the training goals have been accomplished by requiring and evaluating a warning letter written by each supervisor at the end of the training program. Ultimate evaluation is the degree to which the supervisor's letter-writing performance improves on the job.

Training Techniques

Although no single training technique is by nature superior to any other, the goals or objectives of a particular program may be better served by one method than another. This is demonstrated by Table 8-6, which reports the results of a survey of personnel specialists who were asked to rank a limited number of training or instructional methods with reference to how effective they were in helping trainees acquire knowledge, in changing trainee attitudes, in developing trainee problem-solving and interpersonal skills, in gaining participant acceptance, and in trainees retaining the knowledge gained. The higher the ranking (1 is the highest rank), the more effective the specialists felt the technique to be. These results demonstrate that, at least in the opinion of knowledgeable people, there are differences among the methods in terms of how well they serve various purposes.

Among the most commonly used training techniques are lectures, films, audio cassettes, case studies, role playing, on-the-job training, videotapes, simulations (business games), and programmed instruction. Table 8-7 lists various training methods and presents a summary of the most frequent uses to which these methods are put. The table uses two broad classifications of the methods: on-the-job and off-the-job techniques. On-the-job techniques refer to methods that are applied in the workplace, while the employee is actually working. Off-the-job techniques are applied when the employee is not at the workplace. Off-the-job techniques take place in classrooms or meeting rooms away from the workplace. In our earlier example of letter-writing (disciplinary warning) training for supervisors, we established training goals. We decided that supervisors needed to acquire knowledge of what should go into a warning letter, as well as the skill to write one. According to the opinions presented in Table 8-6 and the information in Table 8-7, we might

TABLE 8-6   The Relative Effectiveness of Training Methods:
Expert Opinion and Research

Training Method	Knowledge Acquisition Rank	Changing Attitudes Rank	Problem Solving Skills Rank	Interpersonal Skills Rank	Participant Acceptance Rank	Knowledge Retention Rank
Case study	2	4	1	4	2	2
Conference (discussion)	3	3	4	3	1	5
Lecture (with questions)	9	8	9	8	8	8
Business games	6	5	2	5	3	6
Movie films	4	6	7	6	5	7
Programmed instruction	1	7	6	7	7	1
Role playing	7	2	3	2	4	4
Sensitivity training (t group)	8	1	5	1	6	3
Television lecture	5	9	8	9	9	9

From Stephen J. Carroll, Jr., Frank T. Paine, and John J. Ivancevich, "The Relative Effectiveness of Training Methods—Expert Opinion and Research," *Personnel Psychology*, Vol. 25 (1972), pp. 495-509.

consider programmed instruction or case studies for our knowledge goals and programmed instruction for our skill-building goals.

At this point it might be worthwhile to review selected training methods in greater detail. Those selected for discussion are either commonly used or represent recent and promising innovations. The following methods are discussed: lectures, audiovisual techniques, on-the-job training, programmed instruction, computer-assisted instruction, simulation, case study, and laboratory training.

Lectures are verbal presentations of information. They are considered most appropriate when the goal is to provide a great deal of information efficiently to large numbers of individuals. Some educators are not enthusiastic about the lecture method, pointing out that it represents one-way communication (modified slightly by opportunities to ask questions), and assumes that the lecturer organizes the material effectively and that the audience is so homogeneous that the selected organization, content, and level of difficulty are equally appropriate for everyone. Although lectures are not considered very effective by the training specialists who participated in the survey discussed previously (Table 8-6), there is very little convincing evidence to support the strong negative subjective evaluations found in such surveys of opinion.[15] It would seem, however, that although the lecture method dominates education and training programs, there remain some unanswered questions regarding its effectiveness.

[15]Irwin L. Goldstein, "Training in Work Organizations," in *Annual Review of Psychology* (Palo Alto, California: Annual Reviews, 1980), p. 144. See also Kenneth N. Wexley and Gary P. Latham, *Developing and Training Human Resources in Organizations* (Glenview, Illinois; Scott, Foresman, 1981), p. 130.

TABLE 8-7   Training Techniques and Activities for Which They Are Typically Used

	Orienting New Employees, Introducing Innovations in Products and Processes	Special Skill Training	Safety Education	Creative, Technical, and Professional Education	Sales, Administrative, Supervisory, and Managerial Education
On-the-job techniques					
Orientation training	X				
Job-instruction training	X	X			
Apprentice training	X	X		X	X
Internships and assistantships		X		X	X
Job rotation	X				X
Junior board	X				X
Coaching		X	X	X	X
Off-the-job techniques					
Vestibule	X	X			
Lecture	X	X	X	X	X
Special study	X	X	X	X	X
Films	X	X	X	X	X
Television	X	X	X	X	X
Conference or discussion	X		X	X	X
Case study					X
Role playing				X	
Simulation	X	X	X	X	
Programmed instruction	X	X	X	X	X
Laboratory training			X	X	

From B.M. Bass and J.A. Vaughan, *Training in Industry: The Management of Learning,* Copyright © 1966 by Wadsworth Publishing Company, Inc. Reprinted by permission of Brooks/Cole Publishing Company, Pacific Grove, CA 93950.

Television, videotapes, and films (audiovisual methods) can provide a wide range of realistic examples of job conditions and situations in a condensed period of time. Further, the quality of the presentation can be controlled and will remain equal for all training groups. This method, although similar in some ways to the lecture method (e.g., one-way communication), does not suffer from the effects of instructor availability, instructor fatigue, variations in instructor quality, or classroom limitations (e.g., various locations may be used). It does not, however, allow an opportunity for questions regarding film content (unless coupled with an instructor), nor does it allow for any flexibility of presentation from audience to audience when appropriate.

On-the-job training (OJT) includes all attempts to train personnel in the actual workplace. Table 8–7 provides a list of the various methods that may be classified as OJT training methods. Individuals are trained on the same machines, while doing the same work that will be expected of them when they are fully trained employees. The idea is that OJT will result in *positive transfer* (participation in the training programs leads to improved performance) because many of the conditions for positive transfer are present. For one, the similarity between the training situation and the actual workplace is high. Further, trainees are aware of the relationship between their performance in the training program and their success on the job. Unfortunately, OJT is often haphazardly conducted. Someone is singled out as a trainer and told to show the trainee the ropes. Often the training program is not well planned and systematically conducted by the employee trainer. The teaching skills of these employees may also not be adequate to the task. When the employees selected as trainers are not performing the job as it should be performed, their bad habits become the training model. Perhaps the greatest problem is one of motivation to conduct the training. Not all employees are anxious to teach or to be responsible for teaching someone on the job. This is especially true when time taken out of an employee's workday to train someone is perceived to cost the trainer in terms of his or her own work performance and possible rewards. In addition, a poorly conducted OJT program may create safety hazards, result in damaged products or materials, and pose an unnecessary stress on the trainees.

    Programmed learning and computer-assisted instruction have certain characteristics in common.[16] Both are designed to assist trainees in learning by allowing them to work at their own pace. Further, both methods provide information to the trainee, test the trainee's mastery of the material, and bypass material already learned to concentrate on material with which the trainee is having difficulty. The material is self-contained, so that after an initial orientation to the training materials, the presence of a trainer is not usually necessary. Programmed instruction, in the traditional sense, does not take advantage of computer technology. It combines informational text with paper-and-pencil subject matter tests. In this sense it is similar to traditional training materials. It is in the design or integration of the materials that programmed learning differs from conventional teaching materials. Information is broken down into discrete sections, each building upon the material in the preceding section. The information in a section is studied until the trainee feels that it has been mastered, at which point he or she is tested on it. If the test is passed, the trainee moves to the next section of information. If the test is failed, the trainee is requested to review the material once again or is referred to additional material directly related to the test questions missed. The trainee continues to study the information until a test on it is passed. Some programmed learning materials have a number of tests for each section. This makes it more likely that the material is being mastered rather than the test questions. The materials may also have pretests for each section, so that if the trainee already understands the material, he or she may move directly to the next section. The approach empha-

---

[16]For a thorough discussion of computer-assisted instruction see Franz E. Fauley, "Push-Button Training," *Training and Development Journal*, Vol. 34 (1980), pp. 110–114.

sizes frequent questions, small steps, and specific, understandable, immediate, and accurate feedback.[17] Because trainees move through the material individually, they may do so at their own pace. There are no instructors to become impatient with slow learners, and it is not necessary to adapt to classmates who may learn at a different pace. It is possible to convert a traditional paper-and-pencil programmed learning package for use on a computer. When this is done, the firm is using a form of computer-assisted instruction (CAI).

CAI depends completely upon computer technology, making use of videotapes, videodiscs, light pens, touch screens, computer terminals, and mainframe, mini, and micro computers.[18] Trainees are presented with displays on computer terminals or television monitors. These displays may be similar to programmed learning materials, animated graphics, or video presentations (similar to videotapes). Trainee understanding and skill development are measured and evaluated through responses entered into the computer using a keyboard, light pen, or touch screens. As with traditional programmed learning, each subsequent step is dependent upon the quality of the trainee's response. CAI has the potential to provide a wider range of, and more realistic learning situations than, paper-and-pencil programmed instruction. This is due to the ability of the computer to store a range of alternatives efficiently (eliminating the need for the trainee to deal with bulky stacks of paper), and to the video and audio capabilities of the computer and related equipment. Research has shown that programmed learning and CAI can reduce the training time for some employees; however, there is no clear evidence that the retention of what has been learned is superior to that achieved with more traditional methods such as lectures. Despite its potential, the growth of CAI has not met expectations. Considering its individualized nature, versatility, video, audio, and graphics capabilities, and practically unlimited capacity for information storage and record keeping, this low level of use has disappointed many training experts. It is difficult to explain why CAI has not assumed a more prominent place in corporate training programs, but among the reasons that have been proposed are the following: marketing and distribution problems, the poor quality of off-the-shelf materials (materials are not created by learning specialists), the high cost of materials and equipment, and misapplication of the method (inviting failure)[19]

Interactive videodisc training (IVT) combines all of the advantages of CAI. Although many of the marketing and preparation shortcomings associated with

---

[17]See James Hassett and Sheree Dukes, "The New Employee Trainer: A Floppy Disk," *Psychology Today* (September 1986), p. 33. Jan Meyer, "Interactive Training Systems Offer Choices," *Safety & Health* (August 1991), pp. 56–61, and Anthony O. Putman, "Computer-based Coaching: The Trainer's Missing Piece," *Training and Development Journal* (March 1989), pp. 34–38.

[18]For an interesting discussion of technology-based training, see The Bureau of National Affairs, Inc., "Training: New Way for a New Day," *Bulletin to Management* (March 1, 1990), p. 72. See also Mel Mandell, "Pen-input Aids Illiterate Workers," *ComputerWorld* (September 30, 1991), p. 42.

[19]Mary Jane Ruhl and Keith Atkinson, "Interactive Video Training: One Step Beyond," *Personnel Administrator* (October 1986), p. 66; Dan Siemasko, "CBT Fantasies: The Ground Beckons," *Training* (December 1986), pp. 79–80; Jack Gordon, "Why CBT Isn't Just for Training Anymore," *Training* (April 1986), pp. 42–43.

CAI also characterize interactive videodisc training, training specialists see a bright future for it. IVT offers a considerably richer learning environment than other types of CAI.[20] This is because in addition to a microcomputer, IVT has audio and video storage and presentation capabilities. There are four components to interactive videodisc hardware—the computer (micro, mini, mainframe), the laser videodisc player (similar to those for home use), the laser disc interface, and the television monitor. The laser disc interface is the heart of the interactive system, providing user control of the videodisc player through a computer program operating on the computer. The videodisc looks like a silver 33⅓ phonograph record. One disc can hold 54,000 individual pictures and two audio tracks. Each picture can be randomly accessed. This means that the pictures need not be viewed one after the other in the order in which they occur on the disc. The computer program can go from picture to picture, regardless of where the pictures are placed on the disc. This means that the trainee decides through his or her progress, not the hardware limitations, where the interactive program goes next.

The training situations created using IVT can be very realistically portrayed. Further, the trainee can control the video and audio presentation through a microcomputer keyboard, mouse, light pen, pressure-sensitive writing surface, or voice recognition. The audio track is not synthetic computer speech, but rather standard spoken language stored on the videodisc and presented through the television monitor. Different language tracks can be created for different sets of trainees. Languages other than English can be selected by the trainee through the computer input device. Different levels of information intensity and language complexity can also be selected for the trainee. As with programmed learning, the material is organized so that as a trainee masters a subset of the material (answers questions correctly), the program moves on to another section. If trainees do not answer the questions correctly, they will be branched to a review of the material. The training program contains a number of these branches so that trainee learning can be improved when necessary through repetition. As with other forms of CAI, movement through the material is self-paced. An advantage of IVT, however, is that viewers can stop (freeze frame), back up, and move the video and audio forward at their convenience. This allows them a closer look at the material whenever they wish.

The National Library of Medicine has developed an interactive videodisc medical program that uses voice recognition. Students literally ask questions of the patient (speaking to the video image through the computer) to gather information on symptoms, family history, and even state of mind, in order to diagnose and prescribe treatment. Auto companies, AT&T, IBM, and Jack-in-the-Box restaurants use videodiscs for employee training. Businesses are placing touch-screen interactive videodiscs in stores to answer customers' questions and to help them locate merchandise. Sears Financial Network has created a program to assist people in financial planning and to explain how Sears can help with their plans.

[20]The following discussion of IVT is based on Mary Jane Ruhl and Keith Atkinson, "Interactive Video Training: One Step Beyond," *Personnel Administrator* (October 1986), pp. 66–75, and Ron Peterson, "The Silver Teacher," *Management World* (September-October 1986), pp. 32–33.

The Ford Motor Credit Company, the second largest finance company in the world, replaced most of its classroom training with an interactive video disc system. "Ford Motor Company started a Worldwide Engineering-Release System, translated into five languages, which lists 400,000 automotive parts and more than 300 million pieces of data." There are 25,000 training screens, 1,600 simulations, and 1,500 assessment exercises to teach trainees about the parts.[21]

Expert systems may also be considered a form of CAI.[22] An expert system functions in much the same way a human expert would. Perhaps the easiest type to understand is one that is developed using information provided by a human expert. A human expert would make a decision based upon his or her experience and knowledge. When making a decision, human experts would seek to find answers to specific questions they believe to be important. Suppose that you went to an expert for advice on the purchase of a computer system for your company. The expert would ask you about the purposes for which the computer will be used, the necessary memory and storage requirements, the physical space available for it, and the amount that you are willing to spend, as well as other questions (many designed to probe your initial answers if they do not contain sufficient information). Each answer that you give guides the expert in selecting the system that is right for you. An expert system is designed to do the same thing. Rather than answering the questions of the human expert, you respond to the questions asked by the computer. The software (initial questions, probing follow-up questions, the logic guiding the decision making, the usefulness of your answers) is designed to duplicate the behavior of the human expert. The software is developed by asking acknowledged experts how they would assist someone under similar circumstances. Whenever someone uses the software, it is as though they were having a dialogue with an expert. Some expert systems will actually answer your questions about why they want certain information and exactly how it will be used to make the decision. As people use the software, they become aware of the most important considerations, range of options, and diagnostic reasoning for similar decisions. In short, they become more personally expert as they use the system. An expert system represents an involved programming task with numerous logic rules and constraints. For this reason, expert system shells have been developed by major computer hardware and software companies (e.g., IBM, Carnegie Group).[23] Within a programming shell, a company can develop an expert system uniquely

---

[21]The Bureau of National Affairs, Inc., "Training: New Way for a New Day," *Bulletin to Management* (March 1, 1990), p. 72.

[22]For information on expert systems and artificial intelligence see Frederick Hayes-Roth, "The Knowledge-Based Expert System: A Tutorial," *Computers* (September 1984), pp. 11–28; L. Harris and D. Davis, "AI: What's In A Name," *Unix Review* (August 1987), pp. 33–37; David Kull, "Programming, Not Magic," *Computer Decisions* (September 23, 1986), pp. 41–50; John J. Sviokla, "Business Implications of Knowledge-Based Systems," *Data Base* (Summer 1986), pp. 5–19; P. Harmon and D. King, *Expert Systems: Artificial Intelligence In Business*, (New York: Wiley, 1985). See also, Valdis E. Krebs, "How Artificial Intelligence Assists HR Managers," *Personnel* (September 1987), pp. 58–61. This is a technical article on how to use prolog, a major artificial intelligence programming language, to create expert systems.

[23]David Kull, p. 44.

suited to its needs without the need for specialized and expensive programmers. The more sophisticated and versatile the shell, the larger the computer system needed to run it and the more expensive it is to purchase. Expert system shells for a mainframe computer can range from a few thousand dollars to more than $100,000. A number of expert system shells have been made available for microcomputers. Although comparatively limited in capability, these shells can serve many of the same purposes for which expert systems would be used for training.

The relationship of CAI to the larger area of computer-based training (CBT) should be understood. CBT includes CAI and computer-managed instruction (CMI). The latter refers to a system used to keep track of trainee performance, score trainee responses, or otherwise provide data or control the training process. CMI and CAI may be implemented separately or together as a computer-based training system.

Simulation. Simulation refers to any materials that attempt to create a realistic decision-making environment for the trainee. Simulations present likely problem situations and decision alternatives to trainees. The materials, for example, may try to simulate the activities of an actual organization. The trainee would be asked to make whatever decisions are necessary to support these activities. The results of those decisions are reported back to the trainee with an explanation of what would have happened had they actually been made in the workplace. Trainees learn from this feedback and improve their subsequent simulation and workplace decisions. Simulations can be very sophisticated, requiring the trainee to make highly interrelated decisions. Thus, earlier decisions affect both subsequent problems and alternatives. An example of a sophisticated simulation is a business simulation, where trainees are requested to make marketing, pricing, and production decisions for a product or service for a hypothetical firm. The quality of their decision making (performance feedback) is provided in the form of financial and production reports. The decisions are interrelated, and the success or failure of the firm will depend on each decision and how well all of the decisions were integrated. The more realistic and detailed the situation, and the more interrelated the decisions, the more difficult it is to administer the simulation. This is why sophisticated simulations, particularly business simulations, are computer based. Trainees are requested to enter their decisions on a floppy disk (microcomputers) or through a keyboard (mini or mainframe computer). The simulation administrator processes the decisions, organizes the reports, and presents them to the trainees. These computer-based simulations may also be considered a form of CAI.

Machine simulations are also used for training. Perhaps the best-known mechanical simulation is the flight simulator. Airlines and military services use simulator hours, which are less expensive than actual aircraft hours, to train pilots. Simulators can be used to create unusual situations or, for example, with flight simulators, very dangerous ones. The potential to create critically important but rare situations enhances the value of machine simulators.

A new technology-based approach to training simulations is currently being refined. This technology is called *virtual reality.* It is computer based and requires elaborate software and hardware, including special headgear and gloves. The technology of virtual reality can place someone inside a computer-generated, three-dimensional reality. You could design a home and then, in an almost literal sense, walk around inside it. You could walk through the rooms, turn corners, climb stairs and move the furniture. Very sophisticated training simulations can be created using virtual reality. This technology is not yet commonly available for training, but it is likely to be available in the late 1990s.

Laboratory Training (Sensitivity Training). The goals of laboratory training are as follows: the development of a spirit of inquiry and a willingness to experiment with one's role in the organization and the world; an increased awareness of other people, an "expanded interpersonal consciousness"; improved authenticity in relationships with others, including a reduction in the need to play a role; an increased ability to collaborate with supervisors, peers, and subordinates rather than to use authoritarian approaches; and an increased ability to resolve conflict through developing alternatives and problem-solving techniques as opposed to manipulation, coercion, or compromise.[24]

Laboratory training is conducted in groups under the leadership of an experienced trainer. These groups may be composed of strangers (no association with the organization or each other), organizational members not known to each other, or co-workers. The groups may be very structured, with a written agenda, or unstructured (on occasion even leaderless).[25] The training groups meet in a neutral site away from the workplace. This serves to reduce tensions and break down the formal relationships that may exist in the workplace. Individuals meet face to face in one or more intensive sessions. These sessions are designed to facilitate a sharing of attitudes, perceptions, and personal beliefs. Occasionally, the information shared and the dynamics of the group become very personal, and, in the view of some, dangerously so.[26] Overall, these groups have had considerable success in making people more aware of themselves and the way they interact with others. The major drawback to their use is that often this new awareness, and accompanying changes in behavior, are not supported in the actual work environment. This results in pressures for the employee to revert to the old patterns of behavior and interpersonal interactions that were supported in the past.

Case Study. A case study provides a detailed description of a particular series of real or hypothetical events. The events described in a case study take place over a specified period of time. Case studies might describe the activities of a business organization (e.g., the formative years of IBM) or the interactions of individuals (e.g., a confrontation between a supervisor and a subordinate). Through the study of the case, trainees trace the events of importance and discuss, individually or in groups, what they have learned from them. To the extent that they have sufficient detail to provide realistic and complete information to the trainee, and the trainer is knowledgeable of the case and the technique, case studies can be very useful.

---

[24]E. Schein and W. Bemis, *Personal and Organizational Changes Through Group Methods: The Laboratory Approach* (New York: John Wiley & Sons, 1965), as found in Edgar F. Huse, *Organization Development and Change,* 2nd ed. (St. Paul: West Publishing Company, 1980), p. 367.

[25]Edgar F. Huse, p. 369.

[26]Irwin L. Goldstein, p. 258.

Table 8-8 lists some of the methods discussed here. Not all of the methods or materials discussed in this chapter were represented in the survey upon which this information is based.[27] Videotapes have overtaken lectures as the most commonly used technique. Video and audio teleconferencing are growing in popularity, yet are used by only a small percentage of the firms responding to the survey.

Selection and Training of the Training Personnel

The selection and training of the trainers is very important. The quality of the organizational training effort is heavily dependent upon the ability of the trainer to plan, organize, execute, and evaluate the training program. To some extent, this dependence on trainer skills can be lessened by providing prepackaged materials or a program designed by training experts. However, most organizations depend upon their training staffs to design the entire training program, from needs assessment to evaluation. Hence, they must be aware of how people learn, the most appropriate methods for assessing training needs, how to establish training objectives and integrate them with the diagnosed needs, how to bring together the different training methods to accomplish these objectives, and, perhaps most important, how to communicate effectively. There are a number of alternatives to assist organizations in securing training for their training personnel. University programs, private training consultants, and formal programs established by such organizations as the American Management Association may provide trainers with opportunities for skill development and upgrading and knowledge acquisition.

TABLE 8-8   Use of Instructional Methods and Materials

Instructional Methods/Materials	Percentage of Surveyed Organizations Using the Method
Videotape	90
Lecture	85
Role playing	65
Audiotapes	51
Games/simulations	48
Slides	46
Films	44
Case studies	44
Noncomputerized self-study programs	23
Video teleconferencing	10
Audio teleconferencing	6
Computer conferencing	5

From Chris Lee, "Who Gets Trained in What." Reprinted with permissin from the October 1991 issue of TRAINING Magazine. Lakewood Rublications, Minneapolis, MN. All Rights Reserved.

[27]Chris Lee, "Who Gets Trained in What— 1991," *Training* (October 1991), p. 50.

Two personnel researchers have provided insights into some common trainer pitfalls that may lead to program failure. An understanding of these potential problems should be provided during trainer training. They include the following:[28]

1. *Training and development are regarded as a cure-all for all organizational ills.* The belief that any problem can be solved through some type of training is unrealistic. (For example, to believe that all communication problems can be solved through communications training, that all production problems can be solved through production training, and that inferior recruitment and selection processes can always be offset by some form of employee training is not reasonable.) It must be appreciated that although training can prove a useful solution to many organizational problems, it cannot be applied to all of them with equal effectiveness.

2. *Trainees are not adequately motivated to capture their attention and commitment.* As discussed earlier, failure to motivate trainees is one of the best ways to ensure that a training program will fail. People cannot learn when they are inattentive, and they will not change their on-the-job behavior without reason to do so.

3. *One training technique is assumed to be applicable to all groups, in all situations, with equal success.* A single training technique simply cannot be equally effective in all situations for all trainees. The technique selected must be suitable to the ability of the trainees, the content of the program, and the evaluation criteria selected.

4. *Trainee performance is not evaluated once the employee has returned to the job.* A training program based on performance improvement needs must ultimately be evaluated with reference to the degree of positive transfer that takes place. Under these conditions, accomplishing training program goals can never take the place of improved employee job performance as the evaluation criterion.

5. *Cost-benefit information, in order to evaluate the training program, is not gathered.* The use of organizational resources brings with it certain responsibilities, especially the justification that the expense was merited.

6. *Management support is lacking.* Trainers must get the commitment of management to the training program. Without such commitment, trainees and others may not take the program seriously.

7. *The central role of the supervisor is not recognized.* It is the supervisor who will manage the actual work environment. The success or failure of the training program depends upon whether the work environment supports the results of the program (e.g., changes in work methods, employee behavior, attitudes, and so forth).

8. *Training alone is never powerful enough to lead to long-term, verifiable performance improvement.* Although the supervisor manages the work environment,

[28]This material is drawn from Laird W. Mealiea and John F. Duffy, "Nine Pitfalls for the Training and Development Specialist," *Personnel Journal* (November 1980), pp. 929–931; and Dean Spitzer, "Five Keys to Successful Training," *Training* (June 1986), pp. 37–39.

considerable resistance to change may remain. Training transfer may not be possible if resistance to change cannot be overcome. The trainer must prepare the workplace to accommodate the newly trained personnel by anticipating the forces resisting change.

9. *There is little or no preparation or follow-up.* If you "drop an employee into a training program and plop him back on the job; little will change."[29]

Trainers and those responsible for supervising trainers should be aware of what constitutes unacceptable trainer behavior. A survey of members of the American Society for Training and Development provides insight into those behaviors considered unethical by professional trainers. These behaviors are presented in Table 8-9.

TABLE 8-9   Major Categories of Behavior Considered Improper or Unethical for Training and Development Professionals

Major Categories of Behavior Considered Unethical	Typical Response
Lack of professional development	1. "Not 'keeping up'—expanding their own knowledge." 2. "I've seen lots of 'good old boys' who are not educated in the training profession transferred into training." 3. "Application of 'technology' without understanding concepts, theory, etc."
Violation of confidences	4. "Breaking the trust of classroom participants." 5. "Relating information gathered in the classroom back to the organization." 6. "Identifying client deficiencies to others." 7. "Reporting information given in confidence."
Use of "cure-all" programs	8. "Consultants selling programs without any effort to even estimate the needs of the client." 9. "Continuing use of 'sacred cow' type programs when need for them is no longer valid." 10. "Continuation of programs long after they have served their purpose."
Dishonesty regarding program outcomes	11. "Concealing truth on program results." 12. "The assurance that a training program produced results when in fact it was only a good 'show.'" 13. "Falsifying training records to make results look better than they are."

[29]Dean Spitzer, p. 37.

TABLE 8-9   (continued)

Major Categories of Behavior Considered Unethical	Typical Response
Failure to give credit	14. "Failure to give credit for work done by others (includes materials, instruments, and even whole courses)."
	15. "Not giving credit when using another's research."
	16. "Illegal copies of printed and taped matter from existing suppliers' programs."
	17. "Copyright violations."
Abuse of trainees	18. "Treating course participants as children."
	19. "Treating training participants as 'lesser' individuals of little importance."
	20. "Racist and sexist remarks."
	21. "Use of profanity."
	22. "Unwillingness to obtain input from the trainees."
	23. "Using trainees to practice training techniques and exercises to meet trainer rather than group needs."
	24. "Using sexual relations with seminar participants as a portion of training."
Other improper behaviors	25. "Consultants designing programs that give people what they want rather than what they need."
	26. "We must be trainers, not entertainers."
	27. "Lack of follow-up in order to see that programs are properly implemented after the classroom training."

Application of Selected Training Technique(s)

Once the techniques and personnel have been selected, the next step is to conduct the training. The location of the training, the training facilities, and other operational problems must be determined prior to this point. These considerations should not be an afterthought. The accessibility of the location, the comfort of the facility, and the quality and age of the materials and equipment are all very important to the success of the program. As the training is being conducted, it is important that the progress of the trainees be monitored. This might be accomplished by periodic skill or knowledge tests or periodic observation of the program by the personnel/human resource department. Additionally, there is much to recommend observation as a means for monitoring the training program. Frequently the interactions among trainees and trainer can contribute quite a bit to the understanding of what was accomplished. These interactions are rich in information about trainee learning. This richness cannot be captured by the standard end-of-program evaluation. Regardless of the form of monitoring selected, it is necessary that monitoring be done.[30]

Evaluation of the Training Program

Although the evaluation of a training program takes place after the training has been completed (*posttest*), it is essential that some measure of the skill, knowledge, or attitude of the trainees be determined prior to the program (*pretest*). Evaluation designs that do not allow for pre- and posttraining comparisons of the appropriate attributes do not provide sufficient information to evaluate trainees' progress in the program. Even when a determination of trainee progress can be made, it must still be determined whether the training, or some other events that took place at the same time as the training, caused the measured progress. These two issues (amount of change and source of change) require that an organization consider the evaluation process in depth prior to the actual training program. Figure 8-4 provides some examples of training evaluation designs. The Xs represent the training program(s), the Os represent the observations of some measure of training objectives (e.g., trainee skill acquisition, attitude change, trainee reactions, knowledge acquisition or retention), and the subscripts represent sequential time periods.

The first design (Design One) represents a training program in which no observations are taken prior to the training program. Although the relevant trainee attributes are measured after the training program, it is impossible to determine whether any improvement has been made. No comparison of the level of trainee attributes (knowledge, skills, attitudes) before training (*pretraining*) is known. The only situation in which this type of design may provide useful information on the changes that took place during the training program is when the trainees had *no* relevant knowledge or skill at the start of the training. (Pretraining level of the attribute is zero.) This is a rather weak design and, unfortunately, is used all too often as a result of convenience, ignorance, a deliberate attempt to hide the ineffectiveness of a training program, or some combination of the three.

The second design (Design Two) allows for the critical pre- and posttraining comparison. This design can provide information on the degree of improvement (or change) but not the source of that improvement. Thus, the training program may receive credit for causing changes that are due to other events. Nevertheless, this design represents an improvement over Design One and can be used with slightly more confidence. It is especially effective when the organization can logically eliminate any alternative sources for the changes that took place during

---

[30]There are a number of issues that are not addressed in this and the preceding sections. These issues deal with basic learning variables such as whole versus part learning, overlearning, and practice strategies. See T. T. Baldwin and J. K. Ford, "Transfer of Training: A Review and Directions for Future Research," *Personnel Psychology*, Vol. 41 (1988), pp. 63–105, for a complete discussion of these issues.

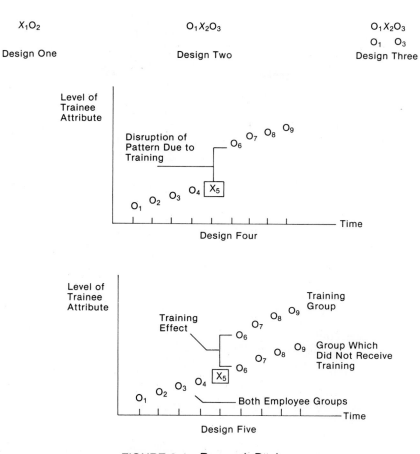

$X_1 O_2$

Design One

$O_1 X_2 O_3$

Design Two

$O_1 X_2 O_3$

$O_1 \quad O_3$

Design Three

FIGURE 8-4 **Research Designs**

training. To the extent that such alternative sources cannot be eliminated, and there is reason to believe that they may have indeed influenced the changes seen, this design is inadequate.

The third design (Design Three) attempts to deal directly with both of the evaluation issues of concern to a firm. In this design the firm divides the trainees into two groups, with one group receiving the pretest, the training, and the posttest, and the other group receiving the pretest and the posttest only. The logic is that the changes in the group receiving the training should be significantly greater than the changes in the group that received no training. Assuming that the two groups are equivalent[31] and that the administration of the pre- and posttests,

---

[31]The issue of equivalence is quite important. The best way to ensure that the employee groups do not differ significantly is to assign employees randomly to the two groups. Whenever multiple groups are suggested for any of these designs, it is safe to assume that random assignment would improve our ability to determine differences between the groups.

when coupled with the training, does not somehow create an impact separate from the training itself, this design will meet the needs of most organizations. Sometimes there are problems in generating two equivalent groups of employees. For example, a firm may compose the two groups from two different shifts or physical locations. This will minimize the contact between the employees who are receiving the training and those who are not. Contact between the two groups might allow for an exchange of information regarding the training and compromise the effectiveness of the comparisons. Unfortunately, many differences can exist between employees on different shifts or in different locations. Those differences may show up as measured change when training effectiveness is being evaluated.

A design that can effectively cope with most of these problems, as well as additional problems not presented in this discussion, requires four groups of equivalent employees. The design is called the *Solomon four-group design*. Because it requires four groups of equivalent employees, it is often impractical for an organization to use. For this reason, the two-group design (Design Three) may be the most practical design.[32]

There is another type of design that may be useful for evaluating training. These designs are classified as *time-series* designs. They require multiple observations of the status of trainee attributes over time. Many of these observations are taken prior to training (*baseline data*), with the remaining observations taken after the training has been completed.[33]

The first of these designs to be discussed (Design Four) uses only one group of employees. This design is referred to as an *interrupted time-series design*. The pretraining observations establish a pattern or baseline for these attributes. The posttraining observations can provide information on whether a pattern has been disrupted by the training. A disruption of this pattern may be considered evidence of a training program effect. Note that this design is similar to Design Two in that observations are made immediately before training (O_4), and immediately after training (O_6). The difference is that with the baseline data to refer to, it is less likely that an observed upward or downward trend in the data would be interpreted as a significant training effect. Design Four can be expanded to include two groups of employees, thereby significantly increasing the power of the design (Design Five). This type of design is referred to as a *multiple time-series design*. There are a number of examples of this type of design in the training literature. Figure 8-5 shows how a design similar to this was used to provide evidence to evaluate a safety training program. In this study, three different groups of em-

[32]The issues surrounding the use and misuse of these designs can become very technical. For a complete discussion, see D. T. Campbell and J. C. Stanley, *Experimental and Quasi-Experimental Designs for Research* (Chicago: Rand McNally and Company, 1963). This text remains the classic work in experimental design. For a more application-oriented discussion, see Jack Phillips, *Handbook of Training Evaluation and Measurement Methods* (Houston, Texas: Gulf Publishing Company, 1983), and Donald Kirkpatrick, *Evaluating Training Programs* (Washington, D.C.: American Society for Training and Development, 1975).

[33]When the training extends over a long period of time, observations (measurements) are sometimes also taken during the training period.

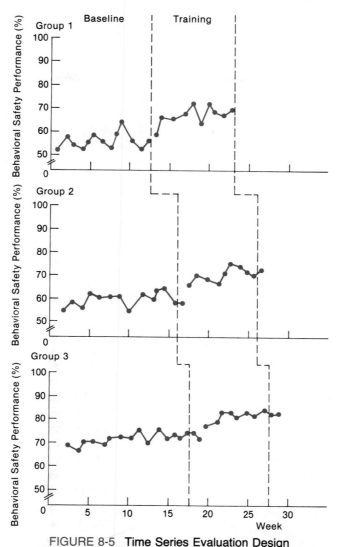

FIGURE 8-5   Time Series Evaluation Design

Source: Robert A. Reber and Jerry A. Wallin, "The Effects of Training, Goal Setting, and Knowledge of Results on Safety Behavior: A Component Analysis," *The Academy of Management Journal* Vol. 27, No. 3 (1984), p. 554. Reprinted by permission.

ployees received safety training at different points in time. The disruption of the data trend for each group, at exactly the time that they received the training, is strong evidence that the training improved the safety performance of these employees. This design is called a *multiple baseline design.*[34]

[34]Robert A. Reber and Jerry A. Wallin, "The Effects of Training, Goal Setting, and Knowledge of Results on Safe Behavior: A Component Analysis," *The Academy of Management Journal*, Vol. 27, No. 3 (1984), pp. 544–560.

A final note on statistical analysis should be added. Simple differences in *observed* employee attribute levels should not be interpreted as meaningful differences. Statistical analyses should be performed on the data. Analyses for Designs Two and Three (Design One cannot be analyzed) are rather straightforward, and guidance may be found in many elementary statistics textbooks. However, statistical analyses for time-series designs can become very complex, and are best left to professional statisticians and others trained in data analysis. Further, statistical significance does not necessarily mean that the differences found are sufficiently large to justify the continued existence of the training program.[35]

Two issues important to the evaluation of training programs have not yet been discussed. Assuming that the training program has resulted in real improvements in trainee skill, how likely is it that other participants in the company will also experience these same skill improvements? There may be something unique about the trainees used in the initial training program. The trainees in the initial program may be volunteers, and may be better qualified and more motivated than later participants, who may be forced to attend the training. For example, some firms have been pleased with the success of training given to self-managed work groups when those groups were composed of hand-picked volunteers. These companies are very concerned that the training may not be as effective when other participants, not hand-picked and not volunteers, are required to participate. Another issue is whether training program success in one organization can be generalized to other organizations. Many things will be different in each company, and those differences may translate into different training program results. This issue is important when, for example, the company is considering using outside consultants with a prepackaged training program. Although the program may have been effective elsewhere, it may not be in this company.

Career Planning and Management Development

Two types of organizational training that merit separate mention are career planning and management development training. When firms intend to provide opportunities for their employees to advance through positions of increasing responsibility, they often share the responsibility for both the planning and preparation of employees for those moves. This planning and preparation may include career planning training and management development programs. Career planning training helps employees define and establish their own roles in the planning of their careers. Employees may meet formally or informally with a representative of

[35]There is an ever-growing literature on the evaluation of training programs. Some of the more interesting and useful articles are J. Kevin Ford and Steven P. Wroten, "Introducing New Methods for Conducting Training Evaluation and for Linking Training Evaluation to Program Redesign," *Personnel Psychology*, Vol. 37 (1984), pp. 651–665, and Donald L. Kirkpatrick, "Four Steps to Measuring Training Effectiveness," *Personnel Administrator* (November 1983), pp. 19–25.

the firm to discuss their personal goals, the skills and knowledge necessary to accomplish these goals, a realistic timetable against which to evaluate goal accomplishment, and how the company can help them achieve their goals. The company representative may also distribute or assist the employee in locating useful career planning materials. This career counseling provides benefits to both the organization and the individual employee. It provides employees with a long-term perspective on their employment with the firm, creates motivation for them to seek out and participate in training programs, and demonstrates the firm's interest in their personal well-being. From the organization's perspective, employees are more willing to identify closely with the firm, more likely to perceive it to be in their own interest to earn high performance evaluations, and more likely to establish realistic personal goals.

Prior to instituting a career planning program for employees, an organization must confront a number of important questions. Table 8-10 provides a list of those questions. They include concerns regarding the components of the program, the employees who should be involved, and the level of resources to be invested. All of the questions deserve serious consideration before an organization commits its resources to a career planning program.

Although career planning training is useful for employees at all levels of the organization, *management development* refers to training reserved for those who currently are or who are about to become managers. A variety of training falls under the management development umbrella. Management development is characterized not so much by training content as by the overall objective—to develop managers.[36] One management researcher has provided an illustrative and useful definition of management development training: "The goals of management development are to support the strategic objectives of the corporation; provide for interdivisional consistency in management philosophy; support the integration of human resource functions, such as career development, appraisals, and encourage an open, flexible, participatory management style."[37]

Consistent with the goals presented previously, development training may take many forms, including university courses and degrees, job rotation (transfers) within lower managerial ranks,[38] and seminars on sexual harassment, motivation, discipline, corporate finance, time management, stress reduction strategies, problem solving, management theories, leadership, strategic planning, and human relations, among other topics. Typically it is very difficult to evaluate the tangible benefits of a management development program. The ongoing nature and future orientation of management development make it difficult to determine when such

[36]Thomas A. Newburg, "Exercises for Better Management Development," *Personnel Journal* (October 1980), pp. 850–852; Richard A. Eastburn, "Developing Tomorrow's Managers," *Personnel Administrator* (March 1986), pp. 71–76.

[37]Julia R. Galosy, "Curriculum Design for Management Training," *Training and Development Journal* (January 1983), pp. 48–51.

[38]John M. Moore, "The Role Relocation Plays in Management Development," *Personnel Administrator* (December 1982), pp. 31–34.

TABLE 8-10   Questions to Be Answered Prior to the Institution
of a Career Planning Program

Why do we want a career planning program and what do we want it to do for us?
For what specific groups of employees do we want to provide career planning?
Should a career planning program be mandatory or voluntary for these groups?
How do we identify members of groups for whom the program might be mandatory?
  Voluntary?
Should our program be generic or custom-tailored to each selected group?
How much responsibility for career planning should be given to that employee? How
  much to the organization?
What should the components of the program be?
  Informal counseling
  Reference assistance
  Career discussions
How much of our resources (people, time, money) are we willing to commit?
Who should have the primary organizational responsibility for a career planning system?
What career planning aids are needed?
  Workbooks
  Career path manuals
  Visual aids
How can training be provided for line managers and how can line management support
  of specialists be assured?
How can we link career planning to our supporting personnel systems?
  Performance evaluation
  Promotion and transfer policies
  Training and development programs
  Job rotation plans
How can we take advantage of new techniques (technology) in human resources
  management?
Can we respond adequately to employees whose expectations are raised?
How can we ensure follow-up accountability in order to encourage commitment and
  determine degree of success?

From Milan Moravec, "A Cost-effective Career Planning Program Requires a Strategy," *Personnel
Administrator* (January 1982), pp. 28-32. Reprinted with the permission of HRMagazine (formerly
Personnel Administrator). Copyright © 1982, The American Society for Personnel Administration, 606
North Washington Street, Alexandria, VA 22314.

benefits should be evaluated. It may take many years before acquired knowledges,
skills, and abilities are necessary on the job. Regardless, 87 percent of organizations participating in a recent survey (Table 8-2) indicated that they provide management development training. They must perceive the return on their investment, however ill-defined, to be worthwhile. Like other types of training,
management development sends a signal to employees that they are valuable and
that the firm is willing to invest in their future.

■ Equal Employment Opportunity Considerations

Whenever some (but not all) employees are selected for training programs, a firm must be sensitive to discriminatory behavior. This is especially true when training programs are a part of the promotion and merit pay processes. For example, when training is a job prerequisite, employers must realize that selection for the training program is in reality a preliminary screening device for job selection. In addition, it should not be more likely that a particular sex or race will have consistently superior performance in the program or be more likely to complete the training program successfully. This may occur because the training materials or machines are designed in such a fashion that one group has an advantage over another.[39]

■ Summary and Conclusions

Training is important to organizations because it can make the accomplishment of organizational goals possible. When organizational and training objectives are accomplished, very important benefits result for the organization as well as the employee. When successfully conducted, training can benefit the organization through increased profitability, improved employee morale and commitment, increased employee awareness of organizational goals, an improved organizational image, improved labor relations, employees who are better able to adjust to technological and organizational changes, and increased flexibility in human resource planning and placement. The employee benefits through increased skill and job knowledge levels (thereby increasing that employee's sense of worth, potential performance, and promotability), improved self-confidence, a sense of belonging and membership in the organization, a sense of control over his or her future, and an opportunity to accomplish personal goals.

This chapter presented an overview of organizational training and development. The intelligent design, implementation, and evaluation of organizational training efforts were emphasized. Special attention was given to organizational and individual needs analysis as the most important step in the training process. Training needs should directly determine the program goals, the trainees and training methods selected, and the design and criteria used for program evaluation. Training and development represent opportunities for the firm to invest in its current employees. Like any investment, training must be viewed in terms of its returns. This chapter discussed the likely organizational and individual returns of a well-designed training program.

[39]For an excellent presentation of these and related issues see C. J. Bartlett, "Equal Employment Opportunity Issues in Training," *Human Factors*, Vol. 20, No. 2 (1978), pp. 179–188.

■ Questions

1. New employees are often trained by other, more experienced employees on the job. Briefly discuss the advantages and disadvantages of this approach to training. What can an employer do in order to ensure that this training is being properly conducted?

2. It is not unusual for employers to begin training programs with only a cursory needs assessment. Explain why needs assessment is so critical to the training process and why you feel that employers often spend less time on needs assessment than might be necessary.

3. An employer is most interested in improving employee job performance through training. How can positive transfer (posttraining improvement in trainee performance) be maximized?

4. Discuss the various types of needs assessment methods presented in the chapter. Assume that you want to conduct a needs assessment for production workers. Which of the methods would provide useful information and which would not? Explain your choices.

5. The growth of IVT has not been as rapid as many experts predicted. What do you think the reasons are for this? What are the advantages of IVT over other forms of CAI? For what topics do you think IVT would be the best training method in this course? Why?

6. Research virtual reality as a potential training method. Consider the application of virtual reality to create training simulations for engineers, airline pilots, combat soldiers, architects, and school bus drivers. What, if any, would be the advantages of virtual reality over other training methods for these occupations?

☐ APPLICATIONS AND CASE EXERCISES

1. Gloria Ruhl is very troubled after a stormy session with her first-line supervisors. She had just agreed to a supervisory training program to be conducted by a local university. She felt that it would help improve their performance and morale. Unfortunately, the firm has not been doing well lately, and a number of hourly employees and some supervisors need to be terminated. The tempers ran high in the meeting as the supervisors charged that the money spent on the training program could be better spent saving the jobs of three supervisors. Ms. Ruhl could not argue with the dollars-and-cents logic of their position, but she knew that the benefits of the training program would result in higher productivity and higher profits for the firm. It was her belief that the training program would go a long way toward preventing another series of firings. She has decided to request that the faculty conducting the training program do an assessment of training needs in order to demonstrate to the supervisors that the training program is necessary.

   As Jordon Mitchell, her assistant, types the request, he cannot help but wonder if the needs assessment should have been done before the training program was planned.

   a. What do you think about the complaints raised by the supervisors? Do you believe that saving three jobs is more important than a training program that could raise productivity and protect the remaining jobs?

   b. Mr. Mitchell has questioned Ms. Ruhl's judgment when she scheduled a training program without a formal needs assessment or a means to evaluate its effectiveness. Do you agree with him? What exactly would you ask of the trainers and the training before scheduling a program?

Performance Appraisal

■ LEARNING OBJECTIVES

After reading this chapter you should understand

1. The importance of employee performance appraisals to other personnel functions and to the careers of individual employees.
2. The EEO requirements for performance appraisals.
3. The common rating errors that can compromise the quality of a performance appraisal.
4. The types and limitations of common performance appraisal methods.

■ INTRODUCTORY VIGNETTE

Digital Equipment Corporation: Team Performance Appraisals

When a company adopts a self-managed work team approach to job design, an important issue is whether to delegate the responsibility for co-worker performance appraisals to team members. As you will see in this chapter, performance appraisals have traditionally been the responsibility of management. Digital Equipment Corporation, one of the largest computer systems manufacturers in the world, has developed a participatory performance appraisal system for its self-managed work groups at its Colorado Springs, Colorado, facility. This system allows co-workers, the individual for whom the appraisal is being written, and management (in the person of the group facilitator) to assemble and share information regarding employee performance.

Digital has decided that its approach to performance appraisal for work group members should emphasize employee self-development and participative goal setting in a collaborative environment. A performance appraisal committee is created, as necessary, for each employee. The employee who is to be appraised is asked to select a co-worker to be the chairperson of the performance appraisal committee. The management facilitator for the work group, and two other work group members chosen at random, join the chairperson and the employee to create the total appraisal committee. The employee is asked to provide each work group member with a statement of personal accomplishments and training over the past year. The chairperson collects the reactions of

The information presented was taken from Carol A. Norman and Robert A. Zawacki, "Team Appraisals—Team Approach," *Personnel Journal* (September 1991), pp. 101–104.

work group members to this statement and forwards them to the employee. The employee is then asked to write a performance appraisal document incorporating the co-workers' input. This document is provided to the members of the appraisal committee. After the committee members have had an opportunity to review the document, the entire committee, including the individual, meets to discuss it. If it is decided that the document needs to be revised, the employee is asked to revise it, and another meeting is scheduled. When the committee accepts the document, a performance rating is determined and goals for the next performance appraisal period are set. The chairperson writes a summary of the meeting(s), including the rating and any personnel recommendations decided upon and, after it is signed by all committee members, including the appraisee, forwards it to the personnel department.

This process creates a high level of involvement across co-workers, management, and the individual employee. The performance appraisal input is job-related, rich in content, fully discussed, and openly dealt with before a performance rating is determined. Obviously, this approach is not for every company. It requires employees and management to be highly committed to the company's goals, to the process, and to each other. Unfortunately, this level of commitment is the exception, not the rule, in American business organizations. The program at Digital shows that there is promise for a highly participatory approach to performance evaluation. It remains to be seen how widespread such an approach will become during the 1990s.

◼ Introduction

Performance appraisal is the process of assessing the quantitative and qualitative aspects of an employee's job performance. Performance appraisals should provide answers to some basic yet important questions for both the employee and the employer: "How well am I doing?", "How can I do better?", "How well are our employees doing individually and collectively?", "What can we do to help our employees do better for us and for themselves?", and "For which employees are various personnel actions appropriate?"

Most organizations have a formal performance appraisal program. This holds true for both large and small, union and nonunion, and manufacturing and non-manufacturing (including nonbusiness) companies. Most employees are involved in these programs as well, with production, office/clerical, professional/technical, first-level supervision, middle, and even top management included.

Performance appraisal is often a difficult and emotion-laden process. An employee's self-image, status in the work group, motivation, promotion and career opportunities, merit compensation, and commitment to perform and improve are all linked to the performance evaluation. Consequently, issues associated with the fairness, accuracy, and use of performance appraisal results are very important, deserving the employer's careful attention. This chapter will highlight considerations important to the design and implementation of fair, accurate, and useful performance appraisal systems.

It should be appreciated that even with the best of intentions, it is unlikely that performance appraisals can ever be made *completely* objective and accurate. One major reason is that we as human beings have limited information processing capabilities.[1] However, completely accurate and objective performance appraisals require the processing without error of complex and occasionally inconsistent information. These demands almost certainly exceed our information processing capabilities. Further, it should be realized that organizations are political in nature, and many decisions, especially evaluative ones, may be heavily influenced by their probable political consequences. A manager may be less interested in providing an accurate appraisal than in motivating or otherwise influencing the behavior of subordinates. Interpersonal dynamics are often more important to a harmonious and efficient workplace than an accurate appraisal for a particular subordinate. In addition, managers may shy away from having candidly accurate evaluations filed in an employee's permanent personnel folder. An employee's motivation, commitment, and possibly entire career may be adversely affected by such statements. These realities make it possible that no organization, however hard it tries, will be able to eliminate political behavior from the appraisal process. Such appreciation notwithstanding, the appraisal process should not be dismissed as merely another example of organizational politics. It is important to realize that performance appraisals will probably always reflect an element of discretion, and that such discretion is not necessarily bad.[2] In spite of the human limitations on the objective processing of information and the political realities of the workplace, it remains possible for performance appraisals to achieve a high level of fairness, accuracy, and usefulness in business organizations.

■ The Performance Appraisal Process

The major steps in the performance evaluation process are presented in Figure 9-1. In this section we briefly discuss each step, reserving more detailed discus-

[1]Jack Feldman, "Beyond Attribution Theory: Cognitive Processes in Performance Evaluations," *Journal of Applied Psychology*, Vol. 66 (1981), pp. 127–148. An important area of research that examines performance appraisal from an information processing viewpoint is quickly developing. Researchers are concerned with why some, as opposed to other, appraisal information is attended to, whether information is stored in long- or short-term memory, how information is organized in our memories, and how we retrieve it and combine it for decision making. The hope is that as we better understand this sequence of cognitive events, we will be better able to create fair, unbiased appraisal systems. An example of this research can be found in Kevin Williams, Thomas Cafferty, and Angelo Denisi, "The Effect of Performance Appraisal Salience on Recall and Ratings," *Organizational Behavior and Human Decision Processes*, Vol. 46 (1990), pp. 217–240.

[2]This discussion of political influences on performance appraisals is drawn from Clinton O. Longnecker, Dennis A. Gioia, and Henry P. Sims, Jr., "Behind the Mask: The Politics of Employee Appraisal," *The Academy of Management Executive* (August 1987), pp. 183–191.

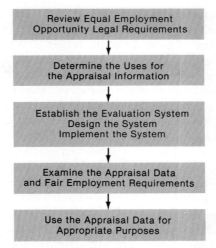

FIGURE 9-1   The Performance Appraisal Process

sions for later in the chapter. To facilitate this discussion, the figure creates the impression of discrete and relatively independent, sequential steps in the performance appraisal process. However, the steps are interrelated, and decisions made at an earlier point may depend on considerations appearing later. The process as we discuss it is somewhat idealized. Many organizations make every effort to approximate the ideal process, resulting in first-rate appraisal systems. Examples include Reynolds Metals, Amoco Corporation, Allstate Insurance Companies, and Xerox Corporation.[3] Unfortunately, many others fail to consider one or more of the steps and therefore have less effective appraisal systems.

The laws and regulations discussed in Chapter 3 are very important, especially when performance appraisals are used to support personnel decisions. They must be considered before the appraisal system is developed. There is little point in investing considerable time and expense to design and implement a formal evaluation system that is likely to result in unfair treatment of employees and run afoul of EEO laws and regulations.

Once the requirements of an EEO environment are appreciated, the organization must consider the purposes to which employee evaluation information will be put. For example, it can be useful for providing performance feedback to individual employees, assessing training and development needs (discussed in Chapter 8), documenting personnel decisions such as merit pay, promotions, and disciplinary actions, and validating selection processes (discussed in Chapter 7).[4] It is unlikely that all these purposes can be adequately served by any single

[3]Advisory Board on Human Resources Management, *Performance Appraisal—What Three Companies Are Doing* (Chicago: Commerce Clearing House, Inc., 1985). See also, The Bureau of National Affairs, Inc., "Personnel Shop Talk," *Bulletin to Management* (April 4, 1991), p. 98.

[4]For a discussion of the various uses of performance appraisals, see Jeanette N. Cleveland, Kevin R. Murphy, and Richard E. Williams, "Multiple Uses of Performance Appraisal: Prevalence and Correlates," *Journal of Applied Psychology*, Vol. 74 (1989), pp. 130–136.

approach to performance evaluation. Decisions must be made regarding purposes important for particular times, levels, and jobs in the organization. Evaluation information that can assist in career development may be very important for entry-level managers, and yet not as important for the housekeeping staff. The evaluation system used for each job should be capable of providing whatever job-related information is considered important. Although any appraisal method used must generate accurate and fair data, it is not necessary, and perhaps not possible, to accomplish everything desired using only one approach and one formal evaluation. The search for the ideal appraisal instrument, suitable for all jobs and personnel decisions, is seldom practical.

Once the purpose(s) to which the evaluation information will be put has been determined, the actual system(s) that will collect it must be designed and implemented. Design issues include the frequency of administration, the form the data should be in, the aspects of performance that should be evaluated, the selection of the individuals who will do the evaluating, the method of evaluation, the materials to be used, a determination of acceptable performance levels, and necessary training for the evaluators.

Implementation begins with the establishment of performance standards for the individual employee. Employees and supervisors should review the evaluation materials (e.g., rating scales) and establish levels of acceptable performance that are sensitive to the specific tasks, duties, and responsibilities of the job. As employees carry out their job duties, those responsible for evaluation should be monitoring performance levels. Routine monitoring is essential if the rater is to have sufficient exposure to the employee's performance prior to evaluating it. An important part of implementation is a review of the completed appraisal with the employee involved. Necessary adjustments in employee behavior should be agreed upon, and future performance goals should be established. Assuming that the evaluation information has met EEO requirements, it may then be used for the purpose(s) for which it was intended.

■ The Equal Employment Opportunity Environment

A discussion of the current EEO environment is a prerequisite to any consideration of appraisal system design and implementation alternatives. A concern for the requirements of an EEO environment prior to the institution of a system will improve the quality and usefulness of performance information and provide the documentation necessary to support any legal challenges.

The majority of appraisal-related litigation during the last few years has resulted from the use of evaluations to support promotion, discharge, layoff, and merit pay personnel decisions.[5] These cases have involved Title VII of the Civil Rights Act

[5]David C. Martin, Kathryn M. Bartol, and Marvin J. Levine, "The Legal Ramifications of Performance Appraisal," *Employee Relations Law Journal* (Winter 1986–1987), p. 371.

of 1964, the ADEA, the Equal Pay Act, and related statutes.[6] With the exception of merit pay allocation, these personnel decisions may be considered selection decisions and may be subject to the same scrutiny by the courts as those selection decisions discussed in Chapter 7.

Employers who base promotion decisions on performance must be prepared to demonstrate valid performance documentation supporting these decisions. The documentation should objectively compare employees on defensible job-related criteria and should appropriately support the relative superiority of the promoted employee over the employees not promoted. For many promotion decisions, performance evaluation information will supplement other types of information used to make the selection decision.

Discharge decisions must be supported by valid documentation establishing that the employee no longer meets, or never met, minimum job performance standards. Discharge documentation should demonstrate one or more of the following: a chronic pattern of unsatisfactory performance, a deterioration of past performance, or serious but previously unnoticed performance shortcomings.[7]

Employers who can demonstrate a carefully conceived, systematic, and well-publicized method of allocating merit pay have had little trouble defending differential awards. However, when merit pay is allocated on the basis of highly subjective grounds, employers will find that where any differences (however unintended) appear to parallel the age, race, sex, or religion (among others) of employees, awards will not be legally defensible. An appraisal system that can provide objective and valid information on defensible, job-related criteria, that compares the performance of employees with one another or with established, mutually agreed-upon standards, will meet the requirements of an EEO environment.

◼ Uses of Performance Appraisal Information

Decisions regarding the design and implementation of the performance system must be consistent with the intended use(s) of the information. It is at this stage that an organization may realize that multiple evaluation systems are necessary. It is entirely possible that information intended for different uses (e.g., promotion decisions or identification of training needs) should be gathered using different methods.

Performance Feedback

Most employees are very interested in how well they are doing at present, as well as how they can do better in the future. They wish to have this information not

[6]David C. Martin, Kathryn M. Bartol, and Marvin J. Levine, p. 371. See also Christopher S. Miller, Joan Kaspin, and Michael H. Schuster, "The Impact of Performance Appraisal Methods on Age Discrimination in Employment Act Cases," *Personnel Psychology*, Vol. 43 (1990), pp. 555–579.

[7]David C. Martin, Kathryn M. Bartol, and Marvin J. Levine, p. 382.

only for the personal satisfaction that positive feedback provides, but also to help them improve their performance in order to qualify for organizational rewards such as promotions and merit pay. Performance feedback is very important to employees, and in the absence of meaningful feedback from the supervisor, employees will resort to informal methods to assess their job performance. Employees may become very sensitive to whether supervisors speak to them, spend time with them, or take them into their confidence regarding departmental affairs. These informal methods can approach superstition, and are the unfortunate consequences of a failure to provide adequate, regular performance feedback.

Performance feedback that is specific, timely, accurate, understandable, and presented in an atmosphere of cooperation and support can improve the quality of subsequent employee performance. It may serve as a source of satisfaction and motivation and, when necessary, as a guide to the adjustments necessary for performance improvement.[8]

Employee Training and Development Decisions

As discussed in Chapter 8, performance appraisal results may be used to determine whether an employee or group of employees will require additional training and development.[9] Deficiencies in performance may be attributable to inadequate knowledge or skills. For example, a word processor operator may improve his or her efficiency by attending seminars designed to show a newly installed machine's full capabilities. A pilot for an air charter service may require training in a new aircraft in order to use its systems safely and efficiently. The performance appraisal system must be sufficiently detailed to isolate specific, trainable performance deficiencies.

For managerial personnel, the performance appraisal process may point to the need for additional development as a means of improving current job performance in areas such as supervisory techniques, interpersonal conflict management, planning and budgeting, and so on. In addition, a manager may be groomed for a higher-level position if the performance appraisal results indicate that he or she has the potential to perform well in an advanced position.

Regardless of the organizational level being evaluated, performance appraisal systems are the primary means of delineating employee weaknesses that can be alleviated through training and development programs. Appropriate appraisal information can be used as a basis for tailoring a specific training and development program to aid employees in reaching their potential.

[8]For an interesting discussion on the positive consequences of feedback, see Sharon Nelton, "Feedback to Employees Can Nourish Your Business," *Nation's Business* (July 1985), pp. 62–63.

[9]Howard P. Smith and Paul J. Brouwer, *Performance Appraisal and Human Development: A Practical Guide to Effective Managing* (Reading, Massachusetts: Addison-Wesley Publishing Company, 1977), pp. 35–42, and Richard Henderson, *Performance Appraisal: Theory to Practice* (Reston, Virginia: Reston Publishing Company, 1980), pp. 228–230.

Validation of Selection Programs

Performance appraisal provides a means of validating both internal (promotions and transfers) and external (hiring new employees from outside sources) selection programs.[10] As discussed in Chapters 6 and 7, organizations spend a great deal of time and money recruiting and selecting employees. Application blanks, interviews, psychological tests, and other measures are used to predict probable applicant performance on the job. Many organizations hire industrial psychologists to construct elaborate selection devices to predict performance as measured by the organization. The definition and measurement of performance are not as difficult with regard to the quantitative aspects of a job (level of sales by a salesperson, error rates, days absent from work, and so on), but the qualitative aspects (ability to analyze complex problems, interpersonal effectiveness, effective delegation of work, and the like) pose much more difficult measurement problems. Nevertheless, measures or scores from the various selection devices given to job applicants must be correlated with job performance measures as a means of analyzing the validity or usefulness of selection devices. When inadequate attention is given to the proper measurement of employee performance, the effort and expense devoted to developing sophisticated selection devices are wasted. An inadequate performance evaluation system used in a criterion-related validation study creates what is called the *criterion problem*. When this happens, the selection device is validated against performance information that does not represent true levels of performance (not a valid measure of performance). Under these circumstances, the validity coefficient is not accurate, useful, or defensible because the company will be predicting something other than future applicant performance.

Documentation and Support of Personnel Decisions

Compensation Decisions

Compensation decisions, to varying degrees, are based on the results of an employee's performance appraisal.[11] Although pay raises are a function of increases in the cost of living, productivity, seniority, and the financial condition of the organization, employee merit (as measured by performance appraisal) is also an important factor. Merit pay is allocated across many different jobs and departments in an organization. Information provided by the appraisal system should be such

[10]A detailed discussion of this topic is presented in Chapter 7. See also Richard D. Arvey and Robert H. Faley, *Fairness in Selecting Employees*, 2nd ed. (Reading, Massachusetts: Addison-Wesley Publishing Company, 1988), pp. 151–164.

[11]A specific examination of the link between performance appraisal and compensation is presented in Chapter 10. See also E. E. Lawler, *Pay and Organizational Effectiveness: A Psychological View* (New York: McGraw-Hill, 1971); Gary P. Latham and Kenneth N. Wexley, *Increasing Productivity Through Performance Appraisal* (Reading, Massachusetts: Addison-Wesley Publishing Company, 1980), pp. 138–142; Richard Henderson, pp. 234–247; and Jerrold R. Bratkovich and Bernadette Steele, "Pay for Performance Boosts Productivity," *Personnel Journal*, Vol. 68 (1989), pp. 78–83.

that employee performance levels across different jobs can be compared. Employees also expect consistency in merit increases across similar jobs when they are being performed equally well.

Pay raises, when based on merit, are often a sensitive issue because they represent a message to the employee regarding his or her value to the organization, as well as a standard of comparison with his or her peers. For this reason, pay raises that are geared to the quality of performance should depend heavily on an objective, unbiased assessment. If subjectivity or favoritism affects the measurement of an employee's job performance and such evaluations are subsequently used to make pay-related decisions, the employee's morale and motivation may be damaged.

Promotion, Transfer, and Layoff Decisions

The selection of one employee for promotion over others who are also eligible is based, in part, on the result of an evaluation of past employee performance. Presumably, an organization wants to promote the best-qualified individual. A rejection for promotion may be based upon the following performance-related reasons: performance shortcomings on the current job, poor performance when given responsibilities directly related to the new job, or superior performance by the employee who did receive the promotion.

Performance appraisal is also useful in making transfer and layoff decisions, especially in a nonunionized environment. Like promotions, transfers often involve changes in job responsibilities, and it is important that employees capable of assuming such responsibilities be clearly identified. Employees may also be rank ordered for layoff, with the weakest performers being the first let go. Like the other personnel actions discussed, the effectiveness of promotion, transfer, and layoff decisions will depend directly upon the quality of the performance information generated by the system.

Grievance and Discipline Programs

Performance appraisal results can be used as an important source of documentation for formal grievances that are filed in connection with employee disciplinary actions.[12] This is especially true in unionized organizations that have highly structured grievance procedures where the final step is binding arbitration (a quasi-legal forum used for resolving many employee-employer disputes).

An organization may attempt to terminate an employee for general incompetence, only to discover that the performance appraisal process is so poor that there is no acceptable documentation of substandard performance. In fact, known marginal employees have received positive performance evaluations simply because supervisors failed to take the process of performance appraisal seriously.

We have discussed in Chapter 3, and again in this chapter, the proliferation of EEO laws, regulations, administrative decisions, and court cases that underscore

---

[12]See Chapter 13 for a more complete discussion of disciplinary issues.

the need for procedural due process and fairness in evaluating employee performance and administering punitive measures. In the event that an employee files a legal suit against the organization, it becomes imperative that an adequate defense is available in the form of valid performance appraisals that clearly support and justify the managerial action.

■ Establishing the Evaluation System

This section deals with the many decisions necessary in establishing the evaluation system. Among these are decisions regarding the frequency of administration of the system, the behaviors or aspects of employee performance that will be evaluated, and the selection and training of the evaluators. This section discusses these and other concerns that must be addressed prior to the establishment of the evaluation system.

Administrative Considerations

A number of administrative considerations may influence the development of the performance appraisal system, including the frequency of administration, computer compatibility of the data, development and maintenance costs, and ease of use.

The frequency with which performance appraisals are administered depends on both practical considerations and the type of employee(s) being evaluated. Generally speaking, more frequent appraisals (shorter appraisal periods) are beneficial for correcting employee performance deficiencies and possibly increasing motivation. Administratively, however, overly frequent performance appraisals may occupy a disproportionate amount of supervisory time, to the obvious detriment of the supervisor's other duties and the quality of the performance appraisal process.

Several factors enter into the decision of how often appraisals should be completed. First, performance appraisals may be geared to the reward cycle. In public sector organizations, for example, pay raises are usually given annually. It makes sense, therefore, to complete performance appraisals prior to granting pay raises if such raises are based in whole or in part on merit.[13] Second, performance appraisals may be based on a task cycle, with the evaluation of job performance being made upon the completion of a specific project. Third, performance appraisals may be completed more frequently on lower-level jobs where good versus bad performance can be discerned in a relatively short amount of time. On the

---

[13]Some companies believe that the performance review and feedback should be completed well before any consideration of merit pay allocation. This belief is based on a desire to focus the feedback session on performance issues rather than on the effect the appraisal will have on pay. See Advisory Board on Human Resources Management, *Performance Appraisal—What Three Companies Are Doing* (Chicago: Commerce Clearing House, Inc., 1985), p. 20, and The Bureau of National Affairs, Inc., "Performance Reviews Revisited," *Bulletin to Management* (January 30, 1992), p. 32.

other hand, the performance of persons working in higher-level, managerial, and executive positions generally requires longer periods of time to evaluate because many actions and decisions made by these individuals cannot be fully and accurately assessed in the short run. Fourth, to prevent bottlenecks where a supervisor must complete numerous performance appraisals at the same time, it may be possible to stagger the dates of employee evaluations over a longer period of time, for instance, on the 6-month or 1-year anniversary of their employment.

Some organizations may also be concerned about the ease with which the appraisal information can be made computer adaptable.[14] This is important when personnel records are kept on computer tapes or disks, as when HRISs are used for personnel decisions. It becomes particularly important when large numbers of appraisals must be entered into the computer. For this reason, some firms may wish to facilitate data entry by using computer-scannable forms, whereas others may require that appraisals be completed on computer screen facsimiles of the appraisal instrument.

The development and maintenance of the selected system are also important issues for some organizations. Elaborate systems requiring considerable time and effort, and perhaps sophisticated statistical analyses in their development, may have higher developmental and maintenance costs. Systems that rely on secret scoring keys may require periodic revisions as the scoring keys become less secret over time. These costs must be considered reasonable within the budget allocated to performance appraisal.

The ease with which alternative appraisal methods can be used may heavily influence the decision to select one method over another.[15] All things being equal, methods that are easier to use will be preferred. Ease of use will reduce not only potential confusion, errors and misunderstandings, but also the time required for training the rater and administering the evaluation.

Performance Criteria—What Should Be Evaluated?

On the surface, the decision regarding what should be evaluated in performance appraisal may appear to be straightforward. Performance appraisal criteria are commonly based on individual traits, cost-related outcomes, and behavioral criteria.[16] However, two major problems pertaining to the criteria used to measure employee performance must be addressed.

First, it is generally assumed that the criteria included in a performance appraisal system are strictly job related and within the control of the individual

---

[14]H. John Bernardin and Richard W. Beatty, *Performance Appraisal: Assessing Human Behavior at Work* (Boston, Massachusetts: Kent Publishing Company, 1984), p. 213.

[15]H. John Bernardin and Richard W. Beatty, p. 214.

[16]See Gary P. Latham and Kenneth N. Wexley, pp. 37–46; M. J. Kavanaugh, "The Content Issue in Performance Appraisal," *Personnel Psychology*, Vol. 24 (1971), pp. 653–669; P. C. Smith, "Behaviors, Results, and Organizational Effectiveness: The Problem of Criteria," in M. D. Dunnette (ed.), *Handbook of Industrial and Organizational Psychology* (Chicago: Rand McNally, 1976), pp. 745–775; and The Bureau of National Affairs, Inc., "Performance Reviews Revisited," *Bulletin to Management* (January 30, 1992), p. 32.

employee.[17] Employees should neither be held accountable for, nor evaluated on, criteria beyond their control. Criteria pertaining to racial, sexual, religious, age, and other personal characteristics that come under the purview of EEO legislation *must* be excluded. Unfortunately, these, as well as certain personal attributes, such as lifestyle, political views, and so forth, that are not related to the job and not directly covered by EEO laws are occasionally allowed to distort performance appraisals. It is crucial that standards of job performance and the criteria used to define job performance are carefully defined. In essence, job performance is a dynamic, multidimensional concept, and performance appraisal methods are designed to evaluate an employee's behavior in fulfilling job requirements. Care should be taken to avoid assessing job performance on a single criterion. In addition, it should be remembered that no universal set of job-related criteria exists for all jobs. Criteria used to appraise the performance of a mechanical engineer differ substantially from those needed to evaluate the performance of a nurse. Job analysis (discussed in Chapter 4) is the major guide to be used in delineating performance criteria for a specific position. If a criterion is not relevant to the job, it should not be part of the performance appraisal.

When irrelevant criteria are used to evaluate performance, the appraisal is considered *contaminated*. When an appraisal is contaminated, employees can be overheard saying such things as "I never type anything in this job, and yet I'm evaluated on how well I perform typing duties." An appraisal is considered *deficient* when relevant criteria are not included. When appraisals are deficient, employees can be heard voicing complaints such as "I spend half my day preparing administrative reports, and yet how well I do them isn't even part of my performance appraisal." Organizations should make every attempt to reduce both deficiency and contamination. Both may be minimized by concentrating on the actual tasks and behaviors required by the job as determined through job analysis.

Second, once the criteria have been selected for assessing job performance, an accurate means of measurement must be found. As previously mentioned, certain aspects of job performance, such as units sold or produced, errors made, and number of customers served, can be measured with relatively little difficulty. Other facets of job behavior, such as initiative, reliability, and the ability to communicate effectively, present greater measurement difficulties that must be overcome in order to minimize biases that creep into the performance appraisal process.

Rater Selection

Performance appraisals should be conducted by those who are most knowledgeable about an employee's work performance and most able to monitor closely job

[17]There is a growing literature emphasizing the situational limitations or constraints placed upon employee performance by inadequate tools, materials, and supplies, inaccurate or limited job information, employee dependence upon others for necessary materials, and lack of sufficient time to complete the task, as well as the limitations of the physical environment. When employees cannot perform to standards or live up to their true potential because of criteria outside of their control, it is counterproductive to hold them responsible.

behaviors. Two major factors determine who the appraiser or appraisers should be. First, appraisers must be capable of eliminating or minimizing biases that arise during the performance appraisal process. Second, appraisers must have the opportunity to observe the employee's full spectrum of job behaviors over an extended time period. With these two considerations in mind, the following types of appraisers are commonly used in evaluating job performance.

Immediate Supervisor

The immediate supervisor works closely with the employee being evaluated and is the one person who should have the complete view of an employee's daily work performance. Therefore, the immediate supervisor is generally best qualified to provide relevant information regarding the performance, deficiencies, and potential of the employee. Major disadvantages in using the immediate supervisor as the sole appraiser are the personal biases, personality conflicts, or friendships that may prevent the objective assessment of employee performance.

Higher-Level Supervisors

In many organizations, a higher-level supervisor will examine and supplement the evaluation made by the employee's immediate supervisor. The use of a concurring or dissenting opinion by a higher-level supervisor may eliminate certain types of biases found in performance appraisals. This is especially true if the employee and his or her immediate supervisor have either developed close personal ties or personality conflicts that make it difficult for the immediate supervisor to make an objective evaluation of the employee's performance. Furthermore, an employee is less likely to feel that his or her pay and promotion prospects are totally under the control of the immediate supervisor if a higher-level supervisor also influences the performance appraisal process.

Multiple Supervisors

Although management theorists and organizational charts generally adhere to the unity of command principle, where an employee reports only to one supervisor, there are occasions when this practice is violated. Matrix organizational structures, for example, are used to manage temporary projects, and persons working in matrix structures often report to more than one supervisor.[18] Even in situations

[18]Research evidence is somewhat inconclusive regarding the increased accuracy of multiple raters. M. J. Kavanaugh, A. C. McKinney, and L. Wolins, "Issues in Managerial Performance: Multitrait-Multimethod Analyses of Ratings," *Psychological Bulletin*, Vol. 75 (1971), pp. 34–39, found that multiple raters increase accuracy, whereas no significant improvement in accuracy was noted in W. C. Borman, "Performance Judgments: The Quest for Accuracy in Ratings of Performance Effectiveness," paper presented at the First Annual Scientist-Practitioner Conference in Industrial-Organizational Psychology, April 1980. The consistency of evaluations from multiple raters is also of interest. See Hannah R. Rothstein, "Interrater Reliability of Job Performance Ratings," *Journal of Applied Psychology*, Vol. 75 (June 1990), pp. 322–328.

where an organizational chart indicates that an employee must report to a specific supervisor, the actual work environment may create informal relationships between the employee and other supervisors.

In the situations described here, it may be beneficial to obtain assessments from some or all of the supervisors who come into contact with the employee. This is especially true if the employee, in the course of his or her job, performs a variety of tasks in different environments. For example, one supervisor may work with the employee when technical aspects of a job are being performed and another supervisor may deal with the same employee in situations where communicative skills are crucial.

Peer Evaluation

Co-workers and colleagues are often able to evaluate certain facets of an employee's job performance that cannot be evaluated by supervisors and others. Contributions to work on group projects, interpersonal effectiveness, the ability to communicate, reliability, and initiative are factors that might be assessed by fellow employees. Often the closeness of the working relationship and the amount of personal contact place peers in a position to make accurate performance appraisals. Generally, performance appraisal evaluations by one's peers are used to supplement supervisory appraisals. Unfortunately, friendships, animosity, and frequency of interaction have all been shown to affect peer evaluations. Further, when reward allocation is competitive and is based in part on peer reviews, a serious conflict of interest can be created. If an employee wishes to make it more likely that he or she will receive the reward, the peer review process provides a means to sabotage the competition.

Organizations with self-managed work groups are more likely to use peer evaluations than those without such groups. Mature self-managed work groups are often given a number of responsibilities usually reserved for managers, including performance evaluation. There are several advantages to peer review in self-managed work groups. The close working relationship among the members ensures that performance is continually monitored and that enough information to support an appraisal is available. The group is committed to specific goals and can assess routinely whether each member is contributing as much as he or she should to those goals. The group can provide performance feedback on a continual basis and influence performance through peer pressure. Reward systems for self-managed work groups are designed to reward the group's productivity, so there is less individual competitiveness to compromise the validity of the appraisal. There is also some evidence that employees perceive peer reviews in a mature self-managed work group as more fair than the traditional supervisory evaluation.[19] Although we have seen that there are advantages to peer evaluations, it is important to realize that in a group that is not mature, or that has a competitive, individual-level reward system, peer evaluations can create many problems.

---

[19]Brad Lee Thompson, "An Early Review of Peer Review," *Training* (July 1991), p. 43.

Those problems may include tension, discord, hard feelings, negative attitudes, lower worker motivation, and reduced productivity.

Subordinate Evaluations

Supervisory personnel may also be evaluated by their subordinates. Subordinate evaluations may be useful in assessing an employee's ability to communicate, delegate work, allocate resources, disseminate information, resolve interpersonal differences, and deal with employees on a fair basis.[20] For subordinate evaluations to be accepted, the supervisor must not feel threatened or intimidated by them, and they must provide useful information. Subordinates should not be identified with their evaluations, and managers should be assured that their evaluation scores will not be shared with peers or others in the organization. IBM, RCA, Syntex, and Libbey-Owens-Ford have all successfully incorporated subordinate appraisals into their evaluation of management personnel.[21] These companies believe that when subordinates evaluate a carefully selected set of supervisory behaviors, the information is very valuable for management development, promotion decisions, and the allocation of work loads. Like peer evaluations, subordinate evaluations are generally used in conjunction with other sources of performance appraisal information. It is especially important not to link a manager's compensation or promotions too closely to subordinates' appraisals. Employees are less likely to be honest when the manager will be punished for any negative feedback.[22]

Self-evaluations

The usefulness of self-appraisals has been debated in the professional personnel literature for many years. Some feel that self-appraisal data are self-serving and, as such, do not present a valid picture of employee performance.[23] These individuals point to the sometimes significant differences between supervisor and self-appraisals as evidence of the inaccuracy of self-appraisals. Others see self-appraisals as capable of providing useful and valid data. It is their belief that where differences appear, they are not inaccuracies so much as reflections of differing opinions regarding which aspects of employee performance are important.[24] Thus, the more employees and supervisors agree on the relevant aspects of performance, the greater the likely convergence of the data from the two types of appraisals.[25] Valid job descriptions and

---

[20]H. J. Bernardin and Richard W. Beatty, "Can Subordinate Appraisals Enhance Managerial Productivity?," *Sloan Management Review* (Summer 1987), p. 69.

[21]H. J. Bernardin and Richard W. Beatty, *Sloan Management Review*, p. 63.

[22]The Bureau of National Affairs, Inc., "Rating the Boss: Theory and Practice," *Bulletin to Management* (July 25, 1991), p. 226.

[23]G. C. Thornton, "Psychometric Properties of Self Appraisals of Job Performance," *Personnel Psychology*, Vol. 33 (1980), pp. 263–272.

[24]H. J. John Bernardin and Jarold Abbott, "Predicting (and Preventing) Differences Between Self and Supervisory Appraisals," *Personnel Administrator* (June 1985), p. 151.

[25]H. J. John Bernardin and Jarold Abbott, p. 156.

supervisor-employee communication regarding important aspects of performance can assist in reaching agreement. Assuming agreement on relevant aspects of performance, differences between self- and supervisory appraisals can be the basis for very useful dialogues regarding employee performance.[26]

Rater Training

Even the best-designed performance appraisal systems will be ineffective unless the managers and supervisors who perform the appraisals are properly trained. At a minimum, persons using the performance appraisal system should (1) understand the importance of performance appraisal and its impact on an employee's pay, promotion, and career opportunities; (2) be familiar with their organization's performance appraisal method(s); (3) be trained to observe and report on the job performance of employees consistently and objectively. It is important that raters understand the importance of reliability and validity as they relate to performance appraisals. *Intrarater reliability* refers to the consistency of the rater as he or she evaluates a group of employees. *Interrater reliability* refers to the consistency of evaluations among different supervisors. If a performance appraisal system is not reliable, it will not be valid. Raters should also (4) understand the importance of post-appraisal interviews as a means of providing feedback to employees on their job performance.

One particular area for which training is useful is in the recognition of the many possible rater errors to which the performance appraisal process is subject. It is imperative to be aware of these errors when selecting, designing, or assessing the merits of a particular performance appraisal method. Perhaps more important is the need to train supervisors to minimize the errors discussed here when evaluating an employee's performance, regardless of the appraisal method used.[27] These errors can undermine the validity of the most carefully thought-out performance appraisal process.

Halo Error

The halo effect occurs when the person completing the performance appraisal (the rater) allows a single attribute or general impression of the person being evaluated (the ratee) to distort or "color" the entire performance appraisal. For example, a ratee who holds a degree from an ivy league institution may receive an artificially high rating (positive halo) because the rater holds such institutions in great esteem. In this instance, the actual job performance may not warrant such favorable treatment, and yet the rater's general perception of ivy league graduates precludes

---

[26]The Bureau of National Affairs, Inc., "Performance Reviews Revisited," *Bulletin to Management* (January 30, 1992), p. 32.

[27]H. J. Bernardin and E. G. Pence, "The Effects of Rater Training: Creating New Response Sets and Decreasing Accuracy," *Journal of Applied Psychology*, Vol. 65 (1980), pp. 60–66, and Gary P. Latham and Kenneth N. Wexley, pp. 99–118.

an objective assessment of job performance. Racial minorities, on the other hand, may be shortchanged (negative halo) as the result of biases.

Past-record Anchoring

Regardless of an employee's current level of performance, if past performance ratings have been high, supervisors will continue to rate the level of performance as high. Even when lower performance appraisals are given, they are rarely more than one level lower than before.[28]

Inappropriate Rating Patterns

Inappropriate rating patterns arise when the rater fails to make necessary and appropriate distinctions among the performance levels of different employees. That is, all or nearly all of the employees receive either good (leniency), average (central tendency), or poor (harshness) ratings even though certain employees are clearly superior to others. Perhaps the most common rating pattern problem is inflated or lenient ratings, where even poor performers receive relatively high ratings.

These rating patterns may be the result of inadequate rater training, rater apathy toward the performance appraisal process, reluctance to make hard decisions that can have a negative impact on an individual's pay, promotion, and career opportunities, or simply the inability of raters to make distinctions in the performance levels of employees. The presence of these rating patterns is extremely damaging because the basic tenet of the performance appraisal process—validly representing individual differences in employee job performance—is destroyed. It then becomes nearly impossible to make the distinctions necessary to ensure an equitable system of rewards, adequate employee training and development, and proper validation of selection devices.

Recency Effect

The recency effect occurs when the performance appraisal process is distorted by recent incidents or employee behaviors that occur shortly before the evaluation. Such events may be disproportionately weighted by the rater. For example, a salesperson may capture an important account 2 weeks prior to the date of his or her performance appraisal. Although the overall performance of this particular salesperson is only average, the fortunate timing of the account acquisition may inflate the performance appraisal. Likewise, an unfortunate blunder at an inopportune time (1 week before the performance appraisal, for example) may place an otherwise good employee at a disadvantage.

When performance appraisals are based on a designated time frame (6 months, 1 year, and so on), the rating given by the appraiser (rater) must encompass the

---

[28]The Bureau of National Affairs, Inc., "Performance Appraisal Presentations," *Bulletin to Management*, No. 1829 (May 2, 1985), p. 8.

entire appraisal period, not just the incidents that have occurred most recently. It is important for the rater to review the employee's composite performance during the appropriate time frame before completing the appraisal. Furthermore, raters should be aware that employees may attempt to improve the odds in their favor by exhibiting positive job-related behaviors shortly before the appraisal, as well as delaying or hiding problems that may be detrimental to their rating.

Performance Appraisal Methods

Numerous methods have been devised to measure the quantity and quality of employee job performance. A recent survey indicated that the most common approaches to performance appraisal are ranking, rating scales, essay evaluation, management by objectives, critical incidents, and weighted checklists. The following figures, drawn from that survey, represent the approximate percentage of organizations using each method: 65 percent rating scales, 57 percent essay, 30 percent checklist, 18 percent critical incident, 36 percent management by objectives (higher percentage use among management and professional employees), and 8 percent ranking.[29] It should be kept in mind that each of the methods discussed can be effective for some purposes for some organizations. None should be dismissed, or accepted as appropriate, except as they relate to the *particular* needs of the organization for a *particular* type of employee.

Ranking Methods

Employee ranking methods emphasize how employees compare with one another. Regardless of the ranking procedure selected, the final result is a rank order of employees in terms of their job performance. The first three ranking methods to be discussed are (1) the simple or straight ranking method, (2) paired comparison, and (3) alternative ranking. All result in the best employee's receiving a rank of 1, the next best a rank of 2, and so on until all employees are ranked. The fourth procedure to be discussed is forced distribution. This technique assigns employees to different performance groups: above average, average, and so on. Thus, employees are rank ordered in terms of their *performance group*, rather than as individuals.

An employee's performance ranking can be determined by using either one global criterion or a number of criteria. When a global criterion is used, the employee's rank on that criterion is his or her final performance ranking. Unfortunately, a global assessment is usually based on an overall general impression that the evaluator has formed regarding the quality of an employee and his or her job performance, and that impression is sometimes rather vague. Therefore, this type of ranking is subject to considerable controversy. Those who follow the college

[29]These figures represent simple average percentage use across various types of employees as reported in The Bureau of National Affairs, Inc., *Performance Appraisal Programs* (Washington, D.C.: The Bureau of National Affairs, Inc., PPF Survey No. 135, 1985), p. 6. Organizations using more than one of the methods were allowed to indicate that fact through multiple responses.

football rankings produced by the national wire services are well aware of the disagreements that arise each week during the autumn months when these polls are discussed. Single-criterion rankings of employee job performance commonly suffer the same fate.

The use of multiple criteria means that the employee's final performance ranking is based on his or her ranking on each of several criteria. The criteria are based on the results of the job analysis. The employees may be ranked on the quality of their typing, knowledge of the job, and relationship with customers. An employee's overall ranking is calculated from the average of the rankings that the employee received across the criteria. For example, an employee who received a rank of 2 on typing, a rank of 1 on job knowledge, and a rank of 3 on customer relations would have an average rank of 2. When this average is compared with the average ranks of the other employees, the final performance rank can be determined. When multiple criteria are selected, they should be carefully based on the job duties. When that is done, the final rankings are considered more accurate than those using vague or highly subjective criteria. Each of the ranking methods to be discussed can make use of single or multiple performance criteria.

When using *simple* (or straight) ranking, an evaluator attempts to process performance information on all employees simultaneously in order to rank them from best to worst. This information processing becomes increasingly difficult as the number of employees being evaluated grows. In order to reduce the information processing task, *paired comparison* and *alternative ranking* are sometimes used. The paired comparison method reduces the information processing to a simple comparison of only two employees at a time. The term *paired comparison* is used because employees are evaluated against each other, two at a time. Table 9-1 illustrates how the paired comparison method works. Essentially, employees are evaluated (compared) against each other on each job-related criterion used, and then a final overall ranking is determined.[30] Table 9-1 compares five employees on one performance criterion (Quality of Work). In this example you can see that when B. Staw (employee 1) is compared to employees 2, 3, 4, and 5, he is not considered superior to any of the other employees. When B. Staw is compared to L. Ward (2), L. Ward has better-quality work performance, so her employee number is entered in the table for that comparison. The number of times each employee's number appears in this table will determine his or her rank on the Quality of Work dimension. For example, J. Walker's employee number (5) appears four times in the table, R. Zammuto's number appears three time, L. Ward's employee number two times, Y. Vardi's employee number appears one time, and B. Staw's zero times. This information and the ranking of the employees on this dimension are provided directly under the Quality of Work table. When multiple

---

[30]The number of comparisons grows very quickly as the number of employees grows. The number of comparisons for any one performance criterion will be equal to $n(n - 1)/2$, where n is the number of employees. If there are 5 employees the number of paired comparisons will be $5(5 - 1)/2$, or 10. When there are 25 employees, however, the number of paired comparisons for just one criterion will be $25(25 - 1)/2$, or 300.

TABLE 9-1   Paired Comparison Method

Performance Dimension: Quality of Work

| Employee | | Employee Comparisons[a] | | | | |
| | | Employee Numbers | | | | |
No.	Name	1	2	3	4	5
1.	B. Staw	—	2	3	4	5
2.	L. Ward		—	3	2	5
3.	R. Zammuto			—	3	5
4.	Y. Vardi				—	5
5.	J. Walker					—

[a]Each employee is compared to each other employee. The employee's number is entered when that employee is the better of the two being compared.

Employee	Number of Favorable Comparisons	Rank
J. Walker	4	1
R. Zammuto	3	2
L. Ward	2	3
Y. Vardi	1	4
B. Staw	0	5

criteria are used, a composite ranking can be calculated by averaging the ranking for each employee across the performance dimensions.

Alternative ranking also reduces the information processing task when there are many employees to evaluate. The evaluator is presented with a list of all employees. He or she is requested to select the best and worst employee from that list. A new list is started, with the name of the best employee at the top and the worst at the bottom. The evaluator then crosses off the two selected names on the original list and then selects the best and worst employees from the remaining names on the original list. The best employee selected this time is placed on the new list directly under the best employee from the last selection. The worst employee is placed on the new list directly above the worst employee from the last selection. This process is continued until all employees have been crossed off the original list and placed on the new list. The employee's location on the new list becomes the rank for that employee. In this fashion the ranking is created from the top down and the bottom up. The evaluator need only select the two employees at the extremes—good or bad—each time in order to build the list. This is considered a less difficult task than processing information on all employees simultaneously, as is required in simple or straight ranking.

The *forced distribution method* of ranking operates under the assumption that the level of employee job performance conforms to a normal statistical distribution—

a bell-shaped curve. For example, the following distribution might be assumed to exist: 5 percent of all employees will be excellent performers, 20 percent will be good, 50 percent average, 20 percent acceptable, and 5 percent poor. Figure 9-2 provides an illustration of this concept.

The ranking methods can be helpful when the results of the performance appraisal are used to distribute rewards such as pay raises under limited financial conditions and promotions in situations where few opportunities exist in relation to the number of qualified candidates. In addition, the use of ranking methods is an effective means of eliminating the problems created by inappropriate rater patterns, including the inflation that often plagues performance appraisal efforts. Finally, performance appraisal methods based on ranking are inexpensive to design and implement compared to other appraisal methods.

Unfortunately, the use of these ranking methods of performance appraisal presents several problems. First, the magnitude of differences in employee performance is not specified. Is an employee who is ranked third twice as good as one ranked sixth? How much greater should the pay raise be for the person who is ranked first than for the individual who is ranked second? Second, ranking large numbers of employees may become a very cumbersome, unwieldy exercise, compromising reliability (intra- and interrater) as well as validity. Third, as a method of evaluation, ranking is not as useful as alternative methods in providing performance feedback or in delineating employee strengths and weaknesses necessary for the development of employee training and development programs.

The major weakness of the forced distribution method in particular lies in the assumption that employee performance levels always conform to a normal (or some other) distribution. In organizations that have done a good job of selecting and retaining only the stronger performers, the use of a forced distribution approach would be not only unrealistic but possible destructive of employee morale.

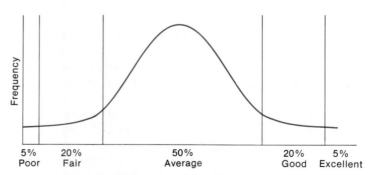

Example: If we have 200 employees to be evaluated,
   10 must be evaluated as excellent
   40 must be evaluated as good
   100 must be evaluated as average
   40 must be evaluated as fair
   10 must be evaluated as poor

FIGURE 9-2   Forced Distribution Method

In addition, the forced distribution method may suffer from the same problem of nebulous criteria that often characterizes the other ranking methods.

Rating Scales

Graphic rating scales are the most prevalent form of performance appraisal. The typical graphic rating scale system consists of several numerical scales, each representing a job-related performance criterion such as quality of work, initiative, job knowledge, and so forth. Each scale or continuum ranges from excellent to poor performance. The rater checks the appropriate performance level on each criterion and then computes the employee's total numerical score. Table 9-2 presents examples of continuous and discontinuous graphic rating scales. A continuous rating scale allows the rater to use any point on the scale line, including those between the numbers, for evaluation purposes. For example, a supervisor may indicate a performance rating for an employee on the rating scale line between 6 and 7. A discontinuous rating scale limits the evaluation to the numbers on the rating scale line; the spaces between the numbers may not be used. Although the continuous rating scale may appear to result in a more precise evaluation, the discontinuous scale can also provide valid ratings. In fact, there is some question as to whether the spaces between the numbers on the continuous scale can be effectively used.

Graphic rating scales offer the advantages of adaptability, relatively easy use, and low cost. Nearly every type of job can be evaluated with some form of graphic

TABLE 9-2 Continuous Graphic Rating Scales

			Need for Supervision					
Minimal		Low		Average		High		Extreme
9	8	7	6	5	4	3	2	1

			Quality of Work					
Excellent		Good		Average		Mediocre		Poor
9	8	7	6	5	4	3	2	1

Discontinuous Graphic Rating Scales

		Initiative and Reliability		
5	4	3	2	1
Exceptional	High	Average	Low	Minimal

		Interpersonal Skills		
5	4	3	2	1
Excellent	Good	Average	Mediocre	Poor

rating scale. In addition, individual scales can be easily constructed and tailored to a specific job. Scales can be created for specific criteria derived from the job descriptions. Table 9-3 provides an example of how different criteria (task dimensions) may be relevant for different jobs. The administrative assistant should be evaluated on the quality of the time sheets and the tabulation, checking, verifying, and computing of cash sums because these are the task dimensions that are part of the job. Likewise, a scale for evaluating how well accounts receivable is maintained may be created for the evaluation of the accounting clerk. Points on each scale can be reviewed with raters to ensure that there is agreement across raters concerning what each point means in terms of actual performance behavior. Due to the simplicity of their design, graphic rating scales generally enable supervisors to evaluate large numbers of employees in a short time.

Graphic scales are summed to create composite scores (points) that may then be used to distribute rewards. For example, if eight separate scales are used (one for each job-related performance criterion, with a maximum score of 9 points per scale), then the highest possible total score that an employee could receive is 72 points ($8 \times 9 = 72$). For an organization that prefers to use an average score, as opposed to a total score, the highest average score would be 9 ($72/8 = 9$). This, of course, assumes that the scales are equally weighted. However, it may be appropriate to weigh important criteria more heavily than less important criteria. This flexibility can result in more valid composite scores. Table 9-4 provides an example of how a performance appraisal average scores would change if the scales were weighted differently. Assume that an individual is evaluated on the two performance dimensions listed in Table 9-4. She received a rather high rating on the first dimension (9) and a moderate rating (5) on the second. If the dimensions are weighted equally she will receive an average score of 7. However, when the first dimension is considered four times as important as the second, the performance score increases to 8.2, a very respectable level of overall performance. On the other hand, if the second dimension is considered four times as important as the first, her performance appraisal drops to a 5.8, only slightly better than average performance.

The negative trade-off for the previously mentioned advantages includes major problems with rating pattern errors. More than any other performance appraisal

TABLE 9-3   Dimensionality of Job Performance

Task Dimensions of Job Performance	Secretary	Administrative Assistant	Accounting Clerk
Maintain accounts receivable			X
Keep time sheets		X	
Tabulate, check, verify, and compute cash sums, and total for accuracy		X	
Maintain petty cash fund	X		

TABLE 9-4   Differential Weighting of Performance Rating Scales

Task Performance Scales	Scale Scores[a]	Equal Weights[b] (50-50) Total Score	Unequal Weights[c] (80-20) Total Score	Unequal Weights[d] (20-80) Total Score
Schedule and approve leave requests	9	7	8.2	5.8
Plan weekly or monthly work schedules and sequences of operation for subordinate technicians	5			

[a]Each scale ranges from 1 (poor performance) to 9 (high performance).
[b]$(9 \times 0.5) + (5 \times 0.5) = 7$
[c]$(9 \times 0.8) + (5 \times 0.2) = 8.2$
[d]$(9 \times 0.2) + (5 \times 0.8) = 5.8$

method, graphic rating scales encourage rating pattern errors, as well as a false sense of precision in the evaluative process.

Behaviorally anchored rating scales (BARS) add a dimension not found in graphic rating scales.[31] Graphic rating scales rely on individual rater judgments as to what constitutes good interpersonal skills or low need for supervision. As a result, interrater reliability is adversely affected: Rater A may claim that a certain employee possesses high job knowledge, whereas Rater B, who is equally familiar with the employee, could conceivably evaluate the same individual as having low knowledge. The different between the two evaluations lies in the two raters' varying interpretations of high versus low job knowledge, as well as in the raters' different evaluative standards.

As a means of alleviating this problem, BARS provide concise narrative descriptions or *examples* of what constitutes excellent quality of work or poor interpersonal skills. Table 9-5 provides an example of a BARS that measures the human relations component of a university departmental secretary's job. Each short description is an example of a relevant behavior for that job dimension. The particular point on the rating scale where an example behavior is placed is based on the collective judgment of job experts. Hence, the example of excellent behavior used on a BARS is a behavior that experts agrees is excellent. In addition to human relations skills, the person holding this job would be evaluated on several other criteria, such as job knowledge, efficiency, job skills, and written and oral communications, among others. Each of the additional criteria would include a scale

[31]See P. Smith and L. M. Kendall, "Retranslation of Expectations: An Approach to the Construction of Unambiguous Anchors for Rating Scales," *Journal of Applied Psychology*, Vol. 47 (1963), pp. 149–155, and J. P. Campbell, M. D. Arvey, and L. V. Hellervik, "The Development and Evaluation of Behaviorally Based Rating Scales," *Journal of Applied Psychology*, Vol. 57 (1973), pp. 15–22. Behaviorally anchored rating scales are sometimes also referred to as *behavioral expectation scales*. This is due to the wording of the behavioral statements, as in Table 9-5.

TABLE 9-5   Department Secretary—Human Relations Skills

Excellent	7	Can be expected to maintain and facilitate harmonious relationships with the most disagreeable professors, students, and staff even under the most trying circumstances
Good	6	Can be expected to command high respect by nearly all professors, students, and staff, most of whom consider the incumbent to be a warm, cooperative individual
Above average	5	Can be expected to maintain composure in difficult situations and is polite to those entering the department office
Average	4	Can be expected to treat the majority of persons with courtesy and resolve minor conflicts that occasionally arise between staff members
Below average	3	Can be expected to exhibit somewhat superficial politeness, with a tendency toward curtness when under stress
Poor	2	Can be expected to exhibit frequent, unprovoked rudeness that occasionally, but significantly, impairs job performance
Extremely poor	1	Can be expected not to get along well with others, and is a significant source of low employee morale and poor relations with other departments

with narrative descriptions. The rater would then evaluate the employee and obtain a composite appraisal score similar to that of graphic rating scales.

The criteria and behaviors are based on a behaviorally oriented job analysis. Job experts are asked to provide a listing of employee behaviors that represent poor, adequate, and high-quality performance. These behaviors are grouped into a smaller number of categories. For example, if behaviors are listed that deal with customer relations, when they are grouped together it would be apparent that customer relations is an important part of the job. Each grouping defines an important criterion for the performance evaluation. The behaviors used to define the various points on each criterion scale are drawn from those behaviors that, when grouped together, originally defined the performance criterion. Job experts are asked to evaluate on a 7- or 11-point scale the quality of the performance behavior. When there is agreement across the various job experts as to the quality of performance represented by a particular behavior, that behavior is used to define a point on the scale.

As previously noted, BARS reduce the semantic problems that plague graphic rating scales. Presumably, this should alleviate difficulties due to rating patterns and to halo and recency effects.[32] BARS are easy to use and minimize many of the errors found in performance appraisal systems.

[32]W. C. Barman and M. D. Dunnette, "Behavior-Based versus Trait-Oriented Performance Ratings: An Empirical Study," *Journal of Applied Psychology*, Vol. 60 (1975), pp. 561–565, and D. P. Schwab, H. G. Heneman III, and T. DeCotiis, "Behaviorally Anchored Rating Scales: A Review of the Literature," *Personnel Psychology*, Vol. 28 (1975), pp. 549–562. It should be noted, however, that there is little empirical evidence to support the superiority of BARS over other methods of performance appraisal; see R. Jacobs, D. Kafry, and S. Zedeck, "Expectations of Behaviorally Anchored Rating Scales," *Personnel Psychology*, Vol. 33 (1980), pp. 595–640.

The major weakness of BARS is the time and expense involved in its design and implementation.[33] A set of BARS must be established for each job or set of jobs. Often the assistance of an industrial psychologist is required, and the final product should be evaluated and tested prior to full-scale use. Performance appraisal committees may be appointed to design a BARS system. The use of an in-house committee is beneficial because the job-related knowledge possessed by individual committee members is essential to the proper selection of factors (criteria) used to design the performance scales of the BARS, as well as in drafting the narrative descriptions (example behaviors) for each criterion. If the job-related performance criteria are not carefully selected and the narrative descriptions carefully drafted, then the BARS may not accurately portray the employee's true performance. Furthermore, raters may have difficulty in discerning any behavioral similarity between the employee's (ratee's) performance and the highly specific behavioral examples used to anchor the scales.

Behavioral observation scales (BOS) overcome some of the difficulties associated with BARS by presenting a clearer picture of the various dimensions of job performance.[34] Behavioral observation scales are also based on a behaviorally oriented job analysis. Critical performance dimensions of a job are determined, and scales are established as depicted in Table 9-6. An employee is rated on a scale of 1 to 5 for each dimension, and a score and overall rating (excellent, good, satisfactory) are determined.

A series of scales may be used for major performance dimensions such as quality of work, interpersonal skills, dependability, and so forth. For example, the performance dimension "dependability" might be structured in a manner similar to that illustrated in Table 9-6. Note that the behaviors listed in Table 9-6 all represent effective performance. Thus, when the rater indicates that the behavior is almost always observed, the employee's total score is increased by 5 points. BOS may use examples of ineffective performance as well. For ineffective performance behaviors the scales range from 1 (almost always) to 5 (almost never). Thus, when an employee almost never exhibits an ineffective behavior, his or her total score is increased by 5 points.

The major advantage of BOS is the clarity and specificity with which they illustrate critical job behaviors; their primary disadvantage lies in the time and expense associated with their development. Other potential problems include invalid rating patterns because of the scale's graphic nature and interrater reliability differences because of the ambiguity of the terms *almost always* and *almost never*. Some organizations attempt to clarify these terms by determining the percentage or number of times the behavior must be seen for each level.

A good BOS performance appraisal system provides an excellent means for thoroughly and specifically evaluating an employee's job behavior. In comparison

---

[33]For a brief discussion on the development of a BARS performance appraisal system, see Donald P. Schwab and Herbert G. Heneman III, "Behaviorally Anchored Rating Scales" in Herbert G. Heneman III and Donald P. Schwab (eds.), *Perspectives on Personnel/Human Resources Management*, rev. ed. (Homewood, Illinois: Richard D. Irwin, Inc., 1982), pp. 73–74.

[34]G. P. Latham and K. N. Wexley, "Behavioral Observation Scales for Performance Appraisal Purposes," *Personnel Psychology*, Vol. 30 (1977), pp. 255–268.

TABLE 9-6 Behavioral Observation Scales—Project Engineer

I. Dependability (Project Engineer)

(1) Manages work time efficiently

ALMOST NEVER   1   2   3   4   5   ALMOST ALWAYS

(2) Promptly meets work/project deadlines

ALMOST NEVER   1   2   3   4   5   ALMOST ALWAYS

(3) Helps meet deadlines by aiding with the work
of other employees, when necessary

ALMOST NEVER   1   2   3   4   5   ALMOST ALWAYS

(4) Is willing to work overtime and weekends when necessary

ALMOST NEVER   1   2   3   4   5   ALMOST ALWAYS

(5) Anticipates and attempts to resolve problems that might
delay the completion of a project

ALMOST NEVER   1   2   3   4   5   ALMOST ALWAYS

13 and BELOW	14-16	17-19	20-22	23-25
VERY POOR	POOR	SATISFACTORY	GOOD	EXELLENT

to other performance appraisal methods, the errors of central tendency, recency, ambiguity, and conflict of interest are probably minimal.

Other Methods of Performance Appraisal

The performance appraisal methods discussed here represent some of the more popular approaches taken in recent years. Much of the popularity of these methods has been based on the flexibility and ease of use that ranking methods and graphic rating scales provide. The pressure exerted by EEO laws and their call for objective, valid measures of job performance have led to greater attention to BARS and BOS. However, several other methods of performance appraisal are widely used and will now be briefly discussed.

Performance appraisals may require that the rater evaluate an employee's performance by describing the performance in his or her own words. *Essay evaluations* are often used in conjunction with the other performance appraisal methods discussed here. In many instances, the rater is given the opportunity to express specific points regarding a particular employee's performance that may not otherwise be covered or noted in the appraisal. That is, essay evaluations may be useful in filling the gaps and covering points that may be missed in a standardized performance appraisal program.

The essay evaluation method has several shortcomings. First, it can be very time-consuming and, therefore, out of the question if numerous employees must be evaluated by a single rater. Second, the usefulness of the essay evaluation depends heavily on the writing skills of the supervisor. Third, the usefulness of an essay evaluation for rewards and validation of selection devices is severely limited.

Management by objectives (*MBO*) is a form of performance appraisal because it involves the establishment of performance objectives and an assessment of how well those objectives are fulfilled.[35] MBO includes the following steps:

1. Subordinate (ratee) proposes goals for the next time period.
2. Subordinate and superior (rater) discuss, modify, and reach an agreement regarding the specific nature of the goals.
3. Periodic formal and informal reviews regarding progress and problems associated with achieving the goals are made.
4. The cycle is repeated.

Performance appraisal under the MBO system permits frequent evaluation and, perhaps more important, enables the employee (ratee) to become involved in the appraisal process. This point is especially useful if employee training and development is regarded as an important by-product of performance appraisal. MBO may be less useful if rewards such as pay raises and promotions are made using appraisal results. Furthermore, MBO is less likely to be used in nonmanagerial or other jobs where employee goal setting is not feasible.[36]

Some persons believe that the use of MBO for performance appraisal has drawbacks. When the results of an MBO system are to be used to allocate organizational rewards, employees may be less likely to establish challenging goals in favor of goals they are confident that they can accomplish. Further, the allocation of merit pay on a semiannual or annual basis may encourage the setting of goals with short time horizons to the disadvantage of important long-term goals.[37]

The *critical incidents* approach to performance appraisal delineates certain criteria or behaviors that are critical to the successful performance of a job. This information is typically obtained from supervisors of the employees to be evaluated. These incidents are next grouped into a smaller number of behavioral categories similar to those found in BARS. The implementation step involves giving each evaluator a list of these general categories and asking him or her to record any positive or negative incidents that occur pertaining to the general categories. An employee's performance on these critical incidents then serves as a basis for rewards and developmental actions.[38]

[35]H. L. Tosi and S. J. Carroll, "Management by Objectives," *Personnel Administration*, Vol. 33 (1970), pp. 44–48, discuss MBO goal setting and performance evaluation.

[36]For more information on management by objectives, see Stephen J. Carroll and Henry L. Tosi, *Management by Objectives* (New York: The Macmillan Company, 1973); Anthony P. Raia, *Managing by Objectives* (Glenview, Illinois: Scott, Foresman and Company, 1974); and The Bureau of National Affairs, Inc., *Performance Appraisal Programs* (Washington, D.C: The Bureau of National Affairs, Inc., PPF Survey No. 135, 1985), p. 7.

[37]For a discussion of these and other drawbacks, see Jeffrey S. Kane and Kimberly A. Freeman, "MBO and Performance Appraisal: A Mixture That's Not a Solution, Part 1," *Personnel* (December 1986), pp. 26–36. See also William W. Scherkenbach, *The Deming Route to Quality and Productivity* (Washington, D.C.: Quality Press, 1990).

[38]See L. L. Cummings and Donald P. Schwab, pp. 85–86.

It may be apparent to the reader that the critical incidents approach is simply an unrefined version of BARS or BOS. BARS and BOS use (or should use) critical job requirements and behaviors to build the scales discussed earlier.

A *weighted checklist* is developed by first obtaining a number of statements about employee performance on the job to be rated from persons familiar with the job. Each statement is then evaluated by a group of persons (usually the supervisors of those being appraised) on how favorable or unfavorable each performance statement is to job success. This item-by-item evaluation is typically done on either a 7- or an 11- point scale, with low values representing unfavorable scores and high values representing favorable scores. Scores are then converted into weights.[39]

Evaluators are generally given copies of the final checklist to use in performance appraisal. Weights are *not* generally known to the evaluators. The evaluator simply indicates whether each ratee (employee) does nor does not engage in the behavior specified in each item. Each employee receives a final score for the appraisal when the scores of each item checked are summed.

Weighted checklists may be especially useful for certain types of jobs where nonperformance of a specific task or behavior is critical. For example, weighted checklists, or a variation thereof, are sometimes used by Federal Aviation Administration flight examiners to evaluate a pilot's ability to handle a specific type of aircraft. A certain score may be required before the pilot is certified for air charter flights. If all weights on a performance checklist are positive, then a rater may be tempted to check as many items as possible in order to inflate the rating. Furthermore, weighted checklists may include statements regarding personal preferences of the employee, the underlying assumption being that the rater knows the employee very well. Such an assumption may not be well founded.

■ The Performance Appraisal Interview

An integral part of any performance appraisal system is the performance appraisal interview. The discussion of an employee's appraisal results is important in providing feedback regarding compensation, job status, disciplinary decisions, and training and development needs.[40] Employees generally are very interested in knowing where they stand within the organization, as well as the justification behind personnel actions that affect their work life.

[39]L. L. Cummings and Donald P. Schwab, pp. 86–87.

[40]See Douglas Cederblom, "The Performance Appraisal Interview: A Review, Implications, and Suggestions," *Academy of Management Review*, Vol. 7, No. 2 (1982), pp. 219–227; R. J. Burke and D. S. Wilcox, "Characteristics of Effective Employee Performance Review and Development Interviews: Replication and Extension," *Personnel Psychology*, Vol. 22 (1969), pp. 291–305; M. M. Greller, "The Nature of Subordinate Participation in the Appraisal Interview," *Academy of Management Journal*, Vol. 21 (1978), pp. 646–658; and W. F. Nemeroff and J. Cosentino, "Utilizing Feedback and Goal Setting to Increase Performance Appraisal Interviewer Skills of Managers," *Academy of Management Journal*, Vol. 22 (1979), pp. 566–576.

Despite the obvious importance of the performance appraisal interview, its infrequent and ineffective use in organizations is widely recognized. Several points have emerged from the literature regarding the effective use of performance appraisal interviews:

1. Supervisors conducting the interviews must be trained regarding the importance of and methods used to conduct the interview properly.
2. The interview must be carefully structured. It may be advisable to split the interview into two separate interviews: the first for counseling on training and development needs with the employee, and the second for discussing pay, promotion, transfer, and other decisions that have been or will be made.
3. Performance appraisal interviews should be structured to follow the criteria (job-related performance dimensions) addressed on the performance appraisal form. As with any interview, there should be a beginning, a middle, and an end. The initial stages of the interview may be used to impress the value of the performance appraisal and subsequent interview on the employee, and the middle section may be devoted to specific job-related factors. Finally, the end of the interview can be used to provide an overall performance assessment, with suggestions for future performance.
4. Subordinates (ratees) should be allowed to participate in the interviewing process. Often, employees may be in a position to offer suggestions that will improve not only their individual performances but possibly the effectiveness of an entire organizational department or unit.
5. The appraisal interview should be undertaken in a supportive, nonthreatening manner whenever possible. Praise and constructive criticism are more likely to achieve positive results. However, the very poor performer whose employment future with the organization is clouded should be so informed with a formal warning. This warning may later preclude an adverse decision in an EEO suit.[41]

An inefficient performance appraisal interview may negate an otherwise superior performance appraisal system. The performance appraisal–related personnel decisions described earlier in this chapter involving training and development, compensation, and discipline must not only be justified by management but must be perceived as being reasonable and equitable by the employee. Performance appraisal interviews are a primary means by which this takes place.

■ Performance Appraisal and Equal Employment Opportunity: Another Look

A poorly designed and administered performance appraisal system may lead to fair employment violations and suits under the state and federal EEO laws. Most

[41]M. G. Miner, *Employee Performance: Evaluation and Control* (Washington, D.C.: The Bureau of National Affairs, Inc., PPF Survey No. 108, 1975).

EEO suits involving performance appraisal programs stem from the failure of the evaluation process to be job related; that is, the appraisal is done in a subjective and inconsistent manner by supervisors. Another problem arises from the failure to use performance appraisal results properly in personnel-related decisions.[42] Although committing these infractions is not illegal per se, if a disparate impact based on race, sex, age, and other protected categories become apparent, then an EEO violation is likely.

The probability of a civil suit's being leveled against an organization can be minimized by adhering to the following practices:

1. Establish explicit performance standards from job analysis and communicate these standards to supervisors (raters) and employees (ratees).
2. Develop performance appraisal systems based on explicit performance criteria and train raters on *both* the importance of the system to the entire personnel function and the need to minimize the problems of central tendency, recency, conflict of interest, and other biases that contaminate the process.
3. Monitor the use of the performance appraisal system after it has been designed and installed. Special attention should be paid to the following:
   a. The statistical distribution of employee performance scores and the reasons for shifts in aggregate (organizational or department) scores over a time period.
   b. Interrater reliability (consistency among raters) when more than one rater is used.
   c. Ambiguous or troublesome sections of the appraisal form, as indicated by inconsistent responses by raters or questions concerning the meaning of certain terms and phrases.
   d. Changes in job tasks and responsibilities that will dictate complete or partial revisions of the performance appraisal system.
4. Conduct performance appraisal interviews using the guidelines mentioned earlier.
5. Provide a specific appeal mechanism if the employee is not satisfied with the appraisal results.

■ Performance Appraisals: A Dissenting View

Because of the many important uses for performance appraisal information, we have discussed performance appraisals as an important human resource activity.

[42]W. H. Feild and H. S. Feild, "Performance Appraisal and the Law," *Labor Law Review*, Vol. 26 (1975), pp. 423–430; G. L. Lubben, D. E. Thompson, and C. R. Klasson, "Performance Appraisal: The Legal Implications of Title VII," *Personnel*, Vol. 28 (1980), pp. 12–21; and H. S. Feild and W. H. Holley, "The Relationship of Performance Appraisal System Characteristics to Verdicts in Selected Employment Discrimination Cases," *Academy of Management Journal*, Vol. 25, No. 2 (1982), pp. 392–406; and Mark R. Edwards and J. Ruth Sproull, "Safeguarding Your Employee Rating System," *Business* (April–June 1985), pp. 17–27.

We have also discussed problems that could result if a company's appraisals are not valid (e.g., not job-related, overly political) or work against important company goals (e.g., teamwork). A number of influential management consultants believe that the performance appraisals conducted by most American companies are extremely counterproductive and should be abandoned. One of the most influential consultants to take this position is Dr. W. Edwards Deming, often credited with playing a major role in the economic rebirth of Japan after World War II. Dr. Deming is convinced that for a company to excel, it must create an atmosphere where workers can take pride in their work and strive for continual improvement in process and product. Dr. Deming believes that performance appraisals destroy teamwork, foster mediocrity, increase performance variability, and focus only on the short term, to the long-term disadvantage of the company.[43]

1. *Destroy teamwork.* Performance appraisal systems are often designed to isolate the performance of departments and individuals. This is done so that the company can decide if person or department A is meeting individual goals and doing better than person or department B. This competitive approach neglects the many cooperative behaviors that must exist, for example, between person A and person B. Cooperative behaviors, according to Dr. Deming, are essential for continual improvement, yet the formal appraisal system discourages those behaviors.

2. *Foster mediocrity.* The highly individualized goals characteristic of many performance appraisal systems help to create a climate of fear in an organization. Fear of failure ensures that no one will take any chances or set truly challenging goals. Initiative and risk taking are necessary for continual improvement and for rising above the mediocre.

3. *Increase performance variability.* The misleading precision attached to performance ratings (e.g., scales of 1 to 7, 43 out of 50 total points) makes it likely that management will overemphasize meaningless differences in employee performance over time and among employees. According to Dr. Deming, many things can affect whether an employee reaches a given level of performance. Some of those things are not within the control of the employee. An employee may work just as hard and just as well for two performance periods, yet have different levels of performance for reasons over which there was no control. Small differences in employee performance ratings over time may be due simply to random factors operating in the environment. However, a manager who treats these rating scale differences as meaningful will encourage employees to improve their performance. This encouragement to change is a dangerous overmanagement of employee performance. To an employee already working well, such micromanagement leads to confusion, frustration, and an attempt to change behaviors that are already high-performance behaviors.

4. *Provide a short-term focus.* The temptation to "make the numbers" at any cost can work against the investment of effort in longer-term but more valuable

---

[43]William W. Scherkenbach, *The Deming Route to Quality and Productivity* (Washington, D.C.: Quality Press, 1990), pp. 47–75.

activities. Any activity, however important, that takes away from the bottom line of the next performance appraisal is risky for the employee. The increasing use of computer status reports can keep management abreast of changes in output or finances on a daily basis. Reacting to daily figures can result in a destructively short performance appraisal cycle.

How seriously should these criticisms of performance appraisal systems be taken? They should be taken very seriously. Dr. Deming's work underscores many shortcomings of appraisal systems as they exist in organizations. Managers must be aware of the destructive potential of a badly conceived and implemented performance appraisal system.

■ Summary and Conclusions

The quality of selection, training, development, compensation, and disciplinary programs depends directly on the performance appraisal process. In addition, a well-designed and administered appraisal system provides an excellent defense in the event of EEO suits.

A great deal of attention and controversy have surrounded the various *methods* of performance appraisal, and much has been said about the strengths and weaknesses of each. Perhaps a more important set of issues includes (1) tailoring performance appraisal to an organization's *specific* set of jobs, (2) training raters to understand the importance of objective, error-free assessment of employee performance, (3) periodically monitoring and evaluating the operation of the organization's performance appraisal program, and (4) creating an atmosphere of teamwork, employee self-development, and continual improvement.

Performance appraisal deserves considerable attention from both management practitioners and scholars. Continued research and analysis will, in all likelihood, lead to improved methods of evaluating employee job performance. Equally important, however, is the need to administer the program properly once it is designed through careful employee appraisal and postappraisal interviews. The role of job analysis is critical to the design of the performance appraisal system, but the role of the personnel manager and rater(s) is equally important to the perpetuation of a high-quality program.[44]

■ Questions

1. What are some of the uses to which performance appraisal information can be put? Is there any single system that could provide all the information necessary for all of these purposes? Explain your answer.

[44]For an excellent discussion of criteria that can be used to rate and assess performance appraisal systems, see Michael J. Kavanaugh, pp. 220–222.

2. Based on your knowledge of EEO matters, how might the use of performance appraisal violate:

a. Title VII of the Civil Rights Act of 1964?

b. The ADEA of 1967?

c. The Rehabilitation Act?

3. Compare and contrast three of the performance appraisal methods discussed in the chapter.

4. What are some of the more common rater errors? How can an organization reduce these errors?

5. Reread the profile on Digital Equipment Corporation at the beginning of this chapter. Contrast Digital's performance appraisal system to the rating and ranking systems discussed in this chapter. Do you believe that Digital's system has advantages over the others for self-managed work groups? If so, what are they?

6. Review and comment on Dr. Deming's remarks regarding the shortcomings of performance appraisals as they are conducted in organizations. Do you believe that performance appraisals that are poorly conceived and implemented can be a destructive activity in an organization? How would you evaluate the appraisal system used for student grading in your school? Does it create an atmosphere of teamwork, self-development, and continual improvement? If not, what changes would you recommend? How do your recommendations tie into the criticisms mentioned by Dr. Deming?

☐ APPLICATIONS AND CASE EXERCISES

1. The First National Bank has decided to computerize as many of its operations as possible in order to increase efficiency and customer convenience. One of their first steps was to place automatic teller machines (ATMs) in the surrounding community. The bank has also started a program that expands on telephone banking by allowing the owners of microcomputers to conduct virtually all of their banking business from their homes.

   These successes have caused the bank to consider the use of microcomputers or terminals in the homes of their employees so that they may work at home. It is believed that this will allow greater flexibility for employees and reduce the need for office and floor space at the main and branch offices. It is clear that technology will stimulate many changes in the bank's current personnel practices as the relationship between work and the individual employee changes. The personnel director has been asked to develop a report outlining the changes that will be necessary in the bank's personnel policies.

   Since contact with immediate supervisors would be eliminated for many employees under this new work arrangement, what type of performance appraisal system would you suggest?

2. Using the job analysis information for the airline captain's job described in Chapter 4, determine the performance criteria that would be useful in establishing a performance appraisal system.

3. As a student, you have been subjected to a form of performance appraisal through the course grades that you have received or earned (depending on your outlook). Discuss whether you feel that the sources of errors present in the performance appraisal process have been encountered in your personal experiences. How might grading systems eliminate such errors?

4. Obtain a copy of a performance appraisal form from a local organization. Critique the form based on

   a. Job relatedness

   b. Potential sources of error

   c. Use in personnel-related programs

5. Do a survey of approximately ten companies in your area. What types of appraisal systems do they use? Which system is most popular? What information does each company wish to collect, and to what specific use(s) do the companies wish to put that information? Given your knowledge of performance appraisal systems, is the system used by each company the best one for that company?

6. Locate an organization in your area that uses self-managed work teams. Interview a representative from the human resources department regarding the performance appraisal system used with the work teams. Compare and contrast that system with the system used by Digital presented at the beginning of this chapter. Discuss the Digital system with the human resources representative and record his or her reactions to the differences between the two performance appraisal methods. Do you believe that the system used by the local organization is more appropriate for that firm than the Digital system? If so, why? If not, why not?

10

The Foundations of Compensation Management

■ LEARNING OBJECTIVES

After reading this chapter you should understand

1. The different categories and types of compensation that organizations use.
2. The important definitions and concepts related to compensation.
3. The impact of economic, organizational, individual, and legal factors on compensation management.
4. The pervasive effect that compensation can have on occupational and job choice, job satisfaction, employee attendance and performance, turnover, and organizational effectiveness.

■ INTRODUCTORY VIGNETTE

Executive Compensation

During the winter of 1992, the American economy was still in the recession that had begun 2 years before. President George Bush traveled to Japan to discuss Japanese exports to the United States and the difficulty experienced by American companies in exporting goods to Japan. The major American auto companies each sent senior executives to accompany the president. It was hoped that hard-nosed businessmen could persuade the Japanese when political figures could not. The trip was, for the most part, a disappointment. Japan did not concede that it was engaged in unfair trade practices, nor were significant export limits established on Japanese autos. The major result of the trip was an increasing disenchantment with the competence and compensation of the major auto executives who accompanied the president. For years, the American auto industry had been in a state of decline. Tens of thousands of employees were laid off during the late 1980s and early 1990s due to low sales. Yet, during that same period, the total compensation received by top auto executives continued to climb. Business magazines, newspapers, and television shows began to focus on the loose link between company performance and executive compensation. To make matters worse, it was revealed during President Bush's visit to Japan that the average American CEO was compensated at a ratio of about

The statistics cited here are drawn from John A. Byrne, "The Flap Over Executive Pay," *Business Week* (May 6, 1991), pp. 90–95. See also, John A. Byrne, Dean Fonst, and Lois Therrien, "Executive Pay," *Business Week* (March 30, 1992), pp. 52–58.

85 times the average employee's pay, while Japanese top executives, with very successful firms, made only 17 times the pay of the ordinary Japanese worker. The annual compensation of Reebok International Chairman Paul Fireman averaged almost $14 million per year during a time when Reebok lost the No. 1 spot in the sneaker business to Nike. In contrast, General H. Norman Schwarzkopf earned $103,927.60 the year he commanded Operation Desert Storm, the successful military operation against Iraq, at a time when Iraq had the third largest military organization in the world. Michael D. Eisner, CEO of Walt Disney, earned in one average day during 1990 what the average Disney employee earned that entire year.

American executive compensation has become a source of embarrassment internationally. It is embarrassing to the companies paying multi-million-dollar salaries while profits fall, and a source of dissatisfaction to shareholders and workers whose jobs or whose friends' jobs have been lost. How did American executive compensation become so far removed from company performance? Most explanations cite the close relationship between the CEO and the board of directors in American companies. For the most part, boards of directors are aligned with management, and their compensation is often recommended by the CEO. The boards hire compensation consultants, who always seem to recommend higher pay for the CEO; consequently, when a CEO's salary is discussed, generosity is assured. Pay for performance is becoming a more important issue at all levels in American organizations. It has become even more important in the executive suite. There may be some changes in the wind, however. Shareholders are putting pressure on companies to link pay and company performance for CEOs, and at least one stockholder organization has taken on the responsibility of finding out who the most overpaid American executives are. One recommendation receiving attention is to pay boards of directors in stock, thereby linking their pay to the performance of the company. Some CEOs have asked for and received contracts that link their pay more closely to corporate performance. It is likely that more and more will do so. At issue is the credibility of executive compensation systems and of the executives themselves.

■ Introduction

Compensation management is an important function within the organization and is typically part of the personnel/human resource manager's responsibility. One of the most important facets of a job in the eyes of most employees is its level of pay. An employee is normally paid in accordance with his or her job-relevant qualifications and the number of people in the labor force who possess these qualifications. Pay is also determined by the skill and effort required to perform a job and the extent to which the job is valued by the organization and society. However, it is still difficult to understand why some jobs pay more than others. For example, why are most over-the-road truckers paid more than high school teachers? Why do business, law, and medical professors in large universities have higher salaries than their colleagues in English, history, and psychology? Why do skilled construction workers earn considerably more than most ministers? How can the high salaries received by many professional athletes be explained? How can physicians often command high fees for medical procedures that sometimes involve only a few minutes of work?

The amount of pay that a person receives is often a personal and sensitive issue. In our society, it is considered socially unacceptable to ask a stranger or brief acquaintance about his or her salary, and it is boorish to boast about our compensation to others. The pay that an individual receives determines his or her standard of living and is commonly considered a benchmark of personal success. Employees are concerned about their level of compensation, not only in an absolute sense but also in how it relates to the salaries of their fellow employees and to persons performing the same job for a different employer. Most employees are also interested in comparing their effort, skills, and pay for their job with those of employees performing different jobs.

Dealing with the total compensation package in an organization that offers a wide variety of pay schedules and employee benefits presents a professional challenge to personnel/human resource managers. Personnel managers must deal with a host of behavioral factors, technical problems, and legal issues when compensation matters arise. Some compensation programs attract high-quality employees and motivate them to put forth their best efforts on the job. Other compensation programs are poorly administered and cause employee turnover, dissatisfaction, and legal problems, all of which are detrimental to employee well-being and organizational effectiveness.

This chapter provides an introduction to the topic of compensation management by discussing the economic, behavioral, organizational, and legal factors that affect compensation programs. A working definition of the various forms of compensation is provided, and key concepts germane to compensation management are analyzed. The concepts discussed in this chapter provide a foundation for the topics presented in Chapters 11 and 12.

■ Compensation: A Working Definition

Compensation is a broad term pertaining to the financial rewards received by persons through their employment relationship with an organization. Generally speaking, compensation is financial in nature because a monetary outlay is made by the employer. Such monetary outlays may be *immediate* (payable within a short period of time) or *deferred* (payable at a later date). An employee's weekly or monthly pay is an example of an immediate payment, whereas a pension, profit-sharing, or bonus plan typifies a deferred payment. Compensation can be *direct*, where money is placed into the hands of the employee, or *indirect*, where the employee receives compensation in nonmonetary forms or has little discretion as to how the compensation will be spent (expense accounts, use of a company automobile, and group life and health insurance). The types of compensation can be categorized as follows:

1. *Wages and salary.* *Wages* typically pertain to hourly rates of pay (the more hours worked, the greater the pay) and *salary* generally applies to a fixed weekly, monthly, or annual rate of pay (regardless of the number of hours worked). Both wages and salaries are usually adjusted annually and are based on the type of job held by an employee, as well as individual seniority and job performance (merit).

2. *Incentive programs.* Additional compensation above and beyond the employee's wage or salary is provided by incentive programs. (Some employees earn all of their pay from incentives.) Incentive programs are geared to providing additional pay based on productivity, sales, profits, or cost-reduction efforts. The major objective of most incentive compensation programs is to encourage and reward employee productivity and cost effectiveness. Incentive programs are of two types:

   a. *Individual incentive programs* provide compensation based on the sales, productivity, or cost savings attributable to a *specific* employee.

   b. *Group incentive programs* allocate compensation to a group of employees (by department, division, or work group) for exceeding predetermined profitability, productivity, or cost savings standards.

3. *Employee benefit programs.* Group life and health insurance, paid vacations and holidays, pension programs, and other benefits associated with an employment relationship or membership in a union are examples of employee benefit programs. Employee benefits now comprise approximately 40 percent of total compensation costs in the United States.

4. *Perquisites.* Employees may receive amenities such as the use of company automobiles, country club memberships, travel allowances, or access to company-owned resorts and airplanes. Perquisites may represent a substantial amount of compensation, especially for highly paid executives.

Nearly all forms of compensation fall into one of the four categories listed here. A detailed analysis of these categories of compensation is presented in Chapters 11 and 12.

■ Major Factors Influencing Employee Compensation

A number of factors influence the amount of money and employee benefits that workers receive. Among these are external labor markets and the firm's demand for labor, organizational factors, individual differences in motivation and job performance, legislation affecting compensation programs, and labor unions.

Economic Influences and External Labor Markets

A firm's demand for labor is *derived* from the demand for and revenues generated by its products and services. Because of the demand for computer equipment, high-tech firms heavily recruited computer science majors during the late 1980s. When fuel prices skyrocketed in the 1970s, the market for large recreational vehicles plummeted. Companies such as Winnebago closed production facilities and laid off employees as sales declined. The same predicament befell the light aircraft industry, which experienced declining product demand and layoffs. The oil-producing states of Texas, Oklahoma, and Louisiana had low unemployment levels during the 1970s, and even relatively unskilled workers found abundant employment opportunities at wages that afforded a comfortable standard of living. By 1982, oil prices began to decline and unemployment in these once prosperous states increased. As petrochemical company revenues dropped, workers were laid off, with little hope of finding comparable-paying jobs.

The supply of labor available to a firm is obtained, in part, from *external labor markets*, a geographical area or occupational group from which an organization recruits employees into the organization. The extent to which a firm taps an external labor market depends on the type and number of employees that are required. External labor markets also regulate the extent to which organizations compete for personnel whose skills are in high demand.

External labor markets are composed of buyers and sellers of labor; employers *demand* (buy) units of labor (employees), and employees are willing to *supply* (sell) their labor to an employer for a certain price (wage or salary). Thus employers hire employees who are willing to avail themselves of the going rate in the labor market. This concept is known as the *exchange value*. Labor markets that are *tight* favor the employee and generate higher pay levels, whereas labor markets that are *loose* favor the employer and result in lower pay levels.[1] Another explanation for establishing pay rates is the *marginal revenue productivity theory*, which says that an employer will hire workers up to the point where the cost of hiring an additional worker (the worker's pay) equals the productivity or revenue added by hiring that worker. Hiring yet another worker will then decrease profits. The exchange value and marginal revenue productivity theories are flawed because both theories assume that employers have a precise understanding of market forces and labor and product costs. In reality, most employers have only a general idea regarding labor supply, demand, and costs, so that although the standard economic explanations may appear to be precise, they depend on data that are imprecise. Regardless, economic wage theories provide valuable insights into the dynamics of establishing pay levels and structures.

Cost of living changes also affect pay levels, especially for organizations with large numbers of unionized employees. *Monetary income* is expressed in absolute dollars, whereas *real income*, the most relevant measure of economic well-being,

---

[1]One way of keeping the labor market terms *tight* and *loose* straight is to remember the following: "If the labor market is tight, tell your employer to fly a kite. If the labor market is loose, saying that will cook your goose!"

is expressed in terms of purchasing power. An employee who receives a pay increase of 3 percent will experience a 3 percent change in monetary income. If the consumer price index changes by 5 percent, however, the employee's real income has actually decreased by approximately 2 percent. Because of the importance of real income, persons contemplating employment in areas with a high cost of living, such as the San Francisco Bay area, Hawaii, Alaska, or New York City, must not underestimate the effects of the costs required to enjoy a decent standard of living in these locations. A $25,000 a year job in Hannibal, Missouri, will provide a substantially higher real income than a $30,000 position in San Francisco. It should be remembered that we are speaking strictly in terms of cost of living, and we are ignoring the cultural and climatological advantages afforded by many high-cost areas.

Organizational Influences and Internal Labor Markets

Even within the same labor market, there are likely to be significant differences in pay levels for the same job. A secretary in a state university may receive 15 percent less than one doing comparable work for a large life insurance company located in the same city. Some organizations attempt to keep labor costs in check by paying less than competing firms in the same labor market. For years, the Boston Celtics of the National Basketball Association allegedly paid their players less than many other teams in the league. Apparently these lower salaries did not impair the ability of the Celtics to win; perhaps the prestige of playing on a team with a strong winning tradition was a form of psychic compensation for the players. Some managers, however, have discovered that a low-wage strategy can be costly in the long run. By paying lower than average wages, some firms get less desirable employees and experience higher than normal rates of turnover, lower productivity, and other problems associated with a less competent and motivated workforce.

Organizations place different values on employees and the knowledge, skills, and abilities that they bring to the job. A university desiring to build a strong chemistry department might be willing to pay high salaries to attract leading professors. A public hospital attempting to install a computer system to handle its massive patient billings and financial data may pay a high salary to obtain the services of a computer expert with a strong background in management information systems. Professional football teams in desperate need of offensive linemen are more likely to provide an attractive contract to talented players in order to fill these positions than would a team with an abundance of good players on the offensive line.

Traditions that are ingrained in the organizational culture also play a role in employee pay levels. Pilots flying small twin-engine aircraft for commuter airlines on short flights are paid much less than their counterparts who fly transcontinental and international flights in jets. Although the latter group usually has more flying experience, commuter pilots frequently have more difficult, stressful, and hazardous routes, and their aircraft contain less navigational equipment and employ a smaller flight crew. In short, tradition in the airline industry dictates that commuter pilots performing more difficult jobs work at one third to one half of the pay received by pilots on the major air carriers. This is true even when both categories of pilots are employed by the same airline. Yet in terms of the knowledge, skills, and abilities of the flight crew plus the stresses of commuter flying, it would appear that such a pay discrepancy is not warranted.

Internal labor markets are a series of related jobs within the organization.[2] For many entry-level jobs, such as the ones recent college graduates occupy for the first few years of their careers, the supply of and demand for labor are often the primary means by which pay is established. College graduates with no managerial experience often find that there is little room for negotiation on starting salaries. Employees are hired for entry-level jobs and then are promoted or transferred within the organization's internal labor market. Internal labor markets tend to develop pay rates that are unique to a specific organization and somewhat isolated from supply and demand forces in the external labor market. Colleges and universities usually hire faculty members at the rank of assistant professor. The salaries for new assistant professors who have recently received their terminal degree (usually a Ph.D.) are dictated primarily by market forces. An assistant professor in operations management, for example, will be hired at the market rate (plus or minus $2,000). Once faculty members become established in an institution and receive tenure, the salary range for associate and full professors will become wider from one institution to another, depending on the individual professor's job performance and college's or university's pay policies. Thus two assistant professors, one of whom is hired by a small state school and one by a large, prestigious university, may start their careers at approximately the same salary. If both professors remain at their respective institutions for 10 years, the professor at the large, prestigious university will, in all likelihood, receive a higher salary than the professor at the small state school. This is an example of how internal labor markets work in academia. The longer a person stays in an organization, the less influence external labor markets have on his or her pay. This is due, in part, to the lack of mobility that employees have as they become tied to an organization because of pension and seniority benefits.[3] As one moves up in an organization, jobs become more specialized and less standardized relative to the external labor market. In addition, employees who remain with an organization for long periods of time become culturally attuned to their organization, more entrenched in their communities, and less willing to leave.[4]

An important factor in compensation management is the organization's *ability to pay* high salaries and wages. Firms that are highly profitable and are predicting

[2]Beverly Kaye and Kathryn McKee, "New Compensation Strategies for New Career Patterns," *Personnel Administrator* (March 1986), p. 61; Paul Osterman, "Choice of Employment Systems in Internnal Labor Markets," *Industrial Relations* (Winter 1987), pp. 46–67.

[3]Caryl E. Rusbult, David Lowery, Michael L. Hubbard, Orly J. Maravankin, and Michael Neises, "Impact of Employee Mobility and Employee Performance on the Allocation of Rewards Under Conditions of Constraint," *Journal of Personality and Social Psychology* Vol. 54 (1988), pp. 605–615.

[4]See David B. Bills, "Costs, Commitment, and Rewards: Factors Influencing the Design and Implementation of Internal Labor Markets," *Administrative Science Quarterly* (June 1987), pp. 202–221.

a strong future demand for their products and services are in a better position to pay lucrative salaries and attract the cream of the crop in the labor market. As mentioned earlier, a high-paying strategy may save the firm money in the long run because of its ability to attract more productive and stable employees. The ability of an organization to pay depends on factors such as the firm's product demand and labor intensity. Companies who sell products or provide services that have an inelastic demand (where product price increases resulting from increases in labor costs can be passed on to the consumer with little effect on consumer demand) are in a better position to pay higher salaries than firms with elastic product demands. A distillery manufacturing a fine (and expensive) brand of scotch probably has an inelastic product demand. The firm can grant a modest wage increase to its workers and pass all or part of the increase on to its customers by raising the price of a bottle of scotch without significantly decreasing the numbers of bottles sold. That is, a 7 percent price increase in the price of a bottle of scotch would result in *less* than a 7 percent decline in business. A firm whose product has an elastic demand, such as a dairy manufacturer producing milk, would find that a price increase of 7 percent would decrease sales by *more* than 7 percent. Finally, an organization's ability to pay is affected by its labor intensity. Service organizations such as hospitals and educational institutions are labor intensive because a high percentage of each's total budget is allocated to personnel costs. If a community hospital spends 60 percent of its total budget on salaries, employee benefits, and other personnel costs, a 10 percent pay increase will result in a 6 percent increase in the hospital's budget ($10\% \times 60\% = 6\%$). A capital-intensive chemical manufacturer whose personnel expenditures are only 15 percent of the firm's total budget will experience only a 1.5 percent budget increase if a 10 percent raise is given.

In recent years, increasing attention has been given to the relationship between organizational strategy and pay policies. An organization's strategy defines its business in terms of product line, quality emphasis, market segment, geographical market limits, diversity, and size. Some firms are expanding and diversifying, whereas others are remaining stable both in size and in terms of product lines. Firms in declining product markets often elect to retrench by eliminating unprofitable products and reducing their workforce. In an extreme case, a firm may divest large segments of its operations or go out of business completely. Firms that are growing and expanding frequently deemphasize low base salaries and benefits and emphasize incentive programs such as sales commissions. Firms in stable or mature markets tend to use competitive base pay and high employee benefits, whereas firms in declining markets may abandon incentive programs altogether.[5]

[5]George T. Milkovich and Jerry M. Newman, *Compensation*, 2nd. ed. (Plano, Texas: Business Publications, Inc., 1987), p. 16. Also see Richard I. Henderson and Howard W. Risher, "Influencing Organizational Strategy Through Compensation Leadership," Stephen J. Carroll, "Business Strategies and Compensation Systems," and Joseph E. McCann, "Rewarding and Supporting Strategic Planning," all in David B. Balkin and Luis R. Gomez-Mejia (eds.), *New Perspectives on Compensation* (Englewood Cliffs, New Jersey: Prentice-Hall, Inc., 1987), pp. 328–363.

Employee Perceptions of Pay

Economic and organizational influences have a general impact on pay rates, but the exact wage or salary paid to an employee is often determined by individual job performance. Because an employee's compensation is usually the single most important employment reward, it can have a significant effect on individual attitudes and job performance. Individual employees place different values on monetary rewards. Some are content to work 40 hours a week, collect a modest paycheck, and enjoy their leisure time. Other employees are motivated to work long hours in order to earn high salaries. Behavioral scientists have examined the effects of various types of financial rewards (wages, salaries, and individual and group incentive programs) on different types of subjects (male, female, young, old, skilled, and unskilled employees) in a multitude of organizational settings. A great deal of behavioral research has focused on the motivational aspects of compensation, the importance of pay to various types of employees, and the relationship among compensation, job satisfaction, absenteeism, employee turnover, and work performance.[6]

Motivational theories are of two types: content theories and process theories. *Content theories* focus on *what* motivates employees to work harder and become more productive. A key question with content theories of motivation is whether money can be used to induce employees to provide additional effort. Individual incentive plans such as sales commissions are based on the assumption that money is indeed a motivator. Anyone who has been accosted by an aggressive and persistent salesperson can attest to the motivating effect that sales commissions can have on some persons. For a large segment of the population, money is the motivator that leads to higher levels of performance. Examples of content theories of motivation include Maslow's hierarchy of needs theory,[7], Herzberg's two-factor theory[8], and McClelland's N-achievement theory.[9]

Process theories of motivation focus on how employees become motivated to work. Two important types of process theories are equity theory and instrumentality-expectancy theory. Equity theory is illustrated in Figure 10-1.[10]

[6]E. E. Lawler III, "Job Attitudes and Employee Motivation: Theory, Research, and Practice," *Personnel Psychology*, Vol. 23 (1970), pp. 223–237; R. L. Opsahl and M. D. Dunnette, "The Role of Financial Compensation in Industrial Motivation," *Psychological Bulletin*, Vol. 66 (1966), pp. 94–118; J. R. Terborg and H. E. Miller, "Motivation, Behavior, and Performance: A Closer Examination of Goal Setting and Monetary Incentives," *Journal of Applied Psychology*, Vol. 63 (1978), pp. 29–39; Clay W. Hamner, "How to Ruin Motivation with Pay," *Compensation Review* (Third Quarter, 1975), pp. 88–98.

[7]Abraham H. Maslow, *Motivation and Personality* (New York: Harper & Row, 1954).

[8]F. Herzberg, B. Mausner, and B. Snyderman, *The Motivation to Work*, 2nd ed. (New York: John Wiley & Sons, Inc., 1959).

[9]D. C. McClelland, *The Achieving Society* (Princeton, New Jersey: Van Nostrand, 1961).

[10]J. S. Adams, "Toward an Understanding of Inequity," *Journal of Abnormal and Social Psychology*, Vol. 67 (1963), pp. 422–435; R. D. Pritchard, "Equity Theory: A Review and Critique," *Organizational Behavior and Human Performance* (May 1969), pp. 176–211.

Focal Person		Referent Person
Outcomes (e.g., pay, benefits, job satisfaction)	:	Outcomes
Inputs (e.g., education, experience, effort)		Inputs

FIGURE 10-1   Equity Theory

Under equity theory an employee (focal person) provides *inputs* to his or her job; these include factors such as education, knowledge, skills, abilities, and effort. In return, an employee receives pay, employee benefits, and other inducements such as job satisfaction, challenge, and the prestige of working for a well-known company. In this example, the focal person (employee) would evaluate his or her *ratio* of outcomes to inputs by comparing it to the *ratio* of a comparison person (referent). The employee would consider all of the inputs and outcomes of the other person to the extent that the employee was aware of them. The employee would calculate a ratio for the comparison person and compare it to his or her own ratio to determine whether he or she is being equitably treated. The other person is usually an individual who is in a position similar to that of the focal person. Thus an accountant working for General Motors (the focal person) might select another accountant at General Motors or, possibly, one working at Ford or Chrysler as the referent person. The accountant at General Motors would then measure his or her salary, benefits, and working conditions against the referent other. At the same time, the General Motors accountant would also compare his or her qualifications and effort (inputs) against those of the other person.[11] If the ratio of outputs to inputs is approximately equal between the focal person and the referent person, the focal person may conclude that he or she is being treated equitably. On the other hand, if the other person is receiving more outputs (e.g., pay) than the focal person (assuming that inputs between the focal and other person are equal), then a state of *underreward* inequity exists for the focal person. An employee experiencing perceived underreward inequity may react in several different ways in an attempt to restore equity (equality of ratios). First, the employee may ask for more rewards, such as a pay raise. This may explain why some organizations attempt to enforce *pay secrecy* policies by insisting that employees not discuss their pay with each other. Second, the focal person may reduce inputs by exerting less effort on the job or, in an extreme case, tender his or her resignation. Third, the employee may find a more realistic referent with whom to make outcome-input comparisons. A police officer who compares his or her pay and employee benefits with those of a corporate executive is probably selecting a referent that will lead the officer to believe that a state of underreward inequity exists. By changing the referent to another police officer (or perhaps a corrections officer or firefighter), a more accurate assessment of personal equity can be made. Fourth, the employee person may rationalize that the inequity is not important and ignore the problem. A

---

[11]Richard W. Scholl, Elizabeth A. Cooper, and Jack F. McKenna, "Referent Selection in Determining Equity Perception: Differential Effects on Behavioral and Attitudinal Outcomes," *Personnel Psychology* (Spring 1987), pp. 113–124.

person may claim that the problems associated with the referent's job are not worth the extra compensation. Occasionally, an employee may discover that a state of *overreward* inequity exists. According to equity theory, employees who perceive themselves as overrewarded will also want to bring the ratios into line. The overrewarded employee might try to reduce his or her ratio by increasing the effort on the job. The employee may also try to increase the ratio of the comparison person by persuading the employer to increase the comparison person's outcomes. As with underreward inequity, the employee can resolve overreward inequity by selecting another comparison person or by leaving the organization. The main lessons to be learned from equity theory are that employees *will evaluate* how equitably they are treated, *are sensitive* to perceived inequities, and will *seek to resolve* them.

The issue of equity is very important to all firms, but especially to those engaged in high-technology activities. Employees who are working in highly specialized and highly technical areas are in a position to make enormous contributions to their companies. Consider the following true story. "A research scientist for a large pharmaceutical corporation develops and patents a successful new drug that produces $100 million in revenue its first year on the market. The executives of the division receive large cash bonuses, and the top salespeople enjoy windfall commissions from the strong demand for the new product—but the scientist receives only a $500 honorarium for developing the drug."[12] Companies must be prepared to develop reward systems that can maintain equity under circumstances such as these. The likely result of a failure to maintain equity is the departure of the employee for greener pastures and a more equitable situation.

The concept of equity in the compensation literature is similar to but more broad-based than that found in the behavioral science literature. The compensation literature defines three different types of equity associated with compensation systems:

1. *External equity* compares the pay of *similar* jobs in *comparable* organizations. An employee working for McDonalds might compare his or her pay with that of a Burger King employee. External equity deals with the concept of *pay levels*. *Wage and salary surveys* are the primary means of collecting information on pay levels.
2. *Internal equity* compares the pay of persons with *dissimilar* jobs within the *same* organization. A checkout clerk in a grocery store might compare his or her salary with that of a produce clerk or a meat cutter working in the same store. Internal equity deals with *pay structures*. *Job evaluation* is the method used to place a value on a job within the pay structure.
3. *Procedural equity* determines the fairness with which pay rates are set and pay changes such as annual raises are made. Pay increases may be made with all

[12]Luis R. Gomez-Mejia, David B. Balkin, and George T. Milkovich, "Rethinking Rewards for Technical Employees," *Organizational Dynamics* (Spring 1990), p. 62.

employees receiving the same dollar or percentage increase, or pay changes may be geared to seniority or job performance.[13]

A second process theory, instrumentality-expectancy theory (Figure 10-2), can be simplified and illustrated as follows:

Effort ⟶ Performance ⟶ Rewards

FIGURE 10-2   Instrumentality-Expectancy Theory

Whether compensation serves as an adequate motivator depends on the effort-performance and performance-reward links.[14] An employee may be willing to work harder only if he or she believes that job performance will improve. By working 60 hours rather than 40 hours a week, the employee may believe that he or she will receive an overall rating of "excellent" on the next annual performance evaluation. On the other hand, there is also the possibility that the extra effort will go unnoticed or unappreciated, in which case the effort-performance link breaks down.[15] By receiving an "excellent" evaluation, the employee might anticipate a generous pay raise. If this does not occur, then the second link (performance-reward) breaks down. Both links break down if the pay raise (reward) is not important to the employee, who instead may covet the additional 20 hours per week of leisure time. Thus, both the effort-performance and the performance-reward links must be strong *and* the reward must be sufficiently attractive to the employee. If any of these conditions are not met, the effectiveness of money as a motivator is diminished.

Laws Regulating Compensation and Employee Benefits

A number of federal and state laws regulate compensation and employee benefits, and it is important that personnel managers and compensation specialists understand these laws, as well as the manner in which they are interpreted by the

---

[13]See Jerald Greenberg, "Reactions to Procedural Injustice in Payment Distributions: Do the Means Justify the Ends?" *Journal of Applied Psychology* (February 1987), pp. 55–61.

[14]Victor H. Vroom, *Work and Motivation* (New York: Wiley, 1964), and J. R. Hackman and L. W. Porter, "Expectancy Theory Prediction of Work Effectiveness," *Organizational Behavior and Human Performance*, Vol. 12 (1968), pp. 417–426. An expanded version of this theory was presented in Chapter 2. See also Walter B. Newsom, "Motivate Now," *Personnel Journal* (February 1990), pp. 51–55.

[15]Robert Drazin and Ellen R. Auster, "Wage Differences Between Men and Women: Performance Appraisal Ratings vs. Salary Allocation As the Locus of Bias," *Human Resource Management* (Summer 1987), pp. 157–168; and "Pay for Performance: The Pros and Cons," *Personnel Journal* (June 1987), pp. 104–111.

regulatory bodies and courts. The major laws affecting compensation management are summarized briefly here:

- *Fair Labor Standards Act* (FLSA) (1938): The FLSA regulates minimum wage and hour provisions that apply to most private sector organizations, federal and state agencies, and labor unions. The FLSA distinguishes between *exempt* and *nonexempt* employees. Executives, administrators, professionals, and outside salespersons are in the exempt category and are not subject to the act's overtime provisions. Nonexempt employees working more than 40 hours per week must be paid one and a half times their normal rate for each hour worked beyond 40 hours. The FLSA regulates the working hours of children under age 16 and also specifies that persons under age 18 cannot work in hazardous jobs. The act requires that employers keep detailed records on employee compensation and enforcement lies with the Wage and Hour Division of the U.S. Department of Labor.
- *Workers' Compensation Laws:* Each state has enacted and administers worker's compensation legislation that provides benefits for employees who suffer job-related injuries. Workers' compensation laws provide disability income payments while the employee is out of work, payments for catastrophic losses (limbs, eyesight, permanent injuries, and so on), burial expenses, and payment of medical bills.
- *Federal Laws Regulating Government Contractors:* Several laws regulate the minimum wages that are to be paid by firms holding federal government contracts. The *Davis-Bacon Act* (1931) requires that construction contractors pay the prevailing wage in the area in which the contract is held, and the *Walsh-Healy Act* (1936) extends the Davis-Bacon Act to most nonconstruction contractors and requires overtime pay (time and a half) for work beyond 8 hours per day and 40 hours per week. In 1965, the *McNamara-O'Hara Act* extended these obligations to service contractors.
- *Social Security Act* (1935): The current Social Security program is composed of four major programs: the retirement program (1935), which provides an income for eligible retirees; the survivorship program (1939), which provides income to the family of a deceased worker (a form of life insurance); the disability program (1956), which pays disability benefits to eligible workers who are totally and permanently disabled; and the health insurance program (enacted in 1965 and better known as *Medicare*) for eligible persons above age 65. These programs are administered by the federal Social Security Administration and are funded through payroll taxes on employees and employers.
- *Unemployment Compensation Laws:* State-administered programs generally provide payments to workers during periods of joblessness that occur for reasons beyond the employee's control. In most states, unemployment compensation insurance is available to an unemployed person for up to 26 weeks. Unemployment insurance is financed by employers in all but three states.
- *Consumer Credit Protection Act* (1968): This law regulates wage garnishments in which an employee has pay withheld by someone to whom he or she owes

money. Under this law, wage garnishments can be obtained only by a court order and limits are placed on the amount subject to garnishment. The Consumer Credit Protection Act also makes it illegal for an employer to terminate an employee for garnishments over a single debt. The Wage and Hour Division of the U.S. Department of Labor enforces the act.

- *Federal/State Child Support Enforcement Program (1975), Child Support Enforcement Amendments of 1984:* This law allows automatic mandatory wage withholding for child support payments. This amendment provides a means of obtaining delinquent child support payments and mandatory payroll deductions to ensure that payments are made on time. State child support enforcement agencies can order employers to withhold pay without the need of a court review. Employers cannot discipline, discharge, or refuse to hire employees who have wages withheld under this law.

- *Employee Retirement Income Security Act* (ERISA) (1974): Retirement programs are regulated under this federal law. The major purpose of ERISA is to safeguard pension funds so that they will be available to employees when they retire. The act sets forth standards on funding, fiduciary responsibilities, vesting, and eligibility to join a retirement program, and it created the Pension Benefit Guaranty Corporation to insure pension funds in the event of program mismanagement or bankruptcy of the employer.

- *Health Maintenance Act* (1973): This act requires firms with 25 or more employees to provide the option of a health maintenance organization (HMO) as part of their health insurance plan if an HMO exists in the local area. HMOs provide comprehensive medical care through a group of health care providers. HMOs have traditionally emphasized preventive medical care. The act is an amendment to the FLSA.

- *Tax Reform Act* (1986): This act makes significant changes in corporate and individual tax structures and imposes a number of changes on the regulation and taxation of employee benefits. (Some of the changes relevant to compensation and employee benefits are discussed in later sections of this chapter and in Chapter 12.) The act is indicative of the federal government's desire to become more involved in the regulation of employee benefit programs.[16]

- *Consolidated Omnibus Budget Reconciliation Act* (COBRA) (1985): This laws allows a continued health insurance protection if an employee dies, is involuntarily or voluntarily terminated (except for gross misconduct), as well as for other "qualified" events that could otherwise terminate health insurance coverage. COBRA provides employees or their families with the option of purchasing continuing health insurance coverage (at the expense of the employee or family) regardless of their insurability.[17]

---

[16]Jack H. Schecter, "The Tax Reform Act of 1986: Its Impact on Compensation and Benefits," *Compensation and Benefits Review* (November-December 1986), pp. 11–24.-

[17]See Stephen A. Huth, "Cobra's 2nd Year: High Costs in a No-Cost Program," in *The Human Resources Yearbook*, 1990 edition (Englewood Cliffs, New Jersey: Prentice-Hall, Inc., 1987), pp. 2.103–2.124, and Muriel N. Feldman, "COBRA Compliance: Guidelines for Employers," *Employment Relations Today* (Spring 1988), pp. 1–8.-

- *Equal Pay Act* (EPA) (1963): This act protects against sex discrimination in pay by mandating equal pay for equal work. Jobs do not have to be identical to be equal, and the factors of responsibility, effort, working conditions, and skills are used to evaluate the equality of two or more jobs to determine pay equity. Unequal pay is permissible for differences in employee seniority, merit, and productivity. The EPA is administered by the EEOC. Pay discrimination can also violate *Title VII of the Civil Rights Act* (1964), the *Age Discrimination in Employment Act* (1967), and other federal and state equal employment opportunity laws.

These laws are designed primarily to protect employees from unfair pay discrimination, loss of employee benefits, and economic hazards such as injury, disease, and unemployment. Some of these laws require that personnel departments maintain records on pay and employee benefits. As noted earlier, personnel/-human resource managers must stay abreast of legislative changes that occur, as well as legal developments applicable to these laws. Many of these laws are discussed in greater detail in Chapters 11 and 12.

Labor Unions and Collective Bargaining

Labor unions are often thought to have a strong influence on pay levels.[18] Because of the profound impact that wage settlements have on the financial condition of the firm and its employees, labor and management negotiators prepare extensively prior to engaging in contract talks. The wage settlements reached as the result of collective bargaining are based on the employer's ability to pay, changes in the consumer price index, wage and benefit trends for other firms in the same industry and labor market, and the bargaining strength and skills of the respective negotiators. The exact impact that unions have on pay levels and structures is difficult to measure because it is not known what employers might pay in the absence of unions, and it is difficult to make comparisons between unionized and nonunionized firms.

Unions probably raise wages in the short run, and they have the greatest impact on pay levels when union bargaining power is high relative to the bargaining power of the employer. Bargaining power is determined by factors such as the degree of unionization within an industry, the economic condition of the employer, the employer's vulnerability to a strike, the availability of replacements for striking workers, general economic conditions, and the bargaining savvy of negotiators. Unions probably affect pay levels most profoundly through their support of the cost-of-living adjustment formulas (COLAs) that were incorporated into many collective bargaining agreements during the inflationary periods of the 1970s and early 1980s. However, a blanket statement that unions increase pay

---

[18]See Thomas A. Kochan, *Collective Bargaining and Industrial Relations* (Homewood, Illinois: Richard D. Irwin, Inc., 1980); Daniel J. B. Mitchell, *Unions, Wages, and Inflation* (Washington, D.C.: Brookings Institute, 1980).

levels by some specified percentage is tenuous because of the uncertainty surrounding the collective bargaining process.

Unions have an important impact on pay structures through their emphasis on seniority in pay decisions and their egalitarian nature. Most union leaders deemphasize merit and job performance in determining individual pay increases and promotions and, instead, use seniority to make these decisions. Labor unions have also been a major driving force behind the expansion of employee benefit programs. Thus it is certain that labor unions *do* make a difference in pay levels, pay structures, and employee benefits. What is more difficult to determine is *how much* of an influence unions have on employee compensation.[19]

◼ The Impact of Compensation on Employee Performance and Organizational Effectiveness

Personnel/human resource managers are primarily interested in the impact that pay will have on individual employee performance and organizational effectiveness. Most compensation programs are designed to attract quality job applicants to the organization, motivate employees to perform to their highest capabilities, and allow the organization to retain its best employees. This section examines the issues of pay equity and job satisfaction and the effects of compensation on job performance, employee attendance, and organizational effectiveness.

Compensation, Occupational Choice, and Job Selection

Conversations with students entering college often reveal a high percentage aspiring to premedicine, business, or law, all of which offer the potential for high salaries and professional status. It is likely that the attractiveness of professions such as medicine, law, and business is based largely on their potential earning power. Discussions among college seniors and graduate students who are in the process of interviewing for jobs also focus on how much a certain company is offering compared to other organizations. Clearly, pay is an important element in both career and job choice.

Persons evaluating the pay of a job offer should consider several factors. First, the cost of living in the location where the pay check will be spent is an important consideration. As noted earlier, cost of living differentials among geographic areas in the United States and in foreign countries can have a profound impact on real

[19]Several excellent labor economics textbooks are available that give an in-depth look at wage theory. See Ronald G. Ehrenberg and Robert S. Smith, *Modern Labor Economics: Theory and Public Policy* (Glenview, Illinois: Scott, Foresman, and Company, 1982); Lloyd G. Reynolds, *Labor Economics and Labor Relations*, 7th ed. (Englewood-Cliffs, New Jersey.: Prentice-Hall, Inc., 1978); and Gordon F. Bloom and Herbert R. Northrup, *Economics of Labor Relations*, 9th ed., (Homewood, Illinois: Richard D. Irwin, Inc., 1981).

income. Variations in property and sales tax rates, the cost of housing, transportation expenses, and the cost of food and entertainment are worthy of serious consideration during the job interview and the selection process. Second, career and job choices should not focus exclusively on the starting salary. Some organizations offer high initial salaries but only modest annual pay raises thereafter. Other organizations offer low starting salaries but have lucrative incentive and bonus plans. Still other organizations have liberal employee benefits and perquisites that may increase take-home pay and provide long-term financial security. Often the employer (and not the employee) pays for group insurance premiums, retirement contributions, and other amenities. Long-term financial security can be provided through tax-sheltered income and retirement programs, and all of these factors have some influence on organizational and job choice.

Pay Equity and Job Satisfaction

The amount of compensation received has a major impact on whether an employee is satisfied or dissatisfied with his or her job. Pay and employee benefits may comprise as much as three fourths of the total budget in labor-intensive organizations such as hospitals, educational institutions, service organizations, and certain public sector entities. Even in capital-intensive firms, the dollar expenditure for pay and employee benefits can be significant. It is therefore safe to conclude that most organizations are (or should be) vitally interested in designing pay packages that encourage high levels of employee job satisfaction and job performance. A progressive view of compensation is that money spent on salaries should be thought of not as a cost, but as an investment in human capital.[20] The dividend reaped from the proper use of this investment is a stable and productive workforce.[21]

Figure 10-3 provides a conceptualization of the factors that determine the relationship between pay and the employee's feeling of equitable treatment and job satisfaction. This model focuses on (1) factors affecting the amount of pay that an employee *perceives* as being equitable, (2) factors affecting the *actual* amount of pay received, and (3) the consequences of an imbalance between perceived pay and actual pay. An attempt is made to integrate several behavioral theories into the model.[22] In

[20]A substantial amount of research has been done on the relative importance of pay. Pay has received various rankings relative to other job-related factors. A summary of the research and importance of pay can be found in Edward E. Lawler III, *Pay and Organizational Effectiveness: A Psychological View* (New York: McGraw-Hill Book Company, 1971).-

[21]Compensation management is interrelated with other personnel/human resource management functions. For example, recruitment and selection programs are affected by compensation policies. Likewise, compensation programs serve as *employee maintenance* functions, as do training and development, performance appraisal, and employee discipline programs.

[22]Figure 10-3 integrates ideas from several behavioral theories. The most obvious contributions, however, are from Adam's equity theory, Katzell's discrepancy theory, and Maslow's hierarchy of needs theory. See R. A. Katzell, "Personal Values, Job Satisfaction, and Job Behavior," in H. Borow (ed.), *Man in a World of Work* (Boston: Houghton-Mifflin Company, 1964), pp. 341–363.

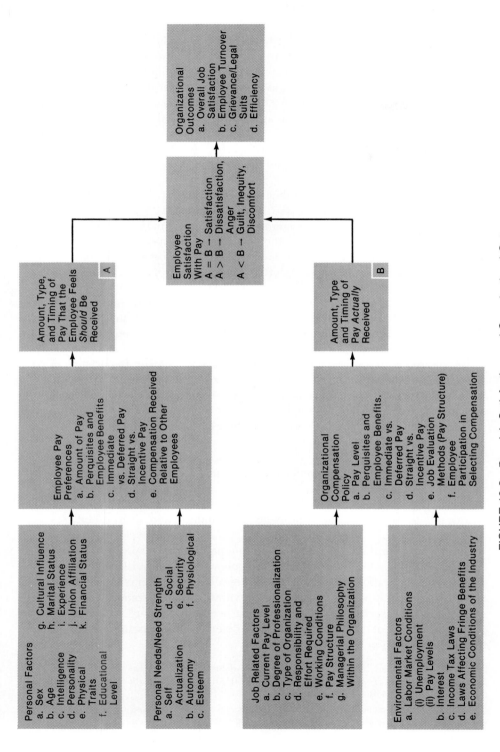

FIGURE 10-3 Pay, Job Satisfaction, and Organizational Outcomes

383

addition, the type of pay, the amount of pay, and the timing with which the pay is administered (immediate versus deferred compensation) are included.

Much of the research on compensation conducted by behavioral scientists has been narrow in both scope and sample. As a result, the findings are often not generalizable to a variety of organizational settings. Lawler, in reviewing the research on pay and its influence on attitudes, concluded the following:[23]

1. Satisfaction with rewards such as pay is a function of how much is paid, how much other employees receive, and the perceptions of what an employee feels should be paid.
2. Satisfaction with rewards can influence overall job satisfaction, as well as employee absenteeism and turnover.
3. The promise of rewards will encourage improved job performance if, and only if, the rewards are important to the individual employee.
4. Depending on how the pay system is treated, it can be a positive or negative force in organizational change efforts.

An examination of Figure 10-3 illustrates several important points. First, different employees attach varying degrees of importance to pay and have different preferences regarding the amount, type (salary versus employee benefits versus perquisites), and timing (immediate versus deferred compensation) of pay received. Research has examined the relationship between the importance of pay and factors such as sex, age, intelligence, personality, and religion.[24] This research has often produced conflicting and uncertain results because of the variety of organizational settings and methodologies. One summary of the research on pay gave the following tongue-in-cheek description of a person who is likely to value pay highly:

> The employee is male, young (probably in his twenties); he has low self-assurance and high neuroticism; he comes from a small town or farm background; he belongs to few clubs and social groups; he owns his own home or aspires to own it; and he is probably a Republican and a Protestant.[25]

Second, organizational job, and environmental factors shape an organization's compensation policies. A compensation policy deals with issues such as the amount an organization will pay its employees relative to other companies (the pay level decision), the manner in which pay within the organization will be determined (the pay structure and job evaluation decisions), the use of incentive programs, the nature of employee benefits and deferred compensation programs, and the administration of the program.

[23]Garnett Stokes Shaffer, "Patterns of Work and Nonwork Satisfaction," *Journal of Applied Psychology* (February 1987), pp. 115–124; and Edward E. Lawler III, *Pay and Organization Development* (Reading, Massachusetts: Addison-Wesley Publishing Company, 1981), p. 27.

[24]Luis R. Gomez-Mejia and David B. Balkin, "Effectiveness of Individual and Aggregate Compensation Strategies," *Industrial Relations* (Fall 1989), pp. 431–445.

[25]Edward E. Lawler III, *Pay and Organization Development*, p. 24.

Third, employees form an opinion of what they personally feel is both an equitable amount and type of compensation. Pay equity is in the eye of the beholder; regardless of what the employer thinks about the fairness of pay levels and pay structures, *employee* perceptions are the most relevant factors in determining pay equity. As Figure 10-3 indicates, a comparison of actual pay with expected pay determines the degree of satisfaction or dissatisfaction. Two pay theories that are relevant to Figure 10-3 are (1) *discrepancy theory,* which indicates that pay satisfaction is the difference between the pay that is desired and the pay that one actually receives, and (2) *equity theory,* which states that pay satisfaction is the result of an individual's comparing his or her job inputs and outcomes to those of fellow employees.[26]

The degree of importance attached to pay depends on an employee's personal characteristics (race, sex, age, family background, and education) and circumstances (financial condition, geographic location, and accustomed lifestyle). Likewise, the extent to which various types and amounts of pay motivate employees to work harder and derive satisfaction from the job are a function of some of the factors depicted in Figure 10-3.

Compensation and Job Performance

High levels of job satisfaction do not necessarily guarantee high levels of employee productivity. Conversely, dissatisfied employees may, on occasion, exhibit high levels of job performance. Thus, there is no completely consistent relationship between job satisfaction (of which pay satisfaction is a major component) and performance. It is probably safe to say that compensation specialists have tried thousands of different combinations of pay and employee benefits to motivate high levels of job performance. In fact, no two organizations have exactly the same philosophy and methods for structuring their compensation packages in an attempt to induce extra effort from employees. An examination of the research coupled with the material presented in Chapter 2 suggests the following:

1. Pay will generally motivate employees if it is believed that good performance will lead to higher pay and if employees value pay.
2. Organizations must continually emphasize the importance of the performance-pay relationship.
3. Negative consequences associated with good performance and higher pay such as adverse peer pressure must be minimized.

Although many organizations and managers pay lip service to tying merit (as measured by the performance appraisal process) to the amount of pay an employee receives, there is some evidence that little attention is given to the performance-

[26]See Allen N. Nash and Stephen J. Carroll, Jr., *The Management of Compensation* (Monterey, California: Brooks/Cole Publishing Company, 1975), p. 75, and E. A. Locke, "The Nature and Consequences of Job Satisfaction," in M. D. Dunnette (ed.), *Handbook of Industrial and Organizational Psychology* (Chicago: Rand-McNally, 1973).

pay link in actual practice. Managers who agree that pay raises should be linked to merit often do not practice what they preach. Rather, factors such as individual seniority, cost-of-living adjustments, and the organization's financial ability to grant pay raises govern most pay decisions. Merit does, however, have an impact on promotions, which subsequently affect pay. Within a particular job level or classification, however, individual merit is not always an important factor.[27]

Some employees may not want their pay tied to performance. This may be due to low individual motivation, fear of unfavorable pressure from fellow employees, or the belief that management will raise performance standards if employees are overly successful at earning too much extra compensation. It is possible that nonmanagerial employees are less favorably disposed toward merit pay plans than those in managerial positions. If this is true, compensation managers may face a major challenge in using pay to motivate employees.

A major hurdle in tying pay to improved job performance is the careful design and administration of a performance appraisal system (see Chapter 9).[28] Performance appraisal is the means by which performance standards can be established, communicated to employees, and used to determine pay. Employee acceptance and trust appear to be crucial factors in determining the success of a merit or incentive pay plan that links quality job performance or high productivity to compensation levels.

Compensation and Job Attendance

Pay can be an important factor in determining whether an employee will attend work on a particular day.[29] Absenteeism may be caused by the desire to avoid the unpleasantness of a work environment (the job, fellow employees, supervisors, working conditions) or disillusionment with the organization's reward structure (pay, promotion, employee recognition). Thus absenteeism may be one way in which an employee may react to a state of underreward inequity in accordance with equity theory. Employees are generally given, through sick days and other forms of leave, the opportunity to miss a certain number of days annually without losing pay. However, some employees are absent even though this decreases their pay.

Tardiness and leaving early from work also impose some of the same costs as absenteeism and are often caused by the same factors. Absenteeism, tardiness, and leaving early may be controlled by using hourly pay rather than a flat salary. However, hourly pay may create dissatisfaction among professionals and white-

---

[27]Jerrold R. Bratkovich, "Pay for Performance Boosts Productivity," *Personnel Journal* (January 1990), pp. 106–110; Thomas Rollins, "Pay for Performance: Is It Worth the Trouble?," *Personnel Administrator* (May 1988), pp. 42–46, and Charles Cumming, "Linking Pay to Performance," *Personnel Administrator* (May 1988), pp. 47–52.

[28]See Frederick S. Hills, *Compensation Decision Making* (Chicago: The Dryden Press, 1987), chapt. 12, and George T. Milkovich and Jerry M. Newman, *Compensation*, 2nd ed. (Plano, Texas: Business Publications, Inc., 1987), Chaps. 8–10.

[29]E. E. Lawler, *Pay and Organizational Effectiveness* (1971), pp. 179–201.

collar workers because of the blue-collar stigma associated with such pay. Hourly pay systems also impose administrative costs because of the added burden of record keeping. Furthermore, overtime pay may encourage job attendance beyond the normal working hours if adequate hourly wages or salary bonuses are given.

The best way to motivate job attendance may not involve pay at all. Rather, the employee's degree of job involvement, peer relations, and self-actualization may have a greater impact on attendance than monetary rewards. Pay plans that are properly designed and administered, however, can make a difference in marginal attendance cases.

Compensation and Employee Turnover

To the extent that an employee's pay determines job satisfaction, it will also have an effect on whether an employee is likely to resign and accept a job elsewhere. The decision to leave an organization involves two considerations: (1) an employee's *desire* to leave and (2) an employee's *ability* to leave. Because the typical employee has more information on internal equity (or inequity), it is likely that dissatisfaction with pay has a greater impact on employee turnover than does the availability of better-paying jobs in other organizations. Except for the exceptionally talented or skilled individual, most employees do not routinely receive unsolicited job offers from other companies. Thus the desire to move may be rooted in job dissatisfaction rather than the availability of a more lucrative job elsewhere.[30]

Most employees realize that there are certain monetary and personal costs associated with changing jobs. Relocating a family that has established bonds in a community can be psychologically and socially traumatic. Unless the new employer bears the financial burden, a middle manager's pay raise in a new job may not be sufficient to offset the moving expenses. Employees entering a new workplace must undergo a period of reorientation and acceptance by fellow employees and supervisors. Even relocation to accept the ideal job has its risks, and leaving the security of a good job is often something employees may be reluctant to do even for a large increase in salary. Nevertheless, pay inequities can result in employee turnover if the level of dissatisfaction is high.

For inadequately paid employees who are trapped in a job because of labor market conditions or obsolescence of knowledge, skills, and abilities, other problems can arise. Employees in this predicament may suffer stress-related problems, psychological withdrawal, and poor physical and mental health. Problems such as these can lead to involuntary turnover if an employee requires medical care or is no longer able to work because of failing health.[31]

[30]Marc J. Wallace and Charles H. Fay, *Compensation Theory and Practice* (Boston: Kent Publishing Company, 1983), pp. 78–79.

[31]James H. Donnelly, Jr., James L. Gibson, and John M. Ivancevich, *Fundamentals of Management*, 7th ed. (Plano, Texas: Business Publications, Inc., 1990), p. 329.

Compensation and Organizational Effectiveness

Personnel/human resource managers and compensation specialists must recognize three major points when designing, implementing, and evaluating a compensation program. First, pay is generally an important factor to employees and will have at least some impact on occupational and job choice, job satisfaction, absenteeism, turnover, and productivity. The importance and impact of pay will vary among employees, depending on variables such as age, sex, income level, family situation, educational level, and other cultural, social, and economic factors. Second, the workforce will continue to change in somewhat predictable ways. Third, organizations change their missions, goals, strategies, and personnel policies. The implication for compensation managers regarding these three points is that pay systems must adapt with changing workforce, organizational, legal, and other environmental threats and opportunities. Figure 10-4 summarizes these changes and provides implications for compensation programs. Three essential points emerge from Figure 10-4:

1. Compensation programs will become increasingly tailored to the needs of the individual employee.[32] One primary reason for this is the increased diversity of the labor force to include more females, minorities, and older workers. EEO laws and a more educated labor force have led employees to insist on more equitable and individual treatment. For example, dual-career couples will have little need for duplicate health insurance coverage but may require high-quality child care facilities. Older workers may desire a comprehensive health insurance plan with high dollar coverage. Highly paid professionals and executives are interested in deferring and sheltering some of their income from taxes. The point is that no single pay plan is equally suitable for all employees. For this reason, many organizations are adopting "cafeteria" and flexible employee benefit plans (Chapter 12).

2. Greater attention may be paid to performance, knowledge, and skill-based pay. For example, under a knowledge-based pay system, a college graduate may receive higher pay for a job that does not require a college degree because of the intangible benefits that accrue from having a better-educated person perform the job. Furthermore, as performance appraisal plans become better designed and validated, it will become more feasible to link pay decisions to job performance.

3. Compensation policies, practices, and decisions must be defensible by those administering personnel/human resource management programs. This means that the issue of comparable pay for work of comparable worth must be addressed (Chapter 11). Job evaluation methods used to measure the value of jobs will be of central concern (Chapter 11). Pay secrecy policies may fall by the wayside as employees force organizations to reveal and justify pay-related decisions.

[32]Bureau of National Affairs, Inc., "Compensation in the Year 2000," *Bulletin to Management* (February 27, 1992), p. 64.

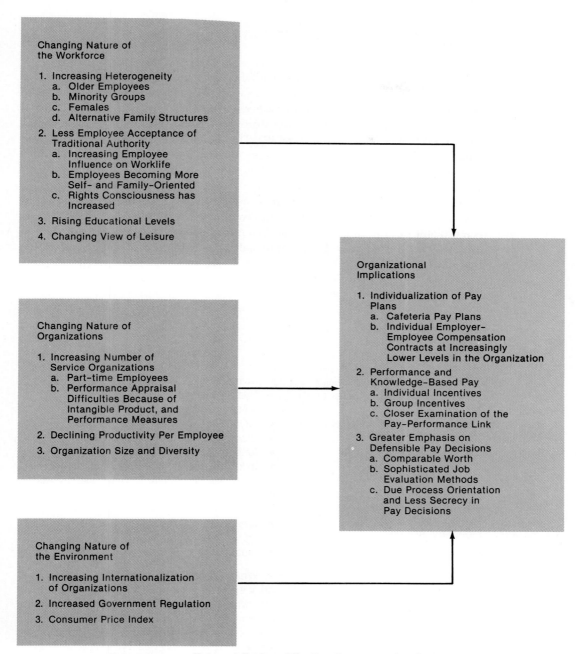

FIGURE 10-4   External Factors Affecting Compensation Programs

Adapted from Edward W. Lawler III: *Pay and Organization Development* (Reading, Mass.: Addison-Wesley Publishing Company, 1981), pp. 216–226.

■ Summary and Conclusions

This chapter has formed the foundation for understanding compensation management. Both the factors affecting compensation decisions and the impact of these decisions have been discussed and are used as a backdrop to a more detailed discussion on establishing and administering the compensation program (Chapter 11) and employee benefits (Chapter 12). The psychological, social, economic, and legal factors affecting pay decisions and outcomes are complex and, at times, imponderable. As a result, compensation management is one of the most challenging endeavors in the personnel field.

The management of a compensation program that meets the needs of professional, skilled, and unskilled employees from a wide range of social backgrounds is a difficult but not impossible task. What is needed is a structured approach to establishing internal and external equity, along with an array of employee benefits that meets the needs of a firm's workforce. These topics are discussed in Chapters 11 and 12.

■ Questions

1. Describe the four major types of compensation.
2. What is the difference between internal and external equity?
3. What is the difference between internal and external labor markets?
4. Briefly define the following:

- Labor demand as derived demand
- Exchange value of labor
- Marginal revenue productivity theory
- Loose versus tight labor markets
- Real versus monetary income

5. What is the difference between content and process theories of motivation?
6. Describe the outcomes-inputs ratio analysis used in equity theory.
7. What are the two important links in instrumentality-expectancy theory?
8. Briefly describe the coverage of the following laws:

- Fair Labor Standards Act
- Worker's compensation laws
- Davis-Bacon Act
- Walsh-Healy Act
- McNamara-O'Hara Act
- Social Security Act
- Unemployment compensation laws
- Consumer Credit Protection Act
- Child Support Enforcement Amendments
- Employee Retirement Income Security Act
- Health Maintenance Act
- Tax Reform Act of 1986
- Consolidated Omnibus Budget Reconciliation Act
- Equal Pay Act

9. What are the differences between discrepancy and equity theory?
10. What two factors must be considered by an employee before he or she decides to resign from the present job and accept employment elsewhere?

☐ APPLICATIONS AND CASE EXERCISES

1. Why is the concept of equity so important in compensation management? Based on a job that you or a close friend or relative has held, examine whether you believe that the compensation for this job was equitable. Be sure to consider internal, external, and procedural equity in your analysis.

2. Visit a local firm and determine what its external labor markets are for unskilled, skilled, and professional employees. How does the firm establish external pay equity? Does the firm pay more than, the same as, or less than its primary competitors?

3. Using the same firm from question 3, describe a segment of its internal labor market. How does the firm ensure internal and procedural equity? Has the firm encountered problems with hiring, attendance, productivity, or turnover that are attributable to the compensation system?

4. Obtain information on the cost of living in your area. Include estimates on what it would take for a family of four (two adults and two children) to enjoy a middle-income lifestyle that includes owning a home with a living area of approximately 2,000 square feet, two automobiles that are approximately 3 years old, plus the normal amounts of food, clothing, and other accessories that a middle-income family normally consumes. How much money would it take per year for your hypothetical family to live comfortably without having excess income for savings? Once you have completed this task, make cost estimates for the amount needed to live comfortably in the Honolulu, San Francisco, or New York metropolitan area. Be sure to include the cost of housing, taxes (real estate, sales, and income), transportation, food, clothing, and entertainment.

5. Select one of the compensation laws briefly discussed in the chapter. Examine its legislative history and provisions. Determine why the law was passed, and discuss its current strengths and weaknesses.

11

Establishing and Administering the Compensation Program

■ LEARNING OBJECTIVES

After reading this chapter, you should understand

1. The manner in which organizations compare their pay policies with those used in other organizations.
2. The factors that determine why some organizations pay their employees more than other organizations.
3. The use of wage and salary surveys.
4. The manner in which an organization decides what pay differences should exist among jobs within the same organization.
5. The use of job evaluation techniques.
6. The criteria used to determine individual pay differences for employees performing the same job.
7. The different types of individual and group incentive programs and the conditions under which such programs should be used.
8. The special compensation issues of executives, employees in high-technology firms, and employees in international organizations.
9. The distinction between the equal pay and comparable worth doctrines and the legal status of each.

■ INTRODUCTORY VIGNETTE

Pay for Knowledge Pays Off

While planning for major capital improvements 3 years ago, union and management at Inland Bar and Structural Company in East Chicago, Illinois, launched a pay-for-knowledge (PFK) system—a wage structure based on the number of skills or jobs an employee masters.

Inland's survival demanded such wide-reaching changes, according to Alan J. Wilgus, manager of human resources. "We saw that successful companies were using, among other strategies, newer forms of compensation. We realized if we didn't adapt to the changes going on around us, we'd go out of business," he says.

The company envisioned a major overhaul: "Taking workers out of fragmented jobs where they may not see how their role fits in the final product and giving them a new perspective of the company—what's 'upstream' and 'downstream' from them," Wilgus says. Thus, as part of the PFK plan, Inland began reorganizing the plant into teams of workers who, after training, would master all the jobs in a sequence and then rotate among jobs, after doing each for, say, a month.

Today much of the plant was converted to PFK. "It's ongoing," says Mike Mezzo, president of United Steelworkers of America, Local 1010. "The goal is to have [the plant] done by the end of '91."

Three factors in particular hamper a quick conversion: money, the large amounts of training required, and the many considerations about how to reorganize the plant. "It's left up to labor to come up with how the work should be organized, how it should flow, how many people are on each job, how they should be rotated, and how much training they need. It's really an extension of collective bargaining, only it's a much more cooperative approach," says Mezzo.

The collective bargaining agreement and seniority determine who is placed in which sequence. Seniority also buffers more experienced workers in a layoff situation, although it plays no part in work assignments or pay. That, according to Mezzo, is a drawback of a PFK system. "Under the old system, you could get on a level or a job you felt comfortable with and stay there by exercising your seniority. Now that jobs are rotated, you may be senior, but still have a crummy job for the day."

One of the pay-for-knowledge system's payoffs is increased wages. "Before, each sequence had four or five jobs in ascending order of earnings; you were only compensated for the tasks you performed," Mezzo says. "In a skill-based

Reprinted from "Pay for Knowledge Pays Off," *Labor Relations Today* (Washington, D.C.: U.S. Department of Labor, Bureau of Labor-Management Relations and Cooperative Programs, July-August 1991), p. 6.

system, once qualified for the job [in a sequence], you are compensated at the top rate, no matter which job you perform."

Adopting pay for knowledge is only one component of Inland's transformation, according to Wilgus. "Currently we're shifting the responsibility for manufacturing and quality to teams of workers. It's scaring people, but if you're serious about empowerment of workers, you need to go beyond PFK," says Wilgus.

Being taken seriously as knowledgeable partners draws an enthusiastic response from workers. He notes a recent innovation by one team that now saves the company $5,000 a week—a suggestion made in part because workers knew it would be considered.

Wilgus cites evidence that PFK is working, although both he and Mezzo admit it's too early to gauge long-term results. "Where implemented, I would say it's been a cautious success. There's evidence it works if both sides want it to," Wilgus says.

◼ Introduction

The previous chapter established a foundation for understanding compensation programs. With this introductory material as a backdrop, the current discussion deals with several major compensation decisions that are faced by nearly all organizations: the pay level decision, the pay structure decision, individual variations in pay, incentive programs, compensation of special employee groups, and the legal problems of equal pay and comparable worth. Figure 11–1 summarizes the major issues associated with establishing and administering the compensation program.

Several issues are important to the administration of compensation programs. First, compensation managers must view decisions regarding the pay level, pay structure, and individual pay as distinct, yet interrelated, facets of compensation. Second, compensation programs are strengthened by sound job analysis and performance appraisal systems. Thorough job analyses that promote internal and external equity in compensation and performance appraisal methods that accurately reflect the nature of the job make it easier to use "performance" as a means of rewarding employees. Third, compensation programs should recognize individual employee needs, whenever possible, in order to enhance job performance and achieve organizational goals.

◼ The Pay Level Decision

The Concept of External Equity

External equity (the pay level) is assessed by comparing similar jobs *between* comparable organizations. Two conditions must be satisfied: (1) the jobs being

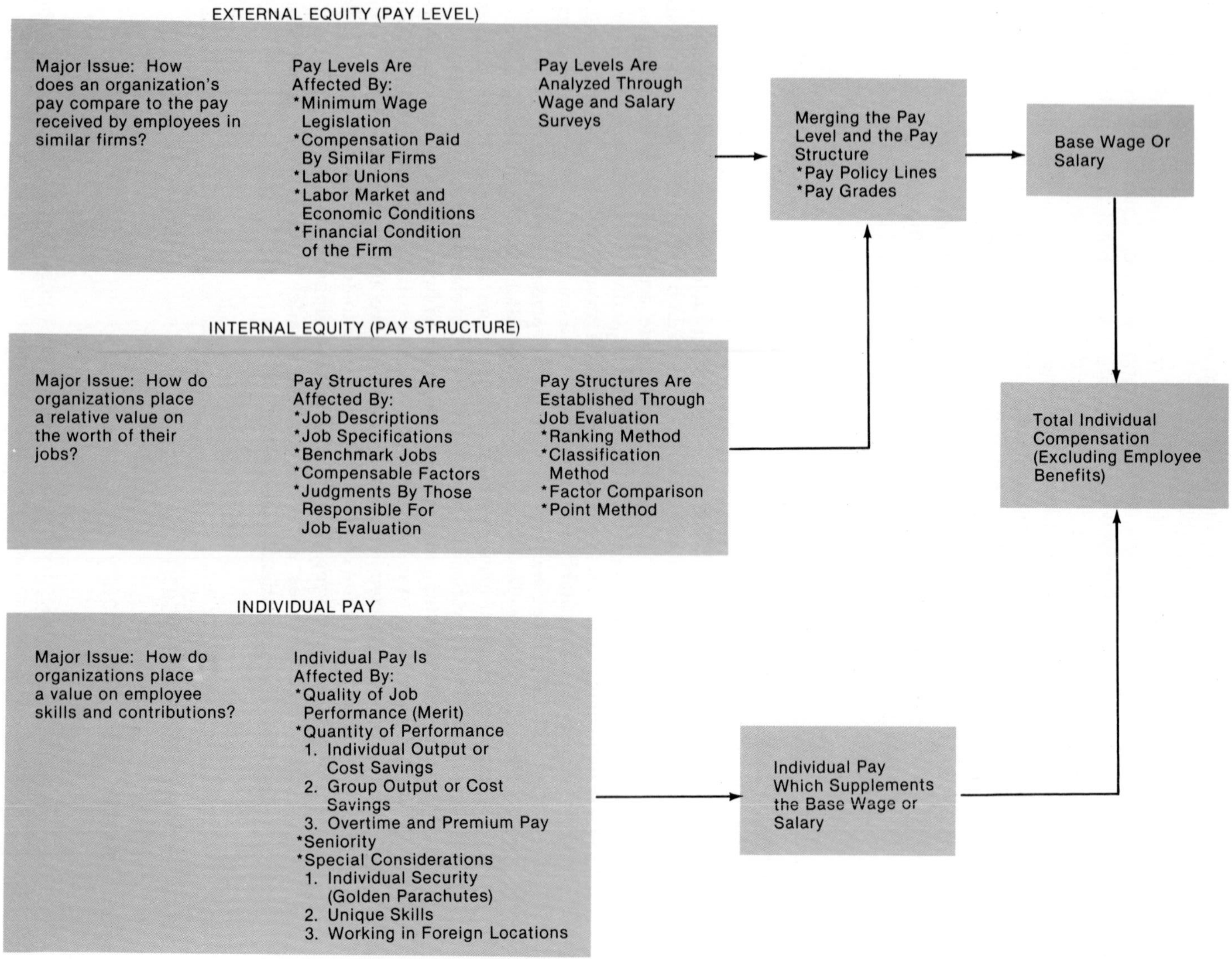

EXTERNAL EQUITY (PAY LEVEL)

Pay Levels Are
Analyzed Through
Wage and Salary
Surveys

Major Issue: How
does an organization's
pay compare to the pay
received by employees in
similar firms?

Pay Levels Are
Affected By:
*Minimum Wage
 Legislation
*Compensation Paid
 By Similar Firms
*Labor Unions
*Labor Market and
 Economic Conditions
*Financial Condition
 of the Firm

INTERNAL EQUITY (PAY STRUCTURE)

Pay Structures Are
Established Through
Job Evaluation
*Ranking Method
*Classification
 Method
*Factor Comparison
*Point Method

Major Issue: How do
organizations place
a relative value on
the worth of their
jobs?

Pay Structures Are
Affected By:
*Job Descriptions
*Job Specifications
*Benchmark Jobs
*Compensable Factors
*Judgments By Those
 Responsible For
 Job Evaluation

INDIVIDUAL PAY

Major Issue: How do
organizations place
a value on employee
skills and contributions?

Individual Pay Is
Affected By:
*Quality of Job
 Performance (Merit)
*Quantity of Performance
 1. Individual Output or
    Cost Savings
 2. Group Output or Cost
    Savings
 3. Overtime and Premium Pay
*Seniority
*Special Considerations
 1. Individual Security
    (Golden Parachutes)
 2. Unique Skills
 3. Working in Foreign Locations

Merging the Pay
Level and the Pay
Structure
*Pay Policy Lines
*Pay Grades

Base Wage Or
Salary

Total Individual
Compensation
(Excluding Employee
Benefits)

Individual Pay
Which Supplements
the Base Wage or
Salary

FIGURE 11-1   The Determination of Individual Compensation

compared must be the same or nearly the same, and (2) the organizations surveyed must be similar in size, function, mission, and sector. A personnel/human resource manager of a medium-sized manufacturing firm would ordinarily compare the wages of the company's production workers with those of a firm that is approximately the same size, competes in the same product market, and is located in the same geographic region. To compare the wages of production workers of medium-sized tool manufacturer in the southeastern United States with those of production workers in a high-tech firm in California's Silicon Valley would be inappropriate and misleading; there are vast differences in the job descriptions and qualifications of the two groups of production workers, as well as in the type of product and location of the firms.

Factors Affecting the Pay Level Decision

Organizations establish wage and salary levels based on a number of factors. Although each organization weighs these factors somewhat differently, all are considered in setting pay levels for different occupational groups. The factors discussed in the following sections directly affect the pay level decision.

Minimum Wage Legislation

The federal minimum wage law, the Fair Labor Standards Act (FLSA) of 1938, sets a minimum wage for workers employed by organizations affecting interstate commerce.[1] In 1985, the U.S. Supreme Court held that all state and municipal employees are also covered under the FLSA.[2] Nearly all states have enacted minimum wage laws.[3] As noted in Chapter 10, the FLSA stipulates that employees must be paid one and one-half times their regular pay rate for working more than 40 hours per week. The act also restricts the employment hours of individuals between the ages of 14 and 18 and prohibits persons in this age group from working in hazardous jobs. Other minimum wage laws applying to federal government contractors are the Davis-Bacon, Walsh-Healy, and McNamara-O'Hara acts. These laws require that the prevailing community wage be paid to eligible workers (often the prevailing wage is well about the federal minimum wage). Federal minimum wages have traditionally been set well below the amount that an average employee earns.[4] The intent of the law is not to raise the general wage

[1]The FLSA also requires an annual sales volume of $362,000 for retail and service establishments and $250,000 for all other firms. At this writing, the federal minimum wage was $4.25 per hour. For employees whose jobs entitle them to customer tips, the employer may count up to 40 percent of these tips toward the minimum wage.

[2]*Garcia v. San Antonio Metropolitan Transit Authority*, U.S. Supreme Court (1985).

[3]The Bureau of National Affairs, Inc., *Personnel Policy and Practice Series*, Wages and Hours (Washington, D.C.: The Bureau of National Affairs, Inc., 1986).

[4]Lloyd G. Reynolds, *Labor Economics and Labor Relations*, 7th ed. (Englewood Cliffs, New Jersey: Prentice-Hall, Inc., 1978), pp. 104–105.

level but to raise the pay of employees who have fallen far behind. Each amendment to the FLSA has set a new minimum at approximately 50 percent of the average hourly earnings in manufacturing.

For many compensation managers, the impact of minimum wage laws is nil because their firm's lowest wage far exceeds the federally mandated minimum.[5] Firms employing a large number of teenage and unskilled employees are affected the most by increases in the minimum wage because such firms adhere to a low-wage policy. Employees who are exempt from the FLSA include professional, executive, and sales employees, as well as some handicapped employees, students, agricultural employees, public transportation employees, employees working in amusement parks, and others.[6] Most exempt employees receive compensation that is well above the minimum wage. However, there has been considerable debate regarding the effects of minimum wage legislation on the young and unskilled worker. Whenever the minimum wage is raised, there is concern that persons with meager job skills and little experience will be displaced by older and better-qualified workers who have, in the past, stayed out of the labor force.

Compensation Levels in Other Organizations

Compensation managers must be cognizant of the wage and salary levels in similar organizations. Labor is a commodity that can be purchased in different quantities and prices. Furthermore, the quality of available labor varies in terms of skill, education, experience, and other personal attributes of the employee. Theoretically, high-quality labor is more likely to migrate to those organizations where the pay level is higher, assuming that working conditions, location, and other personnel practices are about the same.

Pay levels can be monitored by compensation managers and others through numerous sources of wage and salary information available from public and private sources (as discussed later in this chapter). In addition, organizations can conduct their own wage and salary surveys in order to assess the pay levels within a particular industry, segment of an industry, or locale.

Union Influences

Labor unions generally attempt to standardize wages among unionized firms in a particular industry.[7] The phenomenon of pattern bargaining explains why assembly line workers at General Motors, Ford, and Chrysler receive similar wages and

---

[5]Chang Yang-Ming and Issac Ehrlich, "On the Economics of Compliance with the Minimum Wage Law," *Journal of Political Economy* (February 1985), p. 84.

[6]Steven C. Kahn, "Exempt Employees: A Review of the Requirements," *Employment Relations Today* (Winter 1986), p. 317.

[7]Barry T. Hirsch and John I. Neufald, "Nominal and Real Union Wage Differentials and the Effects of Industry and SMSA Density," *Journal of Human Resources* (Winter 1987), p. 138, and Anil Verma, "Union and Nonunion Wages at a Firm Level: A Combined Institutional and Econometric Analysis," *Journal of Labor Research* (Winter 1987), p. 67.

benefits. Within a heavily unionized industry such as automobiles, the wage level settlement between the United Auto Workers and Ford heavily influences the wage settlement for General Motors and Chrysler. One of the traditions in the American labor movement is to "take wages out of competition." When wage levels within an industry are standardized, a low-wage employer cannot undercut a rival company and gain a competitive edge through lower prices obtained by labor cost savings. Standardized pay within an industry, in turn, forces companies to compete on the basis of product quality, production efficiencies, and customer brand loyalty.

Nonunionized firms are also affected by the pay levels negotiated in unionized organizations. Because most organizations wish to attract competent employees and remain nonunion, they often attempt to maintain pay levels that are equal to or perhaps greater than those of their unionized counterparts. Although there are other antiunion strategies that can be followed (some of which are illegal), the equalization-of-pay strategy is both legal (except for giving employees pay raises during union organizing campaigns) and enables nonunion firms to obtain quality labor.

Labor Market and Economic Conditions

Organizations raise wages and salaries when inflation is high, unemployment is low, or a specific type of employee or occupational group is in short supply. Conversely, pay levels rise much more slowly during periods of high unemployment when labor is abundant. Organizations increase pay levels in order to attract employees with scarce and high-demand job skills such as chemical engineers. The successful recruitment of talented employees can sometimes lead to the problem of *pay compression*. Pay compression results from the scarcity of employees with skills that are in high demand. Employers are forced to offer high salaries to skilled individuals in order to attract them to the organization. Many organizations do not have the financial resources to raise the pay levels of other employees in the organization. As a result, the pay differences between employees in entry-level jobs and those in higher-paying jobs becomes compressed. A classic example of pay compression in recent years has occurred among business school professors. Newly hired assistant professors who have recently received their Ph.D.s often make as much as or more than higher-ranking and more experienced professors.[8] The problem of pay compression has evolved into *pay inversion* in some cases; that is, newly-hired employees with highly desirable skills and abilities may command a higher salary than their more experienced counterparts who are performing the same job.

Increases in the cost of living also have a substantial impact on pay levels. Periodic increases in wages and salaries are often tied directly to changes in the consumer price index (CPI). Many collective bargaining agreements in unionized

---

[8]Luis R. Gomez-Mejia and David B. Balkin, "Pay Compression in an Academic Environment: The Case of Business Schools," in David B. Balkin and Luis R. Gomez-Mejia (Eds.), *New Perspectives on Compensation* (Englewood Cliffs, New Jersey: Prentice-hall, Inc., 1987), pp. 124–134.

firms have cost-of-living adjustment formulas (COLAs) that provide an automatic across-the-board pay raise as the CPI increases. A COLA formula does not usually increase pay levels by the same amount as the CPI increase. Thus a 4 percent increase in the CPI might yield a pay level increase of approximately 2 percent.

Organizational Ability to Pay and Strategy

In making pay level increases, firms need to look beyond the immediate profit picture and forecast the financial condition of the company in the future. It is generally easier to avoid large pay increases than it is to cut pay levels later because of financial hardship. Organizations that provide generous pay raises during prosperous times may be planting the seeds of disaster if the firm's business declines. Thus pay level decisions should be made carefully to avoid over-committing the organization's resources. Labor unions are also quick to point out the need to share profits during prosperous times with the employees who made it all possible. However, a dilemma exists for capital stock firms that also have an obligation to shareholders, who likewise expect to share in the firm's profitability.

In recent years, increasing attention has been given to the relationship between organizational strategy and pay policies. An organization's strategy defines its business in terms of product line, quality emphasis, market segment, geographical market limits, diversity, organizational structure, and size. Some companies follow an *algorithmic* pay pattern that emphasizes predetermined, standardized, repetitive measures such as fixed wage scales that can be used to process pay decisions in a standardized fashion, with little concern for individual differences among employees. Private organizations and government entities that are well established and exhibit little change in their mode of operations over a period of time may use an algorithmic approach to pay determination. *Experiential* pay patterns are flexible and adaptive in nature. Companies that are experiencing rapid growth, making significant changes in their product or service lines, or facing environmental uncertainties may be more likely to adopt an experiential pay pattern. An experiential pay pattern might make extensive use of incentive pay, bonuses, and stock options.[9]

Sources of Wage and Salary Data

Wage and salary surveys of comparable firms are the primary tool used to establish pay levels. Once the survey is completed and the wage and salary data are analyzed, the surveying firm can make adjustments to its pay level for individual jobs

---

[9]The algorithmic and experiential pay patterns are discussed in more detail in Luis R. Gomez-Mejia and David B. Balkin, *Compensation, Organizational Strategy, and Firm Performance* (Cincinnati, Ohio: Southwestern Publishing Company, 1992), pp 60–67. Gomez-Mejia and Balkin provide an excellent discussion of the relationship between compensation and organizational strategy, as well as extensive documentation of the compensation strategy literature.

or groups of jobs whose pay is out of line with the labor market.[10] Wage and salary information is generally gathered from two sources: (1) general surveys conducted by third parties such as state and federal departments of labor, consulting firms, or industry associations and (2) surveys tailored to a specific organization that are conducted by personnel specialists and consultants.

Pay Information Gathered by Third Parties

Federal and state governments gather large amounts of wage and salary information that is useful to compensation managers. The U.S. Department of Labor, Bureau of Labor Statistics (BLS), for example, conducts area, industrial, and other surveys covering a variety of jobs and occupations.[11] Private organizations such as The Bureau of National Affairs, Inc., the Society for Human Resource Management, The Hay Group, and various professional, trade, and industrial associations all perform wage and salary surveys.

A major advantage of ready-made or "canned" surveys is their low cost. Most surveys range in cost from $300 to $3,000 per year, depending on the source and the amount of information purchased. These surveys include a wide variety of jobs surveyed across large geographical areas. Ready-made surveys also pose several problems. First, there may be an imperfect match between the jobs surveyed and the job to which the survey information will be applied. Comparing the surveyed salary of an administrative assistant for a chemical manufacturer may be an "apples and oranges" comparison if the firm buying the information employs administrative assistants whose tasks and duties differ from those contained in the survey. There may be a mismatch between the relevant labor market of the employer and the labor market covered by the survey. Many surveys focus on large firms in urban areas and exclude jobs in small organizations and rural communities. Surveys that are industry specific and cover banks, insurance companies, or government organizations may have little relevance to firms outside those industries. Other surveys are geared to specific professions such as accounting, engineering, or health care. Therefore compensation specialists must carefully examine the sample from which a survey is made before applying the data to their organization.[12] Finally, by the time a wage and salary survey has been collected, organized, and published, 6 months to 1 year may have elapsed. Thus it is important to know the month and year the data were collected before they are used to make pay level decisions. During periods of high inflation, it is necessary to compensate for lags between the times when survey data are collected and published, as well

[10]Sara L. Rynes and George L. Milkovich, "Wage Surveys: Dispelling Some Myths About the 'Market Wage,' " *Personnel Psychology* (Spring 1986), p. 71.

[11]John D. Morton, "BLS Prepares to Broaden the Scope of Its White Collar Pay Survey," *Monthly Labor Review* (March 1987), p. 3.

[12]Theodore E. Weinberger, "A Way to Audit Job Matches of Salary Survey Participants," *Compensation Review* (Third Quarter 1984), pp. 47–58.

as for the lag between the times when the data are published and pay level changes will actually go into effect.[13]

Wage and Salary Surveys Tailored to a Specific Organization

Many of the problems associated with third-party wage and salary surveys can be eliminated by designing a wage and salary survey that specifically meets the needs of a particular organization. In essence, a trade-off is made between cost and accuracy when selecting between third-party and tailor-made surveys.[14] Once the decision has been made to perform a wage and salary survey, the personnel/human resource manager can decide whether to use in-house compensation specialists or obtain the services of a compensation consultant. Regardless of the avenue chosen, several important points must be kept in mind:

1. The organizations chosen to participate as respondents in the survey must be carefully selected. Ideally, the firms surveyed should be approximately the same size, offer the same products and services, and be located in the same geographical region.
2. The jobs for which the survey information is being gathered must be carefully chosen. A survey may focus on either *job-based* or *skill-based* systems. To keep the length of the survey reasonable, only those jobs that are essential to the successful completion of the survey should be included. In some industries, such as the airlines, there are number of standard or "benchmark" jobs that have essentially the same tasks, duties, responsibilities, and working conditions from one firm to another. By surveying benchmark jobs, the company can obtain an estimate of how its pay levels compare with those of other firms. An alternative approach is to focus the survey on the skills that employees bring to the job rather than on the job itself. Thus, a survey may ask how much a person with an MBA and 5 years of marketing and sales experience is normally paid (regardless of the job this person holds). The skills-based approach assumes that employers will make every effort to place employees in jobs that are commensurate with their knowledge, skills, and abilities. If employee benefits are to be surveyed, it might be wise to gather information only on the more expensive benefits such as paid vacations, retirement plans, and group health insurance.
3. Wage and salary questionnaires must be carefully constructed and pretested if accurate and timely information is to be obtained. The foundation for designing a survey is a comprehensive and current job analysis system that describes job duties, tasks, and responsibilities and specifies the employee education, experience, and skills necessary to perform the job. Survey data may be collected by personal interview, mail questionnaires, or telephone interviews. Regard-

---

[13]Steven D. Beggs, "The 'Lead-Lag' Problem: Adjustments Needed for Salary Comparisons," *Compensation and Benefits Review* (November-December 1986), pp. 44–54.

[14]Herbert Z. Halbrecht, "Compensation Surveys: Misleading Guideposts," *Personnel Journal* (March 1987), p. 122, and D. W. Belcher, N. Bruce Ferris, and John O'Neill, "How Wage Surveys Are Being Used," *Compensation and Benefits Review* (September-October 1985), p. 34.

less of the method used, survey questions must be clear and concise so that the respondent will understand the type of information being requested.

4. Respondents are more likely to cooperate if a *summary* of the survey results will be shared with them for the time and effort spent in providing wage and salary information. In order to ensure confidentiality, most surveys *do not* reveal salary and benefits data for a specific firm.

5. Wage and salary survey results should be summarized and analyzed in a form that is understandable and useful to those needing the information. Charts, graphs, tables, and illustrations usually enhance and clarify the information being presented.

Table 11–1 provides a summary of the types of information that should be included when designing a wage and salary survey.

Using the Wage and Salary Data

Data collected in a wage and salary survey are usually summarized by calculating the average pay levels for the jobs surveyed and examining the ranges and distribution of pay for each surveyed job. If the average pay for a job within an organization is considerably different from the average pay for the surveyed firms, then further investigation is required. Suppose that the survey reveals that the market rate salary for a clerk typist is $1,500 per month, but the surveying firm is paying $1,800 monthly to clerk typists. It is possible that the clerk typist job in the organization conducting the survey is different (in terms of responsibility, effort, working conditions, and skills) from other clerk typist jobs in the industry.

Summary statistics can be compiled to include the following:

- *Mean wages and salaries:* The average salary for each job surveyed.
- *Median salary:* The salary level for each job surveyed at which half of the surveyed salaries for a particular job are less and half of the salaries are greater.
- *Modal salaries:* The surveyed salary most frequently paid for a particular job.
- *Pay percentiles:* Salaries of the surveyed organizations are ranked for the 25th, 50th, and 75th percentiles. A job paid at the 25th percentile means that 25 percent of the surveyed organizations pay a lower salary or wage for this job and 75 percent pay more. The median salary equals the 50th percentile.
- *Pay distributions:* Considerations such as the range in pay and the shape of the pay distribution for surveyed jobs can be important. Pay distributions may follow the normal distribution of a bell-shaped curve, a bimodal distribution, or a uniform (rectangular) distribution. Figure 11-2 illustrates each of these distributions.

By calculating summary statistics, compensation specialists can obtain a better indication of the appropriateness of their pay relative to what other organizations are paying. Employee benefit statistics can be analyzed in a similar fashion. By plotting pay and employee benefit data on graphs and charts, it is possible to

TABLE 11-1   Information Included in a Wage and Salary Survey

---

I. Data on the organizations surveyed
   A. Number of employees
   B. Major products and services
   C. Financial data: total assets, annual sales, profits
   D. Location of jobs surveyed
   E. Organizational charts
II. Job analysis and pay information
   A. Job description
   B. Job specification
   C. Pay scale of job surveyed
      1. Pay quartiles
      2. Rate ranges
   D. Means by which job incumbent receives pay increases
      1. Merit increases and date of last increase
      2. Seniority increases and date of last increase
      3. COLA formula or general cost-of-living increase and date
   E. Pay incentives
      1. Individual pay incentives (amount, date, and basis for awarding incentive pay)
      2. Group pay incentives (amount, date, and basis for awarding incentive pay)
   F. Perquisites and special allowances
III. Employee benefits
   A. Group life insurance
      1. Total amount of coverage for job incumbent or formulas for calculating life insurance coverage
      2. Average cost per job incumbent
   B. Group health insurance
      1. Dollar limits of coverage
      2. Scope of coverage (e.g., hospitalization, surgical, ancillary services)
      3. Deductibles and co-insurance
      4. Major exclusions and restrictions
   C. Group disability insurance
      1. Definition of disability (in order to receive benefits)
      2. Waiting period
      3. Percentage of gross income paid during disability
   D. Retirement programs
      1. Funding
      2. Vesting
      3. Benefit schedules
   E. Other employee benefits

---

obtain an overview of distributions and trends that are not apparent when raw data and numbers are examined. This information is combined with information on the internal structure of jobs (job evaluation) to determine the final pay level and pay structure for the organization.

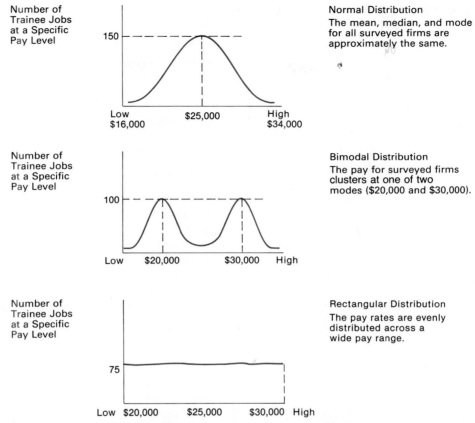

FIGURE 11-2 Hypothetical Pay Distributions for a Sample of Surveyed Management Trainee Positions

---

■ The Pay Structure Decision

The Concept of Internal Equity

Internal equity deals with the variation in pay among different jobs within an organization. The question posed by internal equity is, how much more (or less) should Job A be paid than Job B? Internal equity can have an important impact on employee morale, satisfaction, productivity, and turnover because internal inequities may be more visible, in many instances, than external inequities. Many employees have only a vague idea of what other organizations are paying, but they are usually aware of what their fellow employees are being paid. This is probably true even when an organization has a pay secrecy policy.

Job Evaluation: The Preliminaries

Job evaluation places a *value* on a job. This value may be expressed directly in dollars or indirectly through a ranking, classification, or point scheme. Although numerous job evaluation techniques are available, the following steps are common to most methods:[15]

1. *Sampling benchmark jobs.* Job evaluation systems are often developed and validated on the basis of a select sample of jobs known as *benchmark or key jobs.* Large organizations contain a variety of jobs that can be categorized on the basis of similarities in locations, duties, skills required, and other characteristics. A general hospital that is conducting a job evaluation for all of its jobs may use six broad job classifications: (1) physicians, (2) administrators, (3) registered nurses and licensed practical nurses, (4) laboratory, x-ray, and other technical employees, (5) secretarial and clerical employees, and (6) all others (such as physical plant employees and food service workers).

   Benchmark jobs are then selected from each job classification or cluster based on two important characteristics. First, benchmark jobs have a set of tasks, duties, and responsibilities that are stable over time. Benchmark jobs are often similar in content from one firm to another in an industry (e.g., a flight attendant's job in the airline industry or a welder's job in the automobile industry). Second, the wage and salary survey of benchmark jobs has established a pay rate that is equitable with external labor market conditions.

2. *Establishing compensable factors.* Factors that determine the relative worth of a job (responsibility, mental and physical effort, skill required to perform the job, etc.) are known as *compensable factors.* Compensable factors should meet the following criteria. First, a compensable factor must be found in all (or nearly all) of the jobs being evaluated. Second, the amount of a compensable factor should vary from one job to another. If all jobs within a classification require the same amount of physical effort, then physical effort will not be a good *distinguishing* factor for the jobs being evaluated. Physical effort will be a good compensable factor if some jobs require little physical effort while others are physically demanding. Third, a compensable factor should be measurable. For example, physical effort may be measured by the amount of lifting, bending, walking, and climbing ordinarily done on a job during a typical workday. A compensable factor that is difficult to measure can make the job evaluation process subjective and uncertain. Fourth, the compensable factor should be accepted and well understood by those performing the job evaluation.

3. *Development of a job evaluation system.* Four major types of job evaluation systems exist (ranking, classification, factor comparison, and point methods). The selection of a particular job evaluation method will depend on factors such as the number and complexity of the jobs being evaluated, the amount of accuracy that is desired, the amount of time and money available, and other administrative considerations.

[15]Thomas A. Mahoney, "Compensating for Work" in Kendrith M. Rowland and Gerald R. Ferris (eds.), *Personnel Management* (Boston: Allyn and Bacon, Inc., 1982), pp. 242–248.

4. *Implementation.* Once an evaluation method has been selected, benchmark jobs identified, and the final instrument designed, the job evaluation process begins. Most job evaluations are conducted by a committee familiar with the organization's jobs or by consultants specializing in compensation management.

Job Evaluation: The Nonquantitative Methods

The Ranking Method

The simplest approach to job evaluation is the ranking method. As the name implies, each job within an organization, corporate division, or department is ranked relative to other jobs in the same group. The ranking is usually based on analysis of all components found in a job. In some cases, specific compensable factors may be used to determine rank. The final ranking is, nevertheless, an overall rating, with one job being ranked first in value, one job ranked second in value, and so forth.

The ranking method has the advantages of simplicity and expediency, especially when there are significant differences in the value of the jobs and the number of jobs being evaluated is small. Problems arise with the ranking method when large numbers of complex jobs must be evaluated. The assignment of rankings is a subjective process, and disagreements may arise if several persons evaluate and rank each job. Perhaps the major disadvantage of the ranking method is its failure to determine differences among the values of each job. A job that is ranked third is obviously more valuable than one ranked fourth, but there is little indication as to how much of a pay difference should exist between the two jobs. Other more quantitative methods of job evaluation not only stipulate the ranking of each job but also provide an indication of the proper magnitude of pay differences among jobs.

The Classification Method

Job classifications are established by using a set of general compensable factors. The job descriptions and specifications for each position are compared with the general description of each classification. Jobs are then classified according to the amount of compensable factors present in the job. Classifications are then ranked and compensated according to their relative worth. Some classification methods also incorporate the qualifications of individual employees when determining a pay rate.

Table 11-2 illustrates pay tables that are based on the classification method used by the federal government for white-collar and professional employees. If a person were hired by the U.S. Park Service as an administrator in a job in Yellowstone National Park, that individual would be assigned a General Schedule (GS) rating,

[16]GS ratings are established by the federal government's Office of Personnel Management. The GS ratings are based primarily on the differences in level of difficult among jobs and are determined by nine factors: knowledge required by the position, supervisory controls, guidelines, complexity, scope and effect, personal contacts, purpose of contacts, physical demands, and work environment.

TABLE 11-2 Federal White-Collar Pay Schedules, Effective January 1992

General Schedule (4.2%)

	1	2	3	4	5	6	7	8	9	10
GS-1	$11,478	$11,861	$12,242	$12,623	$13,006	$13,230	$13,606	$13,986	$14,003	$14,356
2	12,905	13,212	13,640	14,003	14,157	14,573	14,989	15,405	15,821	16,237
3	14,082	14,551	15,020	15,489	15,958	16,427	16,896	17,365	17,834	18,303
4	15,808	16,335	16,862	17,389	17,916	18,443	18,970	19,497	20,024	20,551
5	17,686	18,276	18,866	19,456	20,046	20,636	21,226	21,816	22,406	22,996
6	19,713	20,370	21,027	21,684	22,341	22,996	23,655	24,312	24,969	25,626
7	21,906	22,636	23,366	24,096	24,826	25,556	26,286	27,016	27,746	28,476
8	24,262	25,071	25,880	26,689	27,498	28,307	29,116	29,925	30,734	31,543
9	26,798	27,691	28,584	29,477	30,370	31,263	32,156	33,049	33,942	34,835
10	29,511	30,495	31,479	32,463	33,447	34,431	35,415	36,399	37,383	38,367
11	32,423	33,504	34,585	35,666	36,747	37,828	38,909	39,990	41,071	42,152
12	38,861	40,156	41,451	42,746	44,041	45,336	46,631	47,926	49,221	50,516
13	46,210	47,750	49,290	50,830	52,370	53,910	55,450	56,990	58,530	60,070
14	54,607	56,427	58,247	60,067	61,887	63,707	65,527	67,347	69,167	70,987
15	64,233	66,374	68,515	70,656	72,797	74,938	77,079	79,220	81,361	83,502

Senior Executive Service (3.5%)

ES-1	$90,000
ES-2	94,400
ES-3	98,600
ES-4	104,000
ES-5	108,300
ES-6	112,100

Executive Schedule (EX) (3.5%)

level I	$143,800
level II	129,500
level III	119,300
level IV	112,100
level V	104,800

Administrative Law Judges (3.5%)

AL-3/A	$72,865
AL-3/B	78,470
AL-3/C	84,075
AL-3/D	89,680
AL-3/E	95,285
AL-3/F	100,890
AL-2	106,495
AL-1	112,100

Members, Boards of Contract Appeals (CA) (3.5%)

Chairman	$112,100
Vice chairman	$108,737
Other members	105,374

Senior Level (SL and ST)

Minimum	$77,080	(4.2%)
Maximum	112,100	(3.5%)

depending on the nature and complexity of the job.[16] If an employee is hired as a GS-9, Step 1, then that person's base salary would be $26,798.

The classification method provides a practical means of evaluating a large number of jobs, some of which vary considerably in terms of tasks, duties, working conditions, and skill requirements. Distinctions between job classifications rather than individual jobs are emphasized. Two jobs that are placed in the same classification may be completely different (e.g. a civilian accountant working in a military hospital and a border patrol officer working for the U.S. Immigration and Naturalization Service). When the content, responsibility, or qualifications for a job are changed, then it can be reclassified to either a higher or lower classification.

Job Evaluation: The Quantitative Methods

Quantitative methods usually provide a dollar or point value for each job evaluated. Two major quantitative methods of job evaluation are discussed here: the *factor comparison method* and the *point method*.

The Factor Comparison Method

The factor comparison approach to job evaluation places dollar amounts on compensable factors for jobs within a defined classification or cluster. Although there are several variations of the factor comparison method, the following steps are common:

1. *Select benchmark jobs from each cluster or classification.* (Note the definition of benchmark jobs earlier in this chapter.) The base wage or salary rates for benchmark jobs are assumed to be *fixed,* and other wage and salary rates are subject to adjustment based on the pay allocated to benchmark jobs.
2. *Select and define compensable factors that are common to jobs within a cluster or classification.* These factors may include responsibility, mental and physical effort, working conditions, as well as education, skills, and experience requirements. Each compensable factor contributes a certain monetary value to the job.
3. *Allocate the base wage or salary rate for benchmark jobs across each compensable factor.* The sum of the monetary values for each compensable factor will be exactly equal to the rate *currently* paid for the benchmark job. (Remember that the pay rates for benchmark jobs have already been determined to be externally equitable and are *fixed.*)
4. *Compare nonbenchmark jobs on a factor-by-factor basis with the fixed rates for benchmark jobs.* Once the basic structure is determined using benchmark jobs, the basis for determining the internal equity and pay rates for nonbenchmark jobs is established.
5. *Sum the monetary values for each nonbenchmark job.* This produces the *new* and, hopefully, externally and internally equitable wage or salary rates for each job.

Tables 11-3, 11-4, 11-5, and 11-6 illustrate the use of the factor comparison method. The jobs listed in boldface type are the benchmark jobs (Secretary I, Clerk I, and Word Processor Operator). The dollar amount for each compensable factor in the benchmark jobs is obtained by working backwards by spreading or allocating the already *fixed* hourly rates for each benchmark job over each compensable factor. Prior to allocating monetary values to each compensable factor, it was known that the base rates were $10.75 per hour for a Secretary I, $11.60 for a Word Processor Operator, and $6.15 for a Clerk I.

Once the compensable factors have been selected and the monetary values assigned to benchmark jobs, nonbenchmark jobs (whose pay rates are *not* fixed) can be placed into the pay structure. Using appropriate job descriptions and specifications, the nonbenchmark jobs are evaluated relative to the benchmark jobs on a factor-by-factor basis by inserting them into the factor comparison matrix in Table 11-5. The monetary values for each job over each compensable factor are then summed to determine the *new* wage rate for the nonbenchmark jobs. By

TABLE 11-3   A Factor Comparison Structure for Benchmark Jobs

Monetary Value of Each Factor for Each Job	Mental Factor	Physical Factor	Skill	Responsibility	Working Conditions
$4.00/hour					
$3.50/hour	Secretary I ($3.50)		Word processor operator ($3.50)		
$3.00/hour	Word processor operator ($3.10)			Secretary I ($3.00)	
$2.50/hour			Secretary I ($2.25)		
$2.00/hour	Clerk I ($1.90)			Word processor operator ($2.00)	
$1.50/hour		Clerk I ($1.75) Word processor operator ($1.50) Secretary I ($1.25)			Word processor operator ($1.50)
$1.00/hour				Clerk I ($1.00)	Clerk I ($1.00)
$.50/hour			Clerk I ($0.50)		Secretary I ($0.75)

TABLE 11-4 Allocating the *Fixed* Wage Rate of Benchmark Jobs
Over the Five Compensable Factors

Benchmark Jobs	Mental Factor	Physical Factor	Skill	Responsibility	Working Conditions		Wage Rate of Benchmark Jobs
Secretary I	$3.50 +	$1.25 +	$2.25 +	$3.00 +	$0.75	=	$10.75
Clerk I	$1.90 +	$1.75 +	$0.50 +	$1.00 +	$1.00	=	$ 6.15
Word processor operator	$3.10 +	$1.50 +	$3.50 +	$2.00 +	$1.50	=	$11.60

Step 1
These rates are predetermined and fixed

Step 2
The wage rates for each benchmark job are then allocated over the compensable factors according to relative differences among benchmark jobs. The sum of the monetary values for each job related factor must exactly equal the fixed, predetermined wage rate.

applying this method, any previously existing internal inequities (misalignments in the pay structure) are corrected.

Table 11-5 illustrates the relation between benchmark jobs (fixed, predetermined wage rates) and nonbenchmark jobs (new wage rates). By comparing the nonbenchmark jobs to the benchmark jobs on a factor-by-factor basis, the new wage rates for the nonbenchmark jobs are $12.25 for the Administrative assistant, $7.10 for the Typist I position, and $4.95 for the Clerk II position. Table 11-6 summarizes the new wage rates for nonbenchmark jobs.

Once the factor comparison matrix is developed, it provides a reasonably accurate pay structure. As with any job evaluation, an element of subjectivity is present in the assignment of monetary values across compensable factors, and disagreements among persons performing the job evaluation may arise.

The Point Method

The point method, when properly designed and administered, is probably the most detailed approach to job evaluation. Unlike the factor comparison method, the point method does not directly place a dollar value on a job. Rather, each job receives a total point value, and the points are then converted into pay rates.[17]

The preliminary stages of the point method are similar to those of the factor comparison method. First, the compensable factors or dimensions for a job

[17]Edward E. Lawler III, "What's Wrong with Point-Factor Job Evaluation," *Compensation and Benefit Review* (March-April 1986), pp. 29-40.

TABLE 11-5   A Factor Comparison Structure with Benchmark and Nonbenchmark Jobs

Monetary Value of Each Factor for Each Job	Mental Factor	Physical Factor	Skill	Responsibility	Working Conditions
$4.00/hour	Administrative assistant ($4.00)			Administrative assistant ($3.75)	
$3.50/hour	**Secretary I ($3.50)** **Word processor operator ($3.10)**		**Word processor operator ($3.50)**		
$3.00/hour			Administrative assistant ($3.00)	**Secretary I ($3.00)**	
$2.50/hour	Typist I ($2.25)		**Secretary I ($2.25)**		
$2.00/hour	**Clerk I ($1.90)**			**Word processor operator ($2.00)**	
		Clerk I ($1.75) Clerk II ($1.60)			
$1.50/hour	Clerk II ($1.50)	**Word processor operator ($1.50)** **Secretary I** and Typist I ($1.25)	Typist I ($1.50)		**Word processor operator ($1.50)**
				Typist I ($1.10)	
$1.00/hour				**Clerk I ($1.00)**	**Clerk I, Typist I, and Clerk II ($1.00)**
		Administrative assistant ($0.90)	**Clerk I ($0.50)**		**Secretary I ($0.75)**
$0.50/hour			Clerk II ($0.35)	Clerk II ($0.50)	Administrative assistant ($0.60)
$0.00/hour					

TABLE 11-6   Allocating the Nonbenchmark Jobs over the Five Compensable Factors

Nonbenchmark Jobs	Mental Factor		Physical Factor		Skill		Responsibility		Working Conditions		Wage Rate of Nonbenchmark Jobs
Administrative assistant	$4.00	+	$0.90	+	$3.00	+	$3.75	+	$0.60	=	$12.25
Clerk II	$1.50	+	$1.60	+	$0.35	+	$0.50	+	$1.00	=	$ 4.95
Typist I	$2.25	+	$1.25	+	$1.50	+	$1.10	+	$1.00	=	$ 7.10

Step 1	*Step 2*
Compare nonbenchmark jobs on a factor-by-factor basis with the benchmark jobs. Determine the monetary value of each compensable factor for the respective benchmark jobs.	Sum the monetary values to determine the *new* wage rate for each non-benchmark job.

category are specified. Second, each factor must be defined, measured, and weighted. Third, each job is evaluated on a factor-by-factor basis by comparing job analysis information with the compensable factor scales described in step 2 of the following list. The point method of job evaluation does not directly compare one job with another, as in the factor comparison method. Instead, the compensable factor scales are used to determine the final point value of the job. The point totals for each job are then used along with wage and salary survey data to determine the final pay rate.

The following seven steps are typically used in the point method of job evaluation:

Step 1. *Select the category or cluster of jobs to be evaluated,* the final selection being based on a common set of job-related factors.

Step 2. *Select a set of compensable factors common to all jobs being evaluated.* Compose a general statement that defines each compensable factor. Assume that the following factors have been selected and defined:

- Education: The amount of formal training received in elementary, secondary, and higher institutions of learning, as measured by years completed, diplomas, certificates, or degrees received, and credits needed to perform the job adequately.
- Experience: The amount of job-related experience, as measured by the number and variety of managerial positions held and the length of time served on each in order to perform the job adequately.
- Job complexity: The types of thought processes and decisions that are required to perform the job adequately. Types of mental activities might include the

ability to reason in mathematical terms, the use of logical, inductive, and deductive reasoning, and the number of factors affecting job-related decisions.

- Responsibility: Responsibility includes factors such as the number of employees supervised, the amount of money with which the job incumbent is entrusted, and the impact of correct and incorrect job-related decisions on the organization.
- Working conditions: Type of office environment, amount of time spent traveling for job-related reasons, sources of physical and mental stress associated with the job, and hours of work.

Step 3. *Assign a relative weight to each of the preceding factors, with the highest-ranking factor given the weight of 100 percent.* Factors carrying less weight are compared with the highest-ranking factor and then assigned a weight relative to that factor:

Education	100%
Experience	80%
Job complexity	60%
Responsibility	40%
Working conditions	20%

In this particular set of managerial positions, education has been ranked as the most important factor, experience is 80 percent as important as education, job complexity is 60 percent as important, and so forth.

Step 4. *Determine* (a) *the maximum number of points* that a job can receive and (b) *the maximum number of degrees* that each factor should have. Both of these decisions are somewhat arbitrary, the major consideration being to provide a reasonable point spread among the various jobs being evaluated.

For the sake of our illustration, assume that the maximum number of points to be assigned is 1,000 and the number of degrees per compensable factor is 5.

Step 5. Based on the maximum number of points and degrees per compensable factor assigned in step 4, we can now *construct a matrix* that will form the basis for assigning job evaluation points.

Factor	Degree					Factor Weights
	1st	2nd	3rd	4th	5th	
Education	67	133	199	267	333	100%
Experience	53	107	160	213	267	80%
Job complexity	40	80	120	160	200	60%
Responsibility	27	54	82	110	133	40%
Working conditions	13	27	40	53	67	20%
					1,000	300%

The mathematics for this matrix is straightforward. Education is assigned a maximum value (in the 5th degree) of 333 points because (100%/300%) × 1,000 points = 333. Each degree with the education compensable factor is worth 333 points divided by 5 degrees = 66.6, rounded to the nearest whole number. Education in the second degree is worth an additional 66.6 points, education in the third degree another 66.6 points, up to the maximum 333 points for a job requiring an educational level in the 5th degree (which has yet to be defined). Each subsequent factor is treated in the same manner.

Step 6. *Construct written definitions of each compensable factor* (see step 2) by defining what is meant by education, degree 1, experience, degree 3, and so on. No only must each compensable factor have a general definition, but each degree within a given factor must be defined. For example, degrees for the various compensable factors may be defined as follows:

- Education
  Degree 1—Jobs requiring a minimal (eighth grade or less) education.
  Degree 3—Jobs requiring a bachelor's degree or extensive formal training in management.
  Degree 5—Jobs requiring an MBA plus specialized training in a specific area such as accounting, finance, or operations management.
- Experience
  Degree 1—No related managerial experience required.
  Degree 5—A minimum of 10 years' managerial experience at the plant, division, and corporate levels.
- Working conditions
  Degree 1—The job requires little or no travel; air-conditioned private office; day hours only, no weekends.
  Degree 4—Extensive travel required, unstable and often long working hours in stressful and competitive conditions.

The final job evaluation system described here will contain 5 general statements for each compensable factor plus 25 additional statements (one for each degree).

Step 7. The final step involves using the job analysis information along with the job evaluation point matrix (step 5) and compensable factor descriptions (step 6) to *calculate the point value for each respective job.* For example, a financial analyst job for a large bank may be determined as follows:

Education (required)	4th degree	= 267 points
Experience (required)	2nd degree	= 107 points
Job complexity	4th degree	= 160 points
Responsibility	3rd degree	= 82 points
Working conditions	1st degree	= 13 points
Total value of financial analyst position		629 points

It is quite possible that none of the jobs evaluated will approach the 1,000-point maximum. Point totals quantify the relative value or worth of each job to the company. The conversion of points to pay will be discussed later.

Job Evaluation: Some Important Observations

Several important points regarding job evaluation should be emphasized. First, as the name implies, job evaluation is an attempt to assess and evaluate a specific job or category of jobs, not the person holding the job. The latter issue is the function of performance appraisal rather than job evaluation. For this reason, the use of job analysis information is important. Persons responsible for job evaluation will have a difficult time performing this task competently without a detailed knowledge of the tasks, duties, responsibilities, and working conditions associated with a job.

Second, job evaluation is a subjective process. Even when the factor comparison or point method is used, an element of subjectivity is involved in selecting and weighting the compensable factors, as well as designing the comparison or point matrices. If poorly constructed, the quantitative approaches crease a false sense of precision that, in the end, may contribute little to improving the pay structure. It is therefore vital that job evaluations be conducted under the auspices of persons who are familiar with the organization and its jobs.

Third, job evaluation creates a *job hierarchy* that provides a foundation for setting pay rates as long as job content and requirements do not change. If additional tasks or responsibilities are added to a job, then the job should be reevaluated. A job may be overpaid (red-circle job) or underpaid (blue-circle job) relative to what the job evaluation dictates is an equitable pay rate. Employees in red-circle jobs that are overpaid will resent having their pay cut to conform with the job evaluation.[18] For red-circle jobs, it might be wise to wait until the employee is promoted, transfered, or quits and then hire a successor at the new lower rate. Of course, employees who are in blue-circle jobs will be pleased to have their pay increased in order to make an adjustment. Before making a decision to alter the pay rate for a job, wage and salary survey information should also be considered.

Fourth, much of the time-consuming effort spent on maintaining a job evaluation program can be reduced by combining personal computers with job evaluation software. Computer-aided systems simplify the administration of job evaluation information. Job data can be collected from supervisors by using a structured, machine-scorable questionnaire.[19] Computer software can be used to analyze the questionnaire responses and perform the job evaluation.

---

[18]"Red Circle Employees: A Wage Scale Dilemma," *Personnel Journal* (February 1987), p. 92.

[19]Jill Kanin-Lovers, "Salary Practices," in the *Human Resources Yearbook, 1987 Edition* (Englewood Cliffs, New Jersey: Prentice-Hall, Inc., 1987), p. 2.133

◼ Merging the Pay Level and Pay Structure

Once the wage and salary survey and job evaluations are completed, the information is combined to determine the organization's pay policy line, the number of pay grades, the range or monetary spread for each pay grade, and the degree of overlap between pay grades.

Establishing the Pay Policy Line

The pay policy line is derived from wage and salary surveys on benchmark jobs and job evaluation information.[20] Figure 11-3 illustrates the relationship between wage and salary survey data and the pay policy options.[21] Once the market pay line is drawn, an organization's pay for current jobs is plotted and compared to the pay line. An employer has three options when deciding how to compete in the labor market. One option is to be a pay *leader* and offer wages and salaries that are higher than those of most labor market competitors. A second option is to *meet* the competition and pay approximately the same rates as labor market competitors for comparable jobs. Finally, the employer may elect (or be forced because of tight operating budgets) to be a *follower* in the labor market and pay less than most competitors.

If a company's pay rates exceed the market rates, then it is likely that the employer will remain a leader for the time being; instituting an across-the-board pay cut to meet or follow the competition would not be a wise pay strategy unless a financial emergency leaves no alternative. A follower with ample resources might consider raising pay levels to the point of meeting or leading the labor market

---

[20]See, for example, George T. Milkovich and Jerry M. Newman, *Compensation*, 3rd ed. (Homewood, Illinois: Richard D. Irwin, Inc., 1990).

[21]The formula for a straight line is $y = a + bX$, where y is the wage or salary rate, a is the point at which the line crosses or intercepts the y axis, X is the number of job evaluation points for each job, and b is the slope of the wage line. The straight-line formula for a set of job evaluation points and pay rates can be derived through a process known as the *least squares method*, which is a component of regression analysis. Any elementary statistics book will provide the formula for the least squares method. An alternative to using least squares is to plot the wage line by drawing a straight line through the center of the scatter graph and then deriving the linear equation by sampling several points along the line to determine the slope (that is, the change in y divided by the change in x). Suppose that a set annual salary data generates the following straight line for a television broadcasting station:

$$y = \$6,000 + 60X$$

If the job of an electrical engineer working in a local television station is worth 400 points (out of 500 maximum), then the *average* annual salary paid to this position would be

$$y = \$6,000 + 60(400)$$
$$= \$30,000$$

Some electrical engineers would receive a salary above \$30,000 and some would receive less. The \$30,000 represents the approximate *midpoint* salary for all electrical engineers employed by the television broadcasting station.

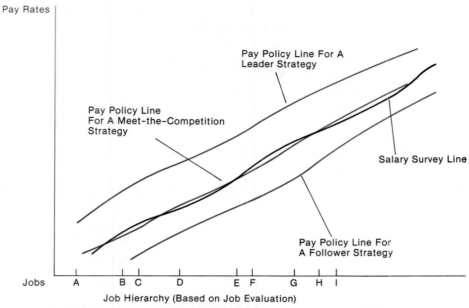

FIGURE 11-3   Leader, Meet the Competition, and Follower Pay Strategies

competition, especially if the organization could attract better employees as a result. However, there is usually more to a pay increase than meets the eye, especially for firms with comprehensive employee benefits. "Roll-up" costs must be considered whenever a pay increase is planned. Pay raises increase not only salaries and wages, but also the cost of employee benefits such as retirement plans, paid vacations, holiday pay, sick leave, overtime, and other benefits. Roll-up costs may comprise an additional 30 percent of a total pay increase. Thus an employer granting a 10 percent pay increase would actually raise total labor costs by 13 percent (10% + [10% × 30%] = 13%).

Determining the Number of Pay Grades

When a variety of jobs are found in an organization, they are often classified into pay grades (also known as *pay ranges*). (Occasionally an organization uses a single pay rate rather than a pay range.) Jobs within a pay grade usually receive the same salary or wage, subject to individual differences in employee job performance (merit), seniority, or productivity. Figure 11-4 illustrates the determination of pay grades using the point method. Point values and a corresponding salary have been previously established for the category of 45 jobs (one dot per job) evaluated under the point method.

For the sake of administrative convenience, six pay grades might be established for the 45 jobs illustrated in Figure 11-4. For example, jobs evaluated as having

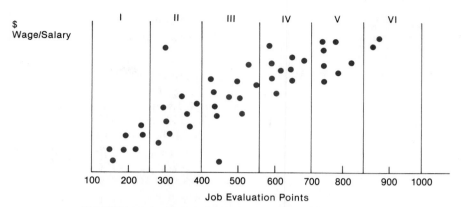

FIGURE 11-4   Determining the Number of Pay Grades

between 550 and 700 points would fall into pay grade IV and would all have the same base salary or wage rate even though there can be a 150-point difference among jobs in this pay grade. Determining the proper number of pay grades is a function of both administrative convenience and the point differences among jobs. Too few pay grades can compromise internal equity and create employee morale problems because jobs with significantly different tasks, responsibilities, and working conditions would be paid the same base salary or wage rate. Too many pay grades, on the other hand, can create pay differentials among jobs that are essentially the same. Equity theory (discussed in Chapter 10) implies that the determination of the proper number of pay grades is an important decision.

The pay grades depicted in Figure 11-4 are spaced at 150-point intervals. Unequal point intervals may be appropriate if the point values of the jobs are not evenly distributed between low and high point values. Gaps in point values or clusters in point values may also require the use of unequal point intervals.

Determining the Range of the Pay Grades

Because jobs within a pay grade receive the same base wage or salary rate (with individual differences in pay being geared to seniority, merit, productivity, shift differentials, or other factors), it is necessary to determine the minimum and maximum pay that can be earned for each pay grade. Jobs at the lower end of the point value spectrum have narrower pay grade ranges than those at the upper end of the point scale. Figure 11-5 illustrates the application of this idea. Note how the height of the pay grade "boxes" increases when moving from the lower to the higher pay grades. Pay grade I has a range of $200 ($1,000 to $1,200), whereas pay grade VI has a range of $525 ($1,175 to $1,700). The primary reason for having "taller" pay grades at the upper end of the structure is that it is possible to have greater variations in employee performance for the higher-value jobs. If an

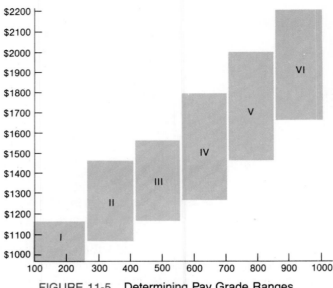

FIGURE 11-5   Determining Pay Grade Ranges

administrative assistant is classified as grade V, a person in this job might have considerable latitude as to how the job is done, and wide variations could exist between good and poor performance among administrative assistants. Therefore, a taller pay grade would be needed to account for differences in performance, assuming that merit is a major factor in determining pay. Taller pay grades also allow room for gradual improvement in competence and job performance over a long period of time. Because of the ever-present "room for improvement" factor in higher-grade jobs, the pay grades have a larger spread between minimum and maximum salaries. Suppose that a file clerk is assigned to pay grade I. A file clerk has little flexibility regarding how the job is done, and there are only small differences between a good file clerk and one who is mediocre. The job of file clerk can be mastered in a short period of time, and any improvements beyond the first month on the job are likely to be insignificant. For this reason, smaller ranges between the minimum and maximum pay rates are justified.

Determining Overlap Between Pay Grades

An examination of Figure 11-5 illustrates that overlap exists between adjacent pay grades. A set of pay grades may have little or no overlap or a high degree of overlap, depending on a number of factors. First, if there are considerable differences between jobs from one grade to another (based on point values), then there will be little overlap between pay grades. For example, if several jobs have widely different point values, we would expect them to be placed in different pay grades. Conversely, small differences denote a great degree of overlap. There may be little justification between paying a job worth 350 points 10 percent more than a job that has been evaluated at 330 points. If the amount of overlap extends beyond adjacent pay grades (e.g., the maximum pay grade of grade III is greater than the minimum pay grade for grade V), then there may be too many pay grades. A high degree of overlap among grades may lead employees to question the fairness of their job classifications. Second, if seniority is used as a primary means of providing pay increases, a greater degree of overlap may be necessary because of the need to increase the absolute height of the pay grades as a means of extending the top of the pay grade to avoid the "dead-end street" phenomenon encountered by long-term, senior employees who are trapped at the top of the pay grade. Furthermore, superior employees who have risen rapidly to the top of their pay grade may lose the incentive to continue performing at a high level.[22]

Individual Compensation Within Pay Grades

Two or more employees doing identical work do not always receive the same level of pay. A compensation system that uses pay grades must have a procedure that allows employees to progress up through a pay range from the minimum to the maximum pay rate. An employee may advance in a pay grade because of seniority, superior performance ratings, or a combination of these factors.

The Use of Seniority in Compensation Decisions

Unless there are significant differences in job performance among two employees performing the same job, the one with greater seniority will probably receive more pay. These are two reasons for using seniority in compensation decisions. First, for jobs in the lower pay grades, differences in the caliber of job performance among employees may be minimal. For example, the difference in quality of performance between an average and a good assembly-line worker may be slight because the job is controlled by the pace of the conveyer line. When it is not possible for employees to engage in distinctive job performance, seniority often plays a central role in determining pay increases.

Second, some organizations have no satisfactory performance appraisal system. The use of seniority in compensation decisions has the advantage of being totally objective and therefore legally defensible; it also takes pressure off supervisors, who must otherwise justify individual performance ratings and compensation decisions. Seniority is an objective and less controversial yardstick for making pay adjustments than merit systems, which are often based on subjective performance appraisals.

---

[22]The overall cost of the pay structure is also affected by the number of employees in each pay grade. If a large number of employees hold jobs in higher pay grades, then the pay structure will be costly even though it is relatively flat.

The Use of Performance Appraisals in Compensation Decisions

A well-designed and administered performance appraisal system can provide a foundation for determining and justifying merit pay increases.[23] Care must be taken to tailor the performance appraisal system to job-relevant behaviors and results. Merit pay increases are based on noteworthy job performance and should be distinguished from pay adjustments geared to seniority or changes in the cost of living.

Table 11-7 provides an example of how pay adjustments are made by combining merit and cost-of-living increases. An employee's pay within a pay grade falls into a percentile or quartile. Suppose that monthly salaries in a pay grade range from $1,500 to $2,300. Assume that employee pay is evenly distributed throughout the pay grade; then the first quartile (0 to 25th percentile) is approximately $1,500 to $1,700, the second quartile (26th to 50th percentile) $1,700 to $1,900, the third quartile (51st to 75th percentile) $1,900 to $2,100, and the fourth quartile (76th to 99th percentile) $2,100 to $2,300. According to Table 11-7, if an organization decides to give employees a 5 percent COLA, then an employee in the *60th percentile* with a *superior* rating would receive a 12 percent increase (7% + 5%). On the other hand, a marginal employee in the same pay grade and percentile would receive only a 2 1/4 percent raise (1% + 5%/4%).

Several factors pertaining to Table 11-7 should be noted. First, employees in the higher quartiles receive a slightly smaller *percentage* increase than those in the lower quartiles because of the higher wage and salary rates in the upper end of a pay grade. Second, the percentage increase in cost of living (denoted by X) is calculated separately from merit increases. Third, employees whose performance

TABLE 11-7   Linking Merit (Performance Appraisal) to Pay Increases

Maximum		Location in Pay Grade	Superior	Good	Marginal	Unacceptable
	− 100th percentile					
		4th quartile	6% + X	3% + X	0	0
	75th percentile					
		3rd quartile	7% + X	4% + X	$1\% + \dfrac{X}{4\%}$	0
	50th percentile					
		2nd quartile	8% + X	5% + X	$1\% + \dfrac{X}{3\%}$	0
	25th percentile					
Minimum		1st quartile	9% + X	6% + X	$2\% + \dfrac{X}{3\%}$	0
	− 0th percentile					

X = percentage COLA.

[23]Robert H. Rock, "Pay for Performance: Measures and Standards," *Compensation Review* (Third Quarter 1984), pp. 15–25.

is marginal will receive little or no merit increase and will run the risk of having their *real* income (income adjusted for changes in the cost of living) reduced. Employees receiving marginal or unacceptable ratings should be evaluated more frequently to detect job performance changes that can be used for compensation adjustments or other personnel actions.

Combining Seniority and Merit

When seniority and merit are combined, management must decide how much weight should be given to each. Even in situations where merit has a strong influence on pay, small seniority-based increases can be used to reward loyalty and recognize that superior job performance associated with seniority is often difficult to measure. For example, an employee who has a long association with a firm understands the internal politics and informal organizational structure, and this may be an aid to better working relationships and job performance. Secretaries and military personnel with considerable seniority have "learned the ropes" and often develop an ability to cut through red tape and the bureaucratic maze in order to get things done in an expedient fashion. Pay increases that are, in part, based on seniority recognize this phenomenon.[24]

An employee moves through a pay grade in an elevator-like fashion based on merit, seniority, or some combination of the two. In general, movement from the bottom to the midpoint (50th percentile) of a specific pay grade is more rapid than movement from the midpoint to the top. When seniority and merit are combined, employees with average job performance may move from the bottom to the middle of the pay grade primarily on the basis of seniority. However, to receive pay beyond the midpoint might require superior job performance. Another alternative is to make seniority a *necessary but not sufficient condition* for pay raises into each quartile or percentile of a pay grade. For example, an organization may decide that 2 years of seniority are *necessary* for an employee to move into the second quartile of a pay grade. However, an employee will not be given a pay raise unless his or her performance is also above average. Under this arrangement, an employee with superior performance must accumulate 2 years of seniority before receiving a raise into the second quartile, but the raise is still contingent on above-average job performance.

Employees who reach the top of a pay grade have limited opportunity to receive additional pay raises. Unless the employee is promoted or his or her job is reclassified to a higher pay grade (because the job is enlarged and given additional tasks, duties, and responsibilities), pay increases may be limited to annual COLAs. As a result, the incentive for superior performance may be diminished for employees who are hemmed in at the top of a pay grade. To combat this problem, pay systems may provide limited merit increases or bonuses for employees who demonstrate superior performance or loyalty. Gold-circle rates are applied to

[24]John E. Buckley, "Wage Differences Among Workers in the Same Job and Establishment," *Monthly Labor Review* (March 1985), p. 11.

superior employees who are at the top of their pay grade and receive a merit wage or salary increase, while silver-circle rates are used for senior employees.[25] Both gold- and silver-circle rates allow specific employees to move above the current pay grade. An alternative to gold- and silver-circle rates are 10-year, 15-year, or 20-year cash bonuses for high-seniority employees who are at the top of a pay grade and display meritorious job performance.

Two-Tier Compensation Systems

In order to contain total labor costs without cutting the pay of long-term, senior employees, some organizations, such as the U.S. Postal Service and the airlines, have adopted two-tier compensation systems.[26] Under a two-tier system, employees hired after a specific cutoff date will receive less pay than employees hired before the cutoff date. New employees often receive fewer employee benefits than senior employees. Two-tier pay systems are most commonly used in unionized organizations and represent a concession to an employer who is financially pressed by high labor costs. Senior employees are able to maintain their accustomed pay levels and standard of living, while job applicants know that, if hired, they will be paid less than current employees. Whether new employees suffer morale problems because of these pay differentials is uncertain. Some organizations gradually phase employees into the higher tier as they accumulate seniority. Two-tier systems began to decline in the late 1980s.[27]

■ Individual and Group Incentive Programs

Incentive programs may be either individual or group plans, and they are usually geared to measurable performance results such as units of production, sales volume, cost savings, or profitability.[28] Performance-based compensation systems that are properly designed and administered can be instrumental in increasing

---

[25]Richard I. Henderson, *Compensation Management: Rewarding Performance*, 2nd ed. (Reston, Virginia: Reston Publishing Company, Inc., 1979), p. 293.

[26]David Wessel, "Two-Tier Pay Spreads, But the Pioneer Firms Encounter Problems," *The Wall Street Journal* (October 14, 1985), pp. 1, and 9; Jane Seaberry, "Two-Tiered Wages: More Jobs v. More Worker Alienation," *Washington Post* (April 7, 1985), pp G1–G3.

[27]*The Wall Street Journal*, Labor Letter (June 16, 1987), p. 1.

[28]Incentive plans differ from merit plans. Incentive pay is directly linked to the amount of work or cost savings, but does not affect an employee's permanent wage or salary. Merit pay is linked to quality of work and generally affects the employee's permanent wage or salary. Also see The Bureau of National Affairs, Inc., *Non-Traditional Incentive Pay Programs* (Washington, D.C.: The Bureau of National Affairs, Inc., May 1991).

productivity and lowering costs.[29] On the other hand, a mismanaged incentive program may have side effects that are counterproductive both to the plan's objectives and to organizational effectiveness.

Individual Incentive Programs

Frederick W. Taylor and his colleagues in the scientific management school paved the way for individual incentive programs by carefully establishing performance standards and linking pay to work output.[30] The *piecework plan* is the most commonly used plan and generally provides a low guaranteed base wage or salary that can be increased as individual output increases. An automobile salesperson, for example, may receive a guaranteed salary of $250 per week plus an additional $200 for each automobile sold.

A variety of individual incentive plans have been used to promote productivity, increase efficiency, and improve employee job satisfaction. Several conditions are important to the successful operation of individual incentive programs, and most pertain to the effort-performance-reward links discussed in Chapters 2 and 10. First, individual jobs must not be too interdependent. Production delays that are not controllable by the employee make if difficult to link effort, performance, and pay. As a result, employee frustration and lower morale are likely if mechanical problems or supply shortages create down time and destroy the opportunity to earn incentive pay.

Second, individual incentive programs require that output be objectively and accurately measured. This requires that employees understand the basis for their incentive pay and trust management to keep accurate records of employee output.

Third, production standards upon which the individual incentive plan is based must be carefully established and maintained. Productivity and incentive standards must be neither too loose nor too tight. A *loose* standard means that an employee can produce at levels that will enable him or her to attain high amounts of pay. *Loose* rates may cut into profitability or, worse, cause financial problems for the organization. Although employees will undoubtedly appreciate a loose rate, the organization's total and unit labor costs may become prohibitively high. If the employer attempts to tighten a loose rate, employee morale will suffer. Tight rates, on the other hand, make it difficult to earn adequate incentive pay and discourage individual effort. Establishing standards that are neither too loose nor too tight requires careful time-and-motion study and adjustments for employee deception (usually slowdowns in the presence of time-and-motion experts), fatigue, and other potential interruptions to the work flow.[31]

[29]Hoyt Doyel and Thomas Riley, "Considerations in Developing Incentive Plans," *Management Review* (March 1987), p. 34, and Jerry McAdams, "Rewarding Sales and Marketing Performance," *Management Review* (April 1987), p. 33.

[30]Daniel A. Wren, *The Evolution of Management Thought* (New York: Ronald Press, 1972), pp. 111–146.

[31]Frederick S. Hills, *Compensation Decision Making* (Chicago: The Dryden Press, 1987), pp. 352–353.

Once the production standards are established, they must be linked to pay rates. Incentive rate scales may be fixed, increasing, or decreasing. *Fixed* scales pay the same amount for each additional unit of output or sales. For example, a realtor who receives a 3 percent commission (after the realty company receives its share) on all real estate sold is on a fixed scale. An *increasing* incentive rate might provide a 4 percent sales commission once a realtor exceeds $1 million in sales in a calendar year, and a *decreasing* scale might provide only a 2 percent commission for sales over $1 million. Because overhead costs per unit typically decrease as production or sales volume increases, an increasing incentive rate allows the employee to share in these cost savings. Decreasing incentive rates also reduce unit costs, but it is the organization rather than the employee who benefits from such cost savings.

A fourth consideration in deciding whether to implement an individual incentive system is the trade-off between quantity and quality of output. Individual incentive systems usually work better than quantity rather when quality is emphasized. A common problem with persons who depend on sales commissions for the bulk of their income is that there is little or no financial incentive for the salesperson to provide customer services after the sale. It may be possible in some instances to design an individual incentive program to overcome this problem by linking monetary rewards to error rates, customer complaints, or product rejections.

Finally, the amount that an employee can potentially earn under an individual incentive system must be significantly high to motivate increased effort and productivity. A basic premise of any incentive plan is that employees value money and are willing to work for additional money. The problem with incentive systems is determining how much additional monetary incentive is necessary to motivate employees to produce more. For most employees, there is not likely to be a noticeable difference in take-home pay when 2 percent is added to base compensation, but nearly all employees will notice a 20 percent addition to base pay. The next question is whether employees are willing to exert the additional effort needed to earn the incentive pay. Research indicates that the amount of additional pay needed to increase productivity varies considerably among individuals.[32] Factors such as pay secrecy policies, inflation rates, and the employee's total compensation level, income tax bracket, and personal perceptions of what constitutes a noticeable pay increment are all relevant to the value that an employee attaches to different amounts of incentive pay.[33]

Examples of Individual Incentive Programs

A common type of incentive program is the *piecework plan*, whereby an employee is paid for each unit produced. The more an employee produces, the more pay he or she receives. Many plans provide a base pay, which assumes that the average

[32]P. Varadarajan and C. Futrell, "Factors Affecting Perceptions of Smallest Meaningful Pay Increases," *Industrial Relations*, Vol. 23 (1984), pp. 278–286.

[33]Edward E. Lawler III, *Pay and Organization Development* (Reading, Massachusetts: Addison-Wesley Publishing Company, 1981), p. 88.

employee will produce at least a standard number of units per hour. Once the employee exceeds the hourly standard output, additional pay is given for each unit over standard. These plans are called *standard hour plans*, and they have been designed a variety of ways.[34]

Sales commissions represent a common individual incentive. Most commissions are based upon the percentage of the selling price of a product or service.[35] Insurance agents, automobile salespersons, and real estate agents are commonly paid on a sales commission. Sales commissions may be *straight* commissions with no minimum guaranteed base salary or, more likely, a *salary-plus-commission* arrangement. Some sales commissions are graduated or multiple-tiered arrangements whereby the commission percentage increases if the salesperson exceeds a specific sales volume. For example, a brokerage firm may pay its stockbrokers a 25 percent commission on total annual sales of $200,000 or less. Once the stockbroker's sales exceed $200,000, the commission is raised to 35 percent and applies to *all* sales for the year. Not surprisingly, such an arrangement is a strong incentive for brokers whose sales are nearing the $200,000 mark.[36] Automobile dealerships typically pay their sales personnel between 25 and 30 percent of the difference between the sales price of a new automobile (the amount paid by the customer) and the invoice price of the automobile. Sales commission plans encounter problems when sales personnel are assigned territories offering different sales potential. An encyclopedia salesperson assigned to an upper-middle-income territory where families value and can afford educational aids is likely to earn more money than would a salesperson assigned to a lower-income area. Similarly, a life insurance salesperson in Dallas will have to spend less time soliciting customers then would an agent working the vast West Texas regions where potential clients live miles apart.

A number of other individual incentive programs are used that do not directly link the employee's productivity to immediate (by the next pay period) financial gain. Managerial and executive *bonuses* are paid periodically when profits or operating expenses are favorable.[37] For example, in 1987 Christie's International, an art auction house, paid $800 bonuses to each of its 1200 employees worldwide to celebrate the record $39.9 million paid for Vincent van Gogh's "Sunflowers." The firm allegedly received between $4 million to $8 million for auctioning off the painting.[38] *Stock option plans* allow employees to purchase company stock at a set price for an extended period and are a valuable benefit when the price of the stock is climbing. An employee may be given the option of purchasing stock at $75 per

---

[34]See Frederick S. Hills, *Compensation Decision Making* (Chicago: The Dryden Press, 1987) for a discussion of the Halsey, Rowan, and Gantt plans, all of which are standard hour plans.

[35]Robert J. Freedman, "How to Develop a Sales Compensation Plan," *Compensation and Benefits Review* (March-April 1986), pp. 41–48.

[36]This example is based on a discussion of multiple-tiered sales commissions discussed in Donald W. Myers, *Human Resources Management: Principles and Practice* (Chicago: Commerce Clearing House, Inc., 1986), p. 791.

[37]James W. Hathaway, "How Do Merit Bonuses Fare?" *Compensation and Benefits Review* (September-October 1986), pp. 50–55.

[38]*The Wall Street Journal*, Labor Letter (July 7, 1987), p. 1.

share for the next 3 years. If the stock is worth $150 a share in 2 years, the employee may exercise the option of buying the stock and reaping the profits. *Employee stock ownership plans (ESOPs)* involve employer contributions to an employee trust that are then invested in company stock. ESOPs provide tax and cash flow advantages to the employer and an incentive to employees because they own stock in the corporation. Payments by the employer into the ESOP trust are tax deductible and serve as a major form of investment capital. Stock-owning employees are provided with an incentive to remain with the firm and help keep it profitable.[39]

Group and Organizational Incentives

Many organizations link pay to the efforts of an employee group. Compensation programs such as the Scanlon plan, a group cost savings plan that is designed to lower labor costs without lowering productivity, and the Lincoln Electric plan, a combined profit-sharing, year-end bonus, and piecework incentive plan, are two noteworthy examples. Profit-sharing programs represent another major form of group and organizational incentive plans designed to allocate a fixed share of organizational profits among its employees based on a predetermined formula.

Group incentive systems may promote productivity and efficiency under circumstances where individual incentive systems are not practical. For example, labor unions generally have not favored the use of individual incentive programs but, perhaps as a compromise during contract negotiations, may agree to a group- or organizationwide plan. In addition, several other factors may preclude individual incentive plans and yet favor group incentives. Organizations that are technologically complex and characterized by a large number of interdependent jobs, such as computer manufacturers, may be better served by group rather than individual incentive plans. However, the success of a group incentive plan is also dependent on a high degree of employee trust within the organization, good communications channels, and explicit organizational goals and performance measures.[40]

The frequency with which incentive pay is given must be determined; frequent payments (more than once per year) can lead to an overemphasis on short-term results such as minimizing costs, to the detriment of long-term concerns such as proper maintenance of equipment and capital expenditures to ensure stable productivity. Longer time spans between incentive payments (less than once per year) can cause the plan to lose its motivational value because most employees do not want to defer monetary rewards for long periods of time. Nevertheless, if an employee waits for a longer period to receive an incentive bonus, the employer has a better chance of paying a larger and more meaningful bonus.

---

[39]Katherine J. Klein, "Employee Stock Ownership and Employee Attitudes: A Test of Three Models," *Journal of Applied Psychology* (May 1987), p. 319.

[40]Edward E. Lawler, *Pay and Organization Development, p. 83.*

Examples of Group Incentive (Gainsharing) Programs

Among the more prominent group incentive or gainsharing systems are the Scanlon Plan, The Lincoln Electric Plan, the Rucker Plan, and Improshare.[41] The Scanlon Plan was developed in 1935 by labor leader Joseph Scanlon and provides a monthly cash bonus for the improved productivity of a plant or employee group. Emphasis is placed on encouraging employees to cut labor costs. A suggestion system and departmental and plantwide production committees are used to explain the plan to employees, and encourage them to submit cost-saving suggestions and to evaluate these suggestions. Bonus systems are established on a formula basis that measures productivity gains and sets a procedure for sharing these gains equitably among workers. Under the Scanlon Plan, bonus payments are based on the ratio of total labor costs to total production costs. For example, if the ratio of the total labor cost to the total production cost is 40 percent, then employees receive a bonus whenever their cost-savings efforts reduce this ratio below 40 percent. The monthly bonus is split three ways: the employer's share, the employees' share, and a percentage placed into the reserve fund. Employers typically receive about 25 percent of the savings and employees 60 percent. The remaining amount is placed in a reserve fund for months when the labor cost ratio is above 40 percent.

The Lincoln Electric Plan combines generous year-end cash bonuses, guaranteed employment (30 hours per week for 49 weeks a year), and an individual incentive system. Tight controls are used to ensure quality control, and employees must correct errors on their own time. In financially strong years, Lincoln Electric employees have received bonuses equal to 100 percent of their base pay. Lincoln Electric employees are among the highest-paid production employees in the United States, and the company has experienced very low employee turnover and cordial labor-management relations.

The Rucker Plan focuses on labor cost productivity. Labor cost productivity is the payroll divided by a concept known as *value added*. Value added is the difference between net sales and costs required to produce the product. If a firm has sales of $4,000,000 and total costs of $2,500,000, then value added is $1,500,000. By examining labor cost data over a period of several years, the firm arrives at an appropriate ratio between labor costs and value added. Suppose that the ratio is 50 percent. Using the preceding figures, assume that labor costs were $525,000, or 35 percent of value added. Employees would reap the benefits of a $225,000 cost savings ($1,500,000 × 50% minus $525,000). As in the Scanlon Plan, the employer receives a share, employees receive the largest share, and some of the savings is set aside in a reserve fund.

An Improshare Plan uses a standard labor hours *per unit* measure to assess employee efficiency and productivity. In essence, Improshare compares a standard

[41]The descriptions for these plans are based on a discussion in The Bureau of National Affairs, Inc., *Compensation: BNA Policy and Practice Series*, (Washington, D.C.: The Bureau of National Affairs, Inc., 1981), Section 321.

productivity per unit measure with the actual labor cost per unit achieved by employees. If employees hold unit labor costs below the standard, they receive a bonus.

Gainsharing and profit-sharing programs have both advantages and disadvantages. A study by the Rutgers Institute of Management and Labor Relations reported that profit-sharing firms are generally more productive than non-profit-sharing firms. A study by the U.S. Chamber of Commerce indicated that employees in firms with profit-sharing plans earn more than those whose firms do not have such plans. Profit-sharing also allows companies greater flexibility during economic downturns. The auto industry, which suffered a large downturn during the early 1980s, used profit sharing as a means of regaining profitability in the mid-1980s. When negotiations on the new collective bargaining agreement took place between the major auto manufacturers and the United Auto Workers, the auto makers asked the union for wage concessions. In exchange for such concessions, the auto manufacturers offered profit-sharing plans to their employees. As the auto industry recovered, the benefits from the profit-sharing plans began to pay off as the auto workers regained lost wages and received large profit-sharing allocations from their companies. Although profit-sharing and gainsharing plans offer a number of benefits, there are employees within firms who make little effort to contribute to the firm's profit picture. Some skeptics of profit sharing believe that management may have too much control over how profits are shared. In addition, employees experience a certain amount of uncertainty as to how much pay will be received since such plans are linked directly to profits, which fluctuate.[42]

Overtime and Premium Pay

Overtime and premium pay schedules are used for two major reasons. First, the FLSA requires that nonexempt employees receive one and one-half times their normal pay for time worked in excess of 40 hours per week.[43] The penalties for failing to comply with the act can be expensive. El Paso Natural Gas Company was ordered by the U.S. Department of Labor to pay $7.6 million to workers who were entitled to overtime wages. These individuals were employed as operators and repair personnel at the company's remote sites in Texas and New Mexico.[44] Second, employers are often willing to pay higher hourly rates or salaries to employees who work during night hours or weekends, as well as those who are exposed to more difficult and hazardous work environments. Companies operating on a 24-hour basis usually pay evening and night shift differentials. Airlines sometimes pay higher rates for crew members who must fly at night or on transcontinental

---

[42]The Bureau of National Affairs, Inc., "Profit Sharing: Pros and Cons," *Bulletin to Management* (Washington, D.C.: The Bureau of National Affairs, Inc., June 20, 1991), p. 190.

[43]Gina Ameci, "Overtime Pay: Avoiding FLSA Violations," *Personnel Administrator* (February 1987), p. 117.

[44]*The Wall Street Journal*, Labor Letter (October 14, 1986), p. 1.

routes. Organizations also provide meal allowances for employees who must work outside the traditional daytime hours.

The purpose of premium and overtime pay is to motivate employees to accept additional and less desirable working hours or, at least, make the acceptance of such work more palatable. Some organizations pay one and a half times the regular pay rate to employees working more than 8 but fewer than 12 hours per day and double time for any work beyond 12 hours. Employees who must remain on call during off-duty hours are often paid a guaranteed minimum number of hours to compensate for the social disruption and uncertainty associated with being on call.[45] Nonexempt employees who must work overtime are sometimes given compensatory time off or additional pay (even though this is not required by the FLSA).

Knowledge-based Pay Systems

Knowledge-based pay (KBP) systems (also known as *pay-for-knowledge systems*) represent a significant departure from the pay systems discussed so far in this chapter. Instead of focusing on the specific tasks, duties, and responsibilities needed to perform a certain job, KBP systems reward employees for knowledge or skills that they have acquired. The knowledge or skills may not be directly relevant to the job performed by the employee, but they may have some indirect relevance.

There are two types of KBP systems: (1) knowledge systems and (2) multiskill systems. Knowledge systems allow an employee to increase his or her pay by acquiring additional knowledge that is germane to the job. For example, public school teachers have traditionally been paid under a knowledge system. A teacher is granted pay increases for earning college credits beyond a bachelor's degree; additional compensation is provided as a teacher earns a masters degree, as well as college course credits beyond a masters degree. The underlying rationale for a knowledge system is to increase an employee's depth of knowledge.

Multiskill systems reward an employee as he or she acquires additional job skills that are deemed important by an organization. For example, an employee who works as a computer programmer may earn additional pay for completing certain computer science courses or training programs. A machinist may receive a pay raise for acquiring the ability to operate more complex equipment. The reason is that multiskill systems increase an employee's breadth of work skills. Thus, the employer has more flexibility in making job assignments and staffing.

Most KBP systems provide specific guidelines for the appropriate knowledge or skills that must be acquired before additional pay is granted. Although KBP systems improve the quality and flexibility of a firm's workforce, such systems may also increase training and total labor costs.[46]

[45]Gary S. Marx, "Is On-Call Time Compensable?" *Journal of Property Management* (November-December 1986), p. 70.

[46]See George T. Milkovich and Jerry M. Newman, pp. 83–87, and Nina Gupta, Timothy Schweizer, and G. Douglas Jenkins, "Pay for Knowledge Compensation Plans: Hypotheses and Survey Results," *Monthly Labor Review* (October 1987), pp. 40–43.

■ Compensating Special Employee Groups

Executives

Talented executives and members of upper-level management are generally not paid in accordance with the standardized compensation policies of the organization.[47] Instead this group is treated separately because of unique problems regarding the structure of the compensation package and timing of the payments. Executives are unique from several standpoints. First, their compensation in terms of absolute dollars is often quite high,[48] averaging $1.2 million for CEOs of major corporations in 1991.[49] Obviously the motivational impact of money takes on a different meaning at such lofty heights. The basic necessities of food, clothing, and shelter are no longer of concern to the highly paid executive, although the quality of what is eaten, worn, or lived in will usually increase drastically. For persons in higher income brackets, salary levels, bonuses, long- and short-term incentives, financial security arrangements, and the value of employee benefits become a scorecard by which success is measured.

Federal and state internal revenue services are most anxious to obtain their share of the top executive's financial fortunes. A major concern is not necessarily how to earn an extra dollar, but rather determining what can be done *legally* to keep those dollars from tax collectors. Over the years, executives have been interested in *deferring* compensation until retirement, at which time they will be in a lower tax bracket. Vehicles such as stock options and tax-sheltered retirement programs afforded tax breaks to both the executive and the corporation.

The Tax Reform Act of 1986 created major changes for executive compensation. A major provision of the act was to lower the top marginal tax rate from 50 percent to 33 percent in 1988. Corporate tax rates were also lowered by the Tax Reform Act, and this provided less incentive for companies to offer tax-deductible benefits to employees.[50] It appears that long-term deferrals of income are now less attractive to executives because there is little or no difference between preretirement and postretirement tax brackets. Incentive stock options that were once attractive to highly paid executives have lost much of their financial appeal because gains on such options are now taxed as ordinary income rather than as capital gains, which had a lower tax rate. However, stock options are still attractive from the incentive standpoint of tying executive performance to corporate performance. Executives

---

[47]W. David Gibson, "Executive Compensation: Tailoring Pay to Turbulent Times," *Chemical Week* (May 14, 1986), p. 36, and L. R. Gomez-Mejia, H. Tosi, and T. R. Hinkin, "Management Control, Performance, and Executive Compensation," *Academy of Management Journal* (March 1987), pp. 51–70.

[48]"Compensation System Called Unfair: U.S. Executive Paychecks Are Too High," *Industry Week* (January 26, 1987), p. 17.

[49]John A. Byrne, Dean Foust, and Lois Therrien, "Executive Pay," *Business Week* (March 30, 1992), pp. 52–58.

[50]*The Wall Street Journal*, Labor Letter (September 30, 1986), p. 1.

are not able to place as much of their income in tax-sheltered retirement plans as was possible before 1987. Restrictions on tax deductions for interest on consumer loans make it less attractive to borrow money from the employer. Reduced depreciation deductions and investment tax credits also offer less incentive for companies to furnish executives with personal automobiles.[51]

Perquisites (or perks) are benefits received by executives that are linked to their corporate position and status. Visible signs of status or prestige among persons occupying the upper echelons of an organization are, in fact, forms of psychic income. Luxurious offices, access to corporate aircraft, expensive automobiles, country club memberships, executive dining rooms, and special parking privileges are common examples of perquisites. Perquisites are generally regarded as taxable income, and items such as free home repairs, personal use of company property, and subsidies on vacation homes have come under closer scrutiny by the Internal Revenue Service.

Executives usually have wide latitude when it comes to negotiating the size and distribution of their base salary, bonuses, long-term incentives, insurance and retirement programs, and perquisites.[52] In addition to salaries and bonuses, executives typically receive stock options that give them the right to buy a fixed number of shares at a specified price. Executive compensation programs may also allocate additional shares of stock if the corporation reaches certain performance goals. Golden parachutes are corporate agreements that protect the job and financial security of executives by guaranteeing them a large financial settlement in the event that they are deposed by a corporate takeover, merger, or acquisition. Golden parachutes also make it easier for corporations to hire top executive talent, retain key executives when takeovers occur, and may actually prevent hostile takeovers in some instances.[53] Most golden parachute arrangements are limited to top executives (senior executives about to retire may get "silver" parachutes and severance pay to middle-level managers is known as a "tin" parachute). Golden parachutes may pay 2 or 3 years of salary and employee benefits. Typically, golden parachutes contain provisions that define what constitutes a change of corporate control, the amount of income protection that will be provided, and the continuance of income protection if the executive finds another job.[54]

During the early 1990s, a great deal of controversy has been brewing over the exorbitant compensation packages that many chief executives have received. A CEO of a major corporation earns, on the average, approximately $2.0 million (an

[51]For a discussion of the impact of the Tax Reform Act on salaries and employee benefits, see Philip C. Hunt, "Tax Reform: Its Impact on Compensation and Benefits," *Employment Relations Today* (Spring 1987), pp. 39–52.

[52]Graef S. Crystal, *Questions and Answers on Executive Compensation: How to Get What You're Worth* (Englewood Cliffs, New Jersey: Prentice-Hall, Inc., 1984).

[53]The Bureau of National Affairs, Inc., Section 325.-

[54]"Golden parachutes can turn to lead weights for executives seeking a new job," says James Challenger, of a Chicago executive placement firm. He says golden parachutes may give an executive "an illusion of security," spur a lazy job hunt, and portray him or her as self centered. *The Wall Street Journal*, Labor Letter (February 2, 1988), p. 1.

average of $1.2 plus stock options), an amount that has tripled over the past decade. Innovations such as restricted stock options, stock appreciation rights, and perquisites such as personal financial consulting have allowed executive pay packages to increase significantly. However, there is concern that some CEOs do not necessarily deserve the multi-million-dollar packages that they receive. There is a growing belief that executive pay should be linked more directly to long-term corporate performance, and that golden parachutes and million-dollar annual pensions should be reduced. Companies such as AT&T, Avon, Citicorp, ITT, and United Airlines have already taken drastic measures to control CEO compensation. Corporate stockholders may also force boards of directors to take a more active role in regulating pay increases and revealing the details of executive compensation to shareholders.[55]

In summary, the primary goals of executive compensation are to attract top managerial talent into an organization (usually through high base salaries).[56] Once top executives are hired, there must be an adequate incentive to motivate performance through short- and long-term incentives (even though research indicates that executives may be more motivated by the challenge of their jobs than by money).[57] Finally, in order to retain blue chip executives, employee benefits, stock option plans, and perquisites are necessary.

Employees in International and Multinational Firms

The concepts of external equity and pay incentives are put to the supreme test in the case of employees working for international and multinational firms. Milkovich and Newman identify three categories of employees in these firms: United States expatriates (USEs), local country nationals (LCNs), and third-country nationals (TCNs).[58] U.S. citizens working in a foreign country (USEs) must receive compensation that will make the acceptance of a foreign assignment financially attractive. The cost-of-living and tax differentials between the United States and certain foreign countries can be both substantial and subject to considerable fluctuation, depending on the value of the U.S. dollar in international markets. U.S. executives assigned to high-inflation countries such as Brazil may require significant pay raises and periodic adjustments in order to maintain their standard of living. Some countries also have extremely high income tax rates and may require U.S. employees to pay the host country's equivalent of their Social Security taxes. Many countries have income tax rates that are considerably higher than U.S. tax rates. For example, Belgium has a maximum marginal tax rate of approximately 70

[55]John A. Byrne, Dean Foust, and Lois Therrien, "Executive Pay," *Business Week* (March 30, 1992), pp. 52–58.

[56]See John R. Deckop, "Determinants of Chief Executive Officer Compensation," *Industrial & Labor Relations Review* (January 1988), pp. 215–226.

[57]*The Wall Street Journal*, Labor Letter (May 6, 1986), p. 1.

[58]George T. Milkovich and Jerry M. Newman, p. 544.

percent. A senior executive earning $100,000 a year in Belgium could cost a company close to $1.0 million in taxes over a 5- to 7-year period. A U.S. citizen working abroad might also be doubly taxed, paying both U.S. income taxes and taxes in the country of assignment.[59] In addition, a foreign assignment may entail living in an unfamiliar and less comfortable environment for the USE.[60]

Problems are encountered in determining equitable rates of pay for LCNs (e.g., a citizen of Portugal working for a U.S. company in the firm's Lisbon office) and TCNs (e.g., a citizen of Portugal working for a U.S. firm in Brazil). Some companies set pay levels for employees working in foreign locations so that they enjoy a standard of living comparable to that of their home country. Under this approach, a U.S. citizen working in Saudi Arabia would receive a higher salary than a citizen of Mexico for performing the same job in Saudi Arabia because Mexico has lower wages and a lower cost of living than the United States. Although this approach (known as the *balance sheet approach*) is equitable from a standard-of-living standpoint, a personnel manager may find it difficult to justify the pay difference to TCNs whose pay lags behind that of their U.S. counterparts. As a result, some companies ignore the cost-of-living issue and opt for the equal pay for equal work approach of paying all employees the same pay for the same job. The latter strategy is more costly for U.S. firms because compensation levels in the United States are among the highest in the world. Internal equity is promoted through the equal pay for equal work approach, whereas external equity is better served by the balance sheet approach.[61] Some firms are "de-Americanizing" their pay scales for TCNs in order to cut labor costs. The 1986 Tax Reform Act also provides an option for companies to reduce the compensation of USEs because less income is needed before taxes to maintain a standard of living comparable to U.S. levels.[62]

Figure 11-6 summarizes the major components that must be taken into account when compensating expatriates. Obviously no standard formula is available to adequately tailor a complex compensation program to a foreign work site, especially where LCNs and TCNs are performing the same work as USEs. Figure 11-6 recognizes the need for compensation to be based on what the employee would be paid in his or her home country, with incentive adjustments being made to encourage the employee to accept the assignment and equalization adjustments being made to ensure external equity and to protect against a loss of real income.

[59]Peter J. Dowling and Randall S. Schuler, *International Dimensions of Human Resource Management* (Boston: PWS-Kent Publishing Company, 1990), pp. 122–125.-

[60]George T. Milkovich and Jerry M. Newman, *Compensation*, 3rd ed. (Homewood, Illinois: Richard D. Irwin, Inc., 1990), p. 544. Also see Michael A. Conway, "Manage Expatriate Expenses for Capital Returns," *Personnel Journal* (July 1987), p. 66, and Arvind V. Phatak, Rajan Chandran, and Richard A. Ajayi, "International Executive Compensation," in David B. Balkin and Luis R. Gomez-Mejia (eds.), *New Perspectives on Compensation* (Englewood Cliffs, New Jersey: Prentice-Hall, Inc., 1987), pp. 315–327.

[61]George T.Milkovich and Jerry M. Newman, pp. 544–548.

[62]*The Wall Street Journal*, Labor Letter (March 10, 1987), p. 1.

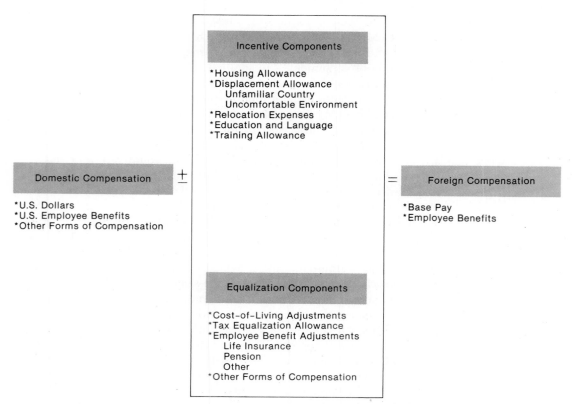

FIGURE 11-6   Factors Affecting Compensation in Multinational Firms

■ Sex Discrimination in Compensation Programs

Compensation programs have been the subject of extensive litigation because females have been paid less than males for performing essentially the same work. There are two types of sex discrimination cases involving compensation management: (1) incidents involving *equal pay for equal work* and (2) the concept of *comparable worth*. Both of these legal issues deal with aspects of internal equity because they are concerned with paying employees (without regard to sex) for the effort they expend and the contributions they make to the organization. However, there are several important distinctions between the equal pay and comparable worth concepts. First, the equal pay for equal work concept is based *explicitly* on the Equal Pay Act of 1963, while the comparable worth concept has been *inferred* from Title VII of the 1964 Civil Rights Act. Second, the equal pay concept is well defined relative to the comparable worth concept, which is still legally uncertain. Third, the equal pay concept involves comparing rates of pay for jobs that have similar tasks, duties, responsibilities, and working conditions and require approximately the same amount of effort and skill to perform. Comparable worth involves comparing jobs with substantially different characteristics that allegedly have the same value to the organization and society.

Figure 11-7 illustrates the comparisons between the equal pay and comparable worth concepts. The equal pay concept involves comparing the pay of a male and a female nurse whereas the comparable worth concept involves comparing the pay of a predominately female group of nurses and a predominately male group of electrical engineers. Thus equal pay issues involve "apples-and-apples" comparisons whereas comparable worth deals with "apples-and-oranges" comparisons.

Equal Pay for Equal Work

The well-established concept of equal pay for equal work has its roots in the fact that males have traditionally earned more than females.[63] As of the early 1990s, females continued to work for the "69-cent dollar." This means that the pay levels for females continue to lag approximately 31 percent behind those of their male counterparts despite the fact that the Equal Pay Act was passed in 1963 to ensure that men and women performing the same job are paid at the same rate.

A man and a woman working at the same job do not have to perform identical sets of tasks for the work to meet the "sameness" test. Rather, the jobs must be similar with respect to *responsibility,* physical and mental *effort, working conditions,* and *skills* required to perform the job satisfactorily. If two jobs are essentially the same insofar as these four compensable factors are concerned, then there should be no significant pay differentials between males and females.

The U.S. Supreme Court held that the Equal Pay Act was violated when a glass company paid male "selector-packers" 21 1/2 cents an hour more than female packers. The company contended that the differential was justified because the men were occasionally required to perform heavier work.[64] Similarly, a bank paid

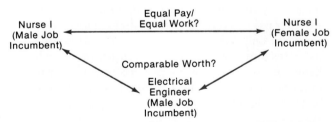

FIGURE 11-7   Equal Pay for Equal Work Versus the Comparable Worth Concept

[63]Robert Drazin and Ellen R. Auster, "Wage Differences Between Men and Women: Performance Appraisal Ratings vs. Salary Allocation as the Locus of Bias," *Human Resource Management* (Summer 1987), p. 157.

[64]*Schultz v. Wheaton Glass,* 9 FEP cases 502 (1970).

its male tellers more than its female tellers, and yet the only extra duties required of the men were to set break periods for outside tellers and "look after them" when they had problems.[65] In both instances, an Equal Pay Act violation was found because male-female pay differentials could not be justified by demonstrating significantly different responsibilities, effort, working conditions, or skills. A health club's practice of paying its male managers a 50 percent greater commission for selling memberships to men than female managers earned for selling memberships to women violated the Equal Pay Act. The health club attempted to justify the higher commission for men on the grounds that the market for women's memberships was considerably larger than the men's and, as a result, the two sexes would ultimately receive the same amount of total compensation for doing the same job. However, the court rejected this argument and held that "sex provided no part of the basis for the wage differentials.[66]

Not all male-female pay differentials violate the act. A group of male physician assistants employed by the State of Georgia who were paid more than a group of predominantly female nurse practitioners did not violate the Equal Pay Act because of different responsibilities associated with the two jobs. Although many similarites between the physician assistants and nurse practitioners were noted, the former group had greater latitude in making decisions as to how to treat patients. Nurse practitioners, on the other hand, "must not diagnose or treat the condition without direct physician involvement.[67] In another case, the U.S. Court of Appeals in Chicago ruled that a university that raised female professors' salaries did not violate the act because the university was trying to restore the salary of women to levels that they would have enjoyed in the absence of such discrimination.[68]

The best protection against equal pay violations is to use a carefully designed job evaluation system and a periodic equal pay audit.[69] However, there are certain exceptions to the Equal Pay Act that permit paying an employee of one sex more than another for *individual* differences that are geared to seniority, merit, productivity, or factors other than sex. Thus, an employee who has longer service, superior job performance, or higher levels of production or sales is entitled to receive greater pay, regardless of sex. Changes in job titles assigned to employees mean very little when the EEOC examines male and female jobs to determine whether pay discrepancies are justified. However, males and females who work for the same employer but in different departments or plants may receive different pay rates under most conditions. Organizations who violate the Equal Pay Act are liable for back pay. It is not permissible to lower the pay of the higher-paid sex in order to comply with the act. (Suppose that females are paid 20 percent less than males for the same work. The less expensive solution would be to lower the pay

---

[65]*Hodgson v. American Bank of Commerce*, 9 FEP Cases 502 (1971).

[66]*Bence v. Detroit Health Corp.*, 32 FEP Cases 434 (1983).

[67]*Beall v. Curtis*, 37 FEP Cases 644 (1985).

[68]*Ende v. Board of Regents of Regency Universities*, 37 FEP Cases 575 (1985).

[69]Frederick S. Hills and Thomas J. Bergmann, "Conducting an 'Equal Pay for Equal Work' Audit," in David B. Balkin and Luis R. Gomez-Mejia, (eds.), *New Perspectives on Compensation*, pp. 80–89.

rates for males to achieve equal pay for equal work. This is not allowed under the act, and the employer must keep the pay rate for males at current levels and raise the rates for women.) Employee benefits are also covered under the Equal Pay Act.

Comparable Worth: The Unsettled Issue

The concept of comparable worth deals with assessing the economic and organizational value of dissimilar jobs. That is, should the Nurse I depicted in Figure 11-7 be paid the same as an electrical engineer working for a large hospital? Should physical plant employees working for a university receive greater pay than the institution's clerical workers? Should state library employees be paid an amount equal to prison guards employed by the state's corrections department? Each of these comparisons involves evaluating the pay of male-dominated occupations (electrical engineers, physical plant employees, and prison guards) in comparison with that of female-dominated occupations (nurses, university clerical employees, state library employees).

The comparable worth debate stems from a phenomenon known as the *dual labor market*. Some occupations such as engineer, accountant, business professor, and other professional jobs have been traditionally dominated by males. Other jobs are almost exclusively occupied by females. For example, 99.1 percent of all secretaries are female, as are 86.2 percent of cashiers, 96.8 percent of registered nurses, 80.1 percent of those who wait on tables in restaurants, and 83.6 percent of elementary school teachers.[70] Traditionally male-dominated occupations are paid, on the average, more than those traditionally dominated by females. Advocates of the comparable worth concept claim that the dual labor market consists of a *primary* segment of desirable, higher-paying jobs and a *secondary* segment of less desirable, lower-paying, dead-end jobs. Females and minorities, the advocates claim, are more likely to be relegated to jobs in the secondary segment of the dual labor market. Even for jobs involving comparable skills and characteristics, proponents of the comparable worth concept believe that females are shortchanged.[71]

Although labor economists and civil rights leaders have cogently argued that the dual labor market phenomenon has increased pay differences between the sexes, the proper solution to the comparable worth problem is a controversial and thorny issue. Traditional job evaluation techniques may not provide a complete answer because the vast differences between jobs may make it impractical to use a common set of compensable factors. A set of compensable factors useful for evaluating nursing jobs would not be useful for evaluating engineering jobs. In

[70]Lawrence Z. Lorber, J. Robert Kirk, Stephen L. Samuels, and David J. Spellman III, *Sex and Salary: A Legal and Personnel Analysis of Comparable Worth* (Alexandria, Virginia: The ASPA Foundation, 1985), p. 7, and Robert S. Smith, "Comparable Worth: Limited Coverage and the Exacerbation of Inequality," *Industrial and Labor Relations Review* (January 1988), pp. 227–239.

[71]Carl C. Hoffman and Kathleen P. Hoffman, "Does Comparable Worth Obscure the Real Issues?" *Personnel Journal* (January 1987), p. 82.

fact, both wage and salary surveys and job evaluation methods have been viewed as culprits that perpetuate and exacerbate comparable worth problems rather than eliminate them.[72]

Recent court cases have provided partial answers, but they have also raised a number of questions regarding the solution and fate of the comparable worth issue.[73] The legal question presented by comparable worth is whether Title VII claims of sex discrimination can be pursued beyond the equal pay for equal work doctrine of the Equal Pay Act. In *County of Washington v. Gunther,* the U.S. Supreme Court decided that *intentional* sex-based pay discrimination that goes beyond the equal pay concept can be challenged under Title VII.[74] The Court said that female employees who claimed that their jobs were undervalued because of intentional sex discrimination may file suit under Title VII even when they do not perform the same work as their male co-workers. Unfortunately, the *Gunther* case focused on the pay of male and female prison guards rather than on radically different jobs and therefore did not provide a stern test of the comparable worth theory. The U.S. Court of Appeals in San Francisco dealt a setback to comparable worth when it reversed a lower court's decision that the State of Washington had engaged in unlawful sex discrimination in its pay practices. The state performed a job evaluation study of 121 job classifications in its personnel system and found that women were paid 20 percent less ($175 per month on the average) than men for performing jobs that received the same number of job evaluation points. A public sector union, the American Federation of State, County, and Municipal Employees (AFSCME), filed suit against the state under Title VII in order to secure remedial pay adjustments and back pay. In ruling against the union, the U.S. Court of Appeals noted that the state's job evaluation "may be useful as a diagnostic tool" but that the state "should also be able to take into account market conditions, [union] bargaining demands, and the possibility that another study will yield different results." Stressing that "[the] economic reality is that the value of a particular job to an employer is but one factor influencing the rate of compensation for that job," the court held that reliance on the free market system to set pay rates in dissimilar female dominated jobs is not in and of itself a violation of EEO laws.[75] The same Court of Appeals in San Francisco also rejected the comparable worth theory when it found that faculty members in the University of Washington College of Nursing could not press a discrimination claim merely by citing statistics indicating that they were paid less than faculty members in other colleges within the university. The fact that the pay rates are different does not

---

[72]See Michael Evan Gold, *A Dialogue on Comparable Worth,* (Ithaca, New York: ILR Press, Cornell University, 1983), pp. 38–54.

[73]See Doug Grider and Mike Shurden, "The Gathering Storm of Comparable Worth," *Business Horizons* (July-August 1987), pp. 81–86.

[74]U.S. Supreme Court, 25 FEP Cases 1521 (1981).

[75]*American Federation of State, County, and Municipal Employees, AFL-CIO, v. State of Washington,* 38 FEP Cases 1353 (1985).

necessarily imply intentional sex discrimination, according to the court. The U.S. Supreme Court decided not to hear an appeal on this case.[76]

The comparable worth debate poses some tough questions that are not likely to be answered in the near future. Even if personnel/human resource managers, civil rights advocates, feminist groups, legislators, and the courts all agreed that comparable worth is a noble goal that should be attained, the means of resolving the issue is difficult to determine.[77] Personnel/human resource managers, however, can do several things to minimize comparable worth problems in their organizations:

1. Use carefully conceived job evaluation systems containing a variety of well-defined compensable factors. Do not use overly broad or narrow job categories. An overly broad category will result in apples-and-oranges comparisons that could lead to comparable worth suits. Narrow job categories may create artificial and unimportant distinctions among jobs; this too could lead to equal pay or comparable worth suits. A job evaluation system should be labeled as "experimental" until experience has shown that it is workable and valid.
2. Identify job classes that are dominated by males or females. The employer may, for example, define a "dominated" class as one that has at least 70 percent males or females. When a job category is predominantly one sex or the other, decide what can be done in terms of recruitment and selection or training and development programs to achieve a more balanced distribution of male and female employees.
3. Stay abreast of federal and state court decisions and legislation that may have an impact on comparable worth.

◼ Summary and Conclusions

Designing a compensation program that is equitable and cost effective, provides incentives to employees, and meets the standards of the federal and state compensation laws is a challenging task.[78] This chapter has illustrated that compensation management is actually a series of separate yet interrelated functions: ensuring external equity through wage and salary surveys, establishing internal equity using job analysis and job evaluation, making individual pay adjustments, and properly using individual and group incentive programs. The compensation manager must also be aware of the special needs of highly paid executives and employees working in foreign countries. Finally, persons responsible for designing

[76]*Spaulding v. University of Washington*, 35 FEP Cases 217 (1984), U.S. Supreme Court, cert. denied, U.S. SupCt, 36 FEP Cases 464 (1985).

[77]Thomas A. Mahoney, Benson Rosen, and Sara Rynes, "Where Do Compensation Specialists Stand on Comparable Worth?" *Compensation Review* (Fourth Quarter 1984), pp. 27–40.

[78]James L. Whitney, "Pay Concepts for the 1990s, Part 1," *Compensation and Benefits Review* (March-April 1988), pp. 33–44.

compensation programs should understand equal pay and comparable worth issues. We hasten to add, however, that equal pay and comparable worth problems will be minimal *if* the job analysis, job evaluation, and wage and salary surveys have been carefully conducted.

Persons with the knowledge and technical skills to design and administer a compensation program are in demand by private and public sector organizations. Although the organization generally has fewer problems with a well-designed and administered compensation program than with one that is poorly conceived, there are several points that should be remembered. First, there is no ideal structure for a compensation program. A program that works well in a young and growing private sector corporation may be poorly suited for a stable corporation whose products are in a declining market cycle. The temptation to borrow or copy the successful compensation program of another organization in a wholesale fashion should be avoided. Of course, examining the compensation programs of other organizations and using elements that appear relevant to your organization is a good idea. Second, even the best-designed and administered compensation programs require frequent fine tuning. Job changes, organizational restructuring, changes in the organization's workforce, and legal developments occasionally require changes in the compensation program. Finally, careful job analysis, accurate and uncontaminated performance appraisal systems, and a willingness to listen to employee suggestions regarding pay policies will help maintain a high-quality compensation management program.

■ Questions

1. What is meant by the concept of external equity and how do organizations ensure external equity in compensation programs?

2. Briefly describe the factors that affect the pay level decision.

3. What is the purpose of the Fair Labor Standards Act? What employees and organizations are covered by the FLSA, and what employees and organizations are exempt from the act?

4. What advantages do tailor-made wage and salary surveys have over pay information gathered by third parties? How should a wage and salary survey be conducted?

5. Why is the concept of internal equity so important from an organizational and legal standpoint?

6. Describe the four major considerations that are necessary for job evaluation.

7. What advantages does the point method offer that make it superior to the ranking, classification, and factor comparison methods?

8. Describe how the pay level and pay structure decisions are merged.

9. Discuss the role of merit and seniority in compensation decisions. Where do you believe the emphasis should be placed?

10. How does a two-tier compensation system work, and what is its major purpose?

11. What are some major organizational and job design prerequisites for an individual incentive program?

12. Under what conditions are group incentive plans most likely to be successful?

13. What impact does the Tax Reform Act of 1986 have on executive compensation?

14. Describe the adjustments that must be made when compensating employees who work in international firms.

15. Discuss the difference between the equal pay for equal work concept and the comparable worth concept. What is the legal status of each?

☐ APPLICATIONS AND CASE EXERCISES

1. An executive in a high-tech firm in the San Francisco Bay area was asked about the perquisites that his firm offered. One of his comments was: "What finally sells isn't the cafeteria gingerbread, it's the pay and the career path."[79] Evaluate this statement. What does it mean? Do you agree with it?

2. "Leisure time—not money—is becoming the status symbol of the 1990s," says John P. Robinson, who directs the Americans' Use of Time Project at the University of Maryland. Many employees with six-figure salaries are either quitting their jobs in an attempt to find less-demanding (and lower paying) work or are refusing opportunities to earn additional income. The additional leisure time might be spent with family or pursuing hobbies. Do you believe this trend will continue? How does the leisure-income trade-off fit in with the concepts of equity and motivation discussed in this chapter and in Chapter 10?[80]

3. Teachers in two Macon, Georgia, schools received bonuses for improved student test scores. The money for the bonuses was supplied by local businesses.[81] Evaluate the wisdom of this bonus system. What are its advantages and disadvantages?

4. The typical sales commission is based *only* on units sold or dollars of sales generated. What problems might be encountered with an incentive program that has such a narrow focus?

5. Each year, the salaries of individual professors (including the name of the professor) at the University of Iowa and Iowa State University are published by a Des Moines newspaper. The salaries of public servants in other states are also published or are a matter of public record. Should private organizations also publish the salaries of their employees? What impact is such publicity likely to have on compensation management? Would you prefer to work in an organization that has open pay information or in one that keeps individual salaries secret? Discuss.

6. A great deal of controversy has surrounded the exorbitant salaries of professional athletes. Major league baseball players have been at the forefront of this controversy because of the multi-million-dollar annual salaries received by the superstars in the American and National Leagues. In 1992, Bobby Bonilla, an outfielder for the New York Mets, topped the list of highest-paid baseball players at $6.1 million. He was followed by Danny Tartabull of the New York Yankees ($5.3 million) and Ruben Sierra of the Texas Rangers ($5.0 million). The top nine players in major league baseball have a combined salary of nearly $40.7 million, almost twice the amount for the nine highest-paid players of 1990.[82] What factors affect the salaries of professional athletes? Are such salaries unreasonably high?

[79]*The Wall Street Journal*, Labor Letter, (February 3, 1987), p. 1.

[80]Carol Hymowitz, "Trading Fat Paychecks for Free Time," *The Wall Street Journal* (August 5, 1991), p. B1.

[81]*The Wall Street Journal*, Labor Letter, (July 1, 1986), p. 1.

[82]Associated Press, "This Dream Team Costs $40 million to Assemble," *Greenville News* (March 31, 1992), p. C1.

12 ■

Employee Benefit Programs

■ LEARNING OBJECTIVES

After reading this chapter, you should understand

1. The various types of employee benefits typically offered by private and public sector organizations.
2. Economic risks faced by employees and some basic rules for dealing with these risks so that an employee receives the best possible protection for each benefit dollar spent.
3. The role of the federal and state governments in providing and regulating employee benefit plans.
4. The major provisions and terms associated with employer-provided benefits, such as group life and health insurance, retirement programs, child-care programs, and others.

■ INTRODUCTORY VIGNETTE

Life Cycle Benefits: How Some Companies Help Working Families

Life-cycle benefits recognize the fact that some workers may have three generations living in the same household. The changing family structure plus the fact that working couples and dual-career families must be away from home at the same time creates problems for the care of children and elderly parents. In addition, life cycle benefits recognize the fact that more individuals are living to advanced ages and will require long-term nursing care.

Lancaster Laboratories has only 380 employees. Yet it has become well known nationwide because of what it does for working parents. The southeastern Pennsylvania company has onsite day care, pays employees who must stay at home and take care of sick children, and guarantees mothers a return to their original job after 3.5 months of maternity leave. Lancaster Lab's day-care center is only a short walk from the firm's main building. Many parents spend lunch breaks with their children, reading stories to them or playing at the day-care center's outdoor park. The day-care center charges employees $55 to $78 per

Compiled from Fawn Vrazo, "Woman Who Pushed for On-Site Day Care Wins Award," Knight Ridder, reprinted in *The Greenville News* (May 30, 1990), p. 7B; Joseph Weber, "Meet DuPont's 'In-House Conscience,'" *Business Week* (June 24, 1991), pp. 62–63; and "Older Women's League Sees Eldercare as Top Women's Issue," *Los Angeles Times*, reprinted in *The Greenville News* (July 24, 1990), p. 3B.

week, and the facility is run by an independent operator. The center requires approximately $5,000 annually in maintenance, but this price is small when the company realizes that it has retained 35 of the 36 female workers who have had children over the past 4 years.

DuPont has spent $1.5 million to build and renovate child-care centers near its major work sites throughout the United States. In its home base in Wilmington, Delaware, DuPont spent $250,000 and enlisted top executives to set up Child Care Connection, a statewide day-care referral service that is used by 75 companies. Working parents can take advantage of the company's family-oriented activities such as job sharing for working mothers and the Flying Colors program, which offers grants to day-care providers to upgrade their services beyond those required to meet the minimums prescribed by law. The company now offers generous and pacesetting leave policies for childbirth and adoptions, including full benefits and up to 6 weeks of paid time off.

At the other end of the age spectrum, the number of corporations offering assistance to employees with aging parents is increasing. Although it costs about $3,000 a year per child for day-care services, the average annual cost to care for an elderly parent is $25,000. Some companies, such as Champion International Corporation and IBM, have elder-care programs. Elder-care programs may provide referral services, assistance in helping employees care for a parent, help from social workers, and psychological counseling. Working women are four times as likely to be caregivers for an elderly parent as working men. According to the Older Women's League, women today will spend 17 years of their lives caring for children and 18 years assisting aged parents. About 89 percent of American women over age 18 will provide care to children, parents, or both, and about 31 percent will care for children and parents simultaneously.

According to The Bureau of National Affairs, Inc.'s survey data, 29 percent of companies provide child care and 45 percent expect to provide the service by the year 2000. Only 11 percent of surveyed companies provide elder-care resources or referrals, but 53 percent expect to have such programs in operation by the end of the decade. Other life-cycle benefits include financial planning, long-term care insurance, and sick child facilities or home-based care.

■ Introduction

Employee benefit programs have become an integral part of most compensation packages. Group life and health insurance programs, retirement programs, paid vacations and holidays, prepaid legal plans, and dental and optical insurance coverage are among the types of employee benefits commonly found in private and public sector organizations. Employee benefits comprise approximately 28 percent of the total compensation package.

Surveys on employee benefit programs have revealed the following, according to estimates by the U.S. Department of Labor, Bureau of Labor Statistics:[1]

1. Nearly all workers are provided with some form of health insurance. Three fourths of the companies bear the entire cost of the health insurance, and nearly all health insurance plans either include coverage for dependents or provide coverage at an additional cost to the employee.[2]
2. Approximately three fourths of the firms surveyed have dental care plans for full-time employees.
3. Nearly all companies surveyed provide retirement (pension) programs. Under most pension plans, the employer pays all expenses and employees are not required to contribute to the plan through payroll deductions.[3]
4. The majority of companies surveyed provide 2 weeks of paid annual vacation for employees who have at least 1 year of service.[4]
5. Nearly all (96 percent) of the companies surveyed provide group life insurance coverage for employees, and employers pay all premiums in 86 percent of these programs.[5]
6. Ninety-two percent of all companies surveyed provide jury duty pay for employees who are summoned to serve.[6]
7. An increasing number of employers are recognizing the need to provide child-care benefits or facilities.[7]

The trend in employee benefits has been clearly toward increasing the amount and variety of programs available to employees.[8] Labor union pressures and spill-over effects into nonunionized sectors (where nonunion employers provide the same benefits as unionized companies) are generally regarded as the primary impetus behind the popularity of employee benefit programs. Employee benefits such as pension programs have traditionally served to defer income until retirement while simultaneously allowing employers and employees to take advantage

---

[1]The Bureau of National Affairs, Inc., *Personnel Policies Forum*, Survey No. 137 (Washington, D.C.: The Bureau of National Affairs, Inc., 1984).

[2]Employees who work on a temporary basis, independent contractors, and workers in small firms often do not have adequate health insurance.

[3]The Bureau of National Affairs, Inc., *Personnel Policies Forum*, Survey No. 134 (Washington, D.C.: The Bureau of National Affairs, Inc., 1982).

[4]The Bureau of National Affairs, Inc., *Personnel Policies Forum Survey*, No. 142 (Washington, D.C.: The Bureau of National Affairs, Inc., 1986).

[5]*The Human Resources Yearbook, 1987 Edition* (Englewood Cliffs, New Jersey: Prentice-Hall, Inc., 1987), p. 2.76.

[6]Ibid, p. 2.77.

[7]Ibid, pp. 2.68–2.71.

[8]Robert E. Perkins, "The Employer's Role in Benefits Evolution," *Personnel* (February 1987), p. 66.

of current tax laws.[9] A comprehensive array of employee benefits is generally believed to aid the organization in attracting high-quality employees, as well as increasing the morale, job satisfaction, and motivation of current employees. In a 1990 survey, the Employee Benefit Research Institute and the Gallup Organization, Inc. found that 39 percent of employees would need at least an additional $9,000 per year before they would choose a job without life, health, or retirement benefits. An additional 25 percent said that they would need at least an annual increase of $5,000 before making such a decision.[10] As employees accumulate seniority in an organization, the employee benefit program may reduce turnover because of favorable group insurance rates and pension vesting arrangements that tie quality workers to the firm.[11] Finally, employees usually discover that benefits such as group life and health insurance are less expensive than they would be if purchased individually from local insurance agents because of lower group insurance rates and employer subsidization of administrative costs and premium payments.

This chapter focuses on the trends, issues, and terminology associated with employee benefit programs. An understanding of employee benefit programs is valuable to persons who are covered under such programs or who are involved in their design and administration.

■ Types of Employee Benefit Programs

Table 12-1 illustrates the types of employee benefits found in many public and private sector organizations. Employee benefit programs have responded to changing employee needs that are dictated by changes in the economy, the tax laws, and the lifestyles of employees. The bottom line for any employee benefits program is to provide the maximum amount of benefits per dollar spent. Unfortunately, although this objective may sound simple, it is not always easy to attain. Organizations and employee groups may be attracted to a specific type of benefit because of its short-term appeal or gimmickry. Although there is some good to be found in nearly every type of employee benefit option, some benefits provide a better "deal" for the employee than others. This is especially true when one recognizes that organizations have only a limited amount of money to spend on employee benefits. For this reason, employee benefits should be viewed from a risk management standpoint in order to assess their usefulness to the individual employee.

[9]Philip C. Hunt, "Tax Reform: Its Impact on Compensation and Benefits," *Employee Relations Today* (Spring 1987), pp. 39–52.

[10]Employee Benefit Research Institute and the Gallup Organization, Inc., 1990. Reprinted by The Bureau of National Affairs, Inc., 1991.

[11]Kevin Anderson, "Workers Staying Put for Benefits," *USA Today* (September 27, 1991), p. 4B.

TABLE 12-1   Examples of Employee Benefits

1. Legally required payments
   a. Old-age, survivors, disability, and health insurance (commonly known as *Social Security*)
   b. Workers' compensation
   c. Unemployment compensation
2. Contingent and deferred benefits
   a. Pension plans
   b. Group life insurance
   c. Group health insurance
      i. Medical expense (hospitalization and surgical)
      ii. Disability income (short and long term)
   d. Guaranteed annual wage (GAW)
   e. Prepaid legal plans
   f. Military leave and pay
   g. Jury duty and bereavement paid leave
   h. Maternity leave
   i. Child care leave
   j. Sick leave
   k. Dental benefits
   l. Tuition-aid benefits
   m. Suggestion awards
   n. Service awards
   o. Severance pay
3. Payments for time not worked
   a. Vacations
   b. Holidays
   c. Voting pay allowances
4. Other benefits
   a. Travel allowances
   b. Company cars and subsidies
   c. Moving expenses
   d. Uniform and tool expenses
   e. Employee meal allowances
   f. Discounts on employer's goods and services
   g. Child care facilities

■ Employee Benefits and Risk Management

During their income-earning years, employees face several risks that have unfavorable financial consequences (we are not dealing here with the mental anguish associated with these risks, although this is of importance in a noneconomic sense). These risks become even more critical when an employee has family members or others who are economically dependent on his or her ability to continue working.

The following risks pose a threat to the economic security of those who work, as well as to their dependents:

1. *Premature death:* A person may die during the years in which he or she is earning an income. Although most persons regard any form of death as premature, we are speaking only of the financial consequences of dying before reaching retirement. Life insurance is the primary means of dealing with the risk of premature death.
2. *Superannuation:* A person may outlive his or her economic usefulness, that is, the individual is still living but is no longer generating an income. Most of us do not worry about the "risk" of living to a ripe old age, but *financially,* those who live well beyond retirement must make provisions for their postretirement years. Public and private pension programs are a primary means of dealing with superannuation.
3. *Interruption or loss of income:* Events such as disability, accidents, illness, or layoff result in either a temporary or a permanent loss of employment and earnings. Disability income insurance, worker's compensation, and unemployment compensation are commonly used to deal with this risk.
4. *Extraordinary medical expenses:* Large medical bills can impose severe financial burdens or lead to financial ruin. Because most employees do not have adequate resources to cover large and fortuitous expenses (e.g., surgery that results in a $50,000 hospital bill), employee benefits such as hospitalization and surgical insurance are used to protect against this risk.

These four categories of risk have two characteristics. First, they impose financially severe consequences that cannot be met through the personal resources of the average middle- or upper-middle-income employee. Second, these risks are contingent or fortuitous in nature. They occur in a somewhat random and unpredictable fashion. Most employees will not die prematurely, but a small percentage will. This is why the term *contingent* benefits is used in Table 12-1. Contingent benefits are paid *in the event* that premature death, disability, or hospitalization occurs. Most psychologically normal people are content never to take advantage of contingent benefits (with the exception of pension benefits and suggestion awards); the real satisfaction of contingent employee benefits is the security of knowing that they are *available if needed* to deal with the risks noted.

In addition to analyzing the *types* of risks faced by workers, the *severity and probabilities* associated with these risks must be assessed. Although events such as premature death, total and permanent disability, and extraordinary medical expenses pose catastrophic financial burdens, they affect relatively few employees. Other occurrences such as routine dental care, jury duty, the need for eyeglasses, and maternity care affect a large percentage of employees. Fortunately, the more common events present the least trouble financially.

From the standpoint of risk management, the dollars used to purchase employee benefits are better spent by insuring against those events that have a *small probability of occurrence* but impose *severe financial losses.*[12] This means that group life, hospitalization, and disability income insurance will afford more protection per premium dollar than items such as dental, eyeglass, or maternity insurance policies. Employee benefits that provide protection against relatively certain yet financially insignificant "losses" are usually not good bargains in terms of cost because the premiums (cost of the insurance) are nearly equal to the benefits received. That is, the company and the employee are merely "trading dollars" with the insurance company. Unfortunately, some employees hold less cost-effective benefits (that require a high insurance premium relative to the amount of coverage received) in high regard. It is probably better for the employer or the worker to pay for the small, high-probability risks out of pocket rather than insuring them.[13] A dilemma is created when employee benefit dollars are used for minor benefits to the neglect of benefits such as major medical insurance or long-term disability income insurance. Responsible employee benefit managers should attempt to convey to employees the importance of securing protection against the potentially severe losses such as major medical expenses and long-term disability.

■ The Government's Role in Employee Benefit Plans

The federal and state governments play two important roles with regard to employee benefit programs. First, they either mandate or provide certain types of benefits. Second, many nonmandatory benefits are regulated through federal legislation or state insurance codes. There is a definite trend toward increased governmental regulation of employee benefits. Perhaps the two most significant federal interventions into employee benefits during the past 20 years are the Employee Retirement Income Security Act of 1974, which regulates pension programs, and the Tax Reform Act of 1986.

Mandatory and Government-Provided Employee Benefits

Table 12-1 includes a list of legally required benefits that most employers must provide to workers. Workers' compensation laws are regulated by the individual states and provide protection against job-related injuries and illnesses. The goals of workers' compensation laws are to help rehabilitate injured workers and to provide them with cash benefits and medical care for disabilities incurred during

---

[12]Emmett J. Vaughan, *Fundamentals of Risk and Insurance*, 3rd ed. (New York: John Wiley and Sons, 1982), p. 41.

[13]As a general rule, insurance coverage policies for eyeglasses, dental care, and even maternity coverage are not good insurance buys because these expenses can be planned and paid for out of pocket.

the course of employment. According to the Bureau of National Affairs, Inc., most state workers' compensation laws have the following objectives:[14]

- Replacement of lost earnings and medical care for those injured while working and income benefits for their dependents, regardless of fault.
- Reduction of court costs, delays, and workloads arising from personal injury litigation, the elimination of legal fees, and the avoidance of court delays.
- Encouragement of employer interest in worker safety and the reduction of preventable injuries.

All but three states have compulsory workers' compensation statutes. Employers are responsible for financing their *workers' compensation* programs (employees do not contribute money to the program). Premiums are paid on an "experience rating" basis that penalizes firms with high rates of worker injuries.[15] The logging industry has historically had one of the highest workers' compensation insurance rates, whereas policies covering office and clerical personnel usually have low premiums because there are few safety hazards associated with white-collar jobs. Organizations typically purchase workers' compensation insurance through private insurance companies or through a competitive state fund. A few states offer workers' compensation through monopolistic state funds. Nearly all states allow employers to self insure their workers' compensation programs if certain standards are met. The amount that a worker receives under workers' compensation depends on the extent of his or her injuries and earnings at the time of injury. Because each state has different workers' compensation laws, benefits vary. However, most states have no maximum on rehabilitative and hospitalization benefits. Most state workers' compensation laws have extraterritoriality provisions for employees such as sales personnel, truck drivers, or construction workers whose jobs involve working in more than one state. Occupational diseases are covered by all state laws, and some jurisdictions now provide workers' compensation benefits for stress-induced occupational illnesses.[16] A major advantage of workers' compensation is that the injured employee avoids the trauma and uncertainty of time-consuming legal proceedings. Determining who is at fault or liable for an employee's on-the-job injury is not an issue—workers' compensation benefits are paid to the employee as prescribed by law. A few states also provide

---

[14]The Bureau of National Affairs, Inc., *Compensation: Personnel Policy and Practice Series* (Washington, D.C.: The Bureau of National Affairs, Inc., 1991), Section 365.

[15]"Wal-Mart Stores Must Pay $16.8 Million for Premiums," *The Wall Street Journal* (July 10, 1987), p. 4; Stephen Tarnoff, "Monsanto Has Coverage for $108 Million Verdict, *Business Insurance* (December 22, 1986), p. 1; James R. Chelius and Robert S. Smith, "Firm Size and Regulatory Compliance Costs: The Case of Workers' Compensation Insurance," *Journal of Policy Analysis and Management* (Winter 1987), p. 193; and Michael L. Murray, "Reducing the Impact of Workers' Compensation," *Risk Management* (February 1986), p. 48.

[16]See Roger Thompson, "Workers' Comp Costs Out of Control," *Nation's Business* (July 1992), pp. 22--24, 28, and 30. John M. Ivancevich, Michael T. Matteson, and Edward P. Richards III, "Who's Liable for Stress on the Job?," *Harvard Business Review* (March 1985), p. 60, and Meg Fletcher, "Employers Facing More Mental Stress Claims," *Business Insurance* (April 13, 1987), p. 34.

state disability insurance for employees who become disabled for reasons other than job-related injuries.

In addition to the perils of death, disability, and extraordinary medical expenses stemming from job-related injuries and illnesses, workers face the risk of loss of income caused by unemployment. Because private insurance companies are not willing to sell insurance coverage for unemployment, the government has established a joint federal-state system of *unemployment compensation*. The basic objective of unemployment compensation is to promote financial security for workers by encouraging employers to stabilize their workforce and avoid repeated layoffs and rehires. Unemployment compensation promotes individual financial security by providing emergency income to workers during periods of high unemployment.[17] The Federal Unemployment Tax Act (FUTA) requires that employers pay unemployment taxes. Individual states must impose a payroll tax on employers (employees do not pay for unemployment insurance) under an experience-rating plan that penalizes firms with high rates of involuntary unemployment rates and rewards firms whose unemployment history is low. Most states require the worker to have earned a minimum income during the year preceding unemployment and to maintain an attachment to the labor force by reporting to a local public employment office. States also vary widely in the amount of unemployment compensation benefits that they offer. Weekly benefit amounts range from a minimum of several dollars to a maximum of several hundred dollars, depending on the state and the income of the employee prior to becoming unemployed. The majority of states provide up to 26 weeks of unemployment benefit payments. During periods of high unemployment, eligible recipients who have exhausted their benefits may receive an additional 13 weeks of unemployment compensation.

Unemployment compensation laws are designed to protect the employee who, through circumstances beyond his or her control, suffers a layoff. States often disqualify employees from receiving unemployment compensation (or limit the amount received) under the following conditions: voluntary resignation without good cause; discharge for misconduct; failure to accept suitable employment through a public employment agency; participation in a strike; receipt of Social Security, workers' compensation, or pension benefits; quitting work to attend school; plant shutdowns for vacation periods; voluntary resignations precipitated by marriage or family obligations; and various types of fraud.[18]

The federal government provides the well-known *Social Security* program (whose proper title is the *Old Age, Survivors, Disability, and Health Insurance* [*OASDHI*] program). The Social Security program provides retirement, life insurance, disability income, and Medicare (health insurance) benefits to eligible recipients. The program is financed through mandatory payroll taxes on both the employer and the employee. In 1992, employees paid a payroll tax of 7.65 percent

---

[17]The Bureau of National Affairs, Inc., *Compensation: Personnel Policy and Practice Series* (Washington, D.C.: The Bureau of National Affairs, Inc. 1992), Section 356.

[18]G. Solon, "The Effects of Unemployment Insurance Eligibility Rules on Job Quitting Behavior," *The Journal of Human Resources* (Winter 1984), pp. 118–126.

on the first $55,500 of wage and salary income and 1.45 percent on wage and salary income between $55,501 and $130,200. Employers match the taxes paid by employees.[19] The more Social Security taxes paid by an employee, the higher the benefit levels to which he or she is eligible. Thus, an employee who pays at or near the maximum tax each year would be entitled to a larger monthly retirement benefit at age 65 than would an employee who pays less Social Security taxes. A qualified employee is currently entitled to receive full retirement benefits at age 65 (or reduced benefits at age 62). However, the age for receiving full retirement benefits will gradually rise to age 66 by the year 2009 and to age 67 by the year 2027. Survivors' benefits (a form of life insurance coverage) are payable to the family of a deceased worker. Eligible survivors include a widowed spouse age 65 (or age 60 for reduced benefits or age 50 if disabled), surviving divorced spouse age 60 or older, dependent parents age 62 or older, unmarried surviving spouse caring for a child under age 16, and unmarried surviving children under age 18 (or under age 19 if a full-time high school student or under age 22 if disabled). Disability benefits are provided to workers under Social Security for workers who are unable to engage in any meaningful employment for at least 12 months. Medicare provides health insurance coverage primarily for persons age 65 and over, as well as persons who are permanently disabled or suffering from a life-threatening illness.[20]

The rationale behind the benefits described in the workers' compensation, state temporary disability programs, unemployment compensation, and Social Security appear to be twofold. First, the federal and state governments have attempted to ensure that workers and their families enjoy at least a minimal level of economic security from the risks of premature death, old age, disability, and unemployment. This line of thought stems from President Franklin D. Roosevelt and the New Deal era, which emphasized antipoverty programs as a means of stimulating economic recovery and growth. Some critics argue that programs such as Social Security only allow benefit recipients to eke out a meager existence. However, the programs would probably impose a severe and politically unpopular tax burden on employers and workers if benefits were substantially increased. Other critics feel that the government should not require employers and employees to participate in programs such as Social Security. Rather, they argue that each worker should be responsible for his or her own welfare. Opponents of the Social Security program claim that it is unfair to persons in higher income brackets because the retirement benefits redistribute income toward workers in lower income brackets. Some employees feel that if they were allowed to invest the amount that is regularly deducted from their paychecks for Social Security, they could obtain better investment results. This argument overlooks the fact that employers match employee contributions to the program. The financial pressures faced by the Social Security program caused by the decreasing number of workers paying payroll taxes into the program coupled with the increasing number of retirees and others

[19]"A Bite Too Big to Swallow," *American Demographics* (March 1987), p. 20.

[20]The Bureau of National Affairs, Inc., *Compensation: Personnel Policy and Practice Series* (Washington, D.C.: The Bureau of National Affairs, Inc., 1992), Section 353.

who are drawing benefits has created uncertainty regarding the future and wisdom of the system.[21]

Second, federal and state governments may provide insurance protection if private insurance companies are either unable or unwilling to do so. This is probably the case with unemployment compensation, but workers' compensation is provided through private insurers in most states. Furthermore, retirement, life insurance, disability, and health insurance coverage as provided by Social Security are also available from private insurers. Some workers, however, may not be able to obtain these coverages from insurance companies because of a poor health history or exposure to occupational hazards. Other workers, if left on their own, would neglect to provide for their retirement or seek life, health, and disability insurance protection; they are therefore forced to obtain protection through the mandatory payroll deductions of Social Security. It should be noted that workers' compensation, unemployment compensation, and Social Security benefits are available only under conditions prescribed by law. Thus, a person requiring large amounts of life insurance to protect the needs of a growing family with young children or a person who suffers a 3-month partial disability because of an off-the-job injury would need protection above and beyond that provided by the government programs described here.

Government Regulation of Employee Benefits

Employee benefit programs are regulated by both federal and state laws. Federal laws regulating employee benefits include the Employee Retirement Income Security Act of 1974 (ERISA), the Consolidated Omnibus Budget Reconciliation Act of 1985 (COBRA), the Tax Reform Act of 1986, and the various EEO laws such as Title VII of the 1964 Civil Rights Act, the Pregnancy Discrimination Act, and the Age Discrimination in Employment Act of 1967. State insurance codes regulate group life and health insurance programs. Most state insurance codes establish the minimum employee group size and set insurance rates, employee participation standards, coverage limits, and other aspects of group insurance.

These laws and their specific applications are discussed individually in later sections of this chapter. However, employee benefits are regulated for three reasons. First, employee benefits that accrue over periods of time (such as pension benefits) can be subject to mismanagement by incompetent or unscrupulous administrators. Second, employers may knowingly or inadvertently engage in unfair sex discrimination (almost always to the detriment of female employees) because of unequal pension and health insurance benefits. The Tax Reform Act of 1986 also focuses on a different type of discrimination: the wide disparity in employee benefits between high-salaried employees and all other employees. Third, state

---

[21]See George E. Rejda, *Social Insurance and Economic Security* (Englewood Cliffs, New Jersey: Prentice-Hall, Inc., 1976), pp. 108–172; William C. Birdsall and John L. Hankins, "The Future of Social Security," *Annals of the American Academy of Political and Social Science* (May 1985), p. 82; and "Slip Sliding Away," *American Demographics* (April 1987), p. 13.

insurance codes focus heavily on the problem of adverse selection—a situation where high-risk (e.g., older or unhealthy) employees participate heavily in group life and health insurance plans, while lower-risk employees choose not to participate. Adverse selection increases the cost of group insurance; by requiring minimum participation standards (e.g., requiring at least 90 percent of all employees to join the health insurance group), state insurance codes negate some of the problems associated with adverse selection. State insurance codes also regulate the management practices and solvency of insurance companies that provide employee benefits. Because the insurance industry is often very competitive, the states regulate the rates set by insurance companies to prevent them from charging rates that are so low that they would run the risk of becoming insolvent and unable to pay claims.

■ Employer-Provided Benefits

Many employees find that government-provided benefits furnish only minimal protection from the risks of premature death, superannuation, extraordinary expenses, and loss of income. For example, most employees faced with retiring and depending *only* on Social Security for an income would be forced into a frugal lifestyle. Many employees also lack the personal resources, such as large savings accounts, to meet these risks. Employers have therefore felt compelled to offer benefits that *supplement* existing government-sponsored programs such as workers' compensation, unemployment compensation, and Social Security. Workers' compensation might be supplemented by disability income insurance, unemployment compensation might be bolstered by supplemental unemployment benefits and guaranteed pay provisions, and Social Security benefits might be enhanced by private pensions as well as group life, health, and disability insurance.

Group Life Insurance

Group life insurance protects the family of an employee against the economic losses that would occur if the worker died during his or her years of gainful employment. An employer typically enters into a master contract with an insurance company (sometimes called the *insurer* or the *provider*). The contract normally provides term life insurance. Term insurance is the least expensive form of life insurance because it contains no savings (cash value) element found in whole life and similar policies. Thus, term insurance provides pure life insurance protection; once the term policy expires, the insured employee has no vested financial interest (cash value) in the policy. Each employee receives a certificate or handbook that explains the type and amount of life insurance protection. Group life insurance as an employee benefit offers several advantages:[22]

1. Premiums usually cost less under a group policy than they would under a comparable individual policy purchased by the employee directly through an insurance company.
2. Group policies usually do not require a physical examination or proof of insurability. Employees who would otherwise have difficulty obtaining life insurance because of poor health or occupational hazards are automatically eligible for group life insurance benefits when they are hired.
3. Employers may receive a business expense tax deduction on the premiums paid for group life insurance.
4. If an employee resigns or is terminated, he or she has the right to convert to an individual life insurance policy at a higher premium (usually within 30 days) without further evidence of insurability.

Group life insurance is an especially important benefit for employees with children or other economic dependents. Many employees who need life insurance the most are often the ones who have the least resources to pay high insurance premiums. For example, a 25-year-old worker with an unemployed spouse and two dependent children, ages 2 and 4, may need $200,000 of life insurance in order to protect the family adequately in the event that the worker suffers premature death. A whole life insurance policy containing a cash value or savings program with a $200,000 face value might cost this 25-year-old worker approximately $3,000 per year, an amount that is prohibitive for most employees. A less expensive term insurance policy providing $200,000 in coverage might cost $500 a year. However, a term policy may expire and not be renewable if the employee's health deteriorates. Group life insurance is often very inexpensive and is often provided without cost to the employee under a *noncontributory* plan whereby the employer pays the entire premium. Even when the employee pays part of the premium, the cost is usually low. Group insurance policies are sold directly to the employer, thereby eliminating sales calls to each employee. Similarly, there is usually no requirement for a medical examination or an extensive insurance application detailing the employee's medical history. Premiums paid by the employer on behalf of the employee are not taxable as ordinary income to the employee for the first $500,000 in life insurance coverage. If the employee had to purchase a life insurance policy personally, the premium would be paid in after-tax dollars—a definite disadvantage.

The primary problem with group life insurance is that an employee may be lulled into a false sense of security regarding his or her life insurance program. Most group programs do not provide an adequate amount of insurance protection to meet all of an employee's life insurance needs, especially for employees with dependent children. It is often necessary for the employee to supplement group

---

[22]The Bureau of National Affairs, Inc., *Compensation: Personnel Policy and Practice Series* (Washington, D.C.: The Bureau of National Affairs, Inc., 1991), Section 339.

life insurance coverage by purchasing additional protection under an individual policy. Employees should therefore determine how much life insurance coverage is necessary to provide their dependents with a comfortable standard of living in the event that they suffer premature death, rather than depending only on the life insurance provided by the employer.

Group Health Insurance

Group health insurance can be divided into three categories: (1) medical expense insurance, (2) health maintenance organizations, and (3) disability income insurance.

Medical Expense Insurance

Medical expense insurance covers charges for surgical, hospitalization, and ancillary services such as x-ray and laboratory services, prosthetic devices, drugs, and other medical items. Plans such as hospital indemnity contracts, Blue Cross and Blue Shield, surgical service plans, major medical insurance, Medicare supplement policies, and various limited health insurance policies covering specific diseases such as cancer all fall under the rubric of medical expense insurance.

Hospital indemnity contracts (also called *cash benefit plans*) are designed to pay a stipulated amount (e.g., $200 per day for a specified number of days) while the insured employee or eligible dependents are hospitalized. The insured is reimbursed up to the policy limits of coverage and is responsible for any charges in excess of these limits. Blue Cross plans (known as *service plans*) maintain contracts with *member hospitals* that have agreed to accept a specific fee schedule as full payment for persons carrying this type of hospitalization coverage. Most group hospitalization plans provide maternity coverage for 10–14 days for workers who have been employed by the organization for at least 9 months.[23] Both hospital indemnity contracts and Blue Cross plans also provide ancillary services. According to The Bureau of National Affairs, Inc., indemnity (cash benefit) plans are generally less expensive than service plans (Blue Cross), but the latter often provides more comprehensive coverage.[24]

Surgical insurance covers the physician's bill for health care services (not just for surgery, as the name implies). Surgical coverage is offered on both an indemnity contract and a service contract (Blue Shield) basis. Indemnity plans reimburse the worker according to a *schedule of benefits* that lists the amounts that the policy will pay for a variety of surgical procedures (e.g., $800 for an appendectomy, $700 for a gallbladder removal, $950 for a hysterectomy, and so on). Surgical service

---

[23]The Bureau of National Affairs, Inc., *Compensation: Personnel Policy and Practice Series* (Washington, D.C.: The Bureau of National Affairs, Inc., 1991), Section 339. Under the Pregnancy Discrimination Act, disabilities arising from pregnancies must be treated in the same manner as other disabilities under a firm's group health insurance plan.

[24]Ibid.

plans generally pay "usual, customary, and reasonable fees" for a physician's services. Most group health insurance policies cover hospital care and surgical services under a single package.

Major medical insurance covers catastrophically high hospitalization, surgical, and other medical expenses. There are two types of major medical plans: one that supplements basic hospital/surgical medical expense programs and one that provides basic coverage that includes regular hospital and surgical insurance along with major medical insurance. The maximum limits on a major medical policy commonly range upward from $10,000 for any single illness or injury. Major medical insurance covers a wide variety of health care costs such as hospital care, physician's fees, surgery, anesthesia, oxygen, drugs, services of a private duty nurse, artificial limbs, ambulance services, and services by radiologists and physical therapists. From a risk management standpoint, major medical insurance is an excellent buy because it protects against severe financial losses that most persons would find devastating. Although it provides a great deal of protection from financially ruinous medical bills, major medical insurance is not prohibitively expensive. The relatively low cost of major medical insurance is a result of its substantial deductible ($50 to $500) plus a co-insurance (or co-payment) provision for amounts above the deductible. A co-payment provision may require that the employee pay as much as 25 percent of the remaining expenses. Co-payments are designed to discourage malingering by covered employees. Major medical benefits are based on a lifetime maximum (e.g., $200,000) that may be subject to a limit (e.g., $30,000) in any given year.

Suppose that a major medical policy has a $50,000 limit, a $500 deductible, and a 10 percent co-insurance clause for medical expenses above the deductible. The insured employee with covered medical bills totaling $23,000 would pay $2,750 ($500 for the deductible plus 10 percent of the remaining $22,500 under the co-insurance provision); the insurance company would pay the remaining $20,250. Although many employees would find the $2,750 payment to be financially inconvenient, this amount pales in comparison to $23,000 — a sum that may force an employee to deplete savings, sell property, borrow heavily, or file for bankruptcy.

The quality of a group medical expense policy such as major medical insurance depends on several factors. It is obvious that the higher the dollar limits of coverage, the better the policy. However, several additional considerations are important. First, persons covered under a group medical expense plan should be aware of the *exclusions* that apply to their policy. Typical exclusions are war-related injuries, self-inflicted injuries (which are intentional and not accidental), expenses payable under workers' compensation, and elective cosmetic surgery. Hospitalization coverage often excludes outpatient care (where the employee is treated at home or in a physician's office rather than being admitted to a hospital). Preexisting conditions are often excluded. A preexisting condition is one that had been diagnosed prior to the employee's eligibility under the group health insurance plan. For example, an employee who is diagnosed with a stomach ulcer on April 3, 1992, and accepts employment with a company on June 18, 1992, may not have health insurance coverage for treatments on the ulcer because the condition existed *prior* to the employee's eligibility under the group insurance plan. All other conditions diagnosed after June 18, 1992, would be covered, however.[25] Medical expense insurance often excludes coverage for mental illness and drug and alcohol addiction. Dental care and prescription eyeglasses are also excluded and can be insured under separate group health policies.

Care should be taken to understand how a deductible provision applies to group health insurance coverage. Most health insurance plans use a deductible that ranges from $50 to $1,000. Deductibles eliminate frequent small claims and reduce the cost of group health insurance. Most health insurance plans use an annual deductible rather than a per-illness deductible. For example, a company may use a maximum $500 annual family deductible, with a $100 deductible for each family member until the $500 maximum is reached. In other group policies, the deductible is more restrictive and applies on a per-illness basis. Thus an employee who is treated for a leg injury in February and then is treated for an eye disorder in July may have to satisfy two $100 deductibles, one for the leg injury and one for the eye disorder.

Medical expense insurance policies that cover *specific diseases or occurrences* such as cancer, confinement to a hospital for at least 30 days, or serious injuries provide catastrophic loss protection only under limited circumstances. These "limited" or "dread disease" health insurance policies do not, however, provide the broad benefits of major medical insurance.

More useful as a limited health insurance policy are supplements that provide coverage for some of the large hospitalization deductibles under the Medicare program. Some companies also provide health insurance to retirees.[26] However, the cost of such coverage can be quite expensive. One consulting firm estimated that a corporation with 200 retired workers will pay $153,000 a year for the retirees' health insurance.[27] With the rapidly increasing cost of health care, health insurance for retirees will undoubtedly continue to increase. There is also concern in Congress that legislation is needed to protect the health insurance benefits of retirees in the event that the employer faces bankruptcy. Congressional concern was precipitated by the adverse publicity associated with the termination of retiree health insurance coverage by LTV Steel Corporation.[28]

Health Maintenance Organizations

For companies and employees who elect not to purchase medical expense insurance, health maintenance organizations (HMOs) are an attractive alternative.

---

[25]Preexisting conditions exclusions may be lifted after an employee has worked a specified period of time.

[26]Daniel L. Klein and Jeffrey P. Petertil, "Health Coverage for Retirees: A Timebomb," *Personnel* (August 1986), p. 54, and Meg Delaney, "Who Will Pay Retirees Health Care?" *Personnel Journal* (March 1987), p. 82.

[27]*The Wall Street Journal*, Labor Letter (March 10, 1987), p. 1.

[28]Richard J. Donahue, "78,500 LTV Retirees Lose Health Coverage: Pensions Safe," *National Underwriter—Life and Health Insurance Edition* (July 26, 1986), p. 3.

HMOs provide a comprehensive array of health care services such as medical examinations, x-ray and laboratory services, maternity care, hospitalization, and surgical services for persons residing in a defined geographic area. The original HMO concept offered comprehensive health care for members within a single organization and encouraged a preventive orientation to medical care as a means of reducing illnesses and controlling health care costs. Most HMOs follow the *group practice model* in which a contract is established with a physician group and area hospitals that provide health care to HMO members. Under this arrangement, physicians are employed by the HMO and members can select a personal physician from within the group and enjoy more personalized medical care. HMOs are funded through premium payments much in the same manner as group health insurance plans; members pay little or no additional fees whenever they consult a physician or are admitted to an HMO member hospital. HMOs are operated as a private business, and there is an incentive for them to reduce costs in order to earn a profit or to at least break even. Supporters of HMOs claim that they offer a more economic and efficient means of health care delivery because of their emphasis on diagnostic services, preventive medical care, and outpatient treatment of illnesses. The traditional modes of health care, on the other hand, focus on the treatment of acute illnesses and inpatient hospital care rather than the prevention of health problems.[29]

The Health Maintenance Organization Act of 1973 was passed to encourage the formation and use of HMOs and to provide grant and loan monies to HMOs that meet federal standards. A federally qualified HMO must provide a wide array of health care services such as physician services, inpatient and outpatient hospital services, emergency medical care, outpatient and evaluative mental health services, treatment and referral services for drug and alcohol addiction, preventive care and immunizations, pediatric care, periodic health evaluations for adults, voluntary family planning services, and children's eye and ear examinations, among others.

Employers with 25 or more employees must offer the option of participating in a qualified HMO. This requirement assumes that the employer offers alternative forms of health insurance and has received a written request from a qualified HMO that operates in the local area.[30] Once the employer has accepted the HMO's request, it must allow the HMO periodic access to its employees, provide employees with the option of joining the HMO, and arrange for payroll deductions to the plan, along with several other requirements.

Disability Income Insurance

Disability income insurance provides protection against a loss of income during periods when an employee is unable to work because of illness or injury. Some

---

[29]The Bureau of National Affairs, Inc., *Compensation: Personnel Policy and Practice Series* (Washington, D.C.: The Bureau of National Affairs, Inc., 1983), Section 339.

[30]See "Employer Perceptions of HMO's: Survey Shows Mixed Feelings on Effectiveness as Cost Savings Vehicles," *Medical Benefits: The Medical-Economic Digest* (April 30, 1987), p. 1.

employee benefit experts argue that protecting against a loss of income is more important than life insurance protection because disability, in an economic sense, is a form of "living death." Disabled workers do not generate an income, but they incur expenses that are equal to or even greater than those of people who are employed. Furthermore, the odds of becoming disabled are higher than the odds of premature death. According to the American College of Life Underwriters,[31]

> At age 35, the chance of experiencing total disability of three months or more before age 65 is about 33%. The average length of disability will exceed five years. Moreover, nearly 30% of all disability cases will be permanent.

From a risk management point of view, disability income insurance should be at or near the top of the employee's priority list of employee benefits. For employees injured on the job, workers' compensation will provide periodic monthly payments up to the maximum specified by law. Some employees will also qualify for disability benefits under Social Security. However, for workers who are not injured on the job or who are ineligible for Social Security benefits, group disability insurance fills an important need. Short-term disability income group insurance policies normally provide protection for up to 1 year and long-term policies may provide protection for 5 years, 10 years, or until the disabled employee reaches age 65. Some long-term policies provide lifetime income protection.

A primary consideration in selecting a disability income insurance group policy is the plan's *definition of disability*. The definition is of the utmost importance because it determines the conditions under which weekly or monthly benefits are paid. Several examples of disability definitions are as follows:

- The inability of the insured employee to engage in *his or her* occupation.
- The inability of the insured to engage in any *reasonable* occupation (commensurate with the employee's education and work experience) for which he or she might become qualified through training within a 2-year period.
- The inability of the insured to engage in *any* occupation.

The first definition of disability is the most liberal because the worker is only required to be physically or mentally incapable of performing his or her occupation. For example, a dentist or surgeon sustaining a broken hand would probably not be able to continue practicing, although there are many other jobs that they could fill. Under a definition similar to the first two given, a surgeon or dentist with a broken hand could collect disability income benefits. However, the third definition is quite restrictive and would not allow payment of benefits unless the worker was severely disabled and incapable of performing any job. Some disability income policies contain a provision of *presumptive disability*. Under such a pro-

---

[31]Emmett J. Vaughan, *Fundamentals of Risk and Insurance*, 3rd ed. (New York: John Wiley and Sons, 1982), p. 256.

vision, a worker who suffers the loss of a limb or eyesight is automatically eligible for income benefits even though he or she is still employable.

Another important feature of a group disability income insurance plan is the *waiting period* (also called the *elimination period*) between the time an employee becomes disabled and the date on which benefit payments actually begin. Short-term disability policies usually require a waiting period of at least 1 week, and long-term policies may require a 1-year waiting period. The waiting period serves as a form of deductible and reduces the cost of the disability income policy by eliminating small claims for very short periods of disability. Most group disability income insurance policies do not pay more than 60 percent of an employee's gross income (because of Social Security disability benefits and to discourage malingering).[32] Under the Tax Reform Act of 1986, disability income benefits are subject to withholding for federal income tax purposes.

Many group disability income insurance plans require that an employee undergo rehabilitative treatments to reduce disabilities and regain employability. Like most forms of health insurance, disability income insurance is subject to certain exclusions under which benefits will not be paid. Benefits may be reduced because of payments made by workers' compensation or Social Security. Preexisting conditions, mental and nervous disorders, and time lost from work for drug and alcohol rehabilitation are frequently excluded. Benefits are also denied for disabilities arising from acts of war, self-inflicted injuries, and injuries suffered while committing a crime.

Health Care Cost Containment Measures

Health care is one of the most expensive employee benefits, and personnel/human resource managers have devoted much attention to keeping employee health care expenditures in check.[33] The cost of health care and health insurance has increased by at least 10 percent in most recent years and has exceeded the rate of inflation by a wide margin. If health care costs continue to increase at the current rate, the annual cost of providing medical benefits would exceed $22,000 per worker by the year 2000, according to John Erb, author of a study for A. Foster Higgins & Company, Inc., a New York employee benefits consulting firm. Medical price inflation, large catastrophic claims by some workers, and an increased use of mental health benefits were cited by surveyed employers as the three major factors contributing to the continued rise in health insurance costs.[34] Most group

---

[32]Carol Cain, "Employer Meddling Can Hasten Mending," *Business Insurance* (January 13, 1986), p. 19.

[33]"Group Health Insurance Survey" (Touche Ross, December 1986). Summarized in *Medical Benefits: The Medical-Economic Digest*, and Regina E. Herzlinger and Jeffrey Schwartz, "How Companies Tackle Health Care Costs," *Harvard Business Review* (July-August 1985), p. 58.

[34]Compiled from Associated Press and *New York Times* reports (January 29, 1991). Also see Robert Kuttner, "Health Care: Why Corporate America Is Paralyzed," *Business Week* (April 8, 1991), p. 14.

health insurance policies are only vaguely understood by employees, who are often content to know little about health care costs as long as "the insurance company takes care of it." Part of this increase is the result of inflationary forces that have affected the price of almost every consumer good. Some of the rising health care costs can be attributed to the improved quality of health care created by advances in medical diagnoses and treatment, technological innovations, and improved pharmaceuticals. Part of the problem with rising health care costs has been created by the lack of market forces affecting prices charged for physicians services, hospital stays, and ancillary medical care. Consumers do not necessarily seek out the least expensive sources of health care and may, in fact, avoid health care providers who offer their services at low rates for fear that they are inferior to their more expensive counterparts. The market mystique of health care prices is compounded by the fact that doctors and other health care providers do not usually advertise their services or prices. Furthermore, persons in need of health care do not shop around for the best buy, as they would for most other goods and services.[35]

Group health insurance policies have traditionally used deductibles, co-payments, and exclusions to contain health care costs and insurance premiums.[36] As employers have become increasingly cost conscious, additional measures have been taken. Employers have begun to analyze closely health care expenditures. Monthly, quarterly, and annual health services data are collected on the length of hospital stays by employees, physician fees, outpatient costs, expenditures on certain ailments, and other items. A number of firms, in cooperation with health insurance companies, have formed coalitions to examine health care costs and establish alternative health care provider systems to contain costs.[37] Some companies audit health insurance claims for accuracy and may save as much as 10 percent in health care costs. Carson Pirie Scott and Company in Chicago started a program urging its employees to examine their medical bills carefully for errors; the employee receives 20 percent of any savings from a billing error. Some states have begun to prosecute individuals who file fraudulent health insurance claims. Other employers and health insurance companies are focusing their cost containment efforts on health care providers.[38] Employers have begun monitoring the hospital stays of their employees to eliminate unnecessary hospital stays and medical services. Health insurance companies are often willing to pay for second medical opinions to determine whether surgical or other expensive medical treatments are necessary. Preadmission certification programs can help reduce hospi-

---

[35]Bruce A. Lepore, "Consumerism and Health Care Costs: It Pays to Shop Around," *National Safety and Health News* (June 1985), p. 63, and James M. Burcke, "Cost No Object: Big Health Care Users Don't Shop Around: Study," *Business Insurance* (November 3, 1986), p. 3.

[36]"Deductibles, Coinsurance Up in Health Care," *Employee Benefit Plan Review* (December 1986), p. 82.

[37]Rick Lee, "Business-Health Coalitions," *Compensation and Benefits Review* (January-February 1986), pp. 18–25, and "Employer Health Care Coalitions Work with Insurers and Providers to Manage Costs, Quality," *Employee Benefit Plan Review* (December 1986), p. 114.

[38]"Guidelines on Diagnostic Testing Will Lead to Cost Savings, Better Patient Care," Blue Cross and Blue Shield Association (March 30, 1987).

talizations by ensuring that less costly alternatives are used whenever possible. For example, some minor surgery can be performed in a physician's office rather than in a hospital. *Preferred provider organizations (PPOs)* work through hospitals and doctors to cut medical fees.[39] *Professional standards review organizations (PSROs)* are used to help eliminate inadequate or inappropriate treatments by physicians and other health care professionals. Catastrophic medical bills associated with cancer, acquired immune deficiency syndrome (AIDS), severe strokes, multiple sclerosis, and other serious diseases and injuries can often be reduced through a concept known as *medical case management,* in which a health care coordinator consults with the patient, the patient's family, and health care providers and then plans a treatment strategy.[40] A treatment strategy might include paying family members to take care of some of the patient's needs (e.g., home care, bathing, feeding, transportation, etc.) rather than hiring a more expensive health care professional to perform these tasks. Health care coordinators may arrange for specialized medical care, home nursing, private transportation (as opposed to the more expensive ambulances), use of generic drugs,[41] and other cost-cutting measures that do not reduce the quality of patient care.[42]

Health care costs may also be contained through employee involvement and education. Some firms have attempted to educate employees regarding group health insurance provisions and cost concerns. Other companies have stressed the use of wellness and fitness programs as a means of preventing heart disease and other health problems.[43] A 4-year study of 15,000 Control Data Corporation employees showed that workers with the worst lifestyle habits had the biggest medical bills. Employers may attempt to control health care costs by either penalizing workers who smoke or are overweight, requiring them to pay larger premiums for health insurance, or reducing their benefits. Employees with health-conscious lifestyles, on the other hand, might have their premiums reduced or their benefits expanded. According to one state insurance commissioner, "It just isn't fair for the person who leads a clean lifestyle to subsidize the debauchery of those who don't."[44]

[39]*The Wall Street Journal,* Labor Letter (February 17, 1987), p. 1; and Eileen McCabe, "Preferred Provider Organizations: PPO's May Offer a New Way to Manage Health Care Costs," *Personnel Administrator* (December 1984), p. 53.

[40]"Managed Care: Effective, Efficient, and Affordable," *Employee Benefit Plan Review* (April 1987), p. 106; and Lynne Tonsfeldt, "Cost Management Through Case Management," *Personnel Journal* (March 1986), p. 74.

[41]Stephen Budiansky, "The Cost of New Drugs Raises the Roof," *U.S. News and World Report* (April 6, 1987); and Alfred J. Haggerty, "Cost Containment Tales: The $15 Dollar Aspirin," *National Underwriter—Life and Health Insurance Edition* (April 13, 1985), p. 12.

[42]See Michael M. Biehl and Linda M. Laarman, "Legal Problems of Health Care Cost Containment," *Employment Relations Today* (Spring 1988), p. 8.

[43]For an excellent discussion on health care cost containment, see The Bureau of National Affairs, Inc., *Compensation: Personnel Policy and Practice Series* (Washington, D.C.: The Bureau of National Affairs, Inc., 1986), Section 339.

[44]Frank E. James, "Study Lays Groundwork for Tying Health Costs to Workers' Behavior," *The Wall Street Journal* (April 14, 1987), p. 1A.

Retirement Programs

Employer-provided retirement (pension) programs represent the primary source of retirement income for many employees, with Social Security and individual retirement plans providing supplementary income. There is considerable variation among retirement programs in terms of funding mechanisms, vesting provisions, and benefit schedules. Furthermore, the Employee Retirement Income Security Act of 1974 (ERISA), as well as Title VII of the 1964 Civil Rights Act and the ADEA, have affected the structure of pension plans. This discussion outlines the basic characteristics of retirement programs and the regulatory structure affecting these programs.[45] Table 12-2 provides a summary of the various plans currently used by workers to fund their retirement programs.

The Concept of a Pension

In its most elementary form, a pension is an *accumulation* of funds during an employee's working years followed by a *liquidation* of these funds once the employee retires (the funds may also be partially liquidated if an employee becomes permanently disabled, resigns or is terminated, or dies prematurely). Figure 12-1 provides an illustration of this concept.

The employer and/or the worker contribute periodic payments (usually every pay period) to a pension program or individual employee pension account. The person or organization responsible for the safekeeping and investment of these funds is known as a *fiduciary*. Over a period of time, the invested funds accumulate interest income. Upon retirement, the amount paid to the employee in a monthly or biweekly retirement check is based on three components: (1) the principal (sum of the employer's and employee's contributions over the years), (2) interest income earned on the principal, and (3) a survivorship element. Although the reader is probably familiar with the principal and interest components, the survivorship component requires further elaboration. The survivorship component is a recognition of the fact that some retirees will live for a number of years after retirement—perhaps well into their nineties—whereas others will survive for only a few years. A retiree who lives to age 97, for example, will probably use up the entire principal and interest income allocated to his or her retirement. On the other hand, a retired person who dies 2 years after retirement will not use up his or her entire principal plus interest. The survivorship component allows pension plan administrators and actuaries to establish benefit levels such that those dying soon after retirement will, in part, subsidize those who live longer.

A retiree's income also depends on the age at which he or she retires; the longer a person waits to retire, the larger the pension benefit. Some employees also elect a *guaranteed benefit option* that provides payments to the survivors of a retiree.

[45]Harry E. Allen, "Recent Developments in Private Pensions," *Management Review* (January 1987), pp. 54–56; Allen Stiteler, "Finally Pension Plans Defined," *Personnel Journal* (February 1987), pp. 44–53; and Judy Olian, Stephen J. Carroll, Jr., and Craig Eric Schneier, *Pension Plans: The Human Resource Management Perspective* (Ithaca, New York: ILR Press, Cornell University, 1986).

TABLE 12-2   A Summary of Employee Retirement Plans

Plan	Funding	Benefits	Vesting	Limitations
Social Security	Employer and employee payroll taxes	Full benefits at age 65 and reduced benefits at age 62. Benefits are low	None	Employee must meet current eligibility requirements
Employer or union-sponsored plans	Either employer or joint employer-employee contributions	Majority of plans are defined benefit and are qualified to provide tax shelters	Minimum of full vesting after 5 years or graded vesting between 3 and 7 years	Limitations on tax-deferred contributins for qualified plans. No deferrals for nonqualified plans
Deferred profit-sharing plans	Primarily employer contributions from profits	Defined benefits	Same as employer and union plans	Same as employer and union-sponsored plans
Cash-or-deferred arrangements (401K plans)	Primarily employee funded	Benefits may supplement employer or union plans or may be used as the sole retirement plan	Immediate and full vesting	Same as employer and union plans
Individual retirement accounts (IRAs)	Primarily employee funded	Used primarily to supplement othe retirement programs	Immediate and full vesting	Contributions limited to persons not covered by an employer or union-sponsored retirement plan or persons whose adjusted gross income is below levels established by law
Tax-sheltered annuities	Primarily employee initiated	Used primarily to supplement other retirement programs	Immediate and full vesting	Limited primarily to educators and other government employees

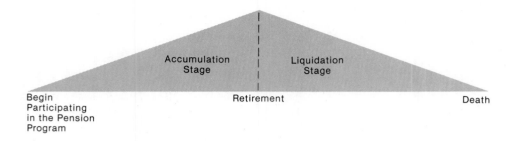

The Pension Fund Builds Up
Through:

1. Employer's Contributions
2. Employee's Contributions
3. Interest Income

Retirement Benefits Are Paid
With:

1. Principal
2. Interest
3. Survivorship Element

FIGURE 12-1   The Pension Concept

For example, a retiree may elect a 10-year certain benefit that guarantees a retirement income for as long as the retiree lives *or* for 10 years, whichever is longer. If an employee dies 6 years after retirement, then benefits are payable to a designated beneficiary for an additional 4 years. One popular form of guaranteed benefit option is a *joint and survivor annuity,* which provides a retirement income for the retiree and his or her spouse. Should the retiree die, the surviving spouse will continue to receive a lifetime income that is the same or slightly less than the amount received before the retiree's death. When a retiree elects a guaranteed benefit option, the biweekly or monthly retirement income is usually less than what would have been received under a straight life annuity with no guaranteed minimum.

The Employee Retirement Income Security Act of 1974

The Employee Retirement Income Security Act of 1974 (ERISA) covers nearly all pension benefit plans sponsored by employers and unions (except for government plans, Railroad Retirement, church plans, and a few others). ERISA establishes standards that protect the retirement benefits of employees from misuse or mismanagement by persons charged with the safekeeping of pension funds so that these funds will be available upon retirement.[46] The impetus behind the passage of ERISA was several pension plan scandals, the most notable being the Central States Fund incident involving the Teamsters Union. Employees have been denied their retirement benefits because of bankruptcies, loans from the pension funds that were never repaid, embezzlement, and investment of pension funds in risky endeavors. ERISA now provides myriad rules and requirements pertaining to employee eligibility to participate in a retirement program, minimum vesting standards, reporting requirements for pension fund administrators, disclosure

[46]Alfred Klein, "Why You Can't Afford to Ignore ERISA," *Personnel Journal* (June 1986), p. 72.

rules, contribution and benefit limits, distribution of plan proceeds, and benefit guarantees.[47]

Companies without private pension plans are *not* required to establish a pension in order to comply with ERISA. In fact, some critics initially argued that the presence of ERISA might discourage the growth of pension plans and possibly lead to the termination of existing plans. This, however, does not seem to have been the case.[48] ERISA was designed to improve the quality of existing retirement programs by providing greater income security to the worker.[49] Despite the presence of ERISA, companies have the right to pay off existing pension liabilities and cancel retirement programs. The rash of corporate mergers and hostile takeovers during the 1980s and early 1990s has created a problem for employees whose company retirement funds contained excess amounts of money that accumulated because of favorable investment results. The excess amounts are the result of a healthy stock market during the 1980s. Some corporate raiders have canceled the retirement program, paid off existing liabilities to employees and retirees, and retained the excess earnings for their own use. Although employees and retirees believe that a corporation has a moral obligation to return the excess earnings to them, a loophole in the federal law allows companies to retain the excess earnings and use them as they see fit.

Retirement Plan Terminology and Provisions

Retirement or pension plans differ from one organization to another. However, they all contain common provisions that are defined and discussed here. These provisions are discussed in light of ERISA and changes mandated by the Tax Reform Act of 1986.

1. *Participation or eligibility standards.* An employer may exclude employees from participating in or making contributions to the company's pension plan until they have accumulated 2 years of service. Employers are required to have a certain percentage of employees participating in the pension plan (e.g., 70 percent of all highly compensated employees must participate).
2. *Contributory and noncontributory plans.* A contributory plan is one in which both the employer and the employee make payments into the pension plan. Under a noncontributory plan, only the employer makes contributions.
3. *Defined contribution and defined benefit plans.* A defined contribution plan fixes the amount of the employer's contribution by a formula, but the level of

---

[47]Pension fund assets are probably nearing the $3.0 trillion level, based on a 1990 estimate of $2.6 trillion. See Scott Shepard, "Private Pension Funds: 'Games' Employers Play," *The Atlanta Journal-Constitution* (March 4, 1990), p. 1.

[48]Johannes Ledoltes and Mark L. Power, "A Study of ERISA's Impact on Private Retirement Plan Growth," *The Journal of Risk and Insurance*, Vol. LI, No. 2, pp. 225–243. Also see Jozetta H. Srb, "Pension Policy for the Eighties," *Industrial and Labor Relations Report* (Ithaca, New York: New York State School of Industrial and Labor Relations, Cornell University, Fall 1981), pp. 7–9.

[49]See Benson Rosen and Thomas H. Jerdee, "Retirement Policies for the 21st Century," *Human Resource Management* (Fall 1986), p. 405.

the benefits paid to the worker upon retirement is not guaranteed. Under a defined benefit plan, the income that an employee will receive is either (a) fixed at a specific dollar amount or (b) determined by a fixed formula (e.g., 50 percent of an employee's average annual income 3 years immediately prior to retirement). Thus, a defined contribution plan holds contributions constant and allows benefits to vary, while a defined benefit plan guarantees benefits but requires that contributions vary. The reason that both contributions and benefits cannot be simultaneously held constant is that contributions to the pension fund accumulate over long periods of time (over 40 years in some cases) and investment results that depend on the state of the economy, interest rates, and so forth cannot be accurately predicted for long time spans.

4. *Funding.* Somewhat related to the previous definitions of defined contribution and defined benefit plans is the concept of funding. ERISA requires that funding be based on a pay-as-you-work basis, with contributions made during the employee's working years. Employers cannot fund pension benefits to retirees from current operating revenues, nor can they design a pension program that purchases a lump sum retirement benefit for an employee who is about to retire. Under either of these arrangements, there is no guarantee to an employee that the funds will be available upon retirement if the company goes out of business or is acquired by another firm.

5. *Vesting.* Vesting refers to the employee's ability to claim all or part of the *employer's* contribution to a pension program that was made on behalf of the employee. Vesting does not pertain to the employee's own contributions because they are always nonforfeitable (i.e., they cannot be taken away from the employee). The issue of vesting becomes important when an employee resigns or is terminated by the employer. Thus, an employee who is 50 percent vested would be entitled to 50 percent of the employer's contributions plus all of the contributions that he or she paid into the plan. If a person resigns or is terminated before becoming fully vested, he or she loses the unvested portion of the employer's contribution (known as a *forfeiture*). Persons who have been employed for several years by a firm may be entitled to a substantial sum of money if they leave the organization, depending on the vesting provisions of a particular pension plan. However, the employer has the option of either paying the worker a lump sum or retaining the vested amount and paying it to the employee upon retirement. Some companies use *portable pensions,* which allow workers to move funds from one plan to another (e.g., when changing jobs) without incurring a tax liability.[50]

The original minimum vesting standards under ERISA were modified by the Tax Reform Act of 1986. Beginning in 1989, employees must be 100 percent vested after 5 years of service. An employee with 4 years of service would have

[50]Employees who cash in retirement funds before age 59½ incur a 10 percent penalty; in addition, they must pay federal and state income taxes on the amount withdrawn. Thus, employees who use retirement funds prematurely may lose over 40 percent of the proceeds in penalties and taxes if they are in a high tax bracket. See Ellen E. Shultz, "Changing Jobs Means Having to Find a New Home for Cash in Retirement Plan," *The Wall Street Journal* (March 9, 1991), p. A1.

no vested pension rights but would go from zero to full (100%) vesting after 5 years of service. Vesting may also be phased in between an employee's third and seventh year of service, with 20 percent vesting after 3 years and 20 percent increases per year such that 100 percent vesting is achieved after 7 years. The latter option provides earlier vesting rights but delays full vesting until the seventh year of service. Plans that condition participation on more than 1 year of service must provide full and immediate vesting rights. Pension administrators are, of course, free to use vesting standards that allow more rapid vesting than is required under federal law.

6. *Qualified and nonqualified pension plans.* A qualified pension plan must meet certain Internal Revenue Service (IRS) requirements that entitle both the employee and the employer to substantial tax breaks. Employers receive a tax deduction for contributions made to a pension plan, and investment income from pension funds is not subject to taxation. Employees do not incur a tax liability on the employer's contributions until pension benefits are paid (usually at retirement). Employee contributions to a qualified pension can be made in before-tax dollars, which provides greater disposable income (take-home pay). Nonqualified plans do not offer the aforementioned tax advantages.

7. *Benefit and contribution limits.* There are dollar limits on the amount that can be contributed annually to a pension plan as well as the amount that can be paid to a worker at retirement. Under a defined benefit plan, for example, the limit on the amount that can be paid at retirement (and still receive tax deferrals) is 100 percent of the final average compensation up to a maximum of $108,963 (indexed to the Consumer Price Index as of 1988). Contributions are limited to 25 percent of compensation up to $30,000 per year; amounts contributed in excess of $30,000 must be made in after-tax dollars. However, highly compensated employees may elect to contribute amounts above the limits imposed by the Tax Reform Act.[51]

8. *Integrated pension plans.* Pension plans that coordinate benefits with Social Security retirement benefits on a formula basis are known as *integrated plans.* There are a number of methods by which retirement benefits may be coordinated with Social Security. For example, employees making more than the Social Security base ($55,500 in 1992) may have their contributions increased to offset the loss of Social Security retirement benefits. The complex integration rules that went into effect in 1988 focus on nondiscriminatory integration between highly paid and other employees.

9. *Fiduciary standards and the protection of pension assets.* Fiduciaries who safeguard, control, and invest pension funds are required to meet "prudent person" standards, as well as numerous record and reporting requirements.

---

[51]According to Hewitt Associates, 95 percent of the top 100 U.S. industrial companies have established supplemental executive retirement plans to make up for losses that executives have faced under the Tax Reform Act. *The Wall Street Journal,* Labor Letter (December 8, 1987), p. 1. Also see Kathleen Wechter, "Compensating the Executive: Supplemental Executive Retirement Plans," *Employment Relations Today* (Winter 1987–88), pp. 355–360.

In the event that pension monies are lost through fraud, embezzlement, or mismanagement, the Pension Benefit Guaranty Corporation (created by ERISA) protects employees through a mandatory plan termination insurance program.[52]

The legal and economic factors affecting retirement plans are complex and are often beyond the expertise of personnel and compensation managers. Assistance from tax experts and pension specialists may be needed to ensure that eligibility requirements, contributions, vesting standards benefits, and other facets of a retirement plan meet the standards of ERISA and the latest changes in the tax laws. The discussion of pension terminology and features in this chapter is brief and does not cover all of the intricacies that affect retirement programs.

Other Forms of Retirement Plans

In addition to the employer-provided pensions just discussed, employees may have the option of participating in other programs that provide tax shelters and supplemental retirement benefits. For workers not covered by employer-provided pension plans, these programs offer an important means for providing income security in later years.

Deferred profit-sharing plans provide a defined benefit pension program that is based on a firm's profitability. These plans may supplement existing pension programs or they can be used in place of a regular employer-provided pension plan. The tax advantages of a qualified deferred profit-sharing plan are essentially the same as those of a qualified pension plan. A major goal of deferred profit-sharing plans is to provide employees with a retirement program while creating an incentive to help keep the firm profitable. Most firms distribute a share of the profits to each employee based on an individual's compensation and some use formulas that consider both compensation and seniority. As of 1987, employers are allowed to make discretionary payments to deferred profit-sharing plans that go above and beyond payments geared to profits. Employees are also allowed to make contributions to the plan much in the same manner as they would under a regular pension plan, but contributions cannot exceed the maximums established by ERISA.

Cash-or-deferred arrangements, individual retirement accounts, and *tax sheltered annuities* differ from regular pension plans and deferred profit-sharing plans in one important respect: they allow an employee to defer and tax-shelter income that would otherwise be included directly in the employee's paycheck. An employee who is a participant in a pension or deferred profit-sharing plan has little control over his or her own contributions or those made on his or her behalf. The decision to participate in one of these plans, however, is done primarily at the

---

[52]In 1988 firms had to pay the Pension Benefit Guaranty Corporation an annual premium of $16 per employee. Firms with underfunded pension plans had to pay as much as $50. *The Wall Street Journal,* Labor Letter (January 5, 1988), p. 1.

employee's discretion, and the amount contributed to these plans is also controlled by the employee.

Cash-or-deferred arrangements (CODAs), also known as *section 401(k) plans* after the section of the IRS code that created them, allow eligible employees to defer receiving compensation and postpone income tax liabilities until retirement.[53] For persons such as independent contractors or construction workers who frequently change jobs or work on an intermittent basis, 401(k) plans offer a means of building a retirement program. If the worker joins a company with an employer-provided pension program, funds from the 401(k) plan can be transferred (known as a *rollover*) into the employer's pension plan without incurring a tax liability. Some employees also use 401(k) plans to supplement the pension plan provided by their employer. These plans are regulated by ERISA.

Individual retirement accounts (IRAs) are designed for workers to set aside funds to provide financial security for themselves and their spouses upon reaching the age of 59 ½ or upon retirement at a later age. Tax-deductible IRAs may be purchased only by workers who are not covered by other retirement programs, as well as by those whose adjusted gross income is below established levels. Employers may also purchase IRAs for their employees as a means of funding a retirement program. Self-employed persons may fund their retirement through the purchase of IRAs or Keogh (H.R. 10) Plans.

Employees who work for public educational institutions or certain tax-exempt organizations are eligible to participate in a retirement arrangement known as a *tax-sheltered annuity (TSA)*. Contributions to TSAs are not taxable until the benefits are withdrawn, usually at retirement. An annual limit of $9,500 is placed on contributions to a TSA, and this amount is reduced on a dollar-for-dollar basis for contributions made to 401(k) or employer-provided IRAs.

Income Maintenance Benefits

Organizations whose production or service levels fluctuate may be forced to lay off and recall employees later as business demands dictate. Income maintenance benefits that supplement state unemployment compensation payments are useful in attracting and retaining workers for employment in cyclical business operations, and they take one of the following forms: guaranteed minimum amounts of work or pay, supplemental unemployment benefits, and severance pay (for employees who are subject to permanent layoff).[54]

Guaranteed work and pay programs ensure that employees can count on receiving a minimum number of work hours or base pay per month or year,

[53]Leonard Wiener, "For Both Young and Old, a New Retirement Plan," *U.S. News and World Report*, Vol. 99 (August 5, 1985), p. 3; Dallas L. Salisbury, "The 401(k) Krunch," *Across the Board* (April 1986), p. 46; and Scott R. Schmedel, "A Bit of Blue Shines Through the Ceiling on '401(k)' Pay Deferrals," *The Wall Street Journal* (December 10, 1985), p. 1.

[54]The Bureau of National Affairs, Inc., *Compensation: Personnel Policy and Practice Series* (Washington, D.C.: The Bureau of National Affairs, Inc., 1982), Section 331.

regardless of their layoff status. Many of the guaranteed work and pay programs only apply to employees who have worked with an organization for a specified number of years. Other programs void the minimum guarantee if an employee refuses assigned work, as well as for work stoppages caused by economic strikes or matters beyond the employer's immediate control such as floods, power outages, or inclement weather.

Supplemental unemployment benefit (SUB) plans provide additional income for laid-off employees above and beyond the amount paid by state unemployment compensation. In some cases, the state unemployment compensation plus the SUB will restore income to 95 percent of the level received when the employee was working, minus a small deduction for incidental work-related expenses. SUB plans fall into two categories: the pooled-fund system and the individual account plan. Employers having SUB plans generally contribute a percentage of the payroll to the plan. The pooled-fund system provides benefits only in the event that no work is available. Individual account plans, on the other hand, allow an employee greater flexibility. For example, the worker may withdraw his or her full amount at termination. In some cases, individual SUB plans also allow employees to withdraw money from the account for reasons other than layoff or termination.

Severance pay (or *separation pay*) may be paid to employees who are permanently terminated. Several reasons may prompt an employer to provide severance pay. First, severance pay allows time for an employee to search for a new job without becoming economically desperate. Second, severance pay may be used to decrease an employee's desire to sue the employer for wrongful discharge or violation of an EEO law. Third, severance pay may be a means of enhancing the employer's social responsibility and improving the corporate image. For managerial employees, the amount of severance pay may be individually negotiated based on a portion of annual income (3, 6, or 12 months of salary, and so on). Other employees commonly receive severance pay based on a length of service and seniority formula. Under this arrangement, the greater the length of service and earnings, the greater the severance pay. Severance pay arrangements often contain payment restrictions. Benefits may not be payable to employees who quit voluntarily, are eligible for retirement benefits, or refuse other work offered by the employer.

Compensation for Time Not Worked

Paid vacations and holidays are a common employee benefit, and the trend over the years has been to increase compensation for time not worked because of union pressures and employer concerns for attracting and retaining employees.[55] Entitlement to paid vacations is often determined by an employee's seniority. As a worker accumulates seniority, the amount of paid vacation time increases. It is common for employees with only 1 year of service to receive 2 weeks of paid

---

[55]The Bureau of National Affairs, Inc., *Compensation: Personnel Policy and Practice Series* (Washington, D.C.: The Bureau of National Affairs, Inc., 1987), Section 335.

vacation, whereas employees with 10 or more years of service are commonly provided with at least 4 weeks. Some industries, such as the steel industry, have provided extended vacation periods of up to 13 weeks at 5-year intervals.

Paid vacations can present a number of administrative problems for employers, as well as uncertainties for workers. Personnel policies on paid vacations should address the following issues. First, computing the length of the employee's service for vacation entitlements can pose problems, especially if the employee has breaks of service for disabilities, layoffs, or leaves of absence. Second, some employees may prefer to work during all or part of their vacation time for personal or financial reasons. Management must decide whether to pay employees double time (paid vacation plus pay for working) or place a ceiling on maximum allowable earnings during vacation periods. Management may also consider not allowing employees to work during vacation time, except under unusual circumstances. Third, management must establish a system for determining *when* an employee will take the paid vacation. Vacation policies should also stipulate whether employees must take their vacation time all at once or whether they will be allowed to take several shorter vacations. If the latter practice is used, then management must decide on the smallest increment of vacation time that it will permit. Management must determine whether employees will be allowed to take vacations during peak business months or only during periods when business is slow. A paid vacation policy must also have a method for resolving conflicts that arise when two or more employees want to take their vacations on the same date (when it is necessary that at least one worker remain on the job).

Most employees also receive about 10 paid holidays per year. Paid holidays pose fewer administrative problems than vacations because their dates coincide with or fall near the observed holiday date. Some companies require that an employee work both the day before and the day after the holiday in order to receive holiday pay. If a holiday falls on a scheduled day off, such as during the weekend or when an employee is on vacation, the employer may elect to provide an alternative holiday such as Easter Monday, compensate employees for the holiday, or simply not count the holiday because it does not fall on a regular working day. Many companies provide premium pay for nonmanagerial employees who work on a paid holiday.

Employees who are ill are ensured continued pay through sick leave policies. Organizations typically grant between 5 and 12 sick leave days per year; some provide all employees with the same number of paid sick leave days, whereas others base paid sick leave entitlement on seniority. About half of the firms surveyed by The Bureau of National Affairs, Inc., allowed employees to accumulate sick leave days from one year to the next, subject to a maximum limit that fluctuates between 30 and 90 days.[56] Some companies allow an employee to elect reduced paid sick leave benefits in exchange for payments over a longer period. In order to discourage short periods of absenteeism, an employee may have to wait several days before drawing sick leave benefits. Many employers pay sick leave

[56]The Bureau of National Affairs, Inc., *Compensation: Personnel Policy and Practice Series* (Washington, D.C.: The Bureau of National Affairs, Inc., 1983), Section 335.

only if an employee obtains a physician's statement certifying illness. Some plans also impose penalties for misuse of sick leave policies. Female employees who use sick leave for maternity-related disabilities must be treated in the same manner as other employees on sick leave in order to comply with the Pregnancy Discrimination Act. Other forms of compensated time off include jury duty leave, bereavement or funeral leave, military leave, and child care leave.

Child Care Benefits

As more women and single parents have entered the labor force and dual-career couples have become more common, providing care for the children of working parents has become an important issue. The growing concern and publicity about the plight of "latchkey" children who must spend time at home without adult supervision while their parents are at work have also prompted corporate action.[57] Employers have incentives for providing child-care benefits because they help to attract and retain employees and provide a tax deduction (as an ordinary and necessary business expense). Some companies establish care centers for the exclusive use of employees' children. Other firms provide employee referral services to qualified child-care centers in the community. Companies that do not provide child care on the firm's premises may purchase services from established child-care services such as Kindercare. The cost of child care may be borne entirely by the employer or the employee or may be shared on some basis. Some firms provide vouchers to parents that cover all or part of child-care expenses at a licensed day-care facility. Firms that elect to establish a child-care facility should carefully study the need for such a center, the services to be provided, the costs involved, and the liability issues that can arise.

Parents who must deal with the guilt and worry of leaving children unattended at home may suffer from low morale and reduced productivity.[58] Personnel policies that allow parents to do some of their work at home, flextime work schedules (where they may either come to work late *or* leave work early), job sharing, and child-care leave policies represent options that enable parents to care for the needs of their children. Suitable child-care arrangements can reduce the safety concerns and other burdens on working parents whose children may range from infants to adolescents. On-site or near-site day-care programs can reduce the amount of commuting required by working parents and reduce absenteeism and tardiness. Child-care arrangements also provide favorable publicity to the sponsoring company.[59]

[57]Mary F. Cook, "Child Care Programs and Options," *The Human Resources Yearbook*, 1987 edition, (Englewood Cliffs, New Jersey: Prentice Hall, Inc., 1987), pp. 2.68-2.71.

[58]Fern Schumer Chapman, "Executive Guilt: Who's Taking Care of the Children? And How Will Kids Raised By Nannies and in Day Care Centers Turn Out?" *Fortune* (February 16, 1987), p. 30; "Child Care Woes," *The Wall Street Journal* (May 14, 1987), p. 29.

[59]In addressing problems at the other end of the age spectrum, some companies are offering to help employees with aging parents. For example, IBM has introduced the Eldercare Referral Service. This service provides IBM employees with consultation and assistance in determining the proper care for elderly relatives. *Employee Benefit Plan Review* (January 1988), pp. 15–16.

Other Employee Benefit Programs

The types of employee benefit programs vary and seem to be limited only by the employer's imagination. In recent years, new and innovative benefit plans have been designed and some are gaining acceptance among corporations. *Prepaid legal plans* are designed to offer affordable legal services to individual employees. Under a prepaid legal plan, employees are able to obtain counseling on matters such as income and property taxes, civil actions, criminal matters, bankruptcy, consumer complaints, real estate matters, adoptions, the preparation of wills, and traffic offenses.[60]

Management's interest in developing a better-educated workforce has led to the use of *tuition-aid plans* for employees. Some companies provide tuition assistance for all courses taken at an approved institution, whereas others grant tuition aid only for job-related course work. Companies may grant total or partial cash advances (or reimbursements), provide educational leaves of absence, or loan employees money for educational purposes.[61]

Some employee benefits are more directly tied to the workplace. For example, travel allowances, moving expenses, uniform and tool expenses, and meal allowances permit employees to perform more efficiently and enhance morale. Suggestion systems provide financial incentives to employees for submitting cost-saving ideas to management. Retail and service firms may provide discounts to employees who purchase their products and services, a tactic that creates brand loyalty and knowledge of the company's products.

Cafeteria and Flexible Benefit Plans

Many employee benefit programs in private and public sector organizations have used a standard package of benefits for all employees. A fixed benefits package often fails to account for individual differences in an employee's age, financial status, family situation, or personal preferences. Young singles may prefer to maximize take-home pay and paid vacation benefits, whereas older, married employees may show more interest in health insurance and retirement benefits. Maternity coverage is important to young couples who plan to start a family but is of no use to an elderly bachelor who might prefer that more money be placed in a retirement plan on his behalf. A married employee with a working spouse may desire few employee benefits if the spouse's employer already provides a comprehensive array of life and health insurance coverage. Employees in higher income brackets may desire to shelter as much income as possible through 401(k) plans or tax-sheltered annuities.

[60]The Bureau of National Affairs, Inc., *Compensation: Personnel Policy and Practice Series* (Washington, D.C.: The Bureau of National Affairs, Inc., 1987), Section 339.

[61]Marvin S. Katzman, "Tuition Benefits: Are They Not Being Used Wisely Because of a Lack of Planning and Counseling?" *Employee Benefits Journal* (September 1985).

Cafeteria and flexible benefit plans allow employees to structure benefit packages to meet their personal needs. In general, the term *cafeteria* describes plans that provide employees with a choice among several benefits consisting of cash and certain nontaxable benefits, whereas the term *flexible* refers to plans that offer benefits only (no cash).[62] Under cafeteria and flexible arrangements, the employer generally provides a minimum "core" of benefits coverage (such as group life and health insurance), and workers select additional benefits from a list of available options. Workers may be able to select benefits worth a defined amount of money, with the cost of benefits above this limit being assumed by the employee. Cafeteria and flexible benefit plans offer several advantages. First, they allow an employee to tailor the amount and type of employee benefits to his or her personal situation rather than accepting a package of benefits that has been prescribed by the employer. Employees may learn more about what benefits are available rather than blindly accepting what the employer has to offer; this may also enable employees to develop a greater appreciation of their benefits. Second, there is evidence that cafeteria and flexible plans can reduce employee benefit plan costs for the employer. Third, the cafeteria plan may give employers greater flexibility in designing a benefits package. New and innovative benefits can be made available without restructuring the entire employee benefit program.

Perhaps the biggest drawback to cafeteria and flexible benefit plans is the problem of *adverse selection*.[63] Adverse selection occurs when employees with specific and immediate needs for certain benefits overwhelmingly select those options. An employee with a life-threatening illness might attempt to buy as much group life insurance as possible, whereas an employee with three teenage children in need of expensive orthodontic care might elect group dental insurance coverage. If adverse selection is not controlled, it can increase the cost of certain benefit options to prohibitive levels. A number of methods can be used to deal with adverse selection, such as allowing employees to enroll in new options only on an annual or biannual basis, packaging a series of options together (such as dental, vision, and eyeglass insurance), or raising the price of options to cover the expenses associated with adverse selection.[64]

The Tax Reform Act of 1986 places certain restrictions on cafeteria benefit plans. Under a cafeteria plan that satisfies the IRS code, amounts contributed by an employer to a nontaxable benefit are nontaxable to the employee even though the employee could have received the benefit in cash. The Tax Reform Act also prohibits an employer from using a cafeteria benefit plan to discriminate between highly compensated and other employees. Statutory nontaxable benefits under a

---

[62]John A. Haslinger, "Flexible Compensation: Getting a Return on Benefit Dollars," *Personnel Administrator* (June 1985), p. 39; Bob Cohn, "A Glimpse of the 'Flex' Future," *Newsweek* (August 1, 1988), pp. 38–39.

[63]M. Susan Marquis and Charles E. Phelps, "Price Elasticity and Adverse Selection in the Demand for Supplementary Health Insurance," *Economic Inquiry* (April 1987), p. 299.

[64]The Bureau of National Affairs, Inc., *Compensation: Personnel Policy and Practice Series* (Washington, D.C.: The Bureau of National Affairs, Inc., 1987), Section 339.

cafeteria plan include group term life insurance (up to $50,000 tax free), accident and health plans, dependent care programs (e.g., child care), CODAs that are part of a profit-sharing or stock bonus plan, and paid vacation days. Benefits that may not be offered under a cafeteria plan include scholarships and fellowships, educational assistance provided by the employer, and some deferred compensation arrangements.

Communicating Employee Benefits

Employee benefit programs are complex because they deal with legal, financial, and tax-related issues. Most employees find that the actuarial assumptions, tax regulations, and behavioral implications associated with certain employee benefits such as pension programs can be complicated. The problem is compounded when one realizes that benefits are often discussed at orientation programs for new employees, a time when the employee is already under stress and is being inundated with other, more pressing information. Most companies provide employees with a booklet or brochure that outlines the benefits program. Such information is frequently ignored because it is difficult to understand and not very exciting to read. As a result, employees often do not learn the facts about their benefits until they need to make a claim. They may then learn, to either their delight or their chagrin, that employee benefits cover certain contingencies but not others.[65]

If a cafeteria benefit plan is used, it is important that employees understand the options available to them. Employees should understand their benefits and how certain choices can affect their personal financial situation.[66] Two key points to remember in communicating employee benefits are that (1) employees must understand the basic coverage and restrictions that apply to their benefit programs, and (2) employees should be personally counseled about their benefits on a periodic basis. Internal memos, newsletters, and brochures can provide up-to-date information on changes in employee benefits. However, such information must be carefully written to avoid an overly detailed and technical presentation that most employees will find difficult to comprehend. Individual benefits counseling should probably be done on an annual basis or whenever requested by the employee. Benefits counseling allows the employee to make changes in his or her benefit program based on changes in family structure (births, deaths, divorces, and so on), income level, tax laws, age, health status, and other factors.

[65]Never Enough: Communications Aids in the Acceptance of Employee Benefit Changes," *Employee Benefit Plan Review* (October 1985), p. 12.

[66]Richard J. Anthony, "A Communication Program Model for Flexible Benefits: Keeping Employees Informed Takes Time, Effort, and Planning," *Personnel Administrator* (June 1986), p. 65; and Peter R. Schleger, "Effective Benefits Communication: Delivery Counts Too!," *Employee Benefits Journal* (March 1988), pp. 24–26.

■ Summary and Conclusions

The employee benefit programs discussed in this chapter represent those typically found in private and public organizations. However, the amount and extent of benefit coverage vary considerably from one company to another. Employees face certain risks such as premature death, outliving one's ability to earn a living, loss of income caused by disabilities and unemployment, and extraordinary medical expenses. Public programs such as Social Security, workers' compensation, and unemployment compensation afford some protection from these risks, but employer-provided programs such as life, medical, and disability insurance and retirement plans enhance the benefits established by public programs and improve economic security for many workers. Other benefits such as paid vacations, holidays, and perquisites enhance the quality of work life and the employer's public image.

Although there is evidence that the growth of employee benefits has reached a plateau, their presence is likely to have an impact on the attraction, retention, motivation, and satisfaction of employees for years to come. Employers must maintain concern over how their limited benefit dollars will do their employees the most good. Employees, on the other hand, must be cognizant of their rights and benefits under the program, as well as of the need to view employee benefits as a risk management tool.

■ Questions

1. Why do employers provide employee benefits, and why has the percentage of benefits relative to total compensation increased over the past 25 years?

2. What fundamental rule of risk management should be followed when selecting employee benefits?

3. Describe the four categories of risk faced by workers.

4. What are the basic objectives of workers' compensation programs?

5. Under what conditions might an employee who is terminated not receive unemployment compensation benefits?

6. What basic benefits are available under the Social Security (OASDHI) program?

7. Why is group life insurance less expensive than purchasing the same coverage individually through a local insurance agent?

8. What are the basic characteristics of major medical insurance coverage?

9. How do HMOs differ from other types of health insurance?

10. Why is the definition of *disability* so important under a group disability income policy?

11. Describe some of the ways in which health care costs might be reduced.

12. How does a pension work? What are the major components of a pension plan?

13. What are the major objectives of ERISA?

14. Why is vesting so important? What are the minimum vesting provisions under the Tax Reform Act, and how are they more liberal than the vesting standards originally contained in ERISA?

15. Discuss the retirement options that employees may elect.

16. Describe the major income maintenance benefits.

☐ APPLICATIONS AND CASE EXERCISES

1. "With 1,500 retirees and only 3,500 active workers in the U.S. Fluor Corp. says it has been forced to quit promising to pay health insurance premiums in full for retired employees. 'I shudder at the coldheartedness this conveys,' a spokesman says, but 'the cost to the company was rising dramatically.' "[67] What can be done to resolve this problem? Do you believe that employers should take the responsibility to offer health care benefits to retirees? According to Buck Consultants, Inc., the typical 65-year-old man can now expect to live until age 81.[68] Discuss the implications that this has for the retiree health care problem.

2. Despite changes in the tax laws, about two thirds of eligible employees are putting a portion of their wages aside in 401(k) plans (CODAs). Only 4 percent are contributing up to the maximum allowed by law, but many others are contributing even though there is an additional 10 percent levy on premature withdrawals.[69] Why do you suppose this is occurring?

3. Visit your nearest Social Security office and determine the benefits to which you are currently entitled. If you have not been employed long enough to have contributed to Social Security, calculate the benefits for a family member or friend.

4. More than half of the workers without health insurance are in the retail trade and service industries. Seventy percent of the uninsured workers who work full time earn less than $10,000 annually.[70] Should the federal government provide health insurance for these employees? What problems does this situation pose for the health care system?

5. "Convinced that workers don't appreciate what they are getting and eager to control costs, 20 percent of major corporations are letting workers assemble their own benefit packages, according to Wyatt Co. At Bankers Trust Co., a worker earning $27,000 a year might get a $1,500 allowance to choose among five medical and three dental plans."[71] How do such plans save money? Will cafeteria and flexible benefit plans satisfy employees?

6. Why should managers who are under age 35 be concerned about retirement programs? Discuss.

[67] *The Wall Street Journal*, Labor Letter (February 10, 1987), p. 1.

[68] *The Wall Street Journal*, Labor Letter (December 10, 1985), p. 1.

[69] *The Wall Street Journal*, Labor Letter (May 5, 1987), p. 1.

[70] *The Wall Street Journal*, Labor Letter (March 31, 1987), p. 1.

[71] *The Wall Street Journal*, Labor Letter (May 13, 1986), p. 1.

PART THREE INTEGRATIVES CASES

■ The Airlines Turn to Training to Address the Pilot Shortage

Representatives from the Federal Aviation Administration (FAA), major flight academies, and universities met to discuss the role of training in the airline industry. Although the major airlines were not yet experiencing a pilot shortage (a Piedmont representative said that his company had 8,000 applications from qualified pilots), the smaller regional airlines were complaining of severe shortages of competent flight crew members. The primary cause of the shortages was simple: the military, once a favorite source of trained personnel, is no longer turning out as many pilots for the civilian ranks.

Representatives of regional airlines told horror stories of pilot turnover that exceeded 100 percent in a year. Some reported that flights were canceled because qualified flight crews were unavailable. Most regional pilots have their career sights set on a job with the major airlines. When they receive notice of an opening, they often provide only a few days notice before resigning; yet it takes from 60 to 90 days for the regional carrier to train a replacement. According to the Future Aviation Professionals of America (FAPA), 42,000-52,000 new airline pilots will be needed over the next decade.

A Northwest Aerospace Training-University of North Dakota (UND) consortium is establishing an ab initio (from the beginning) training program. People with no flying experience will be trained at the University of North Dakota and will emerge from the pro-gram qualified to work as flight engineers and co-pilots (first officers). The Northwest-UND program is modeled on the program used for years by European airlines. Pilot trainees are taught from the start to function as a crew member team, an approach that differs from the training typically encountered in the United States, where civilian pilots learn to fly solo in small single-engine aircraft. Most applicants who apply for airline jobs typically build flying time through work as flight instructors or solo light-airplane flying for small charter operations. Members of the consortium believe that such experience does little to prepare a pilot for airline work. The rationale of the Northwest-UND program is to screen out persons who would be unacceptable for airline flight duty and train qualified student pilots using full-motion Boeing 727 and Douglas DC-9 simulators (the type of aircraft common to major airlines).

Questions

1. What problems might UND encounter as it attempts to assess the training needs of airlines over the next decade?
2. Because of the sophisticated training methods used, the Northwest-UND consortium estimates training costs of approximately $40,000 per student. Who should subsidize this training? Discuss.
3. Based on your knowledge of employee selection procedures, what predictors could be used to select trainees for the program?
4. What evaluative criteria would you suggest using to determine the quality and effectiveness of the pilot training program?

Based on J. Mac McClellan, "Ab Initio Training: Airlines Address the Pilot Shortage," *Flying* (February 1988), p. 93.

■ Performance Appraisal and Salary Administration at Merck & Company, Inc.

When the performance of Merck & Company, Inc., of Rahway, New Jersey, began to fall behind other leading drug companies, management decided to examine the potential causes. Obvious problems included unfavor-able foreign exchange rates, the increased cost of doing business, and several disappointing new products. However, management assembled a task force to look into the less obvious problems that might have been plaguing the company.

Among the 50 recommendations made by the task force were proposals for improving the company's performance appraisal and salary administration programs. The task force suggested revising the performance

Exempt Performance Rating Definitions

Performance Ratings			Performance Definitions		
Rating	Distri-bution Target	Specific Job Measures and Ongoing Duties	Planned Objectives	Management of People	
EX Exceptional within Merck	5%	Far above Merck peers Capitalized on unexpected events to gain superior results	Made significant breakthroughs or exceptional achievements	Outstanding leader Exceptional development/ recruitment of people Superior communications	
WD Merck standard with distinction	15%	Clearly superior to Merck peers in most respects Took advangate of unexpected events to achieve unusually good results	Objectives met and many exceeded	A clear leader among Merck peers Top quality people recruited, developed Excellent communications	
HS High Merck standard	70%	Comparable to Merck peers Made use of unexpected events to achieve very good results	Objectives met	A very good leader Hires very good people/develops people as well as peers Very good communications	
RI Merck standard with room for improvement	8%	Work is not quite as good as Merck peers Contended with unexpected events	Most objectives met Some shortfalls	Adequate leader Hires good people Satisfactory communications	
NA Not adequate for Merck	2%	Work is not up to that of Merck peers Did not fully cope with unexpected events	Missed significant objectives	Poor leader Communications could be better	
PR Progressing	Not appli-cable	Typically this employee is new to the company or in a significantly different assignment. Normally this rating would apply only during the first year in the new job.			

Reprinted with permission of Arthur F. Strohmer, executive director of staffing and development for human resources, Merck & Company, Inc., Rahway, New Jersey

appraisal system for exempt personnel (primarily professional, managerial, and supervisory employees) in order to make better distinctions between performance levels of employees and to improve consistency among the company's divisions and departments. It was also suggested that the compensation program be revised to provide more substantial increases to outstanding performers and smaller increases to less stellar performers. Additional financial incentives were also needed for top employees, according to the task force.

Under the old performance appraisal system, approximately 97 percent of Merck employees had been grouped within a very narrow band of ratings. As a result, salary increases failed to reflect performance differences between average and exceptional employees. To help alleviate this problem, a new performance appraisal system was introduced.

The new system revised and expanded definitions for three major areas of performance: specific job measures and ongoing duties, planned objectives, and the management of people. The last category was added because many managers were compensated only for their technical abilities rather than for the way in which they managed people. A distribution target for performance appraisals was used to help managers rank employees according to their performance and compare their performance with that of their peers. Thus, performance evaluation under the new system is a two-step process: First, an employee's performance is measured against objectives and ongoing duties; second, the employee's performance is compared with the performance of other employees in the same area of the company.

Merck also linked pay increases to the new performance appraisal system. For each category of performance and for each position within a salary range, a salary-planning guideline specifies the amount and frequency of pay increases. Targets within pay grades

are emphasized to guide supervisors in assessing the long-term impact of performance appraisals and their effect on an employee's compensation. Merck also uses a variety of salary surveys each year to ensure that salaries remain competitive with those of other top-paying companies.

Questions

1. According to Arthur F. Strohmer, executive director of staffing and development at Merck, "Under the company's old numerical appraisal system, employees were evaluated in terms of *absolute* definitions of performance. As a result, only about 1.5 percent of employees met the absolute definition of a '5' (the top) rating. The new system requires divisions to identify 5 percent of employees whose performance ranks in the top performance category relative to their peers, and then 15 percent for the next performance category, and so on." What do you think of using a system that uses percentages for each performance category? What are the advantages and disadvantages of this system?
2. What problems must be overcome in implementing a new performance appraisal system?
3. Why is it important to monitor carefully performance appraisal results and their impact on individual pay increase?

■ Female Social Workers and Male Psychologists: A Case of Pay Discrimination?

Ms. Schulte was hired by the New York State Office for Mental Health as a psychiatric

Based on William H. Wagel, "Performance Appraisal with a Difference," *Personnel* (February 1987), pp. 4–6.

social worker in December 1974. On August 10, 1979, she filed a charge with the EEOC alleging that the state's pay scales for the positions of Psychologist I and Social Worker I and II discriminated against females. Ms. Schulte alleged that the positions of psychologist and social worker were similar in duties and responsibilities. However, as of February 4, 1981, there were 1,093 psychologists employed by the New York State Office of Mental Health, 67 percent of whom were male. Of the 1,332 social workers employed on the same date, 70 percent were female. This percentage roughly parallels the percentage of women who receive graduate degrees from social work programs in the United States.

The minimum qualifications for a Psychologist I include a master's degree in psychology and 2 years of professionally supervised experience in psychology (1 year of which must be served after receipt of the master's degree). Employees working in the position of Psychologist II must possess a master's degree and 3 years of supervised experience, 2 of which must be post-master's degree. The minimum qualifications for an Associate Psychologist include a doctorate in psychology and an internship. Male and female psychologists performing the same job are paid the same starting salary and are entitled to the same annual increments.

The position of Psychiatric Social Worker I required a master's degree in social work. The Psychiatric Social Worker II required a master's degree plus 2 years of social work experience (1 year of which must be served after receiving the master's degree). Male and female social workers performing the same job are paid the same starting salary and are paid the same annual increments.

A comparison of the job market for psychologists with the job market for social workers throughout the United States indicates that psychologists are paid a higher starting salary than social workers in every state, including New York. Notwithstanding the different job descriptions, pay scales, and qualifications for social workers and psychologists, Schulte contends that the work actually performed is substantially similar, if not identical.

Questions

1. Is this case an equal pay or a comparable worth case? Discuss.
2. Does the fact that approximately 30 percent of the social workers are male reduce the likelihood that Schulte will win her case?
3. As noted in the case, the qualifications for the psychologist positions are generally more rigorous than those for the social worker positions. In addition, psychologists are paid higher salaries throughout the United States. What impact will these facts have on the outcome of the case?
4. In the case *County of Washington v. Gunther* (discussed in Chapter 11), two separate pay scales were used for male and female prison guards. Does the Gunther case apply to the circumstances discussed here?

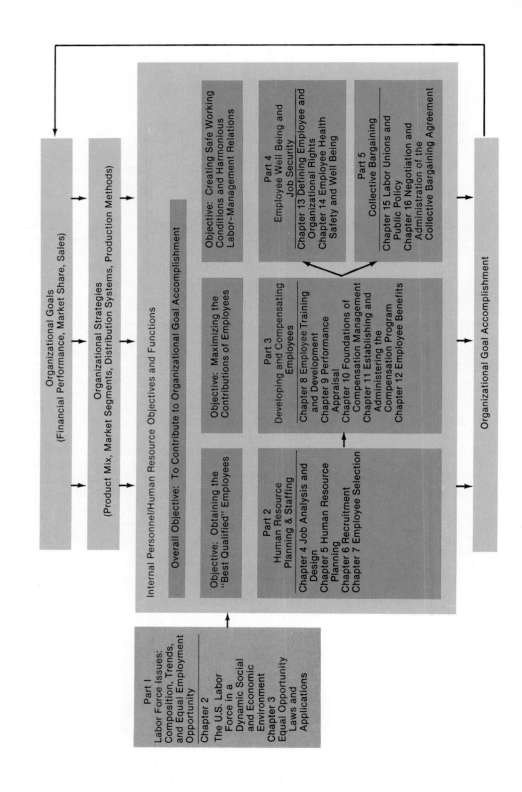

Organizational Goals
(Financial Performance, Market Share, Sales)

Organizational Strategies
(Product Mix, Market Segments, Distribution Systems, Production Methods)

Internal Personnel/Human Resource Objectives and Functions

Overall Objective: To Contribute to Organizational Goal Accomplishment

Objective: Obtaining the "Best Qualified" Employees

Part 2
Human Resource
Planning & Staffing

Chapter 4 Job Analysis and
Design
Chapter 5 Human Resource
Planning
Chapter 6 Recruitment
Chapter 7 Employee Selection

Objective: Maximizing the Contributions of Employees

Part 3
Developing and Compensating
Employees

Chapter 8 Employee Training
and Development
Chapter 9 Performance
Appraisal
Chapter 10 Foundations of
Compensation Management
Chapter 11 Establishing and
Administering the
Compensation Program
Chapter 12 Employee Benefits

Objective: Creating Safe Working
Conditions and Harmonious
Labor–Management Relations

Part 4
Employee Well Being and
Job Security

Chapter 13 Defining Employee and
Organizational Rights
Chapter 14 Employee Health
Safety and Well Being

Part 5
Collective Bargaining

Chapter 15 Labor Unions and
Public Policy
Chapter 16 Negotiation and
Administration of the
Collective Bargaining Agreement

Organizational Goal Accomplishment

Part I
Labor Force Issues:
Composition, Trends,
and Equal Employment
Opportunity

Chapter 2
The U.S. Labor
Force in a
Dynamic Social
and Economic
Environment
Chapter 3
Equal Opportunity
Laws and
Applications

EMPLOYEE WELL-BEING AND JOB SECURITY

■ Some of the most controversial issues affecting personnel/human resource policy involve employee well-being and job security issues. Until recently, organizations had the right to discharge most employees for good cause, bad cause, or no cause at all. Now the employer's discretion in firing has been curtailed in a number of states, and wrongfully terminated employees are suing and winning large judgments from employers. In California, for example, discharged employees are winning an average of $400,000 in suits against their former employers.[1] A *Los Angeles Times* poll estimates that employees win approximately 70 percent of all wrongful termination cases that are tried by juries. Many of these unfortunate incidents could have been prevented with a well-administered employee discipline policy. Chapter 13, Defining Employee and Organizational Rights, covers the causes of disciplinary problems, describes categories of difficult employees, outlines the components of a sound disciplinary policy, and analyzes the legal issues associated with terminations.

Although personnel/human resource managers have long been concerned with employee health and safety, the issues of AIDS, drug testing, and smoking in the workplace have created new and controversial issues. In Chapter 14, Employee Health, Safety, and Well-Being, the history and scope of the Occupational Safety and Health Act and the law's implications for industrial health and safety programs are discussed. Emerging issues in employee health and safety such as stress management, the health hazards faced by women, genetic testing, drug abuse, AIDS, and smoking are analyzed.

[1] *The Wall Street Journal*, Labor Letter (March 1, 1988), p. 1.

13

Defining Employee and Organizational Rights

■ LEARNING OBJECTIVES

After reading this chapter you should understand

1. The need for and the positive effects of a formal disciplinary system in organizations.
2. What characteristics a disciplinary system should have.
3. The various types and causes of employee problem behaviors.
4. The importance of due process in protecting the job rights of employees.
5. The role of the other personnel activities in reducing the incidence of employee problem behaviors.

■ INTRODUCTORY VIGNETTE

Controlling Absenteeism at Mazda

Workers at Mazda Motor Corporation's car assembly plant near Detroit have agreed to work more overtime in exchange for a new policy on absenteeism that includes a perfect-attendance bonus of $1,500. The absenteeism policy was negotiated with Mazda by the United Auto Workers in response to several problems that had arisen in the plant. Unlike other Japanese auto manufacturers, Mazda had experienced unusually high absenteeism rates of between 8 and 10 percent. Workers also complained about the company's attendance and temporary employee policies.

Japanese auto companies operating in the United States have generally been successful at avoiding unionization, primarily by paying competitive wages and allowing workers more autonomy on the factory floor. Auto manufacturers with employees represented by the United Auto Workers have won contracts that are substantially less restrictive than traditional collective bargaining agreements with the Big Three auto manufacturers—General Motors Corporation, Ford Motor Company, and Chrysler Corporation. Such pacts were achieved, in part, by assuring auto workers in Japanese plants that there would be no layoffs.

Mazda's new attendance policy gives workers 60 percent of their regular pay for the first four absences in a rolling 12-month period. Workers are allowed 11

Information on Mazda's Detroit plant is based on "Mazda Workers Reach Pact on Policy Covering Absenteeism," *The Wall Street Journal* (October 12, 1989), p. A1.

additional absences without pay and then are subjected to dismissal for absences beyond this limit. Workers with no absences get a bonus of $1,500 at the end of the year.

Absenteeism has been a chronic problem in many companies. High absenteeism rates may create scheduling problems, force employers to pay for expensive overtime, and create administrative problems for supervisors who must discipline workers with constant attendance problems. The absenteeism program at Mazda represents a philosophical change in the way in which U.S. corporations deal with common disciplinary issues. Instead of punishing workers for undesirable behaviors such as excessive absenteeism, companies such as Mazda are attempting to reward them for positive behavior. With an understanding of the causes of disciplinary problems and the use of innovative policies such as the one at Mazda, managers may be able to reduce the costs of absenteeism and create a more productive and efficient work environment.

◼ Introduction

Organizations employ workers with the expectation that they will perform their jobs in a safe, reliable, and competent manner. Likewise, the employee who accepts and abides by the employer's work rules generally expects entitlement to job security, respect for individual dignity, reasonable compensation, and freedom from unfair or capricious action by management. In the majority of cases, employee and employer fulfill their mutual obligations in a satisfactory manner. Unfortunately, there are instances in which employees either do not conform to organizational policies and rules or create difficulty at work. Examples of such behavior include poor attendance, alcohol or drug abuse, carelessness and negligence, theft, insubordination and abusive language, misconduct, rule violations, and poor performance. Similarly, organizations may violate the expectation employees have of fair treatment. Examples include requesting employees to break the law, terminating employees for off-duty behaviors that have no bearing on job performance, and terminating employees in order to avoid the payment of earned commissions.

Although it is easy to view the employee as the villain when organizational policies and rules are violated or performance is poor, organizations sometimes contribute to the problem. Poor recruitment and selection, inadequate training and orientation programs, sporadic supervision, and lack of communication often add to employee disciplinary problems. Furthermore, management often fails to follow the fundamental precepts of due process and fairness in administering disciplinary measures. As a result, employee trust of management is diminished. Nonunion employees may feel that their only alternative is to seek legal recourse through the EEOC or civil proceedings, while their unionized counterparts press for a hearing under the grievance procedure. Regardless of the outcome, disciplinary problems create disruptions, cost money, and waste time. This chapter discusses the causes of, and appropriate responses for, disciplinary problems and explores the employment rights of employees.

Causes of Employee Discipline Problems

Table 13-1 examines two major sources of employee disciplinary problems: organizational sources and individual (employee) sources. In many cases, the organization's poor personnel practices contribute to discipline problems. For example, persons with a history of unacceptable or troubled work performance may be hired if references are not carefully checked and verified. Careless placement of employees in jobs for which they are not suited generally creates difficulties. Similarly, haphazard and inadequate training programs may lead to employee inefficiencies, feelings of inadequacy and frustration, and safety hazards, all of which represent potential disciplinary incidents. Supervisors may contribute to the problem through unequal application of rules, favoritism, an unduly harsh posture toward employees, and failure to communicate adequately performance standards and expectations. Although most employees are willing to abide by policies and work rules that they perceive to be reasonable and equitable, they may question and test those that appear to be unreasonable or antiquated. Therefore, in dealing with employee disciplinary cases, the personnel/human resource manager would

TABLE 13-1   Sources and Types of Employee Discipline Problems

Organizational Causes	Individual Causes
Poor recruitment and selection	Alcohol and drug use
Inadequate training and development	Financial difficulties
Lack of communication	Domestic problems
Poor supervision	Physical/mental disease or disorder
Unreasonable rules and policies	Personal traits

Types of Employee Problems
Absenteeism and tardiness
Abusive and obscene language
Poor attitude and disloyalty
Carelessness and negligence
Dishonesty, theft, and illegal acts
Insubordination
Misconduct, horseplay, and fighting
Poor performance
Work slowdowns and stoppages
Work rule violations

be wise to investigate whether the organization's personnel practices created or accentuated the problem.

Other discipline problems are rooted in an employee's personal life. Alcohol and drug abuse (or addiction), financial worries, and domestic problems all take their toll and may adversely affect an employee's work performance. Physical and mental disorders can also play an integral part in employee problems at work. Personal characteristics such as an employee's high level of aggression toward others, intolerance for monotony and routine work, and immaturity leading to a lack of reliability and attention to detail, as well as carelessness and poor individual initiative, are common factors that underlie disciplinary problems.[1]

■ Categories of Difficult Employees

Using Table 13-1 as a backdrop, we now examine the most commonly encountered types of employee disciplinary problems.[2] No attempt is made to provide a psychological profile of the typical problem employee. Rather, the objective is to describe the problems that supervisors and personnel/human resource managers must periodically face.

The Attendance Problem: Absenteeism and Tardiness

For many organizations, absenteeism and tardiness are pressing concerns. Although the overall absenteeism rate for organizations in the United States is approximately 2–3 percent of scheduled work time, some organizations experience much higher rates.[3] Furthermore, employees are often absent on either Fridays or Mondays (or both) in order to lengthen their weekend.[4] Periods of high absenteeism may disrupt work schedules and create expensive delays for some companies.

Although nearly all employees are occasionally forced to be late or absent from work, the chronic absentee or tardy employee presents a difficult problem. Although some absenteeism is involuntary and out of the control of the individual employee, other absenteeism and tardiness are clearly voluntary and within the control of the employee. Many employees make every effort to attend work, in spite of illness, family conflicts, or transportation problems that occasionally pose barriers. Other employees seize the opportunity to stay away from work whenever

[1]See Walter Kiechel III, "How to Discipline in the Modern Age," *Fortune* (May 7, 1990), pp. 179–180.

[2]James R. Redeker, *Discipline: Policies and Procedures* (Washington, D.C.: The Bureau of National Affairs, Inc., 1983), pp. vii and viii.

[3]"Job Absence and Turnover," *Bulletin to Management* (Washington, D.C.: The Bureau of National Affairs, Inc., 1985).

[4]Frank E. Kuzmits, "What to Do About Long-Term Absenteeism," *Personnel Administrator* (October 1986), p. 93.

a plausible (or semiplausible) excuse occurs. For example, inclement weather that is likely to slow or delay travel to work may mean leaving the house 1½ hours early for one employee. The chronically late or absent employee will use the same inclement weather as a reason to either arrive late or stay at home. Some employees are willing to come to work with the common cold, whereas others will remain away for several days.

From the perspective of employee supervision and discipline, absenteeism and tardiness present a thorny dilemma. First, the supervisor must determine whether the absence or lateness is legitimate. This forces the supervisor to play the role of detective, for which he or she is poorly suited. Second, personnel/human resource managers must define and establish a reasonable absenteeism policy. Third, the policy should be communicated and enforced in a consistent fashion.

Some companies have instituted *no-fault absenteeism programs*. Under a no-fault plan, the employee accumulates absences (or points for absences or tardiness) and is dismissed if a certain number of absences or points are accumulated during a specified time period.[5] The rationale of a no-fault system is to relieve supervisors of the burden of determining whether an absent or tardy employee has a legitimate excuse. However, no-fault plans may unfairly penalize employees who must experience lengthy absences for a serious illness. In addition, certain employees may view the no-fault arrangement as a permissive limit, and will be absent or late up to the maximum allowed by the system.[6]

The Rule Violators

Employees occasionally violate work rules.[7] In some instances, a rule is violated unknowingly. In other cases, it is broken by an employee who is fully aware of the transgression. Poor training programs and inadequate communications may lead to accidental rule violations. Employees who purposely violate work rules often do so to test what they feel is an unreasonable or outmoded policy. Others intentionally violate rules or fail to follow prescribed work procedures simply for the thrill involved or to show off for fellow employees.

Management can deal most effectively with rule violators by communicating applicable rules to employees and stressing the reasons underlying specific rules. Most employees are willing to abide by purposeful rules. When reasonable policies and rules are violated, employees should be warned or disciplined in a consistent and fair manner.

[5]See Darrell Olson and Ruth Bangs, "No-fault Attendance Control: A Real World Application," *Personnel Administrator* (June 1984), pp. 53–63; and Frank E. Kuzmits, "Is Your Organization Ready for No-Fault Absenteeism?" *Personnel Administrator* (December 1984), pp. 119–127.

[6]A no-fault plan that is used to retaliate unfairly against an employee or as a pretext for illegal discrimination may pose serious problems. See *Knafel v. Pepsi-Cola Bottlers of Akron*, CA 6, No. 89-3208 (1990).

[7]Frans Mulder, "Characteristics of Violation of Formal Company Rules," *Journal of Applied Psychology*, Vol. 55 (1971), pp. 500–502.

Employees with Drug and Alcohol Problems

Alcohol and drug use among employees has the potential to create numerous performance problems. Poor performance, unreliability, absenteeism, interpersonal conflicts, job-related safety hazards, and violations of federal or state laws are common trouble areas. Employees may abuse alcohol or drugs without being addicted. Regardless of an employee's level of dependence on potentially addictive substances, however, the crux of the issue is the impact that alcohol and drug use has on work life.

A great deal of research has been done on employee alcohol and drug use. Some of this research focuses on the causes of abuse and addiction. Factors such as an individual's genetic predisposition to substance abuse, as well as social and organizational forces that contribute to alcohol and drug usage, have been examined. Job-based risks, such as low job visibility, absence of clear goals, freedom to set work hours, occupational obsolescence, stress, on-the-job social drinking with clients and customers, and other factors appear to contribute to alcohol and drug problems. Other research studies have focused on the consequences of illicit alcohol and drug consumption. Alcohol and drug use appears to impair job performance in many, but not all, cases. Some employees develop the ability to cover up even severe alcohol/drug problems, sometimes with the help of close co-workers and supervisors. In recent years, employers have come to regard alcoholism and drug addiction as diseases that should be handled similarly to other medical disabilities.[8] Some organizations have developed programs that combine the identification and rehabilitation of employees who abuse or are dependent upon alcohol or other drugs. In Chapter 14, these programs are discussed in detail.

Alcoholism or drug abuse can serve as a double-edged sword in disciplinary proceedings. First, and most obvious, is that disciplinary proceedings may result against an employee if he or she is either caught using alcohol or drugs on the job (regardless of whether their usage had adverse consequences) or has job-related problems stemming from alcohol or drug use. Second, and less obvious, is that alcoholism or drug dependency may serve as a defense to explain inappropriate on-the-job conduct, thereby avoiding or reducing discipline penalties. That is, alcohol or drug problems can create mitigating or extenuating circumstances in some disciplinary cases.[9] Nevertheless, discharge may still be warranted if an employee commits violations that are either very serious or endanger fellow employees and customers.

Organizations and society in general are more socially tolerant of alcohol than of drug use. Alcohol-induced misconduct is therefore more likely to lead to a

[8]For an excellent treatment of drug and alcohol use at work, see Harrison M. Trice and Paul M. Roman, *Spirits and Demons at Work: Alcohol and Drugs on the Job*, 2nd ed. (Ithaca, New York: Cornell University, New York State School of Industrial and Labor Relations, 1978).

[9]James R. Redeker, p. 81.

greater degree of uncertainty about what constitutes appropriate behavior and disciplinary action than is drug abuse, which is usually illegal and often leads to automatic discharge for first offenders. Specific policies that address the use of alcohol before work, at work, or during lunch breaks or after hours should be promulgated by the employer to reduce uncertainty. For example, if an employee comes to work heavily intoxicated, the employer may use this incident as grounds for immediate dismissal or severe disciplinary action. If an employee comes to work with liquor on his or her breath, the employer may elect to have the company physician, safety officer, or other qualified person administer a breathalyzer or blood alcohol content (BAC) test to determine the proper course of action. Employers may wish to consider the merits of having a policy against drinking alcoholic beverages during off-premises lunch breaks if this will result in improvement in work performance or reduction in safety hazards. The precise nature of the policies will depend on the tasks and responsibilities of the employee's jobs, safety considerations, applicable drinking laws, and the employer's posture on alcohol use.[10]

Numerous organizations are now attempting to help employees with drug and alcohol problems through the use of employee assistance programs (EAPs). EAPs provide either direct counseling or other assistance for employees who abuse or are dependent upon chemical substance.[11] Employees may voluntarily seek assistance from an EAP as part of a disciplinary process. Employee assistance programs are discussed in more detail in Chapter 14.

Participants in Theft and Illegal Acts Against the Employer

Most organizations will move swiftly to dismiss an employee who is caught or found guilty of stealing merchandise, supplies, or money from the employer.[12] However, several important issues can arise when employees are involved in theft or illegal acts. First, companies may prefer not to press criminal charges if an employee admits to the theft or illegal act and accepts an uncontested discharge. Second, when an employee does not admit to such an act, the employer must decide whether to use internal channels to investigate and discipline the wrongdoer or to resort to filing criminal charges. If criminal charges are filed, the

[10]See August Ralston, "Employee Alcoholism: Response of the Largest Industrials," *Personnel Administrator* (August 1977), p. 50; and Carol Durtis, *Drug Abuse as a Business Problem—the Problem Defined with Guidelines for Policy* (New York: U.S. Chamber of Commerce, 1970).

[11]See Martin Shain and Judith Groenveld, *Employee Assistance Programs: Philosophy, Theory, and Practice* (Lexington, Massachusetts: Lexington Books, 1980); N. R. Berg and J. P. Moe, "Assistance for Troubled Employees" in D. Yoder and H. G. Heneman, Jr. (eds.), *ASPA Handbook of Personnel and Industrial Relations, PAIR Policy and Program Management* (Berea, Ohio: American Society for Personnel Administration, 1979), Vol. VII, pp. 1-59–1-77.

[12]See William L. Taylor and Joseph P. Cangemi, "Employee Theft and Organizational Climate," *Personnel Journal* (October 1979); August Bequai, *White Collar Crime: A Twentieth Century Crisis* (Lexington, Massachusetts: D. C. Heath, 1978); and R. J. Healy and T. J. Walsh, "Security Policies, Programs, and Problems," in D. Yoder and H. G. Heneman, Jr., pp. 1-79–1-93.

organization and the employee should be prepared to weather adverse publicity and time-consuming investigatory and criminal proceedings.

An internal investigation, if necessary, may require the employee to submit to a polygraph test or paper-and-pencil honesty test. However, these methods may or may not help find the thief, and the test results will probably not be admissible in court. Although polygraph, or lie detector, tests have been used for many years, they remain very controversial. In recent years, more cases of innocent employees having been dismissed for theft because of polygraph test results have appeared in the courts. Increasingly the employees involved are suing for damages and collecting substantial settlements.[13] The American Psychological Association, American Civil Liberties Union, AFL-CIO, and American Medical Association's Council on Scientific Affairs have denounced polygraph testing as an inaccurate means of assessing honesty.[14] The misuse of polygraph tests in the workplace has also drawn the interest of Congress, which enacted the Employee Polygraph Protection Act in 1988. This act severely restricts the use of polygraphs for preemployment screening, as well as for the testing of current employees. Employers may still test for economic loss or injury, such as theft or other criminal acts on the job, but must do so under detailed procedures prescribed by the law. Kevin McGuiness, the counsel for the Senate Committee on Labor and Human Resources, believes that in addition to the reliability problems associated with lie detector tests, "there is overwhelming evidence that employers are using polygraphs to justify activities that otherwise would be prohibited. Some employers use the test to screen out minority applicants and union sympathizers, or to get rid of employees who aren't liked."[15] Many states also bar the workplace use of polygraph tests.[16]

Polygraph tests are not without their advocates. Days Inn of America has stated that between 1975 and 1985 the use of polygraphs resulted in a reduction of annual employee theft from $1 million to $115,000. Further, the company claims that the tests resulted in $1 million in employee restitutions.[17] In spite of the success of Days Inn of America, polygraph testing in the workplace has been severely curtailed by state and federal legislation.

Sophisticated white-collar crime is a growing concern for organizations. Estimates of white-collar crime run as high as $200 billion per year. This figure seems incredible until you consider that bank embezzlements average $42,000, office

---

[13]One example, of two employees fired for theft at a securities firm, is described in Benjamin Kleinmuntz, "Lie Detectors Fail the Truth Test," *Harvard Business Review* (July-August 1985), p. 36.

[14]"Trends," *Bulletin to Management* (Washington, D.C.: The Bureau of National Affairs, Inc., September 25, 1986), p. 323. See also Lisa J. McCue, "Employee Screening: Who's Behind the Mask?" *Bottomline* (April 1986), pp. 19, 37–38.

[15]"No Future for Polygraphs," *Bulletin to Management* (Washington, D.C.: The Bureau of National Affairs, Inc., November 20, 1986), p. 381.

[16]As of early 1987, 22 states had outlawed lie detector use. Ed Bean, "More Firms Use 'Attitude Tests' to Keep Thieves Off the Payroll," *The Wall Street Journal* (February 27, 1987), p. 1A.

[17]Washington Roundup, "It's A Lie," *Nation's Business* (December 1985), pp. 12–13.

supply scams run at least $50 million per year, insurance fraud costs $4 billion, and a single incident of computer fraud cost investors $1 billion.[18] In fact computer crime is definitely a growth industry. This should not come as a surprise, as the average bank robbery grosses $15,000, whereas the average computer crime yields $400,000. Further, the crime is far less likely to be detected, and the white-collar criminal is less likely to be caught, as well as less likely to spend time in jail if caught, than a bank robber. Although most computer crime is done for financial gain, there are different types of computer crimes: vandalism, theft of information, use of computers for moonlighting, burglary by modem, and financial fraud.[19] Valuable information may be stolen from memory banks to be sold to competitors, computers may be used by employees to support their own private businesses, orders for merchandise may be placed directly through modems from home (bypassing normal ordering and billing procedures), and records of false assets may be created from nothing to dupe unsuspecting investors.

Some organizations have had considerable success in reducing employee theft by instituting an aggressive antitheft program. Elements of those programs include the following:[20]

1. Conscientious preemployment screening.
2. New employee orientation that includes a discussion of the firm's theft policy and the impact of theft on all employees.
3. A strong antitheft policy that is communicated to all employees.
4. Security controls, including computerized inventory control, frequent physical inventories, and routine package checking.
5. Training employees in how to spot and report employee theft.
6. An ongoing show of management concern about the problem and determination to end it.

Employee sabotage is another problem that employers must face.[21] Employees, for a variety of reasons, may seek to destroy the property or disrupt the operations of the firm. Some employees want revenge for real or imagined wrongs at the hands of co-workers or management. Others may resort to sabotage to seek thrills or avoid work. A recent report by Authur D. Little, Inc., a consulting firm

---

[18]Rod Willis, "White Collar Crime," *Management Review* (January 1986), p. 22. See also Ted Gest, "Stealing $200 Billion 'the Respectable Way,' " *U.S. News & World Report* (May 20, 1985), p. 35; and Peter J. Ognibene, "Computer Saboteurs," *Science Digest* (July 1984), pp. 59–61.

[19]Rod Willis, p. 27.

[20]Ron Zemke, "Employee Theft: How to Cut Your Losses," *Training* (May 1986), p. 77. An alternative view is presented by Robert R. Taylor, "A Positive Guide to Theft Deterrence," *Personnel Journal* (August 1986), pp. 36–40. This article describes aggressive antitheft programs as oppressive and suggests a more positive program emphasizing employee dignity, respect, and support.

[21]Michael D. Crino and Terry L. Leap, "What HR Managers Must Know About Employee Sabotage," *Personnel* (May 1989), pp. 31–38; Associated Press, "Study: Pay Cuts Boost Employee Pilfering," *Anderson-Independent Mail* (November 13, 1990), p. 6B.

hired by Union Carbide, indicated that the deadly gas leak at the company's Bhopal, India, plant was the result of employee sabotage. According to the report, the employee wanted to punish a superior who had demoted him. The gas leak killed 2,850 people and injured another 20,000.[22]

In the past, sabotage usually meant the destruction of equipment or inventory. The modern office, however, has created new avenues for sabotage. Computers allow employees interested in sabotage easy and inconspicuous access to important data and programs. As a consequence, employees have found creative ways to alter or destroy company data and programs. For example, employees have planted logic bombs in company software. Logic bombs are unauthorized programming instructions secretly embedded in a computer program. These instructions execute automatically at a specified date in the future or after a certain number of computer operations using the program. The instructions can shut down the system, alter the operation of the program, or print amusing or obscene messages on computer screens.

Employers may reduce the likelihood of sabotage by applying many of the guidelines for the reduction of theft presented in this chapter. In addition, a climate of justice and fair treatment in the workplace should be created through personnel programs.

Participants in Illegal Acts Off Duty

Employees may be charged with criminal misconduct not associated with their employment. Although most organizations do not attempt to influence directly the conduct of an employee's private life, a dilemma is created when off-duty conduct tarnishes the organization's image. Some companies adopt the stance of standing by their employees and assuming their innocence until they are proven guilty, whereas others may suspend or even dismiss employees who are accused of felonies or other instances of serious misconduct. Illegal acts committed outside the realm of employment present a difficult issue to resolve. The nature of the job and the offense generally determine the employer's action. For example, a teacher accused of immoral conduct off the job might be more likely to face suspension than would a machinist because of the potential risk to students. A bank employee accused of armed robbery would probably be removed from the job pending the outcome of a trial because of the nature of the crime, whereas a laborer may not be suspended. An airline pilot found guilty of driving under the influence of alcohol would probably face more severe employment consequences than would a postal worker. The accused employee's rights to retain his or her job must be balanced against the employer's right to protect property, employees, and customers. Unfortunately, such dilemmas are difficult to resolve; clear-cut solutions are rarely apparent. Keeping this in mind, Table 13-2 offers some general guidelines for handling employee off-duty misconduct.

[22]"Report Says Sabotage Led to Bhopal Incident," *The Greenville News* (May 11, 1988), p. 1D.

TABLE 13-2   Disciplinary Guidelines for Off-Duty Misconduct

Establish written prohibitions for specific types of off-duty conduct that management regards as unacceptable. Some organizations have rules that result in automatic discharge for a guilty plea or conviction of a felony. Others list specific behaviors such as drug possession, theft, or assault as grounds for immediate disciplinary action.

Use caution in initiating disciplinary actions that are heavily influenced by the moral or political views of one decision maker. Occasionally an otherwise prudent manager who has no tolerance for extramarital affairs, homosexuality, or unorthodox lifestyles will overreact in suspending or discharging an employee.

Formulate procedures for employees who are charged with a crime and awaiting trial. An employer is not obligated to retain a worker who faces a long period of incarceration before being tried, but employees released on bail may want to return to work. If the nature of the crime makes it inadvisable to allow the employee to work, the company may opt for temporary suspension. Final disciplinary action can then be taken once the case is resolved. As a gesture of good faith, the company may offer to reimburse the employee for lost income if the case is later dropped or there is an acquittal.

Stipulate how the organization will deal with employees who receive suspended sentences. Individuals who either plead guilty or who are convicted often receive suspended sentences, which once again makes them available for work. In some instances, the suspended sentence is contingent upon the employee's having a full-time job. Arbitrators tend to show leniency when the courts do likewise. In the absence of an arbitration award or state statute protecting the employment rights of convicted felons, however, the employer must decide whether reinstatement is advisable by considering factors such as the employee's trustworthiness, the employee's propensity for violence or drug abuse, and the reaction of customers and co-workers.

continued

Adapted from Terry L. Leap, "When Can You Fire for Off-duty Conduct?" *Harvard Business Review* (January-February 1988), pp. 28-37.

Employee Insubordination

Employees are generally expected to comply with reasonable management orders because such compliance is considered essential to the functioning of the employer's business. When an employee willfully disobeys or disregards a supervisor's directive, the organization usually has the right to discipline the employee for insubordination.

In order to establish a case of insubordination, management must show that the supervisor issued a direct order (either orally or in writing), the employee received and understood the order, and the employee refused to obey the directive through an explicit statement of refusal or through nonperformance. Employees who refuse to perform duties that are unsafe or illegal may be entitled to statutory protection and reinstatement if they are discharged. The Occupational Safety and Health Act (OSHA), for example, protects employees who are disciplined for

TABLE 13-2   (continued)

Anticipate the possibility that an employee who is guilty of a serious crime may "beat the system." Employees who avoid criminal prosecution because of legal technicalities in the face of overwhelming evidence of guilt may still be disciplined by management. As one arbitrator stated, "it matters not that the rigorous protection in the criminal law saved the individual from criminal penalties because such fact does not constitute a bar to the employer's right to protect itself or its other employees." Unless the employer has agreed to base disciplinary action on the outcome of a criminal proceeding, then the use of double jeopardy is legally permissible.

Consider the impact that an employee's off-duty acts will have on co-workers and formulate plans for dealing with their concerns. It may be possible to calm co-workers' fears by thoroughly explaining why the employee is being reinstated. Co-workers should understand that the reinstatement is based on an extensive investigation of the off-duty incident and its impact on the employee's job. Care should be taken to set the record straight on exaggerated or distorted stories surrounding the employee's conduct while protecting sensitive information surrounding the case. Management should also consider transferring the employee to a different location if irreconcilable differences and tensions persist.

Decide how much negative public opinion can be tolerated before sacrificing an employee. When customers object to an employee's reinstatement, consider the following points. First, how many customers have complained? One or two complaints out of several thousand potential customers may not be a reasonable basis for disciplinary action. Negative public reaction can be strong, however, when employees holding jobs requiring high moral values engage in off-duty misconduct (especially where contact with children is involved). Second, can a competitor exploit the bad publicity of an unsavory off-duty incident and harm the employer's business? When this is the case, the employer may have little choice other than discharge unless effective public relations tactics can be used to offset the competitor's claims.

refusing unsafe work. In fact, some employees cite this act to justify their refusal to work with co-workers who have AIDS. The protection afforded employees by this act is discussed in Chapter 14.

Another type of insubordination involves the use of abusive language by employees to supervisors and others. A primary consideration with regard to abusive language as a form of insubordination is the context in which the incident occurred. Generally speaking, an employee is more likely to engage in insubordination if (1) the abusive language was not provoked by the supervisor, (2) it was spoken in the presence of other employees or customers, and (3) abusive and profane language is not part of the "shop talk" in the particular workplace.[23] If

[23]James R. Redeker, pp. 170–181.

some or all of these conditions are not met, then management should take a close look to determine if extenuating circumstances exist that might temper the disciplinary penalty.

Incompetence and Carelessness

Employee incompetence often poses a somewhat different dilemma than the previously discussed disciplinary cases, because the employee may not be directly at fault. *Incompetence* refers to inability rather than unwillingness to perform in an acceptable manner. Employees may have been carelessly selected, lack proper training, or possess physical or mental impairments that prevent satisfactory job performance. A good performance appraisal system can be used to document incompetence, and it may also provide a basis for suggesting appropriate remedies. Incompetence, for example, may be eliminated through remedial training or transfer to a less demanding job. Dismissal should be used only as a last resort, especially for older or handicapped employees.[24] Improved selection should be considered as a means to prevent incompetent applicants from becoming incompetent employees.

Carelessness and negligent actions involve imprudent behavior that is either unsafe to employees and customers or is damaging to buildings, equipment, and materials. An act may be deemed inappropriate if it is done by an employee who, by virtue of his or her experience, training, and capabilities, should not have committed such an act. For example, an employee trained in the proper use of a forklift truck who carries an oversized or unbalanced load that results in extensive damage to the cargo when it overturns is guilty of carelessness and negligence. An untrained operator who is requested by a supervisor to drive a forklift with an unbalanced load may, on the other hand, not be guilty of wrongdoing. Personnel policy should also distinguish between careless acts that do not result in injury or damage and acts that carry some negative consequence. Should an organization discipline employees only for unsafe acts that result in damage, or should all acts of carelessness or negligence be punished, regardless of the outcome? The potential severity of the damage is a prime consideration. An employee who places the lives of co-workers in jeopardy (even if no lives were lost or injuries sustained) is probably a prime candidate for immediate discharge. Another consideration is the presence of mitigating factors. For example, an employee who is occasionally required to work a double shift (16 hours) may commit a careless act because of fatigue. In addition, an employee without a history of negligent behavior is generally granted more leniency than one whose record contains previous aberrant behavior.

---

[24]Incompetence is probably the only valid reason for using *demotion* as an employee discipline and control measure.

■ Disciplinary Measures: Some Issues

Positive Versus Negative Approaches to Discipline

The term *discipline* is usually viewed in a negative, punitive vein. Employees are "disciplined," or punished, if they exhibit some of the behaviors and problems discussed in the preceding section. In recent years, increased emphasis has been placed on a more positive approach to dealing with employee problems. One facet of the positive approach is to prevent as many disciplinary incidents as possible through careful selection, training, employee communications, and performance appraisal efforts.

A number of organizations, including Union Carbide, Tampa Electric Company, AT&T, Martin Marietta, Procter & Gamble, Pennzoil, and General Electric, are trying a different approach to positive discipline. Employees who break minor work rules are given a friendly reminder. The next infraction results in a written reminder and the next in a decision-making leave day. During this leave day the employee is asked to reflect on his or her employment with the company and consider whether he or she wishes to continue working there. The next day, the employee is asked to agree, in writing or orally, not to break any work rules during the next year (or other specified time period). The next infraction during the year results in the employee's immediate discharge.[25] Personnel/human resource directors who use this approach are very pleased with the results; morale has improved, grievances and terminations have declined, and employee performance has improved. Overall it appears to be a useful alternative to traditional disciplinary systems.[26] (Traditional disciplinary systems are discussed later in this chapter.)

Another positive approach is the concept of affirmative discipline.[27] Under the affirmative approach, an employee is given a complete set of company policies and rules of conduct appropriate to his or her job. All policies and rules are explained, and the employee is required to sign both a receipt for the documents and an agreement to abide by the policies and rules. Emphasis is placed on a mutual commitment between employer and employee: management agrees to retain the worker as part of the company "family," and the worker agrees to abide by the standards set by the employer. Upon satisfactory completion of the employee's

[25]Laurie Baum, "Punishing Workers with a Day Off," *Business Week* (June 16, 1986), p. 80; Bruce Jacobs, "An Apostle of Non-Punitive Discipline," *Industry Week* (November 10, 1986), pp. 123–124; Gene Milbourn, "The Case Against Employee Punishment," *Management Solutions* (November 1986), pp. 42–43; and Eric L. Harvey, "Discipline vs. Punishment," *Management Review* (March 1987), pp. 25–29.

[26]See Alan W. Bryant, "Replacing Punitive Discipline with a Positive Approach," *Personnel Administrator* (February 1984), pp. 79–87, for a discussion of the positive discipline program at General Electric's Meter Business Department in Somersworth, New Hampshire; and David N. Campbell, R. L. Fleming, and Ricard C. Grote, "Discipline Without Punishment—At Last," *Harvard Business Review* (July-August 1985), pp. 162–178, for a discussion of the program at Tampa Electric Company.

[27]James R. Redeker, pp. 33–39.

probation, the supervisor asks the worker if he or she desires to remain with the company on a permanent basis. If the employee answers in the affirmative, the supervisor once again outlines the company's expectations. Should the employee subsequently violate a policy or rule, the supervisor reminds the employee of his or her previous commitment and, once again, requests that the employee reaffirm his or her desire to remain in the firm's employ. In the event that the worker again violates the rules, the employer assumes that the employee no longer desires to remain with the firm.

Critics of the affirmative approach may feel that it is simply a sugar-coated method of punishment. However, James Redeker summarizes the advantages of the approach as follows:

> The basis of the affirmative approach is to entice an employee into adherence to standards of conduct, rather than drive the employee into conformity through punishment. Rather than try to avoid transgressions, the employee is asked to live up to a standard, which is subtly made the condition of employment. The burden is thus always placed on the employee.[28]

Use of Reasonable Rules, Standards, and Procedures

Employees are more likely to accept and abide by policies, standards, and rules that are perceived as being reasonable. Of course, the definition of what is "reasonable" will vary from one employee to another. Generally speaking, an employee will regard a policy, standard, or rule as being reasonable *if* he or she understands its underlying rationale. That is, why does this policy exist? What benefits accrue from having such a policy? What negative consequences might occur if this policy or rule were violated? For example, employees in retail establishments may not be allowed to carry purses or pocketbooks with them while they are in customer areas as a means of reducing employee theft. Most employees are willing to accept such a rule if (1) it is applied uniformly, (2) it is clearly communicated to each retail employee, and (3) the reasoning behind the policy is understood and accepted.

Policies that were reasonable in the past may become antiquated due to changes in the workplace. Technological advances in security systems, for example, may make the no-purse policy just described obsolete. Therefore, management must periodically assess policies, standards, and rules to ensure that they remain relevant. A prime test for reasonableness is to examine carefully rules that represent employee disciplinary trouble spots. Rules that are repeatedly violated may need elimination, restructuring, or reemphasis to employees regarding their importance.

Some companies are making increased use of computers and electronic devices to keep workers under surveillance. Such measures have been dubbed *technological whips* for keeping workers in line. Employers use electronic devices to

---

[28]James R. Redeker, p. 39.

monitor the content and length of telephone conversations, count keystrokes and gauge the amount of time that workers spend on transactions, observe worker actions through video cameras, and measure the effectiveness of worker-customer relationships. Although management may regard such devices as an extension of their supervisory responsibilities, these measures may create a climate of suspicion and distrust among employees. Thus electronic surveillance devices should be used only when absolutely necessary.

Burden of Proof, Due Process, and Equal Protection

As a general rule, the burden of proof in demonstrating wrongdoing by an employee falls on management. In our loosely structured system of industrial jurisprudence, the employer usually assumes the role of plaintiff and the worker that of defendant. The employer has the responsibility of initiating disciplinary action, collecting evidence, and presenting a case against the employee. This is not to imply, however, that the strict rules of evidence and procedural due process found in the courtroom are used in organizational disciplinary proceedings. Other than with unionized or a few select nonunionized employees who are protected by a formal grievance procedure, the gathering of evidence and application of the tenets of due process may be slipshod, thereby depriving an employee of a fair hearing and disposition of his or her case. The only semblance of due process available to many employees not protected by a collective bargaining agreement or structured disciplinary system is through EEO or other laws protecting employee rights.

Although the concept of due process is somewhat elusive and subject to varying degrees of interpretation, four elements appear essential. First, the employee must be made aware that he or she has committed a violation of the rules. Second, the employer must supply credible evidence that supports whatever accusation is being made against the employee. Third, the employee must be made aware of the nature of such evidence. Fourth, the employee must have the opportunity to question and refute the evidence.

Another hallmark of a sound disciplinary procedure is equal protection or treatment. The term *equal* does not necessarily mean that each employee committing the same offense will receive exactly the same treatment or punishment. Differences among employees in terms of seniority, work record, and past disciplinary incidents will ultimately mean that some employees are treated differently than others. In addition, extenuating circumstances can play a paramount role. The key to equal protection lies in the employees' perception of whether fair treatment was accorded in a specific case. As long as there are no radical fluctuations in punishments for similar offenses and there is the belief that management tailored the disciplinary action to the offense, there should be little controversy over equal protection. The key is not to ignore offenses by some employees while punishing others. Furthermore, the employer should keep records on employee offenses, the circumstances surrounding each offense, and the penalties handed out. By reviewing previous cases, management is better able to handle equitably new cases involving similar facts and circumstances.

Preventive Measures: The Role of the Personnel Functions

As previously mentioned, personnel functions such as recruitment and selection, training and development, performance appraisal, compensation management, and others can prevent or alleviate disciplinary problems when properly conducted. Table 13-3 provides a list of key considerations with respect to such preventive measures. Although the list of possible preventive measures is not exhaustive, they do serve to illustrate a *proactive* rather than a *reactive* approach. Ultimately each organization must tailor the precise preventive approach to its specific situation; factors such as the nature of the jobs, type of employees, work environment, union influences, and local customs should be considered.

TABLE 13-3   Considerations for Preventive Measures

Recruitment and Selection	Training and Development	Performance Appraisal	Other Functions
1. Psychological tests to match employee personality traits to the job tasks and demands. 2. Analysis of application forms and reference checks to determine: • Previous employment problems • Unexplained gaps in employment • Frequent changes in jobs • Lack of career progression or job regression history 3. Medical examinations to determine: • Physical and mental ability • Alcohol and drug problems	1. Communication of policies and work rules. 2. Periodic reemphasis of policies and work rules. 3. Thorough job training. 4. Periodic job retraining to avoid erosion of job skills. 5. Employee development to expand job skills and career horizons.	1. Reasonable performance criteria and standards. 2. Communication of performance criteria and standards. 3. Timely and accurate assessments of performance. 4. Appraisal interviews. 5. Using results of appraisal system for employee rewards (promotions, pay raises, etc.).	1. Adequate and equitable compensation programs. 2. Relevant health and safety rules. 3. Open communication channels that allow employees to discuss grievances and problems with supervisors. 4. Human resource information systems that document instances of favorable and unfavorable job behavior. 5. EAPs

Table 13-3 illustrates a single important point: organizations that have well-designed and competently administered personnel programs are more likely to prevent discipline problems than those that do not.

■ Hierarchical Disciplinary Policy and Procedures

Although an ounce of prevention is worth a pound of cure, there is no absolute guarantee that disciplinary problems will be totally avoided even when the most thorough preventive measures are followed. Therefore, it behooves personnel/-human resource administrators to establish a disciplinary system containing the following elements:

1. Categories of violations.
2. A system of penalties to match the respective violations.
3. An appeal mechanism.

Categories of Violations

As an initial step, an organization should categorize violations as minor, moderate, and serious. For example, serious violations are those that could result in the discharge of an employee on the first offense. Theft, physical attack on a supervisor or co-worker, and acts that endanger the lives of others would likely fall into this category. Moderate violations are those that normally warrant definite disciplinary action but not discharge for a first offense. Neglect of duty, absence without permission, insubordination, and sleeping on the job are typically regarded as moderate violations. Minor infractions are those that generally result in discharge only after repeated violations and warnings. Examples of minor violations might include occasional loafing on the job, tardiness, and minor safety violations.

When categorizing violations, management must consider the skill level and professionalism of its employees, the nature of their jobs, and the impact of the infraction upon safety, workflow, other employees, customer image, and additional factors affecting the organizational culture. Violations that might be regarded as minor in one organization could be regarded as serious in another. For example, a librarian who arrives at work after a night of heavy drinking may not experience a subpar level of job performance that would warrant disciplinary action (in fact, the severe headache and nausea is probably sufficient punishment). An airline pilot reporting to work in the same condition, however, could pose a very serious threat to passenger safety. Under these circumstances, the violation would probably be regarded as serious and would place the employee in a position of being immediately discharged.

Ultimately, each firm must determine how it wishes to categorize various violations. It is not possible to think of and classify every conceivable violation that might occur. Therefore, management may wish to establish a set of criteria that will aid in determining whether a violation should be regarded as serious, moderate, or minor. Table 13-4 provides a possible set of criteria.

The criteria listed in Table 13-4 are intended to categorize offenses only, not to determine the final disposition of a disciplinary incident. Previously mentioned factors, such as extenuating circumstances, the employee's disciplinary and work records, and so forth, are normally used in determining the ultimate outcome of a specific disciplinary case.[29] For example, most companies would not be likely to include, as part of the categorization process, a prohibition against employees bringing fighting gamecocks to the premises for lunch hour entertainment and gambling. Because cock fighting and gambling are at least misdemeanors in most states, such a violation might be categorized as moderate. The criteria in Table 3-3 should serve to guide managers as they categorize a multitude of potential employee offenses. Ultimately, however, the final categorization will depend on the nature of the employees, their jobs, and the organizational culture.[30]

TABLE 13-4   Violations Categories

Minor	Moderate	Serious
1. Little or no disruption to workflow.	1. Moderate disruption to workflow.	1. Severe and expensive disruption to workflow.
2. No damage to products or equipment.	2. Some damage to products or equipment.	2. Severe and expensive damage to products and equipment.
3. Inconsequential safety hazard posed to employee or others.	3. Employee and possible others were exposed to a definite safety hazard.	3. Employee and others are placed in a life-threatening situation.
4. Conduct was unacceptable for this type of worker (skill and professional level), but not grossly "out of line."	4. Conduct was definitely unacceptable for this type of worker. Employee fully understood that actions were wrong.	4. Conduct was outside the scope of that normally expected of a prudent, rational person.
5. Employee's behavior can be corrected by simply discussing it with him or her.	5. Employee's behavior may be corrected by further training and counseling.	5. Employee's behavior is either not correctable or is correctable only through extensive training or psychiatric counseling.
6. No state or federal law was violated.	6. The act committed was a misdemeanor (on the job).	6. The act committed was a felony (on the job).
7. Morale and welfare of employees was not significantly disrupted.	7. Morale and welfare of other employees was disrupted.	7. Morale and welfare of other employees was significantly and possibly irreparably impaired.

[29]See Patrick L McConnell, "Is Your Discipline Process the Victim of Red Tape?" *Personnel Journal* (March 1986), pp. 64–71; and Roger B. Madsen and Barbara Knudson-Fields, "Productive Progressive Discipline Procedures," *Management Solutions* (May 1987), pp. 17–25.

[30]See Brian S. Klaas and Hoyt N. Wheeler, "Managerial Decision Making About Employee Discipline: A Policy-Capturing Approach," *Personnel Psychology*, Vol. 43 (1990), pp. 117–133.

The Penalty Structure

An equitable penalty system has two characteristics; it tailors the penalty to the offense, and it ensures that employees who commit similar transgressions are treated in similar fashion. Table 13-5 provides an example of a penalty structure associated with a progressive disciplinary system.

Table 13-5 portrays a system of increasingly severe penalties, with the ultimate sanction being discharge. Serious violations can result in discharge on the first offense and will result in discharge on the second. Minor violations, on the other hand, do not result in discharge before the third offense and may offer an employee as many as four chances. The use of minimum and maximum penalties for each offense allows management a degree of flexibility to consider both the precise nature of the offense and any extenuating circumstances.

Two additional considerations regarding the penalty structure depicted in Table 13-5 are noteworthy. First, the system should impose time limits between offenses. That is, statute of limitations is necessary. For example, should an employee who committed a minor violation 5 years ago be credited with a second offense if another minor violation occurs? Organizations may decide to expunge an employee's disciplinary record if no further violations occur within 1–2 years. This has the effect of offering employees who improve their behavior a fresh start.

TABLE 13-5   Progressive Discipline Penalty

Serious Violations		
First Offense		Second Offense
Minimum	Maximum	
Suspension (1 month)	Discharge	Discharge

Moderate Violations				
First Offense		Second Offense		Third Offense
Minimum	Maximum	Minimum	Maximum	
Suspension (1 week)	Suspension (1 month)	Suspension (1 month)	Discharge	Discharge

Minor Violations							
First Offense		Second Offense		Third Offense		Fourth Offense	
Min.	Max.	Min.	Max.	Min.	Max.	Min.	Max.
Oral warning	Written reprimand	Written reprimand	Suspension (1 week)	Suspension (1 week)	Discharge	Discharge	

Second, what happens if an employee commits a combination of violations? For example, if an employee is caught loafing on the job (a minor violation) and 6 months later has an unexcused absence (another minor violation), then the absence is generally considered to be a minor second offense and carries more stringent penalties. If an employee commits a minor violation and then follows it with a moderate violation (first offense), then the employer will probably credit the workers with a first moderate offense but may elect to impose the maximum penalty (1 month's suspension). Regardless of how combination violations are handled, the key is to be as consistent as possible. Otherwise, employees will begin to view the entire process as capricious and arbitrary.

Progressive Discipline: The Bottom Line

Organizations that install and carefully administer a progressive discipline system are likely to reap the benefits of improved employee performance, morale, and protection for the employer in grievance proceedings and lawsuits. The underlying rationale of a progressive discipline system is that employees are expected to perform in a safe, competent, and reliable manner; otherwise, they can expect that sanctions will be imposed. In return, the employee has a right to expect fair and consistent treatment from the employer. The essence of progressive discipline is as follows:[31]

1. An adequate *warning system* is established. Incidents of employee misconduct are well documented, and the employee is counseled and fully aware that further incidents will lead to more severe penalties.
2. *Enforcement is consistent* among employees. The employee is assured of equal protection, free from discriminatory application of discipline policies.
3. *The penalties are matched with the offense.* A penalty structure such as the one outlined in Table 13-5 prevents management from overreacting to a specific offense.
4. *Due process* is ensured. Each employee should have a full hearing, cognizant of the evidence brought against him or her. Furthermore, the system should allow the employee to rebut evidence presented by management.
5. Management has *adequate flexibility* to tailor the penalty to a specific violation by considering an employee's work record and extenuating circumstances. Progressive discipline systems with minimum and maximum penalties should provide consistent enforcement and yet allow a certain degree of flexibility when circumstances warrant.

[31]See Jill Hauser List, "In Defense of Traditional Discipline," *Personnel Administrator* (June 1986), p. 42, and Rodney P. Beary, "Discipline Policy—A Neglected Personnel Tool," *Administrative Management* (November 1985), pp. 21–24, for a discussion of some of the listed points. On occasion, employees engage in peculiar or bizarre behaviors both on and off the job. These behaviors create difficult disciplinary problems, and standard approaches to discipline may not provide guidance. For guidelines on dealing with bizarre employee behavior, see Terry L. Leap and Michael D. Crino, "How to Deal with Bizarre Employee Behavior," *Harvard Business Review* (May-June 1986), pp. 18–22.

Appeal Mechanisms

Systems of justice in democratic nations generally provide for courts of appeals. However, many organizational discipline systems in these same countries do not have established appeal mechanisms (or at least ones that employees trust); a noteworthy exception applies to unionized employees, who generally have the opinion of a neutral arbitrator at their ultimate disposal. Even when management does have an appeal mechanism, it is often based on a "trust us to be fair although we've already found you guilty" posture.

Of course, the ideal type of discipline system is one that is never called into use or, if and when it is, one that leaves the employee fully satisfied with the outcome. Unfortunately, disciplinary systems are used (and overused) and the parties involved are not always pleased with the results. Therefore, appeal mechanisms are important.

In nonunionized organizations, an appeal mechanism can be established that is satisfactory to employees if the persons hearing the appeal are totally distinct and separate from those rendering the initial decision. For large organizations, a special appeals committee consisting of middle- and upper-level managers or nonmanagerial employees may be used. If a permanent committee is not seen as desirable, then an ad hoc committee jointly selected by management and the employee may possibly be used. Nonunionized forms can also follow the lead of their unionized counterparts by instituting a formalized grievance procedure complete with binding arbitration. The composition of the appeals body, however, is not as important as its fairness in objectively hearing a case on appeal.

As a means of reducing the caseload on an appeals mechanism, management may elect to limit appeals to discharge cases. An appeals body will generally focus on whether the concepts of due process and equal protection have been followed. They may examine the evidence, testimony, and other documentation to determine whether the discharged employee was treated fairly. A well-conducted appeals process may serve to minimize problems for the company if the employee later files suit under state or federal EEO law.[32]

---

[32]For other useful articles on employee discipline and control, see Wallace Wohlking, "Effective Discipline in Employee Relations," in Mary Green Miner and John B. Miner, eds. *Policy Issues in Contemporary Personnel and Industrial Relations* (New York: Macmillan Publishing Company, 1977), pp. 447–456; Gene Booker, "Behavioral Aspects of Disciplinary Action," *Personnel Journal* (April 1969), pp. 525–529; Rodney L. Oberle, "Administering Disciplinary Actions," *Personnel Journal* (January 1978), pp. 29–31; Lawrence Steinmetz, *Managing the Marginal and Unsatisfactory Worker* (Reading, Massachusetts: Addison-Wesley Publishing Company, 1969); Hoyt Wheeler, "Punishment in Organizations: A Review, Propositions, and Research Suggestions," *The Academy of Management Review* (January 1980), pp. 123–132; B. Rosen and T. H. Jerdee, "Factors Influencing Disciplinary Judgments," *Journal of Applied Psychology*, Vol. 59 (1974), pp. 327–331; E. Walster and G. W. Walster, "Equity and Social Justice," *Journal of Social Issues*, Vol. 31 (1975), pp. 21–44; and J. D. Aram and P. F. Salipante, Jr., "An Evaluation of Organizational Due Process in the Resolution of Employee/Employer Conflict," *The Academy of Management Review*, (April 1981), pp. 197–204.

■ The Employee's Job Rights

Discharge cases often raise the question of what entitlement an employee has insofar as his or her job is concerned. Under what conditions, for example, do employees have the right to contest the employer's decision to discharge them? We have already seen that EEO laws protect persons against unfair job treatment that is rooted in race, sex, religion, color, national origin, age, handicap, or other protected characteristics. However, many individuals who are discharged cannot demonstrate discrimination as part of a protected class. Furthermore, a number of these persons are discharged for flimsy reasons or for no reason at all. In recent years, the courts in some states have begun to take a closer look at questionable discharge cases.

Essentially, an employee falls into one of three categories with respect to employment rights (or lack thereof). First, some employees have *contractual* rights to employment. Second, others are tenured employees. Finally, a large group of employees are employed *at will* and have no specific job security rights.

Contractual Rights to Employment

A worker who signs an employment contract with an employer generally has protection against unjust dismissal during the life of the contract. An employment contract stipulates the terms and conditions of the employment relationship between the worker and the employer. For instance, the employee is expected to perform a specified job in a competent and reliable manner. The employment contract may spell out the tasks, duties, and performance standards explicitly, or it may simply outline the employee's obligations in general terms. Some employment contracts may spell out, in detail, the conditions under which an employee may be dismissed during the life of the contract (e.g., failure to perform, dishonesty, or financial insolvency of the employer). For example, a secondary school teacher may sign a 10-month contract to teach mathematics and physics courses in a public high school. The contract may further require that the teacher act as an assistant track coach. Barring gross incompetence or neglect of duty, the teacher can expect to remain on the job or be paid for the academic year (10 months) unless the contract specifically delineates conditions for early dismissal.

Contracts are not one-way streets. The employer is also generally obligated to provide compensation according to the terms of the contract and must fulfill any other agreements that may have been made. Should the employer fail to allow an employee to work in accordance with the contract terms, the employee may sue for lost wages. Several universities, because of alumni pressure, have fired football coaches before their contracts have expired. In most cases, the universities paid the coaches' remaining salaries. Likewise, a coach who attempts to leave a university for a more prestigious coaching job may be obligated to reimburse the school he leaves behind. The essence of individual employment contracts is that a party may sue for breach of contract if the other party fails to fulfill its contractual obligations.

As already noted, a group of employees covered by collective bargaining agreements in unionized firms enjoy protection against unjust dismissal. Job security provisions, such as seniority clauses, also give certain employees quasi-contractual rights. Unionized employees facing discharge usually pursue their case through the grievance procedure (including arbitration) to determine if any of the collective bargaining provisions protecting job rights have been violated.

Tenured Employees

Probably the strongest form of job security and protection against unjust dismissal is afforded to tenured employees. Tenure is most commonly used in academic institutions; a prime example is college professors, who normally receive tenure after 4–7 years of service if their teaching, research, and total work record are meritorious. Tenure for university professors is awarded as a protection of academic freedom. Once tenure is received, an employee can generally be discharged only for gross incompetence, neglect of duty, or moral turpitude. Many institutions, however, reserve the right to dismiss tenured employees in the event of a financial crisis or emergency.

At-will Employees

Individuals not covered by contractual or tenure arrangements are regarded as *at-will* employees.[33] An at-will employee can be terminated by the employer for good cause, bad cause, or no cause at all. Traditionally, little legal protection for those employed at will has been available. The EEO, health and safety, and labor laws (Wagner Act, Taft-Hartley Act, and the like) prevent employers from engaging in various forms of discrimination and retaliatory actions against workers, but many people are discharged without cause and have no legal recourse. Such individuals are forced to "take their lumps" and must begin looking elsewhere for employment.

Although the common law interpretation of employment at will still favors the employer, recent court decisions and denouncements by employee advocates have created the speculation that the at-will doctrine may be eroding.[34] Unfortunately,

[33]Stephen P. Pepe and Michael A. Curley, "Fire at Will? Not Necessarily," *ABA Banking Journal* (July 1984), pp. 24–33; D. A. Cathcart and M. S. Dichter (eds.), *Employment-At-Will: A State by State Survey*, American Bar Committee on Employment and Labor Relations Law, 1983; W. J. Issacson and G. B. Axlerod, "Employment at Will: An Idea Whose Time Is Done?" *Legal Times of New York* (June 20, 1983), p. 14; I. M. Shepard and N. L. Moran, *Employment at Will: A Personnel Director's Guide* (Washington, D.C.: College and University Personnel Association, 1983); William H. Holley and Roger S. Wolters, "Employment at Will: An Emerging Issue," *Journal of Small Business* (October 1987), pp. 1–6.

[34]Terry L. Leap and Michael D. Crino, "Protecting a Bank from Punitive Damage Suits for Discharging Employees," *Banking Law Review* (May-June 1988), pp. 40–46; David L. Bacon and Angel Gomez III, "How to Prevent Wrongful Termination Lawsuits," *Personnel* (February 1988), pp. 70–72.

some employers have drawn attention to themselves by discharging employees for reasons that appear highly unreasonable and unethical by nearly anyone's standards. Not only were the tenets of due process, equal protection, and progressive discipline not followed, but some discharges were contrary to the public interest or based on malice and bad faith.

Proponents of the traditional employment-at-will position claim that employers should have the right to terminate employees as they see fit; after all, the employee also has the right to terminate an at-will employment relationship if a better employment opportunity arises. To a certain extent, this proposition assumes that an employee has the same degree of power as the employer and that employment on a new job is readily available. Obviously, this is not the case for many employees. Finding new employment may be difficult, if not impossible, for some. Factors such as age, poor economic conditions, and poor health may preclude employees from finding a new job. Although an employer is within proper bounds to discharge employees who are incompetent, unreliable, disloyal, or troublesome, there are instances in which the courts have stepped in and overturned an employer's decision to discharge at-will employees. Employees are appealing discharge decisions in record numbers. In the late 1970s there were 200 wrongful discharge suits pending in state courts. A decade later, there were an estimated 25,000 suits pending.[35] Reversals of employee discharges are usually based on one of the following reasons:[36]

1. The employee was discharged for exercising a right under a statute.
2. The employee was discharged for refusing to disobey a law when requested to do so by his or her employer.
3. The employee was discharged for "whistle blowing" when he or she reported the employer to authorities for breaking a law.
4. The employer's actions amounted to malice, bad faith, or breach of public trust.
5. The employer had created an *implied* contract of employment with the discharged employee and had breached the contract.

The first three exceptions to the employment-at-will doctrine listed fall under the umbrella of employer actions that are contrary to the public interest. These are discussed collectively, while the malice and bad faith as well as the implied contract issues are discussed separately.

Discharges Contrary to the Public Interest

By far the most common exception to the employment-at-will doctrine occurs when an employee is discharged for reasons that contravene the public interest.

---

[35]John Hoerr, "It's Getting Harder to Pass Out Pink Slips," *Business Week* (March 28, 1988), p. 68.

[36]See Sami M. Abbasi, Kenneth W. Hollman, and Joe H. Muray, "Employment at Will: An Eroding Concept in Employment Relationships," *Labor Law Journal* (January 1987), pp. 21–33; and Kenneth L. Sovereign, *Personnel Law* (Reston, Virginia: Reston Publishing Company, 1984), pp. 299–310.

The public interest may include specific statutes, accepted principles of law, high moral standards, or established interests of society. The following are examples of discharge that might violate public policy:

- Lockheed is ordered to pay $45.3 million in damages to three former employees who claimed they were wrongfully fired for questioning the safety of the giant C-5B military cargo plane. The damages were awarded by a California jury in 1990.
- An employee is discharged for filing a legitimate workers' compensation claim.
- An employee refuses to knowingly file false reports to the Environmental Protection Agency (EPA) and is fired as a result.
- An employee is summoned for jury duty, and the employer discharges him or her for missing work for 10 days.
- An employee faces dismissal for reporting details of a company's price-fixing arrangement to the Department of Justice.
- An employee refuses to dump hazardous waste material into a river and is discharged for insubordination.

Most discharges affecting the public interest rest on the issue of employee disloyalty or lack of respect toward management. Steeped in tradition, management has long been accustomed to giving orders and expecting compliant behavior from employees. Those who question management's authority, speak out against management policies and actions, or contact the authorities with details of a company's illegal actions have, in the past, placed themselves in a precarious position. However, the public interest increasingly appears to be taking precedence over management's right to rule the workplace and its employees with an iron hand.

Although an employee has the right to disobey orders that violate the law and speak up when violations occur, there are limits.[37] First, no employee has a right to divulge confidential information about legal and ethical organizational practices. Second, damaging personal accusations or slurs against management in general or specific members of management need not be tolerated if they are unfounded. Third, management still has the exclusive prerogative to plan, organize, direct, and control its legal and ethical operations without acts of insubordination or undue interference of employees. The crux of the issue here is an employee's right to stand up to management when the public interest is threatened.[38]

Malice and Bad Faith

Employee dismissals are occasionally so out of line and repugnant to a normal person's sense of decency that the courts will step in and overturn the dis-

[37]David W. Ewing, *Freedom Inside the Organization: Bringing Civil Liberties to the Workplace* (New York: McGraw-Hill Book Company, 1977), p. 109.

[38]Daniel Farber, "Free Speech Is No Crime, But It Can Still Get You Fired," *Newsday* (February 12, 1990), p. 45.

charge. Examples of discharges made in malice and bad faith might include the following:

- Mass firings of employees because of the misconduct of one employee.
- Discharging an employee for refusing to date a supervisor.
- Discharging an employee to avoid further payment of sales commissions that had already been earned.
- Discharging employees shortly before they achieved full vesting rights under a pension plan.
- Firing an employee who had a legitimate physical need to use the restroom even when the employer had a "no-restroom" policy during working hours.
- Discharging an employee suspected of theft who refused to submit to a strip search.

Organizations with any semblance of reasonable and enlightened personnel practices are not likely to find themselves being accused of malice and bad faith. However, the courts appear willing not only to examine such cases, but to reverse the employer's decision to discharge. What remains to be seen is how the courts will, in the future, interpret malice, bad faith, and actions violative of the public interest. Will the courts continue to reverse more and more at-will discharges or will they retreat to their original hands-off position? The latter seems unlikely, especially in light of legislative proposals at the state level that may give at-will employers statutory protection.[39]

The Implied Contract

Under certain conditions, an at-will employee may be inadvertently transformed into an employee who possesses certain contractual rights. The employer, because of statements made or actions taken, may have unknowingly given an employee more job security than was originally intended. Examples of situations that may create implied contract rights include the following:

- Promising an employee that he or she can expect to work for the company until reaching retirement age.
- Convincing an employee to leave a secure job by promising a better job and then failing to keep the promises after the employee is hired.
- Quoting salaries on an annual basis, which may create an implied employment contract for 1 year.
- Clauses in employee handbooks stating that employees who are not on probationary status may expect an indefinite term of employment.

A contractual relationship need not be secured in writing. If an employee is led to believe that he or she can expect permanent employment if satisfactory

---

[39]See J. W. Fenton and G. Miller, "A Comment and Reply to *Foley v. Interactive Data Corporation:* The Implied Covenant of Good Faith and Fair Dealing," *Labor Law Journal,* Vol. 41 (1990), pp. 307–310.

standards of job performance are maintained, then an implied contract may exist. Ultimately, the court hearing the wrongful discharge case will decide whether an implied contractual relationship exists between the employer and the employee. However, there are two precautionary measures that employers can take to reduce the chances of misunderstanding. First, persons conducting job interviews should be warned to avoid making promises that may not be kept. An overly zealous recruitment and selection effort may cause trouble later.[40] Realistic job previews and expectations should be emphasized. Second, a disclaimer similar to the following should be placed in the employee handbook specifically stating that the terms and provisions of such are not binding on the company and are subject to amendment:

- This manual is not a contract of employment, and we retain the right to alter this manual at any time.
- This policy does not in any way affect our right to terminate an employee for any reason, at any time, nor does it affect your right to leave at any time.[41]

A Proposal for an Employment Termination Act

At-will employees who contest their terminations have experienced different results in different states. For example, an employee in Hawaii who claimed that she was terminated because she testified in an antitrust suit was awarded over $2 million in damages. Had the case been tried in another state, the outcome might have been radically different. The plaintiff might have also been successful if the case was heard by a California, Michigan, or Illinois court. But had the case arisen in Georgia, where the employment-at-will doctrine has eroded very little, the chances of her receiving a favorable judgment would have been low. As a result of the extreme variations in the manner in which at-will cases have been adjudicated among the states, the National Conference of Commissioners on Uniform State Laws has proposed the Model Employment Termination Act (META). The fundamental provisions of META are as follows: (1) the requirement that employers provide "good cause" for termination, (2) the replacement of court (and jury) trials with private arbitration in wrongful discharge cases (the arbitrator's decision is not normally subject to court appeal), and (3) the imposition of strict limitations on employer liability for wrongful discharge Under META, an employer may terminate an employee for good cause based on either improper job-related behaviors or an employer's good-faith business judgment regarding staffing needs.

---

[40]A food service director was fired for abusing her expense account. The company claimed that she was an at-will employee. She claimed that materials provided by the company constituted a written contract and that her discharge violated that contract. A San Francisco jury awarded the employee $1.7 million. *Bulletin to Management* (Washington, D.C.: The Bureau of National Affairs, Inc., February 18, 1988), p. 55.

[41]Andrew M. Kramer, "The Hazards of Firing at Will," *The Wall Street Journal* (March 9, 1987), p. A1; Amy Dockser Marcus, "Courts Uphold Oral Pledges of Lifetime Employment," *The Wall Street Journal* (December 12, 1989), p. B1.

The National Conference of Commissioners estimates that META would cover approximately 60 million workers. Of the 2 million workers who are fired each year, up to 10 percent (200,000) would potentially benefit from a law such as META. Theodore St. Antoine, a University of Michigan law professor and nationally renowned expert on employee rights, has stated that META would represent the most significant change since the enactment of Title VII of the 1964 Civil Rights Act. The proposed law would also be of benefit to lower-income workers who do not have the financial resources to pursue a wrongful discharge suit through the court system.[42]

Worker Adjustment and Retraining Notification Act (WARN)

Plant closings and mass layoffs have become a controversial issue over the past decade. Although a majority of companies have notified their employees well in advance of plant closings and layoffs, an estimated 30 percent of firms failed to provide such notice.[43] Employers have expressed the concern that advance notice of layoffs and plant closings will result in impaired production, sabotage, or a mass exodus of employees before the facility closes. Those advocating advance notice of closings claim that relatively few employees leave before the actual closing.[44] When employees have little or no advance notice of plant closings, they are often unable to make financial and psychological adjustments to losing their jobs, and they are less likely to find new jobs before depleting their personal savings.[45] Advance-notice requirements for firms closing facilities or laying off employees en masse may also save approximately $400 million in unemployment insurance costs and may increase the earnings of displaced workers by more than $1 billion.[46]

As a result of the plight facing displaced workers, as well as the benefits that could accrue from giving advance notice to employees of plant closings, Congress passed the Worker Adjustment and Retraining Notification Act (WARN). WARN requires that companies with more than 100 full-time employees give a 60-day notice of certain plant closings and mass layoffs. Notice is required if a total or partial plant closing will result in the displacement of 50 or more employees at one

[42]Jeremy B. Fox and Hugh D. Hindman, "The Model Employment Termination Act: Provisions and Discussion," unpublished paper (1991), and Aaron Bernstein, " 'Tell It to the Arbitrator,' " *Business Week* (November 4, 1991), p. 109.

[43]U.S. Congress General Accounting Office, "GAO's Preliminary Analysis of U.S. Business Closures and Layoffs During 1983 and 1984," cited in U.S. Congress Office of Technology Assessment, *Plant Closing: Advance Notice and Rapid Response* (Washington, D.C.: U.S. Government Printing Office, 1986), p. 8.

[44]See Paul O. Flaim and Ellen Sehgal, "Displaced Workers of 1979–83: How Well Have They Fared?" *Monthly Labor Review* (June 1985), p. 3.

[45]For a discussion on the impact of plant closings on workers, see Carolyn C. Perrucci, Robert Perrucci, Dena B. Tang, and Harry R. Tang, *Plant Closings: International Context and Social Costs* (New York: Aldine De Gruyter, 1988).

[46]Comments of Conte Sivio, *Congressional Record*, No. 105 (July 13, 1988), p. H5507. Cited in Paul D. Staudohar, "New Plant Closing Law Aids Workers in transition," *Personnel Journal* (January 1989), p. 88.

location. WARN also requires notice for mass layoffs for 6 months or more involving at least 50 employees who constitute more than 33 percent of the plant's workforce, or if the layoff involves more than 500 employees.

■ When All Else Fails: Discharge

Discharge has been regarded as the "capital punishment" of organizational life. Although this term is perhaps too harsh to accurately characterize the fate of an employee who is fired, it is the maximum penalty that an employer can impose. From the preceding discussion, it may appear that the employer is taking a great legal risk in discharging an employee. Generally, this is not true if certain procedures are followed:

1. Make sure that you have supporting evidence and documentation.[47]
   a. Adhere to established progressive discipline procedures.
   b. If your firm is unionized, follow the spirit and language of the collective bargaining agreement.
   c. Put the conditions and terms of the discharge in writing.
   d. Explain your reasons for discharge in a specific fashion. Glittering generalities such as "you didn't work out" will not provide much support in a court of law or with the EEOC. Here is where you can be thankful for good performance appraisal systems and counseling sessions.
2. Respect the dignity of the employee. Avoid anger, personal confrontations, or vendettas. Specifics surrounding a discharge should be treated as confidential information.
3. Suggest other avenues of employment if the reason for discharge will allow. Be extremely careful, however, about writing positive letters or recommendations that are not indicative of an employee's job performance.
4. If a formal grievance procedure exits, make the employee aware that it can be used for possible appeals.

If the above guidelines are followed, the employer will minimize the chances of encountering and perhaps losing a wrongful discharge suit.[48]

When an employee is terminated for misconduct or incompetence, personnel/human resource managers must be especially careful about releasing unfavorable information surrounding the incident. The circumstances surrounding the discharge of an employee should be held in the strictest confidence, and supervisors should be warned to avoid spreading sensitive information to employees who are not involved in a disciplinary incident. Personnel/human resource managers and

[47]Daniel M. Shidler, "Documenting Disciplinary Situations," *Supervisory Management* (July 1989), pp. 15–24.

[48]See Gary S. Marx, "Justifying a Termination," *Management World* (November-December 1986), pp. 20–21, for a discussion of many of these points.

supervisors who pass truthful, but unfavorable, information about a former employee to another firm whose personnel staff has made an inquiry about a job applicant are generally protected. The unfavorable information that is conveyed must be (1) truthful (with documentation to substantiate the veracity of the information), (2) communicated in good faith, with no intent to create unnecessary harm to a former employee, and (3) transmitted through proper business channels and directed only to persons who have a legitimate need for access to such information. During the 1980s and early 1990s, an increasing number of defamation of character lawsuits were spawned by persons who received unfavorable recommendations from former employers. Unfortunately, a number of companies have either stopped providing such information altogether or are only willing to provide verification of an individual's job title and employment dates. Such information is of little help to another firm that is trying to make an informed hiring decision. In addition, firms that hire a person who poses a danger to other employees or to customers may become embroiled in a negligent hiring suit. Such suits have arisen when a company fails to check the background of a person who is later discovered to have a history of assaults. As long as a company is aware of the legal doctrines associated with libel and slander cases in its state, employment information about job applicants can be exchanged with little fear of legal repercussions.[49]

■ Summary and Conclusions

This chapter has presented an overview of the sources and types of disciplinary problems, the mechanisms for dealing with disciplinary incidents, and the legal considerations surrounding discharge cases. Many organizations have adopted a "firefighting" approach to dealing with employee problems as they arise. We have attempted to stress a preventive approach based on sound personnel policies and practices coupled with a progressive discipline system. Emphasis should be placed on selecting, training, and rewarding employees rather than punishing poor performance or unacceptable behavior. The ideal situation would be to establish a well-designed, progressive discipline system that is *never* used.

The discipline and control function in modern day organizations has gone well beyond the dictatorial, "fire now, ask questions later" posture of the 1920s and early 1930s. Labor unions and protective labor legislation affecting unionized employees represented the major first step in protecting employment rights.

---

[49]See J. W. Fenton, Jr., "Negligent Hiring/Retention Adds to Human Resource Woes," *Personnel Journal*, Vol. 69 (1990), pp. 62–73, D. J. Petersen and D. Massengill, "The Negligent Hiring Doctrine—A Growing Dilemma for Employers," *Employee Relations Law Journal*, Vol. 15 (1990), pp. 419–431, R. B. Jacobs, "Defamation and Negligence in the Workplace," *Labor Law Journal*, Vol. 40 (1989), pp. 567–574; C. Atwood and James M. Neel, "New Law Suits Expand Employer Liability," *HR Magazine*, Vol. 10 (1990), pp. 74–75; and D. Yulish and B. Heshizer, "Defamation in the Workplace," *Labor Law Journal*, Vol. 40 (1989), pp. 355–360.

Later, civil service rules, EEO legislation, and other laws expanded and reinforced protection afforded to employees. Common law doctrines such as employment at will have favored the employee in more instances than ever before.

Today, employers as a group seem to be exhibiting greater social responsibility toward employees and their problems than in the past. This trend has been most markedly demonstrated by employee assistance programs, which provide counseling for personal, domestic, financial, and alcohol and drug problems. Perhaps also, spillover effects from the Japanese management concept of lifetime employment are gradually making inroads in the United States, with companies now willing to become involved and to help with employee problems.

Nevertheless, both employers *and* employees occasionally exhibit gross insensitivity toward their responsibilities to each other. Employers, in some instances, still treat workers with a lack of dignity, fail to respect even the most fundamental notions of due process and fairness, and show little concern for employee welfare. Likewise, employees periodically fail to fulfill their job responsibilities, create trouble with supervisors and co-workers, and become a thorn in the side of the company insofar as harmony and productivity are concerned. Under these circumstances, disciplinary concepts and systems are important.

■ Questions

1. What general obligation does an employer have to an employee?

2. What general obligation does an employee have to the organization?

3. Compare and contrast the positive, affirmative, and progressive approaches to employee discipline and control.

4. What is meant by the concepts of due process and equal protection? How would you define these terms?

5. What is meant by an at-will employee? Does the employer have unrestricted rights to fire an at-will employee? If not, what restrictions are there on an employer?

6. In what ways can the organization create its own disciplinary problems? What can the company do to minimize disciplinary problems?

☐ APPLICATIONS AND CASE EXERCISES

1. What is your opinion concerning the status of at-will employees? What reasons have the courts used to overturn at-will employee discharges? Do you believe that these reasons offer legitimate protection to employees or are unnecessary interference with the employer-employee relationship?

2. Discuss the role of preventive discipline practices. Do you feel that a preventive approach is feasible in many organizations? What factors might mitigate against the successful use of preventive discipline?

3. Interview a local personnel/human resource director or small business owner about any disciplinary problems recently experienced and the procedures set down to deal with them. How sound do you feel these procedures are?

4. A San Francisco man who charged that he was wrongfully terminated by Shell Oil Company because he is homosexual was awarded $5.3 million by a superior court judge in Alameda County, California. The judge issued her verdict after a 2-week trial, saying that the man had been fired "for private homosexual conduct occurring away from his employment," not for unsatisfactory job performance. This case illustrates the dilemma that companies and individual employees face when a manager finds certain off-duty conduct to be unacceptable. Do you believe the verdict in this case was reasonable? Why or why not?[50]

5. It is Monday morning and Marcia Foley, the plant personnel/human resource officer, is sitting at her desk considering a disciplinary problem. Recently there have been a number of incidents where employees have been leaving work anywhere from 20 to 40 minutes early on Fridays. Because these early departures violate company policy, and in order to avoid punishment, the employees have asked friends to punch their timecards. This means another employee also is breaking a company rule.

    This behavior has become more and more widespread over the last few months. Reports from supervisors indicate that the location of the plant and traffic patterns at the regular quitting time make it difficult to get across town, where many employees live. It seems that leaving 20 minutes early saves more than 1 hour of driving time on Fridays. This justification makes sense to Ms. Foley, and she is reluctant to discipline these employees. However, something must be done or the credibility of the entire disciplinary system may be compromised.

    Over the weekend she considered a statement made by her assistant that the problem lies not with the employees, although they are clearly violating company policy, but rather with the company in not recognizing an important employee preference for an earlier quitting time on Fridays. Ms. Foley has decided to propose to her boss that 10 minutes be added to each of the other four workdays in order to allow employees to leave 40 minutes early on Fridays.

    This problem has caused Ms. Foley to wonder if there are any other company work rules that could be changed to the advantage of both the company and the employees. She has become intrigued by the idea that some discipline problems could be prevented by a more sensible approach to work rules.

    a. What do you think of Ms. Foley's suggestion? Do you think that she is catering to employees who should know better or suggesting a sensible change in the company's policy?

    b. Are there any examples that you can think of from your own experience, either at work or in the classroom, where rules were unreasonable? What were they? Did they create unnecessary problems? What changes in the rules would you suggest to your supervisor or teacher to solve the problems?

[50]"Man Awarded $5.3 Million," *Los Angeles Times*, reprinted in *The Greenville News* (June 18, 1991), p. 6A.

14 ∎

Employee Health, Safety, and Well-Being

■ LEARNING OBJECTIVES

After reading this chapter you should understand:

1. The importance of safeguarding employee health and safety in the workplace.
2. The protection afforded workers, and the obligations of employers under the Occupational Safety and Health Act.
3. The major emerging issues concerning employee health, safety and well-being.

■ INTRODUCTORY VIGNETTE

Adolph Coors Company: A Nationally Recognized Wellness Program

In 1989, Adolph Coors Company received the Health Action Leadership Award for having the nation's leading employee health program. That same year the company received top honors from the Association for Fitness and Business. These awards were well deserved. Since 1981, when the company first began its wellness program, Adolph Coors Company has created a pretty impressive track record of success. It has done so by making employee physical and mental health a corporate priority.

For many companies, employee wellness is a program separate from daily operations. Employees use the program typically on their own time, and the companies hope for the best. At Coors that isn't the case. The employee wellness program is integrated so well with other aspects of the company's safety and health effort that it is impossible to separate one from the other. The redesign of a work station to reduce injuries is as much a part of the wellness effort as it is a part of the safety program. This corporate wellness culture can be traced back to the efforts of William Coors, CEO of Adolph Coors Company. In 1971, Mr. Coors began to work for a health promotion program. It took 10 years

This profile was drawn from: Shari Caudron, "The Wellness Payoff, *Personnel Journal* (July 1990), pp. 55–60; Paul Perry, "Corporate Cardio-Fitness; Mending Hearts Is Good Business," *American Health* (November 1990), p. 33; Shari Caudron, "Wellness Works," *Industry Week* (February 4, 1991), pp. 22–26; and The Bureau of National Affairs, Inc., "Wellness: Curing Company Ills," *Bulletin to Management* (October 10, 1991), p. 320.

before the company's on-site wellness center opened. Since then it has become clear that health promotion is the primary motivation of the effort. Health promotion is so much a part of the company culture that in 1986 this phrase was added to the corporate values statement: "We . . . encourage wellness in body, mind, and spirit for all employees." The substantial cost savings realized from this successful program speaks for itself. Cost savings appear to be a natural by-product of healthy employees.

Mr. Coors prefers to think of the physical facility as a "learning center" rather than a fitness center. Employees learn how to lead healthier lives, preventing illnesses and injuries. Management believes the program works for a number of reasons: wellness is a stated corporate priority, wellness is considered a family affair, a healthy lifestyle is made convenient for employees, participants are aggressively screened for health problems, and the program is revised as unmet health needs are discovered or at the request of employees. In addition, Coors is not reluctant to request outside evaluation of its program. A recent cost-benefit study by the University of Oregon's Graduate School of Management is an example of the company's interest in obtaining objective data regarding the wellness program.

Those objective data are indeed impressive. Forty percent of its employees regularly use the company wellness program. Health savings to the company approached $3.2 million in 1991. That same year, the program's budget was only about $500,000, including salaries for six full-time staff and a manager. In 1990, Coors's cardiac arrest rehabilitation center returned employees who had suffered heart attacks to work 5 months earlier than average. The early return to work for these employees realized $600,000 in annual savings. By the late 1980s, it was estimated that Coors saw a return of $6.15 for every dollar spent on wellness.

■ A Statistical Summary

As a backdrop to the discussion on employee safety and health, the following statistics should be kept in mind:[1]

- Estimates range as high as 12,000 work-related deaths per year.
- In the United States there are approximately 6.8 million work-related illnesses and injuries per year.
- Approximately 60.4 million work days are lost each year because of occupational injury and illness.

[1]More detailed information can be found in The Bureau of National Affairs, Inc., "New BLS Statistics Show 6.8 Million Workplace Illnesses and Injuries Recorded in 1990," *BNAC Communicator* (Winter 1992), p. 6. Albert P. Opdyke, and Jan M. Thayer, "The Work Environment," *Personnel Journal* (February 1987), pp. 37–42; and William Serrin, "The Wages of Work," *The Nation* (January 28, 1991), pp. 80–83.

- From 70,000 to 80,000 of the workers injured will sustain some form of permanent injury because of an industrial accident.
- Direct and indirect costs associated with industrial accidents total approximately $33 billion for a typical year.
- Approximately 400,000 employees annually develop diseases that were very likely caused or worsened by exposure to various toxic substances on the job, of whom 100,000 will eventually die from their occupationally contracted diseases.
- An untold number of employees will suffer from health problems associated with stress that was created, at least partially, by job-related factors.

■ The Historical Scenario

The Industrial Revolution, with its mechanization, efficient production processes, and factories, unquestionably benefited Western civilization. The harnessing of energy sources, the development of new techniques of mass production, and huge investments in capital equipment created jobs and products that improved standards of living. Unlike capital, however, which was an expensive and scarce resource, labor was inexpensive and abundant. Consequently, some employers took workers for granted and ignored health and safety in the plant. New employees were often young, strong, rapidly trained, and plentiful. Unfortunately, there were instances where human suffering, even when avoidable, was largely ignored. Because of machinery speedups, poor lighting and ventilation, unsafe equipment, employee negligence, and inadequate training, the number of industrial deaths and accidents reached unacceptable levels. Further, those seriously injured often could not find gainful employment, and others were forced to turn to less lucrative employment. Additionally, employers sometimes discharged injured employees without paying their medical bills.

A system of common law redress, developed in England and followed in the United States, assisted employees who were injured on the job. This system required that the injured employee prove employer negligence in order to receive damages from the employer. In response to charges of negligence, three common law defenses that were used by employers proved effective in preventing injured employees from obtaining compensatory damages. The first, the *assumption of risk* defense, acknowledges that some jobs are inherently more dangerous than others and that employees in an explicit or implicit way assume the known, but not hidden, risks. To support such a defense, the courts assumed that employees in high-risk jobs would be paid more than others. The second common law defense was the *fellow servant rule*. Employers are not responsible for the negligence of fellow employees who injure other employees, provided that the former were carefully selected. However, employers could be held responsible for compensatory damages when other employees are negligently selected or when injuries are caused by negligent supervisors. The third defense is known as *contributory negligence.* Employers using this defense admit to being negligent, but escape or minimize legal responsibility because the injured employee was also guilty of negligence.

These defenses made it difficult for an injured employee to collect damages. The common law remedy for injured employees was inadequate for other reasons as well. Proving negligence in court under the strict rules of evidence was difficult, and lawyers, whose legal fees depended upon winning the suit, only reluctantly represented injured employees. Many witnesses, fearing loss of their jobs and blacklisting, would not testify against their employer. Months, and even years, passed before a jury trial could be scheduled. Unable to await the outcome of a lengthy court battle, injured employees would sometimes settle for smaller sums of money than they might have been awarded. When an injured employee won, one third of the award, or more, went to attorneys for legal fees and expenses. Because such fees were not large, it was usually the less capable legal talent that was available to employees.

Because of the infrequency of employee success in the courts and the apparently unlimited supply of labor immigrating to the United States, there seemed little incentive for some employers to take steps to reduce the number of accidents. Furthermore, the large corporation impersonalized the working relationship between stockholders, management, and employees; in such an industrial environment, an injury simply became another statistic. Obviously, for those employers who did not choose to act responsibly regarding employee safety, something had to be done. Reform of the system, however, was complicated by the form occupational maladies could take. Many on-the-job injuries (e.g., chemical explosions) are dramatic, patently visible, and easily linked to the workplace. On the other hand, some occupational disabilities and illnesses, such as cancer and lung diseases caused by chemical carcinogens, develop over an extended period of time, and it is more difficult to prove their link with hazards in the workplace. The development of occupational diseases or disabilities is not usually noticeable at the outset, and employers often cite genetic and environmental factors not associated with the workplace as causes. Only recently have scientists and employers become aware of the many chronic health problems linked to certain jobs. Nevertheless, a great deal of uncertainty surrounds many health problems because conclusively linking occupational disabilities to a job performed years earlier requires careful study. Additionally, these research results are often disputed by other experts in the field.

Respiratory disease and emphysema were risks that many coal miners knowingly accepted to support their families. Coal miners developed black lung disease, and persons working in textile plants often developed brown lung disease. Today, research data have led to the suspicion that many chronic disabilities afflicting older workers are due to exposure on the job; for example, heart disease, lung cancer, and other disabilities are tied to the inhalation of coal, cotton, and chemical dusts. Workers consistently inhaling lead and mercury fumes for several decades developed brain disease. More recently, exposure to continual loud noise has been linked to occupational and stress-related ailments. The chemical revolution of the past 40 years has exposed workers and persons living near petrochemical plants to increasing health risks from toxic materials and pollutants. The magnitude of these (and other) risks is, however, unknown.

In order to compensate workers with work-related injuries, European countries enacted no-fault laws. These laws were sporadically duplicated in the United States. Washington, in 1911, was the first state to enact a no-fault workers' compensation statute, which shifted responsibility for injuries from employees to employers. The idea was that accidents and illnesses are a business expense, and, as such, associated costs should be paid by employers and included in the pricing of the product. Today, all states provide workers' compensation benefits, and in a few instances, federal laws fix responsibility. Workers' compensation benefits cover hospital costs, medical care, prosthetic devices, permanent injuries, and weekly support stipends even when employees are negligent.

As medical knowledge and the political power of unions expanded, occupational disease and illness benefits slowly became available under the workers' compensation statutes. However, occupational disability coverage under workers' compensation laws has been, on the whole, inadequate because of the long period of time that elapses before an occupational disability is recognized. Unfortunately, a few states grant benefits only for specifically listed disabilities. In addition, a few irresponsible employers, spurred by the need to maximize profits, did little to control the working environment and reduce accidents. Safety and health were ignored unless either costs and production were affected or management was forced by law to make improvements. Unfortunately, the costs borne by firms to compensate injured workers were frequently less than the costs necessary to prevent accidents and safeguard health. Unions, through the AFL-CIO, have lobbied for laws to ensure worker safety. International and local unions have also sought to provide additional protection via collective bargaining agreements. Insurance companies have pressured employers to make safety and health reforms and have assisted them in these efforts. The workers' compensation laws entitle injured employees to designated medical benefits and weekly stipends, but employers are not required to hire health-impaired employees, retain the services of those injured on the job, or provide sick leave and health insurance beyond workers' compensation.

■ Causes of Accidents and Occupational Diseases

Figure 14-1 provides an overview of the employee safety and health picture. Job-related injuries can be traced to unsafe conditions in the work environment, unsafe behaviors of employees, or a combination thereof. Neither the presence of unsafe conditions nor unsafe employee behaviors, however, necessarily mean that an on-the-job accident will occur. Employees may manage to survive hazardous conditions at work or unsafe behaviors for months or even years without an accident. Even when accidents occur (defined here as unplanned or unanticipated

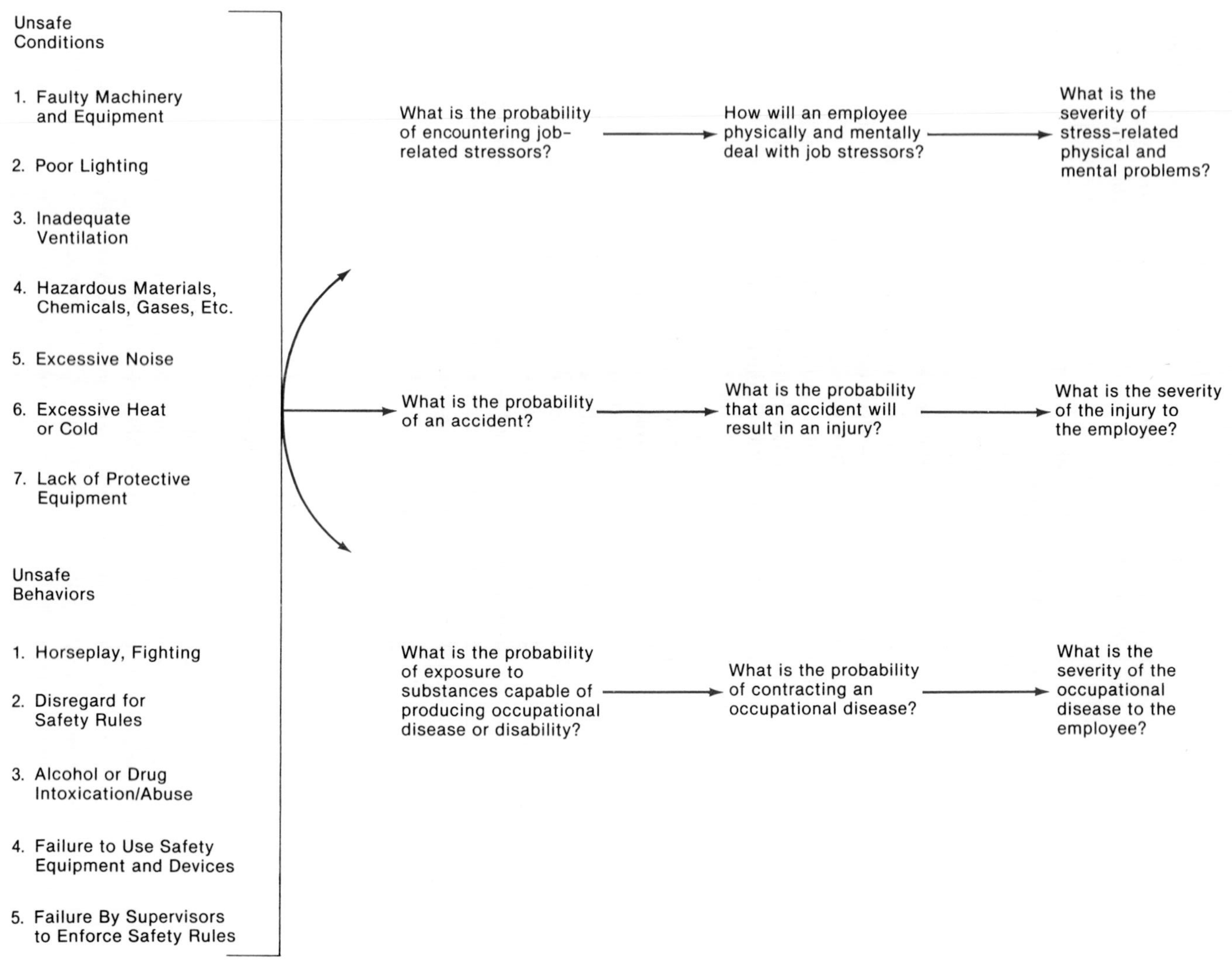

Unsafe
Conditions

1. Faulty Machinery
   and Equipment

2. Poor Lighting

3. Inadequate
   Ventilation

4. Hazardous Materials,
   Chemicals, Gases, Etc.

5. Excessive Noise

6. Excessive Heat
   or Cold

7. Lack of Protective
   Equipment

Unsafe
Behaviors

1. Horseplay, Fighting

2. Disregard for
   Safety Rules

3. Alcohol or Drug
   Intoxication/Abuse

4. Failure to Use Safety
   Equipment and Devices

5. Failure By Supervisors
   to Enforce Safety Rules

What is the probability
of encountering job-
related stressors?

How will an employee
physically and mentally
deal with job stressors?

What is the
severity of
stress-related
physical and
mental problems?

What is the probability
of an accident?

What is the probability
that an accident will
result in an injury?

What is the severity
of the injury to
the employee?

What is the probability
of exposure to
substances capable of
producing occupational
disease or disability?

What is the probability
of contracting an
occupational disease?

What is the
severity of the
occupational
disease to the
employee?

FIGURE 14-1   An Overview of Employee Safety and Health

events causing bodily injury or property damage), the employee may escape without injury. When an injury is sustained, its severity may range from a minor abrasion to death. The severity of an accident can be assessed in a number of ways, for example, medical expenses incurred, work time lost, costs associated with hiring and training new employees to replace those who are injured, increased workers' compensation and health insurance costs, and pain, suffering, and mental anguish.

Poorly designed jobs, faulty equipment, employer and employee negligence, inadequate training, and a lack of safety inspections encourage work-related accidents. Accidents common to the working environment are burns, electric shock, cuts, bruises, broken bones, loss of limbs, eyesight, or hearing, and sprains. Such accidents are often avoided by more experienced, better-trained, and more cautious employees. The causes of industrial accidents and occupational diseases are negligence, fire, explosion, exposure to electrical hazards, airborne particles, aerosols, lifting equipment, heat, vibration, and noise.

Employers and employees share responsibility for many injuries. For example, employees supplied with safety equipment, such as hard hats and goggles, may refuse or forget to wear them. Employers may fail to enforce plant rules or periodically check equipment for safety hazards. The number of accidents is also likely to increase when employees work continually without rest and for long periods of time.

Occupational diseases are often more difficult to deal with than occupational injuries because they develop slowly over a long span of time. Furthermore, workers have different tolerance levels for exposure to toxic substances and are exposed to hazardous substances away from work. Occupational hazards fall into four risk categories:[2]

1. Physical—heat, radiation, low level electromagnetic energy, noise, and vibration.
2. Chemical—carcinogens, dusts, poisonous gases, and toxic chemicals and waste.
3. Biological—insects, fungi, and bacteria.
4. Stress—work, physical, chemical, and psychological pressures faced on the job (to be discussed separately).

We have come to realize, for example, that excessive and constant noise, long ignored as a source of problems in the past, can lead to serious health problems. Noise may lead to neurologic, cardiovascular, and endocrinological changes, and produce signs of stress and fatigue. Many blue-collar employees work in areas where noise levels exceed 90 decibels, which can cause loss of hearing after prolonged exposure. Textile and woodworking facilities are examples of working environments where noise can exceed safe levels. When safety- and health-threatening situations are identified, the firm can replace, modify, or muffle noisy

[2]Nicholas A. Ashford, *Crisis in the Workplace* (Cambridge, Massachusetts: MIT Press, 1976), p. 73.

equipment, provide ear plugs, redesign the job, or shorten exposure time by job rotation. Sometimes the costs of alleviating noise stress may be small, while the returns are considerable.

Occupational exposures may be more frequently associated with the leading causes of death than is generally realized. For example, researchers believe that some cancers and hypertension are due to occupational hazards and stress. Further, the proliferation of chemicals in the working and living environments, particularly chlorinated and synthetic organic chemicals, creates serious long- and short-term problems. Examples include carbon tetrachloride-induced liver and kidney damage in plastics and dry cleaning workers and bladder cancer in paint manufacturing workers and textile dyers from the dye auramine.[3] Because the link between a worker's exposure to toxic substances and health problems is often obscured by the passage of time and events, it may be difficult to establish employer liability when it does exist.

■ The Occupational Safety and Health Act of 1970 (OSHA)

The Inspiration

OSHA, passed by Congress in 1970 and administered by the U.S. Secretary of Labor, was enacted to hold corporations responsible for protecting worker safety and health. This was deemed necessary because existing state and federal laws did not adequately protect workers in the plant. Workers' compensation laws focused on reimbursing employees after they were injured rather than on preventing on-the-job accidents, injuries, and occupational diseases.[4] State regulation of employers operating nationally and internationally often proved unsatisfactory. Federal legislation was very limited in scope and protected few workers. A comprehensive federal law was necessary. OSHA represented the federal government's response to that need. OSHA evaluates the health and safety implications of technological changes, establishes minimum industrial safety standards, promotes research on safety in the workplace, and encourages industry cooperation with state officials. Although OSHA is a federal law, it allows states to regulate workplace health and safety when state standards equal or exceed federal standards.

---

[3]See Robert Lewy, "The Fundamentals of Health," in Donald F. Tapley, Robert J. Weiss, Thomas Q. Morris, Genell J. Subak-Sharpe, and Diane M. Goetz (eds.), *The Columbia University College of Physicians and Surgeons Complete Home Medical Guide* (New York: Crown Publishers, Inc., 1985), pp. 315–319, for information on the relationships between many common workplace chemicals and diseases, illnesses, and injury.

[4]See William P. Curington, "Federal Versus State Regulation: The Early Years of OSHA," *Social Science Quarterly* (June 1988), pp. 341–360.

Coverage and Scope

OSHA established two categories of employer responsibility: a broad duty to provide a working climate free of known and suspected hazards and a specific duty to follow the standards created by OSHA administrators. Employers are obliged under the general duty clause to create a work environment "free from recognized hazards that . . . are likely to cause death or serious physical harm," at least until specific standards are approved.

Legislative history and the broad duty imposed upon employers by OSHA lead to differences of opinion regarding congressional intent and the propriety of regulations designed to implement the act. Looking at the general duty clause, employers are held responsible for "hazards" at work that should be "recognized" as leading to "death or serious physical harm." Employees may refuse to work when death or serious injury is imminent.[5] Employers are not responsible for the prevention or elimination of unknown hazards, nor can they be made responsible for hazards that cannot be reasonably eliminated. Also, employers are not usually held responsible when employees disregard safety rules that are consistently enforced.

Employees or unions can complain to the Department of Labor, which will undertake an immediate investigation. Should the investigation show immediate danger, a court order can be sought to shut down the plant or otherwise remove the danger; the Secretary of Labor, however, is not authorized to order permanent plant closure. Fines are also levied against companies found violating safety and health regulations. In 1986, Union Carbide was fined $1.3 million for 221 health and safety violations, 127 of which were described as "willful disregard of the law," at its Institute, West Virginia, chemical plant. Union Carbide eventually agreed to pay $405,500 for the violations.[6] In 1987, Chrysler Corporation was fined and paid a record $1.5 million for 811 safety violations at its Newark, Delaware, automobile assembly plant. In the words of OSHA Administrator John A. Pendergrass, the Chrysler fine was "the only possible response to a totally unacceptable situation." OSHA said that it found unsafe arsenic and lead levels in several areas, inadequate warnings to employees of the health effects of substances in the workplace, and violations of rules covering safety equipment, fire protection, and electrical protection.[7] In 1988, OSHA agreed to a $975,000 payment and a commitment to redesign jobs to address repetitive trauma disorders from IBP, the nation's largest meatpacker. The original OSHA fine was $5.7 million for hazardous working conditions. Earlier in 1988, OSHA fined John Morrell & Company $4.33 million

[5]The legitimacy of this OSHA regulation, whereby employees can refuse to work when death or serious injury is imminent, was upheld by the Supreme Court in *Whirlpool v. Marshall*, 100 S. Ct. 883 (1980).

[6]"Union Carbide Settles Suit, Agrees to Pay Record Fine," *Anderson Independent-Mail* (July 25, 1987), p. 1c.

[7]"Chrysler Hit with $1.5 Million Fine," *The Greenville News* (July 7, 1987), p. 1D. In response to the record fine Chrysler officials stated that most of the violations were minor electrical and mechanical safeguarding discrepancies.

for many of the same conditions found at IBP.[8] In 1991, CITGO Petroleum Corporation agreed to a $6 million settlement with OSHA after a Lake Charles, Louisiana, refinery explosion that killed six workers.[9]

The most complex and contentious problems involve the thousands of safety and health standards that must be established and the endless task of adding, modifying, and revoking existing standards. The meeting of these standards can place a financial burden on employers. Small- and medium-sized firms are particularly concerned with the costs of meeting many standards because the financial burden can be significant. To assist smaller businesses and those financially unable to meet established standards, OSHA requires the Small Business Administration to provide assistance.

Although not mandated by OSHA, employers believe that a cost-benefit analysis should be required before definitive and realistic standards can be set. In essence, a cost-benefit analysis involves a comparison of the cost of implementing improved health and safety standards with the advantages (e.g., improved worker health, fewer lost-day injuries, etc.) of such standards. It is not surprising that questions relating to cost-benefit analysis came before the Supreme Court in 1980.[10] The Secretary of Labor tightened the standard for exposure to airborne benzene, a carcinogenic agent. According to the Supreme Court, the secretary's action was improper because a determination was not made that the stricter standard was "reasonably necessary." This decision is important, because it requires that specific standards be justified and that evidence be presented to support the unacceptability of an industrial risk. Prior to this decision, the Secretary of Labor had shifted the burden of proof to employers, requiring them to show that the existing level of exposure to known carcinogens was safe for workers. With this decision, the Supreme Court placed the burden of proof upon the Secretary of Labor to establish need for a stricter standard (i.e., lower level) of exposure. In essence, the legislative call for a reasonably safe workplace does not require a risk-free environment. However, the Supreme Court in 1981 recognized the problem and ruled that the Secretary of Labor did not have to undertake cost-benefit analysis to set specific standards for known toxic agents, although the use of the cost-benefit technique of evaluation was not ruled out. Given the current state of knowledge, the Supreme Court noted that cost-benefit analysis provided less protection for employees than had been contemplated by Congress. The Secretary of Labor is required, however, to prove that strict standards are reasonably necessary. Unfortunately, the establishment of specific standards for toxic agents is far from scientific, especially because of the difficulty associated with measuring the long-term effect on exposed employees.

[8]Matt Yancey, "Meatpacker Agrees to Landmark Pact on Job Conditions," The Associated Press, *Anderson Independent-Mail* (November 24, 1988), p. 8D.

[9]The Bureau of National Affairs, Inc., "Workplace Accidents = Costly Mistakes," Bulletin to Management (September 12, 1991), pp. 281–282.

[10]*Industrial Union Department, AFL-CIO v. American Petroleum Institute*, 100 S. Ct. (1980).

Administration and Enforcement

The administration and formulation of OSHA have been assigned to four agencies. It is administered by the Secretary of Labor via the Occupational Safety and Health Administration, which can establish specific health and safety standards, investigate work sites, and rule on complaints. The administration can establish three types of standards—permanent, interim, and temporary (when conditions are dangerous).

An independent agency, the Occupational Safety and Health Review Commission, functions in a quasi-judicial appellate capacity, ruling upon challenges to OSHA decisions. Employers cited or penalized by OSHA have 15 days to contest rulings by petitioning the Review Commission. The Review Commission appoints a hearing officer, who reviews the facts and renders a decision. The hearing officer's report is final unless challenged by one or more members of the Review Commission. Review Commission orders can be challenged in federal court.

The National Institute for Occupational Safety and Health (NIOSH) provides research support, helps to develop specific standards, and trains professional personnel (physicians and other health professionals). NIOSH is also required to list all known toxic substances, and the levels that are damaging to health.

Section 7 of the act established the National Advisory Committee on Occupational Safety and Health (NACOSH), composed of employer, union, public, and professional members. NACOSH advises the Secretaries of Labor and Health and Human Services (HHS) on administrative matters.

Employers must keep accurate records of injuries and disabilities, from which the Secretary of Labor prepares statistical data and develops inspection priorities. Failure to keep accurate records may result in a fine. Originally, federal inspectors, called *compliance officers*, were authorized to inspect corporate premises and machinery at reasonable hours without giving advance notice. However, in 1978, the Supreme Court ruled that unannounced, warrantless inspections violated the Fourth Amendment and placed OSHA compliance officers in the position of having to obtain a search warrant if the company requests one prior to an inspection. After inspection, the compliance officer forwards a report to the area director of OSHA, who has 6 months to decide whether a violation has occurred. When imminent danger exists, the Secretary of Labor can seek an injunction in court before a decision is made. Employers cited must be given an opportunity to correct the unsatisfactory conditions of work. Civil and criminal penalties can be imposed upon employers who continue to violate the law.

Issues and Controversies

The controversy surrounding OSHA at times appears to be limitless. Much of the criticism is based on the strictness and extensiveness of the standards promulgated under the act, the necessity for cost-benefit analysis, and the relationships between OSHA standards, state regulations, and collective bargaining agreements.

Safety Standards

More than 80 percent of the standards adopted (called *consensus standards*) had been endorsed by professional organizations, unions, and employers even before OSHA officials acted; yet employers often criticize them. Some employers claim that the standards have been approved too quickly, unnecessarily, and without considering the remedial costs.

Congress intentionally refused to establish specific standards of health and safety, imposing instead a general duty upon employers to create reasonably safe working environments. By so doing, Congress realized that the scientific and professional communities would have to establish specific standards, a difficult assignment because of constant technological change and the paucity of information regarding certain work hazards. Furthermore, Congress provided little or no legislative direction, a move that was tantamount to delegating legislative authority to responsible administrating agencies and courts. As a result, the authority delegated to OSHA administrators was considerable for the enforcement of the act.

Although OSHA might be improved, regulation by properly organized and staffed administrative agencies appears preferable to regulation through the painfully slow process of filing civil and criminal court proceedings after employees die or become injured on the job.

Although critics will disagree with many OSHA decisions—some standards are extreme, duplicative, conflicting, unjustifiably costly, and improperly promulgated—many criticisms are unfair and needlessly hostile. A charge of unwarranted government interference is always made when costs for correcting years of neglect are high. Many employers take the position that to be profit oriented is rational and healthy for society, and that government regulation is bad and unnecessary. On the other hand, proponents of employee well-being assert that to view health and safety measures as drains on profits is to ignore the welfare of workers, as well as the societal costs (lost wages, and thus tax income to the government, costs of supporting disabled and sick workers). Unfortunately, however, these latter costs do not directly affect the employer.

The congressional record fails to provide guidance, partly because much less was known about industrial health and safety in 1970 when OSHA was passed. The general duty requirement was, at that time, the best congressional guidance to be offered. For example, what is a reasonably safe place to work? Can there be unanimous agreement, except at the extremes, as to what is or is not safe? Agreement is possible where the workplace is obviously dangerous and the cost of correction is minimal. For the most part, disagreement is inevitable, with employer, employee, and union self-interest dictating the position adopted regarding the safety of the work environment. Should employers be cited for violations when no injury is reported? Should specific employers be aware of hazards before being cited by OSHA, or is industrywide recognition sufficient to warrant citation? Should worker safety and health be subjected to cost-benefit analysis, or is such analysis to be regarded as inhumane because one cannot reduce employee health and safety to an economic, dollars-and-cents analysis?

Cost-Benefit Analysis

A concern assuming enormous proportions is the issue of cost-benefit analysis. Supporters of cost-benefit analysis point out that it is used for reasons similar to those when the side effects of new pharmaceuticals are considered by the health profession. In addition, physicians often make such decisions when treating patients. Thus, economists and others feel that such analysis is proper under OSHA. Unions and employees, on the other hand, note that the analysts making these calculations are far removed from the workplace risks. Critics of cost-benefit analysis ask how many lives, limbs, or illnesses should be saved to justify costs. Can the value of life and health be estimated in dollars? How many injuries and deaths are acceptable? Should death or permanent incapacity of family heads be weighed more than that of persons without family responsibilities? Should highly skilled and trained workers be assigned greater value than those less skilled? Attempts to answer these and other questions call for judgments that are not easily made or explained. OSHA does not call for cost-benefit analysis, and the Secretary of Labor cannot be required to make such analysis, according to the Supreme Court. Critics feel that cost-benefit analysis undervalues life and reduces it to a cold and harsh economic proposition.

Relationship with State Regulations

OSHA permits concurrent state and federal regulations, as do the EEO laws. However, OSHA only permits the delegation of responsibility to states with laws that equal or exceed federal standards. Such a dual system of regulation ultimately leads to jurisdictional and philosophical disagreements. Proponents of states' rights favor state or joint state and federal regulation, a costly system to support, whereas critics claim that only the federal government can provide essential uniform regulation when firms operate in interstate commerce. Furthermore, it can be argued that OSHA is unnecessarily duplicative and probably not cost efficient, because four separate agencies hold administrative responsibilities.[11]

Relationship with Collective Bargaining Agreements

An issue as yet unresolved is the proper relationship between OSHA and collective bargaining agreements that insist upon medical care for the injured, the provision of safety equipment, inspections, fire protection, adequate ventilation, and formation of safety committees, to name a few. It is estimated that more than 90 percent of all collective bargaining agreements contain some type of safety and health clause.[12] Furthermore, safety in the plant may be questioned and concerns presented to labor arbitrators for binding decisions. The Supreme Court, in fact,

[11]The Bureau of National Affairs, Inc., "Workplace Safety and Health," *Bulletin to Management* (November 1, 1990), p. 345.
[12]"Holding Unions Liable for Safety and Health," *Business Week* (August 4, 1980), p. 32.

decided that arbitrators could entertain questions pertaining to dangerous working conditions, and that employees facing real, not imaginary, danger could strike before the arbitrator made a final decision.[13] If the danger leading to the work stoppage is later found to be imagined or unwarranted, employees who walk out could lose their jobs. In essence, the Occupational Safety and Health Administration, the courts, and arbitrators can entertain questions of safety in the plant. Does such a state of affairs unnecessarily complicate enforcement?

Another important question is whether employers can legitimately refuse to bargain with unions over safety and health measures falling directly within the province of OSHA regulation. The Wagner Act requires employers to bargain in good faith over working conditions, and it would seem that safety and health are mandatory subjects for bargaining. Yet collective bargaining positions that potentially conflict with OSHA may be regarded as illegal bargaining subjects.

Evaluation of OSHA

The impact and effectiveness of OSHA depend largely on one's viewpoint.[14] Most employers, employees, and unions, as well as others, feel that employee safety and health is worthwhile; the controversy arises when one examines OSHA's impact on this issue. In summary, OSHA has had a positive impact in the following areas:

1. Employer and employee awareness of health and safety issues has increased, as evidenced by the increasing number of formal safety programs that have started since the passage of OSHA.
2. Some studies have indicated that OSHA has led to an improved safety record in the workplace (although research to date is not conclusive on this point).
3. OSHA has encouraged a closer look at job-related hazards and has stimulated research into occupational diseases, toxic substances, and accident reduction.

Critics of OSHA claim that certain negative consequences have also resulted:

1. Some specific safety standards are not based on adequate scientific evidence, or they impose an unreasonable cost burden on employers. Some standards are regarded as trivial.
2. Although employers are held liable for unsafe working conditions under OSHA, employees who engage in unsafe conduct or fail to follow prescribed safety rules are not liable.
3. Because of joint federal and state jurisdiction in ensuring compliance with health and safety laws, enforcement is inconsistent, disjointed, and unpredictable.

---

[13]"*Gateway Coal Co. v. United Mine Workers*," 85 L.R.R.M. 2049 (Sup. Ct. 1974).

[14]Henry R. Moore, "OSHA: What's Ahead for the 1990s," *Personnel* (June 1990), pp. 66–70.

■ Components of a Safety and Health Program

Safety Specialists

A recent survey found that almost two thirds (65 percent) of the companies polled place the responsibility for employee safety and health on the personnel/human resource management department.[15] The time and money devoted to employee health and safety will usually depend on a host of factors, such as the size of the company, whether employees face a wide variety of on-the-job hazards, pressures for improved health and safety in the plant by outside forces such as OSHA inspectors and labor unions, and top management's posture on the importance of employee health and safety.

Many organizations employ safety specialists to design and handle the day-to-day activities of the safety and health program. The Bureau of National Affairs, Inc., notes that the following activities and objectives typically encompass the employee safety and health function:[16]

1. Reduce the frequency and severity of accidents by safety inspections, accident investigations, and safety training and education.
2. Develop and monitor building facility requirements, safety and security requirements, and emergency procedures.
3. Comply with OSHA, state health and environmental regulations and provide engineering services in industrial safety, traffic, noise, water, air, fire prevention, security, and health to reduce accidents.
4. Inspect, survey, and keep records on activities germane to work hazards, workers' compensation, and OSHA compliances.

Safety Committees

Nearly all companies with a formal safety and health program use safety committees of various types. Most of these committees are composed of employees from across the organization. Typically, safety committees serve in an advisory capacity and are responsible for such tasks as reviewing safety procedures, making recommendations for eliminating specific safety and health hazards, investigating accidents, fielding safety-related complaints from employees, and monitoring OSHA compliance.

[15]The Bureau of National Affairs, Inc., "SHRM-BNA Survey No. 56," *Bulletin to Management* (September 26, 1991), p. 3.

[16]The Bureau of National Affairs, Inc., "Personnel Management," *Bulletin to Management* (1982), Section 247.

Communicating Safety Rules and Policies

Although OSHA places the burden of maintaining a safe, hazard-free workplace on the employer, it is the responsibility of the organization to promulgate safety rules, policies, and procedures and convey them to employees. In essence, OSHA polices the firm (to remove unsafe conditions), and the firm, in turn, polices workers (to minimize unsafe behaviors).

The communication of safety rules and policies may be accomplished in several ways. Common methods include personal letters to employees, a discussion of safety in the employee handbook, posters, safety promotion contests, and employee orientation and training programs. Most safety and health programs attempt to communicate the following types of information to employees:

1. The importance of on-the-job safety.
2. A summary of general safety and health policies, with emphasis placed on safety rules, practices, and procedures directly related to each employee's job.
3. Instruction on the recognition of specific hazards that employees may encounter during the course of their work.
4. Specific prohibitions against unsafe behaviors and employer provisions for dealing with employee conduct that jeopardizes the health and safety of the employee or his or her co-workers.
5. Information regarding reporting safety and health hazards and the duty to refuse hazardous work.

Of course, the exact content and scope of communication and training efforts will depend on the employees involved, the nature of their work, and management's commitment to employee health and safety. A key point to bear in mind, however, is that management and supervisory commitment to an employee safety and health program is the most essential ingredient for success. Employee safety and health must become ingrained in the organizational culture for the best results to occur. OSHA, despite its threats of fines and sanctions, is probably at best only a stopgap measure; more permanent improvements in safety and health will be realized if employees and supervisors are constantly alert to safety problems and regard safety as their personal responsibility. OSHA has recently placed additional communication responsibilities on employers. What is known as *right-to-know* regulations have been broadened to include virtually every major workplace in America. This regulation requires employers to tell workers about hazardous chemicals and other toxic substances. It is estimated that this broadening of worker coverage will cost $687 million the first year and $200 million annually in subsequent years as employers keep track of and communicate the existence of all hazardous substances in the workplace. OSHA officials estimate that chemically related injuries, illnesses, and deaths will be reduced by 20 percent by this expansion of coverage to an additional 18 million workers.[17]

[17]Linda D. McGill, "OSHA's Hazard Communication Standard: Guidelines for Compliance," *Employee Relations Today* (Autumn 1989), pp. 181–188.

Measuring the Effects of Employee Health and Safety Programs

OSHA requires that companies compile accident statistics for their operations. Information on aggregate safety and accident trends, as well as the details surrounding individual injuries, are required by the act. OSHA uses the following standardized formula for calculating incidence (frequency) rates of job-related injuries and illnesses:[18]

$$\text{Incidence}^{19} = \frac{N}{EH} \times 200,000$$

where

N = number of injuries and illnesses, or lost workdays
EH = total hours worked by all employees during the calendar year
$200,000$ = 100 full time employees $\times$ 40 hours per week $\times$ 50 weeks per year

The Bureau of Labor Statistics (BLS) uses this formula to allow standardized comparisons among firms and industries. The BLS develops estimates and incidence rates by industry for all work-related deaths, seven categories of nonfatal illnesses, and nonfatal injuries that result in one or more of the following: loss of consciousness, restriction of work or motion, transfer to another job, or medical treatment other than first aid. Safety and health data are published by the BLS based on types of accidents, injuries, and occupational illnesses, as well as by major industries.[20]

Other measures of injury frequency rates are also available. For example, the American National Standards Institute (ANSI) uses a frequency measure of disabling injuries based on 1,000,000 employee hours of exposure. In order to measure differences in the seriousness of accidents, severity rates (SR) can be compiled. ANSI uses the following severity formula:

$$SR = \frac{\text{days lost by injured employee} \times 1,000,000}{\text{employee hours of exposure}}$$

A time charge for an accidental death is 6,000 days, and a sliding scale is used to compute time charges for permanent partial disabilities (e.g., loss of a hand is assigned a charge of 3,000 days).[21] Although frequency measures receive greater attention by OSHA, severity measures may provide better bottom-line measures, because they are based on time lost from work by injured employees.

[18]*What You Should Know About OSHA Recordkeeping* (Washington, D.C.: U.S. Department of Labor, 1980).

[19]This results in the incidence that would be expected if this company had 100 full-time employees working 40 hours per week for 50 weeks. This provides a common base for comparing incidence frequency across organizations.

[20]For more information on the BLS survey, contact the Office of Occupational Safety and Health Statistics, Bureau of Labor Statistics, Washington, DC 20212.

[21]Bureau of National Affairs, Inc., at footnote 13, Section 247.

■ Some Emerging Issues in Employee Safety and Health

Managerial Liability for Employee Health and Safety

In Illinois three managerial employees of a silver recovery firm (the former president, plant manager, and plant foreman) were convicted of murder and sentenced to 25 years in prison.[22] They were charged with the on-the-job death of an employee. It was determined that his death was caused by extensive exposure to cyanide and that the managers had direct knowledge of the danger to employees resulting from the totally unsafe working conditions. In fact, warning labels were torn from the cyanide containers, and workers were allowed to wear cotton gloves when handling the chemical.[23]

This case has caused considerable speculation as to the limits of the criminal liability of managers for employee injury or death. Those who claim that this case represents an anomaly point to that unique aspect of Illinois law that allows a murder charge to be filed if an individual "knowingly creates a strong probability of death and great bodily harm."[24] Unlike other states, no intention to kill need be established in Illinois for the individual to be charged with murder. The maximum charge for this type of behavior in all other states is manslaughter. Further, the degree of personal knowledge and acceptance by management of unsafe conditions, and the appalling lack of safety consideration in this case, make it different from the typical on-the-job injury or death. It is unlikely that any manager who does the job reasonably well would accept the working conditions found in the silver recovery case just discussed. However, there are those who feel that this case will make it more likely that unions, and state and local prosecutors, will seek criminal charges when severe injury or death occurs in the presence of any degree of company negligence.

It will be some time before the national impact of the growing number of local and state prosecutions can be evaluated, but it is likely that the issue of executive liability for worker safety will receive attention and will be cause for considerable speculation.[25]

---

[22]John Burnett, "Corporate Murder Verdict May Not Become Trend, Say Legal Experts," *Occupational Safety and Health* (October 1985), pp. 22, 24–26, 58–59. See also News of the Week, "Unsafe Workplace: Managers Found Guilty of Murder," *C & EN* (June 24, 1985), p. 14; and "Prosecutors Crack Down on Executives Who Endanger Workers," *The Greenville News* (January 18, 1987), p. 1D.

[23]John Burnett, pp. 22, 24–26, 58–59; and Paul G. Engel, "From Pinstripes to Prison Stripes," *Industry Week* (August 4, 1986), pp. 55–56.

[24]John Burnett, p. 22.

[25]See, for example, Amy Dockser and Jose De Cordoba, "Employers Can Face Charges for Endangering Workers," *The Wall Street Journal* (October 17, 1990), p. B5; The Bureau of National Affairs, Inc., "Workplace Accidents = Costly Mistakes," *Bulletin to Management* (September 12, 1991), p. 282; and The Bureau of National Affairs, Inc., "Criminal Liability for Safety Violations," *Bulletin to Management* (May 9, 1991), p. 144.

Employee Stress and Emotional Health

The causes and effects of employee stress have received considerable attention in recent years. Jobs (and life in general) contain stressors that impose physical and psychological demands on the mind and body. Factors such as workloads, quality of supervision, receiving (or not receiving) pay increases or promotions, interpersonal conflicts, and exposure to noise and other physical hazards all represent stressors in the workplace. Stress can accelerate physical and mental deterioration, create job dissatisfaction, performance problems, increased turnover, and absenteeism, lead to addictive narcotic and excessive alcohol use, cause depression and anxiety, and lead to a variety of physical illnesses.[26]

A survey conducted by Northwestern National Life Insurance Company reported that 7 in 10 workers indicated that stress caused frequent health problems and made them less productive. One in three Americans considered quitting their jobs because of workplace stress during the preceding year. One in 10 said they had quit their jobs because of stress, and 46 percent said that their jobs were highly stressful, a figure more than double that found in a similar survey done in 1985.[27] *Business Week* reported that by the late 1980s, the cost to businesses of stress-related problems and mental illness was estimated at $150 billion annually. This figure included health and disability claims, lost productivity, and other expenses.[28] By 1990, stress claims had become the fastest-growing category of workers' compensation cases, accounting for approximately 15 percent of all occupational disease claims.[29] What makes these figures even more alarming is that experts believe that work-related stress is increasing, and that the figures just cited are bound to rise.

Potentially damaging levels of psychological and physical stress can be created by work hazards and pressures, as well as by domestic problems, financial pressures, and personal characteristics. A deterioration of work relationships, personal or family relationships, significant changes in our lives (for better or worse), poor physical condition (and accompanying health problems), compulsive Type A behavior (time impatience, doing multiple tasks simultaneously, free-floating hostility), a perception of helplessness, and low self-esteem can all create stress.[30]

[26]See Philip R. Voluck and Herbert Abramson, "The Work Environment- How to Avoid Stress-related Disability Claims," *Personnel Journal* (May 1987), pp. 95–98.

[27]The Bureau of National Affairs, Inc., "Job Stress, Northwestern National Life Insurance Co.," *Bulletin to Management* (May 24, 1991), p. 153. See also Associated Press, "Survey: 1 in 3 Considered Quitting Job Last Year," *The Greenville News* (May 8, 1991), p. 2A.

[28]Sana Siwolop, Reginald Rhein, and Joe Weber, "Stress: The Test Americans Are Failing," *Business Week* (April 18, 1988), p. 74.

[29]Helen LaVan, Marsha Katz, and Wayne Hochwarter, "Employee Stress Swamps Workers' Comp," *Personnel* (May 1990), p. 61. See also Thomas F. O'Boyle, "Fear and Stress in the Office Take Toll," *The Wall Street Journal* (November 6, 1990), pp. B1, B3; and Michael Trimarchi, *The Washington Post*, "Stress Has Become a Major Business Expense," *The Greenville News* (May 20, 1991), p. 6B.

[30]See William H. Hendrix, K. K. Ovalle, and R. C. Troxler, "Behavioral and Physiological Consequences of Stress and Its Antecedent Factors," *Journal of Applied Psychology*, Vol. 70, No. 1 (1985), pp. 188–201, for a more complete explanation of the causes, reactions, and consequences of workplace stressors.

Although stress is generally regarded as being negative, positive life consequences of stress (known as *eustress* occur from positive events, such as receiving raises, promotions, and so forth. Eustress is the stress of winning, of effectively meeting challenges.[31] However, whether stress or eustress is created may simply depend upon how the individual views the situation. There are employees who would feel increased negative pressure, rather than a sense of achievement, from having past successes. People with different physical disabilities and emotional responses react differently to environmental stressors and stress, so that the individual consequences among different employees will vary.

Although many employers have been more concerned with stress at the executive level, professional, managerial, and blue-collar workers are also affected. In fact, in many instances, executives may experience less stress than lower-level employees who have little control over or variation in their work and who must pay constant attention to their work (such as assembly-line employees).[32] Ironically, some of the most stressful jobs (e.g., those of physicians and hospital administrators) are in the health care industry. Other stressful jobs include those of inner-city school teachers secretaries, assembly line inspectors, police officers, firefighters, public relations personnel, and customer service representatives.

Assigning responsibility for health problems caused by stress may be even more difficult than isolating the causes of other occupational diseases or injuries. When is damaging stress attributable to family and social situations and when is it attributable to the job? In fact, stress at home probably adds to stress on the job and vice versa. For example, to save energy and other costs when expansion is necessary, employers might schedule night work. Such decisions produce stress in the plant and in the home, because working and social patterns are disrupted.[33]

There is no reason to believe that the changes in industry and family responsibilities will be less dynamic in the future. The changing composition of the workforce increases stress both in the home and in the corporate family. Recession and the high probability of layoffs certainly create stress for many employees. When both spouses are wage earners, stress related to income is lessened, but the family adaptation required leads to other stress-producing situations.

To protect employee health, enhance efficiency and the quality of life, and avoid legal problems, employers should recognize the physical and behavioral impacts of stress on employees. Under OSHA regulations, environmental and psychological stressors are factors that are reviewed to ensure worker health and safety. For example, excessive noise, pressure to produce or meet deadlines, fear

---

[31]Karl Albrecht and Hans Selye, *Stress and the Manager* (Englewood Cliffs, New Jersey: Spectrum, 1979).

[32]See Stanley S. Heller and Kenneth A. Frank, "The Effects of Stress on Health," in Donald F. Tapley et al. (eds.), *The Columbia University College of Physicians and Surgeons Complete Home Medical Guide*, p. 335.

[33]See Jane C. Hood and Nancy Milazzo, "Shiftwork, Stress and Wellbeing," *Personnel Administrator* (December 1984), pp. 95–105, for a complete discussion of the effects of shiftwork on employees' work and family relationships and stress.

of working with toxic chemicals, and anxiety associated with unsafe working conditions are all examples of hazards that create physiological and psychological problems. When management has attempted to deal with employee stress it has looked at the workload, the physical workplace (heat, cold, noise, lighting), the relationship among employees, the status of the job, the level of responsibility, the level of supervisor training, and the degree of monotony or variety of tasks, and has then referred employees to the company employee assistance program for counseling and training in stress reduction techniques. (Employee assistance programs are discussed later in this chapter.)

Because of the growing awareness of stress and its deleterious effects, employees with health problems attributable to job-related stress are being compensated by many states under workers' compensation laws. For purposes of workers' compensation, various state courts have recognized three new stress-related classifications for workers: "those who suffer a physical injury that leaves a psychological aftereffect; those who suffer mental trauma that yields a physical ailment, such as an ulcer; and those who suffer mental strain that leads to more serious mental problems."[34] There have been cases where such job conditions as inconsistent job performance evaluations, rejection of an employee's proposals, increase in job duties, overwork, a layoff notice, and inconsistent supervision have been linked to such employee mental disturbances as anxiety, depression, schizophrenia, mental breakdown, and paranoid personality.[35] These cases have led to workers' compensation awards in state courts. Although it may seem that there is no end to such claims, some states have begun to reject automatically all cases where employees claim that mental strain led to serious mental problems. In addition, Massachusetts has forbidden "claims of 'mental or emotional disability arising out of a bona fide personnel action' such as transfer, demotion or layoff."[36] Only time will tell how stress-related workers' compensation claims will be handled by the many state jurisdictions involved.

Reproductive Health Hazards

There is considerable controversy surrounding the occupational hazards discussed in this section. As with the issue of occupational disease, the controversy takes place at two levels. The first level is related to whether a particular hazard is unquestionably linked to such things as an increased likelihood of birth defects, mental retardation, childhood cancers, fertility problems, and miscarriages. The second issue is related to the degree of employer responsibility to minimize employee exposure to the hazard.

[34]Susan Dentzer, John McCormick, and Doug Tsuroka, p. 46. See also "Workplace Stress: Curbing Claims," *Bulletin to Management* (Washington, D.C.: The Bureau of National Affairs, Inc., April 14, 1988), p. 120.

[35]Philip R. Voluck and Herbert Abramson, p. 98. See also Susan Dentzer, John McCormick, and Doug Tsuroka, p. 47.

[36]Susan Dentzer, John McCormick, and Doug Tsuroka, p. 47.

It has become clear during the last few years that human reproductive health is not a uniquely female issue. Although most attention focuses on the issue of exposing unborn children to workplace hazards, there is also potential for damage to the productive health of either parent.[37] "In fact, almost all job hazards found to threaten women's ability to conceive and deliver healthy children also have proven dangerous to men's reproductive health."[38] At present, the potential reproductive health hazards receiving the most attention include radiation, low-level electromagnetic energy, and chemical substances.

Radiation and low-level electromagnetic energy have not been investigated thoroughly enough to allow any clear statements regarding their impact on reproductive health. Obviously, large doses of radiation are dangerous, but at issue is whether limited exposure is still too much exposure. The Federal Aviation Administration issued an advisory in the spring of 1992, telling flight crew members that flying many high-altitude routes might shower an unborn baby with unsafe radiation doses, leading to birth defects, mental retardation, and childhood cancers.[39]

Low-level electromagnetic energy is only now receiving attention as a potential workplace hazard. Electric alarm clocks, electric blankets, television sets, and electric power lines all emit low-level electromagnetic energy. Whether exposure to this energy puts someone at risk for leukemia, brain cancer, or fetal deformities is highly speculative at this point. There is enough concern, though, for the U.S. Office of Technology Assessment to have issued the statement that these fields "may pose public health problems," and to recommend a policy of "prudent avoidance."

In the workplace, radiation and low-level electromagnetic energy come together at the computer terminal. Video display terminals have come under investigation as a potential cause of repetitive motion injury (see the discussion in the following section), but they have also received unfavorable publicity concerning the radiation and electromagnetic energy that they may emit.[40] Although every study linking extensive video display terminal use to miscarriages has acknowledged flaws, the issue is still unresolved. For example, research conducted by Kaiser Permanente in 1988 found that clerical workers who used video display terminals more than 20 hours per week had twice as many miscarriages as clerks not using terminals. However, the researchers acknowledge that other work factors unrelated to computer work may have had an effect. Recent research has been no more conclusive regarding the link between video display terminals and em-

---

[37]For example, exposure to dibro-3-chloropropane in a pesticide plant has been linked to sterility in males. See Robert Lewy, "The Fundamentals of Health," in Donald F. Tapley et al. Robert J. Weiss, Thomas Q. Morris, Genell J. Subak-Sharpe, Diane M. Goetz (eds.), p. 317.

[38]Dr. Maureen Paul, chief of the Occupational Reproductive Hazards Center at the University of Massachusetts, as quoted in Marilyn Elias, "Concerned Workers Find Few Answers," *USA Today* (June 21, 1990), p. 2D.

[39]Marilyn Elias, p. 1A.

[40]Peter Lewis, "Trying to Assess the Potential Hazards of Video Display Terminals (Studies on Effects of Electromagnetic Fields on Working Women)," *The New York Times* (April 21, 1991), p. PF9 (N).

ployee reproductive health.[41] In spite of the uncertainty, computer manufacturers are now creating terminals that shield workers from radiation and electromagnetic energy as a safety precaution.

There is not much debate about how little we know regarding the potential health effects of the over 60,000 chemicals in commercial use in the United States. OSHA has regulated three chemicals because of their reproductive dangers, but overall, we know very little about the reproductive health effects of most of the chemicals we use in the workplace. So, although caution should be exercised regarding exposure of any worker to any chemical substance, our lack of medical knowledge about most chemicals makes it difficult to convince employers and workers that care should be taken routinely. Studies have indicated that there is an increased risk to the reproductive health of workers engaged in laboratory work and in the metal, chemical, plastics, and rubber industries, where exposure to solvents, gases, sterilizing agents, and pesticides is more likely. For example, a 5-year study conducted by the University of Massachusetts's School of Public Health for Digital Equipment Corporation indicated that the rate of miscarriage for workers involved in computer chip production was significantly greater than would have been expected in the general population at large or was found among nonproduction workers at Digital. Although it should be emphasized that this was a preliminary study, it does indicate that there is cause for concern and a need for further investigation into the effects on workers of the chemicals used in the production process.[42]

The issue of what constitutes responsible employer behavior toward workers and reproductive health hazards is fraught with significant controversy as well. For many years, employers attempted to prevent women of childbearing age from being exposed to chemical substances that could damage their reproductive health. These policies were, in general, insensitive to the fact that almost every chemical that compromises the reproductive health of females also endangers males. As noted in Chapter 3, Johnson Controls, an automobile battery manufacturer, adopted a fetal protection policy. The policy prevented all women, except those who could verify that they were sterile, from working at jobs where they would be exposed to lead. Lead is a primary ingredient in battery manufacturing and poses a health risk to unborn children. Lead also poses a danger to male reproductive health, yet under the Johnson Controls fetal protection policy, men could decide for themselves whether they wished to risk exposure. In 1991, the U.S. Supreme Court ruled that fetal protection policies such as the one adopted at Johnson Controls violated Title VII. The Court said that "decisions about the welfare of future children must be left to the parents who conceive, bear, support, and raise them rather than to the employers who hire the parents." Employers must do everything possible to reduce the exposure of all employees to workplace

[41]Carol Hildebrand, "Health Board Rebuts VDT Miscarriage Link," *Computerworld* (March 18, 1991), p. 100.

[42]"Computer Chip Study Finds High Miscarriage Rate," *Greenville News* (December 25, 1986), p. 1D.

hazards. This includes the design of equipment, the venting of work areas, the shielding of workers, and the substitution of less harmful substances wherever possible. As discussed earlier in this chapter, employers who irresponsibly expose their workers to hazardous working conditions may be fined by OSHA and prosecuted on criminal charges in a number of states.

Repetitive Motion Injuries

Thousands of cases of repetitive motion or strain injury are diagnosed each year. Repetitive motion injuries occur when a worker is asked to repeat the same hand or arm motion for extended periods of time. There are a number of jobs that place demands of this type on the worker, including some in auto assembly, textiles, poultry processing, athletics, and computer operation. Ford Motor Company, Chrysler Corporation, and General Motors Corporation all have programs to help automotive assembly workers avoid repetitive motion injuries.

An example of a repetitive motion injury is carpal tunnel syndrome (CTS). Clerks who must use computer keyboards for hours at a time, every day for years, may develop CTS. "The carpal tunnel is the passageway, composed of bone and ligament, through which a major nerve system of the forearm passes into the hand. These nerves control the muscles in this area, as well as nine tendons that allow your fingers to flex. The wear and tear of repeated movement thickens the lubricating membrane of the tendons, and presses the nerve up against the hard bone. This process is called nerve entrapment. CTS usually affects the dominant hand and begins with pain and tingling and numbness."[43] CTS can be disabling if it is severe enough. Most repetitive motion injuries can be prevented with more attention to the design of the work station. CTS, for example, can be eliminated from a computer operator's job by changing the height of the keyboard, providing of rest breaks, and adding specially designed arm rests for the wrists.

Genetic Testing

The United States is in the midst of a very ambitious project designed to map, in detail, each of the human cell's estimated 100,000 genes. This research effort, known as the *human genome project,* will last into the next century. Although the project has an almost unimaginable potential for understanding and treating genetic-based disease, many are frightened of its implications for American workers.[44] One day in the not too distant future, perhaps less than a generation away,

---

[43]University of California at Berkeley, "Preventing CTS," *Wellness Letter* (April 1991), p. 7.

[44]Larry Gostin, "Genetic Discrimination: The Use of Genetically Based Diagnostic and Prognostic Tests by Employers and Insurers," *American Journal of Law and Medicine,* Vol. XVII, Nos. 1 and 2 (1991), pp. 109–144; Kathleen Zeitz, "Employer Genetic Testing: A Legitimate Screening Device or Another Method of Discrimination?", *Labor Law Journal* (April 1991), pp. 230–238; and Richard Smith, "Predisposition and Prejudice," *Science News* (January 21, 1989), pp. 40–42.

the technology will be in place to reveal whether Americans are susceptible to a wide range of diseases, including cancer, heart disease, and Alzheimer's disease.[45] The blood drawn from a small finger prick is all that would be necessary. To some this raises concern about a new form of discrimination—genetic discrimination.

As used in the workplace, genetic testing encompasses two techniques. Genetic screening involves examining individuals for certain inherited genetic traits. Genetic monitoring involves examining individuals periodically for environmentally induced changes in the genetic material of certain cells in their bodies. Genetic screening is creating the most concern because it may make it difficult for some Americans to secure employment. Employers may seek to control potential health care costs by screening out applicants and employees with specific defects in their genetic material. The Council on Ethical and Judicial Affairs of the American Medical Association has issued a report on the use of genetic screening by employers. It is the council's position that genetic tests are poor indicators of disease and even poorer indicators of disability. Many individuals who carry a specific gene will never show a manifestation of that gene. And even if that gene manifests itself, the effects will vary from person to person. To deny someone employment based on an unknown likelihood of a future disease seems inappropriate. Even in cases where the gene is sure to result in significant disability or death, the health problem is often many years in the future, making a negative employment decision unfair.[46] Whether American workers will receive effective protection under Title VII, the Rehabilitation Act of 1973, and the ADA remains to be seen. The council is optimistic that the ADA, which prevents medical testing unrelated to an applicant's ability to do the job, will prove effective in preventing genetic discrimination. The council has recognized the interest employers may have in screening applicants for genetic hypersusceptibility to specific workplace substances. However, given the uncertain predictive value of genetic testing, the council believes that employers would be better off monitoring exposure and the health of all employees coming in contact with dangerous chemical substances.

Substance Abuse and Dependency

The abuse of chemical substances is a major societal problem. It recognizes no social, racial, or economic boundaries.[47] It has been estimated that 60 percent of the world's illegal drugs are consumed by Americans.[48] The abuse of legal and illegal substances has created millions of troubled and dependent individuals, and

---

[45]Larry Gostin, p. 110.

[46]Council on Ethical and Judicial Affairs, American Medical Association, "Use of Genetic Testing by Employers," *Journal of the American Medical Association* (October 2, 1991), p. 1827.

[47]Hope Edelman, "Hooked: When Medical Students Become Addicts," *The Washington Post* (February 19, 1991), p. PWH10; and Michael Isikoff, "Study: White Students More Likely to Use Drugs; High School Survey Said to Contradict View of Substance Abuse as a Minority Problem," *The Washington Post* (February 25, 1991), p. PA4.

[48]"America on Drugs," *U.S. News and World Report* (July 28, 1986), pp. 48–54.

has destroyed relationships, careers, families, and lives. Substance abuse has increased crime,[49] compromised public and workplace safety, and, as we search for a solution, threatened our civil liberties. It should come as no surprise that organizations have made significant efforts to cope with employee substance abuse and dependence in the workplace.

According to the U.S. Chamber of Commerce, drug and alcohol abuse was costing America over $140 billion per year by the mid-1980s.[50] Alcohol abuse alone costs this nation over $85 billion per year in lower productivity, as well as costs due to premature deaths, road accidents, crime, and additional law enforcement.[51] Potential employer costs of substance abuse include lost productivity (including waste, inefficiency, low morale, and poor decision making), turnover costs, increased medical claims, accidents, absenteeism, actions creating criminal liability for the company, and theft of company property. Employee behaviors associated with drug abuse include neglect of personal hygiene, repeated lateness and absenteeism, slowness in performing high-speed tasks such as typing and collating pages, verbal confusion in conversations that require paying attention to detail or absorbing complicated information, faulty memory, difficulty with mathematical computations, and frequent and prolonged trips to the restroom.[52]

With estimates indicating that 10–20 percent of the general population is using drugs, it should not be surprising to find somewhat similar levels of drug use among the workforce. In a recent survey, 22 percent of the 1,007 workers surveyed in a Gallup poll said that illegal drug use is "somewhat widespread" where they work. Forty-one percent believe that co-workers' drug use seriously affects their ability to do their own jobs. Eight percent had been offered drugs at work, and 7 percent had been approached to buy drugs at work.[53] Public testimony of two Conrail crew members involved in a 1987 Maryland accident that killed 16 passengers and injured 130 indicated that it was not unusual for a crew member to drink up to a case of beer while on the job. Further, they painted a picture of widespread alcohol and drug abuse among workers.[54] A Federal Railroad Administration study of 176 major collisions that took place in 1987 indicates that 65 percent of the fatalities suffered involved drugs or alcohol.[55] The drugs most

---

[49]A federal study released by the Justice Department indicated that 79 percent of males arrested for serious crimes in New York City from June through November 1987 tested positive for drugs. "Crime in the Cities: The Drug Connection," *Newsweek* (February, 1988), p. 47.

[50]William Hoffer, "Business' War on Drugs," *Nation's Business* (October 1986), p. 19.

[51]William C. Symonds, James E. Ellis, Julia Flynn Siler, Wendy Zellner, and Susan B. Garland, "Is Business Bungling Its Battle with Booze?", *Business Week* (March 25, 1991), p. 77.

[52]The Bureau of National Affairs, Inc., "Substance Abuse Detection," *Bulletin to Management* (January 4, 1990), p. 8.

[53]The Bureau of National Affairs, Inc., "Workers Support Drug Testing," *Bulletin to Management* (January 4, 1990), p. 2.

[54]Marilyn Rauber, "Conrail Workers: Drug, Alcohol Use Widespread," *The Greenville News* (February 26, 1988), p. 2D.

[55]Jeff Shear, "Rash of Wrecks Puts the Heat on Railways' Federal Overseer," *Insight* (May 9, 1988), p. 19.

commonly used in the workplace are alcohol, marijuana, cocaine, and prescription drugs such as tranquilizers, amphetamines, and barbiturates.

It is obvious that the problem is too widespread, and too costly in human and economic terms, to ignore. Although there is very little disagreement regarding the importance of identifying and rehabilitating substance-abusing and dependent employees or the need for educational programs to prevent others from using drugs, there is genuine controversy over the means and process of identification, as well as over the civil and job rights of the employees involved, particularly those identified as substance abusers.

Increasing numbers of employers are testing current employees for drug use. The majority of American companies currently test employees for drugs. In fact, 63 percent of the companies responding to a major survey conducted by the American Management Association indicated that they conducted drug testing of employees.[56] Larger companies, certain government agencies, and companies with significant potential safety risks for employees or the general community are more likely to have drug testing programs. Examples include Motorola, Inc., which has decided to test all of its 60,000 employees, from receptionist to president, on a random basis.[57] Another example is the construction industry, where contractors implementing effective drug testing programs have seen costs associated with "workers' compensation, theft, accidents, absenteeism, and health insurance drop as much as 25 percent."[58]

As discussed in Chapter 7, the identification of those who abuse chemicals is usually accomplished through the examination of body fluids (urinalysis, blood tests), although alternative means, such as hair analysis, have also been used.[59] Importantly, these tests cannot measure an individual's current degree of impairment, nor can an employer assume that all drug tests are accurate. To ensure accuracy, most employers follow up the initial radioimmunoassay test with the gas chromatography or mass spectrometry test. Both tests are used for both body fluids and hair analysis. Employers should also ensure that they are using a certified laboratory to conduct the tests. Alternatives to drug testing that attempt to determine current impairment are the pupillary reaction test (the pupil will react differently if the employee is under the influence of drugs) and performance testing. The pupillary reaction test must be administered by a trained professional and, if positive, is usually followed up by tests on a body fluid. Performance testing involves a video-based eye-hand coordination test. Employees establish a baseline standard of performance over a period of time, and every time they report to work, the employees must play the video game to determine if they are fit to work that

---

[56]The Bureau of National Affairs, Inc., "Employee Drug Testing Escalates," *Bulletin to Management* (May 23, 1991), p. 154.

[57]Ellen Neuborne, "More Top Firms Test Workers for Drugs," *USA Today* (June 21, 1990), p. B1.

[58]William Hoffer, "A New Focus on Drugs," *Nation's Business* (December 1986), p. 59.

[59]See Michael R. Carrell and Christina Heavrin, "Before You Drug Test . . . ," *HR Magazine* (June 1990), pp. 64–66, and *The Wall Street Journal*, "Employee Drug Tests" (September 18, 1990), p. B8. Hair roots absorb chemicals from the bloodstream. Those chemicals remain in the hair until the hair is cut and discarded.

day. No determination other than current impairment is made. The employee may be impaired because of fatigue, illness, stress, or substance abuse. Subsequent testing is necessary to determine whether the employee is impaired by drug use.

When it comes to drug testing, however, the real workplace issues do not involve the tests per se, but rather the scope of the testing program and the rights of employees before, during, and after the tests. For example, does an employer have the right to demand that an employee, regardless of the nature of his or her work and specific work record, submit to a urine test for drugs (perhaps with the sample given in the presence of another person)? To what extent does testing without specific cause presume that the employee is guilty until proven innocent? What right does an employee have to refuse to submit to a drug test on the basis that it would be an invasion of privacy? And if the employee is discovered to have used drugs, what job rights does that employee have, and to what extent should the nature of the employee's work, his or her performance history, and federal, state, and local laws affect those job rights? These questions are among the many that must be answered before we can resolve the drug testing issue within a framework that will not destroy our unique American guarantees of civil liberty and individual dignity.

The answers to these questions are by no means obvious. Although it is impossible to anticipate decisions yet to be reached by the courts, and legislation to be enacted by state, local, and federal governments, it is likely that drug testing programs that meet the standards presented in Table 14-1 will prove acceptable.

Rehabilitation and education are both important parts of successful drug testing programs. Attempts to accomplish both are made by government (federal, state, and local) as well as privately funded programs, including employee assistance programs.

Acquired Immune Deficiency Syndrome (AIDS)

AIDS has become a serious general health concern that has only begun to make its presence known in the workplace. AIDS is caused by a retrovirus that attacks the body's immune system, eliminating its ability to combat infection and leaving the individual vulnerable to fatal infections and opportunistic diseases.

The Centers for Disease Control estimates that up to 1 million Americans have already been infected by the AIDS virus.[60] Every one of these persons can infect others. By early 1992, the Centers for Disease Control reported over 200,000 cases of AIDS and 133,232 deaths from AIDS in the United States. The first 100,000 cases of AIDS took 8 years to develop, occurring in August 1989. The next 100,000 cases took only 26 months.[61] Although it may seem that AIDS is primarily

[60]Benard Gavzer, "What Can We Learn from Those Who Survive AIDS?," *Parade* (June 10, 1990), p. 4.

[61]Associated Press, "Nation's AIDS Epidemic Reaches 200,000," *Greenville News* (January 17, 1992), p. 2A.

TABLE 14-1   Standards for Drug Testing Programs

Corporate policy regarding the possession, use, and sale of drugs should be clearly specified, consistently enforced, and readily available to employees. Employees must be aware of the company drug policy, especially if it entails any disciplinary action. The development and dissemination of corporate policy must proceed drug testing.

Selective testing of particular employees is based upon reasonable suspicion of drug involvement, and that such involvement would compromise the safety of the employee or others and/or is adversely affecting job performance.

Tests are conducted so as to preserve the dignity and privacy of the employees involved.

Employees are assured of accurate test results, regardless of the expense. This includes a secure chain of custody for the samples, and multiple tests on a given or subsequent body fluid samples. It would not be unreasonable to make a portion of the body fluid sample available to the employee for independent testing.

Employees who refuse to participate in a mandatory drug testing program are provided with an opportunity to appeal their required participation in a manner that assures them due process.

No federal, state, or local laws are violated by the program.

No collective bargaining agreements are violated. In fact joint union-company development and enforcement of a drug testing policy would be advantagous.

Employees who test positive for drug use are provided with an opportunity to participate in a rehabilitation program and will retain their job rights contingent upon the successful completion of the program, assuming subsequent lack of drug use.

Employees who refuse to be or cannot be rehabilitated and are then dismissed from the organization should be assured of confidentiality with reference to the cause of their dismissal.

a disease striking those with unusual lifestyles, it is also a major concern for mainstream America.

Individuals may become exposed to the AIDS virus by coming in contact with the body fluids, particularly the blood and semen, of infected persons. These fluids must gain direct entry into the bloodstream (through a break in the skin, for example) in order for an individual to become infected.[62] Although the AIDS virus has also been found in human tears, breast milk, and urine, the likelihood of transmission through exposure to these fluids is considered remote.[63] Thus far,

[62]*Aids, What Everyone Should Know* (American College Health Association, 1986).

[63]Michael S. Cecere, "AIDS in the Workplace," *Journal of Career Planning and Employment* (Spring 1986), p. 3.

AIDS has been contracted primarily through sexual contact with an infected individual or through the use of a contaminated intravenous needle, although a small number of early exposures have resulted from transfusions of infected blood products and infected tissue transplants.

Although workplace exposure is unlikely for most American workers, there are a number of professions in which employees will be exposed to blood or other body fluids as part of the job. These professions include dentists, dental assistants, nurses, emergency medical personnel, firefighters, police officers, laboratory technicians, prison guards, physicians, and associated personnel. In 1991, OSHA issued a standard on occupational exposure to bloodborne pathogens, including AIDS. Dates were established for various compliance levels through 1992, with all provisions taking effect in July 1992.[64]

Employers who wish to discriminate against those infected with the AIDS virus (the human immunodeficiency virus [HIV]) will find that the federal government and many states define the infection as a protected disability, preventing such action.[65] The ADA expressly extends coverage to those infected with HIV. Many state laws now cover organizations with too few employees to be covered by federal law.

In most workplaces attention should center on AIDS education and the reduction of anxiety for employees, especially the co-workers of an AIDS patient. A formal company-sponsored education program should seek to make employees aware of prevailing medical opinion regarding the nature, symptoms, and means of transmission of the disease, as well as prepare them for the emotional difficulties they are likely to experience when a co-worker contracts a terminal disease. Table 14-2 presents such a policy developed by Bank of America. Other companies have developed similar policies in recent years.[66]

Smoking in the Workplace

In the not so distant past, smoking in the workplace was accepted by smokers and nonsmokers alike. Although smoking might have been annoying to nonsmokers, little was ever said. Recently nonsmokers have begun to assert themselves and have demanded from smokers, company management, and state and local governments that they be allowed to work in a smoke-free environment. This new attitude and militant behavior have resulted in significant hostility and tension in the workplace. As a

---

[64]The Bureau of National Affairs, Inc., "OSHA Activity Regarding New Rules," *Bulletin to Management* (March 26, 1992), p. 89, and The Bureau of National Affairs, Inc., "AIDS Compliance Dates," *Bulletin to Management* (December 12, 1991), p. 385.

[65]The Bureau of National Affairs, Inc., "Economics of AIDS Testing Questioned," *Bulletin to Management* (July 18, 1991), p. 218.

[66]See Michael D. Whitty, "AIDS, Labor Law, and Good Management," *Labor Law Journal* (March 1989), pp. 183–187; and Bill Paterson, "AIDS in the Workplace: Is Your Company Prepared?", *Training and Development Journal* (February 1989), pp. 38–41.

TABLE 14-2   Bank of America:
Assisting Employees with Life-threatening Illnesses

BankAmerica recognizes that employees with life-threatening illnesses including, but not limited to, cancer, heart disease, and AIDS, may wish to continue to engage in as many of their natural pursuits as their condition allows, including work.

As long as these employees are able to meet acceptable performance standards, and medical evidence indicates that their conditions are not a threat to themselves or others, managers should be sensitive to their conditions and ensure that they are treated consistently with other employees.

At the same time, BankAmerica seeks to provide a safe work environment for all employees and customers. Therefore, precautions should be taken to ensure that an employee's condition does not present a health and/or safety threat to other employees or customers.

Consistent with this concern for employees with life-threatening illnesses, BankAmerica offers the following range of resources available through Personnel Relations:

- Management and employee education and information on terminal illness and specific life-threatening illnesses.
- Referral to agencies and organizations which offer supportive services for life-threatening illnesses.
- Benefit consultation to assist employees in effectively managing health, leave, and other benefits.

Guidelines
When dealing with situations involving employees with life-threatening illnesses, managers should:

continued

Reprinted by permission from Bank of America, Corporate Health Programs, San Francisco, CA 94104.

consequence, management is faced with the dilemma of balancing the rights of smokers (29 percent of workers) and nonsmokers (71 percent).[67]

Nonsmokers cite research literature that indicates that sidestream smoke (smoke from the tobacco products used by smokers) is hazardous to their health.[68] According to the Surgeon General of the United States, the Environmental Protection Agency and the Environmental Protection Agency's Scientific Advisory Board, secondhand smoke has been linked to increased rates of cancer and heart disease among nonsmokers. Estimates are that every year secondhand smoke causes 3,000 lung-cancer deaths and triggers 35,000 additional heart

[67]Paul Scelsi, "Smoking: Bad for Business?", *Management World* (November-December 1986), p. 16. See Mary Jo Blackwood, "Health Risks of Smoking Increased by Exposure to Workplace Chemicals," *Occupational Health and Safety* (February 1985), p. 27.

[68]Walter R. Barrus, "Smokers' Nonsmokers' Rights Collide in the Work Environment," *Occupational Health and Safety* (February 1985), p. 32.

TABLE 14-2   (continued)

1. Remember that an employee's health condition is personal and confidential; reasonable care should be taken to protect information regarding an employee's condition.
2. Contact Personnel Relations if you believe that you or other employees need information about terminal illness, or a specific life-threatening illness, or if you need further guidance in managing a situation that involves an employee with a life-threatening illness.
3. Contact Personnel Relations if you have any concern about the possible contagious nature of an employee's illness.
4. Contact Personnel Relations to determine if a statement should be obtained from the employee's attending physician that continued presence at work will pose no threat to the employee, co-workers, or customers. BankAmerica reserves the right to require an examination by a medical doctor appointed by the Company.
5. If warranted, make reasonable accommodation for employees with life-threatening illnesses consistent with the business needs of the division/unit.
6. Make a reasonable attempt to transfer employees with life-threatening illnesses who request a transfer and are experiencing undue emotional stress.
7. Be sensitive and responsive to co-workers' concerns and emphasize employee education available through Personnel Relations.
8. No special consideration should be given beyond normal transfer requests for employees who feel threatened by a co-worker's life-threatening illness.
9. Be sensitive to the fact that continued employment for an employee with a life-threatening illness may sometimes be therapeutically important in the remission process or may help to prolong that employee's life.
10. Encourage employees to seek assistance from established community support groups for medical treatment and counseling services. Information on these can be requested through Personnel Relations or Corporate Health.

disease deaths.[69] Further, they are convinced that allergies and other respiratory problems are aggravated by a smoke-filled environment. In a survey of several thousand Social Security Administration employees, 48 percent of nonsmokers stated that they experienced eye irritation on the job from sidestream smoke, 30 percent complained of throat discomfort, 35 percent complained of nasal irritation, 19 percent experienced eating difficulties, and 25 percent were frustrated and hostile that management allowed smoking in the workplace.[70] Smokers believe that they have a right to smoke and that nonsmokers' claims of potential health hazards are groundless or, at best, greatly exaggerated. The issue is

[69]The Bureau of National Affairs, Inc., "Smoking Rules?," *Bulletin to Management* (May 9, 1991), p. 137; Warren E. Leary, "U.S. Agency Urges Cut in Smoking on the Job," *The New York Times* (July 18, 1991), p. B7, and Geoffrey Cowley, "Poison at Home and at Work," *Newsweek* (June 29, 1992), p. 55.

[70]Cary B. Barad, "Smoking on the Job: The Controversy Heats Up," *Occupational Health and Safety* (January-February 1979), pp. 21–24, as found in Mary Jo Blackwood, p. 27.

further complicated by recent reports that smokers are not as effective and are more expensive to employ than nonsmokers. One research study has estimated the annual cost to firms per smoking employee to be $5,662.[71] If these figures are accurate, it would mean that 100 smokers would unnecessarily cost a firm more than half a million dollars per year. These estimates are based upon the following beliefs:

1. Smokers are absent more often than nonsmokers.
2. Smokers have higher medical costs.
3. Nonsmokers have lower insurance costs.
4. Productivity is reduced due to the time spent on the rituals and habits associated with smoking.
5. Cigarette fumes and burns can damage sensitive electronic equipment and furniture.
6. The expense of cleaning and maintenance of company property is higher due to smoking.
7. Sidestream smoke increases the costs of health care for nonsmokers.
8. A smoke-filled work environment directly and indirectly affects the productivity and morale of both smokers and nonsmokers, in part through tension and hostility created in the workplace.

Three other researchers, using categories similar to those listed here, present a very different estimate of the cost of employing smokers. They believe the cost to be approximately $657 per year (in 1982 dollars).[72] There appears to be little agreement on the cost estimates of workplace smoking.

A category of potential costs appearing in neither of these two studies that represents perhaps the most significant threat to employee safety and well-being is the additive and interactive medical effects of smoke with other workplace pollutants. The World Health Organization stated that smoking is the major source of the following indoor pollutants: formaldehyde, asbestos, carbon dioxide, and sulfur dioxide. There are more than 1,000 identifiable substances in smoke. These indoor pollutants, combined with the reduced effectiveness of smokers' lungs (e.g., excess mucus, reduced dust clearance from the lungs, a reduction in cilia action), the additional pollutants derived from the increased use of synthetic materials in the workplace (e.g., modern office furniture), and the reduction of air exchange with the outside due to energy conservation efforts, present cause

[71]William L. Weis, "Can You Afford to Hire Smokers?", *Personnel Administrator* (May 1981), pp. 71–78, as found in Walter R. Barrus, p. 31.

[72]Donald Kent, Martin Schram, and Louis Cenci, "Smoking in the Workplace: A Review of Human Operating Costs," *Personnel Administrator* (August 1982), pp. 29–33, 83, as found in Mary Jo Blackwood, p. 27. For additional estimates of the cost to an employer of a smoker, see Elaine F. Gruenfeld, "Smoking in the Workplace," *ILR Report* (Ithaca, New York: Cornell University, Spring 1986), pp. 9–16.

for considerable concern.[73] This concern has led to suggestions that those occupations with an unusually high risk of lung cancer should have smoking restricted in the workplace.[74] This set of occupations includes bus drivers, roofers, painters, electricians, auto mechanics, asbestos and insulation workers, and pressmen and plateprinters, among others.[75]

Management has begun to respond to the pressures from nonsmoking employees, recent laws and court decisions, and the ever-increasing medical evidence supporting the potential detrimental effects of smoking on employee health and productivity.[76] The Boeing Company, of Seattle, Washington, announced in April 1984 that smoking was prohibited in restrooms, lobbies, classrooms, auditoriums, medical facilities, and hallways.[77] The U.S. Army prohibited smoking in Army-occupied space since July 1987, "except for designated areas necessary to prevent undue inconvenience" for smokers.[78]

Further, a survey of 833 organizations found that more than 85 percent had some type of smoking policy while 34 percent ban smoking totally.[79]

From 82 to 90 percent of the companies with smoking policies banned smoking in the work area, as well as in hallways, restrooms, conference rooms, and customer/visitor areas. The reasons given for instituting a smoking policy included the following: concerns about employee health and/or comfort (79 percent, complaints from employees (59 percent), state or local law (36 percent), concerns about high health care costs (26 percent), and concerns about productivity and absenteeism among smokers (22 percent). The same survey also asked those companies that did not have a smoking policy why they elected not to have one. The following are the reasons cited most often: lack of employee demand (48 percent), lack of support from top management (44 percent), anticipated objections from smokers (33 percent), and anticipated problems with enforcement (27 percent). Only 2 percent of the surveyed companies hire nonsmokers exclusively, and 8 percent have a stated preference for nonsmoking applicants. Sixty-four percent of all the companies surveyed indicated that they have offered help or encouragement to employees

[73]The Bureau of National Affairs, Inc., "OSHA Focuses on Indoor Air, Secondhand Smoke," *Bulletin to Management* (September 26, 1991), p. 297.

[74]John E. Vena, "Air Pollution as a Risk Factor in Lung Cancer," *American Journal of Epidemiology* (July 1982), pp. 42–56, as found in Walter R. Barrus, p. 31.

[75]Walter R. Barrus, p. 31.

[76]Smokers are three times more likely to die of cancer and two and a half times more likely to suffer acute respiratory illness than nonsmokers. Further, 85 percent of lung cancer fatalities can be attributed to smoking. See Eric Josephson, "Smoking, Alcohol, and Substance Abuse," in Donald F. Tapley et al., Robert J. Weiss, (eds.), pp. 340–359.

[77]Paul Scelisi, p. 16.

[78]"Army Initiates Crackdown on Smoking," *The Greenville News* (June 12, 1986), p. 1D. See Sherry C. Hammond, David A. Decenzo, and Mollie H. Bowers, "How One Company Went Smokeless," *Harvard Business Review* (November-December 1987), pp. 44–45, for an in-depth case study of the smoking program in Blue Cross/Blue Shield of Maryland.

[79]The Bureau of National Affairs, Inc., "SHRM-BNA Survey No. 55, Smoking in the Workplace: 1991," *Bulletin to Management* (August 29, 1991), pp. 1–16.

TABLE 14-3   Smoking Policy Recommendations

Indicate a willingness to accommodate both smokers and nonsmokers.

State that the company wishes to accommodate all concerned employees or, at its discretion, the (preferences of the) nonsmokers.

Designate areas as smoking or nonsmoking.

Request that employees exercise common sense and courtesy, and attempt to resolve smoking-related conflicts when they develop.

Designate a manager to whom any employee may bring a smoking-related complaint without prejudice.

State that the policy is for the comfort of all employess in the plant or office, and not as a means to regulate individual behavior.

Affirm that the company expects reasonable willingness on the part of employees to accommodate each other.

who wish to stop smoking. Fifty-four percent of the companies with smoking bans stated that violators would be subject to disciplinary actions. Eighty-four percent of those companies included discharge as a possible penalty.

A firm that feels it necessary to adopt a smoking policy which would accommodate both smokers and non-smokers would be well advised to consider the suggestions provided in Table 14-3 when developing and communicating that policy. These suggestions should minimize conflict and improve employee acceptance of a new smoking policy. They should also reduce the likelihood of lawsuits by unhappy nonsmokers or smokers.

It is not likely that smoking in the workplace will disappear as an important health-related issue during the next few years. In fact, it is likely that the controversy and conflict will continue to escalate, resulting in more restrictive smoking policies for firms and additional smoking regulations passed by states.[80] This is underscored by the American Medical Association's announcement that it will seek legislation to ban all tobacco advertisements and work to make the United States a smoke-free country by the year 2000, and former Surgeon General C. Everett Koop's statement that nicotine is as addictive as cocaine and heroin.[81]

Employee Assistance Programs (EAPs)

EAPs are designed to "prevent problems that interfere with an employee's ability to perform his or her job and to rehabilitate those employees who are

[80]By mid-1992, 45 states had adopted restrictions on smoking in public places and 400 communities had adopted clean indoor air acts. The Associated Press, "Non-smokers Back Public Smoking Ban," *The Greenville News* (March 25, 1992), p. 2A.

[81]Los Angeles Times, "Surgeon General Calls Nicotine As Addictive As Cocaine, Heroin," *Greenville News* (May 17, 1988), p. 2B.

experiencing problems that affect the employee's performance on the job."[82] As discussed in Chapter 13, troubled employees have a much higher potential for disciplinary problems. Further, they are more likely to be involved in accidents, to be in poorer health, to have below-average productivity, to have reduced quality of work, to have behavioral problems, and to be involved in criminal activity.[83]

Immediate supervisors or managers are usually the ones who are responsible for employee referral to EAPs.[84] It is the supervisor or manager who is in the best position to notice the job performance and behavior of the troubled employee. Also, many EAPs encourage self-referrals, as employees themselves can recognize problems before performance is affected.

EAPs have become routinely accepted in many organizations. Although the idea of providing help for employee personal problems is over 70 years old (R. H. Macy had one in 1920, Hawthorne Works of the Western Electric Company in 1927),[85] EAPs became widespread only during the 1970s and 1980s. For example, there were 500 programs in 1973; by 1977 there were more than 2,400, by 1981 more than 5,000 programs,[86] by 1985 over 8,000 programs and by 1989 over 10,000 EAPs were in existence.[87] A survey conducted by the American Management Association found that the percentage of companies providing EAPs had risen from 39 percent in 1989 to 64 percent by 1990.[88]

Early EAPs were usually housed in the medical department and administered by medical personnel.[89] Today most EAPs, although typically utilizing medical personnel, are the responsibility of the personnel department.[90] Current EAPs differ along three primary dimensions: variety of services available to employees, the qualifications and training of EAP personnel, and the location of the program (in-house, out-of-house, a combination of the two).

[82]D. W. Myers, *Employee Assistance Programs* (Chicago, Illinois: Commerce Clearing House Inc., 1986), p. 4. This excellent text also contains detailed information on the EAPs of Reynolds Metals and Dupont.

[83]D. W. Myers, *Human Resources Management* (Chicago, Illinois: Commerce Clearing House, Inc., 1986), p. 611. See also Phillis Schiller Myers and Donald W. Meyers, "EAPs: The Benefit That Creates New Risks," *Risk Management* (May 1985), p. 46. See also William E. Bailey, "Putting Together the Pieces," *Management World* (March 1986), pp. 32–37.

[84]Mark Ralfs and John Morley, "Turning Employee Problems Into Triumphs," *Training and Development Journal* (November 1990), p. 74.

[85]D. W. Myers, *Human Resources Management*, p. 613.

[86]Carol Turkington, "EAPs: Healthier Employees, Lower cost Spur Growth of Programs," *APA Monitor* (August 1985), pp. 22–23.

[87]Bill Chiabotta, "Evaluating EAP Vendors," *Personnel Administrator* (August 1985), pp. 39–43; and Fred Luthans and Robert Waldersee, "What Do We Really Know About EAPs?" *Human Resources Management* (Fall 1989), p. 386.

[88]The Bureau of National Affairs, Inc., "Employee Drug Testing Escalates," *Bulletin to Management* (May 23, 1991), p. 154.

[89]Keith McCellan, p. 30.

[90]D. W. Myers, *Human Resources Management*, p. 615.

Firms have programs which offer services ranging from psychological counseling, including behavior modification (personal and family), to financial planning and chemical dependency treatment (e.g., alcohol and drugs). The range of services provided is a reflection of the variety of problems currently affecting employees and our increased sophistication with reference to them (See Table 14-4).

These programs, although costing approximately $15 to $30 per employee, can add up to a significant aggregate expenditure.[91] In addition, any firm concerned enough about employee welfare to develop an EAP should, by extension, be concerned with the quality of care provided by the EAP. Employers should be cautioned that the third-party provision of EAPs (providing agents outside the company) has become big business, and there are many firms that may not provide the level and quality of service required. EAP vendors must be selected with the same care as any other vendor.[92]

Two personnel researchers have outlined the risks to employers created by the provision of EAPs. The consequences of improper treatment can be significant for the employee and result in considerable liability for the organization. One case resulted in a $1.9 million settlement when an employee claimed that his depression was misdiagnosed by the company physician and the external EAP provider.[93] The employer may risk excessive treatment costs due to overtreatment, irrelevant treatment, or inefficient treatment. Further, there is an undefined liability if the employee becomes subject to an adverse employment decision based upon participation in the EAP. Employees may file grievances or suits or take other action.[94] Perhaps the best way to reduce these risks is to take considerable care in the selection of the EAP provider.

The company should also consider what combination of internal and external locations of the programs and program personnel are most appropriate. This decision should be based on where the treatment can be best provided, the combinations of personnel qualifications and medical capital required, and employee privacy. An employee should feel comfortable in seeking help for

---

TABLE 14-4 Types of Services Prevalent in Companies with EAPs

Alcohol or drug abuse counseling	Career counseling
Preretirement counseling	Marital counseling
Emotional or stress counseling	Financial counseling
Termination counseling	Legal counseling

---

[91]Carol Turkington, pp. 22–23.

[92]Bill Chiabotta, pp. 39–43.

[93]Phillis Schiller Myers and Donald W. Myers, p. 49.

[94]Lloyd Loomis, "Employee Assistance Programs: Their Impact on Arbitration and Litigation of Termination Cases," *Employee Relations Law Journal* (Autumn 1986), pp. 275–287; and Richard I. Lehr and David J. Middlebrooks, "Legal Implications of Employee Assistance Programs," *Employee Relations Law Journal* (Autumn 1986), pp. 262–274.

personal problems. Often confidentiality of participation and treatment is a very important issue for a troubled employee. If the employee feels that he or she may be seen using the services or that EAP employees will record personal material in his or her employment file, and worse yet, that those making employment decisions may consider such information, little participation can be expected.[95]

The effectiveness of the program should be an ongoing concern. Careful planning of the original program and care in the selection of the EAP provider will contribute to an effective program, while good record keeping can provide the means to evaluate it.[96] Motorola and AT&T have evaluation processes for their EAPs that include cost-benefit analyses. Motorola estimates and compares the training/replacement costs associated with the turnover expected without the EAP to the actual costs incurred with the EAP in place. The difference is considered the savings attributable to the EAP. For Motorola and other companies that estimate the costs and benefits of EAPs, the data indicate significant savings resulting from their use. One estimate from the insurance industry suggests a return of $5 for every $1 invested in an EAP.

Because supervisors play a critical role in the EAP referral process, they should be sensitive to employee problem behaviors and their reaction to them. Unfortunately, many supervisors deal with troubled employees in an unproductive fashion. They may deny the problem, become angry at the employee, become resentful, or feel guilty and blame themselves for the problem behaviors. Supervisors should fully understand the company's EAP functions and programs, as well as the nature of common employee problems such as alcohol and drug abuse. They must learn to document problem behaviors objectively, and to work through their personal feelings of anger, guilt, or resentment when a troubled employee needs assistance.

Employee Wellness Programs

Nearly all the laws, measures, and methods associated with employee health and safety have emphasized the prevention and elimination of hazards that could lead to injuries or illness. Employee wellness programs approach health and safety from a different perspective—improving and enhancing the current health status of employees. The underlying premise of employee wellness programs is that workers who are in better physical condition and have a lifestyle that minimizes common health hazards will be more productive, satisfied, and reliable employees.

---

[95]Phillis Schiller Myers and Donald W. Myers, p. 50. There is also a potential financial liability for breaches of confidentiality. "A federal regulation (42 C.F.R., Section 2.1 et seq.), subjects employers to fines for confidentiality violations in EAPs that receive federal funding." An excellent discussion of an employer's confidentiality obligation is contained in Martin K. Davis, "Privacy Rights and Medical Disclosures: An Employer's Dilemma," *Employee Relations Today* (Spring 1987), pp. 65–74.

[96]Donald W. Myers, *Employee Assistance Programs*, p. 12.

A survey of 832 organizations by the Hay Group indicated that over 90 percent of those surveyed had some formal health, physical fitness, or recreational programs.[97] The list of major U.S. corporations having wellness programs is considerable and includes Adolph Coors Company, Pepsico, Johnson's Wax, Xerox, Kellogg Company, Tenneco, IBM, Sentry Insurance Company, Conoco, Mesa Petroleum, Pitney Bowes, Mannington Mills, Levi Strauss, Quaker Oats, and Johnson & Johnson.

Most employee wellness programs have three components. The first component is health screening and assessment. A typical health screening involves a physical examination plus several tests that measure, among other things, the employee's cholesterol and blood sugar levels, hemoglobin, and liver function. Stress tests (running on a treadmill while being monitored) are often part of the health screening process. Once the health assessment has been completed, the second component involves a physical fitness program that usually includes stressful aerobic activities such as jogging, bicycling, swimming, and aerobic dance. In addition, weight training may be part of the exercise regimen. The program is usually monitored by the wellness program staff. The third component of the program, educational activities, is designed to inform employees about common health risks such as hypertension, obesity, smoking, high cholesterol, and stress. Educational activities are directed primarily at bringing about lifestyle changes.[98] The company profile that begins this chapter describes the wellness program put into place at Adolph Coors Company.

Some firms sponsor health fairs in place of wellness programs. These fairs take place on specified days each year, have screening and educational components, and usually refer employees to off-site fitness centers for physical fitness programs, workshops, and counseling.

Companies have used a number of incentives to encourage employee participation in wellness programs. They have provided awards for physical fitness and health, cash bonuses for miles walked, run, swam, or cycled, compensation for nonabsenteeism, discounts at local health clubs, competitions for weight loss or physical fitness, and recognition for special wellness achievements.[99] U-Haul International, Inc., began a program in 1990 that encouraged its 13,000 workers to stop smoking and lose or gain weight, depending upon what their ideal weight was. The hope was to reduce the company's $17 million annual health

[97]The Bureau of National Affairs, Inc., "Wellness Programs Quite Common," *Bulletin to Management* (April 25, 1991), p. 127.

[98]See, for example, The Bureau of National Affairs, Inc., "Healthy Workers Make World of Difference," *Bulletin to Management* (June 7, 1990), p. 177.

[99]Lisa Gettings and Nick Maddox, "When Health Means Wealth," *Training and Development Journal* (April 1988), p. 82. See also Barbara Scherr Trenk, "Corporate Fitness Programs Become Hearty Investments," *Management Review* (August 1989), pp. 33–37; Edward J. Cooper, "Wellness Programs Slow Rising Costs," *Safety and Health* (April 1990), pp. 46–48; and Albert R. Karr, "The Carrot: More Firms Use Financial Lures to Foster Healthy Living," *The Wall Street Journal* (March 26, 1991), p. PA1.

insurance bill. Unlike other plans, though, U-Haul's deducted $5 every week from the paychecks of employees who smoked or were overweight or underweight.[100]

Until recently, little hard evidence was available on the effectiveness of employee wellness programs. Several companies have noted substantial savings in health care insurance costs, while others have claimed that absenteeism and sick days have been reduced.[101] Eight thousand Johnson & Johnson employees who participated in a "Live for Life" program were followed for 3 years. The program included stress management, fitness, cessation of smoking, weight control, and informational activities. Johnson & Johnson made a comprehensive study of the costs and benefits of the programs. The conclusion was that the program saved $378 per employee by lowering absenteeism and by slowing the rise in health-care expenses. The program cost per employee was $200.[102] Johnson & Johnson Health Management, Inc., is marketing the Johnson & Johnson program to about 60 companies and their 840,000 employees. Prudential Insurance Company measured the cost savings associated with the wellness program at its Houston office and found that disability days were reduced by 20 percent. This resulted in a savings of $1.93 for every dollar spent on their program and facility. In addition, the company's major medical costs dropped from $574 to $312 for each participant in the study.[103] "At Control Data Corporation, employees who maintained their weight, did not smoke, and exercised regularly filed significantly fewer health claims over $5,000 than those who were overweight, who were inactive, and who smoked."[104] It is estimated that over a 10-year period the wellness program at Control Data Corporation returned $4 for every $1 invested.[105] In other cases, companies have not documented tangible cost savings but believe that job satisfaction, morale, productivity, and general well-being among employees have been enhanced.[106]

[100]Rhonda Rundle, "U-Haul Puts High Price on Vices of Its Workers," *The Wall Street Journal* (February 14, 1990), p. B1.

[101]See, for example, "Health Promotion Brings Dollars-and-Cents Return," *The Wall Street Journal* (September 18, 1990), p. PB1; Karen M. Conrad, John Riedel, and James O. Gibbs, "Effect of Work-site Programs on Employee Absenteeism," *AAOHN Journal* (December 1990), pp. 573–579; and "Wellness Programs at Work: A Healthy Return For Employees—and the Bottom Line," *Mayo Clinic Nutrition Letter* (February 1990), pp. 2–4.

[102]Neal Templin, "Johnson & Johnson 'Wellness' Program for Workers Shows Healthy Bottom Line," *The Wall Street Journal* (May 21, 1990), p. B1.

[103]See Dennis Thompson, "Wellness Programs Work for Small Employers, Too," *Personnel* (March 1990), pp. 26–28, for a description of this study and of studies at The Canadian Life Assurance Company and Johnson & Johnson.

[104]Norma R. Fritz, "Wellness Programs Thrive," *Personnel* (March 1988), pp. 7–8.

[105]The Bureau of National Affairs, Inc., "Wellness: Curing Company Ills," *Bulletin to Management* (October 10, 1991), p. 320.

[106]See The Bureau of National Affairs, Inc., "Wellness Programs Are a Good Investment," *Bulletin to Management* (February 7, 1991), p. 39, for the results of a survey conducted by Coopers & Lybrand.

■ Summary and Conclusions

Employee safety, health, and well-being are important issues. Managers have the responsibility of ensuring that workers are not unnecessarily endangered, and that they are fully aware of and properly trained and prepared for unusual workplace risks. OSHA was passed by Congress to assist employers in the determination of workplace safety standards and to protect workers from employers who chose to ignore or otherwise compromise workplace safety. OSHA can regulate work environments, inspect the workplace, and administer fines for failure to comply with its regulations. In addition, state and federal court decisions have established in common law an expanded basis for managerial financial and criminal liability for damages to workers resulting from workplace hazards.

As society has experienced such problems as chemical substance abuse, AIDS, and the ever-increasing stresses on the individual (and their resultant emotional toll), so too have employers. Further, there is a growing recognition that work is an important part of life and that organizations, by providing more than simply a safe place to work, can have a positive impact on the physical and psychological well-being of employees. This has led organizations to investigate and establish employee-oriented programs, and policies such as wellness programs and EAPs. These programs, where established, appear to have benefited both the employee and the organization.

This appreciation of the well-being of employees represents a change in the early historical relationship between employer and employee. Thus far it has worked to the advantage of both. There is every reason to believe it will continue.

■ Questions

1. Common law suits that were based upon employer negligence proved to be an inadequate remedy for injured workers. Why? In passing OSHA, Congress empowered it to perform certain regulatory and administrative duties in order to ensure a safe workplace. What were these duties, and how well do supporters and critics of OSHA feel that it has carried them out?

2. Smoking policies are becoming more common in the workplace. What are some characteristics of an effective smoking policy? How would you set up a policy if asked to do so by your employer?

3. Do you believe that EAPs are a good idea? What should be considered by an employer when establishing an EAP? Outline how you would establish an EAP for a large organization.

4. Employee wellness programs are becoming very popular. What are the characteristics of employee wellness programs? What are they designed to accomplish? What reasons do you believe might be responsible for the increased interest in these programs?

☐ APPLICATIONS AND CASE EXERCISES

1. There is general agreement that managers can be held responsible for worker safety if they have personal knowledge of unsafe working conditions. Do you think that this is reasonable? Does this place managers in a position where they may have to "blow the whistle" on superiors in order to protect themselves from prosecution? What general procedures and policies would you establish to ensure that the workplaces you supervise are safe?

2. Recent workers' compensation decisions in state courts have created three new stress-related classifications for workers. Explain each classification and provide work-related examples of each. Do you believe that they are reasonable classifications of legitimate work-related injuries? Why or why not? Do you believe that they will lead to an explosion of frivolous workers' compensation cases or to justifiable awards for long overlooked worker injuries?

3. No one questions the promise of genetic testing for improving the safety and health of employees. Many people are concerned, however, over the potential for this technology to create a group of Americans permanently denied employment because of a genetic predisposition to cancer or some other costly disease. Do you believe that an employer should have the right to deny employment to someone because he or she has a greater than average likelihood of developing an expensive disease? Outline the positions on both sides of this issue as part of your response.

4. At the turn of the century it was not uncommon for paternalistic employers to attempt to influence or regulate the off-duty behavior of their employees on moral or religious grounds. In Chapter 13 we saw that some employers are attempting to influence the off-duty behavior of employees through disciplinary actions in order to avoid public embarrassment and to preserve their business images. In a controversial move in 1987, USG Acoustical Products in Chicago banned smoking by workers both at home and at work. The company's justification for banning smoking at home was the need to protect the company from future liability from occupational hazard claims based on the research showing that the interactive effects of smoke (as a pollutant) and smoking (physical effects on lung functioning) with many indoor pollutants is a major contributing factor to occupational diseases. Although this research cannot be disputed, do you believe that an employer should regulate the off-duty behavior of employees in order to lessen the risk of occupational diseases? At what point should an employer's responsibility for, or power over, employees end?

5. His company has just developed an EAP, and J. C. Smith is wondering whether he should become involved in it. Smith knows that he has a drinking problem, but he is unsure as to whether he is an alcoholic. In fact, he isn't quite sure what an alcoholic is. He knows that he drinks far more than his friends. Since he has always been able to hide his drinking at work, he feels that his problem isn't that bad.

   Yesterday Mr. Smith came dangerously close to severely injuring himself and another worker while he was driving a forklift in the warehouse. Since no one was hurt, they both decided not to report the incident. However, Smith knows he was at fault and is worried that he might not be able to prevent a similar incident from occurring again. He wants to stop drinking, but he cannot seem to manage it on his own.

The company EAP might allow him to receive the help that he feels that he needs. Smith's biggest worry is that if he enrolls in the program the company will find out about his problem and use it against him. He needs this job, and being labeled an unreliable drunk will not help him keep it or find another job. In addition, he is not sure if his supervisor will have access to his medical records if he enrolls, nor does he feel comfortable seeking out the program because it is run through the personnel/human resource department and everyone will see him talking with the program administrator.

Smith is becoming resigned to trying to cope with his problem himself. There is too much uncertainty involved in the company's program. He will just have to be more careful when he's been drinking on the job.

Do you feel that Smith has some legitimate concerns? What are they? How would you design an EAP that would take care of them and make it more likely that he would seek help?

PART FOUR INTEGRATIVE CASES

▨ The Wellness Program at Nissan Motor Manufacturing Corporation, U.S.A.

In 1983, Nissan Motor Manufacturing Corporation U.S.A. opened its Smyrna, Tennessee, production facility and, over the following 3 years, increased the annual production capability of the $848 million plant to 265,000 vehicles. By mid-1988, Nissan's 3,300 employees were working two shifts, manufacturing trucks and Sentras in one of the most technically advanced automobile plants in the world. A tour of the Smyrna plant also reveals Nissan's commitment to employee wellness. The company's wellness philosophy states: "The quality of our product is only as good as the quality of life for our employees." Nissan defines wellness "as the progressive realization of a personal pre-determined worthwhile goal in any of six areas: spiritual, mental, physical, occupational, social and familial." The objective of the Nissan wellness program is "to achieve individual excellence through team support and to create a wellness work place culture that reinforces quality lifestyles." Because of its commitment to wellness, Nissan received the first "Wellness In the Workplace" award during the national Wellness in the Workplace Conference in 1986.

Nissan provides several programs to help employees identify their personal wellness needs and achieve individual goals. The core of the wellness program, the Wellness in Nissan (WIN) system, provides individual consultations, work-group meetings (4–25 employees per group), fitness center screening and training programs, educational classes, and recreational activities for employees and their spouses. With the assistance of trained group facilitators, WIN focuses on creating a wellness culture in the workplace that facilitates individual positive lifestyle change. Workshops and educational materials are used to help employees make lifestyle changes and set fitness goals.

Nissan initially constructed a 12,500-square-foot Fitness Center at the Smyrna plant for all employees and their spouses and then later expanded the field house (40,000 square feet, costing $3.9 million). The new field house, known as the *Nissan Activity Center*, is a two-level structure. The lower level contains a regulation basketball court, locker and shower facilities, a lobby area with ping pong, pool, and chess, an aerobics area with specially designed floors, and a wellness library. The second level houses a track and a large area for Nautilus training. Outside the activity center, Nissan has provided an Olympic-sized pool with six lanes and a diving well, four tennis courts, two softball fields, a jogging trail, practice golfing facilities, and an archery field.

In order to participate in the Fitness Center programs, employees and spouses complete a group health habit assessment (HHA) and preentry screening (PES) that includes a medical screening to determine health risks. Employees also have the option of participating in strength, flexibility, structural analysis, body composition, and aerobic capacity assessments. After successful completion of the screenings, employees and spouses may participate in one of the following training programs: Nautilus training, general fitness training, and major motion (aerobics, strength, flexibility, balance, and coordination).

Nissan also offers wellness educational programs in nutrition and weight management,

Based on information supplied by Nissan Motor Manufacturing Corporation, U.S.A.

smoking cessation, stress management, hypertension control, healthy back, and general wellness. Employees may request individual consultations with the wellness staff. In addition, Nissan offers employees a variety of recreational programs such as softball, basketball, volleyball, bowling, tennis, golf, fishing, and badminton. Many of the recreational activities are conducted during lunch breaks. Employees also form intramural teams and competitive leagues.

Questions

1. Why are an increasing number of corporations establishing fitness centers for employees? Discuss.
2. What long-term impact might a fitness center such as the one at Nissan have on group health insurance costs, absenteeism, and on-the-job accidents?
3. Discuss some of the general considerations that need to be addressed in designing, staffing, and running a comprehensive employee fitness program.

■ A Hunting Episode That Backfired

David Swanson, a locomotive engineer with 21 years of seniority, and Timothy Summers,[1] a locomotive brakeman with 19 years of seniority, were operating a 96-car ore train for the Erie Mining Company. After a 3-hour trip to an unloading site and a 30-minute wait during the unloading operation, the pair was en route on the return trip down the company's main railroad line. This line traversed a large wilderness area containing wild game. For safety reasons, the company had issued special notices approximately 10 years ago that prohibited hunting along this route. Employees who disregarded this rule were subject to disciplinary action. To amuse themselves during trips along the railroad line, however, crew members occasionally engaged in "dry hunting" by taking imaginary shots at wildlife that they would spot from the cab of the locomotive. Such activities were accompanied by shouts of "I'll get that deer" or "I just shot that bear."

Earlier that day, Mr. Summers drove his automobile to a rendezvous point where he was to meet Mr. Swanson, who would then drive the crew to the location where the train was to depart. During his drive to meet Swanson and the other crew members, Summers noticed a loaded 22-caliber, model 66 German 8-cylinder hunting pistol on the floor of his automobile. The gun had been left in the car by Summers' son. Fearing that it would be stolen, Summers decided to take the gun with him rather than leave it in the automobile. He then placed the weapon in a handbag of the type commonly used by railroad crews for their lunches and sundries.

After the return trip was underway, Summers sat back in his locomotive seat, lit a cigarette, and decided to shoot crows if he had the opportunity. Reaching in his bag, he checked the pistol, spun the chamber, and saw that it was "all brass." When he spotted a crow, Summers reached into the bag to get the pistol and intended to open the door behind Swanson, who was at the controls of the locomotive, and take a shot. Summers told Swanson that "he was going to get that crow." But as he attempted to pull the gun from the bag, the weapon snagged. Summers then pulled the gun out barrel first with the weapon pointed at his throat. The gun fired, striking Summers and injuring him seriously. At this point Swanson administered first aid, and then stopped the train at a nearby crossing where an ambulance transported Summers to the hospital.

[1]The facts in this case are true, but the names of the parties involved have been changed.

Citing his irresponsible and reckless conduct, the company fired Summers. Swanson received a 3-day suspension for failing to follow operating rules and take proper measures to protect his crew and the train.

Questions

1. Both Summers and Swanson had good employment records prior to this offense. Should the company have considered this fact before taking disciplinary action?
2. Because the accident occurred so quickly and Swanson did not realize that Summers was carrying a loaded weapon, was the company's relatively minor punishment of Swanson justified?
3. Although the company had prohibited hunting along the railroad right of way, there was no specific rule against crew members carrying weapons while operating a locomotive. Should the company have such a rule, or does common sense dictate that loaded weapons have no place in the cab of a locomotive?
4. What penalties do you believe are appropriate in this case? Discuss.

■ Fired for Dating a Competitor: An Invasion of Privacy?

Virginia Rulon-Miller was hired by IBM in 1967 as a receptionist in the Philadelphia Data Center. At the time of hiring, she was told that "career opportunities are available to [employees] as long as they are performing satisfactorily and are willing to accept new challenges." During her employment at the Data Center she attended night school and earned a bachelor's degree.

Ms. Rulon-Miller's career at IBM progressed rapidly as she mastered one job after another and received several promotions. After working as a receptionist in Philadelphia, she was promoted to equipment scheduler and received her first merit award. She was subsequently transferred to Atlanta, Georgia, where she worked as a data processor. From there, she was assigned to the position of marketing support representative in San Francisco, where she trained IBM customers to use newly purchased equipment. In 1973, Ms. Rulon-Miller was promoted to the position of product planner, a job that involved transfers to Austin, Texas, and then Lexington, Kentucky. At the urging of her managers, she enrolled at the IBM sales school in Dallas and, upon graduation, was transferred back to San Francisco.

Ms. Rulon-Miller's performance at her IBM position in the financial district of San Francisco was exemplary. After her first year on the job, she was given the highest possible performance rating by her manager. One year later, IBM reorganized its office products division and Ms. Rulon-Miller was assigned to office systems. As in the past, her performance was rated at the top of the appraisal scale. She was very successful at selling office equipment, and received a number of prizes for her efforts. She was then put into the "Accelerated Career Development Program." This was IBM's way of indicating that Ms. Rulon-Miller had management potential and, in 1978, she was named marketing manager in the office products branch.

During her time in San Francisco, Ms. Rulon-Miller was dating Matt Blum. Mr. Blum was a former account manager for IBM who left the company in 1977 and took a position with QYX, an IBM competitor in office products. Ms. Rulon-Miller's superiors were aware of her relationship with Blum and did not initially object. Throughout 1979, Ms. Rulon-Miller continued to flourish in her management position and earned a $4,000 merit raise. One week later, her manager, Phillip

Callahan, left a message for Ms. Rulon-Miller stating that he wanted to see her. When she entered his office, Mr. Callahan confronted Ms. Rulon-Miller and wanted to know whether she was dating Blum. Callahan continued by telling her that the dating constituted a conflict of interest. He then gave her a "couple of days to a week" to think about it. He also made it clear that she would lose her job if she insisted on continuing her relationship with Mr. Blum.

Rather than allowing Ms. Rulon-Miller to contemplate the dilemma, Callahan called her back into his office the following day. He told her that "he had made up her mind for her," and when she protested, he ordered her to turn in her company ID card and office keys and terminated her. Callahan later claimed that he was not dismissing Ms. Rulon-Miller but was simply transferring her to another division.

Ms. Rulon-Miller filed charges against IBM for wrongful termination and intentional infliction of emotional stress. A California court awarded her $200,000 in punitive damages and an additional $100,000 in compensatory damages.

Questions

1. Did IBM have a right to discharge Ms. Rulon-Miller because of her at-will status? What exceptions to the employment-at-will doctrine might have aided Ms. Rulon-Miller in her case? Do you think a different verdict might have been rendered in a less liberal state than California?

2. IBM did not demonstrate that Ms. Rulon-Miller's relationship with Mr. Blum actually posed a conflict of interest. How would the company prove such a conflict? If a conflict of interest existed, then would the company have a right to fire Ms. Rulon-Miller?

3. What factors should a company consider when drawing the line between an employee's off-duty conduct and work-related conduct? In what ways can a company violate an individual employee's right to privacy?

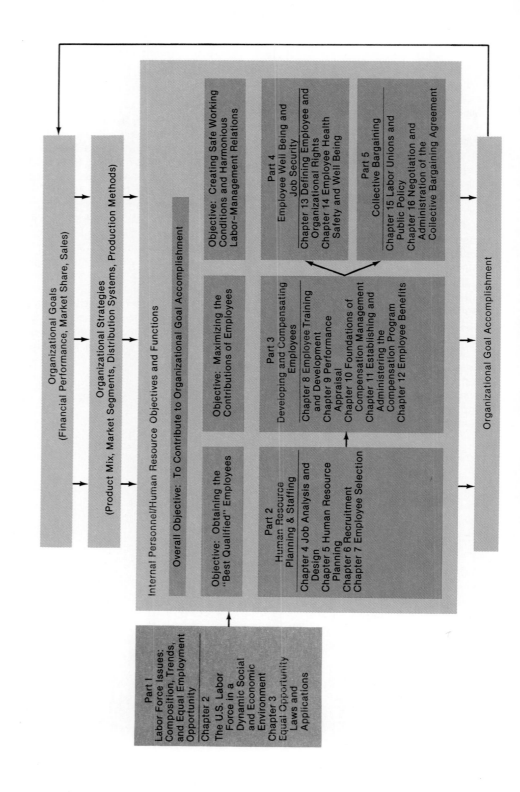

Organizational Goals
(Financial Performance, Market Share, Sales)

Organizational Strategies
(Product Mix, Market Segments, Distribution Systems, Production Methods)

Internal Personnel/Human Resource Objectives and Functions

Overall Objective: To Contribute to Organizational Goal Accomplishment

Part I
Labor Force Issues: Composition, Trends, and Equal Employment Opportunity

Chapter 2
The U.S. Labor Force in a Dynamic Social and Economic Environment
Chapter 3
Equal Opportunity Laws and Applications

Objective: Obtaining the "Best Qualified" Employees

Part 2
Human Resource Planning & Staffing

Chapter 4 Job Analysis and Design
Chapter 5 Human Resource Planning
Chapter 6 Recruitment
Chapter 7 Employee Selection

Objective: Maximizing the Contributions of Employees

Part 3
Developing and Compensating Employees

Chapter 8 Employee Training and Development
Chapter 9 Performance Appraisal
Chapter 10 Foundations of Compensation Management
Chapter 11 Establishing and Administering the Compensation Program
Chapter 12 Employee Benefits

Objective: Creating Safe Working Conditions and Harmonious Labor–Management Relations

Part 4
Employee Well Being and Job Security

Chapter 13 Defining Employee and Organizational Rights
Chapter 14 Employee Health Safety and Well Being

Part 5
Collective Bargaining

Chapter 15 Labor Unions and Public Policy
Chapter 16 Negotiation and Administration of the Collective Bargaining Agreement

Organizational Goal Accomplishment

PART FIVE

COLLECTIVE BARGAINING

■ Labor-management relations is a primary concern of personnel/human resource administrators. In unionized firms, personnel managers must bargain in good faith with the union designated by the employees as their exclusive bargaining representative. Part V presents two chapters on collective bargaining. Chapter 15, Labor Unions and Public Policy, provides an overview of the labor movement in the United States. Unions have helped many workers attain better wages, hours, and working conditions than they might have otherwise. The U.S. labor movement has been guided by dedicated and sometimes colorful individuals; it has also been marked by struggles that occasionally turned violent. Today, labor unions are run by leaders who work hard to meet their members' needs. Unfortunately, their efforts have been overshadowed by the bad press associated with labor disputes that have received widespread publicity and charges of infiltration by organized crime in a few unions. Chapter 15 presents a brief history of unions and then discusses the extensive federal regulation of labor-management relations. Unions as organizations are also examined, along with their organizing strategies and the impact that organized labor has on the workplace. In recent years, a great deal of attention has been given to management's response to union-organizing efforts. Management tactics, both legal and illegal, are also discussed in Chapter 15.

Chapter 16, Negotiation and Administration of the Collective Bargaining Agreement, presents an analysis of how union and management negotiators prepare for and conduct contract talks. The various stages of the collective bargaining process are discussed, along with the tactics that are employed at the bargaining table. Strikes, the most publicized aspect of union-management relations, are examined in terms of their frequency, impact, and legal status. Contrasts between private and public sector labor relations are also briefly analyzed. Finally, the administration of the collective bargaining agreement and the institution of labor arbitration are discussed. Sources of grievances, the manner in which arbitrators evaluate grievances, and the union's duty of fair representation are among the topics covered.

15 ∎

Labor Unions and Public Policy

■ LEARNING OBJECTIVES

After reading this chapter you should

1. Understand the historical roots and current state of the U.S. labor movement.
2. Have an overview of the federal labor laws that directly affect union-management relations.
3. Understand the structure of unions and their mode of operation.
4. Gain insights into union organizing campaigns and the tactics employed by union and management.
5. Understand the impact of unions on organizations and their employees.

■ INTRODUCTORY VIGNETTE

The United Auto Workers' Organizing Campaign at Nissan, U.S.A.

The summer of 1989 was a milestone in U.S. labor-management relations as the United Auto Workers (UAW) neared a showdown certification election with Nissan, U.S.A. The UAW sent 30 organizers to Smyrna, Tennessee, in an attempt to capture a union certification election victory. The UAW's efforts promised a handsome payoff in future union dues revenues if they could win the election because the plant employed 2,400 workers at the time of the organizing campaign. The following excerpt from *The Wall Street Journal* captures the atmosphere prior to the election.

> But Nissan is pulling out all of the stops. It airs slick messages over the plant's closed circuit television system, such as the one that blames the union for layoffs at GM and shows Mr. Benefield [Nissan USA's president] noting that Nissan has never had a layoff. "Do you want job security at Nissan," he asks workers, "or do you want job security UAW style?"

. . .The union, for its part, has shipped in 30 professional organizers. They put ads in the local papers, hand out leaflets to workers as they enter and leave [the plant], and make housecalls. Some 1,700 of the 2,400 workers have received visits.

The heated atmosphere has made the factory a house divided. In the cafeteria, "they sit at their own tables, and we sit at ours," says Stanley Tribble, 57, who opposes the UAW. "You don't eat with your enemies."

Jerry C. Waldrop, another foe of the UAW, has a friend who favors the union. They don't discuss it. "I still consider the young man my friend," he says, "although sometimes I'd like to choke him."

Workers wear their hearts on their sleeves. Pro-union forces in shirts that read "Vote Yes for a Safer Workplace" work alongside people wearing shirts saying "I Can Speak for Myself." Both sides try to appeal to patriotism: Anti-union workers have adopted the American flag as their symbol at rallies, while a pro-union T-shirt seemingly tries to tap anti-Japanese sentiment by proclaiming: "Unite! The 13 Colonies did it."[1]

This excerpt illustrates the emotionalism that often accompanies union efforts to organize a group of employees. UAW lost the election at Nissan by a 2:1 margin. All of the time and money spent by the union appear to have been for naught (under federal law, the union could not seek another certification election for at least 12 months and has not done so for over 2 years). Perhaps even more damaging was the fact that the UAW's defeat in Smyrna, Tennessee, received nationwide media attention. Labor advocates regarded the defeat as a major setback from which they could recover, but other observers such as CNN's Patrick Buchanan (who later became a presidential candidate) pointed to the defeat of the UAW at Nissan as proof of the demise of organized labor. The campaign is an excellent illustration of how effective management tactics can be used to defeat a union in an organizing campaign. As we will see in this chapter, management has adopted an aggressive stance to prevent unions from organizing their employees. We will also see that unions are beginning to take new initiatives to maintain their viability.

■ Introduction

The terms *union-management relations* and *collective bargaining* conjure up images of tense negotiation sessions in smoke-filled rooms, strong-arm tactics, and violent strikes. Although the relationship between union and management is generally adversarial, the days of table pounding and shouting during negotiations,

[1]Gregory A. Patterson, "The UAW's Chances at Japanese Plants Hinge on Nissan Vote," *The Wall Street Journal* (July 25, 1989), p. 1. Reprinted with permission of *The Wall Street Journal* 1989 Dow Jones & Company, Inc. All rights reserved worldwide.

mass worker rallies, and strikes that resemble miniature wars have largely been replaced by a more cool, calculating, well-informed, and intelligent approach to labor relations.[2]

Personnel/human resource managers in unionized firms must deal with unions and be especially cognizant of labor laws affecting union-management relations. Unions have helped their members achieve a number of economic and social benefits. Today, approximately one of six nonagricultural employees is a union member. For personnel/human resource directors working in unionized firms, the task of designing and administering personnel programs and policies offers the additional challenge of coping with a *collective bargaining agreement* that is jointly negotiated by union and management. The collective bargaining agreement is a written contract covering many of the personnel policies that affect recruitment and selection, training and development, performance appraisal, compensation, and employee benefits, disciplinary matters, and health and safety. Once the collective bargaining agreement is negotiated, the union acts as a watchdog to ensure that the letter and spirit of the contract provisions are followed. Through a process called *contract administration* the union and management use a grievance procedure and binding arbitration to resolve disagreements over the interpretation and application of contract terms.

Events involving collective bargaining and labor relations also affect our society and economy. Strikes and lockouts associated with labor-management disputes occasionally pose inconveniences for customers and suppliers. On a broader level, collective bargaining can affect wages, prices, technological change, and unemployment levels.

■ The History of Labor Unions

Nineteenth-century unions were grass-roots organizations that were forced to deal with strong opposition by companies, a lack of support by judges and legislators, and an economy that was in transition from one that was agriculturally based to one in which work life was centered in industrial factories. Early unions were responding to the subpar wages and deplorable working conditions that characterized industrial life in the 1800s. Workers, some of whom were children, were often forced to work long hours in unsafe working conditions. Inhabitants of the early factories had no *individual* power to improve their compensation and working conditions; unions represented a way in which employees could use the power of *collective* action to improve life at work. Many of the early labor organizations also had short life spans. The first union formed in the United States was the Philadelphia Cordwainers (shoemakers) in the late 1700s. It was not until after

---

[2]Unfortunately, the labor disputes and strikes that make the news often represent the worst that collective bargaining has to offer and are not representative of the more responsible but less sensational events that typify labor-management relations.

1830, however, that an interest in unions on a national scale began to surface. Labor-saving technology, politically inept immigrants from Europe, adverse publicity created by employers, and suppressive public policy curtailed the success and growth of unions throughout most of the nineteenth century. During this period, several national unions were permanently established, but attempts to form stable labor federations proved unsuccessful.

Prior the landmark court case *Commonwealth v. Hunt* (1842), unions were regarded as illegal criminal conspiracies.[3] Even after this decision, labor organizations were still regarded as civil conspiracies if they damaged an employer's business. This led to the use of the injunction as a weapon to prevent unions from organizing workers and bargaining collectively with the employer. The use of labor injunctions to stop economic strikes was criticized because a temporary injunction could be granted without a full court hearing, and employers frequently turned to the injunction to avoid bargaining with the union. By interrupting strikes or other concerted union activities with injunctions, employers could dampen workers' enthusiasm for organized labor and dilute the union's bargaining power. In fact, unions were sometimes broken when courts issued injunctions to curtail strikes.

The Early Unions

The Knights of Labor

Organized in 1862 to represent garment cutters and reorganized in 1869 to welcome all workers, the Knights of Labor represented a variety of occupational groups.[4] The Knights were interested in increasing wages, forcing employers to pay weekly rather than monthly wages, changing what they perceived as unfair labor laws, supporting equal pay for men and women, and an 8-hour day. Although these goals are not unusual by today's standards, they were considered radical during the latter half of the nineteenth century. In fact, Terence V. Powderly, the Knights' best-known leader, opposed economic strikes and naively favored negotiation and employer persuasion rather than economic threats and sanctions. The Knights functioned not only as a union, but also as a social club, political group, and education society.

The Knights' influence and membership diminished by the end of the nineteenth century due to a poorly designed organizational structure, bad publicity caused by strikes, and Powderly's overly intellectual ideals, which the Knights of Labor members found difficult to comprehend.[5] Despite the fact that their success was short-lived, the Knights are historically important because they demonstrated

---

[3]4 Metcalf 3 (1842).

[4]See Terence V. Powderly, *Thirty Years of Labor: 1859–1889* (Columbus, Ohio: Excelsior Publishing House, 1889); Joseph G. Raybeck, *A History of American Labor* (New York: Macmillan Book Company, 1968); Norman J. Ware, *The Labor Movement in the United States, 1860–1895* (Gloucester, Massachusetts: Peter Smith, reprinted 1959); Leon Fink, *Workingmen's Democracy: The Knights of Labor and American Politics* (Urbana, Illinois: University of Illinois Press, 1983).

[5]Powderly insisted that Knights members listen to intellectual speeches and refrain from drinking beer at picnics in order to prevent them from being distracted from the business at hand.

the potential power of federating unions on a national level, organizing skilled and unskilled workers in the same union.[6]

The American Federation of Labor (AFL)

The era of the potentially powerful Knights of Labor was marked by organizational and jurisdictional friction among its member unions. Samuel Gompers of the Cigarmakers Union and other leaders decided that it was time to consolidate national unions into a federation while simultaneously respecting the jurisdictional sovereignty of unions. Unlike the Knights of Labor, Gompers focused on the concept of business unionism, which emphasized improving the wages, hours, and working conditions of *skilled workers*. He regarded the socialists with disdain and he viewed the unskilled masses of illiterate and docile immigrant workers as politically powerless. The AFL was founded in 1887. The early going for the fledgling federation was rocky, but it survived for nearly 70 years before merging with the Congress of Industrial Organizations (CIO) in 1955.

The AFL under Samuel Gompers operated on the basis of the following strategies:

1. Collective bargaining with employers over wages, hours, and working conditions.
2. Backing of political candidates who were supportive of organized labor. Gompers did not believe that a separate labor party should be established because of its potentially divisive effect on the political system.
3. Working within the capitalistic system to achieve better conditions for workers.
4. Establishing unions with sound organizational structures and financial policies.
5. Use of the economic strike to pressure employers into meeting the demands of unions.
6. Organizing efforts that focused on skilled craft workers rather than the unskilled masses that worked in factories.[7]

Many of Gompers' ideas on organized labor are found in the operation of modern-day labor unions.

The Industrial Workers of the World (IWW)

The IWW, founded in 1905, took the Marxist position that workers must overthrow the capitalist society. IWW's ultraradical leadership under the direction of

---

[6]Perhaps the single most damaging event to the Knights was the infamous Haymarket Square riot that occurred in May 1886 in Chicago. What started as a mass rally by striking McCormick Harvester Machine Company employees resulted in bloodshed when someone threw a bomb into the crowd. The Knights were indirectly blamed for the incident, in which 10 people died. Eight persons were convicted of murder, of whom four were hanged.

[7]See Samuel Gompers and Nick Salvatore (eds.), *Seventy Years of Life and Labor: An Autobiography* (Ithaca, New York: ILR Press, Cornell University, 1984); Frank L. Grubbs, *The Struggle for Labor Loyalty: Gompers of the A.F. of L. and the Pacifists, 1917–1920* (Durham, North Carolina: Duke University Press, 1968); and Harold G. Livesay, *Samuel Gompers and Organized Labor in America* (Boston: Little, Brown, and Company, 1978).

the one-eyed "Big Bill" Haywood[8] condemned the support of capitalism, which they considered detrimental to the welfare of labor. The IWW was too radical for the majority of workers and was, for the most part, ineffective. Many IWW members were unemployed itinerant workers who did little to provide a solid membership base. Financial corruption within the organization undoubtedly weakened the IWW's position, and the labor organization was never able to muster the strength and resources necessary to have a strong or lasting effect on the American labor movement.[9]

The Congress of Industrial Organizations (CIO)

Some leaders within the AFL were critical of the federation's commitment to the organization of skilled craft workers. Supporters of industrial unions composed of unskilled workers sensed that the natural community of interest of workers employed by the same firm created a collective bargaining power that could be successfully harnessed; a strike by all workers in a plant should cause more damage to a company than a strike by a small group of skilled workers. The political tension within the leadership ranks of the AFL reached a breaking point at the 1935 AFL convention when the United Mine Workers president, John L. Lewis, punched the carpenters' union president, William Hutcheson, in the mouth in full view of the press and convention delegates. The renegade industrial unions were expelled from the AFL in 1938 and formed the CIO. After nearly 30 years of tension between the two organizations, a merger of the AFL and CIO was achieved in 1955. At this time, George Meany assumed leadership of the AFL-CIO and remained in office for the next quarter of a century.

Early Employer and Union Tactics: The Need for Federal Regulation

The questionable and sometimes violent tactics employed by management and labor during the late nineteenth and early twentieth centuries led to the passage of a series of labor laws that began with the Railway Labor Act in 1926, followed by the Norris-LaGuardia Act in 1932, the Wagner Act in 1935, the Taft-Hartley Act in 1947, and the Landrum-Griffin Act in 1959.

Government neutrality during union-management disputes is supportable when opponents possess approximately the same amount of strength, but the balance of power originally favored the employer. Although unions were not large and powerful at the turn of the century, they were thought to impede the flow of commerce and restrict economic forces by setting artificially high wage rates in violation of the Sherman Antitrust Act. The Sherman Act was originally passed by Congress to control large corporations that were suppressing competition through their monopoly power. Unions, despite their lack of size or economic influence,

---

[8]Haywood was later jailed and released on bail. He fled to the Soviet Union, where he died in 1928.

[9]Derek C. Bok and John T. Dunlop, *Labor and the American Community* (New York: Simon and Schuster, 1970), pp. 67–68.

were also liable under the Sherman Act. This meant that unions could be subjected to three penalties—a criminal charge against union leaders, a civil suit for treble (triple) damages under which rank-and-file workers could be held financially liable, and court injunctions to stop union activities when the employer could demonstrate that irreparable damage would result from union organizing efforts.[10]

In addition to being curtailed by the Sherman Act, unions were forced to deal with employers who hired private detectives, supplied weapons to antiunion employees, discharged strikers, enforced lockouts, blacklisted union supporters, insisted upon yellow-dog contracts as a condition of employment,[11] and used the police to stop peaceful picketing. Unions, on the other hand, called strikes and resorted to sabotage and destruction of property, consumer boycotts, and threats of physical and economic harm to those who did not support union goals and tactics. Widespread violence occurred in the railroad and coal mining industries. For example, a secret organization in Pennsylvania that was not a union, the Molly Maguires, destroyed property and engaged in physical violence. Responding to this and other adverse publicity, employers hired Pinkerton agents to contain legitimate unions. As violence accelerated, the public as well as employers unfortunately viewed legitimate unions in the same vein as the Molly Maguires. Violence in the garment, copper, and other industries was also common, and union leaders claimed that tough tactics were necessary for survival.[12]

Primary picketing directed at the company involved in the labor dispute was regarded as legitimate by public policymakers. Secondary picketing, however, was regarded by many as unfair because neutral employers not involved in the primary labor dispute were unfairly forced into a conflict that they had not instigated. Jurisdictional disputes between unions over whose members would perform certain jobs occurred frequently, and led to strikes and boycotts that unfairly damaged innocent employers. Even those supporting unions found jurisdictional disputes intolerable because the maximization of union power, and not the interests of employees, was often the primary goal.

■ The Regulation of Union-Management Relations

The U.S. economy fell into a depression in the early 1930s, a condition that led President Franklin D. Roosevelt to develop domestic reforms known as the *New Deal*. One aspect of the New Deal was the regulation of union-management

[10]*Loewe v. Lawlor*, 208 U.S. 274 (1908). This case is commonly refered to as the *Danbury Hatters* case.

[11]Employers forced workers to sign a yellow-dog contract in which they agreed not to join a union while employed with the firm. A violation of the yellow-dog contract usually led to firing and blacklisting of the employee. The yellow-dog contract was ruled to be a valid agreement in *Hitchman Coal & Coke Company v. Mitchell*, 245 U.S. 229 (1917). Later the Norris-LaGuardia Act (1932) made yellow-dog contracts unenforceable, and the Wagner Act (1935) then declared that such contracts were illegal.

[12]See Sidney Lens, *The Labor Wars: From the Molly Maguires to the Sitdowns* (Garden City, New York: Doubleday, 1973).

relations. Public policymakers hoped that labor disputes could be reduced and the economy stimulated by increased employment opportunities and higher wages. Prior to the New Deal, the passage of the Railway Labor Act in 1926 had already demonstrated that the union-management relationship could be regulated successfully without major hardship to the railroad industry and unions representing railroad employees. This set the stage for further legislative attempts to regulate labor-management relations. The Norris LaGuardia Act was passed in 1932 to restrict the use of injunctions against labor unions. In 1935, the Wagner Act was passed and brought considerable protection and strength to unions. Despite cries that the law was unconstitutional, the Wagner Act was upheld in a surprising five-to-four decision by the Supreme Court, a decision that established the legitimacy of regulating employer-employee relations affecting interstate commerce.[13] As a result, the federal power to control industrial relations was expanded and solidified.

The Railway Labor Act (1926)

To minimize the impact of labor disagreements and to secure government help to discourage company-dominated unions and to promote collective bargaining, rail carriers and associated unions supported federal labor legislation. Because railroads (and air carriers) transport passengers and freight across state lines and affect interstate commerce, they are subject to federal regulation. The Railway Labor Act originally covered railroad employees and, in 1936, brought airline employees under its jurisdiction.[14] Labor disputes involving contract negotiations are handled by the National Mediation Board, and disagreements over the interpretation and application of labor contract provisions are settled by the National Railroad Adjustment Board and the National Air Transport Adjustment Board. Both mediation and voluntary arbitration are provided under the act to ensure that rail and airline labor disputes are minimized.

The Norris-LaGuardia Act (1932)

Excessive use of the labor injunction by employers was a frequently criticized but potent weapon for suppressing unionism. The issuance of injunctions in federal courts was deliberately curtailed by the Norris-LaGuardia Act in 1932.[15] A temporary injunction can be secured when the employer proves that a union's actions will cause irreparable damage, violence, or harm to innocent parties. However, the temporary injunction is good for only 5 days, after which a full hearing must be held in order to secure a permanent injunction. The act also provides for civil

[13]NLRB v. Jones & Laughlin Steel Corp., 301 U.S. 1 (1973).
[14]44 Stat. 577, as amended (1926).
[15]47 Stat. 70 (1932).

damages against the person or organization seeking the injunction if it is later found to have no legitimate basis and is damaging to the union.

The Wagner Act (1935)

The passage of the Railway Labor Act suggested that collective bargaining was not a threat to labor-management harmony, and the Norris-LaGuardia Act stopped the unwarranted use of labor injunctions. However, the Norris-LaGuardia Act did not outlaw other forms of antiunion activities detrimental to unions and collective bargaining. Tactics by employers such as firing union sympathizers, blacklisting, and spying on union activities were still permissible prior to 1935.

The Wagner Act[16] was aimed only at *employer* abuses and contained the following provisions:

1. The National Labor Relations Board (NLRB) was established to enforce the provisions of the Wagner Act. NLRB decisions may be appealed to a U.S. court of appeals.[17]
2. Section 7 of the Wagner Act gave employees the right to join, form, or assist labor unions. An individual also was given the right to refrain from engaging in union activities if he or she so desired.
3. Provisions for certification elections were established to determine whether a group of employees desired to have a union act as their exclusive bargaining representative. Certification elections are conducted under NLRB auspices.
4. Five unfair labor practice charges could be brought against *employers* (only) under Section 8. The NLRB is authorized to hear the following unfair labor practices:[18]

   - *Employers cannot interfere, with, restrain, or coerce employees in the exercise of their Section 7 rights.* This means that management cannot threaten to fire union supporters, spy on union activities (or pretend to spy), or threaten to relocate a plant if the union wins a certification election to represent employees. Section 7 has been broadly construed to protect

---

[16]49 Stat. 449 (1935). See John T. Delaney, David Lewin, and Donna Sockell, "The NLRA at Fifty: A Research Appraisal and Agenda," *Industrial and Labor Relations Review* (October 1985), pp. 46–75.

[17]The reader should note that appeals regarding NLRB decisions bypass federal district courts and are heard by a U.S. court of appeals. However, appeals of other federal administrative agency decisions such as those of the EEOC are initially made to a federal district court. In recent years, the NLRB has been plagued with a backload of cases. See Edward B. Miller, *An Administrative Appraisal of the NLRB*, 3rd ed. (Philadelphia: Industrial Research Unit, The Wharton School, University of Pennsylvania, 1981); Donald L. Dotson, "Processing Cases at the NLRB," *Labor Law Journal* (January 1984), p. 9; and *Delay, Slowness in Decision-Making, and Case Backlog at the NLRB* (Washington, D.C.: U.S. Government Printing Office, 1984).

[18]Kenneth C. McGuiness and Jeffrey A. Norris, *How to Take a Case Before the NLRB* (Washington, D.C.: The Bureau of National Affairs, Inc., 1986).

employees engaging in *concerted activities* such as striking and protesting against poor working conditions.

- *Employers cannot dominate or interfere with the operation of a union.* This unfair labor practice outlaws company-dominated unions and "sweetheart" arrangements in which union and management officials collude to the detriment of union members. For example, it is an unfair labor practice for management to bribe union officials or promise a payoff to union negotiators in exchange for lowering bargaining demands.

- *Employers cannot discriminate against employees "in regard to hire or tenure of employment or any term or condition of employment" for the purpose of encouraging or discouraging membership in a labor organization.* Refusing to hire employees who are known union sympathizers, firing employees who have encouraged others to join a union, and assigning union members less desirable jobs than are given to nonunion employees are examples of violations under this unfair labor practice.

- *Employers cannot retaliate against individuals who file unfair labor practice charges with the NLRB.*

- *Employers must engage in good-faith bargaining with a legally certified bargaining representative.* The duty to bargain in good faith (discussed in Chapter 16) is complex and has been the subject of extensive debate and litigation. Employers must meet at a reasonable time and place to negotiate with the union, must supply union negotiators with information that is relevant to the bargaining process, and must make proposals and counterproposals that create movement toward a settlement. However, management is not required to reach a settlement with the union or sign a collective bargaining agreement.

The Wagner Act accomplished the congressional goals of increasing union membership and promoting collective bargaining. Because their membership levels and financial resources increased dramatically, unions began to have influence on Capitol Hill. Unions not only aided organized employees but, in addition, indirectly helped other employees because of the spillover effects of bargaining into nonunionized firms. Furthermore, the political influence generated today through the AFL-CIO has resulted in legislation that benefits both unionized and nonunionized employees.[19]

The Taft-Hartley Act (1947)

The Wagner Act constrained the unfair actions of employers, but no such sanctions were imposed on unions. The craft versus industrial union schism within the AFL that led to the formation of the CIO added to the already intense jurisdictional

[19]See Charles J. Morris (ed.), *American Labor Policy: A Critical Analysis of the National Labor Relations Act* (Washington, D.C.: The Bureau of National Affairs, Inc., 1987); and Kenneth C. McGuiness and Jeffrey A. Norris.

rivalry between some unions; prices and wages were decontrolled after World War II, and labor restlessness led to a relatively large number of strikes in 1946. Negative publicity was directed at the closed and preferential shops that restricted the employer's ability to hire the best-qualified job applicants. Secondary boycotts, race and sex discrimination, and other union practices of dubious social value also attracted public attention. Employers resented having their hands tied by the Wagner Act while unions asserted their recently acquired rights.[20] The Wagner Act was amended by the Taft-Hartley Act in 1947[21] and unions were placed under the regulatory eye of the NLRB. Congressional support for the Taft-Hartley Act was substantial, and the law was passed despite a veto by President Harry S. Truman.

The Taft-Hartley Act includes the following provisions:

1. Employees cannot be required to join a union as a condition of employment unless a valid union security agreement is negotiated between the employer and the union. In essence, an employee's right to join or not join a union is protected unless a legal union security agreement (such as the union shop provision requiring union membership with 30 days after hiring) is included within the collective bargaining agreement.[22] The closed shop (which requires that *only* union members are hired) is declared illegal under the Taft-Hartley Act. States enacting right-to-work legislation can outlaw all forms of union security, including the union shop.

2. Employers, as we have seen, were held responsible for unfair labor practice violations (known as Section 8(a) after the Taft-Hartley Act was passed); Section 8(b) of the Taft-Hartley Act enumerates unfair labor practice charges that can be levied against *unions*. The following are some of the more prominent unfair labor practice charges that can be brought against unions (also referred to as *labor organizations*):

   • *Unions cannot restrain or coerce employees with regard to joining or supporting a labor organization.* Section 7 gives employees the right to support

---

[20]Unions were given a number of rights in 1935 by the Wagner Act that were initially difficult to assert. Until 1937, when the constitutionality of the act was affirmed, many lawyers did not take the law seriously and believed that it would be ruled unconstitutional. Then, between 1941 and 1945, unions were compelled to cooperate in the war effort. Thus, it was not until 1946 that unions were finally clear of all restrictions and allowed to develop fully their organizing and bargaining strategies.

[21]61 Stat. 136, as amended (1947). The NLRB, in its decisions, commonly refers to the *combined* Wagner and Taft-Hartley Acts as the *Labor-Management Relations Act* (the original name of the Taft-Hartley Act). To further complicate matters, the act is also known as the *National Labor Relations Act* (the original name of the Wagner Act).

[22]Union security provisions are contained in many collective bargaining agreements. Their purpose is to help unions gain membership and financial support. Union security agreements include the *union shop* clause described previously, the *agency shop*, which requires that employees pay union dues even if they elect not to join the union, and the *maintenance-of-membership shop*, which requires that current members remain in the union but does not require that new employees join. Twenty-one states currently have *right-to-work laws* that outlaw most forms of union security. In addition, the *closed shop*, described previously, and the *preferential shop*, which requires that union members be given first consideration in hiring, are illegal under the Taft-Hartley Act and are banned in all 50 states.

as well as reject unions. Threats by union members or officials of bodily injury or loss of jobs for employees who cross a picket line during a strike is an example of such an unfair labor practice charge. Refusing to process the meritorious grievance of a union member who has spoken out against the union leaders is another example.

- *Unions cannot restrain or coerce an employer in the selection of a bargaining representative.* Employers have the right to designate whomever they deem appropriate to bargain on their behalf with the union.

- *Unions cannot force an employer to discriminate against an employee in order to influence union membership.* For example, a union cannot require an employer to hire only union members (closed shop) or give hiring preference to union members (preferential shop). Unions cannot force an employer to discharge or reduce the seniority of employees because they circulated a petition protesting a union policy.

- *Unions must bargain in good faith with management.* This obligation is similar to that imposed on employers. Unions cannot insist on an illegal provision (e.g., a closed shop or a racially discriminatory seniority system) in a collective bargaining agreement. It is also a violation for unions to adopt a "take-it-or-leave-it" posture with the employer at the bargaining table.

- *Unions are prohibited from engaging in certain types of strikes and boycotts.* It is illegal for a union to prevent suppliers from making deliveries to a firm as a means of forcing the company to recognize the union as the employees' bargaining representative. Likewise, a union cannot engage in a *secondary boycott* by applying pressure on a neutral employer not directly involved in a labor dispute to, in turn, put pressure on a primary employer.[23] For example, a union representing a manufacturer cannot strike or picket a supplier during a strike as a means of forcing bargaining concessions. In this case, the supplier is a neutral party to the dispute unless work normally performed by striking employees is subcontracted to the neutral firm. Strikes over *jurisdictional disputes* between two or more unions that are vying for the right to perform specific work are also illegal. Jurisdictional disputes occasionally arise in the construction industry when one union, such as the bricklayers, has a disagreement with another union, such as the carpenters, over who should build a wooden support to be used during the construction of a brick wall. The NLRB allows 10 days for the unions involved to settle the dispute on their own. If they fail to do so, the NLRB will decide which union members should perform the work.[24]

- *Unions cannot charge excessive or discriminatory initiation fees and dues.* Dues structures must be in line with area practices, custom, and the wages

[23]See Ralph M. Dereshinsky, Alan D. Berkowitz, and Philip A. Miscimarra, *The NLRB and Secondary Boycotts*, rev. ed. (Philadelphia: Industrial Research Unit, The Wharton School, University of Pennsylvania, 1981).

[24]The AFL-CIO's Building Trades Department is available to help resolve jurisdictional disputes in the construction trades.

paid to union members. Dues or fee differentials cannot be based on a member's race, sex, or age.

3. The Federal Mediation and Conciliation Service (FMCS) was established to help union and management negotiators establish collective bargaining agreements and minimize labor disputes and work stoppages. The FMCS provides mediators who assist negotiators in resolving bargaining deadlocks. Mediators, however, are not authorized to force an agreement between private sector employers and unions.

4. The act permits civil suits if either the union or management violates or ignores the terms of their agreement.

5. The act authorizes the NLRB to seek a temporary court injunction when an unfair practice violation is suspected. However, employer use of the injunction remains limited because of the Norris-LaGuardia Act.

6. Management has a "free speech" right to discuss the advantages and disadvantages of unions as long as they do not threaten to retaliate against union supporters or promise pay raises or other benefits to employees who remain loyal to the company and campaign against the union.[25]

The Landrum-Griffin Act (1959) and Union Corruption

As a result of investigations by the congressional McClellan Anti-Racketeering Committee, the Landrum-Griffin Act[26] was passed to ensure internal union democracy for members and to weed out corruption among union officers.[27] To enhance democracy within unions, a "Bill of Rights" pertaining to labor organizations was enacted by Congress. The Bill of Rights provisions stipulate that unions must have a constitution and by-laws, members must have the right to speak out against the policies of union officials without fear of retaliation, and union officers must periodically face reelection. Detailed financial and other union reports have to be supplied to both the union members and the U.S. Department of Labor. Trusteeship arrangements in which the international union headquarters seizes managerial control of a corrupt or mismanaged local union must be conducted without damaging the financial position of the local union. The Landrum-Griffin Act also regulates employers who hire labor consultants; attorneys and others who assist employers in defeating union organizing drives are required to register and submit reports to the Department of Labor. The act also regulates financial transactions involving union funds.

[25]For an analysis of the role of the NLRB in enforcing the Wagner and Taft-Hartley acts, see Charles J. Morris (ed.), *American Labor Policy: A Critical Analysis of the National Labor Relations Act* (Washington, D.C.: The Bureau of National Affairs, Inc., 1987).

[26]73 Stat. 519 (1959). The Landrum-Griffin Act also modified some provisions of the Taft-Hartley Act.

[27]Martin H. Malin, *Individual Rights Within the Union* (Washington, D.C.: The Bureau of National Affairs, Inc., 1988).

The infiltration of organized crime in some labor unions has been a problem for decades and, in recent years, has attracted considerable attention by the President's Commission on Organized Crime.[28] Labor racketeering has been defined as "the infiltration, domination, and use of a union for personal benefit by illegal, violent, and fraudulent means.[29] The report issued by the President's Commission on Organized Crime focuses on the "big four" unions: the International Longshoremen's Association (ILA), the Teamsters, the Laborer's International, and the Hotel Employees and Restaurant Employees International Union.[30] Most labor racketeering in the United States is conducted by organized crime families and syndicates that raid workers' employee benefit funds, enter into various sweetheart deals with employers that are not in the best interests of union members, and exact "insurance" payments from companies whose businesses could be irreparably damaged by an untimely strike. Labor unions controlled by organized crime can create monopolies in certain industries; as a result, businesses owned or run by criminals and crime syndicates gain an economic advantage over their competitors. Business practices such as price fixing, bid rigging, and other practices are used to destroy fair competition in an industry.

Former U.S. Attorney General Benjamin Civiletti estimated that approximately 300 local unions were severely influenced by racketeers. Despite the relatively small number of locals affected (there are approximately 65,000 local unions in the United States), the impact of organized crime in labor unions can be significant. For example, New York construction businesses cooperating with organized crime have formed a cartel, with the union serving as the enforcing agent. General contractors are told what suppliers and subcontractors to use. If a general contractor does not comply, he will either not get the job or will be unable to complete it without major disruptions. Contractors who are not part of the cartel have told the President's Commission on Organized Crime that they are unable to obtain projects in the New York construction industry. Other industries such as the garment, trucking, and retail meat industries have also been plagued by strike insurance and other forms of extortion by organized crime. As a result of organized crime's pernicious influence in some areas, the President's Commission on Organized Crime is currently proposing legal measures and a national plan of attack to reduce the impact of racketeering on unions and legitimate businesses.

◼ Union Membership Statistics and Trends

Union membership increased rapidly after 1937, the year the constitutionality of the Wagner Act was upheld by the Supreme Court. Membership quadrupled

---

[28]President's Commission on Organized Crime, *The Edge: Organized Crime, Business, and Labor Unions* (Washington, D.C.: U.S. Government Printing Office, 1986).

[29]President's Commission on Organized Crime, p. 9.

[30]"Trade Unions: The Usual Suspects," *Economist* (May 4, 1985), p. 29.

between 1937 and the end of World War II. In 1945, the percentage of nonagricultural employees who were unionized reached a peak of 35.8 percent.[31] By the mid-1980s, this percentage had decreased to approximately 16 percent. However, in absolute numbers of members, unions continued to grow until the mid-1970s because the size of the labor force continued to increase. Since 1976, unions have been losing members as well as considerable dues revenues. Major reasons for the decline in union membership are the industrial shifts away from the union strongholds in the heavy manufacturing industries of the Northeastern and Midwestern states to the lighter service and manufacturing industries in the Sunbelt, the increasing proportion of white-collar workers who are more resistant to union organizing campaigns, and the passage of legislation protecting employee rights and working conditions (e.g., health and safety, EEO, and pension reform laws such as ERISA).[32]

The decline in union membership might have been more severe had it not been for the increasing number of federal, state, and municipal employees who began unionizing in the 1960s. Favorable laws in a number of states have allowed public sector employees to join unions and bargain collectively, and President John F. Kennedy's 1962 Executive Order 10988 for federal employees paved the way for the unionization of federal government employees.

Union membership is typically concentrated in a few very large unions such as the Teamsters, National Education Association (NEA), Food and Commercial Workers (UFCW), American State, County, and Municipal Employees (AFSCME), and United Auto Workers (UAW). Nearly two thirds of all unionized employees are concentrated in fewer than 20 unions. This suggests that of the approximately 200 national unions that currently operate in the United States, many are relatively small. Unions such as the Composers and Lyricists Guild of America, the National Hockey League Players Association, and the International Horseshoers of the United States each have fewer than 1,000 members.

The Structure of U.S. Labor Unions

There are three levels of unionism in the U.S. labor movement: the *federation level*, which is dominated by the (AFL-CIO), the *international unions*, and the *local unions*. At each of these levels, distinct functions are performed that serve

[31]Chester A. Morgan, *Labor Economics*, 3rd ed. (Austin, Texas: Business Publications, Inc., 1970), p. 354.

[32]See The Bureau of National Affairs, Inc., *Unions Today: New Tactics to Tackle Tough Times* (Washington, D.C.: The Bureau of National Affairs, Inc., 1985); Doug Kalish, "The New Collar Workers and Unions' Changing Roles," *Personnel Journal* (December 1986), p. 10; "Shrinking Unions," *American Demographics* (October 1986), p. 14; "Union Membership of Employed Wage and Salary Workers," *Monthly Labor Review* (May 1986), p. 44; and Lee P. Stepina and Jack Fiorito, "Toward a Comprehensive Theory of Union Growth and Decline," *Industrial Relations* (Fall 1986), pp. 248–264.

not only union members, but also nonunion employees. Figure 15-1 outlines the basic functions for each of the three levels of unionism.

The American Federation of Labor and Congress of Industrial Organizations (AFL-CIO)

Ninety affiliated national unions comprising approximately 14 million union members and more than 60,000 local unions belong to the AFL-CIO (see Figure 15-2). Contrary to common belief, the AFL-CIO is not a labor union; it does no collective bargaining or contract administration. Its primary function is to promote the interests of labor by coordinating a wide range of joint union activities involving AFL-CIO member unions. An important mission of the AFL-CIO is to serve as the political lobbying arm for labor (both unionized and nonunionized).[33] Every 2 years, representatives of the AFL-CIO affiliated national unions meet and establish a policy to be followed until the next convention. Day-to-day AFL-CIO operations are under the control of the president and secretary-treasurer, who are elected at the convention. Leadership within the AFL-CIO and national unions has been stable and, since its inception in 1955, the federation has had only two presidents (George Meany and Lane Kirkland). When necessary, the president can convene the members of the Executive Council to discuss matters of urgent concern. Although almost 90 percent of all unionized workers in the United States belong to AFL-CIO member unions, there are some large unions that have not been affiliated with the federation, but have recently joined. The 2-million-member Teamsters Union was expelled in 1957 because of corruption found in the union's ranks by the McClellan Anti-Racketeering Committee. However, on October 24, 1987, the executive council of the AFL-CIO voted unanimously to allow the Teamsters to rejoin its ranks.[34] The United Mine Workers also recently became an AFL-CIO affiliate.

AFL-CIO headquarters are in Washington, D.C., a location that suggests the importance that it attaches to being near influential political figures. Although the AFL-CIO attempts to persuade Congress to pass laws that have a direct impact on unionized employees (such as the ill-fated Labor Reform bill in 1978, which would have made it easier for unions to organize nonunion workers), the federation also supports legislation that benefits workers from all occupations. The AFL-CIO has long supported EEO and safety legislation. Legislation that might be considered

[33]Roger Thompson, "What Labor's Agenda Could Cost You," *Nation's Business* (May 1987), p. 20; Bruce Ingersoll, "Labor Leaders Ask Congress to Stop Rash of Takeovers," *The Wall Street Journal* (April 9, 1987), p. 56 (W), p. 21 (E), col. 1; and Mitchell W. Fields, Marick F. Masters, and James W. Thacker, "Union Commitment and Membership Support for Political Action: An Exploratory Analysis," *Journal of Labor Research* (Spring 1987), p. 142.

[34]AFL-CIO, Teamsters Heal 30-Year-Old Rift," *The Greenville News* (syndicated by the *New York Times*), October 25, 1987, p. 1-A. Some of the Teamsters' motivation to realign with the AFL-CIO was based on the U.S. Justice Department's attempt to seize control of the union because of its domination by organized crime. The AFL-CIO membership estimates used here include the addition of the 2 million Teamsters' members and the fact that the U.S. Census Bureau estimated that there were 16.9 million union members in the United States in 1985.

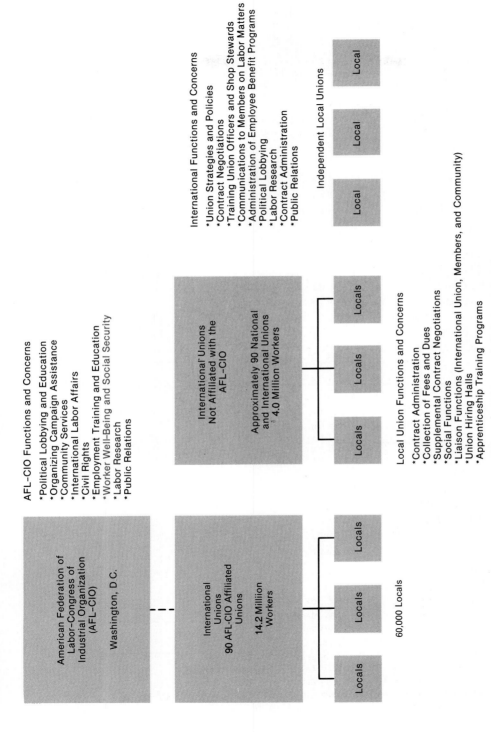

AFL–CIO Functions and Concerns

*Political Lobbying and Education
*Organizing Campaign Assistance
*Community Services
*International Labor Affairs
*Civil Rights
*Employment Training and Education
*Worker Well-Being and Social Security
*Labor Research
*Public Relations

International Functions and Concerns

*Union Strategies and Policies
*Contract Negotiations
*Training Union Officers and Shop Stewards
*Communications to Members on Labor Matters
*Administration of Employee Benefit Programs
*Political Lobbying
*Labor Research
*Contract Administration
*Public Relations

Local Union Functions and Concerns

*Contract Administration
*Collection of Fees and Dues
*Supplemental Contract Negotiations
*Social Functions
*Liaison Functions (International Union, Members, and Community)
*Union Hiring Halls
*Apprenticeship Training Programs

American Federation of
Labor-Congress of
Industrial Organization
(AFL–CIO)

Washington, D.C.

International
Unions
**90 AFL-CIO Affiliated
Unions**

**14.2 Milliion
Workers**

60,000 Locals

International Unions
Not Affiliated with the
AFL–CIO

Approximately 90 National
and International Unions
4.0 Million Workers

Independent Local Unions

FIGURE 15-1   Structure of the United States Labor Movement

589

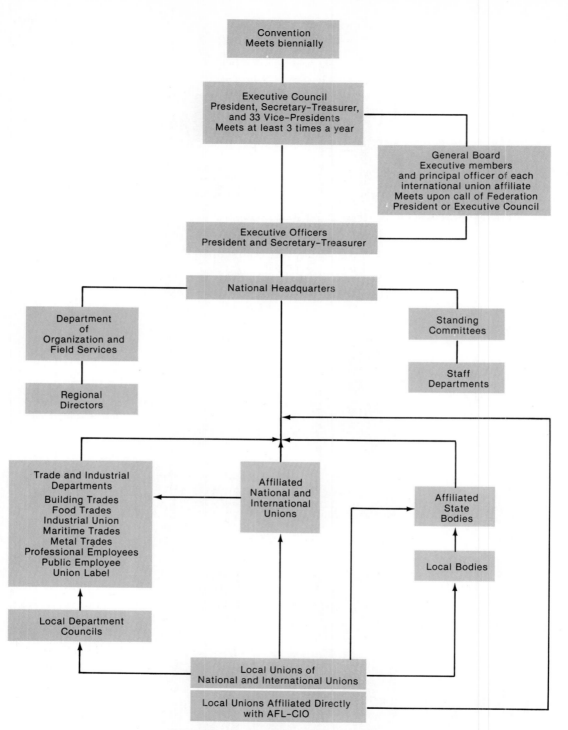

FIGURE 15-2   Structure of the AFL-CIO

Source: Courtney D. Gifford, *Directory of U.S. Labor Organizations* (Washington, D.C.: The Bureau of National Affairs, Inc., 1988), p. 2.

remote to the concerns of working people, such as forestry regulations, also receives the attention of the federation. In short, the AFL-CIO adopts a position on nearly every law that is even remotely related to labor and then attempts to sway the vote of key members of Congress through political lobbying. The federation is also involved in labor research, international labor issues, disaster relief, and other societal concerns.

International (National) Unions

Although the AFL-CIO occupies the top rung in the U.S. labor movement, the international unions are the most powerful level of organized labor. The AFL-CIO's power is informal and is confined to its ability to persuade labor leaders at the international level to adhere to the goals and objectives of the AFL-CIO. International unions establish union policy for their member locals and govern in a fashion similar to that of the headquarters of a large corporation. International unions perform a multitude of functions. These functions vary from one international to another, but most internationals are responsible for organizing nonunionized workers, negotiating collective bargaining agreements, educating union officers and agents about union matters, communicating with members on recent developments, and political lobbying efforts at the state and federal levels.[35]

The international union provides the major impetus in union organizing campaigns. Most union organizers are employed by and use international union headquarters as their operations base. In many cases, union officials at the international level select the target group of nonunion employees and plot the strategy for the organizing campaign. Representatives from the international are usually responsible for recruiting and training local employees and union members who will assist in the organizational campaign. Planning of mass meetings and distribution of union literature are also frequently coordinated through international union officials. Because of their legal expertise, employees of the international are usually responsible for initiating unfair labor practice charges against employers that arise during organizing campaigns.

Negotiation of the collective bargaining agreement is another important function for many international unions. The increasing complexity of collective bargaining agreements requires expertise at the bargaining table. Thus negotiating contracts has become a primary responsibility of the international, which often employs a cadre of professional negotiators, economists, compensation specialists, health and safety experts, and labor lawyers. When collective bargaining agreements are negotiated on a multiplant or industrywide basis, the international union becomes the focal point for contract talks with the employer. In many

---

[35]For an excellent discussion of union functions, see James Wallihan, *Union Government and Organization* (Washington, D.C.: The Bureau of National Affairs, Inc., 1985).

instances, the international negotiates a master agreement with the company and the local unions supplement the master contract with contracts that deal with single-plant or local concerns. International unions also collect vast amounts of data germane to the collective bargaining process for use by union officials and negotiators. Because the international union often negotiates collective bargaining agreements that cover employees at multiple locations, it also administers employee benefit programs. In addition, internationals establish strike funds that provide union members with an income during work stoppages.

Internationals are governed by elected officials whose authority is established by the union's constitution and bylaws. The supreme governing body for most internationals is the annual or biennial convention, which sets policy and regulates other union matters. International union presidents generally wield considerable power in making decisions about bargaining strategy, organizing campaigns, interpreting of the union's constitution and by-laws, and other operational matters. Once in office, most international union presidents manage to thwart political opposition successfully and may remain in at their posts for long periods of time by repeatedly winning the Landrum-Griffin Act-mandated elections every 5 years.[36] Although many top union officials receive annual salaries in excess of $100,000, their compensation is modest compared to that of most corporate CEOs.[37]

Mergers and acquisitions have become common growth and expansion strategies for corporations.[38] A similar although less publicized trend is also occurring among unions. For example, recent mergers include the Teamsters and the International Typographical Union (ITU),[39] the Brewery Workers Local 9 (Milwaukee) and the United Auto Workers, and the Upholsterers' International Union and the United Steel Workers Union. Union mergers have been used to pool operational costs, match and offset increasing employer size and power, accommodate rapid technological change, limit jurisdictional rivalries among unions, and adapt to the decline of old industries and the creation of new ones. Corporations usually merge or acquire another corporation to expand markets, bolster financial strength, and spread risk. However, union mergers cannot be measured in terms of profits, revenues, and cost savings; this fact has led labor experts to question the wisdom of some union mergers. Whenever a merger occurs, some union leaders gain power while others are forced to step aside or accept a less prominent role in the newly merged union. Dissidents from within the union's rank and file may also

[36]Steven L. McShane, "A Path Analysis of Participation in Union Administration," *Industrial Relations* (Winter 1986), p. 72.

[37]Jonathan Tasini, "How Much Labor Leaders Made in 1986," *Business Week* (May 4, 1987), p. 96; and Bert Spector, "Transformational Leadership: The New Challenge for U.S. Unions," *Human Resource Management* (Spring 1987), p. 3.

[38]Larry T. Adams, "Labor Organization Mergers 1979–1984: Adapting to Change," *Monthly Labor Review* (September 1984), p. 21.

[39]"Union Merger Developments," *Monthly Labor Review* (November 1985), p. 64.

create problems after a union merger. An unsuccessful or ill-advised union merger can lead to turmoil and dissension within the union ranks. Political infighting among union officials can also create problems for personnel managers who must negotiate with a union whose leadership and methods of operation have changed.[40]

Local Unions

The local union serves as the most accessible and immediate point of contact for union members. Most locals are chartered by internationals and are ultimately governed by the constitution, by-laws, and policies that are established at the international level. Local unions are responsible for dealing with the concerns of employees in a large plant, citywide area, or county. Some local unions negotiate collective bargaining agreements (or supplements to master agreements) with individual firms or a group of firms within a metropolitan area.

Local unions can be categorized into factor and nonfactory locals. As the name implies, factory locals serve union members who work in a plant (or a group of plants). That is, members of factory locals work in a permanent location, whereas nonfactory local union members move from one work site to another. The construction unions are a prime example of a nonfactory union; skilled carpenters, for example, move from one site to another and may work for more than one general contractor. Industrial local unions are composed of unskilled and semiskilled workers with different occupational skills and employment situations, whereas craft locals consist of skilled workers whose jobs and skills are homogeneous. The variety of unskilled and semiskilled workers employed in a factory might be organized by an industrial union. Skilled carpenters, masons, and electricians are usually organized on a craft union basis.

Local union members elect their presidents and secretary-treasurers at least once every 3 years, as required by the Landrum-Griffin Act. Craft unions commonly employ full-time *business agents* to conduct local union affairs such as contract negotiations and administration. Many local leaders serve on a part-time basis and receive little or no compensation for union duties. Local union leaders must be politically responsive to the concerns of rank-and-file employees. The duties of local officials include negotiating contracts, collecting membership dues and initiation fees, enforcing the collective bargaining agreement, adjusting grievances, and arranging social events. *Shop stewards* are typically regular, nonsupervisory employees who are appointed by local union officials (or elected by local union members) to take care of daily union matters in the workplace. The only difference between stewards and other employees is that stewards are authorized by the union to deal with members' grievances, answer questions

---

[40]Also see Jack Fiorito, Daniel J. Gallagher, and Cynthia V. Fukami, "Satisfaction with Union Representation," *Industrial and Labor Relations Review* (January 1988), pp. 294–307.

about the collective bargaining agreement, and oversee other official union business. Collective bargaining agreements usually grant stewards superseniority so that they are the last employees to be laid off during company reductions in force.[41]

Union Organizing Campaigns

In order to represent employees and secure the right to bargain collectively with the employer, a union goes through an organizing campaign.[42] An organizing campaign is a controversial event for management and employees, and it can create excitement, tension, and hard feelings in the workplace. Employee loyalty may be divided as the union tries to pull them toward union certification while employers are trying to convince their workers to vote against the union.[43] However, the ultimate choice of whether to select a particular union as the exclusive bargaining representative rests with employees who comprise the bargaining unit designated by the NLRB. Public concern, as outlined in the Wagner and Taft-Hartley acts, centers on ensuring that employees have *freedom* of choice in supporting or rejecting unions. Threats, bribes, or other coercive action by either management or the union that stifles the employee's ability to select or reject unionism during an organizing campaign is a violation of federal law.

Factors Affecting an Employee's Desire to Join a Union

Nearly everyone has an opinion about labor unions. Young people are often influenced by family views in supporting or rejecting unions. Later, peers, personal experiences, education, and choice of profession influence one's reaction to labor organizations. Personal experience with employer hostility, union violence, good or bad working conditions, availability of jobs, and discrimination all foster positive or negative feelings toward unions. Thus, an employee's decision to join and support a labor union during an organizing campaign is based on a number of factors, some of which are not well understood. Table 15-1 summarizes the major factors that affect the degree of employee attraction to labor unions. Some of these

---

[41]For a more detailed examination of the AFL-CIO, international unions, and local unions, see Terry L. Leap, Collective *Bargaining and Labor Relations* (New York: Macmillan Publishing Company, 1991), pp. 174–219.

[42]Alan Kistler, "Union Organizing: New Challenges and Prospects," *Annals of the American Academy of Political and Social Science* (May 1984), p. 96.

[43]See Edward J. Conlon and Daniel G. Gallagher, "Commitment to Employer and Union: Effects of Membership Status," *Academy of Management Journal*, Vol. 30, No. 1 (1987), pp. 151–162.

TABLE 15-1   Factors Affecting Employee Propensity
To Join and Support Unions

Factors in the Work Environment

Low wages and inadequate benefits
Favoritism or inconsistent conduct by supervisors
Lack of due process in disciplinary actions
Internal inequities in the pay structure
Poor and unsafe working conditions
Increasing job duties and responsibilities without commensurate pay increases
Lack of adequate communication channels between management and employees
Inadequate grievance mechanisms
Race, sex, or other forms of discrimination
Uncertainties associated with job security
Inequities in pay and promotion decisions

Personal and Demographic Factors

Socioeconomic background
Education level
Race, sex, and religion
Family and peer influences
Geographic locaton (sector of the country)
Urban versus rural residence
White- versus blue-collar orientation
Image of labor unions
Instrumentality perceptions (perceived costs versus benefits) of unions
Employee commitment to the job
Industry in which the union is organizing
Presence of right-to-work laws
Personal desire to exert more influence on the job
Peer pressure to support unions
Organizational size

Union and Management Tactics During Campaign

Union organizing tactics
Countermeasures by management
  Proactive measures
  Reactive measures

---

factors are based on empirical studies, whereas others are based primarily on the opinions and experiences of labor relations practitioners and scholars:[44]

1. Workers are more likely to join a union if there is a significant degree of dissatisfaction with wages, hours, and working conditions.

2. The primary impetus behind the unionization of white-collar workers is to obtain more *influence* over job-related conditions rather than to actually change these conditions.

3. Nonunionized blacks and other racial minorities are more willing to support unions than are unorganized white workers.

4. Female white-collar workers are more receptive to unions than their male counterparts.

5. Blue-collar workers in the South are not significantly different from blue-collar workers in the Northeast insofar as their interest in joining unions is concerned. However, white-collar workers in the South are significantly less willing to join unions than are their counterparts in the Northeast.

6. Employees working in intermediate-sized organizations are more receptive to unions than employees in very small or very large establishments.

[44]Examples of the research on employee propensities to unionize include: Herbert R. Northrup, "The AFL-CIO Blue Cross–Blue Shield Campaign: A Study of Organizational Failure," *Industrial and Labor Relations Review* (July 1990), pp. 525–541; Satish P. Deshpande and Jack Fiorito, "Specific and General Beliefs in Union Voting Models," *Academy of Management Journal* (December 1989), pp. 883–897; Gary Florkowski and Michael Schuster, "Predicting the Decisions to Vote and Support Unions in Certification Elections: An Integrated Perspective," *Journal of Labor Research* (Spring 1987), p. 191; Timothy P. Summers, John H. Betton, and Thomas A. DeCotiis, "Voting for and Against Unions: A Decision Model," *Academy of Management Review* (July 1986), p. 643; John G. Kilgour, "White-Collar Organizing: A Reappraisal," *Personnel* (August 1986), p. 14; Clive Fulligar, "A Factor Analytic Study on the Validity of a Union Commitment Scale, *Journal of Applied Psychology* (February 1986), p. 129; H. L. Angle and J. L. Perry, "Dual Commitment and the Labor-Management Relationship Climate," *Academy of Management Journal*, Vol. 29 (1986), pp. 31–50; S. M. Hills, "The Attitudes of Union and Nonunion Male Workers Toward Union Representation," *Industrial and Labor Relations Review*, Vol. 38 (1985), pp. 179–194; W. Clay Hamner and Frank J. Smith, "Worker Attitudes as Predictors of Unionization Activity," *Journal of Applied Psychology*, Vol. 63, No. 4 (1978), pp. 415–421; Henry S. Farber and Daniel H. Saks, "Why Workers Want Unions: The Role of Relative Wages and Job Characteristics," *Journal of Political Economy*, Vol. 88, No. 21 (1980), pp. 349–369; Richard B. Freeman, "Why Are Unions Faring Poorly in NLRB Representation Elections?", in Richard L. Rowan (ed.), *Readings in Labor Economics and Labor Relations* (Homewood, Illinois: Richard D. Irwin, Inc., 1985), pp. 129–141; Thomas A. Kochan, *Collective Bargaining and Industrial Relations: From Theory to Policy and Practice* (Homewood, Illinois: Richard D. Irwin, Inc., 1980), pp. 142–150; Richard B. Freeman and James L. Medoff, *What Do Unions Do?* (New York: Basic Books, Inc., 1984), pp. 26–33; Stuart A. Youngblood, Angelo S. De Nisi, Julie L. Molleston, and William H. Mobley, "The Impact of Work Environment, Instrumentality Beliefs, Perceived Labor Union Image, and Subjective Norms on Union Voting Intentions," *Academy of Management Journal*, Vol. 27 (1984), pp. 576–590; J. M. Brett, "Why Employees Want Unions," *Organizational Dynamics* (Spring 1980), pp. 47–59; Herbert G. Heneman III and Marcus Sandver, "Predicting the Outcome of Union Certification Elections: A Review of the Literature," *Industrial and Labor Relations Review* (July 1983), pp. 537–559; and Julius Getman, Stephen Goldberg, and Jeanne Herman, *Union Representation Elections: Law and Reality* (New York: Russell Sage Foundation, 1976).

7. No specific race, sex, or socioeconomic group was found to be uniformly hostile toward labor unions. A likely exception would be members of management, who are normally not targets for union organizers.

8. An estimated one third of the nonunionized labor force is willing to join a labor union under the proper circumstances.

9. Workers generally do not remember a great deal about the substance of preelection campaign statements by union organizers or management. When they do remember, however, they are more likely to vote for the side from whom the information was obtained.

10. Unions generally do not persuade large numbers of undecided or antiunion employees to support them during organizing campaigns. A union's success is usually based on obtaining a substantial number of authorization card signatures (in which the employee claims to want the union as his or her bargaining agent) before the campaign is fully developed.

11. Employees who are undecided about whether to support the union usually vote against certification.

12. The more an employer uses antiunion tactics (both legal and illegal), the more likely it is that the union will lose the certification election.

Although much has been said about individual tendencies to accept or reject labor unions, the research is somewhat limited. Younger workers, women, and blacks seem more likely to vote for unions in certification elections than other groups. A possible explanation is that these workers have traditionally held lower-paying, less desirable jobs and have exerted relatively little control over job-related matters. Moreover, blacks and women historically have experienced greater employment discrimination, a factor that could enhance their interest in unions. Blue-collar workers have been more receptive to labor unions, although the white-collar sector has taken an increasingly strong interest during the past 25 years. Much of the white-collar membership in labor unions is among government employees. A person's educational level does not appear to have a strong impact on his or her willingness to join a union. Also, regional labor force differences (most notably North versus South) regarding employee willingness to join or support unions have largely disappeared.

Workers in the United States are pragmatic and normally need to be convinced that a union will provide greater pay, better benefits, and an improved quality of work life before they will vote for and financially support a labor organization. An employee is more likely to support a union if he or she believes that the perceived benefits of unionization will exceed the costs of membership. The most obvious costs of belonging to a union are the initiation fees and monthly dues assessments. There are also other less obvious employee "costs" to union membership such as acquiescing to the desires of the bargaining unit majority, attending union meetings, and possibly opening a rift between personal friends who are working in a supervisory or managerial position.

Some labor experts claim that an employee is more likely to support a union if he or she has a long-term commitment to remain at a particular firm. Employees who view a job as temporary may be less likely to support a union during an organizational campaign. The presence of right-to-work legislation (currently existing in 20 states) may also reduce union support because these laws forbid compulsory union membership. Right-to-work laws allow an employee to refuse to join a union that has been certified as the exclusive bargaining representative; yet the same employee remains in the bargaining unit and receives all of the benefits and protection afforded under the collective bargaining agreement.

The policies and actions of employers and unions help to shape employee attitudes toward unions. Examples of unenlightened management are often not hard to find, and they can create an atmosphere that makes employees more vulnerable to union organization campaigns. Companies may literally invite union organizers to approach employees by operating without grievance procedures, providing inadequate employee benefits, creating more than the usual employee turnover and layoffs, failing to improve working conditions, and following inadequate or outdated rules. According to Bernie Trimbull, executive director of CUE, the National Association of Manufacturers' educational unit, "It's not unions that organize employees; it's poor management."[45] Personnel/human resource managers in nonunion plants periodically need to make comparisons with their unionized counterparts to see if improvements in compensation and personnel policies are necessary.

Professional union organizers use persuasion, peer group pressures, mass meetings during off-duty hours, media publicity, individual and small group question-and-answer meetings, telephone calls, and home visits to generate worker enthusiasm for the union. Furthermore, union organizers may help employees with personal or work-related difficulties, promise economic rewards, engage in organizational picketing, and publicize past successes to bolster their cause. Table 15-2 outlines the steps that union organizers use to target a group of nonunion employees and conduct a union organizing campaign.

Union and Management Strategies During Organizing Campaigns

International unions employ organizers who spend a great deal of time targeting potential union members. Once a nonunionized employee group has been targeted, union organizers launch a campaign designed to convince them to vote for the union in the certification election conducted by the NLRB. Union organizers use a variety of tactics to convince employees to support the union. Organizers also gather information on the industry, the employer targeted for unionization, and the geographical area where the employees reside.[46] The primary strategy of union organizers is to capitalize on issues that are important to most employees

[45]The Bureau of National Affairs, Inc., *Unions Today: New Tactics to Tackle Tough Times* (Washington, D.C.: The Bureau of National Affairs, Inc., 1985), p. 13.

[46]Paula D. Voos, "Union Organizing Expenditures: Determinants and Their Implications for Union Growth," *Journal of Labor Research* (Winter 1987), p. 10.

TABLE 15-2 Measures Taken by Unions During Organizational Campaigns

Establishing Organizational Targets →	Making the Initial Advances →	Obtaining the "Critical Mass" of Employee Support →	The NLRB Certification Process
Identifying potential targets • AFL-CIO data on unorganized workers • Type of employees and workers preferred by a particular union • Financial and time constraints of the union • Economic, social, and industrial factors • Other factors Telephone surveys directed at worker targets to obtain a more accurate measure of their propensity to unionize	Gathering data on the target group's compensation and working conditions Formulating an organizing platform and agenda Enlisting the support of prounion employees to assist in the organizational campaign Holding training sessions for organizing committee members Obtaining organization charts and diagrams of the workplace in order to better define employee contact points and the appropriate election unit	Gaining access to the target group • Personal visits at home or outside of work • Oral or written solicitation during working hours by employee organizers • Small group meetings • Mass meetings • Use of news media Conveying the union's message to the target group Responding to employer countermeasures Obtaining employee authorization card signatures	Clarification of the election unit Filing the certification election petition Obtaining a current list of employees in the election unit The NLRB-supervised, secret-ballot election Postelection matters • Final certification • Resolution of any challenged ballots • Resolution of any unfair labor practice charges

such as subpar wages, poor supervisor-employee communication, recent injustices, or threats of layoff in the company in order to encourage union membership. A skilled union organizer obtains information on the internal affairs of a company through employee handbooks, diagrams of plant layouts, financial statements, and rumors that circulate through the workplace.[47] Employees who are sympathetic to the union often supply such information. Organizers may also pose as job applicants and even allow themselves to be hired by an unsuspecting employer in order to obtain inside information for the organizing campaign. Information on general

[47]See Thomas F. Reed, "Do Union Organizers Matter? Individual Differences, Campaign Practices, and Representation Election Outcomes," *Industrial and Labor Relations Review* (October 1989), pp. 103–119.

economic and industrial conditions in the area is also helpful and is usually supplied by the national union or local sources.

Union organizers are usually prohibited by management from visiting targeted employees on company property. In the past, the NLRB occasionally permitted organizers to enter the company premises if employees were otherwise not accessible because of the location or layout of the workplace. A January 1992 U.S. Supreme Court decision appears to have made it even more difficult for union organizers to gain access to employees during an organizing campaign. The Court ruled that organizers should be able to enter an employer's property only in "the rare case" when the union could demonstrate that "unique obstacles" prevented it from reaching potential members in any other way. Justice Clarence Thomas, who wrote the Court's opinion, said that it would apply only to "those employees who, by virtue of their employment, are isolated from the ordinary flow of information that characterizes our society." Thomas said that "classic examples" of such workplaces would include logging and mining camps and mountain resort hotels.[48]

Because management will not allow union organizers on company property, they frequently solicit the support of employees who are sympathetic to union representation. By using sympathetic employees as go-betweens, union organizers can contact employees who have been targeted for a union organizing campaign. Employees who assist the union organizer can legally solicit union support from their fellow employees during nonworking times (e.g., rest breaks) and in nonworking areas such as cafeterias and locker rooms.

The Taft-Hartley Act allows employers to inform employees of the disadvantages of unionization as long as there are no threats or economic coercion. Table 15-3 outlines the measures and countermeasures that are taken by management during the organizing campaign in order to discourage employee support of the union and increase the likelihood of its defeat in the certification election. Two categories of managerial antiunion measures—proactive measures and reactive measures—are illustrated in Table 15-3. *Proactive measures* are used to prevent or discourage employee interest in unions by creating a work environment that makes unions unnecessary or by developing a workforce that is antiunion. Proactive measures taken *before* union organizers approach a firm's employees often focus on improving wages, hours, and working conditions or eliminating problems that might encourage employees to unionize. Other (potentially illegal) proactive measures that can be taken by management include discriminating against former union members during the hiring process or indoctrinating employees via threats against organized labor soon after they are hired.[49] Once the employer is aware that a union is interested in organizing a group of its employees, then reactive measures are often taken to either stop the campaign or defeat the union in the certification election. Table 15-3 distinguishes between legal and illegal reactive

[48]*Lechmere v. National Labor Relations Board, No. 90-970* (January 28, 1992). See Linda Greenhouse, "Union Action Restricted on Employers' Property," *New York Times* (January 28, 1992).

[49]Terry L. Leap, William H. Hendrix, R. Stephen Cantrell, and G. Stephen Taylor, "Discrimination Against Prounion Job Applicants," *Industrial Relations* (Fall 1990), pp. 469–478.

TABLE 15-3   Measures and Countermeasures by Management to Prevent Unionsim

Prior to a Union Organizing Campaign	After a Union Organizing Campaign Is Underway	
Proactive Measures	Legal Reactive Measures	Illegal Reactive Measures
Adequate and equitable wages and salary programs Comprehensive employee benefits Favorable supervisory-employee relationships Open channels of communication Safe working conditions Job security measures Grievance mechanisms that afford due process and equal protection Equitable promotion and transfer policies Periodic communications on the organization's success and benefits in a nonunion environment Organizational structure • Small plants (fewer than 200 employees) • Establishing operations in rural Southern areas • Designing facilities to limit access by union organizers Screening out prounion job candidates during the hiring process (generally illegal) Employee attitude surveys	Nonthreatening, noncoercive, and factual antiunion propaganda • Letters to employees • Speeches to employees • Information posted on bulletin boards • Lobby or cafeteria displays • Film and slide shows "Vote no" committees composed of antiunion employees Hiring labor consultants to provide advice during union organizing campaigns Forming supervisory committees to ensure that work activities are not disrupted Banning union organizers from soliciting on company property (unless there are special circumstances) Forbidding employees from distributing union literature	Threatening to discharge employees who support the union Threatening to close or relocate a plant or facilities if the union wins the certification election Spying on union activities or meetings Making job assignments based on whether an employee supports a union Circulating antiunion propaganda that: • Emphasizes that it is futile to elect the union because compensation and working conditions will not change • Predicts strikes and turmoil in the workplace if the union is certified as the employees' bargaining representatives • Otherwise violates an employee's Section 7 rights Holding captive audience speeches within 24 hours of the certification election Providing support to a company dominated or favored union in order to exclude an outside union

measures. Legal reactive measures are those that the employer can use without violating the Wagner Act. Whether a specific reactive measure is legal depends on a number of circumstances, as witnessed by the controversies surrounding many of the NLRB and court cases stemming from employer tactics during union organizing drives. Several of the more troublesome and controversial management actions are employer speeches prior to the certification election, statements made by supervisors and management during the organizing campaign, and the banning of employee solicitation for the union on company premises.

Employers can inform employees that unions will not necessarily prove beneficial. Statements about a union's strike history, its ineffectiveness in securing favorable terms for its members at the bargaining table, or instances or internal union problems are permissible as long as such statements are not coercive or threatening. Employers may ask employees to withhold a decision until they have had an opportunity to evaluate union and employer presentations. The law states that "[t]he expressing of any views, argument, or opinion [written or oral]" is permissible "if such expression contains no threat of reprisal or force or promise of benefit." Employers who threaten or promise economic benefit (e.g., giving employees a pay raise during the organization campaign) interfere with rights guaranteed in Section 7 of the Wagner Act and may be guilty of an unfair labor practice.

The dividing line between protected and illegal speech is not always clear. Views expressed by management may be labeled as coercive by the NLRB even if management did not intend for such statements to be coercive. To guard against coercion, employers should advise employees that they can join or not join a union without reprisal; following this rule of thumb softens the impact of subsequent remarks that could otherwise be considered threatening. The NLRB considers the context, surroundings, and tone in which management statements are made. In addition, a firm's labor relations history is considered by the NLRB when evaluating the impact (threat potential) of an employer's remarks. A remark such as "Unions are not in the best interest of the employees" may be regarded by the NLRB as nonthreatening when made by the management of a firm that has not previously committed unfair labor practices or other actions that are hostile to organized labor. The same remark made by a manager for J. P. Stevens, a Southern textile firm with a long history of labor violations, might be viewed in a different light by the NLRB. The likelihood of a violation also increases when employees are called into a supervisor's office and interrogated about union organizing activities. Otherwise nonthreatening speeches made by management before a captive audience of employees are illegal when made less than 24 hours before a certification election. The 24-hour rule was instituted because the union often does not have an adequate opportunity to respond to management comments before the election is held. Management should not suggest that employees form an independent union; favoritism and support for another union, particularly an independent, is viewed suspiciously by the NLRB.

The following threats or interference generally constitute unfair labor practice violations:

1. Blacklisting employees who are known union adherents.
2. Discharging employees who appear to support the union.
3. Hiring labor spies to observe union organizing meetings.
4. Spying on employees after working hours.
5. Showing favoritism to one union during an organizing campaign while discouraging employees from joining another union (if more than one union is attempting to organize a firm's employees).
6. Threatening to close or move a business operation or facility if the employees unionize.

One of the more controversial issues in union organizing campaigns is what employer behaviors or statements constitute a threat in violation of the Wagner Act. Employers are usually aware of the illegality of direct threats and adopt more subtle approaches for sending antiunion messages to their employees; in fact, some of the most chilling threats may be delivered in a very cordial manner. For example, a young union supporter who worked in a plant along with his grandfather was approached by a company supervisor. After exchanging pleasantries, the supervisor smiled and asked: "How long has your grandfather worked here?"[50] Although the supervisor did not directly threaten the young man or his grandfather, the supervisor's seemingly innocent question was a thinly veiled threat that discouraged the employee from continuing to support the union. In instances such as these, the NLRB must carefully examine the total conduct of the employer and the context in which the remarks or threats were made. If a threat is made by the employer or supervisor, the person issuing the threat must be in a position to make good on the statement. A first-line supervisor who threatens to fire an employee for his or her union activities may violate the law if the supervisor has the power to hire and fire. However, many supervisors have little or no authority in such matters. Employers generally do not have the legal right to question employees about union organizing activities. Questions that may violate the Wagner Act include "How do you (the employee) feel about unions?", "Which way will you vote in the election?," or "How many people in your department have signed authorization cards?"

Management occasionally makes "predictions" about what will happen if the union wins the certification election. If such predictions are both adverse to the employees' interests *and* within the control of management, the statements are probably in violation of federal labor law. For example, if management predicts plant closings, then a violation is a virtual certainty. But if management says that the union will cause increased labor costs that could harm the company's business, then such a prediction is beyond the control of management and it is probably permissible under the law. Finally, an employer who indicates that it is futile for employes to vote for the union because wages and working conditions *will not* be changed has probably violated the Wagner Act. In essence, the NLRB is concerned with the impact of management's statements on the free selection or rejection of a bargaining representative without placing employees under duress. The NLRB is also concerned with protecting the free speech rights of management. The following employer statements are regarded as legitimate and nonthreatening under most circumstances:[51]

1. The company believes that unions are not in the best interests of the employees.

---

[50] This incident is based on the personal experience of a colleague who once worked as a summer employee.

[51] James W. Hunt, *Employer's Guide to Labor Relations* (Washington, D.C.: The Bureau of National Affairs, Inc., 1979), pp. 45–47. Also see Stephen I. Schlossberg and Judith A. Scott, *Organizing and the Law*, 4th ed. (Washington, D.C.: The Bureau of National Affairs, Inc., 1991).

2. Wages and benefits paid by the company are competitive with those of other firms in the local community or industry.

3. Superior employees may be handicapped by the seniority and promotion clauses found in many union contracts.

4. The union that is attempting to secure certification has been involved in several lengthy strikes during the previous year.

5. Union dues will average $20 per month for each employee.

6. Employees do not have to sign authorization cards.

7. The only guarantee of improved wages, benefits, and job security is good business conditions, not labor unions.

8. The company is required by law to bargain in good faith, but there is no guarantee that the union will be able to live up to all of its promises. Collective bargaining, rather than promises made during an organizing campaign, determines what the union will achieve.

9. A strike will not necessarily force the company to accede to union demands. In fact, the company has the right to continue operations during a work stoppage and may hire permanent replacements to fill jobs previously held by striking employees.

10. An employee is not required to vote for the union in a secret ballot election even though he or she has signed an authorization card.

The Appropriate Bargaining Unit

Union organizers do not normally attempt to represent all employees in an organization or plant. Rather, they focus their efforts on a segment of employees who work in a specific department(s) or occupational grouping within a firm. The subset of employees to be represented by a labor organization is called a *bargaining unit*.[52]

The bargaining unit is established by the NLRB and is influenced by a number of factors, such as the employer's organizational structure and method of operation, the nature of the employees' jobs, pay scale, and employee benefits, the type of union seeking representation and its membership requirements, the history of collective bargaining in the firm, and the desires of the employees being organized. The size and composition of the bargaining unit are important considerations and may determine which union (if any) wins the certification election. If a union is certified, then the composition of the bargaining unit influences the negotiating power and strike effectiveness of both the union and management, as well as the ease or difficulty of administering the collective bargaining agreement. Only those employees whose jobs fall within the bargaining unit designated by the NLRB are represented by the union that wins the certification election. When

[52]See John E. Abodeely, Randi C. Hammer, and Andrew Sandler, *The NLRB and the Appropriate Bargaining Unit*, rev. ed. (Philadelphia: Industrial Research Unit, The Wharton School, University of Pennsylvania, 1981).

union and management subsequently negotiate the collective bargaining agreement, the wages, hours, and working conditions apply only to bargaining unit employees; other company employees may have a different set of pay schedules, employee benefits, and work rules than those who are included in the bargaining unit.

The NLRB is guided by Section 9(b) of the Taft-Hartley Act when formulating the bargaining unit. The following are some of the more important guidelines used by the NLRB in drawing the bargaining unit lines:

1. Supervisory and managerial personnel are excluded from bargaining units containing nonsupervisory employees. In fact, these employees are not protected under federal labor law. Employees having access to confidential company information who are involved with labor relations and agricultural employees are also excluded from protection. Part-time employees are covered by the act, but casual employees who work on an intermittent basis are not.
2. Professional and skilled craft workers may be included in the same bargaining unit with nonprofessional and unskilled workers, or they may opt to form a separate bargaining unit of their own.
3. Security guards, confidential employees, or nonmanagerial employees who have family ties with the firm's ownership are not included in the same bargaining unit with other employees.

Beyond these specifics, the NLRB is endowed with considerable discretion and the bargaining unit can be departmental, company, or plantwide, skilled or unskilled, or some combination thereof. For example, skilled craft workers and nonsupervisory professional employees may be placed in a separate bargaining unit from other employees. The NLRB may establish a single bargaining unit that covers employees in a single plant or, if the employer operates several plants, the bargaining unit may cover employees working at more than one location. Thus, an employer with five plants in three states may be covered by a single collective bargaining agreement that encompasses all five locations. Some companies bargain as an *employer association* in which they band together and engage in contract talks with a union. This arrangement is common in the underground coal mining industry, where small mining firms pool their resources and strength to bargain with the United Mine Workers. In such instances, a multiemployer bargaining unit may be used. Thus, one collective bargaining agreement would apply to employees who work for different companies.

The NLRB has established a *presumptively appropriate bargaining unit* for some organizations. For example, the appropriate unit for department store employees includes both sales and nonsales personnel, whereas for automobile dealers the NLRB separates sales and office employees from service department employees. Similarly, the NLRB favors a fleetwide bargaining unit in the shipping industry and a systemwide unit for public utilities. The NLRB will make exceptions to these practices when circumstances warrant.

The Certification Election

A union can acquire the right to represent employees in one of three ways. First, bargaining unit employees may sign authorization cards signifying an interest in a particular union. If management is satisfied that a union represents a majority of the employees in the bargaining unit, then it may recognize the union as the exclusive bargaining representative. However, an employee who signs an authorization card is not legally obligated to vote for the union in a certification election. A second method is for the employer or union to request an NLRB election. This approach enables union and management to resolve any issues regarding the appropriate bargaining unit, and it ensures that the employees have freedom of choice in selecting the union through a secret ballot election. Employees who sign authorization cards because of pressure from union organizers or fellow employees may later decide to vote against the union in the certification election. Under extenuating circumstances, a third method has been provided by the NLRB and endorsed by the Supreme Court: a union losing an election will be certified if the employer resorts to *grossly* illegal tactics and a second election appears futile because the employees are too intimidated or discouraged to "vote their conscience."[53] Before the NLRB will automatically certify a union without a second election, the union must demonstrate that it once had the support of the majority of employees. In addition, the unfair labor practices of the employer must have been so outrageous, flagrant, and of lasting impact that the possibility of majority support for the union has been destroyed.

The union requesting an election must have authorization card signatures from at least 30 percent of the employees in the bargaining unit. Additional unions are put on the ballot if they represent 10 percent or more of the voting employees. Employers and unions appoint representatives to monitor the polls and screen employees as they arrive to vote. If they believe that an employee is not eligible to participate in the certification election (i.e., not employed in a job that falls within the bargaining unit), the employee's ballot can be challenged. As a general rule, bargaining unit employees who were on the payroll prior to the certification election are eligible to vote. In addition, seasonal employees who expect to return to work and employees on military or sick leave are often eligible. Representation decisions are occasionally challenged if an unfair labor practice was allegedly committed during the union organizing campaign. The eligibility of employees to vote in an election may also delay final certification, especially if the outcome was decided by a narrow margin. Once the ballots have been counted and any alleged improprieties have been resolved, the election results are certified. A majority of those *voting*, and not a majority of those eligible to vote, determines which union (or no union) represents the employees. A runoff election is conducted between the two highest vote getters when more than one union is seeking certification and none of the choices on the ballot receives a majority of the votes cast. By the early

---

[53]*NLRB v. Gissel Packing Co.*, 395 U.S. 575 (1969).

1990s, unions were winning less than one half of all certification elections.[54] Once the representation issue is decided the NLRB cannot hold another election for at least 12 months. Such a policy favors the employer and prevents the frequent disruptions in the workplace that normally accompany an event as important as a certification election. If the bargaining unit employees become disenchanted with their union, they may *decertify* it through an NLRB-conducted decertification election.[55]

Some Important Statistics on Union Organizing Campaigns

According to The Bureau of National Affairs, Inc., unions won 47.6 percent of certification elections in 1990 and 46.8 percent in 1991. Elections involving fewer than 50 employees had a higher win rate for unions (almost 52 percent).[56] A study of 189 certification elections between July 1986 and April 1987 by the AFL-CIO, Department of Organization and Field Services, revealed some interesting statistics.[57]

- As the number of employees increases, the likelihood of a union victory decreases significantly. In units of 250 to 500 employees, the union wins only 21 percent of the time.
- The manufacturing sector is the most difficult to organize, whereas the health care sector is the easiest.
- The New England states are the least hospitable to union organizing campaigns, while the western and southwestern states are more receptive.
- Once a union has won a certification election, it obtains a collective bargaining agreement (written contract) in 73 percent of the cases. However, the odds of obtaining a contract decrease as the size of the unit increases (only 40 percent of units over 150 employees were able to obtain a contract).
- Union organizers believe that an effective representative committee and the extensive use of visits to an employee's home are the most important factors in a successful organizing campaign.
- Although the federal law only requires that 30 percent of the unit employees sign authorization cards, it is not until the union has at least 75 percent of the signatures that it has more than a 50 percent chance of winning the election.

---

[54]See the Bureau of National Affairs, Inc., *NLRB Representation and Decertification Election: Year-End Statistics for 1991* (Washington, D.C.: The Bureau of National Affairs, Inc., 1992).

[55]Ellen R. Peirce and Richard Blackburn, "The Union Decertification Process: Employer Do's and Don't's," *Employee Relations Law Journal* (August 1986), pp. 205–220. The 12-month election rule also applies to decertification elections. Thus, if employes support a union in a certification election, they must wait at least 12 months before a second election can be held decertifying the union.

[56]The Bureau of National Affairs, Inc., *NLRB Representation and Decertification Elections: Year-End Statistics for 1991* (Washington, D.C.: The Bureau of National Affairs, Inc., 1992).

[57]The AFL-CIO, Department of Organization and Field Services, *AFL-CIO Organizing Survey 1986-87 NLRB Elections*, unpublished report.

- There is a direct correlation between the number of persons who attend mass meetings before the election and the union's win rate. If 50 to 60 percent of employees attend mass meetings, the average win rate is 72 percent.
- The three most effective issues during an organizing campaign are working conditions, grievance procedures, and the individual dignity of the employee. When wages are the primary issue, the union wins only 33 percent of the time.
- A union is more likely to win an election when the employees being organized are low-wage, female, minorities (especially undocumented immigrants), less than 35 years of age, and living in a small town.
- If the employer does not wage a significant campaign against the union, the win rate is 80 percent. But when the employer wages an intense antiunion campaign, the win rate declines to 35 percent. The use of delay tactics by management to postpone the date of a certification election is an especially effective antiunion tactic.

According to the Bureau of National Affairs, Inc., 558 decertification elections were held in 1990 and 539 in 1990. The unions managed to prevent decertification in 27.2 percent of the 1990 elections and 31.9 percent of those held in 1991. Thus, unions lose approximately two-thirds of the decertification attempts held by disgruntled bargaining unit workers.[58]

The Three Levels of Union-Management Interaction

Contract Negotiations

If the union wins the certification election, it becomes the exclusive bargaining representative for all employees working in the bargaining unit. The employer is legally obligated to bargain in good faith with the union over wages, hours, and working conditions covering bargaining unit employees. However, the federal law does not require that the sides reach an agreement (about one third of the certification elections won by unions never result in a written collective bargaining agreement with the employer). The negotiation of a collective bargaining agreement representing the diversified interests and skills of bargaining unit members is a complicated and time-consuming task. Large companies require sizable personnel and industrial relations staffs and extensive legal support to deal with union-management relations. Negotiation of a comprehensive collective bargaining agreement requires considerable preparation, skill, and knowledge. Chapter 16 discusses the contract negotiation process in detail.

[58]The Bureau of National Affairs, Inc., *NLRB Representation and Decertification Elections: Year-End Statistics for 1991* (Washington, D.C., 1992).

Contract Administration

Once a collective bargaining agreement has been negotiated, employers and unions are expected to comply with the letter and spirit of its provisions. Because of the size and complexity of the typical collective bargaining agreement, it is almost inevitable that disagreements will arise between labor and management over the meaning of specific provisions and terms. These disagreements are not necessarily signs of bad faith or attempts to disrupt labor relations. Rather, genuine differences of opinion arise because of misunderstandings, unclear draftsmanship, and unexpected turns of events in the workplace. Disputes regarding the interpretation and application of the agreement are resolved through *contract administration*. Local union officials and shop stewards are usually responsible for ensuring that the employer follows the terms of the agreement. Management, on the other hand, uses first-line supervisors and the personnel/human resource management department to protect the company's rights under the contract.

The centerpiece of contract administration is the *grievance procedure*. Grievance procedures are designed to deal swiftly and fairly with disputes over the application of the collective bargaining agreement without resorting to work stoppages or other disruptions. Most grievance procedures allow union and management officials ample opportunity to resolve contract problems. If the two sides cannot reach an accord, then the dispute is usually submitted to an arbitrator who is jointly selected by both sides. The arbitrator then makes a final and binding decision that the parties must accept. The process of contract administration is discussed in Chapter 16.

Informal Joint Consultation and Union-Management Cooperation

Because of the difficulties of negotiating complex provisions such as job evaluation systems, retirement programs, and health and safety rules, union and management may elect to meet and discuss issues of mutual concern in an informal, nonnegotiating session known as "informal joint consultation. This arrangement allows each side to explore complex issues without the pressure-cooker atmosphere of contract negotiations. Joint consultation can be used to pave the way and lighten the burden for future bargaining, as well as eliminate potential problems and major roadblocks that could lead to a lengthy labor dispute.

Union and management have also engaged in formal cooperative efforts. For example, Xerox Corporation has entered into an agreement with the Amalgamated Clothing and Textile Workers Union (ACTWU) to form problem-solving teams. Quality of work life and productivity programs have been used to improve the work environment, boost productivity efficiency, and improve company profitability. Measures such as these are designed to enhance labor-management harmony, reduce absenteeism and turnover, improve job security, and place the company in a better position to raise pay levels. Joint health and safety programs help employers avoid legal entanglements under OSHA and reduce workers' compensation costs. Health care cost containment measures that are jointly controlled by labor and management reduce medical insurance premiums and offer employees improved medical care coverage. For the first time, many unions and members of management find themselves working together, rather than as adversaries. Although many union and management leaders regard cooperative programs with a certain amount of skepticism, these relationships offer the potential to limit labor disputes and improve communications between the sides.[59]

Labor-management cooperative committees have been referred to by such names as *work teams, quality circles, quality of worklife committees*, and *employee involvement programs*. At the time of this writing, the legality of these programs in unionized firms is being challenged before the NLRB involving Electromation, Inc., of Elkhart, Indiana, a manufacturer of small electrical items. Labor-management committees were used to discuss specific workplace issues. The NLRB ruled in 1990 that Electromation had violated the act's ban on interfering with a labor organization (a potential violation of Section 8(a)(2) of the Wagner Act). The case is pending before the NLRB's Washington, D.C., five-member board.[60]

■ A Comparison of Union and Management Organizational Structures

The relationship between union and management has been depicted as a power struggle between adversaries. As a result, the organizational structures of both unions and management have evolved to provide a system of checks and balances. Figure 15-3 illustrates the organizational counterparts that exist in most union-management relationships.

At the lowest level is the relationship between first-line supervisors and shop stewards, sometimes referred to as the *shop floor level*. The primary concern at this level is enforcement and administration of the collective bargaining agreement. The union shop steward is responsible for ensuring that management adheres to the spirit and terms of the labor agreement. When complaints or formal grievances arise, the first-line supervisor and shop stewards are often the first

---

[59]See Charlotte Gold, *Labor-Management Committees; Confrontation, Cooptation, or Cooperation?* Key Issues, Number 29 (Ithaca, New York: ILR Press, Cornell University, 1986); and Michael Schuster, "Problems and Opportunities in Implementing Cooperative Union-Management Programs," in Barbara D. Dennis (ed.), *Proceedings of the Thirty-fifth Annual Meeting, Industrial Relations Research Association* (Madison, Wisconsin: Industrial Relations Research Association, 1983), pp. 189–197.

[60]"Labor Laws Challenge Employee Involvement," *AQP Report: The Newsletter for Quality and Participation* (February-March 1992), p. 3; and "Federal Decision May Imperil Employee Involvement," *AQP Report: The Newsletter for Quality and Participation* (December-January 1992), pp. 1, 3.

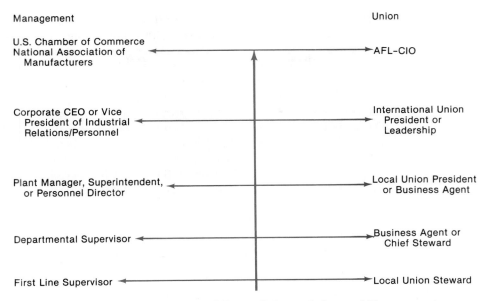

FIGURE 15-3   **The Balance of Power Between Labor and Management**

points of contact for employees. First-line supervisors and stewards usually have an intimate knowledge of working conditions and employee concerns; if they handle grievances in a competent and timely fashion, they can minimize conflict before it escalates and leads to chronic productivity and morale problems.

In large organizations, a department supervisor is the counterpart of the business agent or chief steward. When contract negotiations are conducted at the local level, these individuals may be members of their respective bargaining teams. Departmental supervisors, chief stewards, and business agents also deal with grievances that are not resolved by first-line supervisors and shop stewards.

Plant managers or superintendents usually deal directly with the local union president and leadership. When bargaining is done at the local level, they may be the chief negotiators for their respective sides. If bargaining is done at the companywide level, plant managers and local union officials may have significant input into bargaining preparations. Furthermore, plant managers and local union leaders must convince bargaining unit employees to approve a companywide contract once a settlement has been reached between the union and management bargaining teams. The most serious grievances also receive attention by plant managers and local union leaders. Often such grievances are precipitated by confusing contract terms and have important long-term implications for both the union and the employer.

At corporate headquarters, the CEO and vice-president of personnel establish industrial relations policies that regulate personnel/human resource management. Many contract negotiations take place between international union leaders and their counterparts at corporate headquarters. Union bargaining teams may consist of the international president, who is the chief negotiator, along with various international leaders and staff experts. The vice-president for personnel/human resources or the industrial relations director may serve as management's chief negotiator and is assisted by personnel experts in compensation, employee benefits, and other functional areas. Corporate and international union leaders do not generally become involved with grievances unless the grievance is both exceptional and has important managerial or financial ramifications.

At the pinnacle of Figure 15-3 are the organizations that represent the common interests of organized labor and business. As noted earlier, labor's principal advocate is the AFL-CIO. The vast interests of business are represented by a variety of groups. Perhaps the best known are the U.S. Chamber of Commerce and the National Association of Manufacturers (NAM). Both organizations lobby on behalf of business interest groups to achieve a number of goals. Among NAM's recent concerns are the federal deficit and tax reform measures.[61] Business and labor leaders occasionally clash openly over important issues such as plant closings.[62] However, the two groups normally pursue their objectives independently without direct confrontation.

■ The Impact of Unions and Collective Bargaining on Employers

The negotiation of a collective bargaining agreement and the establishment of a mechanism for contract administration have several important implications for management, especially for those individuals involved in the personnel/human resource management function. A brief summary of the most probable effects of unionization on an organization follows.

1. *Loss of unilateral discretion on personnel matters.* Management's ability to make unchallenged decisions about pay, promotions, transfers, dismissals, and other personnel matters is often curtailed significantly under a collective bargaining agreement. *Management rights* is perhaps one of the most controversial issues in labor-management relations. Most collective bargaining agreements stipulate that management retains the right to make decisions about corporate strategy, product lines, plant locations, and pricing policies. But when such decisions affect unionized personnel, there is a greater probability that the union will challenge managerial prerogatives. Table 15-4 outlines the impact that unions typically exert on personnel functions and policies. Some

---

[61]NAM Will Have No Narrow 'Wish List' Under Pace," *Industry Week* (January 7, 1985).

[62]Mark Sfiligoj, "Union Chiefs, NAM at Odds on Plant Closing Notice Bill," *American Metal Market* (May 20, 1985), p. 32.

TABLE 15-4   The Influence of Unions on Major Personnel Functions and Policies

Functions that differ little between unionized and nonunionized firms	Employee recruitment and selection Training and development Absenteeism control
Personnel policies specifically favored by unions	Promotions, transfers, layoffs, compensation, and job rights based on seniority Apprenticeship training Grievance procedures and arbitration Checkoff of union dues Subcontracting restrictions Protective work rules (e.g., prohibiting supervisors from performing bargaining unit work)
Personnel policies specifically disfavored by unions	Merit pay plans Individual and group incentives Behavioral or output-based performance appraisal systems
Personnel policies in which the union wants joint control with management	Safety and health programs Plant closing decisions Quality of work life programs Employee benefits Wage and salary administration Employee discipline and control

personnel functions differ little between nonunion and unionized firms, while in other instances the differences are more pronounced.[63]

2. *Greater uniformity in personnel practices* is often achieved as the result of a collective bargaining agreement that standardizes wages, hours, and working conditions. One of the beneficial by-products of unionization is that a company may be forced to improve the way in which it administers its personnel functions. Employee morale, productivity, and harmony may actually improve when the transition is made from a nonunion setting with poor personnel practices to a unionized setting with a comprehensive collective bargaining agreement.

3. Perhaps the most common fear of employers is that the unionization of their firm will place them at a *competitive disadvantage* relative to their nonunionized competitors. The assumption is that unions will increase labor costs and force the employer to either accept reduced profits or raise prices and lose

[63]For an analysis of the differences in personnel policies between union and nonunion firms, see Fred K. Foulkes, *Personnel Policies in Large Nonunion Companies* (Englewood Cliffs, New Jersey: Prentice-Hall, Inc., 1980) and Terry L. Leap, *Collective Bargaining and Labor Relations* (New York: Macmillan Publishing Company, 1991), pp. 220–251.

customers. A unionized firm in a highly competitive industry in which most competing firms are nonunion will probably be placed at a disadvantage. However, in many other situations, unions do not create a competitive disadvantage for the employer. For example, in heavily unionized industries, the effects of pattern bargaining (where one company reaches an agreement with the union and thereby establishes a bargaining precedent for other firms in the same industry) may standardize wages among firms. This is typically the case in the U.S. automobile industry, where the United Auto Workers (UAW) may target the Ford Motor Company for the first round of negotiations. Once Ford and the UAW reach a settlement, a precedent is set for negotiations with General Motors and Chrysler.[64] Furthermore, an employer is not legally obligated to agree with the union on a compensation package or other personnel policy that would place it at a competitive disadvantage if the firm is willing to endure a possible strike.

4. Another source of apprehension regarding unionism is the *fear that collective bargaining agreements will not allow employers to take full advantage of technological advances.* Unions are naturally concerned with the job security of their members, and computer technology, robotics, and automation represent threats to jobs. Collective bargaining agreements may illegally promote featherbedding (a situation in which the employer must either pay union members who perform no work or perform work that is of no use to the company). Restrictive work rules may prevent employees from performing tasks that are not included in their job description or require slavish adherence to inefficient work practices. Most union leaders are receptive to technological advances that will either promote safety or reduce monotony in the workplace. In addition, unions are generally receptive to technological advances that increase worker productivity and company profitability because the unions can point to these gains as reasons for granting pay increases. However, technological changes that result in the layoffs of union members may be bitterly contested by organized labor.

◼ The Impact of Unions and Collective Bargaining on Employees

Employees working in unionized firms may be affected in a number of ways that set them apart from employees in nonunionized companies. Among the more prominent differences are the following:

1. *Favoritism and uncertainty regarding pay, hours, and working conditions is reduced.* A uniform compensation and employee benefit package and a set of

[64]UAW's Beiber Lists Aims for Future Negotiations," *The Wall Street Journal* (April 13, 1987), p. 11 (W), P. 5 (E), col. 4; and Harry C. Katz and Charles F. Sabel, "Industrial Relations and Industrial Adjustment in the Car Industry," *Industrial Relations* (Fall 1985), pp. 295–315.

work rules will leave less room for misunderstandings between employees and the employer. For example, a forklift operator with 9 years of seniority on the evening shift will know precisely what rate of pay he or she is entitled to, as well as other work-related considerations such as safety shoe allowances, premium pay, and vacation pay. Any unilateral breach of these collective bargaining provisions by either the company or the employee is resolved through the grievance procedure.

2. *Employees are more likely to receive due process and equal protection in the workplace.* Capricious and unfair treatment or dismissal of employees is comparatively rare in unionized settings because of the grievance procedure. Employees can generally be dismissed only for just cause in unionized firms. Contrary to the beliefs of some, however, incompetent or troublesome employees cannot hide behind the protective shield of the union. Most grievance procedures provide for careful evaluation of employee discipline cases. Employers are contractually bound to adhere to the grievance procedure, and unions are legally obligated to process all meritorious grievances in a competent manner.

3. *Unions provide strength in numbers.* As *individuals,* employees possess little bargaining power, but they can acquire bargaining power through the *concerted* activities of unionization. The ultimate weapon of the employee group is the *economic strike.* Although an employer may permanently replace economic strikers, it is often difficult to replace several hundred or several thousand striking employees. This is especially true during periods when there are labor shortages or when strike replacements are reluctant to cross a union picket line. Thus unions represent the means by which employees can fuse their meager individual power into formidable group power.

4. *Unions may make it difficult for some employees to exercise individual initiative and demonstrate exceptional performance.* Because of their emphasis on equality among employees, unions encourage contract provisions that deemphasize the use of individual merit and performance appraisals. This "one for all and all for one" philosophy often means treating superior employees the same as average or mediocre employees. For example, an employee who is a superior performer may deserve a promotion in a short period of time; yet he or she may be frustrated by seniority systems, restrictive promotion policies, and work rules that dampen employee initiative and make personal advancement difficult or impossible.

■ The Future Viability of Unions

The decline in union membership in the United States has prompted questions about the future of organized labor. Once the guardian of workers' rights, unions are now viewed by many as self-serving organizations that have outlived their usefulness. A number of social, economic, and legal factors appear to be working against organized labor. In addition, some firms hire antilabor consultants to prevent successful union organizing campaigns, and others are willing to risk labor law violations to prevent unions from organizing their employees.

Factors Leading to the Decline in Union Membership

According to the Bureau of National Affairs, Inc., there are six major factors that have heralded the decline of organized labor over the past quarter of a century.[65] First, much of the unionized segment has been tied to the declining steel, rubber, and other smokestack industries. Drastic declines in membership have also occurred in the construction industry. Second, since 1974, unions have had a losing record in NLRB certification elections. Compared to the 1960s and 1970s, the 1980s witnessed fewer NLRB certification elections involving fewer employees. Third, decertification attempts are succeeding more often. Decertification attempts by employees have tripled since 1970, and unions have been ousted in three of every four decertification elections. Fourth, unions have been increasingly forced to make economic concessions in exchange for job security for their members. Concession bargaining was common in the early 1980s for unions representing employees in financially strapped firms in the automotive and steel industries. Fifth, nonunion employees have recently received larger pay increases than unionized employees. However, unionized employees still have higher pay rates than nonunion workers in comparable jobs. Finally, public opinion of unions has been on the decline. Public opinion polls show that the majority of the public still approves of labor unions, but the percentage of those approving was at an all-time low in the early 1980s.[66]

According to Donald Ratacjczak of Georgia State University, the primary reason for the drop in union membership is that union strength "is in the wrong part of the economy." The decaying industrial sector has been faced with increasing foreign competition, and unions have been unable to assist heavy manufacturing firms in responding to threats from abroad. Management, often with the help of consultants, has become increasingly sophisticated in employing antiunion tactics to thwart organizing campaigns and defeat the union in NLRB elections. These tactics often circumvent and manipulate the Wagner and Taft-Hartley acts. Deregulation of industries such as trucking and the airlines has also hurt organized labor. Former Teamsters president Jackie Presser said that nearly 100,000 Teamsters members had lost jobs in the trucking industry because of deregulation.[67]

[65]The Bureau of National Affairs, Inc., *Unions Today: New Tactics to Tackle Tough Times* (Washington, D.C.: The Bureau of National Affairs, Inc., 1985), p. 1.

[66]Ibid., pp. 9–10.

[67]Ibid., pp. 12–14.

The Response by Organized Labor

Unions have begun to intensify their efforts to organize workers and have looked to new and growing industries such as information processing, communications, and computer manufacturing in order to bolster their membership levels.[68] The AFL-CIO has helped its member unions with organizing efforts in locations where there is rapid population growth, as well as in the public sector, health care, retail, manufacturing, and construction trades. Unions are also making a concerted effort to organize women, who have been rapidly entering or reentering the workforce in recent years. Contrary to organizing drives of the past, some unions are now willing to organize smaller groups of employees such as those found in the cable television industry.

Unions are expanding their organizing budgets and using current union members to help identify targets for organizing campaigns. Some unions are joining with nonunion organizations to form associations that provide information on job openings, health care benefits, and consumer goods. One example of such an association in the High Tech Network, which serves nonunion workers in high-tech firms in the Boston area. The High Tech Network was formed with help from the Communication Workers and the United Electrical Workers unions to help members deal with issues concerning pay, promotions, health and safety, and legislative lobbying. Unions are also trying to improve their public image in an attempt to appeal to potential members.[69]

In order to deal with firms that are intent on violating labor laws to suppress unions, organized labor is using two weapons: underground campaigns and corporate campaigns. *Underground campaigns* involve quietly forming a committee of workers who are strongly committed to the union. Once a group of union sympathizers has been formed and trained in organizing tactics, the union publicizes the fact that it has targeted a company for an organizing campaign. The rationale behind the underground campaign is that an employer who would feel safe in firing 1 or 2 workers would not risk a labor law violation by firing a group of 20 union sympathizers. In a *corporate campaign*, the union attempts to pressure the company through stockholders, banks, customers, and others who have an impact on the firm. Unfavorable publicity, consumer boycotts, or involvement by public figures is used against a recalcitrant employer to resolve a labor dispute or prevent unfair labor practices.

At the bargaining table, unions are focusing on increased job security, flexible work-sharing arrangements, and greater access to company financial information. In addition, labor negotiators are reexamining their positions on incentive pay plans, early retirement alternatives, health care cost-containment measures, child-care benefits, and other issues.[70]

---

[68]Ibid., pp. 95–121.

[69]Marcus Mabry, "New Hope for Old Unions?" *Newsweek* (February 24, 1992), p. 39.-

[70]Also see Stephen J. Cabot and Rusch O. Dees, "The Reemergence of Unions," *Employment Relations Today* (Spring 1988), pp. 37–42.

Unions are also using the news media to communicate with their members and the general public. Comedy, music, and professional actors are being used to illustrate union positions and concerns. The United Food and Commercial Workers union prepared an advertisement aimed at a dispute with the Albertson's grocery chain in New Mexico. Although it was never aired, the threat of the union's doing so allegedly forced Albertson's to settle the dispute.

■ Summary and Conclusions

This chapter has provided a summary of labor history and the mode of operations of unions in the United States. Among the key points concerning the U.S. labor movement are the following:

- Unionization preceded industrialization in the United States, but the Industrial Revolution fueled the growth of labor organizations.
- Employers took whatever measures they felt were necessary to stunt the growth of unions as a means of protecting their managerial autonomy and business interests.
- Labor leaders who attempted to appeal to workers on an ideological level were unsuccessful.
- Labor leaders who attempted to build unionization based on short-range material goals of improving wages, hours, and working conditions (known as *bread-and-butter* or *business unionism*) were more likely to be successful.
- Until the 1930s, public policy was not conducive to a rapidly expanding labor movement. With the passage of protective legislation and the creation of a more amenable legal environment, union membership increased.
- Unions have attempted to enlarge their sphere of influence by organizing professional, white-collar, and government employees. They have also attempted to do this by expanding the number of items addressed at the bargaining table.
- In recent years, unions have suffered from declining membership and reduced political clout. Labor leaders have been forced to use new and innovative strategies to help their organizations retrench and regain momentum.

Chapter 16 provides insights into how union and management negotiate and administer a collective bargaining agreement. An examination of bargaining preparation, issues, and tactics is discussed, along with an analysis of how the grievance procedure and labor arbitration are used to enforce and clarify the terms of the contract.

■ Questions

1. Why were early labor organizations such as the Knights of Labor and the IWW not successful?

2. Describe some of the tactics that were used by management to suppress labor unions prior to 1935.

3. Describe the major provisions of the following labor laws:

- Railway Labor Act (1926)
- Wagner Act (1935)
- Taft-Hartley Act (1947)
- Landrum-Griffin Act (1959)

4. Discuss the major functions of the AFL-CIO.

5. Why is the international (national) union so influential in the U.S. labor movement?

6. What are the basic functions of local unions, and how are they related to the international?

7. List five factors that you believe are most influential in an employee's decision to support a union.

8. Discuss three major tactics that employers use to prevent unions from successfully organizing employees. Are any of these tactics illegal?

9. Outline the tactics used by union organizers.

10. Why is the bargaining unit structure critical to the certification election and union-management relations?

11. Outline the steps normally followed in a certification election.

12. Describe the three levels of union-management interaction.

13. What impact do unions have on employers and employees?

14. Why have unions suffered declines in their membership base?

☐ APPLICATIONS AND CASE EXERCISES

1. In an attempt to unionize workers at Nissan Motor Company's Smyrna, Tennessee, plant, the UAW assigned four full-time staff members to the organizing campaign.[71] What steps should the union take in order to organize Nissan's employees? What steps should Nissan take to counter the UAW's efforts?

2. Union membership among health care workers increased 6 percent between 1980 and 1985 and now stands at 20 percent, according to an American Hospital Association report. During the same period, union membership in other private sector industries dropped from 23 percent to 18 percent.[72] The National Union of American Physicians and Dentists is organizing physicians and dentists by warning that health care professionals will soon be "owned" by health corporations if they are not represented by responsible negotiators.[73] What factors might explain the increasing interest in unions by doctors, dentists, nurses, and other health care workers?

3. According to a study edited by sociologist Daniel Cornfield of Vanderbilt University, management tends to wield increased power over employees when automation comes to industries with weak or no unionization, or when workers do not believe that their job security is threatened. The U.S. Postal Service, for example, dropped some jobs by one pay grade after new equipment was introduced. In highly unionized industries, however, new technology has led to increased labor-management cooperation.[74] Do you agree with this conclusion? Why or why not?

[71]*The Wall Street Journal*, Labor Letter (July 21, 1987), p. 1.

[72]*The Wall Street Journal*, Labor Letter (February 3, 1987), p. 1.

[73]*The Wall Street Journal*, Labor Letter (December 10, 1986), p. 1.

[74]*The Wall Street Journal*, Labor Letter (June 30, 1987), p. 1.-

4. The Culinary Workers and Bartenders, Local 814 (Los Angeles) attempted to organize the dining room, kitchen, and housekeeping employees of the Westwood Horizons Hotel. Several prounion employees threatened to beat up anyone who did not vote for the union in the certification election. On the day the election was held, the prounion employees physically forced employees to go to the polls and cast their ballots for the union. The Culinary Workers and Bartenders union won the certification election, but the hotel management moved to have the NLRB set aside the election results because of the intimidation tactics by prounion employees.[75] Do you believe that a second election should be held? What factors should the NLRB consider in this situation?

5. A job analysis for a union organizer might include the following: "Organizing is the most difficult job in unions. Rejection is nearly a daily occurrence and some prospects are belligerent and insulting. There is a strong likelihood that the organizer will be arrested and convicted for, at least, trespassing, and as a consequence, find it difficult to obtain personal credit. While not as prevalent as in the 1930s, there is still the danger of violence, enough so that some organizers feel compelled to carry a handgun. Frequent overnight travel is common. Organizing is very uncertain; there is no formula for guaranteeing success. The organizer must become immune or, at least, accustomed to rejection and, more important, proceed to the next prospect with the same enthusiasm as he or she had the first day on the job."[76] Would you be willing to work as a union organizer? What training would be necessary to prepare union organizers for the job?

6. After organizers from the United Food and Commercial Workers were arrested for trespassing at Smitty's Super Valu, Inc., a Phoenix, Arizona, supermarket, the union abandoned traditional tactics and sent undercover organizers into the store to videotape alleged safety and child-labor law violations. Unions have used similar tactics against other companies.[77] Do you believe that such tactics will help unions organize employees? Are employers more likely to cooperate with unions if they fear that organized labor will notify state or federal regulatory agencies of workplace problems? Discuss.

[75]*Westwood Horizons Hotel*, 116 LRRM 1152 (1984).-

[76]Ken Gagla, *Union Organizing and Staying Organized* (Reston, Virginia: Reston Publishing Company, Inc., 1983), p. 95.

[77]Robert Tomsho, "Unions Search for Regulatory Violations to Pressure Firms and Win New Members," *The Wall Street Journal* (February 28, 1992), p. A1.

■ 16

Negotiation and Administration of the Collective Bargaining Agreement

■ LEARNING OBJECTIVES

After studying the material in this chapter you should

1. Obtain an overview of the variety of provisions contained in many collective bargaining agreements.
2. Appreciate the role of bargaining theory as it applies to labor relations.
3. Gain insight into the duty of good faith bargaining.
4. Obtain an overview of the various stages of contract talks.
5. Understand the legal, economic, and social dynamics of labor disputes and work stoppages.
6. Understand the components of a typical grievance procedure.
7. Possess insight into how grievances arise and how they can be prevented.
8. Gain a working knowledge of labor arbitration, including the arbitrator's qualifications, the factors arbitrators consider in making a decision, and the legal status of labor arbitration.
9. Have a basic understanding of the union's duty of fair representation.
10. Gain an appreciation for the role of grievance procedures and arbitration in resolving disputes over the interpretation and application of the collective bargaining agreement.

■ INTRODUCTORY VIGNETTE

Labor-Management Cooperation

The need to adapt to increased global competition, new technology, deregulation, and changing workforce demographics has spurred growth in the number of companies and unions forming collaborative relationships.

While some union officials and managers look upon cooperative agreements with a wary eye, more and more are receptive to and even enthusiastic about the concept. Consequently, the last decade has seen a rise in the number of employee involvement plans varying from limited problem-solving quality circles to total transformation of the workplace from traditional assembly lines to autonomous work teams.

While parties must tailor cooperative programs to fit individual needs, several elements are key to any successful plan, according to John Stepp, president of Bill Usery and Associates of Washington, D.C., and former deputy undersecretary for the Department of Labor's Bureau of Labor-Management Relations and Cooperative Programs. These include the following:

- Employee involvement, permitting workers to share decision-making responsibilities with management.
- Employer reciprocity, under which management, in exchange for workers' commitment, addresses concerns such as job security and work and family needs.
- Training and retraining needed to keep pace with competitors.
- Remuneration systems that treat everyone as a stakeholder. Gainsharing, profit sharing, and stock ownership plans are among the methods of rewarding employees for their talents and contributions.

Cooperation based on mutual respect and trust is the topic of a recently released report by the Collective Bargaining Forum, a group of experts representing labor, industry, government, and academia. The panel was formed in 1984 by the Department of Labor's Bureau of Labor-Management Relations and Cooperative Programs "to explore ways in which management and labor can work together to achieve their individual goals and those of society." The underlying premise of the Forum is that U.S. companies that are able to compete globally will prosper, thus providing jobs and a rising standard of living for workers.

Innovative labor-management programs require companies and unions to share the responsibility of manufacturing products and supplying services to meet quality standards that match or surpass those of competitors. To attain competitiveness, the Forum suggested that

- economic goals and work rules be geared to marketplace realities and the needs of the public, while a safe, healthy work environment and reasonable work practices are maintained;

- management reflect these realities in such internal operations as compensation, organizational structure, pricing, and investment decisions;
- the parties develop ways to promote teamwork and employee involvement in the workplace.

Labor's commitment to improve management's economic performance hinges on a company's acceptance and support of a union and the collective bargaining system in general, the report noted. Such acceptance should manifest itself by the two sides' sharing information, refraining from public criticism, and agreeing on how the question of representation at new facilities will be handled.

Employment security is the "key policy and program" for enhancing the use of new technology and workforce motivation and competence, the Forum stressed. Top management must be committed to job security "as a major corporate value and policy objective," and laying off employees must be "an action of last resort." In addition, the parties must work together to provide training and development.

Worker involvement at all levels also is essential. Participation programs must be carefully planned, with the union engaged in each step.

Noting that even in a highly cooperative relationship conflicts will arise, the Forum advised that "maximum resolution of conflicting goals should be encouraged without destroying or jeopardizing the common bonds between the parties."[1]

Two examples of successful labor-management cooperative programs are as follows:[2]

- The United Auto Workers has worked with General Motors's Saturn plant and with Ford Motor Company's Sharonville, Ohio, transmission plant. At Saturn, the basic automobile production processes have been altered and replaced with systems that borrow heavily from the Japanese. All employees are paid on a salary basis, they work in small groups, and production workers are paid bonuses that are tied to the company's profitability (but their base pay is approximately 80 percent of that found in the Big Three auto manufacturers—GM, Chrysler, and Ford). At Sharonville, Ohio, Ford uses self-managed work teams to deal with productivity objectives, disciplinary actions, and safety issues.
- LTV Steel Company and the United Steelworkers (USW) have formed labor-management participation teams aimed at improving quality, productivity, and profitability. Work teams make cost-savings suggestions, and management and union leaders believe that the program has increased trust between the company and the union. It is also believed that these participative efforts helped

[1]From The Bureau of National Affairs, Inc., "Labor-Management Cooperation," *Collective Bargaining Negotiations and Contracts* (Washington, D.C.: The Bureau of National Affairs, Inc., May 16, 1991), p. 4.

[2]The Bureau of National Affairs, Inc., "Cooperative Labor-Management Programs," *Collective Bargaining Negotiations and Contracts* (Washington, D.C.: The Bureau of National Affairs, Inc., 1991), Section 16.

LTV weather the depressed conditions that plagued the steel industry during the 1980s.

■ Negotiating the Collective Bargaining Agreement

- A 2-year contract calling for a 5 percent retroactive pay raise was overwhelmingly ratified by members of Local 1199 of the Drug, Hospital, and Health Care Employees Union. The contract covers 20,000 workers at 28 New York City private agencies that administer home health care services. The increase raised the hourly pay rate from $5.90 to $6.20, retroactive from January 21, 1992, to July 1, 1991.[3]

- A strike-averting agreement at United Air Lines, Inc., was overwhelmingly ratified by members of the International Association of Machinists, representing 27,000 mechanics and other ground service workers. The new 3-year contract grants a series of wage increases over this period. Employees will receive more life insurance and pension benefits, but they will be required to pay higher deductibles on their health insurance.[4]

- After 5 months of negotiations, the United Auto Workers reached an agreement with Saturn, a General Motors Corporation subsidiary. The agreement provides 4,700 Saturn employees with a 15.8 percent pay boost and a modified system under which 20 percent of the workers' pay depends on achieving quality and production goals. The pay increase raises the rate for operating engineers from $13.45 to $15.57 an hour; skilled technicians' pay rose from $15.59 to $17.91 an hour.[5]

- A 40-month contract with the Food Employers Council, Inc., covers 5,000 employees at Northern California supermarkets. The agreement provides for a series of pay raises, and in 1995 increases will be made in pension fund payments.[6]

The preceding examples represent the most publicized aspect of union-management relations: the *contract negotiations* process. Often labor-management negotiations are viewed as a life-or-death struggle in which the union and the employer attempt to carve out their respective interests in a hostile,

---

[3]The Bureau of National Affairs, Inc., "New York City Home Health Care Workers Agreement," *Collective Bargaining Negotiations and Contracts* (Washington, D.C.: The Bureau of National Affairs, Inc., February 6, 1992), pp. 1–2.

[4]The Bureau of National Affairs, Inc., "Airline Contract Ratifications," *Collective Bargaining Negotiations and Contracts* (Washington, D.C.: The Bureau of National Affairs, Inc., January 9, 1992), p. 1.

[5]The Bureau of National Affairs, Inc., "Saturn-UAW Contract Amendment," *Collective Bargaining Negotiations and Contracts* (Washington, D.C.: The Bureau of National Affairs, Inc., November 28, 1991), pp. 1–2.

[6]The Bureau of National Affairs, Inc., "UFCW Supermarket Contracts," *Collective Bargaining Negotiations and Contracts* (Washington, D.C.: The Bureau of National Affairs, Inc., November 14, 1991), p. 1.

no-holds-barred environment. A common image of contract talks is one in which negotiators use slick and evasive bargaining tactics in a pressure-cooker atmosphere, with tensions mounting as the strike deadline nears. Although contract talks are occasionally marked by turmoil, most are very calm and businesslike. Successful collective bargaining depends not on theatrics and table pounding but on a thorough understanding of contract provisions and the factors affecting wages, hours, and working conditions. Collective negotiations require extensive preparation, a knowledge of bargaining strategy, and an ability to assess the costs of labor disputes.

The final product of contract negotiations is the *collective bargaining agreement*, which spells out wages, hours, and working conditions for bargaining unit employees. Table 16-1 presents an outline of the topics commonly found in collective bargaining agreements in the United States. As the extensive list of provisions suggests, collective bargaining agreements can be as lengthy as a small book. Such agreements are often contain extensive and detailed provisions that are drafted in legalistic language.

■ A Look at Bargaining Theory

A Behavioral Theory of Negotiations

Theories or models of the collective bargaining process range from descriptions of what occurs at the bargaining table to complex theories that make extensive use of mathematical and economic models. A number of bargaining models have their roots in social psychology.[7] Perhaps the best-known of the behavioral theories is that of Walton and McKersie.[8] Walton and McKersie view collective bargaining as four subprocesses: distributive bargaining, integrative bargaining, attitudinal structuring, and intraorganizational bargaining. *Distributive bargaining* applies to situations in which union and management goals are in conflict. Negotiations over wages and overtime pay typify distributive bargaining because concessions over economic issues usually represent a monetary loss to the company and a gain to the union and its members. *Integrative bargaining*, on the other hand, refers to bargaining issues that are not necessarily in conflict with the those of the other party. Negotiations over subjects such as the quality of work life and employee safety and health are examples of integrative bargaining. The issues, rights, and obligations to which distributive and integrative bargaining pertain are often written into the collective bargaining agreement.

[7]See Jeffrey Z. Rubin and Bert R. Brown, *The Social Psychology of Bargaining and Negotiation* (New York: Academic Press, Inc., 1975); Richard E. Walton and Robert B. McKersie, *A Behavioral Theory of Labor Negotiations* (New York: McGraw-Hill Book Company, 1965); and Max H. Bazerman and Roy J. Lewicki (eds.), *Negotiating in Organizations* (Beverly Hills, California: Sage Publications, 1983).

[8]Richard E. Walton and Robert B. McKersie, *A Behavioral Theory of Labor Negotiations* (New York: McGraw-Hill Book Company, 1965; currently published by ILR Press, Cornell University).

TABLE 16-1 The Prevalence of Major Collection Bargaining
Agreement Provisions

1. Base wage or salary scale (nearly all contracts)
   a. Two-tier wage systems (17%)
   b. Variable rate ranges (45%)
   c. Single rates (55%)
2. Provision for general wage increase
   a. Deferred wage increases (80%)
   b. Cost-of-living adjustments (42%)
   c. Wage reopeners allowing renegotiation of wages during the life of the contract (10%)
3. Supplementary pay
   a. Second and third shift differentials (86%)
   b. Reporting pay (when no work is available) (74%)
   c. Call-back pay (premium pay to cover call-in of the employee outside of regular working hours) (68%)
   d. Pay for temporary transfer (62%)
   e. Hazardous work premium (11%)
   f. Travel expenses (31%)
   g. Work clothes (33%)
4. Overtime (96%)
   a. Premium pay for weekend work (70%)
   b. Double pay for Sunday work (76%)
   c. Meals during overtime (34%)
5. Job classification procedures (57%)
6. Employee benefits
   a. Life insurance (96%)
   b. Accidental death and dismemberment insurance (74%)
   c. Sickness and accident insurance (86%)
   d. Supplemental occupational accident insurance (26%)
   e. Long-term disability insurance (21%)
   f. Hospitalization insurance (79%)
   g. Surgical insurance (77%)
   h. Major medical insurance (74%)
   i. Miscellaneous medical expense benefits (61%)
   j. Maternity benefits (54%)
   k. Health care cost containment measures (55%)
   l. Dental care (79%)
   m. Prescription drugs (35%)
   n. Optical care (40%)
   o. Alcohol and drug abuse benefits (32%)
   p. Retirement programs (pensions) (almost all contracts)
7. Grievance procedures (100%)
   a. Binding arbitration (99%)
8. Income maintenance (52%)
   a. Guarantees of work or pay (13%)
   b. Severance (separation) pay (41%)
   c. Supplemental unemployment benefits (16%)
9. Daily work schedules (83%)
10. Holidays (99%)
   a. Holiday pay (88%)
   b. Pay for holidays worked (97%)

11. Layoff, rehiring, and work sharing
    a. Layoff arrangements (91%)
    b. Recall after layoff (82%)
12. Leave of absence
    a. Personal leave (72%)
    b. Union leave (77%)
    c. Maternity leave (36%)
    d. Funeral leave (84%)
    e. Civic duty leave (82%)
    f. Paid sick leave (28%)
    g. Unpaid sick leave (52%)
    h. Military leave (72%)
13. Management restrictions and union rights (nearly all)
    a. Restrictions on management rights (89%)
    b. **Subcontracting restrictions or plans (54%)**
    c. Supervisory limitations on performance of bargaining unit work (59%)
    d. Restrictions on technological change in the workplace (25%)
    e. Plant shutdown and relocation provision (26%)
    f. Access to plant by union representatives (56%)
    g. Union access to bulletin boards (69%)
14. Seniority (90%)
    a. Employee probationary period (82%)
    b. Conditions under which loss of seniority may occur (80%)
15. Promotion and transfer criteria
    a. Seniority is sole factor in promotions and transfers
    b. Most senior *qualified* employee (most frequent)
    c. Seniority is given equal consideration (least frequent)
    d. Posting of job vacancies (60%)
    e. Transfer based on seniority (53%)
16. Strikes and lockouts (95%)
    a. **No-strike pledges by the union during the life of the contract (94%)**
    b. **No-lockout pledges by the employers during the life of the contract (90%)**
17. Union security (nearly all)
    a. Union shop provisions (60%)
    b. Dues checkoff provisions (90%)
18. Vacations (92%)
    a. **Vacations based on length of service (90%)**
    b. Vacation pay (84%)
    c. Pay for employees who work during vacation (55%)
    d. Vacation scheduling (87%)
19. Occupational safety and health (33%)
    a. First-aid supplies (23%)
    b. Physical examinations (21%)
    c. Investigation of on-the-job accidents (19%)
    d. Employee safety responsibilities (41%)
    e. Hazardous work (26%)
    f. Joint union-management safety and health committees (49%)
20. Guarantees against various forms of discrimination (96%)

Compiled from The Bureau of National Affairs, Inc., *Basic Patterns in Union Contracts*, 11th ed. (Washington, D.C.: The Bureau of National Affairs, Inc., 1986), based on a sample of 400 contracts from industries throughout the United States. The percentages in parentheses indicate the frequency with which a provision appears in the sample of collective bargaining agreements.

Walton and McKersie recognize an additional function of collective bargaining, *attitudinal structuring*, which describes how the union and management influence each other and build a relationship. *Attitudinal structuring* is the means by which bargaining parties cultivate friendliness, trust, respect, and cooperation. Unlike some bargaining relationships, labor-management relationships often continue for years and even decades. This suggests that the personal attitudes and reputations of negotiators and key union and management figures are crucial to the bargaining relationship and should be incorporated into a behavioral theory. The final subprocess in Walton and McKersie's theory is *intraorganizational bargaining*. Most observers of collective bargaining focus their attention on the interaction *between* the union and management. However, before the union and management negotiating teams can meet at the bargaining table, each side must determine its own bargaining goals and priorities. These four subprocesses interact to help shape the final outcome of contract negotiations, as well as the long-term relationship between union and management.

Bargaining Range Theory

Bargaining range theory began with the late Professor A. C. Pigou, who formulated a model of short-run wage determination during the 1920s.[9] Pigou's bargaining range theory explains the process by which labor and management establish upper and lower wage limits within which a final settlement is made. Figure 16-1 illustrates Pigou's range theory under conditions that should result in a wage settlement between union and management. The union's upper limit (point *A*) represents the union's ideal wage. Management will offer a wage that is well below that acceptable to the union (point *D*). From these two extremes, the union and management negotiating teams will normally proceed through a series of proposals and counterproposals. The union will gradually reduce its wage demands, while the employer will raise its wage offer. Both sides, however, have established limits as to how far they are willing to concede. The union establishes a sticking point (point *B*) at which it is willing to endure the lost wages and hardship of a strike rather than accept a lower wage rate. Management is also willing to accept the costs of a work stoppage before it grants a wage concession greater than point *C*.

Both the union and management regard their sticking points as confidential, and they may go to great lengths to avoid revealing this information to the opposing side. Because the employer and union sticking points overlap in Figure 16-1, a settlement without a work stoppage is likely. Suppose that the union's sticking point is a 3 percent wage increase, while management is willing to provide a maximum increase of 6 percent. A wage settlement somewhere between 3 and 6 percent is likely. According to the bargaining range theory, the exact settlement point will depend on the bargaining skills and strengths of the union

[9]A. C. Pigou, *The Economics of Welfare*, 4th ed. (London: Macmillan and Company, Ltd., 1933), pp. 450–461.

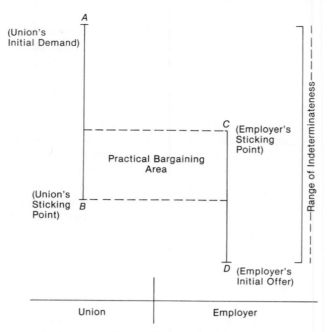

FIGURE 16-1   Pigou's Bargaining Range Theory

and management negotiators. If the union's sticking point is higher than the employer's sticking point, then there is no overlap and no area of practical bargaining. In this situation, a strike is likely unless at least one alters its sticking point.

The Hicks Bargaining Model

The Hicks bargaining model focuses on the length and costs of work stoppages. Professor Hicks proposed that union and management negotiators balance the costs and benefits of a work stoppage when making concessions at the bargaining table. Each side makes concessions to avoid a work stoppage. Because of miscalculations, unrealistic expectations, or political reasons, strikes occasionally happen. Once a strike occurs, further concessions are determined by union and management estimations of the strike length and cost of the strike.

Hicks's model is diagrammed in Figure 16-2. In the absence of a need to negotiate with the union, the employer would prefer to pay the wage indicated by the point W_1. On the other hand, the union would prefer wage W_2 if it can be obtained without calling a strike. As negotiations progress, both the union and the employer modify their demands along their respective concession curves in order to avoid a work stoppage. The union gradually makes concessions and lowers its wage demands, while management makes higher wage concessions until their positions intersect at wage W_3. A primary difference between the Hicks model and bargaining range theory is that the Hicks model pinpoints a precise wage settlement, while the range theory does not.

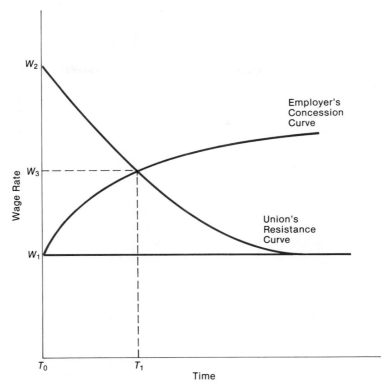

FIGURE 16-2   **The Hicks Bargaining Model**

Similarities Among Bargaining Theories

The discussions of the three bargaining theories are brief and represent only a sample of the existing depictions of bargaining behavior. However, a number of common threads exist among bargaining theories. By describing these common elements, a more realistic picture of collective bargaining will begin to emerge.

Settlement Points and Ranges

A number of mathematical and economic bargaining theories establish a point or range within which the parties will reach a settlement. Exact wage settlements cannot be predicted with great accuracy. We may be able to predict that the United Auto Workers and General Motors will reach a settlement that falls between a 4 and a 6 percent wage increase, but predicting the exact settlement is difficult. The more information that is available on past negotiations, economic and industry conditions, and collective bargaining settlements at the other major automobile manufacturers, the more accurate our predictions will be for future UAW-GM negotiations.

Costs of Agreeing and Disagreeing

Models that emphasize the concept of collective bargaining power often stress the costs of agreeing and disagreeing. A party should be willing to reach an agreement once the costs of disagreeing with an opponent exceed the costs of agreeing. Unfortunately, both union and management negotiators find it difficult to predict the costs of a work stoppage. In addition, not all costs are monetary. Noneconomic consequences such as tarnished working relationships and lingering animosity between labor and management officials are also important in assessing the costs of disagreeing.

The Rationality Assumption

Nearly all economic models of the collective bargaining process assume that negotiators are engaging in rational behavior. Occasionally an observer will make the accusation that union and management negotiators do not behave rationally. Such arguments are bolstered by pointing to the pecuniary damages caused by a work stoppage. In some cases, these damages far exceed the costs that would have been incurred had the parties settled earlier. Union and management negotiators, however, must make decisions with incomplete information, while the critics who evaluate contract talks have the advantage of 20/20 hindsight. Furthermore, actions that appear irrational from a short-term economic perspective may be rational in the long term from a social or organizational standpoint. For example, President Ronald Reagan's firing of the air traffic controllers in 1981 may have been irrational in the short term. However, the President may have decided that such drastic action was necessary in order to discourage other federal employees from striking illegally in the future.

The Element of Timing

Nearly all theories of the collective bargaining process recognize that the actual negotiations between union and management require time in order to reach a settlement. An important element that sets collective bargaining apart from some other types of negotiations is the time pressure under which most contract talks take place. Deadlines imposed by contract expiration dates force union and management negotiating teams to reach an agreement within a stipulated period of time. Failure to settle before the deadline may lead to a work stoppage. For this reason, collective bargaining sessions often reach a frenzied pace just prior to the deadline.

Communications Issues

Most economic bargaining models assume unbiased communications and perfect knowledge of the factors relevant to collective bargaining. Neither the union nor management, however, has a complete understanding of its opponent's preferences and sticking points. Because of the rapid exchange of information and abundance of talking in a bargaining session, the probability of misunderstanding among negotiators is high and communications are far from perfect.

During collective bargaining sessions, negotiators try to camouflage sticking points and gain tactical advantages through bluffing and deceptive behavior. Most negotiators stop short of outright dishonesty; to do so can lead to charges of bad-faith bargaining. The degree of familiarity and trust between union and management also has an effect on bluffing. Parties who have been successfully negotiating agreements for years may not try to mislead each other; being caught in a deceptive act can damage an otherwise trustful relationship.

Bargaining Tactics and Concessions

Nearly all models of the collective bargaining process depict negotiations as a series of proposals, concessions, and counterproposals. The parties often initiate contract talks by making offers or demands that they know the other side is likely to reject. For example, the union chief negotiator may request a 20 percent wage increase—a demand that management will view as ludicrous. Management may counter by offering no wage increase for employees under the new collective bargaining agreement. Both sides realize, however, that they will need to make reasonable proposals and counterproposals. The rate at which the parties are willing to concede is a key concern in bargaining behavior. Conceding to the opponent's demands too quickly may indicate a weak bargaining position, while conceding too slowly may trigger a work stoppage.

Another aspect of bargaining behavior is the use of threats. For a threat to be effective, it must be taken seriously by an opponent, and negotiators who threaten too frequently may lose credibility. Thus, threats should be used sparingly and only in crucial situations. Still another bargaining tactic is the "good guy, bad guy" ploy, in which one negotiator appears to be unreasonable; after the bad guy has negotiated for a while, the good guy from the same bargaining team steps in and, by comparison, seems reasonable. After enduring the theatrics perpetrated by the bad guy, the opposing team not familiar with this tactic is often ready to accept the good guy's proposals, which is precisely what the side using the tactic intended.

■ Bargaining Subjects and the Concept of Good-faith Bargaining

One of the most complex legal issues in labor-management relations is the *duty of good-faith bargaining* that is imposed on union and management negotiators. The Wagner Act imposes the duty of good-faith bargaining on the employer and the Taft-Hartley Act imposes a similar duty on unions. Both management and labor must bargain in good faith over *mandatory* bargaining items until an *impasse* is reached. Mandatory items have been defined by the NLRB and courts as those that have an impact on wages, hours, and working conditions. Subjects falling into the broad mandatory category include wages, salaries, incentive pay, shift differentials, vacations, pensions, rest and lunch periods, job duties and work assignments, and seniority provisions. Other mandatory items include subcontracting arrangements, rental of company housing, and vending machines on company property. If either the union or management wants to discuss a mandatory bargaining subject, then the opposing side must discuss it or risk an unfair labor practice charge of bad-faith bargaining. However, there is no obligation to bargain over *permissive* (sometimes called *voluntary*) bargaining subjects. If a negotiating team wants to discuss a permissive bargaining subject, the other side has the right to refuse. Furthermore, neither union nor management can strike over a permissive subject. Permissive subjects include employer-provided performance bonds for employees, use of the union label on company products, strike insurance plans, and changes in pension benefits for employees who have already retired. Finally, neither side can bargain over illegal bargaining subjects such as racially discriminatory seniority clauses or closed-shop provisions.[10]

Over the years, the concept of good-faith bargaining has been refined by the NLRB and courts. An overriding consideration when deciding whether the employer or union has engaged in bad-faith bargaining is to look at their *total conduct*, both at the bargaining table and in other aspects of the labor-management relationship. A company that has committed several unfair labor practices in the past is more likely to have its bargaining behavior viewed with suspicion than would a company that has enjoyed harmonious relations with the union. Although the Wagner and Taft-Hartley acts do not require that negotiators reach a settlement, negotiators are required to maintain an open mind and manifest a sincere desire to reach an agreement. Determining whether talks at the bargaining table are constructive and open often hinges on evaluating the entire conduct of the parties rather than focusing on specific incidents that may be misinterpreted when taken out of context or viewed in isolation. The following general guidelines have been used by the NLRB and courts in determining whether bad-faith bargaining has occurred:

1. *The duty to furnish information relevant to the negotiations.* Employers are obliged to furnish union negotiators with information such as financial statements, data on employees, production and operations information, and other information that is germane to the subjects being negotiated. The U.S. Supreme Court has ruled that employers must furnish financial information if they claim an *inability* to grant concessions to the union because of financial conditions.[11]

---

[10]*NLRB v. Borg-Warner, Wooster Division*, 356 U.S. 342 (1958), was the landmark case that delineated mandatory, permissive, and illegal bargaining subjects. Also see E. J. Dannin, "Statutory Subjects and the Duty to Bargain," *Labor Law Journal* (January 1988), pp. 44–52, and Terry L. Leap, *Collective Bargaining and Labor Relations* (New York: Macmillan Publishing Company, 1991), pp. 298–303.

[11]*NLRB v. Truitt Manufacturing Co.*, 351 U.S. 149 (1956). Also see James T. O'Reilly, *Unions' Right to Company Information* (Philadelphia: Industrial Research Unit, The Wharton School, University of Pennsylvania, 1980).

2. *Surface bargaining and dilatory tactics* are often indicative of bad-faith bargaining. Surface bargaining occurs when a party goes through the motions of negotiating without making a sincere effort to reach an agreement. Dilatory tactics are used to delay meeting an opponent at the bargaining table.

3. One primary indication of good-faith bargaining is a *willingness to compromise during negotiations*. The key for negotiators is to maintain a flexible attitude and a willingness to listen to proposals submitted by the other side and to make counteroffers on those proposals. A take-it-or-leave-it attitude during contract talks is indicative of bad-faith bargaining,[12] as is making a large number of new demands just prior to the end of negotiations, bypassing union negotiators and appealing directly to employees, or making unilateral changes in the terms of the collective bargaining agreement by management without joint consultation with the union.

When irreconcilable differences arise between the positions of the parties after exhaustive good-faith negotiations, the law recognizes that an *impasse* exists. Once an impasse occurs, the obligation to bargain in good faith is suspended and management may unilaterally make changes in wages, hours, and working conditions that are not inconsistent with previous proposals made by the union. That is, if the union requested a 7 percent pay increase during negotiations and management later provided employees with a 10 percent raise during the impasse, then management's actions are inconsistent with the union's earlier demands and may constitute bad-faith bargaining.

Stages of the Collective Bargaining Process

Contract negotiations between union and management can be divided into four stages: (1) preparation for negotiations, (2) the initial proposal stage, (3) the primary bargaining stage, and (4) the eleventh-hour bargaining stage.

The preparation stage occurs before the parties meet for formal negotiations. Often the preparation stage is the most time-consuming and important part of collective bargaining. When the collective bargaining agreement is lengthy and covers a large number of employees or when difficult contract talks are anticipated, preparation may take as long as 2 years to complete.

Once the parties meet at the bargaining table to formally open contract talks, the pressure and excitement begin to build. Union and management negotiators exchange initial demands and proposals and then get down to the business of agreeing on the terms of the collective bargaining agreement. It is difficult to describe a typical sequence of events once the parties meet. In some instances,

---

[12]This bargaining tactic has, in part, been attributed to Lemuel R. Boulware, former vice-president of General Electric. See *NLRB v. General Electric Company*, 418 F. (2d) 736 (1969), and Herbert R. Northrup, *Boulwarism* (Ann Arbor, Michigan: Graduate School of Business, University of Michigan, 1964).

the union and management bargaining teams start slowly and cautiously. There are other bargaining relationships in which the union presents its demands, management comments on what it describes as the ridiculous nature of the union's requests, and both sides start negotiations with "both barrels blazing." Depending on the complexity of the collective bargaining agreement, negotiations normally span a period of several months. The parties do not necessarily meet every day during this period, nor do the meetings always turn into marathon sessions. As the contract deadline nears, however, the negotiating sessions are likely to increase both in frequency and in duration. At the eleventh hour, negotiations may turn into all-night, pressure-packed sessions as both sides attempt to reach a settlement and avoid a strike or lockout.

Figure 16-3 summarizes the various bargaining stages. As noted, collective bargaining starts with the preparation stage and continues through the initial demands, primary bargaining, and eleventh-hour bargaining stages. If the parties reach an impasse, a mediator may be called in to help union and management negotiators regain their bargaining momentum and avoid a work stoppage. Most union and management bargaining teams achieve an agreement before the contract deadline. If the parties are unable to reach an agreement, then the union may elect to call a *strike*, the employer may engage in a *lockout*, or the parties may choose to forsake a work stoppage and continue negotiations. In the last case, negotiations may have reached the point where a settlement is near and a work stoppage would serve no useful purpose. Once the collective bargaining agreement is negotiated and approved by union members, the compensation and benefits of the new contract are often retroactive to the original contract expiration date.

Preparation for Collective Bargaining

A critical aspect of collective bargaining involves prenegotiations preparation. First, preparation allows each bargaining team to determine its *bargaining objectives* and the limits to which it is willing to concede before enduring a work stoppage. Figures 16-4 and 16-5 provide an overview of the factors that affect union and management bargaining goals. The impact of these factors in shaping the objectives that each bargaining team brings to the contract talks will vary among negotiating teams, as well as from one round of contract talks to the next. Second, preparation enables a negotiating team to *defend its proposals*. By collecting and organizing information germane to collective bargaining, negotiators can quickly refer to economic, industrial, and financial information that has an important bearing on contract talks. Third, prenegotiations preparation enables a negotiating team to *anticipate the opponent's demands* and minimize the chances for surprises at the bargaining table. Thus the preparation stage forms the foundation for everything that takes place during actual contract negotiations. Preparation allows skilled negotiators to get the most mileage out of the tactics used at the bargaining table. When both sides carefully prepare for negotiations, they may

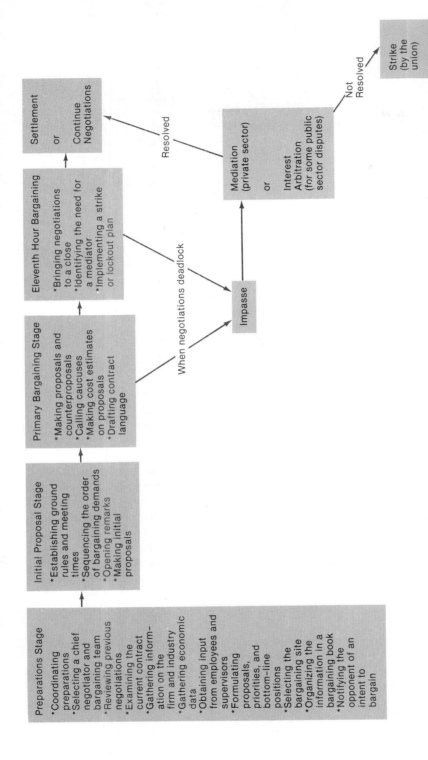

FIGURE 16-3   Stages of the Collective Bargaining Process

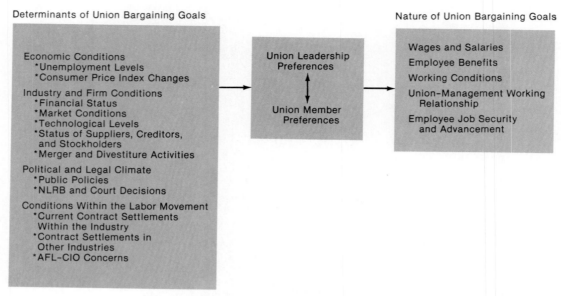

Determinants of Union Bargaining Goals

Economic Conditions
  *Unemployment Levels
  *Consumer Price Index Changes

Industry and Firm Conditions
  *Financial Status
  *Market Conditions
  *Technological Levels
  *Status of Suppliers, Creditors,
   and Stockholders
  *Merger and Divestiture Activities

Political and Legal Climate
  *Public Policies
  *NLRB and Court Decisions

Conditions Within the Labor Movement
  *Current Contract Settlements
   Within the Industry
  *Contract Settlements in
   Other Industries
  *AFL–CIO Concerns

Union Leadership
Preferences

Union Member
Preferences

Nature of Union Bargaining Goals

Wages and Salaries

Employee Benefits

Working Conditions

Union–Management Working
Relationship

Employee Job Security
and Advancement

FIGURE 16-4   Union Goals in Collective Bargaining

adopt a more realistic outlook on contract negotiations, thus reducing the possibility of a strike or lockout.

Among the more important steps to prenegotiation preparations are the following:

1. *Coordinating preparations* among the persons responsible for gathering and analyzing information relevant to the bargaining process. Work should be delegated to persons(s) who will be responsible for obtaining information on different segments of the collective bargaining agreement. For example, one committee might be formed to gather data on wage and salary proposals, another committee might be responsible for employee benefits, and still another might be assigned to work on contract proposals for management rights, union security clauses, or work schedule changes. Deadlines for the completion of each task must be established so that all information is available when needed. It is also important to allow ample time to gather the necessary information.

2. *Selection of a chief negotiator and bargaining team members.* A critical concern in collective bargaining is the composition and size of the negotiating team. The bargaining team is ultimately responsible for making proposals and counterproposals to the opposing bargaining team, and it also has the power to tentatively approve a contract settlement. Members of the negotiating team must have the expertise to draft proposals, analyze counterproposals made by the opponent, present persuasive arguments to back their proposals,

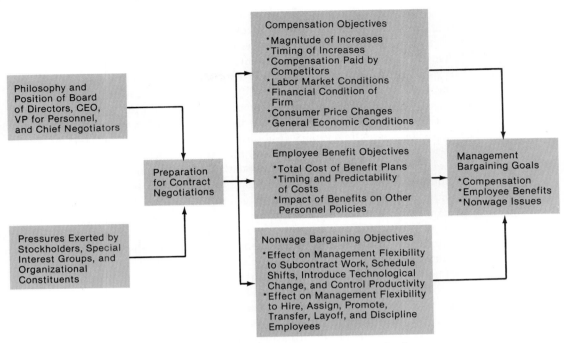

FIGURE 16-5   Management Bargaining Goals

and obtain a settlement that is acceptable to their constituents. Members of the bargaining team should understand the dynamics of labor-management relations and have a firsthand knowledge of industry conditions and the company's operations; some of the negotiators should also be experts on making cost estimates and drafting contract language.[13] Bargaining teams should employ enough members to ensure sufficient expertise for dealing with a wide range of bargaining subjects. However, an excessive number of negotiators may prove cumbersome and increases the likelihood that confidential information will be leaked to the opposing side or to the news media. The chief negotiator for management may be the top personnel/human resource executive or an outside person who is hired to negotiate on management's behalf. The union customarily selects a professional negotiator who is employed by the international union. In some instances, a local union president or business agent may serve as a chief negotiator. Regardless of who is chosen, the chief

---

[13]For an excellent discussion of the details and dynamics underlying the collective bargaining process, see Charles S. Loughran, *Negotiating a Labor Contract: A Management Handbook* (Washington, D.C.: The Bureau of National Affairs, Inc., 1992). Also see Thomas R. Colosi and Arthur Eliot Berkeley, *Collective Bargaining: How It Works and Why*, 2nd ed. (New York: American Arbitration Association, 1992).

negotiator usually speaks for the entire negotiating team, and has the final authority on the acceptance or rejection of contract proposals.[14]

3. *Reviewing previous negotiations* between the union and company is important because it provides insights into the opponent's bargaining tactics and probable demands. If union negotiators failed to secure a union shop clause during contract talks 2 years ago, then they may try again. It is also important to recall how quickly the opponent made concessions during previous negotiations. For example, management negotiators may have conceded begrudgingly on increasing group disability insurance coverage but settled much faster on child-care facilities. The union must decide what implications this behavior has for the upcoming negotiations. Finally, an analysis of the tactics and personalities of previous negotiations may prove useful if the same individuals are expected to be present at the next round of contract talks.

4. *Examine the current contract with an eye toward change.* A key consideration in preparing to bargain over the terms and conditions of a new collective bargaining agreement is to determine what changes should be made in the current contract. Some provisions may have outlived their usefulness and need to be eliminated. Other provisions may have created administrative problems during the life of the collective bargaining agreement and are in need of modification. Provisions involving pay scales and employee benefits may require updating because of changes in economic conditions, tax laws, or health care costs. Other provisions may require little or no alteration. Conversations with first-line supervisors and shop stewards, as well as an analysis of the types of grievances filed by bargaining unit employees, often provide insights into which contract provisions require change.

5. *Gather data on the firm and the industry.* Information on the internal operations and personnel policies of the firm are an important factor in collective bargaining. Such information should include a chronology of wage and employee benefit changes during the previous 10 years, labor cost ratios (per unit of production), employee benefit costs per employee, the amount of overtime worked by employees in each job classification, the age, sex, job, and seniority status of bargaining unit employees, information on work schedules by shift and department, and summaries of employee promotions, transfers, resignations, terminations, and disciplinary actions. Wage and salary surveys for the firm's industry should also be included, along with recent contract settlements involving similar firms.

6. *Gather economic data germane to collective bargaining.* General data on local, regional, national, and even international economic conditions should be collected and analyzed prior to negotiations. Information on inflationary trends, unemployment rates, consumer spending, investment trends, and government spending are all relevant to the bargaining process. Specific information on the company's product and labor markets is also important.

---

[14]The principle of "unseen authority" can be used to justify not using the highest-ranking union and management officials in contract talks. This tactic allows a chief negotiator to consult with a higher authority in order to buy additional time to contemplate a proposal or save face and avoid excessive debate over an unwanted contract term by stating that the higher official "won't buy" the proposal.

When gathering economic data, union and management negotiators must be cognizant of how trends in consumer price changes, unemployment, government economic policies, and international economic forces will affect upcoming negotiations. A key point to remember is that a firm's demand for labor is derived from the demand for its products and services. As a firm produces and sells more, it is usually willing to hire additional employees and pay them better wages. Firms in declining product markets may be forced into layoffs and less attractive levels of compensation for their employees, a problem that reached its peak in 1982 in the automobile and steel industries. Finally, changes in the consumer price index play a prominent role in the compensation demands made by union negotiators.[15]

7. *Obtain input from employees and supervisors.* Shop stewards and local union officials may poll bargaining unit members in an attempt to determine their needs. This process typically yields a list of reasonable demands, along with individual pet peeves, complaints, and unrealistic requests; the list is then reduced to one containing demands that are sensible and realistic. Management may also decide to conduct an employee attitude survey and solicit opinions from supervisors in order to anticipate what the union will demand at the bargaining table. It is important to remember that not all negotiators are intimately acquainted with the working conditions of bargaining unit employees. Input from bargaining unit members is vital for three reasons. First, with this input, the contract is likely to be more reflective of the needs and concerns of bargaining unit employees. Second, it increases the likelihood that the contract will be approved (ratified) by bargaining unit members once it is negotiated. Third, a contract that satisfies bargaining unit employees should be easier to administer and more conducive to harmonious labor-management relations.

8. *Formulate proposals, priorities, and bottom-line positions.* Before negotiating team members are ready to meet the opposing team at the bargaining table, they must formulate bargaining objectives that are understood and accepted by the entire team. By establishing a bargaining agenda, negotiators gain a better understanding of what they want to achieve, are less likely to disagree among themselves during contract talks, and have a better understanding of what concessions and trade-offs they are willing to make. When formulating bargaining demands, negotiators may decide to rank or classify their preferences. Bargaining items can be classified as "must" items, "important, but not vital" items, and "nice to have if we can get them" items. Chief negotiators may not be willing to make concessions on "must" items; in fact, they may be willing to endure a strike before conceding on certain "must" issues. However, negotiators may make wholesale trades on "nice to have" items. Of course, the categorization of bargaining subjects is a tightly held secret; to reveal one's *true* preferences to the other side is a cardinal sin in labor negotiations because it reduces a negotiating team's ability to bluff and make trade-offs with the opposing team.

---

[15]The U.S. Department of Labor, Bureau of Labor Statistics, publishes a wealth of economic and wage and salary information. See the discussion of wage and salary surveys in Chapter 11.

9. *Select a suitable site for negotiations.* Both union and management negotiators need to select a site that is physically comfortable and will allow them to endure long sessions at the bargaining table. In addition, the site should be free from unnecessary distractions posed by interested bargaining unit employees and members of the news media. A neutral site such as a hotel conference room is often a good choice because these sites are usually comfortable and allow negotiators to retreat easily to private suites for conferences.

10. *Organize the relevant information in a bargaining book.* Large volumes of information are usually collected as the bargaining teams prepare to negotiate a complex collective bargaining agreement. It is therefore important that this information be organized for easy access at the bargaining table. A common method for organizing information is a *bargaining book.* A well-organized bargaining book allows the quick retrieval of materials that, if kept in binders, can be easily removed, copied, and shared with the other side. In addition, the latest proposals and counterproposals can be added to the bargaining book as negotiations progress.

11. *Notify the opponent of an intent to bargain.* Private sector firms and unions covered by the Wagner and Taft-Hartley acts, respectively, must notify the other party within 60 days prior to the time that they wish to terminate or modify an existing collective bargaining agreement (this limit is 90 days for health care institutions). Federal law also requires that the parties notify the Federal Mediation and Conciliation Service (FMCS) and any state or territorial mediation agency 30 days after notice to modify or terminate has been given unless an agreement has already been reached. The 30-day notice allows the FMCS to monitor the negotiations and offer the services of federal mediators if it appears that an impasse or work stoppage is likely.

The Initial Proposal Stage

At the outset of contract talks, the sides meet and establish ground rules for the negotiations. Union and management chief negotiators jointly establish a schedule of proposed meeting times that will hopefully allow adequate time to complete contract talks without the need for extended marathon bargaining sessions or the unnecessary risk of a work stoppage. Chief negotiators should decide how they want to sequence the topics for bargaining; they may, for example, elect to negotiate all monetary items together. Provisions for recordkeeping, calling time-outs (caucuses), and the manner in which proposals will be approved should also be determined.

Once the preliminary ground rules are established, both chief negotiators usually make a brief opening statement, much of which is ceremonial and symbolic. Each chief negotiator usually emphasizes the seriousness of the contract talks, along with his intent to bargain in good faith in order to reach a mutually satisfactory settlement. After the opening ceremony is concluded, the union normally presents its lists of demands to management. To avoid surprise proposals that could result in bad-faith bargaining charges, the chief negotiators may decide to restrict proposals on new bargaining topics once the initial demands have been made.

The Primary Bargaining Stage

Most of the progress made at the bargaining table occurs during what will be referred to as the *primary bargaining stage*. During this phase of negotiations, union and management make proposals and concessions, debate points of contention, make cost estimates on proposals, call caucuses to discuss bargaining matters privately, consider the possible ramifications of work stoppages, and gain insights into the opponent's thoughts and willingness to accept a final offer. Several important points are relevant to the primary bargaining stage:

1. *Avoid threatening behavior and ultimatums.* The table-pounding, profane, and threatening negotiator is largely a relic in modern labor-management relations. Most negotiators communicate with the other side through the chief negotiator. A chief negotiator who attempts to cover up inadequate prenegotiation preparations with an aggressive hard-driving stance at the bargaining table is usually doomed to defeat at the hands of sophisticated and experienced negotiators. Ultimatums and extreme statements force a confrontation that can often be avoided if a more conciliatory tone is adopted. Suppose that management tells the union that it will never *under any circumstances* agree to a companywide seniority system. An extreme statement of this nature has placed management in a predicament because it will later be difficult for them to use the companywide seniority system to obtain a concession from the union without casting doubt on the integrity of management negotiators.

2. *Carefully formulate proposals and counterproposals.* The traditional system of collective bargaining used in the United States usually starts with the union making unrealistically high demands and management countering with an unrealistically low offer. Once the initial demands are made, the parties begin to make more reasonable proposals. The manner in which proposals are made provides signals regarding a party's credibility and willingness to reach an agreement. There are three general rules of thumb regarding concessions at the bargaining table. First, counterproposals should not be offered without carefully considering the implications of the opponent's proposal. Some proposals appear, at first glance, to be harmless and of minor consequence. However, the long-term consequences of a proposal may have a profound impact. For example, a plan that provides 5 weeks of vacation for employees with 10 years of seniority may seem inconsequential to the management of a newly opened plant where employees have little seniority. However, such an agreement can become a financial and operational nightmare over the next decade. A second rule of thumb is that concessions should not be made too rapidly.

Rapid concessions create the impression that a party is anxious to settle, and the opponent may take advantage of this condition by increasing its demands. Once a concession is made, it is difficult to retract and reduces the flexibility of a negotiating team in making subsequent proposals. The third rule is to obtain something in return for every concession that is made. In return for raising its wage level, for example, management may ask the union to reduce its demand for expanded health insurance coverage. Proposals should be put in writing to avoid any misunderstandings and presented to the other side in a tone that stresses its positive aspects and encourages acceptance.

3. *Make intelligent use of caucuses.* A caucus occurs when either the union or management adjourns for a private conference. Caucuses are often called to discuss a proposal made by the other side. They are also used to plan bargaining strategy and tactics, draft contract proposals, obtain additional data and information, make cost estimates, and obtain approval from a higher union or management official on a pending contract proposal. The number and length of caucuses taken by a bargaining team can send important signals to the opponent. Too many caucuses or caucuses of excessive length convey the impression that the bargaining team is unsure of itself. The length of a caucus also indicates the importance of an issue to a bargaining team, a point that is not lost on the opponent. On the other hand, a failure to caucus following a complex proposal may lead to a premature and disastrous concession by a bargaining team.

4. *Assess the cost of a proposal or concession.* Management negotiators, perhaps more than union negotiators, must have methods for making cost estimates on contract proposals.[16] Cost estimates are largely a matter of knowing how much money will be spent and when the expenditure will be made.[17] An important element to consider when making cost estimates is "rollup" or "loading" costs. Rollup costs occur because wage increases lead directly to cost increases for some employee benefits. If a collective bargaining agreement calls for a 6 percent increase in wages or salaries, costs for overtime, holiday and vacation pay, and sick leave will also increase, as will payments for Social Security, unemployment compensation, and pension contributions. Noneconomic provisions such as seniority clauses also have a cost impact. Suppose that a new contract provision is negotiated that gives the most senior employees first refusal rights to overtime. As a general rule, senior employees have higher wage rates than less senior employees. This means that overtime costs can be quite high if most senior employees elect to work at one and a half or two times their normal wage. Chief negotiators often use accountants to make cost calculations. The person performing this task should have some understanding of

[16]See Michael H. Granoff, *How to Cost Your Labor Contract* (Washington, D.C.: The Bureau of National Affairs, Inc., 1973).

[17]Many negotiators incorporate the present value or time value of money into their calculations. Simply stated, a dollar today is worth more than a dollar at some future time. From management's standpoint, it is better to defer wage and benefit increases as long as possible. The union, of course, wants to receive their increases at the earliest possible date.

the collective bargaining process, as well as familiarity with the financial condition of the firm. An accountant who mechanically computes costs without appreciating their impact on the firm, combined with a chief negotiator who does not understand the basis on which cost estimates are made, can lay the foundation for expensive mistakes.

5. *Carefully draft the contract language.* The written word of the collective bargaining agreement determines the rights and responsibilities of union and management. It is therefore important that the contract language be drafted carefully so that it reflects the intentions of the negotiators. Contract language should be written with an eye to clarity. Some collective bargaining agreements are drafted by lawyers who use incomprehensible legal prose. Unfortunately, such provisions are not understandable to supervisors, shop stewards, and employees who must interpret the contract on a daily basis. Once a contract provision is drafted, it should be carefully examined by someone who can anticipate possible problems and ambiguities that could later lead to contract administration problems.

The Eleventh-hour Bargaining Stage

Negotiators reach the eleventh-hour stage of bargaining when they realize that the contract expiration date is near and a number of issues remain unresolved. At this point, negotiations evolve into marathon sessions that are often accompanied by heated discussions, strike threats, final offers, and last-minute maneuvering to reach a settlement and avoid a work stoppage.[18] The following important decisions must be made at this point:

1. *A chief negotiator needs to take steps to bring negotiations to a close.* An experienced negotiator may detect that the opponent is attempting to conclude negotiations when the opposing chief negotiator makes concessions at a faster rate than before, drops unimportant demands, proposes final package offers, or agrees to concessions without obtaining a concession of equal value in return. Negotiators should avoid making "final" offers and then asking for further concessions; such a tactic undermines their integrity and credibility. Negotiators occasionally become deadlocked on an unreasonable matter of principle that can lead to an impasse. For example, rigid adherence by the union to having the company provide a full range of safety equipment such as hard hats, steel-toe shoes, and safety glasses to *all* bargaining unit employees may be unnecessary if the workplace and jobs have changed such that only a few employees are exposed to safety hazards. Thus a demand that was reasonable 10 years ago may be unreasonable today. When negotiators issue premature or

---

[18]See Henry S. Farber and Max H. Bazerman, "Why Is There Disagreement in Bargaining?" *American Economic Review* (May 1987), p. 347.

ill-advised ultimatums based on a matter of principle, the opposing negotiator can often salvage the situation by repackaging proposals to allow a settlement without either side losing face.

2. *The need for a mediator should be considered.* At some point the parties may realize that a settlement is not likely without the help of an outside third party known as a *mediator*. Mediators are commonly provided by the Federal Mediation and Conciliation Service (FMCS) or the state mediation agency and have been successfully used for decades to help the parties resolve negotiation deadlocks and prevent work stoppages. Mediators have no legal authority over union or management negotiators, and their use is strictly voluntary. The primary responsibility of a mediator is to help the parties help themselves; a mediator does not attempt to impose a settlement, but rather conciliates, persuades, and assists the parties in breaking an impasse.

Mediators perform their work in a number of ways.[19] In some instances, the mediator will propose to schedule meetings in an attempt to bring the parties back together without requiring that either chief negotiator lose face or appear to be the weaker party. When contract talks become heated, a mediator may suggest that the parties recess for several days. Sometimes a mediator will suggest changing the meeting site or the order in which bargaining subjects are discussed to help the parties regain momentum. Union and management chief negotiators often allow the mediator to be the sole contact with news media in order to prevent conflicting reports on the progress of negotiations. The mediator may help the parties establish their priorities and, in some cases, attempt to deflate unreasonable positions that block a settlement. In short, a labor mediator serves as a catalyst for the parties as they attempt to reach a settlement. Mediators must be careful not to favor one side or the other, and they must be especially careful not to leak confidential information that an opponent could use to gain an advantage in contract talks.

3. *Negotiators should have a plan on how to deal with a work stoppage.* Bargaining preparations should include a plan for failure. That is, both sides should have a plan that can be implemented in the event that a work stoppage occurs.[20] Management's strike or lockout plan usually addresses issues such as whether to maintain full or partial operations during a work stoppage, arrangements to obtain supplies and serve customers, plant security, availability of jobs to bargaining unit employees who do not wish to participate in the strike, and strike replacements for workers who do participate. The union's strike plan includes staffing picket lines, making strike fund payments to eligible union members, and keeping international union officials abreast of pertinent events.

---

[19]For an excellent discussion of mediator functions and tactics, see William E. Simkin and Nicholas A. Fidandis, *Mediation and the Dynamics of Collective Bargaining*, 2nd ed. (Washington, D.C.: The Bureau of National Affairs, Inc., 1986).

[20]See Charles R. Perry, Andrew M. Kramer, and Thomas J. Schneider, *Operating During Strikes* (Philadelphia: Industrial Research Unit, The Wharton School, University of Pennsylvania, 1982).

■ The Strike

- The Teamsters Union called a strike at 15 Consolidated Rail Corporation (Conrail) intermodal freight terminals in six states. The Teamsters acted to protest Conrail's plan to hire new contractors at intermodal facilities. As a result, the rail carrier's intermodal operations were disrupted throughout the Northeastern and Midwestern sections of the United States.[21]
- The Service Employees International Union called a strike against seven Kaiser Permanente hospitals and more than 30 satellite medical facilities in Southern California. The strike lasted 8 days before an agreement was reached, which provided wage and longevity increases to 11,000 workers.[22]
- A bitter strike by *New York Daily News* employees ended after 146 days. The strike threatened the survival of the 71-year-old newspaper and cut in half its prestrike circulation of 1 million. Efforts by the paper's owner, the Tribune Company of Chicago, to continue publishing, using replacement workers and union members who crossed picket lines, were severely hampered by a union boycott and a public sympathy campaign.[23]
- Two days after the United Auto Workers rejected what Caterpillar, Inc., called its final contract offer, the union expanded its strike against the company to an engine plant in Mossville, Illinois. This strike expansion added 2,750 workers to the 8,000 who had been idle for almost 4 months. The union further threatened to call as many as 16,000 additional workers out on strike if no agreement was reached.[24]

The preceding incidents illustrate the types of labor disputes that occur in the United States. Although peaceful and uneventful contract settlements between labor and management do not make headline news, strikes called by unions or lockouts instigated by employers are another matter. Unfortunately, newspaper, radio, and television accounts often overstate the frequency and ferocity of work stoppages. The statistics on strikes indicate that they are infrequent and less damaging to society than might be supposed. Instances of violence precipitated by strikes and lockouts do occur, but "violence" associated with the vast majority of labor disputes is limited to verbal taunts and idle threats. From an economic standpoint, however, strikes can be costly to the company, bargaining unit

---

[21]"Teamsters' Strike Disrupts Conrail Intermodal Service," *Journal of Commerce and Commercial* (February 25, 1992), p. 1.

[22]The Bureau of National Affairs, Inc., "Strike-Ending Kaiser Permanente-SEIU Contract," *Collective Bargaining Negotiations and Contracts* (April 19, 1990), p. 1.

[23]The Bureau of National Affairs, Inc., "Strike-Ending Daily News Contracts," *Collective Bargaining Negotiations and Contracts* (Washington, D.C.: The Bureau of National Affairs, Inc., April 4, 1991), p. 1.

[24]The Bureau of National Affairs, Inc., "Expanding Caterpillar Strike," *Collective Bargaining Negotiations and Contracts* (Washington, D.C.: The Bureau of National Affairs, Inc., March 5, 1992), p. 1.

employees, and the union.[25] In many instances, customers and suppliers who do business with the struck firm also suffer inconveniences and economic losses.

The overall impact of strikes can be assessed in a number of ways, all of which lead to the conclusion that strikes are not responsible for much of what has troubled industrial society over the past half century:[26]

1. The largest number of strikes involving more than 1,000 employees since 1947 occurred in 1952, when 470 work stoppages were recorded. In 1990, only 45 strikes involving more than 1,000 workers occurred.
2. A more significant statistic is the number of employees involved in a strike. In 1952, a record 2.7 million workers were involved in work stoppages, whereas in 1990 only 202,000 workers participated in work stoppages.
3. The largest number of working days lost, 60,850,000, came in 1959 in 245 strikes, whereas in 1990, 45 strikes resulted in only 6.6 million lost working days.
4. Perhaps the most telling statistic is the percentage of working time lost. In 1959, approximately four tenths of 1 percent (.0043) of total work time was lost to work stoppages. A low of four one-hundredths of 1 percent (.0004) was lost in 1982. Thus, work stoppages associated with labor disputes have not had a crippling impact on the flow of commerce.[27]

The downward trend in strike activity in the United States can be attributed to a number of factors. First, both management and labor realize that foreign competition is a major threat in traditionally unionized industries, such as auto manufacturing, steel, and rubber. Unions recognize that when a plant is closed by a strike, customers frequently take their business to domestic or foreign competitors. Second, more companies are willing to use elaborate strike plans that will allow the firm to operate during a work stoppage. A General Accounting Office report issued in 1990 indicates that up to 25 percent of firms faced with a strike are willing to use replacement workers as part of an effort to maintain operations. Many firms have trimmed their middle and lower-level management ranks and can no longer rely on this group to perform work during a strike. Therefore, the hiring of strike replacements becomes much more attractive. Furthermore, firms that are highly leveraged (debt-ridden) cannot afford to close down productive facilities for fear that they will miss debt repayments. Third, many union-management relationships have existed for a number of years and have reached a state of maturity that allows them to resolve their differences without striking. Fourth, the decline in the size of the unionized sector has also meant fewer strikes. Finally, many workers have a middle-class orientation and income and may be

---

[25]Michele I. Naples, "An Analysis of Defensive Strikes," *Industrial Relations* (Winter 1987), pp. 96–105.

[26]The Bureau of National Affairs, Inc., *Labor Relations Yearbook, 1984* (Washington, D.C.: The Bureau of National Affairs, Inc., 1985), p. 522.

[27]See Stanley J. Modic, "Striking Statistics: Work Stoppages Fewer, But the Cost Is High," *Industry Week* (March 23, 1987), p. 18; and David A. Dilts, "Strike Activity in the United States: An Analysis of Stocks and Flows," *Journal of Labor Research* (Spring 1986), p. 187.

reluctant to strike. As one observer noted: "When people are making only a few bucks an hour, they don't have much to lose by striking, but when they're making $17–$18 an hour they think twice about it."[28]

The Economic Strike

The economic strike usually occurs when contract talks are unsuccessful and the union is attempting to put pressure on the employer to reach an agreement.[29] Not surprisingly, most work stoppages are precipitated by demands for wage increases. The strike must be directed against the primary employer and not at neutral or secondary employers such as suppliers or customers (this is the aforementioned secondary boycott). Other than the Taft-Hartley Act's ban on secondary boycotts, few restrictions have been placed on the economic strike.

Economic strikers can lose their jobs if the employer decides to replace them permanently.[30] If an economic striker is not permanently replaced, he or she is entitled to reemployment once the strike ends. Employers can also refuse to reinstate economic strikers who fail to return to work within a recall period stipulated by the employer and union. Economic strikers who have been permanently replaced must be placed on a recall list and considered when there is a job opening for which they are qualified. Employees who engage in serious misconduct during a strike may be terminated by the employer and lose reinstatement rights. Serious misconduct includes assaulting and injuring a supervisor, setting fires, or forcing a vehicle carrying strike replacements off the road.[31] Profanity, throwing gravel at trucks crossing a picket line, or assaults that do not result in bodily harm are not normally regarded as serious misconduct; instead, such acts normally occur in the heat of a labor dispute and have been labeled by the NLRB as "anticipated animal exuberance."[32]

Economic strikers that are permanently replaced still have a right to vote in certification or decertification elections held within 12 months of an economic strike. Temporary strike replacements are not allowed to vote in an NLRB-

[28]The Bureau of National Affairs, Inc., "Declining Strike-Lockout Rate," *Collective Bargaining Negotiations and Contracts* (Washington, D.C.: The Bureau of National Affairs, Inc., February 21, 1991), p. 4.

[29]See Kern O. Kymn and Catherine A. Palomba, "The Strike Experience Model: Adaptive Expectations Applied to Strikes," *Journal of Behavioral Economics* (Spring-Summer 1986), p. 135; W. Stanley Seibert, Philip V. Bertrand, and John I. Addison, "The Political Model of Strikes: A New Twist, *Southern Economics Journal* (July 1985), p. 23; and Joseph S. Tracy, "An Investigation Into Determinants of U.S. Strike Activity," *American Economic Review* (June 1986), p. 423.

[30]John P. Kohl and David B. Stephens, "Replacement Workers During Strikes: Strategic Options for Managers," *Personnel Journal* (April 1986), p. 93. In 1991, a bill was introduced in Congress that would protect the employment rights of striking workers. To date, this bill has not been passed.

[31]See Paul G. Engel, "Picket Line Violence: Should It Be a Federal Offense?" *Industry Week* (June 11, 1984), p. 47; and Cora S. Koch, "Clear Pine Mouldings: The NLRB Adopts a Stricter Standard for Strike Misconduct," *Employee Relations Law Journal* (Winter 1985), pp. 493–507.

[32]For an excellent discussion of the legal aspects of strikes, see Bruce Feldacker, *Labor Guide to Labor Law*, 2nd ed. (Reston, Virginia: Reston Publishing Company, Inc., 1983), pp. 221–236.

conducted election. After 12 months only permanent replacements and economic strikers who have not been permanently replaced may vote.

The Unfair Labor Practice Strike

Workers who strike in protest of an unfair labor practice by the employer are engaging in an unfair labor practice strike. Unfair labor practice strikes might be precipitated when an employer refuses to hire union supporters, fires union members, spies on union activities, or fails to bargain in good faith. Unlike economic strikers, employees engaging in unfair labor practice strikes cannot be permanently replaced. Although an employer can continue operations during an unfair labor practice strike by hiring strike replacements, these replacements can be hired only on a temporary basis. Occasionally an economic strike is reclassified as an unfair labor practice strike if an employer incites violence on the picket line or refuses to rehire striking employees.

Other Types of Concerted Activities

Sympathy strikers are employees who elect to support a work stoppage of employees who work in another bargaining unit. Suppose that a bargaining unit consisting of plant production and maintenance employees is on strike. Employees working in other departments within the plant may decide to support the production and maintenance workers by refusing to cross their picket line. As long as the other employees are free to cross the picket line without intimidation or threats by striking production and maintenance employees, the sympathy strike is legal. A picket line, however, cannot become a "picket fence" in which employees, suppliers, customers, or others are physically barred from entering company property.[33] A worker may also engage in a limited sympathy strike. For example, a truck driver assigned to make deliveries at several plants for a soft drink bottling company may refuse to stock vending machines in a plant where a strike is in progress. Sympathy strikers responding to an economic strike can be permanently replaced, whereas those responding to an unfair labor practice strike can be only temporarily replaced.

A *wildcat strike* occurs when employees walk off the job without union approval.[34] Such strikes often violate the *no-strike clause* of a collective bargaining agreement that prohibits strikes during the life of the contract. A union may be

---

[33]Employees who do not cross a picket line because they have a reasonable fear of bodily harm are not regarded as sympathy strikers. Disciplinary actions taken by the employer in such instances are usually not based on just cause and are likely to be regarded by a labor arbitrator as unreasonable. Section 502 of the Labor-Management Relations Act also protects an employee's right to quit work in good faith because of dangerous working conditions.

[34]Dennis M. Byrne and Randall H. King, "Wildcat Strikes in U.S. Manufacturing, 1960–1977," *Journal of Labor Research* (Fall 1986), p. 387.

liable for damages incurred by the employer if the union authorized the wildcat strike. Otherwise, unions are not liable for the impromptu actions of their members.[35] Employers can obtain an injunction to end a wildcat strike and individual employees who participate can be discharged.[36] In addition, employees can be disciplined or discharged for engaging in *sitdown* or *slowdown* strikes.

As noted in Chapter 15, union leaders are also using *corporate campaigns* to put pressure on companies during organizing campaigns and strikes. Picketing banks that do business with the employer, disrupting stockholders' meetings, and placing ads that reflect negatively on the company are prime examples of the tactics used in corporate campaigns. The first major campaign was launched by the textile workers against J. P. Stevens. The United Food and Commercial Workers, Local P-9, which represented employees of the Geo. A. Hormel & Company's Austin, Minnesota, plant also used such tactics before being ordered to stop by the National Labor Relations Board.[37]

Some unions have employed in-plant actions such as slowdowns or work-to-rule measures as an alternative to economic strikes. Under the work-to-rule strategy, employees perform only the minimum tasks required of them by company rules and regulations. Employees can also follow work rules to the letter and create slowdowns and delays. Eastern Airline pilots used this strategy during their labor turmoil of 1990. By adhering fully to Federal Aviation Regulations without taking any of the shortcuts that are allowed under the regulations and by requesting the full array of services from air traffic controllers, Eastern pilots were able to cause delays at major airports.[38]

Strike Costs

Strikes impose costs on employers primarily because they force a total or partial shutdown of the firm and an accompanying loss of sales and customers. Employees also suffer lost jobs and financial hardships. The union strike fund may be depleted by a lengthy work stoppage and lowered employee morale, and ill-will between employee factions and company supervisors may arise during strikes that are marred by harsh accusations and violence.[39] In essence, the decision to endure a

---

[35]*Carbon Fuel v. United Mine Workers of America*, 444 U.S. 212 (1979).

[36]*Boys Markets, Inc., v. Retail Clerks*, 398 U.S. 235 (1970).

[37]For a summary of major events associated with the Geo. A. Hormel-Local P-9 strike, see William H. Holley, Jr., and Kenneth M. Jennings, *The Labor Relations Process*, 3rd ed. (Chicago: The Dryden Press, 1988), pp. 123–127.

[38]See The Bureau of National Affairs, Inc., "Union In-Plant Actions," *Collective Bargaining Negotiations and Contracts* (Washington, D.C.: The Bureau of National Affairs, Inc., September 5, 1991), p. 4, and Robert L. Rose, "How Pilots Hope to Slow Air Travel," *The Wall Street Journal* (March 7, 1989), p. B1.

[39]Julian Barling and Jill Mulligan, "Some Psychological Consequences of Striking: A Six-Month Longitudinal Study," *Journal of Occupational Behavior* (April 1987), p. 127; and Charles R. Stoner and Raj Arora, "An Investigation of the Relationship Between Selected Variables and the Psychological Health of Strike Participants," *Journal of Occupational Psychology* (March 1987), p. 61.

work stoppage involves weighing the costs of agreeing against the costs of disagreeing with the opponent. A union that agrees to a 4 percent wage increase avoids the problems associated with a work stoppage, but at the same time passes up the opportunity of forcing the employer to endure a strike and thus possibly winning an even greater increase. An employer who accedes to a union's demands avoids a work stoppage but may be saddled with an undesirable and expensive settlement.

Employers may find ways to reduce strike costs. A few corporations purchase strike insurance, and numerous others stockpile inventory to avoid disruption of sales and customer service. Some firms train nonunion and managerial employees to operate the plant. In addition, work normally done by striking employees may be subcontracted to other firms.

Striking employees lose pay and benefits and are usually not eligible for unemployment compensation. Strike benefits paid to union members, however, allow the worker to purchase essentials such as food and clothing and to pay rent. Because of the increasing number of dual-career couples, many strikers are able to survive through part-time jobs until the labor dispute is resolved.

Employers must deal with the following costs during a work stoppage:

1. Plant shutdown and startup costs.
2. Lost sales and customer goodwill.
3. Lowered profits and damage to stockholders' interests.
4. Reduced employee morale and harsh feelings after the work stoppage has ended.
5. Expenditures required to train strike replacements.
6. Overtime costs and scheduling problems.
7. Fixed costs such as rent and maintenance that continue during work stoppages.
8. Potential vandalism and sabotage by striking workers that necessitate hiring additional security personnel.
9. Refusals by customers and suppliers to make pickups and deliveries at a facility where a strike is in progress.

Unions or employees incur the following strike costs:

1. Loss of wages for employees and depletion of the union's strike fund.
2. Loss of revenue for the union because employees do not normally pay dues during a strike.
3. Permanent replacement of economic strikers, which causes a membership loss for the union that can jeopardize its status as the employees' exclusive bargaining representative.
4. Interruption of the accumulation of employee vacation, sick leave, and pension credits.
5. Public ill will toward the union.

■ Public Sector Collective Bargaining

The Wagner and Taft-Hartley acts regulate private sector labor relations but have ignored collective bargaining among federal, state, and municipal government employees. The rationale for this exclusion is that the government is a sovereign authority empowered by the citizenry; elected public officials, not labor unions, were expected to make personnel decisions pertaining to government employees. Unlike many employees in private industry, public employees held well-paying, secure jobs and were guaranteed equitable treatment under civil service regulations. However, a new line of thinking began to emerge in the early 1960s as teachers and other government employees turned to organized labor. The concept of public sector collective bargaining has spread to the point where approximately one fourth of the AFL-CIO membership is composed of public employees.[40] Some of the largest unions in the United States—the National Education Association (NEA), the American Federation of State, County, and Municipal Employees (AFSCME), the National Education Association (NEA), and the American Federation of Government Workers (AFGE)—have memberships that are dominated by public sector employees.[41]

Private sector labor relations are regulated by federal legislation (the Railway Labor, Wagner, and Taft-Hartley acts). By contrast, public sector labor relations are regulated by a patchwork quilt of federal, state, and municipal laws. Federal government employees are covered by the Civil Service Reform Act of 1978 (CSRA), and postal employees are regulated by the Postal Reorganization Act of 1970. The bargaining rights of state and municipal employees are rooted in a multitude of state and local laws, executive orders, and legal opinions. Some of these laws are constructed along the same lines as the Wagner and Taft-Hartley acts, have provisions for certification elections and unfair labor practices, and create an administrative agency similar to the NLRB to enforce the law.[42]

Many public sector employees, including those employed by the federal government, have the right to join, form, or assist unions and bargain collectively with their employers. However, there are some important differences between public and private collective bargaining. Often services provided by public sector employees such as police and fire protection are not widely available from private sector sources. As a result, most public sector employees do not have the right to engage in economic strikes or can engage in such work stoppages only on a limited basis. The most widely publicized and controversial public sector strike occurred

[40]Michael A. Pollack and Jonathan Tasini, "The Public Sector Is Labor's Success Story," *Business Week* (September 22, 1986), pp. 28–29.

[41]See Michael T. Leibig, *Public Employee Organizing and the Law*, 2nd ed. (Washington, D.C.: The Bureau of National Affairs, Inc., 1987).

[42]See Benjamin Aaron, Joyce M. Najita, and James L. Stern (eds.), *Public-Sector Bargaining*, 2nd ed., (Washington, D.C.: The Bureau of National Affairs, Inc., 1988).

in August 1981 when 12,000 air traffic controllers struck in violation of federal law.[43] President Reagan issued an ultimatum to the controllers: either return to work within 48 hours or lose your jobs. Unlike most professionals, air traffic controllers are employed only by the Federal Aviation Administration. Thus air traffic controllers who failed to return to work and were discharged lost both their livelihood and their profession. In addition, the Professional Air Traffic Controllers Organization (PATCO) was decertified. The ranks of the air traffic controllers have been gradually replenished, and in June 1987, the National Air Traffic Controllers Association (NATCA) won bargaining rights for the nation's air traffic controllers.[44]

Other public employees participate in illegal strikes without losing their jobs, however. The position that society is entitled to the uninterrupted service of government offices, schools, hospitals, transportation, and sanitation workers is often viewed with skepticism by public employees and their union representatives in light of the right to strike that exists in the private sector. Employees of privately owned air carriers can strike, whereas city transportation workers in most locales cannot. Private school employees and health care professionals in private hospitals can strike, but their public sector counterparts, who perform essentially the same services, are forbidden to engage in work stoppages. Banning strikes among government employees who perform essential services, such as police, fire, and sanitation workers, appears reasonable. However, most government employees provide services that are either not essential or can be obtained from private sector organizations.

The lack of a strike threat in public sector collective bargaining changes the complexion of contract talks. Public sector laws often require that impasses arising at the bargaining table be settled through a combination of mediation,[45] fact finding, and interest arbitration. If the union and management are unable to negotiate a collective bargaining agreement on their own, the terms and provisions of the contract may be ultimately decided by an arbitrator or panel of arbitrators.[46]

---

[43]See Arthur B. Shostak and David Skocik, *The Air Traffic Controller's Controversy* (New York: Human Science Press, 1986); and Herbert R. Northrup, "The Rise and Demise of PATCO," *Industrial and Labor Relations Review* (January 1984), pp. 167–184. The latter article generated an interesting series of exchanges. See Richard W. Hurd and Jill Kriesky, "Communications," *Industrial and Labor Relations Review* (October 1986), and Herbert R. Northrup, "Reply," *Industrial and Labor Relations Review* (October 1986), pp. 122–127.

[44]The Bureau of National Affairs, Inc., *Collective Bargaining Negotiations and Contracts* (Washington, D.C.: The Bureau of National Affairs, Inc., June 18, 1987), p. 2. The FAA trained new controllers, but it was not until the late 1980s that the number of air traffic controllers again reached pre-1981 levels.

[45]Arnold M. Zack, *Public Sector Mediation* (Washington, D.C.: The Bureau of National Affairs, Inc., 1985).

[46]See Peter Feuille, John Thomas Delaney, and Wallace Hendricks, "The Impact of Interest Arbitration on Police Contracts," *Industrial Relations* (Spring 1985), pp. 161–181.

■ Administration of the Collective Bargaining Agreement

Introduction

The previous sections focused on the *negotiation* of the collective bargaining agreement. The final product of the negotiation process is a collective bargaining agreement, a document that often contains a large number of provisions and clauses covering compensation, hours, and other conditions of employment. Regardless of the exacting efforts of the most experienced negotiators and labor lawyers, the final agreement is likely to contain flaws and ambiguities that, when interpreted and applied on a daily basis, will create what is termed a *dispute of rights*. Disputes of rights arise when either management or the union is believed to have violated the substance and spirit of a provision in the collective bargaining agreement. Nearly all collective bargaining agreements contain a grievance procedure under which rights disputes are submitted and resolved.[47] The following case provides an example of a typical grievance.

The Trent Engineering Company is a subsidiary of the Parker Pen Company. Employees are represented by the United Rubber Workers union, Local 891. Shortly after the company activated a third shift in its operations, a dispute arose with respect to the proper rate of pay for regularly scheduled hours worked by third-shift employees who began their shift at 11 P.M. on Saturday and continued until 7 A.M. on Sunday. The union's grievance is as follows:

> Members of Local 891 request that third-shift employees be paid double time for all hours worked on Sunday.

One month later, the company made the following reply:

> Grievance denied for the reasons contained in Article, Section 6.1. The Wage and Hour Act indicates that twenty-four (24) hours constitutes a work day. Our work week begins at 7:00 A.M. Monday, which is the first work day of the week. This work day is completed at 7:00 A.M. and is completed at 7:00 A.M. on Tuesday. Likewise, the sixth work day begins Saturday at 7:00 A.M. and is completed at 7:00 A.M. Sunday. This is considered the sixth work day, or Saturday work.

---

[47]The Bureau of National Affairs, Inc., *Grievance Guide*, 7th ed. (Washington, D.C.: The Bureau of National Affairs, Inc., 1987).

Section 6 of the collective bargaining agreement defines the normal work day as being 8 hours, and work beginning after midnight constitutes the third shift. Section 6.2 of the contract stipulates the following:

> Time and one-half the regular rate shall be paid for all hours worked in excess of eight (8) hours in a work day and forty (40) in a work week. Double time will be paid for all hours worked on a Sunday.

The union insists that the last sentence of Section 6.2 is clear and unambiguous; the company is clearly obligated to pay employees at double-time rates for all hours worked on a calendar day, which begins at midnight on Saturday night. The union also claims that there was full and complete agreement on the meaning of Section 6.2 by both sides during contract negotiations. Furthermore, there was no second or third shift in operation during the period in which negotiations were underway, and there was no thought that additional shifts would be activated at Trent Engineering during the life of the contract. The union argues that the company is attempting to nullify or modify a clearly stated contract provision, which an arbitrator has no power to modify.

The company argues that the Saturday night-Sunday morning third shift should be paid in accordance with Saturday wages, rather than at the double-time Sunday rate. Thus, the company argues that the Sunday work day does not begin until 7 A.M. on Sunday. The company, like the union, argues that the provisions of the agreement with respect to premium pay for Sunday hours worked are clear and unambiguous. In addition, the company claims that at no time during the negotiations did it agree with the union to pay double time for hours worked by employees on Sundays prior to 7 A.M.

Figure 16-6 outlines a typical grievance procedure. Although grievance procedures vary, most contain the following components:

1. *Definition of what constitutes a grievance:* Most grievance procedures define what types of grievances may be processed through the grievance procedure. Usually any violation of the collective bargaining agreement is subject to the procedure, although there may be exceptions. In some companies a separate grievance procedure is established for disciplinary cases. Also, it should be noted that there is a distinction between an employee *complaint* and a grievance. If a supervisor glares at an employee and addresses him or her in an abrasive and surely fashion, the employee may have a legitimate complaint from the standpoint of human dignity. However, this is not a grievance unless it can be demonstrated that the employee's contractual rights were violated. The key to determining whether a valid grievance exists is twofold: (a) Does it violate the terms, conditions, or spirit of the collective bargaining agreement? (b) Is this type of grievance specifically excluded from the grievance procedure? If the answer to (a) is affirmative and the answer to (b) is negative, then a legitimate grievance probably exists.

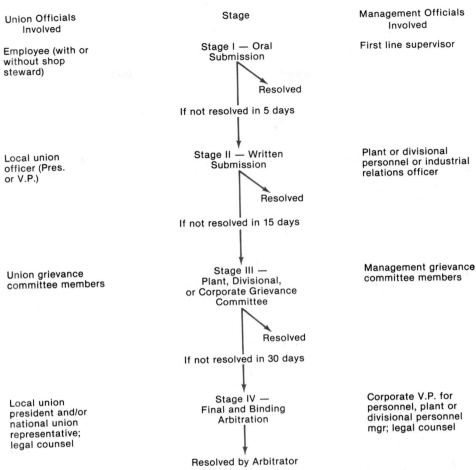

FIGURE 16-6   A Grievance Procedure with Final and Binding Arbitration

2. *Beyond the first step, nearly all grievances are put in writing:* The grievance should be written to ensure clarity and provide specifics on dates, the contract provisions in question, and other supporting documentation. By formulating the grievance in writing, the parties are more likely to present a clear picture of why the contract provisions were allegedly violated. Furthermore, when forced to put a grievance in writing, the parties are occasionally amazed to discover that they have no legitimate grievance after all.

3. *Time limits between stages of the grievance procedure:* An examination of Figure 16-6 will reveal that time limits between each stage of the grievance procedure have been established. This prevents the grievance from "dying on the vine" by forcing a resolution at the earliest possible time. A sound

grievance mechanism allows the parties to settle their differences quickly and economically.

4. *Persons involved:* As the grievance progresses to its more advanced stages, higher-level union and management officials become involved. If the grievance mechanism is functioning properly, only the more important, complex, and precedent-setting issues will rise to the upper levels of the procedure. Such grievances will require the scrutiny of higher union and management officials for two reasons. First, these grievances usually have no easy solution because of their complex nature. Second, they may uncover weak or troublesome areas in the collective bargaining agreement that require change.

5. *Final resolution:* Unless the grievance is settled at an earlier stage, the proverbial buck stops at the point of binding arbitration. An arbitrator is a neutral, disinterested party who is jointly selected by union and management to hear, decide, and finally resolve the grievance. Both sides have agreed in advance to accept the arbitrator's decision as *final* (it will not normally be appealed to a court of law) and *binding* (the parties agree to abide by the decision, regardless of whether they agree with it). Arbitration eliminates the threat that the rights dispute will escalate into a possible strike or lockout. A properly administered grievance procedure not only ensures compliance with the collective bargaining agreement, but can also help to nip labor relations problems in the bud, channel employee frustration properly, and improve morale.

Sources of Grievances

A number of events can prompt an employee or union official to file a grievance. An examination of the hundreds of published arbitration cases indicates that grievances generally arise from the following sources:

1. Contract terms that are too general, contradictory, or ambiguous.
2. Working conditions and pay arrangements that are, in some manner, unsatisfactory to employees.
3. Supervisors who fail to abide by and administer the contract properly.
4. Employees who fail to live up to conditions set by management or who neglect to adhere to the terms of the contract.

Grievances are commonly filed over employee disciplinary incidents,[48] disputes over seniority issues, work assignments, job classifications, scheduling, transfers, promotions, layoffs, and recalls, the subcontracting of work normally performed by bargaining unit employees, and employee entitlement to benefits.[49]

---

[48]Donald M. Wollett, "What an Arbitrator Looks for from Management in Discharge Cases," *Employee Relations Law Journal* (Winter 1983–84), pp. 525–534; and John R. Phillips, "Their Own Brand of Industrial Justice: Arbitrators' Excesses in Discharge Cases," *Employee Relations Law Journal* (Summer 1984), pp. 48–63.

[49]See Sam Kagel, *Anatomy of a Labor Arbitration,* 2nd ed. (Washington, D.C.: The Bureau of National Affairs, Inc., 1986), for a practical approach to preparing a grievance for an arbitration hearing.

Ambiguous Terms in the Collective Bargaining Agreement

The collective bargaining agreement is the source of rights and responsibilities for employers, unions, and employees. At the same time, the agreement contains the seeds of future disputes, due in part to the climate of negotiation under which the collective bargaining agreement is created. Compromises made between union and management negotiators, the fog that surrounds the last-ditch, all-night bargaining sessions, the history of bargaining within the firm, past practices, prior arbitration awards, and the myriad subjects contained in agreements all have an effect on contract administration. Unclear phrases in the agreement such as *discipline for just cause, and so forth, management's prerogative,* and the interchangeable use of the terms *employee, individual,* and *person* can create confusion and ambiguities. Unlike other contracts, the labor contract is entered into between two principals (union and management) for the benefit of the third person (the employees). In a large, diversified bargaining unit, workers' interests often differ and conflicts may arise. All collective bargaining agreements contain clauses of a *general* nature covering safety, discharge, layoff, recall, promotion, night shifts, vacations, pensions, holidays, seniority, bumping, rights during layoffs, and health insurance benefits that must be interpreted when *specific* violations are charged.[50]

The following contract clause illustrates the ambiguities that can lead to a grievance:

> Being absent from work for four (4) working days without reporting to the Company shall be reason for discharge. However, in such cases where an employee is unable to call in or report due to a condition beyond his control, this section does not apply.[51]

This clause presents several problems for management. First, the phrase *reporting to the Company* does not specify exactly to whom the employee must report. Is it a supervisor or a department head? Is it permissible for the employee to notify the company through a co-worker or spouse? The text that is especially troublesome is *however, in such cases where an employee is unable to call in or report due to a condition beyond his control, this section shall not apply.* Suppose that an employee does not come to work because of a common cold and does not call his supervisor. The employee claims that he did not call the company because the telephone company had disconnected his service for nonpayment. Is this "a condition beyond his control"? The employer might argue that the worker has no legitimate excuse for failing to call in, whereas the union could insist that no disciplinary action is warranted. Thus the seed for a grievance is planted in what appears to be an ordinary contract provision.

Even the most airtight collective bargaining agreements fail to anticipate all of the possible legal, social, economic, and ethical questions that can arise. Given the multitude of union and management interests and the variety of contract clauses, grievances are sometimes difficult to avoid because contract preparation is not an

---

[50]Sheri L. Bocher, "Contract Interpretation in Arbitration," *Employment Relations Today* (Summer 1987), p. 181.

[51]This clause was taken from a collective bargaining agreement in the food service industry.

exact science. When contract language is *not clear,* the outcome of the grievance may hinge on past practices, local customs, and industrywide policies. If the contract language relevant to a particular grievance is *nonexistent,* then the employer may have unilateral control over the final disposition of the problem.[52]

Compensation Practices

The application and coverage of pay and employee benefit policies may also represent potential grievances. For example, an employee or the union may file a grievance to protest the job evaluation and pay classification of his or her job. The assignment of overtime work that is paid at a higher rate than the initial 8 hours of work might be contested if assignments are not made in accordance with the collective bargaining agreement. Unions may contest the employer's choice of a health insurance company that provides group hospitalization coverage for bargaining unit employees, especially if the insurance carrier does not promptly pay claims. The list is almost endless, but the preceding examples are illustrative of the types of pay-related grievances that may arise. Even when wages and benefits are, on the surface, clearly spelled out in the collective bargaining agreement, the interpretations of such are rarely "chiseled in stone;" and controversy and grievances can arise.

Problems Associated with Working Conditions

Working conditions, or *other terms and conditions of work,* cover a wide array of contract provisions pertaining to work rules, work loads, seniority, layoff, and health and safety conditions. A multitude of potential grievances may arise that affect working conditions. For example, the union-management tug of war over management's right to control operations, change production standards, hire employees, introduce technological improvements,[53] schedule work, and subcontract work to employees outside of the bargaining unit all shape the working conditions within a firm and represent potential topics for the grievance procedure.[54]

Safety and health issues are an important facet of working conditions in some plants. Grievances might arise over an employee's refusal to perform an unsafe task. Controversies also arise when employers attempt to introduce technological improvements, schedule work, and subcontract work to employees outside of the bargaining unit. These and other issues shape the working conditions within a firm and represent potential topics for the grievance procedure.

Other grievances that have an impact on working conditions might include employee moonlighting activities and other outside business interests that potentially conflict with work in the bargaining unit, personal appearance and grooming

[52]Clyde Scott and Trevor Bain, "How Arbitrators Interpret Ambiguous Contract Language," *Personnel* (August 1987), p. 10.

[53]Richard D. Sibbernsen, "What Arbitrators Think About Technology Replacing Labor," *Harvard Business Review* (March-April 1986), p. 8.

[54]Marvin F. Hill, Jr., and Anthony V. Sinicropi, *Management Rights: A Legal and Arbitral Analysis* (Washington, D.C.: The Bureau of National Affairs, Inc., 1986).

standards, accommodation of an employee's religious beliefs, fraternization and intermarriage of employees, and listening to personal radios while at work.[55]

Supervisors Who Fail to Administer the Contract Properly

Immediate or first-line supervisors occupy an integral position in contract administration. A supervisor who fails to abide by the terms, conditions, and spirit of the collective bargaining agreement can be the source of numerous grievances filed by employees and union officials. Supervisors can precipitate grievances when they demonstrate favoritism among employees, fail to supervise and direct subordinates in their work, and overreact in taking disciplinary action. Grievance procedures also provide a means for checking up on the decisions and practices of first-line supervisors. Immediate supervisors who are in daily contact with employees are often in the best position to either create or halt a grievance. In addition, first-line supervisors are the initial point of conflict for most grievances and employee complaints.

Employee Disregard for Company Rules and Contract Provisions

The single largest category of grievances arises over employee discipline and discharge cases. Employees are disciplined and terminated for a host of reasons, including absenteeism, tardiness, assault, fighting with other employees, insubordination, alcohol and drug abuse, dishonesty and theft, incompetence, damage to company property, negligence, and safety violations.

The grievance procedure is used to determine whether the employee was properly disciplined in accordance with company rules and the applicable provisions of the collective bargaining agreement. Due process and equal protection for the employee filing a grievance can be maintained by examining the individual offense, possible extenuating circumstances, the employee's work and disciplinary record, and similar disciplinary cases that have arisen.[56]

■ The Final Step of the Grievance Procedure: Binding Arbitration

Selecting the Arbitrator

For grievances not resolved at an earlier stage, the collective bargaining agreement usually specifies that an arbitrator(s) is to be selected to make a final and

---

[55]An excellent treatise on labor arbitration is Frank Elkouri and Edna Asper Elkouri, *How Arbitration Works*, 4th ed. (Washington, D.C.: The Bureau of National Affairs, Inc., 1985). The types of grievances listed here are discussed in detail in Elkouri and Elkouri.

[56]See Chapter 13 for details on how factors affecting employee disciplinary cases should be analyzed.

binding resolution.[57] Most agreements call for the appointment of an ad hoc arbitrator, that is, the arbitrator is jointly selected by the employer and union on an as-needed basis when disputes arise. A small percentage of contracts contain provisions for a permanent arbitrator. In addition, tripartite arbitration panels are occasionally used in which the employer and the union each appoint an arbitrator; once selected, the two arbitrators then jointly select a third neutral arbitrator.

The names of ad hoc arbitrators can be obtained from the American Arbitration Association (AAA), the Federal Mediation and Conciliation Service (FMCS), or a state agency. AAA and FMCS procedures permit the selection of arbitrators by employers and unions from a list, with each side eliminating names until one arbitrator remains.

Although there is no law, licensing requirement, or minimum qualifications for arbitrators, they are usually competent, knowledgeable, and well educated. Arbitrators often hold law degrees or advanced degrees in business, economics, or associated disciplines. Some arbitrators specialize in areas such as discipline or subcontracting cases, whereas others are willing to hear nearly every type of grievance.[58] In some instances, an arbitrator may work only in a specific industry. For example, an arbitrator may hear cases primarily in the aerospace industry, where he or she has become familiar with the jobs, work practices, and production methods peculiar to that industry.

There are also cases where employers and unions select arbitrators for predictability of opinion rather than for expertise. To determine the direction that arbitrators are likely to take, employers and unions sift through published awards for further information about the arbitrator's track record, types of cases heard, and decision-making tendencies.[59]

Factors Affecting the Arbitrator's Decision

Five major factors normally control the outcome of an arbitration hearing: the language of the collective bargaining agreement, the submission agreement, the evidence brought forth at the hearing, past practices in the firm and industry, and prior arbitration awards.[60]

[57]Jack E. Steen, "How to Win Arbitration Decisions," *Personnel* (March 1986), p. 66; and David E. Bloom and Christopher L. Cavanaugh, "An Analysis of the Selection of Arbitrators," *American Economic Review* (June 1986), p. 408.

[58]John Smith Herrick, "Profile of a Labor Arbitrator," *Arbitration Journal* (June 1982), p. 18.

[59]See Courtney D. Gifford and William P. Hobgood, *Directory of U.S. Labor Arbitrators* (Washington, D.C.: The Bureau of National Affairs, Inc., 1985).

[60]See Sam Kagel, *Anatomy of a Labor Arbitration*, 2nd ed. (Washington, D.C.: The Bureau of National Affairs, Inc., 1986); William W. Notz and Frederick A. Starke, "Arbitration and Distributive Justice: Equity or Equality?" *Journal of Applied Psychology* (August 1987), p. 359; Max H. Bazerman and Henry S. Farber, "Analyzing the Decision-Making Processes of Third Parties," *Sloan Management Review* (Fall 1985), p. 39; and Orley Ashenfelter and David E. Bloom, "Models of Arbitrator Behavior: Theory and Evidence," *American Economic Review* (March 1984), p. 111.

The Collective Bargaining Agreement

First and foremost, the arbitrator considers the relevant contract provisions in evaluating a case. Arbitrators examine the contract language and the negotiating history of the applicable contract terms in order to determine the intent of the parties when the provisions were initially drafted. Often, however, the contract language is either vague or too general to offer adequate guidance to the arbitrator. In addition, the specific circumstances surrounding the incident and the employee's work record frequently play an important role. Thus, arbitrators must often walk a fine line between the *legalistic approach*, which emphasizes that the arbitrator is a creature of the collective bargaining agreement and must make a decision strictly on its terms, and the *clinical approach*, which attempts to go beyond a literal interpretation of the contract to examine social, economic, and legal factors that have a bearing on the grievance.

The Submission Agreement

Submission agreements are prepared by the employer and union to pinpoint the specific question or questions to be decided by the arbitrator. By this practice, the arbitrator's authority to hear and decide a dispute is clearly defined. The arbitrator cannot exceed the submission agreement by considering other issues or questions that were not included in the grievance. Thus, the arbitrator's decision simply answers questions raised in the submission. In the absence of an agreement between union and management, arbitrators answering questions not raised in the submission can be challenged in court for exceeding their authority. For example, the submission agreement may ask: "Did the Broughton Company discharge Larry Smeltzer for just cause?" The arbitrator's charge is to determine the relevant circumstances surrounding this discharge and to render a decision. If during the hearing the arbitrator discovers that another employee, Joe Willis, was actually more deserving of discharge than Mr. Smeltzer, the arbitrator cannot order Willis to be terminated. To do so would exceed the arbitrator's authority *in this particular case*.

Evidence

The arbitrator usually determines the admissability and weight to be given to evidence at the hearing.[61] Arbitrators vary in the manner in which they admit and weigh evidence, but most are constantly on guard to ensure that both the union and management are allowed to disclose fully whatever they feel is necessary to argue their case. Evidence may consist of testimony by witnesses, documents, exhibits, drawings, and the collective bargaining agreement. Few arbitrators follow the exclusionary rules of evidence developed and used in the courts. The legal rules of evidence were designed to meet judicial needs in criminal and civil cases and strictly limit the admissibility of evidence. The philosophical underpinning for

---

[61]See Marvin Hill, Jr., and Anthony V. Sinicropi, *Evidence in Arbitration*, 2nd ed. (Washington, D.C.: The Bureau of National Affairs, Inc., 1987).

the legal rules of evidence is that only the best evidence should be considered by a jury of *laypersons,* who, because of their lack of legal training, might otherwise make decisions based on irrelevant and unreliable information. Because arbitrators are not normally regarded as laypersons, the formal rules of evidence may be relaxed and are less stringent than those encountered in a court of law. Furthermore, arbitrators act as both judge and jury; they can evaluate evidence and separate the important from the unimportant and the reliable from the unreliable.[62]

In summary, the following points apply to the use of evidence in arbitration:

1. The more *tangible* the evidence, the greater its credibility. For example, in a discipline case involving tardiness, the employee's time cards for the days in question are a more tangible form of evidence than a supervisor's recollection that the employee was late.
2. Evidence must be *relevant* to the case. If an employee is accused of stealing from the employer, then the fact that he or she has also incurred numerous moving traffic violations is probably of no value to the arbitrator and should not be considered.
3. Observations that are *firsthand* carry greater weight than secondhand versions of what has been said or observed. For example, testimony of witnesses who observed an employee vandalizing company property is given more credibility than the testimony of employees who merely heard what happened from a firsthand witness (hearsay evidence).
4. The testimony of witnesses is usually confined to observations and recollections of *fact* rather than *opinion.* However, recognized authorities, such as physicians, safety experts, and other expert witnesses, may include their *opinions* in the testimony as long as it remains within the realm of their expertise.[63]
5. Testimony of witnesses must be *credible* if it is to be given weight. Witnesses may be discredited if they were not in a position to know or observe certain facts, have faulty memories, exhibit bias or prejudice, make contradictory statements during their testimony, or have previously acted in a manner that would raise doubts about their honesty.

Industry and Company Past Practices

Collective bargaining provisions that are intentionally or inadvertently vague may allow arbitrators to turn to company or industry tradition and past practices to resolve grievances. Examples of past practices might include allowing employees to arrive at work late during inclement weather, sponsoring an annual employee

---

[62]See Brook I. Landis, *Value Judgments in Arbitration: A Case Study of Saul Wallen* (Ithaca, New York: Cornell Studies in Industrial and Labor Relations, Cornell University, 1977), for insights into the logic and reasoning of preeminent arbitrator Saul Wallen.

[63]See Edward Levin and Donald Grody, *Witnesses in Arbitration: Selection, Preparation, and Presentation* (Washington, D.C.: The Bureau of National Affairs, Inc., 1987).

picnic, providing free coffee in offices and work areas, giving each employee a ham or turkey at Thanksgiving, paying for counseling and rehabilitation for employees with alcohol and drug problems, and giving an inexpensive gift to newly wed employees. Thus, arbitrators often base their decisions on past practices unless the agreement specifically outlines another course of action. Arbitrators occasionally face claims by employers and unions that past practices control the outcome of the grievance even when they conflict with the agreement. This places the arbitrator in a dilemma, but usually the written collective bargaining agreement is given greater weight.[64] Arbitrators are permitted to turn to past practices to justify their awards if the contract is not clear or if both parties have unequivocally resorted to the new custom or practice.

If the union and management wish to change a past practice, they must clearly demonstrate such intent in the agreement. Unfortunately, intent is not always clearly expressed in the agreement, and testimony presented during the hearing may be less than convincing. For example, has a company that has given a small Christmas bonus to employees over the past several years established a past practice that can be enforced by an arbitrator? In the absence of contractual guidance or financial hardship, the arbitrator may rule that the company must continue this practice.

Previous Arbitration Awards

Judges in the state and federal judicial systems often follow precedents established in earlier, related court cases. Arbitrators may also examine arbitration awards made by others, but these awards are not given as much weight as the courts are likely to give prior judicial decisions. Published arbitration awards are used by arbitrators for insight and guidance rather than as the controlling factor in the outcome of a case. The reason for less reliance on previous arbitration awards stems from the previously mentioned fact that arbitrators are creatures of the collective bargaining agreement. For example, an arbitrator facing the same type of case with the same set of facts may make two totally different decisions *for two grievants covered by two different contracts*. Differences in the content and language of two collective bargaining agreements can make a complete difference in the outcome of the grievance.

When a grievance involves complex factors and the contract language is not clear, arbitrators may research other cases in order to acquire insights that may help them in rendering the award. Greater weight may be given to similar cases decided under the same collective bargaining agreement. When prior cases are

---

[64]The *parole evidence rule* dictates that the written word of the collective bargaining agreement takes precedence over practices that the union and employer might follow that are contradictory to the contract. For example, if the contract stipulates that overtime will be awarded based on seniority, but both the union and management have deviated from this rule in daily practice, the arbitrator, under the parole evidence rule, will adhere to the written contract in rendering a decision over a dispute involving seniority and overtime.

decided under different agreements, the arbitrator will weigh them according to their relevance to current contract provisions and case facts.[65]

■ The Legal Status of Arbitration

Although there is no federal law governing labor arbitration, a series of U.S. Supreme Court decisions has bestowed a great deal of power on the arbitrator. As a result, the courts are extremely reluctant to alter or reverse an arbitrator's ruling.

The essence of an arbitrator's power is as follows:

1. If the collective bargaining agreement contains a grievance procedure with binding arbitration, then the parties must abide by the agreement. Should either party (usually the employer) resist presenting a case to an arbitrator, then the other party (usually the union) can seek court enforcement.[66]
2. Arbitrators generally have the final word in determining whether a particular grievance is both subject to arbitration (this is known as *arbitrability*) and has merit insofar as the collective bargaining agreement is concerned.[67]
3. The NLRB will defer disputes to arbitration in cases where the issue could be decided either through arbitration (because of the collective bargaining agreement) or by NLRB ruling (because it alleges an unfair labor practice).[68] However, the NLRB will not defer unfair labor practice cases to arbitration where an employee's rights to join, assist, or form a union (and bargain with the employer) have been violated.[69]

The courts may overturn an arbitration award if the arbitrator is found to have a conflict of interest in a particular case (e.g., if the arbitrator is discovered to be a close relative of the grievant or has financial interests in the company involved in the grievance). Furthermore, arbitrators may be reversed if they grossly misweigh or ignore important evidence or if they exceed their authority under the collective bargaining agreement. One notable exception to the final nature of

---

[65]For an excellent discussion of how to conduct an arbitration hearing, see Ronald W. Haughton, "Running the Hearing," Edgar A. Jones, Jr., "Selected Problems of Procedure and Evidence," and Robben W. Fleming, "Due Process and Fair Procedure," all in Arnold M. Zack (ed.), *Arbitration in Practice* (Ithaca, New York: ILR Press, Cornell University, 1984), pp. 37–78.

[66]*Textile Workers v. Lincoln Mills*, 353 U.S. 448 (1957).

[67]*United Steelworkers v. American Manufacturing Co.*, 80 S.Ct. 1343 (1960), *United Steelworkers v. Warrior and Gulf Navigation Co.*, 80 S.Ct 1347 (1960), and *United Steelworkers v. Enterprise Wheel and Car Corp.*, 80 S.Ct. 1358 (1960). Collectively, these cases are known as the *Steelworkers' Trilogy of 1960*.

[68]*Collyer Insulated Wire*, 192 NLRB 837 (1971), and *Spielberg Manufacturing Co.*, 112 NLRB 1080 (1955).

[69]See *International Harvester Co., Columbus Plastics Operation*, 271 NLRB No. 101 (1984).

arbitration decisions occurs in cases involving race, sex, religious, and other forms of discrimination. The Supreme Court has ruled that such civil rights cases heard by the arbitrator can be tried again by the EEOC and federal courts.[70]

In 1987, the U.S. Supreme Court unanimously ruled that courts are not free to overturn an arbitrator's award in the absence of proof of fraud or dishonesty. This decision stemmed from the case of a machine operator who was fired after being apprehended on company property in the back seat of a car in which a marijuana cigarette was found burning in the front seat ash tray. Finding insufficient evidence that the employee either possessed or smoked marijuana, the arbitrator subsequently ordered reinstatement. However, a federal court overturned the arbitrator's award and stated that reinstatement of the employee would violate public policy "against the operation of dangerous machinery by persons under the influence of drugs." The U.S. Supreme Court overturned this decision and noted that the courts have limited power to reverse labor arbitration awards and may not do so simply because they disagree with an arbitrator's findings, contract interpretations, or choice of remedies. The Supreme Court also said that an arbitrator's decision can be overturned only if it violates some explicit public policy that is grounded in "laws and legal precedents." However, courts may not reverse arbitration decisions that involve "general considerations of supposed public interests."[71]

The Union's Duty of Fair Representation

Under normal circumstances, unions control the submission of grievances to the formalized procedure. Employees often encourage unions to process a host of grievances, some of which have little or no merit. The union must then determine whether a particular grievance has merit and whether it has the option not to process those that are frivolous.[72]

Making a distinction between meritorious and frivolous grievances is often difficult. The terms of the collective bargaining agreement and the facts of the grievance are key considerations in making this judgment. If a grievance has merit, then the union must process it competently, enthusiastically, and in good faith. To do otherwise constitutes a violation of the union's *duty of fair representation* and opens the door to legal intervention. Unions are expected to handle grievances fairly because they *exclusively* represent the workers in a particular bargaining unit and are their primary source of protection in rights disputes. However, if the union is forced to process ill-founded cases, costs will skyrocket and the entire grievance mechanism could become helplessly backlogged. As a

---

[70]*Alexander v. Gardner Denver Co.*, 7 FEP Cases 81 (1974).

[71]*United Paperworkers v. Misco, Inc.*, US SupCt., 126 LRRM 3113 (1987).

[72]See Jean T. McKelvey (ed.), *The Changing Law of Fair Representation* (Ithaca, New York: ILR Press, Cornell University, 1985).

result, the duty of fair representation has become one of the thornier legal issues in labor relations.

The case *Hines v. Anchor Motor Freight Co.*[73] involved several long-distance truck drivers who were discharged for padding motel bills on their company expense accounts. An arbitration panel supported the firings, and the drivers then hired an attorney. Upon investigation, it was discovered that a motel clerk had overcharged the drivers and pocketed the difference between the actual room rate and the higher rate charged to the truckers. Had the union agent acted fairly or diligently, the innocence of the drivers could have been established before the arbitration panel had met. (Note that the arbitrators made the decision in good faith based upon available evidence, and the employer was also innocent of wrongdoing.) The Supreme Court ruled in favor of the drivers, finding the union representation to be unfair. In attempting to uphold the sanctity of the arbitrators' award, however, the Supreme Court decided that evidence uncovered after an award is made is not always an adequate reason to reverse an award. The Court reasoned that no system of justice, including labor arbitration, can operate error free; the fact that errors occur does not necessarily justify review. However, when the plaintiff can convince the court that the union acts dishonestly, discriminatorily, or in bad faith, the courts can intervene. The Supreme Court also ruled in *Hines* that arbitration awards involving grievants who are incompetently represented may be reversed. Critics feared that the *Hines* decision would open the door to greater interference with arbitration decisions by the courts. To date, there is little evidence to support the fear that wholesale reversals of arbitration awards will become common.

Unions can be held liable for damages when they fail to carry out their duty of fair representation. In *Bowen v. United States Postal Service*, an international union refused to arbitrate an employee's discharge case even though the employee's grievance was supported by lower levels of the union hierarchy.[74] The Supreme Court held that the union failed to fulfill its statutory obligation of fair representation when it refused to submit the case to arbitration. As a remedy, the Court ordered the union to pay $30,000 of the total $53,000 in back pay (with the employer paying $23,000).

◼ Under What Conditions Are Grievances Most Likely to Occur?

The ideal situation with respect to contract administration is to have a well-drafted collective bargaining agreement with no weak spots *and* a bargaining unit environment in which there is rarely, if ever, the need to file a grievance. However,

[73] *Hines v. Anchor Motor Freight*, 96 S.Ct. 1048 (1976).
[74] *Bowen v. United States Postal Service*, 459 U.S. 212 (1983).

grievances do occur and, in some cases, they occur at what might be termed an unhealthy rate.

The incidence rate of grievances in a bargaining unit is a function of the following factors:

1. A higher than usual number of grievances are likely to be filed if the negotiation history of the parties has been marked by hostility and work stoppages.
2. Grievance rates are more likely to increase if the contract language is vague, overly general, and poorly written.
3. The greater the change in technology for a particular industry or company, the higher the grievance rates.[75]
4. Technologies requiring high levels of worker responsibility and close supervision usually result in higher grievance rates.
5. The more centralized the management structure, the higher the grievance rates.[76]
6. Firms that either lack formalized personnel policies or fail to enforce these policies consistently and fairly are more likely to have higher grievance rates.[77]
7. Supervisors who fail to emphasize communication, respect, and trust when dealing with their subordinates increase the chances of having employee grievances.[78]
8. Poor performers tend to use the grievance procedure more often than good performers.[79]
9. Part-time or short-term employees are less likely to file grievances.[80]
10. Union activists, highly educated workers, workers with a high incidence of absenteeism, and workers in lower job classifications tend to file more grievances than other employees.[81]

Although these research findings provide insight, the key point to remember is that firms with stable union-management relations, sound personnel/human resource policies, and well-trained supervisors are more likely to have fewer grievances filed by employees.

---

[75]David Peach and E. Robert Livernash, *Grievance Initiation and Resolution: A Study in Basic Steel* (Boston: Graduate School of Business Administration, Harvard University, 1974).

[76]Ibid.

[77]Ibid.

[78]A. Fleishman and E. F. Harris, "Patterns of Leadership Behavior Related to Employee Grievances and Turnover," *Personnel Psychology* (Summer 1962), pp. 43–56.

[79]Howard Q. Sulkin and Robert Pranis, "Comparison of Grievants and Non-Grievants in a Heavy Machinery Company," *Personnel Psychology* (Summer 1967), pp. 111–119.

[80]Ibid.

[81]Ibid.

■ Criteria for Evaluating Grievance Procedures

The courts, in empowering the arbitrator with final and binding decision-making power, noted that the grievance procedure and labor arbitration are "socially desirable."[82] Grievance procedures allow rights disputes to be settled quickly and economically relative to either pursuing a civil suit in court or risking a work stoppage until the grievance is resolved. In essence, the courts noted, a quid pro quo relationship exists between labor and management; the union give up its *right to strike*, while management transfers to the arbitrator its *right to make a unilateral decision*. For example, if management discharges an employee for just cause and the union questions the discharge by filing a grievance, then management relinquishes its right to control the employee's fate once the case reaches the arbitrator's hands. Should the arbitrator reinstate the discharged worker, management must accept the decision, regardless of whether it feels the action is just.

Several criteria have been used to monitor the effectiveness of the contract administration process. First, the speed with which grievances are resolved is important. Grievances that are resolved quickly have less opportunity to smolder and create underlying tensions and hostility. For better or worse, rights disputes can be resolved without lengthy court battles, allowing the parties to turn their attention to other matters.

Economy is a second often cited advantage of the grievance procedure. The cash outlay, excluding that percentage of union and management's salaries for the time they spend dealing with a particular grievance, is relatively small. If a case is processed through the arbitration stage, the total cost may vary from $2,000 to $5,000, depending on the complexity of the case, whether briefs and transcripts were used, the expense of the arbitrator, and other incidental costs associated with investigations, witnesses, and evidence. Compared to the time and expense of a typical civil suit, most consider the grievance procedure and arbitration to be a bargain.

A third consideration when evaluating grievance procedures is to examine the aftermath of different types of cases. Many grievances are zero-sum in the sense that one party emerges as the victor and the other loses. Research results on the postsettlement phase are scant. Studies involving discharged employees reinstated by arbitrators have indicated that a number of employees did not return to work even though they won their case.[83] Those returning to their job faced various reactions from the employer and fellow employees. Undoubtedly, some reinstated employees were subjected to retaliation, while others continued as productive employees. In other instances, reinstated employees continued to perform poorly and were chronic malcontents who filed grievances whenever the opportunity arose. Whether the impact or shock effect of arbitration awards makes a subsequent impact on changes in personnel/human resource policy or on the content of

---

[82]*Textile Workers v. Lincoln Mills*, 353 U.S. 448 (1957).

[83]See Thomas J. McDermott and Thomas H. Newhaus, "Discharge-Reinstatement: What Happens Thereafter," *Industrial and Labor Relations Review* (July 1971), pp. 526–540.

the collective bargaining agreement is difficult to determine. However, personnel/human resource managers and union officials should use the information and experiences derived from grievance procedures and arbitration hearings when formulating or changing policies or preparing to negotiate the collective bargaining agreement. Otherwise, the underlying problem is likely to reoccur.

A fourth item of importance is whether the outcome of a grievance or arbitration case conflicts with a public law.[84] Some experts argue that the proliferation of health and safety, EEO, compensation, and other personnel laws have eroded the influence of labor arbitration. Prior to the 1960s, employees did not have the legal recourse that is available today and therefore were more dependent on unions and grievance procedures for protection. A dilemma faced by arbitrators is what to do if a contract provision forces an award that is contrary to public policy. Three schools of thought on this matter have emerged. First, some arbitrators feel that they must ignore public policy and, right or wrong, enforce only the terms of the collective bargaining agreement. A second view holds that the arbitrator may incorporate public policy into the decision if the contract is either vague or silent on the matter. The third view stipulates that arbitrators should enforce public policy even if it conflicts with the collective bargaining agreement. At this point, the arbitration profession is somewhat divided regarding the extent to which laws should be incorporated into arbitration decisions. However, a fine line between encroaching on the jurisdiction of administrative tribunals (e.g., the EEOC) and courts versus diminishing the influence of the institution of labor arbitration must be dealt with if the grievance procedure and labor arbitration are to remain prominent in resolving industrial disputes.

■ Summary and Conclusions

The dynamics associated with negotiating and administering a collective bargaining agreement pose a challenge for personnel/human resource managers who operate in unionized settings. Preparing to negotiate with a labor union can consume hundreds of hours of personnel staff time, and the outcome of collective bargaining can determine the competitive posture and ultimate success of the organization. Thus personnel/human resource managers who deal with labor unions must possess a knowledge of bargaining preparations and tactics. This chapter attempts to provide insights into the major issues associated with the successful negotiation of the collective bargaining agreement.

Of equal importance is management's ability to deal with the collective bargaining agreement after it has been negotiated. Effective contract administration is vital to the health of the union-management relationship. A collective bargaining agreement whose provisions and language are carefully and cautiously drafted

[84]See Raymond L. Britton, *The Arbitration Guide* (Englewood Cliffs, New Jersey: Prentice-Hall, Inc., 1982), pp. 130–147.

with an eye to clarity is likely to reduce contract administration problems. In addition, both union and management must be determined to live with and abide by the terms of the agreement. A constant stream of grievances can be precipitated when one side or the other repeatedly attempts to challenge the opponent's rights and authority. Successful administration of the collective bargaining agreement depends on mutual respect among employees, management, and union officials. Rights disputes that arise should be resolved at the earliest possible stage of the grievance procedure, with only the more complex and difficult cases being brought to arbitration. Although mediators and arbitrators are used to resolve bargaining impasses and grievances, respectively, the ideal form of conflict resolution in labor-management relations is mutual agreement without third-party intervention.

■ Questions

1. Describe the duty of good-faith bargaining for both management and the union.

2. Briefly outline the four major stages of the negotiation process.

3. Describe the difference between an economic and an unfair labor practice strike.

4. Under what conditions can an employee lose his or her job during an economic strike?

5. What major costs are imposed on an employer during a strike? What costs are incurred by the union and bargaining unit employees?

6. Describe the major functions of a labor mediator.

7. Why are grievance procedures and the institution of labor arbitration so important in maintaining industrial peace?

8. What are the major characteristics of a typical grievance procedure?

9. How do most grievances arise? Discuss the four major sources of grievances.

10. Describe how labor arbitrators are selected.

11. What factors affect an arbitrator's decision?

12. Why does the union have a duty to represent all employees fairly (members and nonmembers alike)? What implications does the duty of fair representation have for the grievance mechanism?

13. Discuss why most decisions by arbitrators are final.

14. Which employees are most likely to file grievances?

☐ APPLICATIONS AND CASE EXERCISES

1. Addressing the Air Transport Labor Relations Conference in Washington, D.C., American Airlines CEO Robert L. Crandall said that airline deregulation has gone far beyond what "anyone had dreamed." Crandall said that low-cost carriers have taken advantage of deregulation to take labor relations "far beyond the bounds of cost control." He criticized the government for allowing low-cost carriers to get away with abusing employees. The airline CEO asserted that "it's time for all of us—labor, management, and government—to join forces and make it clear that our society will no longer tolerate an

airline, or for that matter any company abusing its employees in order to beat the competition." Taking aim at Continental Airlines, Crandall noted that they do not provide medical benefits for retirees and require employees to bear most of the cost for medical coverage. He then noted that American Airlines spends $1,666 per employee for such coverage, or $80 million annually for current employees plus $16 million for retirees. Discuss the implications of Mr. Crandall's statements and the dilemmas posed by deregulation of an industry for union-management relations.[85]

2. On August 19, 1987, the AFL-CIO called off its 10-year boycott of Coors beer when a settlement agreement called for a union election at the Adolph Coors Company's brewery in Golden, Colorado, and the use of union contractors to complete construction of the firm's new $70 million plant in Elkton, Virginia.[86] Do you believe that corporate campaigns by unions will increase in the future? Why or why not?

3. Employers who do not plan for possible strikes when they are embroiled in bargaining disputes may end up making expensive mistakes, according to one labor lawyer. Although many employers do no strike planning at all, others make the equally critical error of drawing up a strike plan without relating it to what is occurring at negotiations. What factors should be considered when establishing a strike plan?[87] Discuss.

4. Assume that the union's business agent is inexperienced or unprepared when appearing at an arbitration hearing on behalf of a grievant who was fired after an off-duty fight with a supervisor at a local bar. The arbitrator evaluates the evidence and testimony given and rules in favor of the employer. Later it is discovered that the supervisor provoked the fight with scurrilous remarks about the virtue of the grievant's wife. It is also discovered that the local union president was aware of the supervisor's remarks to the grievant *before* the case came to arbitration. Can the arbitrator's decision be reversed? Why or why not?

5. Most arbitrators are legally trained. In your opinion, does this background aid or handicap the arbitration process? Discuss.

6. An arbitrator is a creature of the contract in that he or she must fashion an arbitration award in accordance with the terms of the collective bargaining agreement. What advantages and disadvantages does the creature of the contract posture have on the institution of labor arbitration and the "law of the shop"?

[85]The Bureau of National Affairs, Inc., *Collective Bargaining Negotiations and Contracts* (Washington, D.C.: The Bureau of National Affairs, Inc., July 2, 1987), p. 4.

[86]The Bureau of National Affairs, Inc., *Collective Bargaining Negotiations and Contracts* (Washington, D.C.: The Bureau of National Affairs, Inc., August 27, 1987), p. 3.

[87]The Bureau of National Affairs, Inc., *Collective Bargaining Negotiations and Contracts* (Washington, D.C.: The Bureau of National Affairs, Inc., May 21, 1987), p. 4.

The Organizing Campaign at Conair Corporation

The Conair Corporation is engaged in the manufacturing, sale, and distribution of hair care and personal grooming products. The company maintains administrative offices, manufacturing operations, and distribution facilities in Edison, New Jersey. Over three fourths of Conair's employees are Spanish-speaking.

In March 1977, the International Ladies' Garment Workers' union (ILGW) began an organizing campaign at Conair's Edison plant. Shortly after becoming aware of the union's efforts, the company conducted a series of management-employee meetings. Meetings of this type had not been held previously and were called in direct response to the organizing campaign. Conair vice-presidents John Mayorek and Jerry Kampel held a meeting for all 300 bargaining unit workers in the plant cafeteria on April 4. At that meeting, Mayorek indicated that the company knew of the organizing campaign. He then pointed out the benefits provided by the company in the past and cautioned that certain benefits would be lost with unionization. Mayorek also promised that, in the future, the company would provide a variety of new benefits, many of which were in response to employee complaints aired at the meeting. Mayorek further informed the group that the company had an "open-door" policy, which apparently was unknown to most Conair workers. The open-door policy would allow employees to bring their complaints directly to management. Mayorek then cautioned the workers that direct access to management would be lost with unionization.

On April 6, Conair President Leandro Rizzuto addressed a second mass meeting of the employees that was held in the firm's production area. Rizzuto reiterated the earlier comments of Mayorek and warned that if he had to pay the increased wages demanded by the union, Conair would close the Edison plant. Later in the day, Rizzuto, Mayorek, and Kampel held several meetings with groups of 10–15 employees, during which they again spoke of current and future benefits and of the open-door policy. Rizzuto stated at the small-group sessions that if a union came in, it would be cheaper to move the operations to Hong Kong, where Conair was already involved in a joint venture.

In response to Conair's statements at these meetings, the union called an unfair labor practice strike on the morning of April 11. Approximately 125 to 140 of the 300 employees participated in the strike, and more than 100 remained at the plant to picket. The first 2 days of the strike were marred by incidents of picket-line violence that included a physical assault on a trucking firm employee, the setting of several small fires, vandalism to company property, rock and bottle throwing, verbal abuse and threats to nonstriking employees, and minor injuries and damage to the automobiles of nonstrikers. Conair secured injunctions to contain further violence and filed unfair labor practice charges against the union.

On April 13, the union petitioned the NLRB for certification as the employees' bargaining representative and simultaneously filed an unfair labor practice charge against the company based on the early April meetings. An election was scheduled for May 6 but was postponed pending the outcome of the unfair labor practice charges. One week later, the company sent mailgrams to the striking workers announcing that they would assume that the workers had quit their jobs unless they returned to work by the 22nd of the month.

Several months later, Conair sent another letter to strikers indicating that their group medical and life insurance programs had been canceled.

During the summer months, Conair hired a bilingual personnel director and instituted a number of improvements such as a job bidding system, a set of salary and performance evaluation standards, an employee credit union, hot food in the company cafeteria, formal termination and layoff procedures, and an employee newsletter, among other things. The union made an unconditional offer to return striking employees to their jobs, effective September 28. Although most of the strikers were reinstated, the company required them to fill out job applications. Furthermore, 13 strikers were not reinstated and 5 others were offered jobs that were less desirable than the ones they held prior to the strike.

The NLRB resolved the unfair labor practice charges filed by the company and then scheduled a certification election for December 7. During the 2 weeks prior to the election, Conair supervisory personnel repeatedly stated to various employees that the Edison plant would be closed and moved to Hong Kong if the union won the election. Supervisors also warned employees on several occasions that, in the event of a union victory, they would not receive their Christmas bonuses. "Raffle tickets" inundated the plant warning that a vote for the union was a vote for plant closure. Conair distributed campaign literature (printed in both Spanish and English) and "Statements of Account" declaring that the company's profit-sharing plan was for nonunion employees only.

The union lost the election by a vote of 136 to 69 (41 ballots were challenged). On March 8, the NLRB regional director filed a complaint in which he consolidated the union's previous unfair labor practice allegations against Conair with the ILGW's later challenge to the December 7 election.

Questions

1. Did the employer's initial worker meetings and statements made in connection with these meetings constitute "outrageous" and "pervasive" unfair labor practices that could warrant a bargaining order?
2. What is the legality of the employer's letter of ultimatum to the striking employees?
3. What impact would the picket-line violence have on the employees' job reinstatement rights?
4. What factors contributed to Conair's wide margin of victory in the December 7 election? Do you believe that the company jeopardized its cause by making threatening statements 2 weeks prior to the election? Would Conair have still won the election in the absence of these threats?
5. In your opinion, what are the odds that the union could win a second election?

■ The National Football League Players Strike

Whether the union or management gained the upper hand as a result of a strike is often difficult to determine. There are cases, however, when a clear-cut victor emerges. The 1987 strike by the National Football League Players Association (NFLPA) is a prime example.[1] A consensus of experts in labor relations is that the NFL players lost badly. For four Sundays during the latter part of 1987, the regulars in the NFL did not play because

[1]This case is based on Martha I. Finney, "Owners Play Hardball, Win Football Strike," *Resource* (Arlington, Virginia: American Society for Personnel Administration, November 1987), p. 18.

the NFL team owners refused to negotiate over the NFL's pivotal issue of free agency.

Perhaps the NFL players were bolstered by the 1982 strike, which caused team owners to cancel games and lose millions of dollars in television and ticket revenues. For the 1987 strike, however, the owners used a different strategy; they replaced striking players, and the games were played and broadcast as scheduled. By using replacements, the owners saved approximately $98 million. A number of striking players returned and played alongside the replacement players. Once the strike ended, players lost hundreds of thousands of dollars in income and failed to receive the benefits for which they were striking. There is also speculation that the fans' spirit and enthusiasm were lost. Furthermore, hard feelings between the NFL owners and players are likely to continue long after the strike. According to one veteran NFL player:

> Management wanted it [the settlement] and they got it. They squeezed the players to a certain point, and I really don't think the NFL will be the same until you get a whole new crop of players in who haven't gone through this situation. I think there's a lot of bitterness still going on between players. Players are back doing their jobs, but I don't think things will be the same again in the NFL for a while.

Labor professionals point to the poor strike strategy of NFLPA Executive Director Gene Upshaw as the downfall of the players' cause. There was no clear definition of the issues that concerned all players. The choice of the free agency issue was a mistake because no more than 3 percent of the players would have benefited from being allowed to be free agents after 4 years in the league. The union

also made a mistake in assuming that the players were irreplaceable. One veteran professional football player noted that there are a number of people "out on the street" who are capable of playing in the NFL. According to one labor expert: "If I was Gene Upshaw I would have realized that there are hundreds of guys out there willing to play for nothing." Of course, the replacement players not only were paid, many were given bonuses when their teams later made the playoffs.

Questions

1. If you were Gene Upshaw, how would you plan for a strike if the need should arise in the future? What mistakes would you avoid?
2. Do you believe that there will be long-term repercussions for players and fans because of the strike? Discuss.
3. Even after the players agreed to abandon the strike, the NFL team owners made them wait 1 week to play and get paid. Do you believe that the owners unnecessarily rubbed salt into the players' wounds? What implications might such a display of power by the owners have for team morale?

■ The Corporate Campaign Against Campbell Soup Co.

In August 1978, 2,000 migrant workers walked out of the tomato fields of northwest Ohio.[2] The walkout was organized by the Farm Labor Organizing Committee (FLOC), a Toledo-based union, and it was directed at the

---

[2]Condensed from The Bureau of National Affairs, Inc., *Unions Today: New Tactics to Tackle Tough Times* (Washington, D.C.: The Bureau of National Affairs, Inc., 1985), pp. 62–66.

Campbell Soup Company. Although 30 percent of the tomato crop was reportedly lost, the walkout apparently did not hurt Campbell's. The union then organized a consumer boycott against the Campbell Soup Company, with only spotty results. At this point, the FLOC hired the services of Corporate Campaign, Inc., a New York labor consulting firm that specializes in divide-and-conquer strategies that bring pressure to bear upon a company through its outside directors.

The FLOC wants Campbell's to recognize it as the collective bargaining agent for migrant laborers who come north from Texas and Florida to pick tomatoes and cucumbers each summer. Once union recognition is achieved, the FLOC wants to negotiate a contract with the company that would provide sufficient wages, safer working conditions, and better housing. Foremost among the FLOC's goals is a minimum wage that equals or exceeds the federal minimum wage. Migrant farm workers are paid a piece rate that varies according to the individual farm's contract with the Campbell Soup Company. In a nutshell, the average migrant worker has an estimated hourly wage that is well below the federal minimum wage.

The Campbell Soup Company claims that it does not employ migrant workers; it simply contracts for produce with the farms, and it plays no role in hiring or paying seasonal workers. The FLOC believes that this argument is a ruse because Campbell's sets the price that it will pay for the crops and this, in turn, has a direct and immediate impact on what the migrant workers are paid. The union also contends that Campbell's attempted to break the union in Ohio by insisting that growers buy mechanical pickers in order to guarantee the harvest. The Campbell Soup Company claims that it is sensitive to the plight of migrant workers and points to the subsidies that the company has made to child-care centers, housing, and college scholarships for the

children of migrant workers. In addition, the company points to the fact that half of the firm's 38,000 employees are represented by nine different unions, proof that the Campbell Soup Company is not antiunion.

The FLOC has targeted three interlocking companies as part of its corporate campaign against Campbell's: the Philadelphia National Bank, which owns interest in the company; Equitable Life; and Prudential Insurance. These companies were selected because Campbell executives and board members are also board members of the Philadelphia National Bank and Equitable Life, while the chairman of Prudential sits on the Campbell Soup board. The objective of the corporate campaign is "to shake up the relationships of these corporations in public." As part of the corporate campaign, the FLOC has also distributed leaflets in front of the Philadelphia National Bank (PNB) that describe the plight of migrant workers. Because PNB is only a short distance across the Delaware River from Campbell's Camden, New Jersey, headquarters, winning public sentiment is very important. According to Hillary Horne, national coordinator for the FLOC corporate campaign: "People always seem to be looking for a reason to hate a bank." By 1985, a postcard and letter campaign was instituted asking Prudential and Equitable Life policyholders to protest Campbell's treatment of migrant workers. The idea of the corporate campaign is to draw these companies into the dispute "until it is in their self-interest to convince Campbell's to negotiate or to sever their ties with Campbell."

The Campbell Soup Company claims that the FLOC's corporate campaign has not hurt the firm's image or its earnings. It claims that only a very small percentage of the correspondence that it receives from consumers is in reference to its stance on migrant labor. When Campbell's called for a secret-ballot election among migrant workers in the fields, the FLOC refused to cooperate.

Questions

1. Do you believe that corporate campaigns such as the one leveled by the FLOC at Campbell Soup are simply a passing fancy or a strategy that organized labor can successfully pursue in the years to come?

2. Because Campbell's is already heavily unionized, what role (if any) should the nine unions that have organized approximately 19,000 of the firm's employees have in the corporate campaign?

3. How can the FLOC determine whether the corporate campaign against Campbell's has been successful?

4. Do you believe that the FLOC is being fair in attacking the Campbell Soup Company? What alternatives might the FLOC pursue in order to improve the wages and working conditions of migrant workers?

Personnel/Human Resource Management: Organizational Strategy, Ethical Concerns, and Future Developments

■ LEARNING OBJECTIVES

After reading this concluding chapter, you should

1. Understand the importance of personnel strategy to the organization's general strategy.
2. Gain insights into some of the ethical issues confronted by personnel/human resource managers.
3. Have a preview of developments that will have an important impact on personnel/human resource management at the dawn of the twenty-first century.
4. Develop an awareness of how to stay abreast of current developments in personnel/human resource management.

■ Introduction

In the previous 16 chapters, we have attempted to illustrate some of the major functions, issues, and complexities associated with the personnel/human resource management function. The personnel function has a potentially strong impact on employment outcomes such as employee absenteeism and turnover levels, employee job satisfaction, compliance with personnel-related legislation, employee health and safety problems, grievances, and disciplinary incidents. On a larger scale, the personnel/human resource management function must be responsive to the organization's mission, objectives, and strategies. Because people are the lifeblood of the organization, typical organizational goals such as market share, profitability, stockholder earnings, cost effectiveness, social responsibility, and growth and survival are tied directly to the effectiveness of the personnel function.

This concluding chapter discusses the link between personnel management and the organization's mission, goals, and strategies. One important matter is the increasingly important ethical aspects of personnel management. Major trends that will have an impact on personnel managers at the turn of the twenty-first century are summarized. Finally, a brief discussion is presented on how personnel managers can stay abreast of changes in this rapidly changing profession.

■ Linking Personnel/Human Resource Management with Organizational Missions, Goals, and Strategies

Perhaps the principal concern of personnel professionals is the contribution that the personnel/human resource management function can make to help the organization fulfill its mission, goals, and strategies. The organization's *mission* is usually top management's statement or description of the organization's overall purpose. *Goals* are statements regarding what specific market, financial, and production standards a firm desires to attain. For example, a goal of an automobile manufacturer might be to capture 12 percent of the U.S. market for subcompact cars. Similarly, the market objective of the second leading car rental agency might be to become the leading firm in terms of the number of automobiles rented. Goals may also be stated in financial terms such as profitability or percentage return on investment. Personnel/human resource managers set specific goals regarding staffing levels, affirmative action, employee benefit costs, and absenteeism and turnover levels. An organization's *strategy* is the means by which the goals will be achieved. Strategic decisions include product mix, customer targets, production methods, capital expenditures, and a host of other decisions, all of which describe *how* the organization intends to achieve its goals. Among the personnel/human resource strategies discussed in this book are the following:

1. *Recruitment and selection strategies:* Examples include internal versus external recruitment sources, successive hurdles versus compensatory selection procedures, and formal versus informal selection. The exact recruitment and selection strategies chosen by an organization will depend on factors such as the type of employees needed, the amount of money available for recruitment and selection, whether the organization's goals include expanding its product and services, labor market conditions, and affirmative action obligations.

2. *Personnel planning strategies:* Examples include formal versus informal planning, short- versus long-term planning, centralized versus decentralized planning, and integrative versus piecemeal planning. Some organizations use sophisticated planning models and attempt to project personnel needs precisely several years in advance. Other organizations find extensive personnel planning to be of little help because of the uncertainties associated with the demand for their product, the competitive nature of their business, and international economic developments.

3. *Training and development strategies:* Examples include skill versus developmental training, individual versus group training, on-the-job versus off-the-job training, and narrow versus broad career paths. The selection of specific training and development strategies might include factors such as the caliber and skill levels of recently hired employees, the degree to which the organization's products and services are changing, the philosophy of top management toward

employee career development, and the costs associated with training and development.

4. *Performance appraisal strategies:* Examples include formal versus informal appraisals, general versus job-specific appraisals, reward-oriented versus developmental-oriented appraisals, the mix of trait, behavioral, and productivity performance criteria, infrequent versus frequent appraisals, and global versus critical incident appraisals. Performance appraisal strategies often depend on the extent to which the organization has experienced employee performance problems, management's concern with EEO issues, and the extent to which elaborate selection predictors have been developed that require careful validation. In addition, extensive performance appraisal systems are more likely to be used when an organization ties merit to compensation decisions.

5. *Compensation strategies:* Examples include emphasis placed on internal versus external equity, low versus high starting salaries, follower versus leader strategy (external equity), low versus high merit pay increases, low versus high influence of seniority in pay changes, standard versus flexible pay, few versus numerous incentives, individual versus group incentives, and limited versus comprehensive employee benefits. Compensation strategies often depend on whether a firm is growing, remaining stable, or declining. For example, growing firms might emphasize incentive pay to encourage high levels of individual productivity. Unionized firms, as noted in Chapters 15 and 16, tend to shy away from incentive and merit pay plans in favor of seniority-based pay. Organizations that wish to emphasize individual competence and creativity might use a skill- or knowledge-based pay plan.

6. *Employment relations strategies:* Examples include cooperative versus antagonist posture toward unions, proactive versus reactive posture toward union organizing campaigns, low versus high job security, informal versus formal discipline policies, and indifferent versus paternalistic orientation toward employees. A firm with high labor costs might adopt a combative strategy with union organizers. Some unionized firms with low labor costs may elect to cooperate with organized labor, preferring to bargain in good faith and reach a contract settlement rather than risk an expensive work stoppage. Companies with highly technical production processes and operations that require heavy plant security and attention to safety may adopt a strict posture on employee disciplinary measures.

The Relationship Between Organizational Strategy and Personnel/Human Resource Management Strategy

Business strategists have categorized organizations in a number of different ways. These categorizations typically distinguish between organizations that are growing and those that are stable or declining. The strategic orientation of organizations may be categorized in terms of their profit orientation, the size and scope of their product lines, whether they are trend setters or followers, the speed with which they must adapt to change in order to survive, the type of organizational structure, the risk proneness or aversion of key decision makers, and other factors.[1]

Once the strategic posture of an organization has been identified, the next step is to determine the personnel strategies that will enable the organization to achieve its mission, goals, and objectives. For example, Schuler discusses five types of corporate strategies[2] and business concerns, one of which is the *entrepreneurial strategy*. The entrepreneurial strategy is characterized by high risk taking, minimal policies and procedures, multiple priorities, and insufficient resources to satisfy all customer demands. In short, the basic objective of the entrepreneurial strategy is to see that the business is successfully launched. In order to achieve this basic objective, the following personnel strategies might be appropriate:

1. Use broad and multiple career paths that encourage employee creativity and initiative.
2. Establish performance appraisal systems that are future oriented (such as management by objectives) and stimulate the taking of risks.
3. Compensation programs should emphasize external equity in order to attract high-caliber employees. Compensation should be flexible, contain many perquisites and long-term incentives, and encourage high levels of employee participation and assumption of responsibility.
4. Training and development programs should focus on broad development of individuals and quality of work life.

In contrast to the entrepreneurial strategy, personnel policies would be substantially different in a declining organization that is in the *liquidation/divestiture* mode. In the liquidation/divestiture mode, the focus is on selling off assets, cutting further losses, and reducing the workforce as much as possible. Examples of personnel policies that conform with the liquidation/divestiture mode are the following:

1. Use of limited and narrow career paths.
2. Performance appraisal systems that focus on remedying employee weaknesses and problem areas and involve little or no employee participation.

---

[1]See, for example, Randall S. Schuler, "Personnel and Human Resource Management Choices and Organizational Strategy," *Human Resource Planning*, Vol. 10, No. 1 (1987), p. 3; and Raymond E. Miles and Charles C. Snow, "Designing Strategic Human Resources Systems," *Organizational Dynamics* (Summer 1984), pp. 37–38.

[2]The other corporate strategies and business concerns identified by Schuler are the dynamic growth strategy, extract profit/rationalization strategy, and the turnaround strategy.

3. Compensation programs that foster a short-term orientation. Such programs employ a standard fixed package, few perquisites, and no incentives.
4. Training programs that are either nonexistent or have a narrow application.[3]

These examples illustrate how personnel programs can have a strategic fit with the organization's broader strategies. However, linking personnel strategies to the organization's strategies is not done with a great deal of precision, and there is room for a variety of personnel strategies for a particular organizational strategy. Even though the link between an organization's goals, objectives, and strategies may be loose, it is possible for an inappropriate personnel strategy to hinder the entire organization. Likewise, an appropriate personnel strategy can contribute to organizational effectiveness and goal attainment.[4]

The Personnel Manager's Role in Strategy Formulation

There is evidence that personnel managers do not take an active role in strategic planning. As a result, personnel strategies may not fully complement organizational strategies. Typically, personnel managers are requested by top management to respond after strategic plans have been formulated. According to one expert, personnel professionals can contribute to the strategic management process by doing the following:[5]

1. Establishing a professional image and a competent staff within the personnel function that top managers will respect and view as an important resource.
2. Learning as much as possible about the organization's mission, goals, objectives, and strategies.
3. Being aggressive in helping management formulate strategies. Do not allow a project or priority to be dropped because of human resource management issues.
4. Avoiding the following excesses:

---

[3]Randall S. Schuler, pp. 1–17. Also see George G. Gordon, "Getting in Step: HR Executives Must Get in Line with Strategy Leaders," *Personnel Administrator* (April, 1987), pp. 44–48; John A. Hooper, Ralph F. Catalanello, and Patrick L. Murray, "Shoring Up the Weakest Link: A Tool for Meshing People-Planning with Business Issues," *Personnel Administrator* (April 1987), pp. 49–55, 134; Lee Dyer, "Linking Human Resource and Business Strategies," *Human Resource Planning*, Vol. 32 (1984), pp. 70–84; Richard Gould, "Gaining a Competitive Edge Through Human Resource Strategies," *Human Resource Planning*, Vol. 7, No. 1 (1984), pp. 31–46; Lloyd Baird and Ilan Meshoulam, "The HRS Matrix: Managing the Human Resource Function Strategically," *Human Resource Planning*, Vol. 7, No. 1 (1984), pp. 1–21; and Elmer H. Burack, "Corporate Business and Human Resources Planning Practices: Strategic Issues and Concerns," *Organizational Dynamics* (Summer 1986), pp. 73–87.

[4]See Randall S. Schuler and Susan E. Jackson, "Linking Competitive Strategies with Human Resource Management Practices," *The Academy of Management Executive* (August 1987), pp. 207–219.

[5]Adapted from Lee Dyer, "Linking Human Resource and Business Strategies," *Human Resource Planning*, Vol. 32 (1984), pp. 83–84.

- The tendency of personnel administrators to feel that all human resource issues are theirs.
- The parochial attitude that all issues must be viewed from a personnel rather than a business point of view.
- Constantly taking the negative position that something will not work.

According to a survey conducted by two prominent personnel/human resource management consultants, chief executives of major corporations expect the personnel/human resource management function to assume a broader role in the future.[6] The survey indicates that the personnel/human resource management function will help increase profitability through productivity improvements and quality of staffing. In addition, the personnel function will continue to train department heads and first-line supervisors to deal with personnel matters before they become major problems; this will become especially important in decentralized organizations where employees are geographically dispersed.

■ Ethical Considerations in Personnel/Human Resource Management

Some Major Ethical Issues

Personnel managers deal with people at work. For millions of individuals, work represents one of the most important facets of their lives. Work life not only provides economic security but also affects a person's social and psychological well-being. Decisions related to personnel/human resource management, therefore, have a potentially profound effect on individual lives. Hiring, promotion, and compensation decisions affect careers and career choices, determine one's self-esteem, and enhance or diminish job satisfaction.

Because personnel policies and decisions are so intertwined with employee well-being, actions by personnel managers and supervisors must be above reproach. Ethical behavior is a standard espoused by all professional groups, and the integrity of an entire group can be tarnished by the actions of a few unscrupulous members. While most managers aspire to ethical behavior, the determination of what constitutes either ethical or unethical actions is not always clear. For example, the term *organizational politics* conjures up images of dishonest, unsavory, and behind-the-back maneuvering of an unethical nature. Yet nearly every managerial and nonmanagerial employee engages in organizational politics to some degree. We may view our own political behavior as legitimate while regarding with disdain the actions of those more political than ourselves. According to Joanne B. Ciulla, who designed an ethics course at the Wharton School, the complexity

[6]James W. Walker, and Gregory Moorhead, "CEO's: What They Want from HRM," *Personnel Administrator* (December 1987), pp. 50–59.

surrounding business ethics makes it difficult to separate right from wrong. "By comparison, medical ethics are simple, since it's a basic, universally accepted principle that human life is valuable—whereas business ethics are metaphysical, more like dealing with religious beliefs."[7]

Velasquez, Moberg, and Cavanaugh discuss three basic approaches to moral issues in organizations:[8]

1. *Utilitarian approaches* judge policies and behaviors in terms of their effects on the general welfare. That is, policies grounded in the philosophy of the greatest good for the greatest number of people are based on the utilitarian approach. For example, Chapters 6 and 7 discuss recruitment and selection procedures that use job-relevant predictors to select the best-qualified employees. In so doing, some employees are not hired who would have proven competent if given the chance (you may remember these as false negatives). Yet the overall impact is positive to more people and negative to the relatively small number of rejected (yet qualified) applicants. Similarly, affirmative action programs and the use of reverse discrimination to favor minority applicants over nonminorities have been attacked, in part, on the basis of the utilitarian approach. In a similar vein, layoffs are obviously detrimental to some but possibly necessary for the majority of employees when the layoffs spell the difference between bankruptcy and organizational survival.

2. *Approaches based on rights* emphasize the personal entitlements of individuals. Employees, as human beings, are entitled to be treated with respect by their employers, as well as provided with safe working conditions, a reasonable and equitable pay system, and relevant and unbiased evaluations of job performance. Organizations generally respect an individual's personal privacy, integrity, and freedom to criticize conscientiously the ethics and legality of corporate actions. Problems arise when an organization disregards individual dignity or human rights. A classic illustration of this is the current controversy over drug testing in the workplace (Chapter 14). Many employees regard random urinalysis testing as an invasion of their personal privacy and as a personally degrading experience; their anger is often intensified when they hold jobs that have no bearing on public or personal safety. Much of the erosion of the employment-at-will doctrine (Chapter 13) is attributable to organizations that insisted on violating individual rights by discharging employees under conditions of malice and bad faith.

3. *Approaches based on justice* focus on the fairness of the benefits and burdens imposed by a personnel policy or action. The chapters on EEO (Chapter 3) and employee and organizational rights (Chapter 13) deal with organizational justice. The issue of justice arises when we deal with equal treatment, due process, and consistent application of policies and rules. In addition, the discussion

---

[7]Cheryll Aimee Barron, "Tainted Times?," *Business Week Careers* (Spring-Summer, 1988), pp. 45–51.

[8]Manuel Velasquez, Dennis J. Moberg, and Gerald F. Cavanaugh, "Organizational Statesmanship and Dirty Politics: Ethical Guidelines to the Organizational Politician," *Organizational Dynamics* (Autumn 1983), pp. 13–19.

of pay equity or fairness relates directly to approaches that emphasize organizational justice.

Personnel policies should be written and applied with these three approaches in mind. When considering the ethical quality of personnel policies and actions, attention should be given to (1) the extent to which the policy or action satisfies the greatest number of people, (2) the extent to which the policy or action respects the rights of individuals, and (3) the extent to which the policy or action distributes benefits and burdens in a fair manner.

Unfortunately, some personnel decisions pose conflicts or contradictions with these three ethical approaches. For example, a woman subjected to sexual harassment at work may be reluctant to press charges for fear of the gossip and adverse publicity that such a sensitive case could generate. She might forgo her right to file charges with an internal grievance committee or the EEOC (the approach based on justice) in favor of maintaining her personal privacy and minimizing embarrassment (the approach based on rights). Furthermore, by not filing charges, she may ultimately encourage others to sexually harass female employees, thereby posing a conflict with the utilitarian approach.

Ethics Policies: Personnel/Human Resource Management's Role

Personnel managers, as knowledgeable and intelligent professionals, must be prepared to make difficult choices that pose ethical dilemmas. Clear-cut policies are rarely available to guide and support tough decisions involving people and their jobs. The problem is compounded when conflicts arise *within* the three approaches. For example, restructuring the employee benefits program to favor older employees may penalize the young (a conflict with the utilitarian and justice approaches). Similarly, the comparable worth issue presents a conflict between valuing one job in terms of its responsibilities, skills, and value to society relative to other comparable jobs (a possible conflict with both the rights and justice approaches).

A survey by Bentley College of the 1984 Fortune 500 industrial and service companies found that almost 75 percent of these firms had a code of ethics, 35 percent were providing training in ethics, 14 percent had ethics committees, and 6 percent had ethics ombudsmen.[9] Codes of ethics are often drafted by the corporate legal department and communicated and monitored by the personnel department. Ethics codes may address issues such as dealing with confidential information, conflicts of interest, reporting illegal acts by company personnel, professional judgment, integrity, and truthfulness.

Several points are important regarding ethics codes. First, a committee of managers from across the organization should be used to assist in drafting ethical guidelines to ensure both a broad perspective and acceptance to the guidelines.

[9]This discussion is based primarily on Gary Edwards and Kirk Bennett, "Ethics and HR: Standards and Practice," *Personnel Administrator* (December 1987), pp. 62–66.

Second, the cooperation of organized labor is important in unionized firms. Third, the code of ethics must be communicated to employees. To ensure that employees understand the code and take it seriously, some companies request that each employee sign a statement that he or she had read the code, understands it, and is willing to abide by its provisions. Fourth, company newsletters may publish articles on ethical issues and pose hypothetical ethical dilemmas and discussions on how to resolve these dilemmas. Fifth, top management must set the tone for ethical behavior; when employees realize that the code of ethics is disregarded by top corporate executives, they too will ignore it.

Employee ethics training can play an integral role in ensuring compliance with an ethics code. Such training programs help to emphasize the importance of ethical behavior, specify forms of ethical conduct and identify key ethical issues, increase awareness of pressures that may lead to unethical conduct, alert employees to the importance of avoiding ethical misconduct and the need to report unethical practices and publicize the consequences of unethical behavior by employees.

■ Trends and Issues Affecting Personnel/Human Resource Management at the Dawn of the Twenty-first Century

A review of the recent personnel/human resource management literature illustrates the rapidly changing nature of the field. Some of the more prominent trends present complex and often perplexing problems with which personnel practitioners and academicians must deal as the twenty-first century draws to a close. Among these are the impact of corporate mergers and acquisitions, along with the deregulation of some industries on human resources. In addition, a number of operational aspects of the personnel/human resource management function are changing.

Keeping Corporations Competitive in the Global Economy

Much has been said and written about the influence of global competition because of the strong influence of Japanese corporations on U.S. businesses and, more recently, because of the unified economy of 12 Western European countries (EC'92). Human resource managers in U.S. companies must deal with two issues. First, large companies typically have foreign subsidiaries that require unique and different approaches to personnel/human resource management. When U.S. firms operate in foreign locations, they must be knowledgeable about different labor market conditions and laws that affect the recruitment, training, compensation, health and safety, and labor relations functions.

Second, the personnel/human resource management function must play a primary role in helping corporations improve the quality of their goods and services. Terms such as *total quality management, employee empowerment, quality circles, team building, competitive benchmarking,* and *total quality control* are part of the quality movement that has swept U.S. corporations over the past several years.[10] An underlying theme to the three-part series on *Quality . . . or Else* produced by PBS is the importance of human resources for an organization's quality programs.[11] In delineating the six characteristics of world-class companies, Armand V. Feigenbaum of the General Systems Company points to the need for "progressively better utilization of existing resources." Feigenbaum says that this is "especially true in human resources at all levels."[12] Thus, any attempt by U.S. corporations to enhance the quality of their products and services in order to compete with foreign firms must rely heavily on developing first-rate recruitment, selection, training, and reward systems for employees.

The Impact of Mergers and Acquisitions on Human Resources

Corporate mergers and acquisitions increased dramatically during the 1980s and reached the point where few companies can safely assume immunity from some sort of business combination. In most cases, the dominant firm seeks a financial advantage through increased market share or economies of scale. However, mergers and acquisitions that occur without fully considering the impact on human resources may fall short of their financial objectives.[13] Mergers and acquisitions may present the following problems:[14]

1. Reduced productivity because of the anxiety and sense of betrayal experienced by employees.
2. Staff reductions, transfers, and promotions that are either based on quick and superficial evaluations of personnel or those that fail to consider the goals of the new organization.
3. Unwanted turnover by the organization's superior employees who want to abandon what they perceive to be a sinking ship.
4. Unexpected employee benefits costs such as underfunded retirement programs, as well as lawsuits filed by employees over contractual rights and EEO issues.

[10]See "Questing for the Best," *The Quality Imperative*, special edition of *Business Week* (October 25, 1991), p. 9.

[11]This series was aired on public television in early 1992.

[12]Armand V. Feigenbaum, "World Class Companies Are Remarkably Similar," *Quality and Participation* (March 1992), p. 11.

[13]David Robino and Kenneth DeMeuse, "Corporate Mergers and Acquisitions: Their Impact on HRM," *Personnel Administrator* (November 1985), p. 3.

[14]John D. Gridley, "Mergers and Acquisitions, 1: Premerger Human Resources Planning," *Personnel* (September 1986), p. 28.

5. Dysfunctional leadership struggles as top and middle managers jockey for position in the newly reorganized company.
6. Stress on employees and their families that can lead to health problems or even suicide.[15]

When a corporate merger or acquisition is likely, early involvement of the personnel/human resource management executives from the firms involved may eliminate or reduce a number of problems. Merging companies may have different organizational cultures that can clash unless action is taken to make the transition as smooth as possible; a "we-they" attitude between employees of the merging companies can be destructive. The merging firms may wish to consider a merger-integration team (MIT).[16] This team should initially consist of the CEOs and all vice-presidents of the merged companies. They should redefine the organization's culture and structure and assign new responsibilities as necessary. Employee turnover and anxieties can be reduced by announcing layoffs and other personnel changes as early as possible. In fact, communication may be the most important aspect to a successful merger or acquisition.[17] For employees who receive a transfer or promotion that requires a relocation, the personnel department can establish programs that will ease the displacement and uncertainties associated with moving. Stress management programs may also help safeguard employee health.[18]

Personnel/Human Resource Management in Deregulated Industries

Organizations in regulated industries are constrained with regard to their operation and prices that they charge to consumers. For example, public utilities, railroads, airlines, trucking, and insurance companies have all been regulated to varying degrees. One benefit of being a regulated company is that competition is either limited or controlled. As a result, regulated companies may become very bureaucratic in their mode of operation, with heavy reliance on extensive rules, regulations, and personnel policies. In recent years, there has been a trend toward deregulation. Deregulated industries such as the airlines have suddenly been inundated with competition as rival companies have sprouted and have competed directly with the established carriers. Typically, the upstart competitors have

[15]David L. Schweiger and John M. Ivancevich, "Human Resources: The Forgotten Factor in Mergers and Acquisitions," *Personnel Administrator* (November 1985), pp. 47–61.

[16]Philip L. Hunsaker and Michael W. Coombs, "Mergers and Acquisitions: Managing the Emotional Issues," *Personnel* (March 1988), pp. 56–63.-

[17]David Robino and Kenneth DeMeuse, p. 44. Also see Robert M. Fulmer, "Mergers and Acquisitions, 2: Role of Management Development," *Personnel* (September 1986), pp. 37–49; Michael A. Conway, "Mergers and Acquisitions, 3: Ten Pitfalls of Joint Ventures," *Personnel* (September 1986), pp. 50–52; and Kirkland Ropp, "Restructuring: Survival of the Fittest," *Personnel Administrator* (February 1987), pp. 45–47.

[18]See David L. Schweiger and John M. Ivancevich.

drastically undercut their fares and have offered no-frills service in order to compete effectively.

Deregulation within an industry forces a firm to adopt a more flexible competitive posture. This, in turn, requires a more flexible approach with regard to personnel policies and practices. Employees may be required to make frequent lateral moves, some of which could require relocation. In addition, employees may be required to learn several jobs to permit the rapid completion of assignments. A classic example of this occurred at People Express Airlines, a low-fare carrier, where associates (employees) were trained to perform at least four jobs.[19] Deregulated companies may also offer lower pay and few employee benefits in an attempt to reduce labor costs and achieve a competitive edge. As a result of these practices, deregulated companies may clash with each other and with organized labor.

The Changing Operational Aspects of the Personnel/Human Resource Management Function

The personnel/human resource management function is undergoing a number of changes in terms of its importance to the organization as well as in the way it operates.[20] Among the major changes in the operational aspects of the personnel function are the following:[21]

1. *The influence of the personnel/human resource management function is continuing to increase.* Most top management teams realize that the management of human resources is a vital organizational function. A survey of personnel managers indicates that the personnel/human resource management function has gained influence and has the potential to continue doing so in the near future. Personnel managers are becoming more involved in general business decisions and more aware of the impact personnel programs have on organizational goals.[22]

2. *Personnel policies will be centrally formulated, but implemented on a decentralized basis.* The legal and economic complexity of many personnel policies requires that they be centrally formulated by personnel specialists at the corporate level. However, improvements in management information systems will allow these policies to be applied on a decentralized basis. Management development programs will also be required to enable line managers to acquire the background and skills needed to implement personnel policies.

---

[19]Douglas B. Gehrman, "The Deregulated Employee," *Personnel Administrator* (January 1986), p. 36.

[20]Edward E. Lawler III, "Human Resource Management: Meeting The New Challenges," *Personnel* (January 1988), pp. 22–27; and Michael J. Driver, Robert E. Coffey, and David E. Bowen, "Where Is HR Management Going?," *Personnel* (January 1988), pp. 28–31.

[21]Derived, in part, from L. James Harvey, "Nine Major Trends in HRM," *Personnel Administrator* (November 1986), pp. 102–105, 108–109.

[22]Edward F. McDonough, "How Much Power Does HR Have, and What Can It Do to Win More?," *Personnel* (January 1986), pp. 18–25.

3. *The use of automation and human resource information systems (HRIS) will increase.* As is the case for nearly all organizational functions, such as accounting, finance, marketing, and production, computer technology will continue to permeate the personnel/human resource management function. Software programs for microcomputers have been developed to plan, monitor, and evaluate human resource programs.[23] HRIS are being used to manage recruitment, selection, training, performance appraisal, compensation, and other personnel programs. However, this means that organizations must deal with the problem of "computer anxiety" among employees.[24]

4. *Personnel departments will be more accountable for their contributions to the organization's mission, goals, and objectives.* As noted earlier, there is a trend toward integrating personnel strategies with global organizational strategies. As corporations in the United States attempt to compete with Japanese and other foreign producers, the personnel/human resource management function will be expected to make greater contributions to productivity and efficiency.[25] Personnel managers use "hard" quantitative measures to monitor absenteeism rates, employee turnover, and on-the-job accidents and injuries. In addition, personnel managers use reliability and validity coefficients, base rates, and percentage of correct decisions to assess the utility of employment selection predictors (Chapter 7). Training and development programs can be evaluated by using either simple or sophisticated research designs that provide assessments of learning, retention, and behavioral changes among trainees (Chapter 8). Initially some of the hard measures of the personnel department's effectiveness were precipitated by legal requirements (such as the record-keeping requirements of OSHA and the EEO laws). Additional measures were devised to determine the cost effectiveness of personnel programs, and these efforts will undoubtedly be expanded to examine the impact of the personnel function on the organization's strategies and contributions to bottom-line financial and market measures.[26]

5. *Personnel/human resource professionals must be increasingly cognizant of the attitudes of employees and their desire to be creative.* The education levels and knowledge of the labor force have increased. This trend is attributable to additional formal schooling, as well as the greater individual awareness that comes with constant exposure to the news media. As a result, employees are

[23]Albert S. King, "How 'Micros' Are Changing HR Information Management," *Personnel* (May 1985), pp. 67–69. Also see Donald Harris, "Beyond the Basics: New HRIS Developments," Personnel (January 1986), pp. 49–56.

[24]Paul H. Faerstein, "Fighting Computer Anxiety," *Personnel* (January 1986), pp. 12–17. Computer anxiety may be precipitated by an employee's need for control or autonomy, resistance to change, need for status or power, fear of the unknown, feeling of isolation, and role identity problems.

[25]Louis A. Mischkind, "Seven Steps to Productivity Improvement," *Personnel* (July 1987), p. 30; and Phil Nienstedt, and Richard Wintermantel, "Restructuring Organizations to Improve Productivity," *Personnel* (August 1985), pp. 34–40. See also, George E. Biles, "Auditing HRM Practices," *Personnel Administrator* (December 1986), pp. 89–94.

[26]See George E. Biles, "Auditing HRM Practices," *Personnel Administrator* (December 1986), pp. 89–94.

often more critical about the manner in which business is conducted in the workplace, and, in many instances, they also want a chance to demonstrate their creativity. Personnel managers must help the organization maintain a pulse on current employee attitudes in order to eliminate problems before they escalate into serious matters. Thus personnel directors must be able to use employee attitude surveys skillfully.[27] Encouraging and channeling employee creativity is important for two reasons. First, employees may have suggestions for improving productivity, cutting costs, or new product and service ideas. Second, employees who are allowed to demonstrate their intelligence and ingenuity are more likely to be satisfied and fulfilled in their jobs. Quality circles and participative management techniques have helped in this respect. In addition, suggestion systems and patent policies should be integrated into compensation programs.[28] Finally, personnel managers must help devise methods for fostering employee creativity, especially when group norms are stifling.[29]

6. Personnel/human resource management is a pervasive function that requires the cooperation and efforts of supervisory employees at all levels. Even when personnel/human resource management policies are created on a centralized basis, they are applied in a decentralized manner. Middle-level managers and first-line supervisors are all responsible for understanding and implementing a variety of selection, training, performance appraisal, compensation, employee discipline, health and safety, and other personnel/human resource management policies. Supervisors, for example, often make the final decisions on which employees are hired, how and when they will be trained, the quality of their performance appraisals, and the amount of their pay raises. Unlike organizational decisions affecting production facilities, finances, or marketing, personnel/human resource management decisions are often widely shared. It is therefore important that all supervisory employees appreciate the importance of personnel/human resource management and its various functional areas.

■ Goals and Challenges in Human Resource Management

A survey by The Bureau of National Affairs, Inc., revealed a number of challenges and concerns faced by personnel/human resource managers. The results indicate the following human resource management priorities in order of importance: (1) training and development, (2) employee benefits, (3) recruitment and selection, (4) compensation administration, and (5) employee/labor relations. A closer look at

[27]See Martin Wright, "Helping Employees Speak Out About Their Jobs and Workplace," *Personnel* (September 1986), pp. 56–60; and Norman Smallwood and Joe Folkman, "Why Employee Surveys Don't Always Work," *Personnel* (August 1987), pp. 20–28.

[28]Robert H. Meehan, "Programs That Foster Creativity and Innovation," *Personnel* (February 1986), pp. 31–35.

[29]Robert R. Blake and Jane Srygley Mouton, "Don't Let Group Norms Stifle Productivity," *Personnel* (August 1985), pp. 28–33.

TABLE 17-1A   Personnel/Human Resource Executives' Concern About Ongoing Issues

	Percent of Respondents			
	Very Concerned	Moderately Concerned	Not Very Concerned	Not Applicable/ No Response
Costs				
Health care costs	82%	16%	1%	-%
Workers' compensation costs	57	33	9	1
Wage/salary costs	51	43	6	-
Personnel/HR department costs	19	53	25	3
Employee Relations				
Employee morale	77	21	1	-
Employee communications	60	40	-	-
Employee litigation	32	38	23	7
Grievances	25	40	25	10
Drug testing	24	38	32	7
Labor contract negotiations	23	24	18	35
Employee Performance and Behavior				
Employee productivity levels	59	34	7	1
Performance standards	58	36	6	-
Management training/development	57	36	5	1
Performance appraisals	53	41	6	-
Occupational injuries and illnesses	51	31	16	2
Non-management training/development	45	47	7	1
Absenteeism	33	51	16	-
Discipline and discharge	33	49	18	-
Employee theft	21	28	49	2
Organizational Impact of Human Resources				
Personnel/HR department's role	57	35	5	3
Organization development	46	42	10	3
Organization downsizing/restructuring	34	25	29	13
Automation in personnel/HR management	32	37	24	7
Mergers and acquisitions	10	23	35	32

the survey results in Table 17-1 indicates that personnel/human resource executives are very concerned about health care costs. There is also concern for issues affecting organizational performance and understanding the recently passed ADA. Somewhat surprisingly, there is relatively little concern about employee theft. Other personnel/human resource management issues appear to have a much wider variation in importance to personnel executives.[30]

[30]The Bureau of National Affairs, Inc., "Goals and Challenges in Human Resource Management: A BNA Policy and Practice Series Survey," *Bulletin to Management* (Washington, D.C.: The Bureau of National Affairs, Inc., January 24, 1991).

TABLE 17-1A (continued)

	Percent of Respondents			
	Very Concerned	Moderately Concerned	Not Very Concerned	Not Applicable/ No Response
Compensation and Benefit Programs				
Insurance benefit programs	54	33	11	2
Competitiveness of wage structure	53	37	10	1
Internal pay equity	40	47	13	1
Pension/retirement plans	26	47	21	6
Employee services	21	60	19	-
Post-retirement health plans	19	28	35	18
Employee assistance plan	18	46	34	3
Investment plans	10	32	34	24
External Concerns				
Compliance with government regulations	54	35	7	4
Changing economic/market conditions	50	38	8	4
Affirmative action program/EEO compliance	36	43	17	4
Technological changes	22	45	27	6
Staffing				
Retaining current employees/reducing turnover	33	39	25	3
Non-management recruiting	23	49	25	3
Recruiting for management positions	21	45	29	5
Succession planning	21	41	30	7
Career planning	18	49	28	5
Testing	18	40	33	8

Note: Percentages are based on responses from 136 personnel/HR executives. Percentages may not add to 100 due to rounding.

From The Bureau of National Affairs, Inc., "Goals and Challenges in Human Resource Management: A BNA Policy and Practice Series Survey," *Bulletin to Management* (Washington, D.C.: The Bureau of National Affairs, Inc., January 30, 1992). Reprinted with permission.

■ Staying Abreast of Developments in Personnel/Human Resource Management

As in many professional fields, developments and knowledge expand at an alarmingly fast rate. Personnel/human resource managers must maintain an awareness of facts, figures, innovations, and regulatory changes. Anyone who attempts to stay abreast of the field will soon realize that it is impossible to digest the plethora of articles and information available today.[31] The day of the "personnel expert" has

[31]See Jeffrey P. Davidson, "Mastering Your Professional Reading," *Personnel* (January 1986), pp. 46–48.

TABLE 17-1B   Personnel/Human Resource Executives' Concern About Legislative and Regulatory Issues

	Percent of Respondents			
	Very Concerned	Moderately Concerned	Not Very Concerned	Not Applicable/ No Response
Americans with Disabilities Act of 1990	61%	30%	7%	1%
Proposed health care reform legislation	54	36	8	2
Proposed family and medical leave legislation	38	39	22	1
Civil rights legislation	33	51	15	2
Proposed striker replacement legislation	25	19	25	31
Proposed pension simplification legislation	23	45	24	8
FASB accounting standards for retirees' health benefits	18	36	30	16
Proposed OSHA rules on motor vehicle safety	13	36	34	16
Non-discrimination rules and other requirements for pension and retirement plans	11	55	27	7
Older Workers Benefit Protection Act of 1990	11	48	36	5
IRCA rules on foreign workers and work authorizations	4	42	43	11

Note: Percentages are based on responses from 122 personnel/HR executives. Fourteen organizations did not respond to this section of the survey. Percentages may not add to 100 due to rounding.

TABLE 17-1C   Personnel/Human Resource Executives' Concern About Selected Broad Issues

	Percent of Respondents			
	Very Concerned	Moderately Concerned	Not Very Concerned	Not Applicable/ No Response
Organization performance	73%	25%	2%	-%
Economic/business downturns	49	31	16	4
Basic work skills	41	43	15	1
Discrimination claims/employee litigation	38	45	15	1
Changing work force demographics	37	46	15	2
Personal lifestyle issues	36	51	13	-
Work and family	32	58	9	1

Note: Percentages are based on responses from 136 personnel/HR executives. Percentages may not add to 100 due to rounding.

passed; today most personnel practitioners and academicians who study the field can only hope to stay on the leading edge of a relatively specialized area such as health and safety, EEO laws, job evaluation, retirement programs, and so forth. Even specialists may find it difficult to remain abreast of all of the latest developments.

The key to remaining current may require that personnel managers do the following:[32]

1. Set aside several hours each month for quiet, uninterrupted reading.
2. Scan a large amount of material, but selectively read only that material that is most relevant to your job.
3. Join professional associations such as the American Society for Personnel Administration, the American Management Association, or the American Psychological Association; these associations publish journals and newsletters that highlight recent developments and provide an in-depth analysis of current issues.
4. Subscribe to looseleaf reporting services that deal with personnel practices. The Bureau of National Affairs, Inc., Commerce Clearing House, Inc., and similar organizations offer a wealth of pertinent information at a modest price.
5. Attend seminars and training programs on a regular basis. Not only do such programs offer valuable insights and information, they also provide the opportunity to interact with other personnel professionals who hold different and sometimes intriguing viewpoints.
6. Identify individuals with specialized expertise in various areas of personnel and use them as sources of information and advice.
7. Maintain an open mind about new ideas that may be helpful to your current job and professional development. Learn to keep a balanced perspective on major developments in the field. Although many new ideas and techniques may not be adaptable to your organization on an "as is" basis, they may be quite valuable when modified to suit the needs of a specific setting.

■ Questions

1. How can personnel/human resource managers help strengthen the link between organizational and personnel strategies?
2. Describe the utilitarian, rights, and justice approaches to ethics.
3. Describe the effects that corporate mergers and acquisitions can have on human resources.

4. What basic differences might exist between personnel/human resource management in deregulated and regulated industries?
5. What major changes are likely to occur in the operation of personnel/human resource management departments during the next decade?

[32]See Georgianna Herman and Gwendolyn Lloyd, "PAIR Literature: Keeping Up to Date," in Dale Yoder and Herbert G. Heneman, Jr. (Eds.) in *ASPA Handbook of Personnel and Industrial Relations: Professional PAIR* (Washington, D.C.: The Bureau of National Affairs, Inc., 1979), Ch. 8.5.

☐ APPLICATIONS AND CASE EXERCISES

1. Select a large corporation that is of interest to you. Based on the discussion of organizational and personnel strategies in this chapter, evaluate the strategic fit between the corporation's personnel strategy and its overall mission, goals, and objectives.

2. Analyze the potential human resource problems that might occur between two corporations (of your choosing) that are currently contemplating a merger. How would you attempt to alleviate or eliminate these problems?

3. Select two organizations—one that is in a heavily regulated industry (such as a public utility) and one that is subjected to relatively little regulation. What differences, if any, are there between the personnel policies of these organizations? Are their differences solely attributable to the extent of their regulation? Discuss.

4. Professions such as psychology, medicine, and labor arbitration have developed a code of ethics by which those working in these professions must abide. Using these codes as your guide, draft a code of ethics for the personnel/human resource profession.

5. Of the major trends in personnel/human resource management that will occur over the next decade, which will have the greatest impact? Why? Are there other trends that you believe may arise that are not noted in this chapter?

6. Evaluate how you would deal with the following ethical dilemmas:

   - You are a first-line supervisor in a large department store. An employee in your department approaches you and tells you that a theft ring involving 20 employees is operating in the store. He begs you not to report the incident because he fears for his safety if the leaders of the theft ring discover that he has discussed the matter with you.
   - You are the assistant vice-president for financial operations in a large manufacturing firm. After working late one night you discover that your boss, the vice-president of finance and chief comptroller, is providing inside information to several wealthy investors about your company's planned merger with another large manufacturer.
   - A co-worker and friend has been drinking heavily. She has repeatedly asked you to cover for her and lie to your supervisor about her whereabouts while she continues her alcohol abuse.
   - After a business trip, you begin to file an expense report. A co-worker who accompanied you on the trip files a report that is nearly twice the amount of the expenses actually incurred. He asks you to file a similar report and tells you that "everybody around here pads his travel expenses."
   - While having lunch with the sales representative of a company that is trying to sell your firm nearly $1 million of electrical equipment, the sales representative offers you $5,000 in cash if you see that his company gets the contract.
   - In an attempt to obtain a more reasonable wage demand from union negotiators, a member of the management bargaining team tells the union negotiators that the company paid nearly $3.5 million to employees (both union and nonunion) in group incentives. As the firm's compensation manager, you know that the firm paid only $350,000 in group incentives.

INDEXES

Name Index

Name Index

◼ Organization Index

Subject Index